PERSONNEL MANAGEMENT

Personnel Management

THIRD

EDITION

BY MICHAEL J. JUCIUS, Ph.D.

PROFESSOR OF BUSINESS ORGANIZATION

THE OHIO STATE UNIVERSITY

1955

RICHARD D. IRWIN, INC.

HOMEWOOD, ILLINOIS

THIRD EDITION

First printing, January, 1955

Library of Congress Catalogue Card No. 54–12597

TO

U. Y. J.
B. H. J.
B. A. J.
C. U. J.
E. G. J.

Preface

The basic aim of the first edition of *Personnel Management,* published in 1947, and of the revised edition of 1951, was to supply the collegiate student with a realistic study of principles and practices of personnel management. And it was hoped that others, too, in various fields of, or related to, business might find value in it.

To these ends, the fact was kept in mind that the average college student usually possesses limited business experience and a small but acceptable appreciation of the problems of business administration. Effort was bent, therefore, to provide him with materials which, with the aid of good college teaching, would serve to give him a reasonably clear and usable insight into the field of personnel management without belaboring him with excessive and mechanical details. The emphasis was upon principles of personnel management, interspersed with digested descriptions of good practices and selected examples of generally accepted solutions to common problems.

The favorable reception accorded this text has been gratifying evidence that the basic assumptions upon which it was written and revised were correct. The preparation of the present, the third, edition has been undertaken with the same assumptions as guiding principles. Revision is again deemed necessary because, on the one hand, various users have kindly noted a number of changes in style, order of presentation, and emphasis which would serve to improve the text for the student and the instructor. These suggestions the author has accepted with gratitude, and they have been incorporated throughout the text.

The need of revision has been suggested, on the other hand, in order to record changes in federal legislation, labor-management relations, and practices in personnel management. New interpretations, refinements, and revisions have been made in such basic laws as the Social Security Act, the Fair Labor Standards Act, and the Labor Management Relations Act. Labor-management relations show signs of change from warfare to maturing acceptance of each other's rights and responsibilities. The importance of such practices as programming, executive development, communications, and research has increased in the past several years. The recent contributions of psychology and sociology to interpersonal group dynamics have also been deserving of greater attention. And the developments in automation and atomic power have called for a re-examination of the role of personnel management.

With such significant changes in the making, the timeliness of this revision is apparent. Moreover, it was felt that some revision of the questions at the end of each chapter and the inclusion of new case problems at the end of the text would serve to increase the student's understanding of personnel principles and practices. To this end, some questions are designed to review the specific materials of the text, and others to open new vistas whose exploration requires study of materials outside the scope of the text.

The chapter outline is based primarily upon the broad functions which personnel management must perform in order to build an effective working force. To begin with, however, attention is directed to the scope of personnel management, major factors in personnel problems and labor relations, and the organization of personnel work. Here are stressed the managerial functions, procedures, and relationships which are universally significant in personnel work.

Attention is then turned to the major tasks of procuring, developing, maintaining, and using an effective working team. Specifically, such detailed topics as specifying job and labor requirements, screening and interviewing employees, training employees and executives, evaluating jobs and employees, handling grievances and disciplinary cases, collective bargaining with employees, and research and control of personnel functions are taken up. Much material in connection with these topics has been taken from industry, but pertinent examples in the fields of distribution and office work were not overlooked.

In regard to the detailed topics, the discussion is concerned with (1) factors to be considered, (2) organizational relationships involved, (3) purposes to be served, (4) principles and policies to be followed, and (5) techniques, tools, and devices to be used. Of course, it has not been possible to establish absolute boundaries in the outline of the text. An important reason for this is that some functions, such as interviewing, are related to a variety of tasks—for example, selection, guidance, and disciplinary action. Moreover, some problems, such as those of a morale nature, are widely ramified and may find their source in poor supervision and bring on such other problems as grievances. And, finally, some devices, such as job analysis, have multi-uses and can be used in connection with training, job evaluation, and employee selection. Therefore, a certain amount of crisscrossing is inevitable, yet pedagogically desirable.

Throughout the text, concern is felt for the problems which confront the personnel manager. The realistic and challenging nature of these problems is recognized. Were it not for the numerous problems which face him or which are likely to arise, there would be little need for the personnel manager or for the personnel function. Yet, the existence of such problems is not cause for pessimism. Indeed, when management is willing to face issues squarely rather than to seek to hide them, or to hide from them, it is a hopeful sign. As the challenge is met, the solutions will reduce the frictions which might otherwise lead to grave breakdowns.

So the student in this field who seeks to serve the cause of better labor-management relations may best do so by preparing to tussle intelligently with its problems and by avoiding a dissipation of his efforts in idealistic or wishful thinking. In these efforts, scientific personnel management has much to offer; and it, along with other specialized fields of human knowledge, constitutes one of the most hopeful avenues to the goal of better labor relations.

It is to be expected that various teachers will desire to follow somewhat different sequences of materials than that followed in the present chapter outline. There is no reason why those so inclined should not do so. For example, some might prefer to take up the materials on grievances earlier than presented in the text. Or the material on job evaluation and classification might be taken up after that on job requirements. Such preferences are within the realm of personal choice; and such flexibility of arrangement is easily possible with the materials of this text.

The author also wishes to note that there are details which this text does not cover. Times and conditions change too rapidly to be able to incorporate improvements being made in so many scattered locations and companies. Besides, it is felt that the teacher is in the best position to assay the latest developments as they occur and to use the best ones to spice his own lectures and discussions. Moreover, the author believes that an "encyclopedia" does not make for an effective textbook. But with basic good practices of the text, and a good teacher's zest, the student can be provided with an analysis, a personal touch, and a philosophy that no textbook can ever expect to achieve alone.

In short, this third edition is offered as an adjunct to—not as a substitute for—the good teacher. It is offered in the hope that his efforts of teaching will be more productive and satisfying to the student, and ultimately to those whom the student will serve. And it is offered with the understanding that times and conditions in the field of personnel management will change, but always, it is hoped, for the better.

It is impossible to list here all of those to whom the author is indebted for aid in the preparation of the original and revised editions of this book. Among those who were of assistance, it is a pleasure to mention Professor Ralph C. Davis, of the Ohio State University, whose ideas on organizational and morale matters were invaluable; Mr. Cloyd Steinmetz, of the Reynolds Metals Company, who took time to give constructive suggestions on a number of the chapters; Professor Frank Luken, of Villa Madonna College of Covington, Kentucky, who contributed a number of case problems from his store of business experiences; and the members of the Central Ohio Personnel Association, who provided unlimited access to their practical fund of personnel practices and principles. Thanks are also due to those who submitted critical readings of the earlier editions and to the large numbers of instructors who offered suggestions and comments for use in the revision. To all these the author expresses his fullest gratitude, while at the same time absolving them of any connection with such shortcomings as the text may have.

MICHAEL J. JUCIUS

COLUMBUS, OHIO
December, 1954

Table of Contents

Table of Cases

CHAPTER 1

The Field of Personnel Management

THE CHALLENGE OF HUMAN RELATIONS

From many sides, in numerous ways, we are constantly being reminded of the overwhelming importance of labor-management relations. All forms of news agencies carry reports on conditions in such relations; governmental officials and politicians make them matters of prime concern; and business and union leaders agree that they constitute a field of first magnitude.

Even were one disinclined to believe the findings of the foregoing groups, one's own personal experiences from childhood to old age would be impressive proof of the contention that getting along with others in business or industry comprises a large segment of one's life. With many people, their jobs take up most of their time. Moreover, personal aspirations, interests, fears and joys, and matters of family and community discussions and problems are often tied into the job one holds.

Since human relations in business (and in other areas of human endeavor, too) are so pervasive, it is easy to understand why, in recent years, so much attention has been directed to the consideration of problems arising in this area. Moreover, it takes no great prophet to forecast that even more attention will be directed to them in the coming years. This is not an admission that conditions here are on the downgrade. Rather, it is based upon the fact that more and more groups, as well as the individuals themselves, are realizing that there is no greater challenge than that of learning how to live and work together in greater harmony and with greater satisfaction to all concerned.

PROBLEMS OF HUMAN RELATIONS

Many problems beset this challenge. Their breadth and importance may be quickly seen in the following classification of who is interested in labor problems:

1. The efforts of labor to improve its economic, political, and social position by means of—

1

    a) The personal powers of the individual worker
    b) Organized groups as contrasted with individual efforts
    c) Industry-wide as contrasted with company-wide activities

2. The efforts of employers to direct, utilize, and control labor in terms of—
    a) The individual worker
    b) Organized groups of workers
    c) The confines of a given factory, office, or other business enterprise
    d) Industry in general as an institution of production and distribution

3. The multilateral relations between labor, employer, government, and the general public in terms of—
    a) Economic aspects
    b) Social aspects
    c) Psychological aspects
    d) Political aspects
    e) Legal aspects

There is little uniformity in applying particular terms to any of the subjects outlined above. "Industrial relations," for example, has been used to refer to multilateral relations between employers, labor, and government. To other users it means the relations between labor and management within the confines of a given factory or office. The term "labor relations," in the language of one user, may refer to collective bargaining, and, in that of another, it may refer to the "human" aspects which are significant in a given situation as opposed to the mechanical skills. And still others have tagged some of these subjects with such terms as "human engineering," "labor management," "personnel services," "personnel administration," and "manpower management." Because of the absence of standard definitions, the reader must make certain that he is aware of the meanings of particular terms in any given case. Only in this way can the student make certain whether or not two persons who are using the same term, such as "industrial relations," are really using it in the same sense. Unfortunately, as yet, the field of personnel management suffers from semantic difficulties.

SCOPE OF PERSONNEL MANAGEMENT

It is now pertinent to inquire into the precise nature of personnel management. What is presented here is done solely as a springboard for analysis and not with the claim that the final word is being said on the subject. The discussion in Chapter 2 will serve as sufficient warning that this area is one that is in constant flux. With this in mind, personnel management is described here as follows:

The field of management which has to do with planning, organizing, and controlling:

various operative functions of procuring, developing, maintaining, and utilizing a labor force, such that the—

a) objectives for which the company is established are attained economically and effectively
b) objectives of all levels of personnel are served to the highest possible degree
c) objectives of the community are duly considered and served

1. MANAGERIAL PHASES. This broad statement emphasizes, to begin with, that personnel management is a responsibility of management. This does not preclude others from participating in consideration of matters important to them. It does mean, however, that management must assume constructive leadership in personnel work, else the principle of specialization of effort is violated. Such managerial specialization encompasses three specific functions: planning, organizing, and controlling.

The planning functions pertain to the steps taken in developing a personnel program and in specifying what and how operative personnel functions are to be performed. Such plans are often unwritten, but it is usually preferable to set down such programs in printed form.[1] More is said on this subject in Chapter 3.

After plans have been developed, organizing is next in order. This step calls for procurement of necessary staff to carry out the plan, selection of necessary equipment, and establishment of lines of authority and communication between the various parties working with, or receiving benefit from, the personnel plans. Which aspects of plans will be handled by the personnel department and which by the line executives must be determined in this managerial phase. In Chapter 4, various schemes of organizing personnel work will be discussed.

It is of interest that some companies are assigning the study and planning for organization structures to the personnel division. This is being done because key personnel are such an important part of developing good structures, because job and duty analysis is an accepted part of personnel work, and because organizational changes often involve numerous hirings, layoffs, transfers, and promotions—all in the province of the personnel division.

By means of control, management first gives active direction to the personnel program and, second, evaluates results in comparison with desired objectives. The first phase of control is like the navigation of a ship. Controls guide the personnel ship along the lines laid out in the

---

[1] American Management Association, *How to Establish and Maintain a Personnel Department* (Research Report No. 4) (New York, 1944), pp. 18–23. This report contains an excellent example of such a plan.

program. When the ship docks (at the end of the program year, let us say), controls are exercised to determine how effectively desired personnel objectives were attained. Thus through direct observation, direct supervision, as well as reports, records, and audits, management assures itself that its organization is carrying out planned personnel programs.

2. OPERATIVE PHASES OF PERSONNEL WORK.   In the second place, the foregoing definition places emphasis upon four broad and fundamental phases of personnel work. These arise out of the fact that a working force must be procured, developed, maintained, and utilized. Each function must be performed effectively.

Each involves, of course, many detailed duties and tasks. "Procurement" calls for performance of such functions as locating sources of supply, interviewing applicants, giving physical and mental tests, and guiding selected applicants. "Development" calls for training and education, morale building, good communication between executive and worker levels of the organization, promotion and transfer plans, suggestion systems, and similar plans. "Maintenance" encompasses aspects of all activities in so far as they serve to support the skills and favorable attitudes of employees. Adequate wages and working conditions, supervision, grievance machinery, recreational and social programs, and housing plans are cases in point. Of course, all of the foregoing impinge upon the "utilization" of labor. Here lies the focal point of all personnel effort because the key to the success or failure of all personnel plans is the working effectiveness of the employee.

A discussion of operative functions is out of place at this point, but, merely to illustrate their nature, the following list is worth scanning:

    I. Employment
        1. Source of labor supply
        2. Reception of applicants and interviews
        3. Investigation of references
        4. Physical examinations
        5. Employment tests
        6. Final selection and placement
        7. Introduction to the job
        8. Provision for equipment, locker facilities, etc.
        9. Continued contact
       10. Personnel records
       11. Transfers and promotions
       12. Exit interviews and terminations

   II. Wages and hours
        1. Wage scales
        2. Salary and wage standardization

      3. Incentive plans
      4. Overtime pay
      5. Profit-sharing or bonus plans
      6. Hours
      7. Holidays
      8. Vacations

III. Working conditions

      1. Plant housekeeping
      2. Ventilation and lighting
      3. Sanitary facilities
      4. Rest periods
      5. Eating facilities

IV. Training and education

      1. Training on the job
      2. Company courses, conferences, and lectures
      3. Co-operation with outside agencies
      4. Employee manuals
      5. Employee publications
      6. Bulletin boards
      7. Library
      8. Facts about the company
      9. Suggestion system

V. Safety

      1. Safeguarding hazardous occupations
      2. Safety education
      3. Workmen's compensation

VI. Health

      1. Physical examinations
      2. Health education
      3. First aid in company hospitals
      4. Home visiting
      5. Laboratory studies

VII. Economic security

      1. Steady employment
      2. Unemployment insurance
      3. Life insurance
      4. Accident and health insurance
      5. Retirement plan
      6. Hospitalization plan
      7. Thrift and savings plan
      8. Housing program

VIII. Contacts with employees

      1. Opportunities for personal contacts between management and employees
      2. Open channels for grievances

3. Consultation with employees on matters of mutual interest
4. Collective bargaining

IX. Service activities
1. Athletics and recreation
2. Social activities
3. Employees' clubs
4. Discounts on employees' purchases
5. Legal aid
6. Charities

X. Research and statistics
1. Job analysis
2. Accident records
3. Labor turnover studies
4. Absenteeism and tardiness
5. Analyses of personnel policies
6. Wage levels and cost of living
7. Personnel programs and methods
8. Labor legislation

To perform these tasks, management must employ a variety of tools, devices, forms, records, and procedures. As a consequence, these forms sometimes seem to be the substance of personnel work. They are a means to an end, however, and should be viewed as such. To allow forms to become the keystone of a personnel program is to convert personnel management into a clerkship.

3. OBJECTIVES. The description of personnel management, in the third place, stresses the point that personnel work is intended to attain a number of important objectives. High place must at once be given here to success in producing a service or commodity which earns a reasonable profit. The success achieved in producing a commodity or service and in earning, in turn, a profit is patently dependent upon the effectiveness with which the various members of the business team work together. Personnel management must seek, therefore, to make labor as effective a contributor to the success of the enterprise and its owners as possible. Unless a particular enterprise is successful, it can neither continue to exist nor have use for labor or management.

The foregoing definition recognizes clearly and unequivocally that the performance of personnel duties must also keep in view the best interests of labor itself. Although it is not always possible to determine accurately what the best interests of labor are and although the interests vary from time to time, nevertheless, personnel management must face this issue fairly and squarely. Indeed, management must seek more earnestly than ever before to assure labor that it is receiving a fair deal. Else others will be more than eager, in ways which may run counter to those considered good by the employer, to help labor attain desired goals. And, finally, personnel management must seek to preserve and advance the general welfare of the community. No company operates in an economic world alone; each company must make adequate contributions and adjustments to the social and political aspects of community life.

In summary, this analysis of personnel management may seem somewhat idealistic. After all, few companies are performing all the personnel functions cited here, and all companies do not take the views toward labor proposed here. Nevertheless, the practices and viewpoints of companies which have had the best results from their personnel activities tie in closely with the foregoing suggestions. And in the future, even more so than at present, a total program must encompass carefully considered practices of personnel if a given company expects to retain its position in our economic world.

RESPONSIBILITY FOR PERSONNEL MANAGEMENT

To whom shall responsibility for this field of personnel management be assigned? In the minds of many, the answer may be the personnel manager or some individual with a similar title having reference to the head of a formal personnel department. Without doubt, this is a popular and growing conception.

However, in the final analysis, and in terms of actual labor-management problems, personnel management should be viewed as a major phase of every member of management. From the lowest supervisor to the topmost executive position—whether a man be in production, sales, accounting, or what not—he must be considered a personnel manager, and he should so conduct himself.

To carry out his responsibilities in this area, an executive soon realizes how heavy is the burden that is added to the load which his specialized assignment entails. He therefore welcomes the assistance and advice which a competent personnel department can provide. Because line executives are turning more and more to such departments for help, the personnel department has grown in stature in recent years. This growth may sometimes seem to place responsibility for personnel work in such a department. The idea should never be allowed to gain acceptance, however, that line executives have consequently been relieved of personnel responsibilities. To repeat, line and other executives are in positions from which personnel relations cannot be removed; what help they can receive from a personnel department should supplement their efforts, not supplant them.

The formal personnel department is the accessory rather than the main vehicle of labor-management relations. Whatever is said about a personnel department in this textbook should be related to the work of line executives, who ultimately are the keys to successful personnel activities. Indeed, it is the manner in which first-line supervisors apply personnel policies which will usually make or break any personnel program.

THE PERSONNEL EXECUTIVE

The foregoing review has served to point out the general area of personnel management. Another view of the field may be had by commenting upon the qualifications which a person should possess if he aspires to an executive position in this field.

Very frequently one hears from those seeking to prepare themselves for personnel work that they made the choice because they "like to work with people." This is highly commendable but should scarcely be the deciding factor. After all, one must "like to work with people" in almost all fields of professional and technical endeavor. Moreover, the words "working with people" are too indefinite—they may mean such things as helping others out of trouble (of which there are many kinds, and not all are of interest to the business enterprise); simply liking to work side by side with others (no more than ordinary gregariousness); and telling people what they should or should not do (often a mere desire for power). Hence, desirable as it may be to possess the quality of liking others, there are other qualities which are more significant and found less often in aspirants to positions in personnel work.

The degree of success which an executive can hope to attain is dependent largely upon his managerial and technical skill and ability. In the case of personnel executives, technical skill most certainly must be buttressed by managerial skills. In the case of line executives, to their functional technical skills must be added those pertaining to personnel relations. In either case a premium is placed upon the ability to plan, organize, and control the work of others. The emphasis is upon managing the work of others, not upon doing the work oneself. To be sure, one's qualities of leadership are in part determined by how well one knows the problems and techniques of one's subordinates. But technical skill is much more commonly found than that which calls for ability to direct others, to co-operate in the work of other executives, and to fit one's department into the procedural and organizational structure of the enterprise.

The need of managerial training in personnel work is being increasingly recognized by business, as may be seen in the following statement on the subject by the American Management Association:

It is difficult to prescribe absolute or inflexible requirements of specialized education, training and experience for personnel work. However, the broad pattern of a desirable background may be outlined:

1. Regardless of the extent of the candidate's formal education, he should have completed at least a few courses bearing directly on personnel work. Basic preparation for a personnel position should include some training in psychology (primarily abnormal, industrial, and social), labor problems, labor legislation, sociology, statistics, economics, personnel administration, and general management. Personnel practice of an advanced nature requires familiarity with the specific techniques involved in interviewing, employment testing, personnel record-keeping and personnel research. In the modern personnel setup a further knowledge of job analysis and evaluation, merit rating, and collective bargaining is daily growing in importance.

2. Previous industrial or business experience in the ranks and in an executive capacity is valuable in developing an understanding of the problems of general management as well as a realistic attitude toward personnel problems. (Some personnel executives also cite experience in teaching, vocational guidance, educational personnel work, and social work as providing a good background for specialization in industrial personnel work.)

3. A period of apprenticeship in a personnel department supervised by an able executive is especially advantageous in developing the required insight into human relations and sound concepts of personnel practice.

4. Most valuable is a record of *successful* organization and development of a personnel program for one or more companies.[2]

The executive and professional aspects, perhaps even more than the technical, are stressed in the foregoing statement. This is to be expected because, more and more, the personnel executive is being given a job which calls for, first, technical study and training beyond the borders of mere trade knowledge; second, large responsibilities toward the individuals he is expected to serve; and, third, a high level of ethics in dealing with labor and management. As long as personnel work is viewed as a routine skill, it has no claim to professional status. But when personnel executives themselves establish high standards of performance for themselves and adopt high standards of ethical conduct, labor and the general public will not be long in according them the professional status to which they legitimately aspire.

EDUCATION OF PERSONNEL MANAGERS

It is undoubtedly true that many executives performing functions of personnel management either as a phase of their regular job or as a staff service to others learned about personnel work on the job, by self-experience and by self-education. Acquiring competence in this school

---

[2] "The Qualified Personnel Director," *Personnel,* November, 1945, p. 141.

of hard knocks is invariably time-consuming, costly, and full of hazards, although it is sometimes the only course available.

Because the "graduates" of this school of experience themselves advise the acquisition of formal training when possible, it is understandable why more and more companies are seeking to fill their personnel staffs with individuals who have had such training. For example, in a recent survey[3] of practicing personnel executives, it was reported that the executives recommended that such courses as the following be included in a college training program: English, economics, psychology, statistics, public speaking, industrial management, time and motion study, personnel management, labor relations legislation, labor problems, job evaluation, and psychological testing. And it would be remiss not to add to this list such courses as industrial sociology, ethics, and business policies and management.

A recommendation such as this does not imply that formal education is the only answer to preparing for a career in personnel work. It does carry weight in the recognition it gives to the coming professional status of personnel management. Here, as in other fields, competence to serve in personnel work will be better achieved if formal education and working experience are combined in the best proportions. And education need not stop with a college degree and may continue through postgraduate courses and certainly should include personal self-education.

QUESTIONS AND PROBLEMS

1. Look up the definition of the term "problem." Does the definition imply a criticism of anyone when it is applied to the field of labor-management relations? Explain.

2. By what means can the attention of labor and management be directed to the solution of problems rather than to recriminations against each other?

3. How can a number of groups be at one and the same time "responsible" for labor-management relations? Indicate in what respects the term "responsibility" is being used in connection with a specific group.

4. Check the definition of personnel management given in this text against personnel practices in the companies in your community or in companies with which you are acquainted. Explain any differences which you may note.

5. How would you proceed to prove the contention that personnel management is a specialized phase of management?

6. How are the managerial phases of personnel management related to the functional phases?

---

[3] Donald S. Parks, *Occupations*, February, 1948, p. 288.

7. Illustrate concretely examples of planning, organizing, and controlling personnel functions.

8. Some believe that a favorable attitude toward a broad and liberal program of personnel management is inconsistent with the profit motive. What is your position on this issue? Explain.

9. Does industry have social responsibilities? If so, what are they? Have the obligations changed much in the past fifty years?

10. Who, in the final analysis, is the personnel manager in an industrial or business enterprise? Upon what grounds do you justify your answer?

11. Why is training so essential to the devolpment of those interested in entering the field of personnel management? What is the alternative to formal training? What is the major shortcoming of the alternative?

12. What qualifications should be possessed by a personnel executive? How much weight would you give to the quality of "liking to work with people"?

13. Discuss the importance of leadership qualities in a job specification for personnel managers. Contrast leadership qualities with those of technical requirements.

14. Is personnel management a profession? What are the fundamental requirements of a profession?

15. In the light of how personnel departments have grown in the past quarter of a century, how do you explain the labor unrest which so often reaches the newspaper headlines?

16. Make a list of various sciences and arts which have contributed to better labor-management relations. After each, indicate the contributions made.

17. Make a list of subjects about which the personnel manager should keep informed by reading or attending conferences. Isn't the list formidable? How can the personnel manager keep abreast of developments and still do his daily work?

18. To what types of organizations, professional and social, do you feel the personnel manager should belong? Explain.

19. What would you consider to be the best means and way of introducing those interested in entering personnel management into this type of work? If you have an acquaintance or can conveniently contact a person engaged in personnel work, ask his opinion on this question.

20. What have such groups as the American Management Association and the Society for the Advancement of Management to offer the personnel manager? Review some of the literature before submitting your answer.

CHAPTER

2

A Perspective of

Personnel Management

IMPORTANCE OF PERSPECTIVE

It must be apparent from the discussion in the foregoing chapter that personnel management is of great significance to many groups. To learn how its work may best be done requires a backward as well as a forward look. One cannot understand present and future prospects unless he is acquainted with the background of labor-management relations, with the major trends of historical development, and with basic forces operating in this field. Hence the major concern in this chapter will be with, first, historical factors in personnel management and, second, present and future prospects.

HISTORICAL CHANGES

Many impressive changes have taken place in the status and position of labor in the United States, particularly since the Civil War. Of course, comparisons with earlier periods and with conditions in foreign countries would be even more startling. For present purposes, however, a brief description and study of important changes during the period specified will suffice. Even for this period, however, desired information is not always available, which is evidence, by the way, of how recent is the development of interest in the general field of labor relations.

As certain interpretations are made here, it may seem that the intent is to criticize those in responsible positions of labor, management, and government. This is not so. The wisdom of hindsight surpasses that of foresight. Rather, the intent here is to note some of the lessons of changing labor conditions so that the student, first, will not view personnel management in the light of conditions that no longer exist; second, will see more clearly the forces that have brought about changes; and, third, will learn to be alert for signs of significant changes.

The forces that have been and are at work in the field of labor and management relations are closely intertwined. Hence, within the limited scope of these pages, any attempt to unravel the threads of cause and

12

effect must perforce be arbitrary and no more than suggestive. In the following discussion, a study of historical changes is based (with the knowledge that the classifications are not mutually exclusive) upon the following general classes or types of changes:

1. The cultural and social background of labor
2. The technological conditions of industry and commerce
3. The relations of government to business and labor
4. The relations of labor to management

CULTURAL AND SOCIAL BACKGROUND

In dealing with labor, it is essential to know the cultural and social background of labor. This follows because the attitude that labor (and, for that matter, any group of people) assumes toward its interests depends upon its conditioning background. In this respect, some significant changes have taken place in the United States since the Civil War. Although many forces are at work in this connection, study of trends in public education, urban and rural population, and immigrant versus native-born population as sources of workers, as well as the sociological pattern of labor, will be sufficient to illustrate how the make-up of labor has changed and continues to change.

1. EDUCATIONAL BACKGROUND. In regard to education, for example, a much larger percentage of the population is now enrolled in school. In the age group from five to twenty years, for example, the percentage of the population which attended school was under 60 in 1910, but over 70 in 1950. Another bit of evidence of interest along these lines is that almost six times as many enlisted men in military service during World War II had completed high-school training as those during World War I. Obviously, as the base of education broadens, the working population is bound to gain a new outlook that makes it question the status quo.

2. FACTORS OF IMMIGRATION. Changes in the population make-up, too, are also striking. For example, the relation between native-born population and that due to immigration has changed drastically. Immigration provided a major source of the population increase from 1880 to 1910. This fact is of great significance because the immigrants usually fall into the working-age group of the population, whereas the native-born figures also include those too young to work. Since 1910, however, the wave of immigration has fallen off rapidly. Indeed, during the decade starting with 1930, emigration exceeded immigration. Since the late thirties, however, immigration has slightly exceeded emigration.

Such changes in the working population are of vital consequence to the student of personnel management. Gone, except for insignificant numbers, are the immigrants who viewed working conditions here as far superior to those of the lands from which they came. Gone are those who had a standard of comparison (or at least their standards have been changed after long years in the United States) based upon undesirable and sometimes despotic living and working conditions. In their place is largely a working population whose framework of reference and comparison makes them unwilling to accept the word of the "boss" as final and unequivocal. Labor wants to know what is going on and often wants to have a voice in affairs affecting its interests. In short, the fact that immigration has virtually stopped should be enough to warn the alert student that one is no longer dealing with employees who are willing to accept without question any working conditions.

3. RURAL AND URBAN POPULATION.   Another trend of population change of interest here is that relating to changes in the rural and urban population. These changes are impressive. From 1850 to 1950, the percentage of the population living in rural areas has decreased from about 85 per cent to about 35, a decrease of almost 60 per cent. On the other hand, the urban areas have been growing. A striking example of this may be seen in the fact that there were no cities of a million in 1850; but in 1950, 12 per cent of the population lived in such centers.

As greater numbers of workers congregate in large cities, they become less independent than they once were. They are affected more directly by the business cycles and less by the cycles of agricultural plenty and scarcity. Less and less can they fall back upon their own resources when depression hits. Their views consequently revolve with increasing intensity around the need of attaining economic security. Perhaps for this reason, the contention is heard frequently that business must accept certain social responsibilities, which is another way of saying that business must be prepared to support labor during bad, as well as good, times.

4. SOCIOLOGICAL PATTERNS OF LABOR.   Perhaps the most significant change in the background of labor is that pertaining to its sociological status in the community and, as a consequence, in its place of work. At one time, labor enjoyed relative stability regarding its place in the community and in industry. Most workers had a sense of security deriving from this relative stability. From the job a worker held, he was accorded a definite place in the eyes of his fellow workers and his neighbors. This scale of prestige values was informal, yet was recognized and respected by all concerned. A worker knew that, if his current job was low in the scale of values, there was a ladder of jobs of greater prestige

and status which he might climb through the years. Thus the existence of an established and relatively unchanging framework provided a basis of security and satisfaction which served to engender a minimum of individual discontent and class warfare.

But, for a number of reasons, this rigid structure began to change. Technological mass production, concentration of financing in a few large cities, and improvements in communication brought telling changes in the mode of living in almost all our urban areas. As a consequence of these, the worker saw his chance to move upward through a well-organized series of trades destroyed by technical changes which leveled most jobs to a uniform status of repetitive mechanization. He saw his "boss," once owner of the plant with power to decide, a significant member of the community, become an employee like himself. New owners, who were established elsewhere far from the worker's everyday problems and little concerned, if at all, with the affairs of his community, decided his working conditions. He saw the departure of younger members of the community who might have tended to continue and respect the social practices of old; and he saw them replaced by influxes of strange workers who cared little for community traditions or existing relationships.

As this change proceeded, the relative harmony which had prevailed in labor-management relations was replaced by increasing degrees of discontent. As the sense of security of social and economic status was being reduced, uncertainty entered more and more into the worker's thinking and actions. He became restive because his job gave him neither prestige nor security, he could not look to his boss as a pillar of the community, and his faith in the future was shaken. And, while once he had felt that his place of work was a contributor to his well-being, he began to conclude that it was perhaps his enemy. So case after case materialized in which a pattern of harmonious community relations was replaced by suspicion, antagonism, and non-co-operation.

This factor of the impact of sociological patterns upon labor-management relations cannot be overestimated. How any employee feels about his job and his company is greatly influenced by how his neighbors rate and respect them. The status accorded him has a strong effect upon his sense of satisfaction and stability. Unfortunately, the forces at work in our modern society seem to portend more unsettled, rather than more settled, trends in our social and group relations. Hence the student of personnel management should be prepared to recognize these disturbing factors. Nor need he become unduly pessimistic about the future, because there is good reason to believe that, having recognized the existence of disturbing sociological forces, a big step is taken in also recognizing that something must be done about them if better labor-management relations are to be developed.

TECHNOLOGICAL CHANGES

Technological changes in industry, commerce, and communication have also played a leading role in the growth of personnel management. From a system of manufacturing in which various products were made in the home, there has evolved one in which large numbers of workers are brought together under the immense roofs of modern factories. Ac-

TABLE 1

ESTIMATED RELATIVE SUPPLY OF "WORK ENERGY" FROM MINERAL
FUELS AND WATER POWER, WORK ANIMALS, AND HUMAN
WORKERS, 1850–1960, IN PERCENTAGES*

Year	Mineral Fuels and Water Power	Work Animals	Human Workers
1850	5.8	78.8	15.4
1860	6.5	79.2	14.3
1870	11.5	73.1	15.4
1880	17.2	68.6	14.2
1890	27.5	60.5	12.0
1900	37.8	51.7	10.5
1910	56.9	34.7	8.4
1920	73.5	20.8	5.7
1930	83.7	11.7	4.6
1940	90.0	6.4	3.6
1950	94.0	3.0	3.0
1960	96.3	1.3	2.4

* Source: J. Frederic Dewhurst and Associates, *America's Needs and Resources* (New York: Twentieth Century Fund, 1947), p. 787.

companying this change has been a transition from manufacturing operations carried on manually with the aid of simple tools to operations that are complex, integrated, and in which power-driven equipment predominates. These changes may be seen more dramatically in the figures in Table 1. It is shown here that the contribution of human energy to the total supply of work energy is estimated to have decreased from 15.4 to 3.0 per cent from 1850 to 1950. The estimate for "mineral" energy shows an increase of from 5.8 to 94.0 per cent for the same period. In other words, within this relatively short span of time, the physical work of manufacturing has been largely turned over to the machine.

As might be expected, such technological changes have left their impact upon labor. Instead of large numbers of craftsmen, the working population is now made up largely of machine tenders, desk workers, and service employees. Instead of jobs in which employees have opportunities for initiative and craftsmanship, the average factory job, in and of itself, is repetitious and more restrictive. Instead of experiencing the satisfactions of planning and creating in their jobs, the workers too often were "cogs" in a machine. Moreover, the workers have been separated from their tools and have lost a strong link with pride in this work. Of course, there are offsetting social gains of mass production. Nevertheless, the worker has lost something in the working situation which must be gained elsewhere (as some believe, in the structure of unions) if his working days are to be anything more than an uninspiring round of drudgery.

When such technological changes take place suddenly, as they often have, many workers find themselves replaced by machines. That such changes may be beneficial in the long run provides little satisfaction to the workers suffering from "technological unemployment." And the effects of technological unemployment may well be accentuated in the current beginnings of automation. This refers to the attempts to develop and operate self-regulating, mechanized manufacturing operations. So far, success has attended efforts to achieve automation in producing major parts of products. As this trend gains momentum, new problems of human relations will develop: how to develop the needed large numbers of engineers, maintenance employees, and technicians; how to provide for employees displaced by machines; how to provide incentives for employees who themselves are subject to the control of machine speeds; and how to design supervisory and organizational techniques to meet these new challenges. These are major questions which changes in technology have raised regarding the relations between management and labor, some of which will be touched on shortly in this chapter.

THE ROLE OF GOVERNMENT

Momentous changes have also taken place in the relation of government to labor and business. This may be seen in (1) government attitudes to labor and management, (2) the growing strength of unions, and (3) legislative changes.

1. GOVERNMENTAL ATTITUDES. From an earlier attitude of general disinterest and passiveness, government has in some cases taken giant steps in the direction of positive intervention. And from a role in which it tended invariably to side with capital, government has turned more and more in the direction of becoming a protagonist and guardian of the interests of labor. Perhaps the increasing proportion of votes that are coming from the side of labor has much to do with this change.

About the time of the Civil War and for some time afterward, labor possessed few powerful friends in governmental circles. The concept of interstate commerce had not been extended to cover manufacturing, so that the legislative branch of the federal government was in no position to interest itself in the problems of the workingman. The state assemblies were preoccupied with such matters as expansion and state versus federal rights and therefore had little time to become concerned with labor matters. Moreover, the nation was as yet largely an agricultural, pioneering, and maritime country, so that labor problems arising in industry and commerce were in the minority and so were easily passed over.

Then, too, the executive branch of the federal government had not yet attained any real measure of political strength. It was without the power to have helped labor, even had it been disposed to do so; and the judicial branch was preoccupied with precedent and historical views of property rights, so that it sided more often than not with capital interests whenever arguments with labor arose. Indeed, court injunctions were a favored and easily obtained weapon of employers to combat picketing and boycotts, to stop strikes, and to limit union activities.

2. GROWING STRENGTH OF UNIONS.   However, the hand of labor gradually gathered political and economic strength. Evidence of growing strength may be found in the trends of membership in unions. A few unions, such as those of the typographers, stonecutters, and hat finishers, were in existence about the time of the Civil War, but the membership was relatively small. Perhaps the first real strength of unions was displayed in the growth of the Knights of Labor, which reached a peak membership of about 700,000 in the 1880's. For various reasons, however, it went into a decline from which it never recovered. Nevertheless, this group left its imprint upon subsequent union activities.

Believing that the Knights of Labor were wrong in participating in political activities, others in the labor movement took steps to form the American Federation of Labor. The growth of this federation of local and autonomous unions has been slow but steady. Its membership has grown as follows:[1]

1881	45,000	1920	3,970,000
1890	220,000	1930	2,950,000
1900	550,000	1940	4,250,000
1910	1,580,000	1950	8,000,000

To these figures must be added membership in other unions in order to obtain a complete picture of union strength. As of 1950, total union

[1] R. A. Lester, *Economics of Labor* (New York: Macmillan Co., 1941), p. 550, and estimates of the U.S. Department of Labor.

membership has been estimated at sixteen million. Of this number, the Congress of Industrial Organizations, formed in 1935 to unionize workers on a vertical or industry basis as compared with the horizontal or craft basis of the American Federation of Labor, has somewhere in the neighborhood of six million members. Independent unions not included in the AFL and the CIO account for the other two million. Prominent here are the United Mine Workers of America, the International Association of Machinists, and the Railway Brotherhoods.

3. LEGISLATIVE CHANGES. As a consequence of the growing strength of unions, of disclosures by various groups of poor working conditions, of several costly strikes at the turn of the century, of an overly cautious restriction of labor by the courts, and of the more concentrated voting power of labor, the federal congress and some state assemblies began to take notice of labor matters. Various legislation was enacted, covering such subjects as restrictions upon the use of injunctions, outlawing of yellow-dog contracts, removal of labor unions from the scope of the antitrust laws, and the protection of the economic interest of labor in industrial disputes. Most labor legislation (with the exception of that relating to industrial compensation) traveled a rough road, especially through the courts; hence very little was actually accomplished until after World War I.

Beginning with a liberalization of the interpretation of the powers of the government in the field of public utilities, the movement to side with labor gained adherents. The Railway Labor Acts of 1926 and 1934 were a far step in this direction but were limited to public transportation. Not until the depression after 1929, which brought on the New Deal, however, did the government change its attitude in regard to helping labor. Quickly there came forth such legislation as the National Recovery Act, the National Labor Relations Act, the Social Security Act, the Fair Labor Standards Act. And after World War II, the significant Labor Management Relations Act was passed in 1947.

Most of this legislation was predicated upon changed concepts of interstate commerce and industry's social responsibilities. On the one hand, the federal congress proceeded upon the assumption (with which the courts largely concurred) that manufacturing and labor matters came within the province of interstate commerce. As such, they were consequently subject to federal regulation. On the other hand, there was a growing feeling that the economic security of labor was more or less a responsibility of industry. This view found favor, not because industry was necessarily at fault for economic crises, but because it was considered best able to assume the burden that the crises brought on.

Thus the federal government in all its branches—legislative, judicial, and executive (the latter in particular in recent years)—and many of the state assemblies have moved in the direction of strengthening the position of labor. The growth in number and strength of regulatory bodies is disturbing to some. They see the struggle over labor problems taking on more of the aspects of a continued fight between such agencies and management. They would prefer that such matters be handled by labor and management themselves.

Some contend that there is an undue bias in favor of labor. Perhaps this is so, because there are signs that the federal government, tiring of watching labor and management become overbearing at times, tends to view labor disputes more from the viewpoint of the public interest. Be that as it may, the point of this section, that the government has thrown much more weight to the side of labor, is abundantly evident.

RELATIONS OF LABOR TO MANAGEMENT

In the course of the foregoing changes, there has naturally come a significant change in labor's relation to the employer. The era of unquestioning acceptance of the decisions of the employer is on the wane. So, too, is the era of subservient labor. In their place looms a scene in which the working population is more or less articulate, highly organized, and politically potent. Labor not only has strong views regarding what it wants and the position to which it aspires but also has shown that it knows how to and can achieve its objectives. This does not mean that labor and employer are destined to an era of warfare. On the contrary, it might well be argued that equalization of strength is a prerequisite to more co-operative effort and mutual understanding of each other's problems. Indeed, labor-management relations that have developed in such industries as clothing, printing, and the steel industry on such matters as joint job evaluation, for example, are highly encouraging that co-operation is not a dreamer's ideal.

And it is important to repeat that these descriptions of change are intended, not to arouse arguments regarding the relative merits of the positions of labor and the employer, but to warn the student of personnel work that it is necessary to be alert to changes in fundamental conditions. Unless information on such changes is gathered and assimilated, it is impossible to establish effective personnel policies and programs.

CONCEPTS OF LABOR

Another perspective of this field may be taken by examining the attitudes which employers have taken toward labor. Although there have been historical trends, there is much overlapping, so that it cannot be said either that one concept was held until such and such a date or that all are agreed upon a particular point of view at the present.

Until the turn of the present century, the most widely held view of labor was undoubtedly that it was just another factor of production. As such, it was to be handled like any other technical or economic resource of production. The main considerations were costs and returns. This meant, of course, that the emotional and social needs or characteristics of the individual were not the concern of the entrepreneur. Indeed, where these aspects were not actually frowned upon as being alien to the business scene, they certainly were disregarded. Perhaps something could be said for this concept if the emotional and social characteristics of labor could be segregated from, and did not influence, the working situation. Such, however, is obviously and simply impossible. Hence this attitude toward labor has proved untenable, although occasionally some employers may be seen casting longing glances in that direction.

As the weaknesses of the "factor-of-production" concept became more apparent, consideration began to be given to the human aspects of labor. This has taken a number of directions. Some employers have contended that, while human needs must be considered, they themselves are the best judges of how this should be done industrywise. And so, soon after 1900, a number of companies initiated personnel departments incorporating recreational, pension, and insurance programs. Where this approach has been sponsored in terms of what the employer thought was good for the employee, it has been given the name "paternalism."

Many who adopted this concept, however, found that the employees did not appreciate their well-intended efforts; some employees even went out on strike. As a result, two divergent paths have been taken. On the one hand, some companies have followed a hands-off policy. While they recognize that human values are involved in production, they contend that, because good wages and working conditions are provided, each employee will be in a position to take care of himself according to his own standards of what is "good" for him. Unfortunately for those who hold such views, pressures of competition, community practices, and union demands force them away from the course they would like to pursue.

On the other hand, there is a strengthening trend in the direction of co-operation between labor and management in attacking the human problems of labor. This co-operation may be on an individual or union basis, and it may be on a small scale or on an over-all basis. In any event, it represents an acceptance by industry of its "social responsibilities." To this end, the employer not only takes no steps which might harm the social and economic interests of labor but also takes positive steps to provide adequate bases of security and personal satisfaction. The assumptions here are that, if the personal and emotional needs of labor are assured and if this is done with the concurrence of labor, the technical skills of labor will be applied more effectively for the benefit of all.

In recent years the "human" aspect of labor has been expanded to stress sociological factors. There is growing recognition of the fact that labor must be "handled" not only in terms of individual characteristics but also in terms of its group reactions and needs. Thus lack of success in the past is ascribed to a failure to recognize that effectiveness and loyalty are conditioned as much by what an employee feels his fellow employees feel about his status in a group as by what he individually might like to do or say. From such studies as have been made of conditions where this concept has not been and has been followed, it seems to possess much in its favor as a desirable viewpoint to take in working with labor.

Another concept of labor which has pushed itself into the foreground is derived from the political power of labor. At one time this concept had little weight. In the case of the Knights of Labor, entrance into the political arena helped to bring about its decline. But since the 1930's the political power of labor cannot be doubted. Both the CIO with its Political Action Committee and more recently the AFL with its Labor's Educational and Political League give indication that, in addition to other political methods, the movement of labor both directly and indirectly in politics is likely to accelerate rather than slow down. And this applies to local and state levels as well as the federal level.

Political action in national and local politics finds its counterpart within the business enterprise. Certainly the term, "industrial democracy," which is often heard, refers to more direct participation in industrial affairs that affect the interests of labor. This goes beyond the normal role and mode of operation of the union. It implies a movement in the direction of a "partnership," in which many, if not all, major decisions in a business will be a matter of direct concern to labor as well as management. This has been formalized under the designation "codetermination" in Germany, where labor has by law been given a significant place on the board of directors of business concerns. Although the movement has not gained much headway here, it nonetheless represents a concept of labor which cannot be discounted.

In summary, management may approach its dealings with labor from any one of several viewpoints: the economic or "factor-of-production," various shades of the human and social, and various degrees of political and partnership. All have some bearing upon the matter of how to "get along" with labor in the best interests of all. It does seem that those who are giving greater weight to the human, social, and democratic aspects are more likely to be successful in their labor-management solutions. At least, this appears to be true for the foreseeable future.

PRESENT AND FUTURE PROSPECTS

Our present relations between labor and management stem from the past and will change as time goes on. By being aware of the forces that make for these dynamic changes, personnel management will be better prepared to deal with current problems and future uncertainties. What can be done in these matters can perhaps best be examined in terms of the following:

1. Possible approaches to personnel problems
2. Obstacles to completely satisfactory solutions
3. Factors contributing to better relations
4. Changing philosophies

APPROACHES TO PERSONNEL PROBLEMS

A number of approaches may be used by management in tackling the problems with which it is confronted. These may be classified into two large groups according to, first, the extent to which problems are anticipated and, second, the nature of facts brought to bear upon labor-management problems.

1. CURE AND PREVENTION. Looking, first, at the extent to which problems are anticipated, personnel management can tackle problems after or before they develop. For example, after an employee expresses resentment or belligerence, after a work stoppage occurs, or after a supervisor is faced with non-co-operation, steps are taken to correct the situation. Unfortunately, personnel management has been characterized largely by the use of curative methods.

There is a distinct trend toward the use of preventive measures. Management is attempting more frequently to anticipate possible sources of trouble or irritation and to take steps to minimize or eliminate the development of problems. Job evaluation and merit rating plans, to be discussed later in this book, are cases in point. By working out the relative value of various jobs in a company, it is possible to show employees why their respective jobs are worth a given amount in comparison with others. Thus grievances about wage rates that would otherwise arise may be minimized. Or, by making periodic ratings of employees, it is possible currently to show employees why they are or are not making progress. This helps reduce the number of situations in which some employees, to their disappointment, are unexpectedly informed that they cannot expect to progress any further in the company.

There are also those who are cognizant of the need of positive measures to maintain the equilibrium when relations between labor and management are said to be good. Such a desirable state of affairs is not looked upon as a lucky occurrence or one over which no control may be exercised. Rather it is considered important to study the signs, conditions, and causes of such a happy state of affairs so that its maintenance may be positively influenced. For example, recent studies of companies that have experienced long years of relatively satisfactory relations may provide personnel management with better suggestions than can the studies which stem from cases in which trouble has occurred. The analogy to this is the matter of studying healthy individuals as well as those who are ill. Certainly the general tenor of labor-management relations would be improved if those involved here were to raise their sights so that a healthy body of relations was the accepted standard of attainment.

Since problems seem to be the focal point of so much thinking in the field of personnel management, the question of prevention or cure will always be with us. Preventive measures, when they can be used, are obviously to be preferred to curative measures of personnel management. They are generally less expensive than curative measures, and they are more effective because they reduce the number of problems that must be handled. For example, careful selection of employees will reduce, among other things, the amount of training that need be given and the number of dissatisfied employees on the payroll. Moreover, preventive measures reduce the seemingly inevitable recriminations that flow from the application of curative solutions to such problems as grievances, disciplinary action, and hit-or-miss spot transfers when vacancies "unexpectedly" occur.

On the other hand, preventive measures call for a high degree of planning ability, foresight, and positive leadership in the personnel executive. These qualities can be cultivated and are worth cultivating. Although it is admitted that all problems of personnel cannot be anticipated and that, therefore, curative or "after-the-act" methods of solving personnel problems cannot be entirely discarded, nevertheless a significant test of a personnel executive is his ability to detect areas of friction and to develop plans to forestall their growth. Indeed, when personnel management assumes a dynamic, positive approach, looking toward constructive improvements in labor-management relations and interests, it will meet constructively the challenge of the future.

Thus it is important, when talking about a specific personnel problem, to know whether it is one that has developed or is likely to develop and is, therefore, to be headed off, if possible. The emphasis, type of thinking, and qualities of leadership to be exercised will differ. For example, what should be done after a strike occurs differs from what should be done to try to prevent a strike. What might have worked in the prevention of a strike would likely be futile after a plant is struck. In short, the adage of "crying about spilled milk" is applicable to personnel management. What can be done in a given situation depends upon whether we are looking forward or backward, and which view we take depends upon the nature of the problem. Has it happened? Or is it likely to happen?

2. FACTUAL BASIS OF LABOR PROBLEMS. Another way of looking at the approach to labor problems which personnel management employs is to note the basis used to solve problems. Such solutions may be founded upon one's own experiences, upon the experiences of others, or upon "scientific" analysis of problems.

Under the first-mentioned plan, the personnel executive reaches decisions in terms of his own experience, which are subject, therefore, to the wisdom which a limited personal experience can provide. When a problem is encountered, a decision is reached that the executive hopes will work; if it does not, then it is a case of "try something else." This is, in other words, a cut-and-try, hit-or-miss, or rule-of-thumb system. It is very simple and quick in execution but highly unpredictable in results. Nevertheless, it is undoubtedly the most widely used plan in personnel as well as other fields of management. This is unfortunate because such methods have so small a logical basis of explanation. Moreover, labor can have little confidence in a management that uses such an approach because it cannot check whether or not the decisions being taken are wise and justifiable.

Next, the executive may add the experience of others to his own before reaching a decision on labor problems. By means of attendance at conventions, discussions with various experts, visits to the plants of others, and study of business literature, the executive broadens the horizons of his limited experience. When a problem arises, the executive attempts to find in his files or his memory a plan or solution which someone else has used with success in similar circumstances. The selected plan is then applied to his own problem. This scheme for solving labor problems is relatively simple, not too expensive to use, and hence rather frequently applied. But finding plans of others that will fit one's own problems is often equivalent to looking for the proverbial needle in a haystack. Conditions in the plants or offices of others are seldom quite like one's own, and insignificant differences in conditions of application are enough to cause significant differences in ultimate results. And when one tries to explain to labor why the plan of a given company was selected, one may find a counterproposal that the plan of some other company should be chosen.

Finally, some executives attempt to solve their problems by scientific methods. Under this method, solutions are sought by gathering, analyzing, classifying, and interpreting pertinent data. Starting with a careful statement of the problem, the scientific system includes such major steps as establishing a working hypothesis, collecting data, reaching a tentative solution, checking the solution, and then applying the solution. Obviously, such an approach to problems of labor is time-consuming, often costly, and invariably calls for close attention to details. Hence this approach, though the best in theory, is the hardest to apply and hence the least frequently used. Yet it represents the line along which attempts must increasingly be made, since it is the only one that has a logical basis for continued success. And it is the only one in which both labor and management can join forces without fear that a solution prejudicial to the other is being sought. Since the emphasis is upon facts and logical analysis, the attention of both parties can be centered upon problem solving rather than upon watching each other and detecting the "tricks" that might be played to gain a personal and undeserved advantage.

In this connection, too, it is well to note that various sciences and arts have made and are likely to make even more significant contributions to better solutions to problems. As noted in the next few pages, such areas as psychology, sociology, and economics have been giving increased attention to more precise measurements and interpretations of labor-management relations. Hence there are firmer grounds for concluding that the future will bring better and improved methods of dealing with such problems.

OBSTACLES IN THE PATH OF PERSONNEL MANAGEMENT

It is well to recognize that the problems that confront personnel management are by no means simple. It is not child's play to tussle with such issues as fair wages, the way in which labor should exercise its voice in matters of interest to it, reactions to the political activities, and how far one has a right to go into matters pertaining to private lives and community affairs.

Complex though these problems are themselves, their solutions are made even more difficult by the following obstructions:

1. Precise methods of measuring labor's interests or contributions are lacking.
2. The human factor is difficult to interpret, and its probable future actions are difficult to forecast.
3. The common human shortcomings of ignorance, selfishness, and prejudice interfere with the applications of logical methods

If these obstructions could be removed, a long stride would be taken in reducing labor problems. For example, how much room for argument between management and labor could there be if a measuring device were available that could determine precisely what labor in a given case was worth? Imagine how quickly wage disputes could be settled with a "thermometer of wage rates." But such a device is non-existent, and it is improbable that one will be developed in the foreseeable future. Of course, methods of giving approximate answers are available, but they all leave much to be desired. Is it any wonder, therefore, that disputants over wage matters have recourse so often to tests of power in order to reach decisions in their quarrels? And is it any wonder, then, that labor-management problems, handled thus, have a habit of recurring?

The human factor also is a source of perplexing problems. On the one hand, it acts in ways that are often difficult to understand, let alone forecast. On the other hand, even the fairest of people is not above some selfishness or ignorance—sometimes reasonably so and sometimes not. Although it may be argued that the human race is improving in these matters, we still have a long way to go in learning how to live together peacefully and equitably.

These difficulties are cited as a warning to the student to be realistic about personnel matters. It would be much better if "logic" could alway be used by the personnel manager. Unfortunately, the perversity of nature and man must be considered. When "hit-or-miss" methods must sometimes be used, this should not give rise to cynicism; rather, it is only realistic to recognize the complete nature of things as they are. Moreover, there is no reason under such conditions why improvement rather than artificial perfection should be the test of results achieved.

FACTORS CONTRIBUTING TO BETTER RELATIONS

At this juncture it is well to stop for a moment and give credit to a number of fields of human knowledge which have contributed greatly to the improved solution of problems with which personnel management must deal. For example, from the area of psychology have come many of the principles and techniques applied in such fields as testing, interviewing, counseling, research, training, and motivation. To students of scientific management, personnel is indebted for contributions pertaining to the organization, direction, and administration of labor-management relations. From sociology, anthropology, and ethnology in recent years has come invaluable assistance in terms of group reactions and relationships, the influence of cultural and community patterns, and the significance of dynamic changes in such areas. To such fields as medicine and engineering, personnel management has for a long time been indebted for effective contributions in the areas of health, safety, accident prevention, and improved working conditions. And there are specialists such as statisticians, economists, and political scientists, whose very titles are sufficient to evoke clear pictures of the services they perform. From all these have come in recent years such advancements as operations research, cybernetics, and linear programming, which can aid in improving personnel planning and control.

A mere enumeration of these various areas of specialization is impressive evidence of the caliber of science and advanced art which is being brought to play in the area of personnel management. It indicates, on the one hand, the resources which can be brought to bear upon personnel problems. It indicates, on the other hand, the heavy responsibility which a personnel manager assumes in being sufficiently well acquainted with these subjects that he may use wisely the competence available in these fields. In short, the wise personnel manager seeks the aid of experts; he does not try to "do it all himself." He is aware of their capacities for service and is grateful for them.

A CHANGING PHILOSOPHY

From the perspectives that have been taken of the field, it is apparent that there is a striking change in the philosophy of management toward labor-management relations. How far or how fast this change will progress, no one can forecast. But it seems obvious that there is a trend in the direction of building personnel programs more and more in terms of labor's interests, labor's participation, and labor's characteristics.

While this change in direction has been accelerated by the pressures of union organization, impetus has also been provided by a change in fundamental management philosophy. As little as twenty-five years ago the prevailing attitude toward labor problems was that management alone should decide how these were to be handled; and this point of view was generally supported by a hit-or-miss method of solving such problems as management cared to consider.

Now one sees both a new attitude and a new methodology gaining managerial adherents. Labor problems are, on the one hand, being examined in the light of their emotional, sociological, and political implications. Such examinations are being extended beyond the borders of what happens in a particular company to the implications for the community, the nation, and even other countries. And the examinations are being based more and more upon factual analysis and scientific study. This changes the basis of solution from a personal one to a concerted attack upon problems by both labor and management. As an example, there are cases in which labor, as represented by unions, and management are jointly recognizing and attacking such problems as the need for cost reduction, thus eliminating the previous wrangles over attempts to undercut one another when cost reductions were sought.

There seems little doubt that the future will find increased participation by labor in labor-management relations. If this participation is to be of a high level, labor must be educated in the implications of these relations. Personnel management can do much in this regard. Through better communications between labor and management and through education in economics—which a number of companies have already undertaken—future relations can be improved. But more companies must adopt such programs. And more must seek to determine how all segments in our business enterprises can work together toward common objectives. The future must bring effective co-operation and less emphasis upon tests of strength.

QUESTIONS AND PROBLEMS

1. Are there evidences of historical change in your own community relative to labor-management relations? What are they, and what is their significance?

2. Not until recent years has any considerable number of students or practitioners of personnel management given much weight to the sociological aspects of labor-management relations. What is your opinion of this belated recognition?

3. How has the cultural and social background of labor in the United States changed since the Civil War? What effect have such changes had upon labor-management relations?

4. Explain the influence of immigration and size of communities upon the problems of labor relations.

5. If the "status" a person has depends upon so many factors apart from what has usually been considered "the normal working situation," what right has industry to interest itself in such matters? Cite some of these "factors" in your discussion.

6. If modern industrial conditions and modern community conditions have such an unstabilizing effect upon workers, what hope is there for the future?

7. What suggestions have you in regard to the problem of how to create interest for the worker in his job, which at present seems to be repetitive, monotonous, and uninspiring?

8. How have technological changes affected the growth of personnel management?

9. Indicate the differences to labor of the short-run and long-run effects of "technological unemployment."

10. It has been estimated that the average investment in equipment per employee is $10,000 in some industries. What has this to do with labor-management relations?

11. Do you view the greater role of government in labor-management relations with favor or disfavor? Cite examples of trends that please or displease you.

12. How has the relation of government to labor and business changed since the Civil War? To what causes would you attribute such changes?

13. When were the AFL and the CIO formed? How would you describe the times when they were formed and the growth which they have experienced?

14. The concept that industry should accept responsibility for labor's economic security is based upon what grounds? Do you expect this concept to be extended in the future? Why or why not?

15. Can you cite any labor legislation which indicates that some employee wants must be protected by statutes?

16. Why is it that most managements seem to prefer the use of curative methods? Is it due to the ineffectiveness, relatively speaking, of the preventive methods?

17. What obstacles stand in the way of perfect solutions to labor problems? What room is there for optimism even though perfect solutions are never obtained?

18. Since "logic" cannot always be brought to bear upon the solution of labor problems, what are the alternatives? What safeguards or warnings would you suggest for the alternatives?

19. When the personnel manager avails himself of the services of various experts, such as statisticians and psychologists, how does that affect his own status? Does he become less important or not? Why?

20. What do you expect will be the status of personnel management a quarter of a century hence? You might find it of interest to write out your forecast and save it, to be checked at that later date.

CHAPTER

3 | Personnel Programming

A personnel program is a plan designed to aid in the accomplishment of desired objectives of business and of labor. It would seem a commonplace that the various phases of personnel work should be tied together into an integrated plan. Yet no better suggestion than this could be followed by anyone who works in the field of personnel management. Throughout one's associations in this field, this advice should be a guiding rule. Its importance is soon apparent to anyone who operates without such a plan. In such instances there are contradictions between objectives and policies, gaps in functions, and incorrectly staffed functions. The results are confusing and frustrating to all concerned.

On the other hand, a well-knit program is like a completed jigsaw puzzle. Each function of personnel relations complements the others. Good selection procedures, for example, reduce excessive training and abet good training. Or the disciplinary policies followed by a supervisor in one department are the same as those followed by others. As a consequence, consistency and uniformity characterize disciplinary cases. Again, such work as employee merit rating is restricted to what it can do and is not used as a shaky substitute for a poor job evaluation program or an ill-advised promotional system. And auditing of personnel work is not an afterthought but is planned for at the same time as the activities which the auditing procedure is intended to check.

Programming is, therefore, a recognition of the very important fact that all parts of personnel work are interacting. What happens in a given phase of personnel work sooner or later has an effect upon other phases. Hence, when one contemplates following a particular personnel course, one must weigh what affect it will have upon, and how it is affected by, other functions. It is not feasible in a textbook to show in each chapter the effect of the materials in other chapters. Yet this idea of interrelationships is a practical truism and must be constantly remembered by the practitioner in personnel relations.

To aid in understanding this idea of interrelationships, this chapter is devoted to programming. It must be noted at once, however, that the technical functions blueprinted by a program will be taken up in detail in subsequent chapters. Attention here will be turned to the parts of programming and the work that must be done in preparing a program. In particular, the discussion here on programming is taken up under the following headings:

1. Objectives to be sought through the program
2. Functions to be performed in seeking desired objectives
3. Assignment of responsibility for performance of functions
4. Policies guiding those responsible for programs
5. Principles upon which programs are based
6. Research needs of programming.

OBJECTIVES

THE IMPORTANCE OF OBJECTIVES

Perhaps the most fundamental factor in a personnel program is that of objectives. It is impossible, on the one hand, to establish effective personnel plans until one has definite ideas of what results one hopes to accomplish. For example, an effective hiring procedure cannot be designed until an estimate is obtained of the kinds and amounts of labor to be hired. Or a morale-building program cannot be designed just to raise morale; it must be based upon some definition of the amount or degree by which it is hoped to increase the willingness to co-operate. To cite but one more example, a pension plan, to be successful, must tie in with definitely stated employee desires as well as company goals.

On the other hand, it is difficult to prescribe remedies for personnel troubles that have developed if one does not know what the results should have been. Practical problems are often difficult to handle because frequently no one seems to have bothered in advance to determine, for instance, what a satisfactory wage rate is, how much a given employee should produce in a given day, or upon what basis transfers would be made. Unless definite goals are predetermined, it is difficult to determine what should be done after trouble develops. Moreover, when objectives are established after trouble ensues, employees often become very suspicious because they invariably conclude that the executives are making a case to suit themselves.

CLASSES OF PERSONNEL OBJECTIVES

To develop a concept of personnel objectives, it is necessary to study the objectives of the company of which personnel is a part. In general, the aims of most companies can be summed up as follows:

1. Primary objectives
    a) Produce and distribute an acceptable product or service
    b) Continuously yield satisfactory wages and salaries and other personal values to employees and satisfactory profits to investors
    c) Meet community and social obligations
2. Secondary objective
    a) Attain the primary objectives economically and effectively

1. SERVICE OBJECTIVES. At the outset, it is imperative to recognize the fundamental importance of the objective of service. Upon the successful attainment of this objective depends the attainment of all others. The performance of personnel functions must be directed, therefore, with a view to their ultimate influence upon the efficient and economical production of goods and services. A program directed toward educating all concerned about this relation is highly desirable. Otherwise, employees, and executives as well, are likely to forget that business, industry, and commerce are institutions developed by society for the purpose of satisfying the desires of its members for goods and services.

This may sound somewhat idealistic, but, if a given enterprise fails in this regard, it will be removed very realistically from the productive field by the liquidating process of bankruptcy. In other words, resources will no longer be allocated to it to continue unsuccessful operations. Looked at from the positive side, society rewards those who successfully produce goods and services by permitting them to continue to derive personal rewards and satisfactions from the business enterprise. In short, the successful servants of society—the successful producers—tend to make very satisfactory profits.

Some individuals try, shortsightedly, to misuse the business institution or take advantage of various interested groups in the institution. There is ample evidence of attempts to palm off inferior and shoddy merchandise, to cut wages unfairly, to employ cheap child and female labor to the ultimate disadvantage of the individuals concerned and of the community, and to charge exorbitant prices. Such practices eventually bring on punitive action—labor may organize to protect its interests, consumers may turn to other producers, and the government may enact restrictive regulations. Though the mills of the gods grind slowly, they grind with certainty, and the producer who cuts corners, no matter how cleverly, eventually cuts one too many.

Through all of its plans and programs, therefore, personnel management should seek to instill in employees an understanding of the significance of service and profits. Unfortunately, this has not been done enough. Even in cases where an attempt has been made to impart knowledge on these subjects, the need for such education too often has not been recognized until after labor trouble has occurred or is about to occur. Discussion of service and profits at such times smacks too much of "making cases." Hence it is far more effective to discuss these issues with employees while conditions are undisturbed; then the message is much more likely to gain acceptance and do good.

Of course, the objectives of service, efficiency, and profits do not take precedence over the personal goals that employees seek, nor vice versa. Obviously, the goals of employees also must be attainable, or trouble will ensue. Hence personnel management must give due consideration to the desires of employees. But what are the personal goals which must be satisfied?

2. PERSONAL OBJECTIVES. It is not difficult to list the kinds of goals that are generally in the minds of employees; but the question of how much of each kind is desired is another matter. Detailed comments on this aspect will be made in subsequent chapters. The wants of employees may be classified as follows:

1. Fair wages, hours, and working conditions
2. Economic security
3. Opportunity for advancement and self-improvement
4. Recognition and feeling of worth-while accomplishment and individual significance
5. Positive group feeling

a) Fair Wages and Working Conditions. The keystone of any personnel program is an acceptable wage structure. Unless employees are reasonably satisfied that their wages are fair, it is invariably futile to expect much good from other parts of a personnel program, such as recreational plans, company periodicals, suggestion systems, training plans, and insurance plans. Hence it is imperative, first, to establish as fair a wage policy as possible and, second, to seek to convince the employees of the intrinsic fairness of the plan. Even the best of wage plans will not meet expectations if employees, for one reason or another, will not accept it or do not understand it and therefore are suspicious of it. The inherent fairness of a number of wage plans is offset by their complexity, and hence their use is inadvisable.

In the matter of hours of work, there is less probability of trouble so long as rules governing working periods, rest periods, holidays, vacations, and shift rotations are definitely stated, uniformly applied, and conform to general community practice. Unfortunately, these matters have often been considered only after grievances have stemmed from them.

Working conditions also can be handled without too much difficulty, so that employee morale is affected constructively. At least this is true of the physical aspects of working conditions, such as heating, lighting, equipment, safety devices, maintenance, and clean workplaces. However, supervision—the nonphysical or human aspect of working conditions—is more difficult to manage and generally has caused trouble. Undoubtedly, many complaints of employees arise out of the failure of supervisors to work smoothly and capably with their subordinates. Yet the amount of attention required to clear up such situations is not excessive. It is, however, a mistaken attitude that human aspects of supervision are easy to handle.

b) *Economic Security.* Another group of personal objectives in which the employees are interested is that of economic security. It is a real fear that loss of work due to such events as accidents, seasonal or cyclical depressions, or inability to hold a job will reduce or remove income. To be sure, federal and state legislation has been enacted that serves to alleviate some of these losses, but a long road must be traveled before substantial relief is obtained.

c) *Opportunity for the Employees.* Less tangible than the foregoing, and for that reason perhaps less frequently considered, is the desire of employees for the opportunity for self-improvement and advancement. There is a subtle distinction here that must be grasped. Obviously, all employees do not want advancement and promotions; to many the responsibilities of new jobs are too great and the feeling of self-assurance in their present positions is too satisfying to give up. But there are very few employees who do not like to think that, if they wanted to get ahead, the opportunity for such development would be open to them. So long as the "open-door" policy is maintained, employees do not develop into less efficient workers by reason of the repressive feeling caused by having lost a rightful privilege.

d) *Individual Feeling of Significance.* Perhaps modern business has been most negligent in the matter of making employees feel that their individual accomplishments are significant and worth while. The pat on the back, the word of encouragement, and the smile of sincere appreciation are employed infrequently. Yet such rewards have their place along with financial compensation. Of course, insincere or ineptly given compliments are not suggested here; but experience in World War II indicated that when employees were shown the contributions they were making to the prosecution of the war, morale and output improved noticeably. Obviously, there is no use to pretend that employees can be convinced by such methods that their work is unalloyed pleasure. Nevertheless, employees on many routine jobs would be much more satisfied and hence more effective if they were shown in various personal ways that their jobs are significant and that their efforts are appreciated.

e) Group Feeling of Significance. There is growing recognition, too, that personnel management must build the feeling of significance that arises from group acceptance and status. How an employee feels about his job, for example, is vitally influenced by the opinions that fellow workers hold of his job. If a job is "inferior," the man holding it will feel inferior. That he may react negatively or "retaliate" against management should not, therefore, be surprising. Hence management should consider how status can be built into jobs so that this desired goal of employees can be attained.

3. COMMUNITY AND SOCIAL OBJECTIVES. The final category of primary objectives is that of community and social obligations. Here a remarkable change has been in the making. Business is discarding the attitude of "It's none of our business," and adopting the attitude contained in an affirmative answer to the question, "Am I my brother's keeper?"

Many forces for many years have been at work to bring about the realization that what happens within the walls and during the working hours of a business organization has an effect upon the community and, in turn, upon the efficiency of the business. For example, overworking employees, failure to provide safe working conditions, taking advantage of child labor, or sweatshop wage rates adversely affect the community. Eventually, there is a reaction against all business as well as the individual enterprise. Legislation requiring compensation for losses arising out of accidents and health hazards is a case in point. It is not implied that industry in this case was callously unaware of these losses. Nevertheless, the failure of enough employers to do something constructive did lead eventually to the enactment of such legislation by all the states. In recent years, the passage of federal legislation creating unemployment insurance and old-age pensions is additional evidence of what happens when business itself has not (and, it can be argued, for good reason) accepted such social obligations itself.

The extension of such legislation may not be at an end, as may be seen in the recurrent pressures on the federal government to underwrite programs to cover health and accident losses, dental care, and socialized medicine. Unless a particular enterprise concerns itself with the degree of responsibility that it should accept in the light of social ethics and community needs of the moment, it will only hasten the day of mandatory acceptance of obligations or of some form of retribution unfavorable to it.

4. SECONDARY OBJECTIVES. All the foregoing objectives must invariably be attained effectively and economically. This follows for the simple reason that society's resources are not unlimited. Therefore, the secondary objectives must always be considered along with the primary.

In summary, the various objectives which the employer seeks and the interests which are of concern to employees may well be sought jointly through a good personnel program. This relation between objectives and the program is aptly illustrated in Figure 1, developed by Professor Mee.

FIGURE 1. Relation of Objectives, Personnel Program, and Leadership*

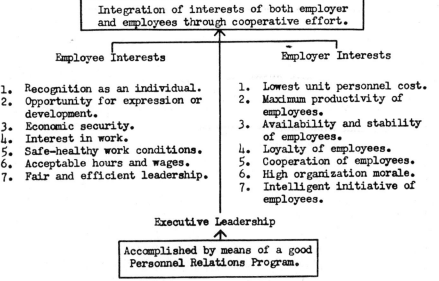

* Source: John F. Mee, *Management Organization for a Sound Personnel Relations Program* (Bulletin 2) (Bloomington: Bureau of Business Research, School of Business, Indiana University, 1948), p. 2.

FUNCTIONS

NATURE OF FUNCTIONS

Having established the objectives of personnel management, the next important question to be settled is that of how desired goals are to be attained. One of the prime factors in this connection is that of functions to be performed.

"Functions" are the activities by the performance of which it is hoped to attain desired goals. Hence the kind and quality of functions chosen in any given case are affected by the objectives which a company seeks to attain. For example, in a company that lays great stress upon such personal objectives of employees as the desire for opportunity to get ahead or the desire for economic security, a number of duties will have to be undertaken that would be unnecessary if these objectives were not considered. Or in a company that is conscious of the secondary objectives of economy and effectiveness of its personnel programs, control and audit functions will be installed which others would ignore. And a company that proposes, for example, to set wages upon community levels must undertake surveys which are of no interest to those that follow a traditional or hit-or-miss system of setting wage differentials. Indeed, it may be concluded that the number and kind of functions performed in any company are dependent upon, first, the kind and quality of its personnel objectives and, second, the economy and effectiveness with which it desires to attain these goals.

Although details of actual practice vary considerably, the general outline of personnel functions is much the same among progressive companies. These functions fall into two major classes: operative and managerial. Since they have been described in the first chapter and will be taken up in detail in succeeding chapters, only a brief comment on each is needed now. The operative functions of personnel management include the activities specifically concerned with procuring, developing, utilizing, and maintaining an efficient working force. The managerial functions pertain to the activities concerned with planning, organizing, and controlling the work of those performing operative personnel functions.

It is essential to grasp the significance of this dual division of personnel functions if the mistake of becoming preoccupied with the demand of detailed problems to the neglect of managerial duties is to be avoided. It is easy, as many executives have learned to their regret, to become so busy with such tasks as hiring, transferring, counseling, and training that they fail to foresee shifting conditions which call for changes in operative functions, they fail to organize the work of subordinates satisfactorily, and they fail to keep a good check upon the work of subordinates.

ASSIGNMENT OF RESPONSIBILITY

The personnel program should also specify who is to be responsible for its preparation, execution, and control. In particular, three areas of responsibility need to be marked out. First, the exact role of the staff personnel division needs to be noted. To what extent should it prepare programs and what line approval of its programs must it seek are questions that need answering here. Second, the duties and responsibilities of each member of the management team must be designated in regard to planning and executing the program. And, third, the relationship between the staff and line executives needs to be clearly indicated as to their specific areas of authority, responsibility, and conditions of co-operation and consultation.

These organizational relationships will be discussed more fully in the next chapter. Hence only a few comments on this aspect of programming are needed now. Of great import is the fact that the personnel division cannot and should not be made solely responsible for the personnel program. Indeed, the greatest obligation must fall on the supervisors and executives who deal with people in their respective functional units. Moreover, it is increasingly apparent that responsibility for carrying out a program depends upon gaining the co-operation of union leadership in the objectives sought and in the personnel procedures utilized. And, finally, and perhaps most crucial, is the support—financial and administrative—that top management gives to the program and to those immediately concerned with carrying it out.

PERSONNEL POLICIES

NATURE

The performance of personnel functions specified in a personnel program is significantly conditioned by personnel policies. Policies are basic rules established to govern functions so that they are performed in line with desired objectives.[1] They are a managerial device to restrain employees from performing undesirable functions or from mishandling specified functions. As an example of the former, a policy which states that unauthorized collections among employees shall not be permitted upon company premises upon penalty of discharge serves to prevent such activities from being performed. Or, as an example of the latter, a policy which states that candidates for employment shall be selected only from those who possess a grammar-school education or its equivalent serves to screen those who would, in the opinion of the company in question, fail to succeed, if employed.

In other words, policies are fundamental guides to action. They serve to provide an answer to questions or problems that recur frequently. Hence they make it unnecessary for subordinates to refer to their supervisors a problem covered by a policy. Consider, as an example, the policy

---

[1] To some, the term "policies" has reference to the basic principles or philosophy upon which an organization is built or operated. While such principles or philosophy are basic to policy making, it is preferred here to follow the more restricted connotation of "policy."

that all employees will be evaluated every four months to determine which deserve raises. This policy is restrictive, to be sure, in that the subject of raises is to be taken up only at specified time periods; but it states definitely when each employee can expect to have his record reviewed, which certainly is not true in the absence of such a policy. As a consequence of this policy, when an executive is asked about raises, he can give a definite answer to a question which occurs frequently. And, of course, neither does he need to waste time in going to his superior to get an answer, nor, in turn, is the superior's time wasted in taking up these repetitious questions.

EXAMPLE OF POLICIES

The importance of personnel policies is evidenced by the number of companies that have prepared booklets covering their policies. Normally such booklets are entitled "Company Rules and Regulations." They carry the policies to which employees, supervisors, and executives are to conform while in the employ of the company. For example, the booklet of one company has the following index of subject matter of rules, regulations, and directions:

Absence	Hours of Work . . . .
Accidents	Ideas and Suggestions . . . .
American Legion	Interpreters . . . .
Appearance	Lateness . . . .
Associated Hospital Plan	Layoffs . . . .
Attendance	Legal Advice . . . .
Bells	Library . . . .
Cafeteria	Lockers . . . .
Check Room	Luncheon . . . .
Consultation with Executives	Members' Mutual Benefit Association .
Contributions	Members' Relations Committee . . . . .
Credit Union	Overtime . . . .
Discount	Pass
Dismissals	To Resume Business . . . .
Dress Regulations	To Hospital . . . .
Elevators	Out of Building . . . .
Employment Guarantee	Personnel Policies . . . .
Employment Policies	Personnel Review . . . .
Entrances	Problems
Financial Assistance	Financial . . . .
Gifts	Legal . . . .
Grievances	Personal . . . .
Health	Promotions . . . .
Holidays	Ratings . . . .
Home Early	Records on Job Performance . . . .
Hospital	Recreation Rooms . . . .

Re-employment	Social Security ....
Re-instatement	Sponsors ....
Relief or Rest	Suggestions ....
Return to Work after Absence	Telephones ....
Review Method, Personnel	Termination of Employment ....
Salaries Policy	Time—Recording of ....
When Paid	Training ....
Unclaimed	Transfers ....
Savings	Vacations ....
Security on the Job	Visitors ....
Shopping	Weddings ....
Smoking	

1. CLASSES OF PERSONNEL POLICIES. The kinds and number of policies are many and varied. For purposes of ready reference they may be classified as follows:

1. According to the level of the organization structure to which they apply—
   a) General company policies are broad rules to which all other policies must conform.
   b) Administrative policies are those established for the guidance of the top executive levels of the company.
   c) Operative policies are those established for the guidance of the lower-level executives who carry out the plans and programs of the top executives.
   d) Functional or staff policies are those which govern the personnel activities of specialized departments, such as accounting, engineering, and inspection.

2. According to the subject matter covered by the policies, e.g., hiring, testing, health, safety, grievance handling, service, and recreational policies.

2. TESTS OF PERSONNEL POLICIES. Inasmuch as personnel policies should be established with great care, it is desirable to adopt a standard set of tests by which to judge whether or not any given policy possesses the qualifications that make for a good policy. Among the tests which have been suggested are the following:

1. Is the policy based upon a careful analysis of the objectives and ideals of the company?
2. Is it definite, unambiguous, complete, and accurately stated?
3. Is it reasonably stable and not subject to change because of temporary changes in existing conditions?
4. Does it have sufficient flexibility to handle normal variations in conditions?
5. Is it related to policies of other sections of the company so that a proper balance of complementary policies is established?

6. Is it known and understood by all who must work with it or are affected by it?

In order that policies be maintained, as well as established, in line with such tests, it is invariably desirable to have a plan for continually auditing and appraising rules and regulations. Such a plan might incorporate some or all of the following: (1) review by committees; (2) suggestion systems; (3) customer complaints; (4) periodic audits; (5) employee grievances; and (6) executive reports.

PRINCIPLES OF PERSONNEL MANAGEMENT

NATURE

Another important factor affecting the establishment and attainment of personnel objectives (and, for that matter, the entire personnel program) is the set of principles which a company follows in labor relations. By this is meant the standards of fairness, the basic attitudes of how to deal with people, and the basic knowledge which is brought to bear upon the topics encompassed within personnel management. Without such principles, the solution of personnel problems becomes a matter of expediency, uncertainty, and inconsistency—qualities certainly not conducive to the development of satisfactory morale.

Unfortunately, there does not exist a set of principles that can be adopted without further thought and applied to one's problems. Each company must set for itself the task of establishing such principles. As conditions alter, as time and experience reveal, and as executives change, it will be found that principles should be modified or amended. But, in any case, where no conscious attempt is made to set such principles, imperfect though they may be, personnel management sails an uncharted sea in a rudderless craft.

SUGGESTED PRINCIPLES

Without implying that the list is complete or should be adopted in all cases, the following discussion is illustrative of the lines along which a set of principles could be built.

1. Establish fair levels of wages, hours, and working conditions. Although unassailable standards of fairness are not available and although everybody would not agree as to the exact meaning of fairness, nevertheless the basic watchword of personnel management is fairness. Exhaustive steps must be taken to establish levels of wages, hours, and working conditions which management, without reservation, feels are fair to all parties concerned. Anything less, sooner or later, will under-

mine a personnel program and the confidence of labor in management.

2. Add to fairness the appearance of fairness. Be fair, but also appear to be fair. This rule seems to have escaped the attention of many industrial leaders. What does it avail to attempt to be fair if that attempt is not placed in its true light or is overshadowed by an unfair appearance? For example, it may be company policy to pay, let us say, 10 per cent more than other employers. This, it would seem, lends itself to fairness. But the appearance of fairness can readily be spoiled by, first, selecting a complex plan of paying wages or, second, being niggardly in other matters.

It is not argued here that appearance of fairness takes precedence over being fair (although some seem to follow the inversion of the rule). Were an inverted policy adopted, the ultimate and certain discovery of unfairness would make irreparable the breach between labor and management. The maxim as stated here recognizes the simple truth that all of us are influenced more or less by how things are presented to us, as well as by what is presented.

3. Supply employees with relevant information. There is little reason for believing that important information can be kept from employees. As a permanent policy it cannot be done. Attempts to do this merely antagonize employees. Sooner or later the "hidden" information turns up, often in a form which tends to weaken the confidence of employees in their company.

Consider in this connection the case of a supervisor who, in order to answer a question of an employee regarding the profits of his company, turned to the superintendent for information. The latter, after inquiring up the line, told the supervisor that such data were neither available nor any of his concern. The supervisor returned empty-handed to the employee, who later obtained the desired information from outside sources. As a consequence, he assumed that management was attempting to hide exorbitant profits, and the grievance which eventually resulted was handled to the disadvantage of the company.

It does no good to argue that employees cannot understand and, therefore, are likely to misinterpret, for example, a profit-and-loss statement. Whether they can or not is irrelevant (for that matter, no one except the accountant who drew it "really" understands it), because that is not the issue in the minds of the employees. To them, the availability of such a statement (and particularly one drawn in a form designed for their benefit) is assurance that the company has nothing to hide.

4. Make employees feel worth while and related. "Men do not live by bread alone" is a saying that applies to personnel. Of course, all of

us are anxious to get our pay envelopes; that is a morale booster, particularly when it is bulging. But what about the intervals between pay-days? What is there then to maintain a favorable attitude?

During this interlude there is a rich opportunity for morale building. Here is the time during which the employee must have encouragement that cannot be found solely in the pay envelope. Here is time during which a feeling of worth-while contribution, of the spirit of craftsmanship, and of the satisfaction of accomplishment must be developed if levels of output are to continue high.

It is important to re-emphasize that feelings of worth-whileness and relatedness are tied in not only with individual accomplishments but also with how well individuals are identified with their working groups. Hence personnel management should build and operate its programs so that such significance can be achieved. This means that group reactions, group customs, and group traditions are of great importance.

In short, anything that serves to identify the worker with his company or its products is a factor that lends itself to building the indispensable quality of worth-whileness.

5. Eliminate all traces of "gift giving." Gift giving is not the province of industry, it is not wanted by employees, and it is rarely appreciated. When labor has earned something, then it is theirs without any strings attached. Moreover, gifts freely given often come to mean something that must be continued as an earned obligation.

Gifts are almost worthless as morale builders. Strong evidence of this may be found in the experience of so many industrial leaders who, finding themselves with disturbances on their hands, wonder why their employees can be ungrateful after all that has been given to them. There is no need for employees to feel grateful to the employer when they have done their jobs effectively. To disguise portions of actual earnings as gifts is to invite trouble when such practices are discovered in their true light.

6. Build programs in terms of labor's reactions to them. In other words, do not treat workers as children. This rule is easier to state than to apply. Nevertheless, an executive who fails to appreciate in large measure how employees feel about their problems cannot reach highly satisfactory agreements with them. And this appreciation should relate to group, as well as individual, feelings.

A case in point arises when employees post a grievance. Management must then seek to discover the motives and reasoning which led to the disagreement. In this search, the analysis must be made in terms of how the employees, and not solely how executives, think about labor's position. And it does not help to assume that employees are acting illogically. Unless an educational program can be brought to bear immediately, the supposed irrationality must be accepted realistically; then every effort must be bent to reach a compromise solution rather than to continue the strife and make labor "see" the problem as management would, were it in labor's shoes.

7. The intelligence or strength of labor should not be underestimated. In dealing with labor, organized or not, it is courting trouble to assume that employees are neither strong nor generally intelligent. Sometimes management so assumes because labor is often slow to move. And such mistakes have surprised many executives. Indeed, much labor unrest can be laid to a mistaken appraisal of the powers of labor. Once aroused, labor has shown that it knows not only what it wants but also how to get it.

The results in the national scene find their counterpart in the individual company. It is much wiser for the employer to measure correctly the strength of labor than to risk the repercussions that stem from an underestimation of its powers. Moreover, when dealt with upon such a high plane, the employer protects himself from vindictive action when labor is in the saddle.

An interesting point can be made here relative to the question of whether or not labor should have a voice in decisions affecting its interests. The question, though often debated, is irrelevant. Labor exerts an influence upon every decision that management reaches. When labor has no voice in bargaining, for example, it may "soldier," it may seek employment elsewhere, or it may have recourse to the ballot box. In short, it acts indirectly when not invited to do so directly. Hence the question should be stated in terms of how and by what means labor should be brought into the mechanism of joint action.

8. Allow enough time to transmit, as well as to develop, programs. It should appear obvious, yet apparently does not, that policies and programs that have taken perhaps months to develop cannot be assimilated by employees in the time it takes to read a notice on the bulletin board or time clock. On what grounds is it reasonable to assume that employees can understand the implications of a posted notice over which the top executive struggled in reaching some semblance of agreement? Of course, there are none.

Perhaps some might argue that it is not the place of employees to think of how or why—theirs but to "do and buy." In rebuttal it can be said that so long as employees are interested in the policies, it makes no difference whether they should or should not be interested. The realistic position to take depends entirely upon the action which is likely to stem from their interest.

Let there be no doubt that employees think, or think that they think, about such programs. And where there is thought, there is bound to be action. The action may be helpful or harmful, depending, in the case of labor relations, upon the degree to which management has taken steps to clarify the reasons for and implications of policies to the satisfaction of all interested parties.

9. Select carefully oral and written expressions. This warning constitutes perhaps a subheading under the preceding principle. Nevertheless, it deserves emphasis because many of management's communications are practically unintelligible. In this connection, there comes to mind a conference of foremen recently conducted by the writer. The topic for discussion at the time was that of wage incentive plans. One of the conferees volunteered to describe the plan used by his company. He took about ten minutes in this attempt and failed to make clear the nature of the plan to the experienced foremen present. How, then, could a "green" hand, let us say, have confidence, let alone understand, a plan which a supervisor could not describe? Thus it seems patent that it is not enough for management to have a clear understanding of proposed plans or policies; these must be expressed in terms known to the man at the bench or the machine.

10. "Sell" personnel policies to the employees. If a company has a worth-while purpose, if its standards of fairness are high, in short, if it attempts to follow the best practices of human relations, then these programs and ideals should be "sold" to the employees. Training, education, yes, even indoctrination, are justifiable. After all, if a company refrains from undertaking the task of education, that does not mean that its employees will remain in a happy state of suspended educational balance—if not progressing, at least not retrogressing.

On the contrary, the process of education continues willy-nilly. The issue really is what are the employees learning, how, and from whom? Since that is the issue, then the employer pays for a program of education whether or not he has a "formal" program. If he does pay for the education, he may as well establish a thoroughly considered program.

11. Activate one's principles. In the last analysis, the real significance of one's principles will be found in whether or not they are a part of daily routines and executive acts. All the talk in the world is ineffective unless backed with action. Hence management should make its principles a part of all it does, so that employees can see before them the example which is preached and stated in oral and printed words.

In short, the "good" life must be lived by management in order that labor can be sure that what is said is really meant.

APPLICATION OF PRINCIPLES

The foregoing tests or rules, then, should be of help in the development or appraisal of any personnel program. Let us assume, for example, that a company desires to install a wage incentive plan under which employees would be paid, in addition to base rate for hours actually worked, a bonus of 100 per cent of time saved under standard task time. Without attempting to appraise the plan here, the scheme of analysis proposed would require a searching examination of this wage payment plan in terms of each of the foregoing statements.

Some might object that such an analysis of every proposal would be expensive and time-consuming. To this objection, there are two answers. First, every proposal need not be examined with the same degree of care; the degree would depend upon the importance of the proposal. Second, and far more important, it is invariably cheaper to prevent than to cure labor disturbances. Who can gainsay that the immediate and long-run losses of one strike exceed the cost of a well-rounded organization and program of personnel work?

RESEARCH NEEDS OF PROGRAMMING

It should be apparent by this time that much information will be required in programming personnel work. How well this job of collecting information is done will determine how successfully responsible executives can reach decisions on personnel objectives, functions, policies, and principles. Reliance in such matters is often placed upon personal experience or the experience of others. Yet it is contended here that much more emphasis will have to be placed upon logical, scientific research for needed information.

A number of research tools are already available for these purposes and will be touched upon in later chapters. It is worth noting here, however, a few examples of information gathering through research. Such techniques as job analysis and man specifications, merit rating and job evaluation analysis, procedural analysis, turnover and absenteeism studies, morale and attitude surveys, wage and salary surveys, and policy audits and evaluations can provide indispensable information basic to program development. Such investigations need not be perfect analyses of these subjects. Of course, the more thorough, the better. But, for all practical purposes, much data can be gathered with a minimum of fanfare and expenditure. There is needed only the sincere desire to seek facts for decisions in the place of personal hunches and limited experience.

The purpose of this chapter has been to call attention to certain basic factors to which consideration must be given early in the study or development of any personnel program. Decisions must be reached on such matters as objectives, functions, assignment of responsibilities, policies, and principles in building an effective personnel plan. Some believe that such matters may be resolved by "cut-and-try" methods. But there is no short-cut solution to the complex problems of human relations. The only hope, in the long run, to fair and equitable solutions is along the path of facts and information. Hence the subject of research has been given special emphasis in this chapter of programming. Research is without doubt the key to effective planning of personnel activities.

QUESTIONS AND PROBLEMS

1. What are the purposes of a personnel program? Are the purposes solely for the interests of the company?
2. Can you illustrate the argument that a personnel program serves to tie together various personnel activities?
3. Make a list of personnel objectives. Which do you think are the most difficult to attain?
4. How do secondary objectives differ from primary objectives? Why are both necessary?
5. How would you prove in a given case that the investment in a personnel program was justified?
6. How would you classify the wants of employees? Can you cite specific illustrations in support of your classification? To what extent are these wants selfish?
7. List some constructive suggestions as to how economic security may be achieved by employees. By efforts of employers.
8. Do you believe it feasible for any company to include in its personnel program all the activities listed in the pages of this chapter? Which ones do you believe are performed less frequently and which more frequently?
9. What are the purposes of personnel policies? Do employees have a voice in their determination?
10. What is the relation between personnel policies and employee booklets of rules and regulations?
11. How would you go about testing a policy in order to determine whether it was a "good" one?
12. What is meant by a "principle" of personnel management? Distinguish

between policies and principles. Is it possible, except by luck, to establish policies without pre-establishing principles?

13. If significance and worth-whileness are such important factors of motivation, why are they not used more often? Are there any ways by which executives might be encouraged to use them more often?

14. An executive desires to be friendly with his employees to assure them of his sincerity and interest in them. He fears, however, that employees may take advantage of him if he so acts. What suggestions do you have to offer him?

15. Can such principles as those stated in the text be practiced in either a non-union or unionized shop with equal ease? Explain.

16. How far would you go in supplying employees with company information? Would your answer be the same during a strike as during a period of relative peace?

17. Why must personnel management seek to make employees feel worth-while and significant members of the company team? Can employees see this for themselves?

18. Illustrate the truth of the statement (or contradict if you can) that employee morale cannot be purchased.

19. Is it necessary to "talk down" to employees? Distinguish between "talking down" and expressing oneself clearly.

20. For a long time the owner of a medium-sized plant viewed his labor force as a technical factor of production and dealt with it as such. One of his fellow businessmen convinced him that he should be more of a humanitarian, so he decided to do something for labor. He installed and maintained an expensive recreational, athletic, and social program. In spite of this, the employees went out on strike not long afterward. When the strike was settled, the owner threw overboard all personnel activities except those concerned directly with wages, hours, working conditions, and collective bargaining. As he expressed it, "I got along without these frills when I first started. They didn't do any good; and, besides, labor is really not interested in anything much besides wages." What is your critical opinion of this case?

Organization Structure

of Personnel Management

IMPORTANCE OF ORGANIZATION STRUCTURE

When one notes the number of employees, executives, and specialists whose efforts must be co-ordinated, it sometimes seems surprising that so much is actually accomplished in the average business concern. A partial, yet significant, explanation of this may be found in the contributions made by the mechanisms of organization structure. This structure provides an invisible framework by which the work of various individuals is fitted into an effective team. It provides a means for assigning authority and responsibility to individuals, for communicating between experts at various levels, and for enforcing accountability. In short, it helps make possible the large and effective aggregations of employees we know today.

If personnel management is to function correctly in such aggregations, organizational understanding on the part of staff, as well as line, executives is a prerequisite. Such understanding is usually gained in casual fashion through the give-and-take of daily experiences. Better still, however, is understanding based upon a firm grasp of the theory and principles of design and operation of organization structure. When the personnel executive masters these matters, he not only can reduce disagreements that arise regarding his place on the company team but also can help instruct others on their logical personnel duties and relationships.

SCOPE OF DISCUSSION

The fundamental question to which organization structure is expected to supply an answer is: How much and what kind of authority should be allocated to each person in the organization? For example, should a personnel department have complete authority over everybody in regard to personnel functions? Or should it have only the right to suggest how personnel functions should be performed by others? Or should it seek to develop and awaken appreciation of personnel responsibilities but leave the design of functions to the executives themselves? And should there be any differences in authority to be exercised during normal times as opposed to emergency periods? Unless these and similar questions are answered in advance, they will arise to plague all concerned at times when the attention of executives should be concentrated on more urgent issues or those that could not have been foreseen.

These aspects of authority and responsibility have three major areas or directions of flow. They include an executive's relation, first, to the group he supervises; second, to his superiors; and, third, crosswise to other specialists in the company. The discussion that follows considers the variables in these personnel relations under the following headings:

1. Formal types of organization structure
2. Informal aspects of organization structure
3. Relations between line and staff executives
4. Factors in specific structural designs

FORMAL TYPES OF ORGANIZATION STRUCTURE

Although the formal organization structures of various companies differ from each other, for purposes of study it is possible to classify them into three major groups—the line, the line and staff, and the functional types of organization structure. Of the three, the most widely used is the line and staff type. It is discussed last here, however, because its characteristics stand out more clearly if the other two types are examined first.

THE LINE FORM OF STRUCTURE

The line form of organization structure (sometimes misnamed the "military" form because of the clear lines of authority) is the simplest and oldest type. A diagram of this type is shown in Figure 2 (p. 52).

1. CHARACTERISTICS. The distinguishing characteristics of this form of organization are few in number but, nevertheless, of great significance. In the first place, as may be seen in Figure 2, each person reports to one and only one superior. Thus each worker is responsible solely to the foreman of his department, who, in turn, is specifically responsible solely to his superintendent. As a consequence of this undivided line of authority, each individual is given complete charge of the work assigned to him, subject only to the authority of the superior to whom he reports.

In the second place, but not obvious on the face of an organization chart for the line type, the work of each person or executive revolves directly around the production of goods and services, their distribution, or the financing of the business. Work assignments and executive assignments are based upon divisions of these functions. As may be seen in Figure 2, in the sales part of the organization, for example, there are only sales executives and salespeople. It is obvious that each person or executive must perform for himself, subject only to whatever advice he can get from his superiors, all other duties (such as personnel functions of hiring, training, wage determinations, etc.) which may be helpful to the performance of his primary tasks.

2. ADVANTAGES. What are the advantages of the line form of organization structure? First, it lends itself to a minimum of "buck passing." When a supervisor has been given complete charge of his department, he cannot blame someone else if things go wrong. Since he is also his own personnel manager, for example, he is in no position to claim that he failed to receive adequate assistance in forestalling grievances that may arise. Second, so long as problems do not become too complex, decisions can be reached more quickly when problems arise. This fol-

FIGURE 2.   The Line Form of Organization Structure

```
                         ┌──────────────┐
                         │  PRESIDENT   │
                         └──────────────┘
        ┌────────────────────┬────────────────────┐
┌────────────────┐  ┌────────────────┐  ┌──────────────────┐
│   PRODUCTION   │  │ SALES MANAGER  │  │ FINANCIAL MANAGER│
│    MANAGER     │  │                │  │                  │
└────────────────┘  └────────────────┘  └──────────────────┘
┌────────────────┐  ┌────────────────┐  ┌──────────────────┐
│     SHOP       │  │DIVISIONAL SALES│  │    TREASURER     │
│ SUPERINTENDENT │  │   MANAGERS     │  │                  │
└────────────────┘  └────────────────┘  └──────────────────┘
┌────────────────┐  ┌────────────────┐  ┌──────────────────┐
│    FOREMEN     │  │  LOCAL SALES   │  │   SUPERVISORS    │
│                │  │   MANAGERS     │  │                  │
└────────────────┘  └────────────────┘  └──────────────────┘
┌────────────────┐  ┌────────────────┐  ┌──────────────────┐
│    WORKERS     │  │   SALESMEN     │  │     CLERKS       │
└────────────────┘  └────────────────┘  └──────────────────┘
```

lows because the person involved, if he has questions at all, need refer them only to his superior and not to a number of experts before it is decided how to handle a particular problem. Third, since the number and variety of executives are reduced to a minimum, the line type is relatively simple to understand, and hence it is easier for each person to know where he fits into the company's structure.

3. DISADVANTAGES. However, there are offsetting disadvantages. For one thing, it is difficult to find and train enough supervisors and other executives who can capably manage not only their primary work

assignments but also all the subsidiary tasks that are related to the main task. A foreman may be a good technical man, for example, but it is asking a lot to expect him also to be an expert in human relations, employment, training, and motivation. Yet that is what the line form of organization presupposes. The usual result in such cases is that most supervisors and executives fall into the category of a "Jack-of-all-trades but master of none."

4. SPHERE OF BEST USAGE. When, then, is the use of the line form desirable? The advantages of the line form tend to outweigh the disadvantages when, first, a company is relatively small; second, the executives at all levels and in all parts of the company are well seasoned; and, third, the problems of the company are neither complex nor changing rapidly. Obviously, its sphere of usefulness is limited.

THE FUNCTIONAL FORM OF STRUCTURE

Of a nature quite different from the line form is the functional form of organization structure. This form is shown in Figure 3. In this dia-

FIGURE 3. The Functional Form of Organization Structure

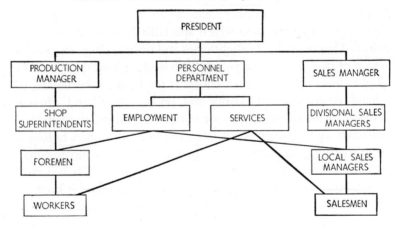

gram the higher divisions of the structure, as well as complete details, have been omitted for sake of simplicity.

1. CHARACTERISTICS. The distinguishing feature of the functional form is striking—each person, except those at the top levels, in the production and distribution divisions reports to several superiors. When the lines of responsibility are traced, it is found that each person reports to each superior for only a specified phase of his work. For example, the local sales managers report to the divisional sales managers on sales matters, to the employment section on hiring problems, and to the per-

sonnel service section for such matters as personnel programs. Of course, if a complete chart had been drawn to include other functional experts, it would have shown that the sales managers also reported to an accountant, a commercial research director, and a traffic manager.

2. ADVANTAGES.   The significant advantage of the functional form is that each person has the opportunity to become an expert in his field of specialization. This division of functions among various specialists leaves the shop foreman, for example, free to concentrate upon his main job of directing and supervising operative employees. Another advantage is that subordinate personnel and executives are assured of better technical supervision, because each person to whom they report is supposed to be an expert in his field of specialization. For example, the shop foreman looks to the personnel department for leadership on personnel problems and not to the shop superintendent. Finally, it is easier to find people who are trainable in a few lines than it is to find and train supervisors in a wide variety of tasks.

3. DISADVANTAGES.   This form of organization structure, however, suffers from serious disadvantages. Foremost is the evil of divided lines of authority. Although there is apparent clarity on paper in the lines drawn from a particular subordinate to his several superiors, it is not always easy to determine to which specialist to turn when in need of guidance. The inevitable twilight cases and overlapping functions throw a burden of choice upon the person who is often least qualified to make the right choice. When a poor choice is made, the subordinate, on the one hand, receives poor guidance and, on the other hand, often incurs the enmity of the other experts for not having turned to them.

Another disadvantage flows from the normal human failing of experts to work together smoothly when all seemingly have "equal" authority. Each is prone to feel that his specialty is actually not receiving attention equal to its importance. The inevitable result is futile squabbling when the personnel director, for example, concludes that his authority to enforce labor policies is being nullified by the lack of appreciation which other experts, such as engineers, often have toward labor relations.

Finally, the divided lines of authority are conducive to "buck passing." When an employee spoils a part on a machine, for example, is this due to poor training, faulty materials, or inadequate machine maintenance? Each of the experts would likely think it is due to shortcomings in the work of the other specialists.

4. FIELD OF USAGE.   Wherever the functional plan has been tried upon a broad scale, it has eventually failed. It seems that otherwise

well-trained and reasonable people cannot avoid running afoul of the divided lines of authority of the functional form. When several people exercise authority over the same subordinates, but in different fields of specialization, they tend to dissipate their efforts in jurisdictional disputes.

Then why discuss this form? First, because it serves to clarify the operation of the line and staff form, which is, in one sense, a cross of the line form and the functional form. Without a knowledge of the theory of the functional form, it is easy to miss the meaning of the line and staff form. Second, this form deserves discussion because its use upon a restricted or temporary basis is sometimes desirable. There are occasions when the personnel departments of given companies are delegated functional authority over line departments. This is an efficient way of handling emergency personnel problems or duties imposed by federal and state labor regulations. And, third, with the growth of automation, it may be practically necessary to place authority for such functions as communications and instructions in the hands of a centralized, functional expert.

THE LINE AND STAFF FORM OF STRUCTURE

As already noted, the most widely used form of organization structure is the line and staff form. A simple diagram of it is shown in Figure 4.

FIGURE 4. The Line and Staff Form of Organization Structure

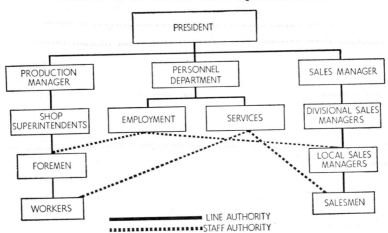

1. CHARACTERISTICS.   Perhaps the most striking feature of the line and staff form is that in it each person reports to one and only one su-

pervisor, yet receives specialized service and help from various experts. To illustrate, let us examine the hiring procedure, which is operated by the employment section of the personnel division, as shown in Figure 4. This unit screens applicants for jobs and then directs those selected as desirable employees to the supervisors for their acceptance or rejection. Since the employment unit cannot compel supervisors to follow its recommendations, the line of authority between the foreman and the superintendent remains undivided and the allegiance of the former to the latter is not placed in question. Of course, the personnel department should be operated so that its services will seldom be rejected; but, even though they never are, this should not lead to the conclusion that staff departments have any authority over those they serve.

2. ADVANTAGES.   The advantages of the line and staff form are readily apparent. First, the staff departments provide expert service, a matter of significant importance in this age of specialization. Second, since the specialists have no right to interfere with the authority of those they serve, the line and staff form has the advantage of a single line of accountability. In short, experts are available for service, but their services need not be accepted merely upon the recommendation of the staff executives. Obviously, it would ordinarily be foolish to refuse to avail oneself of such services, hence the line and staff form, in the third place, frees line executives so that they may concentrate upon their primary responsibilities.

3. DISADVANTAGES.   As for disadvantages, the line and staff form has a few possible, but not necessarily unavoidable, shortcomings. In the first place, staff specialists, instead of offering their services on a voluntary basis, attempt sometimes to force their suggestions and services upon others. In that event, subordinate executives become uncertain as to whether they should obey their immediate superiors or the dictates of the staff. This leads to the "divided-line" weakness of the functional form, but this difficulty can be avoided if staff experts are expressly warned against exceeding their assigned scope of activity. On the other hand, strict adherence to this rule may render the line and staff form ineffective under certain emergency conditions. For example, during the war years it was impossible to train large numbers of supervisors in all matters that ordinarily came within their jurisdictions. Many companies found it desirable, therefore, to turn such rights as that of discharge over to the personnel department. These allocations of authority are usually intended to be temporary, for it is hoped to return such rights to the supervisors as soon as they can handle their responsibility adeptly.

Certainly, if the line and staff principle had been kept inviolate in such cases, enough foremen could not have been trained to handle required duties within the limits of available time.

4. AREA OF USAGE. Except in small-sized enterprises, in which the line form of organization seems best suited, the line and staff has evolved as the best all-around type of organization structure. Of course, this form would seldom be as simple as that shown in Figure 4. Ordinarily, there are numerous staff personnel—engineers, public relations experts, office help, accountants, lawyers, etc.—scattered throughout an organization. In any event, the key to this form of structure is that experts should be brought into the organization when such services are needed and can be obtained at reasonable cost, but that they should not be permitted to intrude in the lines of authority of those whom they presumably serve.

INFORMAL ASPECTS OF ORGANIZATION STRUCTURE

Although the lines between various positions in the foregoing diagrams are usually single and occasionally double, actual examinations of the workings of particular companies will disclose much more complicated and "extralegal" relationships. For example, on the one hand, it is often found that, while two executives may seemingly be on the same level in the formal organization chart, one of them may actually be held in higher esteem by colleagues and subordinates; or one of them may be referred to frequently while the other is avoided or bypassed. Again, it is also found that some employee to whom no formal grants of authority have been made whatsoever, nonetheless is looked upon as the natural leader of a given group. To this person, various individuals "declare" their allegiance by their acts, though by the organization chart they seemingly report to someone else. And, finally, employees in the case of unionized situations turn for help to their stewards, who are not in the company organization structure. Yet there exists here a definite organizational relationship that, for all practical purposes, is often more significant than the relationships shown on the company chart. The first two of these nonformal relationships are now discussed, and the third is taken up in a later section of this chapter.

INFORMAL EXECUTIVE AUTHORITY

Even casual observation is usually sufficient to show that there are differences between the formal authority an executive has and that which he actually possesses. Some executives have high titles but wield little power, whereas others of lower status in the organization chart exercise authority beyond their assigned station.

More careful studies disclose such differences even more strikingly. Of particular interest here are sociometric studies that seek to show graphically various types of working relationships between members of an organization. An example of this is shown in Figure 5. The light

FIGURE 5.   Sociometric Analysis of an Organization Structure*

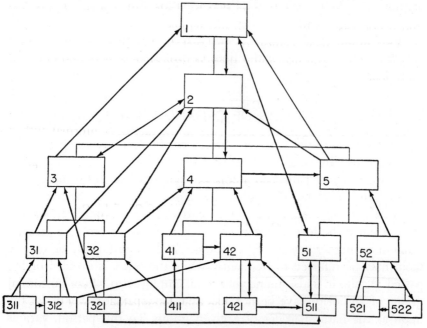

* From C. L. Shartle, "Leadership and Executive Performance," *Personnel*, March, 1949, p. 6.
Source: The Ohio Leadership Studies, Personnel Research Board, Ohio State University.

lines depict the formal lines of relationship between levels of the organization structure. The heavy lines show the relationships based upon a study of the question with whom most time is spent in getting work done. It is clear from the heavy lines running to the positions marked "4," "42," and "511" that, because of their respective levels in the structure, their significance is greater than that of the other positions.[1]

Although the existence of such differences between actual and assigned authority is beyond dispute, how they develop and change are

[1] It is to be noted that such sociometric measurements are superimposing procedural analysis upon structural elements and are not solely making examinations of structural importance.

topics about which too little is known. Nonetheless, the significance of such informal authority relationships cannot be overestimated. To the personnel executive who feels that staff position in an organization is perhaps inadequate, developing his services so that more and more people rely upon his organization is a real possibility along informal lines. Or the personnel executive who is wondering why his services are not being accepted may make a sociometric study to see if other executives are being consulted more than he on personnel matters. Moreover, by knowing who the "real" leaders are in an organization, the personnel executive can make sure that he deals with the significant cogs and is not wasting his time with just names.

This might seem cynical on the surface, but it is not. If a system operates in a certain way and if there is little chance of changing it, one who does not adapt himself to it is naïve and unrealistic. Certainly, in the field of personnel management some of our failures can be laid to the fact that we have idealistically tried to work through formal structures alone. Had cognizance been paid to the fact that informal authority relationships exist, there would have been fewer mistakes—such as dealing with the wrong executives, having good plans and policies rejected, obtaining insufficient funds to carry on needed functions, and being obstructed in the execution of otherwise good programs.

Without then seeking to judge whether or not informal structures should be allowed to exist, the point made here is simply that they do exist and are likely to continue to do so. Hence, in the performance of various functions of personnel management, it is essential to try to know as much about informal relationships in a group as we seem to know about formal relationships. And then such knowledge should be used so that the personnel functions, on the one hand, can be performed as effectively as possible and, on the other hand, will suffer as few unexpected obstructions as possible.

INFORMAL EMPLOYEE AUTHORITY

Wherever groups of people organize, the careful observer will soon note that unofficial cliques form among employees. Each clique will have a structure of leaders and led as rigid as any put down formally on paper. The "appointment" of the leaders in such cliques comes about in a number of ways. Some become recognized because they are "born" leaders of men; they naturally are accepted because of an aptitude to perform leadership functions. Others are accorded leadership status because of some institutional factor, for example, seniority, type of work, position in a line, pay received, age, or special technical skills.

These informal structures, also, are composed of a hierarchy of positions of prestige. There is not just one leader, but usually several of varying importance or of specialized areas of significance. Thus the group may look to a particular employee on matters pertaining to wages, to another for advice on how to deal with recalcitrants, and to still another when a spokesman is needed to talk to the supervisor. In a way, each member of the group is assigned some place that determines his status. Thus it is that one observes an employee being "put in his place" by a second employee, who feels that the first has not earned the right to be heard as yet. And the other employees will support the second, or reject him, depending upon the status of leadership which the first has not, or has, attained.

These hierarchies carry duties as well as privileges. The informal leaders are, on the one hand, expected to lead the employees in their "assigned" specialties. The "old-timer" is expected to counsel those in need of advice. The "spokesman" is expected to present to supervisors the thoughts which need to be conveyed in that direction. And the "organizer of social gatherings" is looked up to as the arbiter in these matters. As noted earlier, it is usual to find several leaders of specialized character, although occasionally the various duties are embodied in one person.

On the other hand, varying types and degrees of rights and privileges are accorded the natural leaders. Perhaps the most significant is that of the esteem in which they are held. Thus they possess a "status" in the group of considerable prestige value. Such status not only is recognized within the working areas but also is often extended into the community itself. Consequently, the employee himself, and at times his wife and family, are accorded respect that is not the lot of the "average" employee. In addition to this social status, it will also be found that the natural leaders are considered to be immune from performing menial tasks or are permitted various liberties which others are not.

While these hierarchies are informal, they nonetheless are well fixed in the minds of employees. The newcomer in a group, for example, is soon made aware of the need for respecting the informal social systems, or he is placed outside the pale; and failure to be accepted by a group is a penalty that few wish to pay. Indeed, it is felt by some that the pressures of the informal social system are much more important than the so-called "logical" factors of individual motivation.

If this be true—and some events in labor-management relations seem to indicate that there is merit to the argument—then the student of personnel management should give heed to this phase of human relations. To begin with, the wisdom of taking such social systems into consideration when developing any personnel program is evident. For example, in developing a recreational program, the character of existing informal patterns of recreational relationships or alignments had better be known and taken into account. Moreover, such informal structures may be utilized for such purposes as communications, for making sample surveys of employee attitudes, and for feeling the pulse of employee reactions. To cite one example, the company that stopped an unfounded but spreading rumor in its tracks, by getting in touch with a few key employees, made use of the informal structure to its own advantage as well as that of its employees.

To sum up, there is in every formal organization, a series of informal and unofficial structures. They develop spontaneously, they exist at the grass roots, and they certainly cannot be stamped out. One may as well be realistic, recognize their existence, and at least do nothing to arouse antagonism if one cannot make good use of them. It is worth underlining again the contention of some that these informal systems are perhaps more important than the formal in achieving more effective and satisfying labor-management relations. Certainly, this seems true in the negative sense, for where companies have run roughshod over the informal structure, the results have been far from happy.

RELATION OF LINE AND STAFF EXECUTIVES

The basic kinds of organization structure have now been described. The predominant use of the line and staff form of structure has been noted. It is now pertinent to inquire into the particular roles of line executives and of staff executives in personnel matters. This may perhaps best be done by examining who has authority over, and who is responsible for, personnel work. It is impossible here to establish boundaries of authority and responsibility in every case. All that can be done is to note, first, the application of these terms to line and staff executives (taken up in this section) and, second, some factors which tend to change the boundaries of authority and responsibility in different cases (taken up in the next section).

AUTHORITY IN ORGANIZATION STRUCTURE

1. DEFINITION AND SOURCE. "Authority," in its broadest sense, means the right to command performance of others. It implies the right to give orders to others and to expect obedience from those to whom the orders are given. These comments give authority a harsh sound, but in

actual practice "giving orders" and "expecting obedience" can and should be tempered with understanding, personal interest, and common rules of courtesy.

But what is the source of authority, and how far does authority extend? In a formal sense, any executive obtains authority by delegation from a superior. Hence, the right to command and over whom are determined by the wording of the delegation. Thus a personnel director may be empowered by the vice-president, first, to organize and operate a personnel department and, second, to render personnel services to various other groups in the organization. The first part of this delegation gives him authority over the staff and the workings of his organization unit. The second part of the delegation indicates that his direct line of authority stops at the borders of his own department. Beyond these limits, his authority is advisory, which, in the final analysis, means no authority.

Those served by the personnel department have direct authority over personnel matters. A shop supervisor, for example, has the right to accept or reject candidates sent over by the employment section. Or he has the right to recommend discharge of employees from his department, to recommend wage increases, to decide whether or not a given employee should be disciplined, etc. These rights are, of course, subject to the decisions of his own superior and circumscribed by company policies and by clauses in the union-management contract.

2. EARNING AUTHORITY.   In an informal sense, the authority derived by delegation may be strengthened and the borders of authority may be extended by earning the right to lead. Indeed, long-run success is dependent perhaps more upon earned leadership than upon delegated rights. Herein lies the great opportunity of such staff departments as personnel. Although its relation to other departments may be advisory, the personnel department can wield great power for good by gaining the respect of those it serves. This may be accomplished, first, by being technically proficient and, second, by performing services of interest to management and labor better than the latter could for themselves.

When the quality of the services of a personnel department is of such a nature as to earn the respect of line executives, its influence and status will rise to a high point. It will have so many calls on its services that it will never need to worry about prestige, power, or "authority." Personnel executives should therefore concern themselves with superior service. All else will come to them as a natural result.

Another aspect of earning authority may be noted by examining the contention that the personnel executive should sit in the highest councils of the company. The bald statement implies that high authority should be given to this staff specialist. While it is not denied that labor matters are of paramount and growing importance in the average concern, it is nevertheless true that the importance of a problem does not of itself mean that the executive who is supposed to be handling the problem deserves authority to handle it. Before such authority is granted, the executive should prove his ability to handle important issues. Unfortunately, in the past, many of the executives who carried high-sounding personnel titles did not possess the training, skill, or experience to merit large measures of authority.

RESPONSIBILITY IN ORGANIZATION STRUCTURE

If an executive in the organization structure has authority, he also has responsibilities. Sometimes it seems that the burdens of responsibilities outweigh the rights of authority. Why this is so may have various explanations, but one lies in the nature of responsibility.

1. MEANING OF RESPONSIBILITY. By "responsibility" is meant, first, the obligation to do an assigned task and, second, the obligation to someone for the assignment. But what is meant by "obligation," and how far does it extend? This implies a willingness to accept, for whatever rewards one may see in the situation, the burden of a given task and the risks which attend in the event of failure. Because of the rewards and penalties involved, it is highly essential to specify the limits of responsibility. Let us examine briefly the case of the personnel director in this connection. According to the definitions just given, he is responsible not only for the work he does but also for the work of his subordinates. Assume that in a particular company the personnel director holds a staff position, as defined earlier. Assume, further, that one of his subordinates helps in selecting a candidate for a job in the factory and that, after a month or two, the employee proves to be an inefficient worker. Should the personnel department be held responsible? Of course, the personnel director may and should take steps to prevent a recurrence of similar mistakes in the future. However, since the personnel department holds a staff position in this instance and since veto powers of hiring were in the hands of the shop department, does the blame lie upon the staff department that suggested the hiring or the line department that had the final word on hiring?

2. DEFINING RESPONSIBILITY LIMITS. There is no organizational "law" which indicates the one answer to these questions. All that can be said about such cases is that responsibility could have been placed upon one or the other. The important thing is to be sure to define as

explicitly as possible how far each person's responsibilities extend. This is not intended primarily for the purpose of "saving the skins" of employees, although this is significant to the feeling of fairness and security which all of us seek. Of greater importance is the strength which this adds to the organization structure by discovering gaps in responsibility assignment that need filling, and by providing a definite basis for comparing performance against expected results. In the second place, if a formal statement of responsibilities is not made, informal boundary lines with uncertain borders will nevertheless be established. Such demarcations, since they are not studied, are not likely to be good; and, since they are informal, they are bound to encourage "buck passing," recrimination, and "witch hunting" when things do go wrong. Hence, where formal limits of responsibility are defined, an answer to the question posed in the foregoing paragraph would have been a routine matter.

Since personnel matters are subject to "split" responsibilities, it is very important to have clear statements of the obligations of all concerned with these matters. For what is the personnel department responsible in hiring, training, wage determinations, promotions, collective bargaining, and research? And in these matters, for what are line executives responsible? Better to debate these limits at the outset than to recriminate and indulge in personalities later. Moreover, when this is done, all levels of management and the personnel division as well can concentrate on doing their respective jobs. They need not divert their energies to preparing excuses and accusations.

RELATIONS OF AUTHORITY TO RESPONSIBILITY

Having discussed the terms "authority" and "responsibility" separately, it is now appropriate to note how they may be related. Of particular interest here are the following three phases of these terms: first, need of unity of authority and responsibility; second, coequality of authority and responsibility; and, third, importance of lines of communication.

1. UNITY OF AUTHORITY AND RESPONSIBILITY. From what has already been said, it should be apparent that each phase of personnel work should be clearly assigned to a given individual or organization unit. Take training as an example. Training phases, such as program development, teaching methods, and training aids may well be assigned to a training section in the personnel division. Actual trainers—who will use these services and aids—may be assigned to each supervisor. Here there is a clear division of authority and responsibility for particu-

lar phases of training. Delineation of obligations for all other personnel functions should be made in the same manner.

2. EQUALITY OF AUTHORITY AND RESPONSIBILITY. One frequently encounters the statement that authority and responsibility should be coequal. This contention holds true, however, only when the person on a given job is capable, first, of accepting responsibility and, second, of handling authority. Any executive is justified in being reluctant to place authority over personnel in untried or inexperienced hands because of the losses occasioned by misused authority. It is usually less likely that responsibility will be mishandled. We often see people made responsible for something but given little or no authority in connection therewith. However, as these people "prove" themselves, authority is gradually increased; it is made coequal with responsibility for personnel matters.

Of course, there are examples of executives who, through fear or ignorance, refuse to delegate authority beyond the bare minimums, but such individuals have nothing to contribute to the theory of good management practice. On the other hand, most executives are willing to delegate authority to subordinates as the latter prove themselves, because such delegations serve to free the time and energies of the superiors for other matters.

3. IMPORTANCE OF LINES OF COMMUNICATION. Authority and responsibility for a given job may also be related by the lines of communication which are established between upper and lower levels of the organization. To begin with, such a line invariably runs between any subordinate and his superior. This is used to assign particular tasks or plans and to specify limits of authority and responsibility.

In addition, there are lines of communication running between the subordinates just cited and various technical experts. Through such channels, specialized service of various kinds is made available. To illustrate, a sales supervisor may be authorized by his superior to add salesmen to his unit, but the additions may be selected by the personnel department, thus freeing the sales supervisor's time for other duties.

The lines of responsibility, on the other hand, run upward, though they, too, may be several in number. The main line of obligation is, and always should be, except in emergency cases as noted earlier, to one's immediate superior because this insures single and undivided accountability. Lines of information may be established, however, to various staff experts. For example, if a sales supervisor sends a report to his superior regarding the number of people who left his unit and their reasons for leaving, it would be in order to send a copy of this report to the personnel department. In this way, the results will be examined not only by the line executive but also by staff experts. This does not mean that the sales supervisor reports to two executives or that his efforts are being scrutinized with a view to showing him up. Rather, it should be understood that the line of single accountability remains inviolate and that the added line of communication offers a means of gaining expert advice which will provide suggestions on how poor results can be prevented and good results attained.

FACTORS IN SPECIFIC STRUCTURAL DESIGNS

The discussion thus far has presented the theory and fundamental principles of the subject; it is now appropriate to note practical applications and what lessons may be learned from actual practices. The place in the organization structure that is given to personnel in any particular case is determined by a number of factors. Among the more important ones are:

1. Degree to which top management considers personnel factors important
2. Size of company and location of its offices and plants
3. Influence of such outside factors as legislation and labor unions
4. Types of labor or production problems calling for solutions

Of course, these are more or less interrelated, but, for the sake of simplicity, the foregoing list will be used as an outline of exposition.

1. ATTITUDE OF MANAGEMENT. The opinion of top management toward the importance of personnel is undoubtedly the most compelling factor in determining its place in the organization structure. In some companies (and this is true of some of the largest) there is no personnel department worthy of the name, whereas other companies, operating under very similar conditions, have elaborate and high placed personnel divisions. The explanation for the difference lies solely in top management's recognition of this function. An explanation of the reasons why some executives are not convinced of the wisdom of adding such a division to their organization structure is beyond the scope of this text, but a suggestion or two are in order.

In some cases, slowness to recognize personnel stems from a common tendency of line executives to restrict all staff functions to a minimum. Line executives are prone to believe that their prime responsibilities are much more important than all others. Moreover, they are inclined to have unbounded confidence in the solution of labor problems, for example, by sheer intuition. Until they see the losses that flow from their shortsightedness, a personnel department worthy of the name is unlikely to be established.

In other cases, failure of personnel departments to be awarded an important place can be ascribed to the inability of those placed in charge of personnel functions to convince top management of the importance of their work. It is an elementary principle of business that requests for expenditures should not be authorized unless counterbalancing savings or returns can be shown, and such results cannot be shown by many who carry the title of personnel manager.[2] Unable to see the potentialities of their jobs, they are obviously unable to prove to top management that personnel is an important function and that it should be awarded a high organizational position. Of course, one may ask why, in such instances, top management has appointed low-caliber men to these positions; and the source of trouble is found to be in top management itself.

In instances in which top management takes a comprehensive and understanding view of the subject, a personnel division approximately along the lines of that shown in Figure 6 (p. 68) would be the result. It should be noted that this chart is a composite developed from actual practice and not just a theoretical conception.

2. PHYSICAL FACTORS.   As suggested earlier, size of company, location of offices and plants, and the importance of labor problems affect the specific place which such a division would be given in a particular organization. For example, a medium-sized company with one plant and no unusual labor problems might get along very well with the setup shown in Figure 7. As illustrated there, an employment section has been installed in the production division to serve its needs, whereas employment functions apparently are performed by the sales manager himself. In the case of personnel matters affecting all employees, central units have been established in the accounting department to handle social security records and in the treasurer's department to handle pension and insurance programs. But as an enterprise grows and all parts of an organization require the services of a specialized staff, there is a tendency to centralize authority over performance of personnel functions, as illustrated in Figure 4 (p. 55). A centralized staff department is usually preferred because it is more economical and results in the application of uniform plans and programs.

---

[2] This does not mean that returns must be immediate or measurable in dollars or cents. Much that good personnel work accomplishes comes only after years of effort and often in terms of intangibles whose value is significant, though not always expressible in monetary terms.

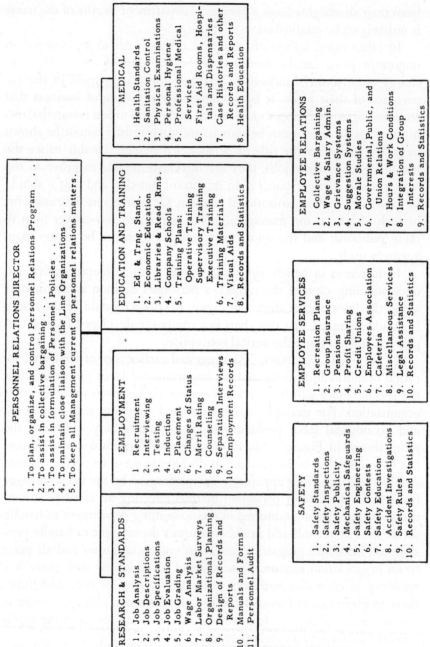

FIGURE 6. Composite Personnel Relations Functional Chart*

PERSONNEL RELATIONS DIRECTOR

1. To plan, organize, and control Personnel Relations Program . . .
2. To assist in collective bargaining . . .
3. To assist in formulation of Personnel Policies . . .
4. To maintain close liaison with the Line Organizations . . .
5. To keep all Management current on personnel relations matters.

RESEARCH & STANDARDS

1. Job Analysis
2. Job Descriptions
3. Job Specifications
4. Job Evaluation
5. Job Grading
6. Wage Analysis
7. Labor Market Surveys
8. Organizational Planning
9. Design of Records and Reports
10. Manuals and Forms
11. Personnel Audit

EMPLOYMENT

1. Recruitment
2. Interviewing
3. Testing
4. Induction
5. Placement
6. Changes of Status
7. Merit Rating
8. Counseling
9. Separation Interviews
10. Employment Records

EDUCATION AND TRAINING

1. Ed. & Trng. Stand.
2. Economic Education
3. Libraries & Read. Rms.
4. Company Schools
5. Training Plans:
   Operative Training
   Supervisory Training
   Executive Training
6. Training Materials
7. Visual Aids
8. Records and Statistics

MEDICAL

1. Health Standards
2. Sanitation Control
3. Physical Examinations
4. Personal Hygiene
5. Professional Medical Services
6. First Aid Rooms, Hospitals and Dispensaries
7. Case Histories and other Records and Reports
8. Health Education

SAFETY

1. Safety Standards
2. Safety Inspections
3. Safety Publicity
4. Mechanical Safeguards
5. Safety Engineering
6. Safety Contests
7. Safety Education
8. Accident Investigations
9. Safety Rules
10. Records and Statistics

EMPLOYEE SERVICES

1. Recreation Plans
2. Group Insurance
3. Pensions
4. Profit Sharing
5. Credit Unions
6. Employees Association
7. Cafeteria
8. Miscellaneous Services
9. Legal Assistance
10. Records and Statistics

EMPLOYEE RELATIONS

1. Collective Bargaining
2. Wage & Salary Admin.
3. Grievance Systems
4. Suggestion Systems
5. Morale Studies
6. Governmental, Public, and Union Relations
7. Hours & Work Conditions
8. Integration of Group Interests
9. Records and Statistics

* Source: Edgar G. Williams, "Indiana Personnel Executives—Their Programs and Practices," *Booklet of the Indiana State Chamber of Commerce* (1952), p. 5.

FIGURE 7. Personnel Functions in a Medium-Sized Company

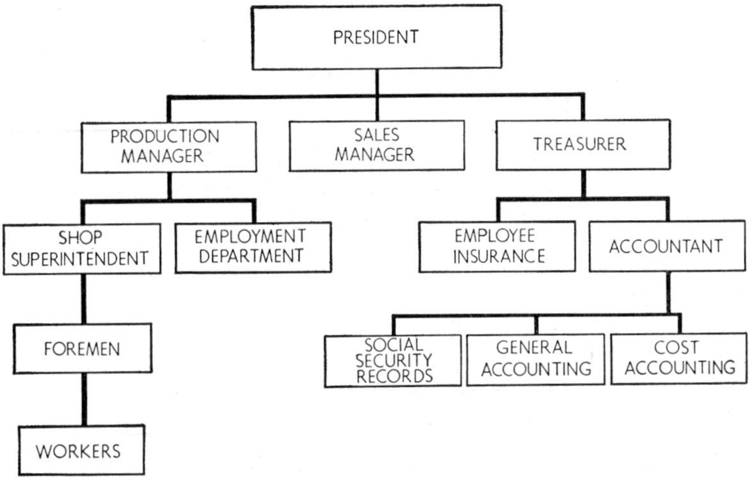

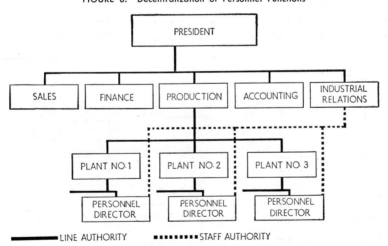

When growth of an enterprise takes place by establishing additional locations, the question arises as to where and by whom personnel functions should be performed. One answer is illustrated in Figure 8. A personnel department, subject to the plant manager, is established at

FIGURE 8. Decentralization of Personnel Functions

each location. In addition, there is a central personnel unit to which each may turn for expert advice and from which uniform plans and policies are derived. By this arrangement, local autonomy with its advantages is secured, yet uniform practices are assured for the company. In some instances, the foregoing arrangement is changed by making the local personnel units responsible to the central personnel unit instead of to the respective plant managers. This relationship is used because of the more specialized direction which is given to the local personnel units. This advantage is attained only at the cost of lowered co-operation between the local personnel units and the plants which they serve. Another answer to the question of multiple-plant units is to centralize the authority and performance of personnel functions, notwithstanding. This arrangement, illustrated in Figure 9, is usually unwieldy and gives way to some decentralization of performance, if not authority over personnel work.

FIGURE 9.   Centralization of Personnel Functions

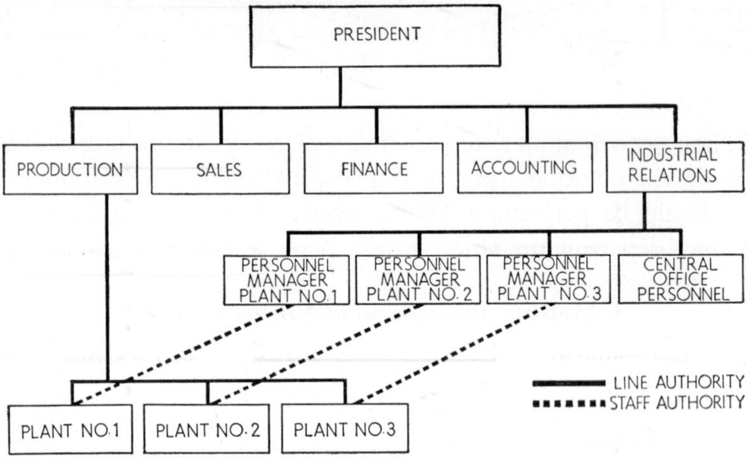

3. EFFECT OF LEGISLATION AND UNIONS UPON STRUCTURE. Such factors as legislation and labor unions have also influenced the design of organization structures. For example, the installation of such units as safety and unemployment compensation can be ascribed almost entirely to legislative regulations or requirements. Also, the rights of employees to organize and bargain collectively have resulted in the addition of organization relationships as illustrated in Figure 10.

4. PROBLEMS FACED. In the last place, the type of personnel functions performed depends largely upon the problems to be solved. This explains why personnel management usually developed first in the production divisions of most companies. Here, labor problems among large aggregations of workers have been encountered. Another excellent example of the force of special problems is provided as recently as World War II when many companies established personnel units for the sole purpose of dealing with the large numbers of women workers

who were entering industry's ranks for the first time. Additional proof of the tendency to create personnel units to handle particular problems is illustrated in Figure 11 (p. 72). This shows the existence of units to take care of such war-created activities as fingerprinting, rationing and transportation services, and night-shift counseling.

FIGURE 10.   Structure of Collective Bargaining

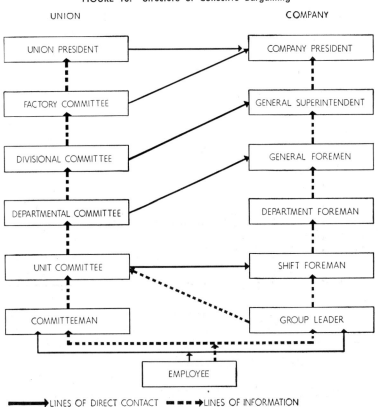

UNION   COMPANY

LINES OF DIRECT CONTACT ▬ ▬ ▬▶LINES OF INFORMATION

TESTS OF GOOD STRUCTURE

The foregoing discussion of the theory and practice of organization structure has been undertaken with a view to providing the student with a background of material essential to an understanding of the place of personnel management in an enterprise. In conclusion, it is worth pointing some remarks toward the matter of tests by which it may be possible to determine whether or not a given personnel department is well organized. In general, a good personnel department should possess the following characteristics:

1. Stability, or the ability to replace key personnel executives or employees with a minimum loss of effectiveness
2. Flexibility, or the capacity to handle effectively short-run changes in the volume of personnel work or in the personnel problems encountered
3. Growth, or the feature of being prepared with advance plans to handle permanent changes in personnel problems or in underlying labor conditions
4. Balance, or the feature of having authority and resources adequate in amount to handle the functions and problems for which the personnel department is made responsible
5. Simplicity, or the feature of keeping personnel lines of relationship to other departments clear and simple
6. Objectivity, or the feature of having definite objectives for each unit in the personnel department

FIGURE 11. A Personnel Department

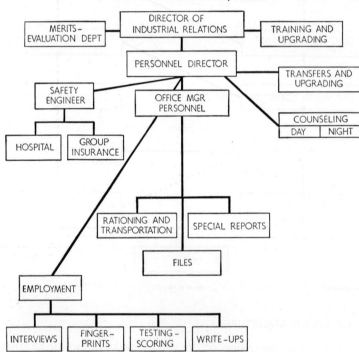

QUESTIONS AND PROBLEMS

1. What answers can be given to the question of the kind and amount of authority and responsibility that may be accorded to the personnel manager? Which answer do you consider to be most nearly correct?
2. Why is a limited use of the functional form of organization structure desirable during periods of emergency? Illustrate this in connection with the

conditions that exist during wartime or when much legislation is being enacted. Use personnel situations in your illustrations.

3. Essentially how much authority does a staff executive, such as the personnel manager, have in a pure line and staff structure? Where and how does he ever build any influence over personnel matters?

4. What must be done to keep the channels of line command and staff advice from running afoul of each other?

5. What are the sources from which authority may be derived? What moral is there here for the personnel manager?

6. In the course of selecting a given employee, some differences of opinion arose between the personnel department, the factory superintendent, and the legal department. The trouble came to a head when a foreman refused to accept a candidate sent to him by the personnel department. The latter attempted to force the factory superintendent to make the foreman take the man in question. The personnel department brought in the company lawyer, who said that the selection of the personnel department had to be followed because it (the legal department) had decided that, unless the candidate in question were hired, the company would be subject to a lawsuit for having failed to take on a man that the personnel department had hired.

   a) What kind of authority did each of these departments think it had?

   b) What authority should each have?

   c) Is the legal department right?

7. Of two executives on the same plane organizationally, it was found that, during a given period of time, one was contacted by subordinates and other executives on an average of thirty times a day, and the other, five. What are the possible explanations?

8. Is it desirable or undesirable to encourage each executive to develop his informal powers as much as he can? Explain.

9. What is the moral of informal authority for the personnel manager himself?

10. If employees appoint informal leaders among themselves, why doesn't industry seek out these leaders and put them on the management team?

11. Why not suppress informal organizations among employees and require all relationships to conform to the formal chart of organization structure? Explain.

12. In what ways may the informal organization be used by the company?

13. Can you cite any actual examples of how employees use the informal structure among themselves? If you cannot from your own experience, ask some "old-timer" about this subject, but don't use the term "informal structure" when talking to him.

14. Upon what factors does the place accorded the personnel department in a company organization structure usually depend? Illustrate by concrete examples.

15. Why has top management been more prone in recent years to give greater recognition to personnel departments?

16. What is meant by "centralization" of personnel functions? Distinguish between the aspects of authority and performance as related to centralization. Illustrate how one may be centralized and the other decentralized.

17. As communication facilities are improved what would you expect to happen in the case of centralizing personnel work? What factors tend to centralize, and what factors to decentralize, personnel work?

18. In future years, would you expect personnel departments to increase or decrease in importance? Why?

19. How would you determine whether or not a given personnel department had been accorded sufficient resources and authority to carry on its assigned tasks effectively?

20. During a conference between the plant manager, the personnel manager, and the chief shop steward (union representative) of a given company in regard to a proposed pension plan, a number of disagreements became apparent. The plant manager stated that pension plans did no good so far as younger employees were concerned; the personnel manager stated that he was going to have one put in regardless; and the chief steward insisted that the benefit payments as stated in the proposal be doubled. Discuss this case from the viewpoint of organizational and managerial principles.

CHAPTER

5 | Job Requirements

In the preceding chapters, broad background and managerial aspects of personnel were studied. It is now pertinent to turn attention to the operative functions of personnel management. These, as will be recalled, are concerned with procuring, developing, maintaining, and utilizing a labor force. Each of these involves detailed activity, specific methodology, and careful application of principles. As a consequence, it will be necessary to devote the next several chapters to a discussion of the first of these; the others will be studied in subsequent chapters.

It is worth repeating the statement made earlier, however, that all functions of personnel are interaffecting. While procurement, for example, is taken up now as a separate function, it affects and is affected by such other operative personnel functions as training, wage determination, and collective bargaining. But to keep the textbook within practical limits, it is not feasible to show these interactions in each chapter.

"Personnel procurement" may be defined simply as the task of hiring labor to fill current or future job vacancies. This simple statement hides a number of important questions that must be answered if the task of hiring is to result in successful placements. Among these questions are the following:

1. What are the requirements and the content of jobs to be filled?
2. What kinds of and how much labor must be procured?
3. From what sources may the required labor be procured?
4. What procedures should be adopted in order to screen desirable from undesirable candidates?
5. What is the use of such tools as interviewing and testing in the selection procedure?
6. What is the place of transfers and promotions in the procurement function?

The present chapter is devoted to the first of these questions; the other questions are considered in the next several chapters.

75

DEFINITIONS

The terms used in connection with job studies are several in number and differ in connotation; therefore, it is desirable at the outset to have some agreement on usage and definitions. It is well to point out that the definitions suggested here are not universally adopted. Unfortunately, common usage of terms does not exist. Hence, when terms are encountered in other sources or actual cases, it is well to ascertain what meaning is given in each instance. In this section on definitions, the material is taken up under the following headings:

1. Meaning of job requirements
2. Terminology of job studies
3. Definition of job terms

1. MEANING OF JOB REQUIREMENTS. One of the easiest mistakes to make about jobs is to assume that what a job is or requires is readily understood. For example, if one were asked what a stenographer does, the answer most likely to be given is that she takes dictation, transcribes the "shorthand," and types. This obvious answer really reveals very little about the job so far as filling a vacancy is concerned. How fast, for example, must the stenographer be able to take dictation or type? And what about a candidate who is not now a stenographer but who would like to become one?

These two questions point up the need for specifications of job requirements that are defined in terms of the experience that a company will require of candidates. On the one hand, the policy may be that of hiring experienced labor. In that case, job requirements can be usefully stated in what activities are performed on each job. A listing of typical duties of a typist's job, of sales duties of a salesman, or of the work activities of a production machinist would suffice. In each case, a candidate's work experience could be checked against the stated requirements.

On the other hand, it is often necessary to hire inexperienced and untrained persons. Then a statement of job requirements in terms of duties is of little help. Assume, for example, that the specification for a vacancy on a drill press job stated that the operator drills holes in various classes of metal. Such a statement would be of little service in determining whether or not an inexperienced candidate possessed the potential qualities to become a good drill press operator.

Job requirements, in such instances, must be translated from physical or mechanical terms to those of human characteristics. Thus, in the case of the drill press operation, such specifications as the following would have to be derived:

1. Finger dexterity requirements
2. Physical strength components
3. Hand-eye co-ordination requirements
4. Spatial relationship requirements

Then, as candidates presented themselves, their potential ability to fill vacancies could better be measured in terms of these basic requirements.

What a job requires may be described either in terms of what duties are performed on the job or of what characteristics are required to perform the duties. Invariably the first of these descriptions must be provided before the latter can be derived. Although the personal characteristics are more fundamental and, therefore, of more lasting value, many companies provide only the first type of job specifications.

2. TERMINOLOGY OF JOB STUDIES. A "job specification," pure and simple, is a written description of a job and its characteristics. Ordinarily, however, job specifications are also used to cover the abilities and qualities that an individual should possess in order to hold the job in question. The latter is perhaps better described as a "man specification," although commonly it is included in the job specification.[1]

While on the subject of definitions, it is well to anticipate a few other terms. "Job analysis," by which specifications are obtained, refers to the process of studying the operations, duties, and organizational aspects of jobs. From such analyses, more or less general statements about jobs are obtained, which are known as "job descriptions." After the descriptions are further refined, specifications are derived. Another term of interest is "job classification," which refers to a system of relating jobs with similar or family characteristics into a logical order of groupings. The term "job evaluation," which subject is studied in a later chapter, has reference to a plan of monetary measurement of job values.

It is well to note here that, although interest in these tools at present is in relation to hiring, they are also of use in connection with other personnel tasks. For example, training, counseling, safety work, job evaluation, promotion plans, and personnel research are scarcely possible without a good plan of job analysis, descriptions, classifications,

---

[1] "Man specifications" are discussed more fully in the next chapter.

and specifications. Their use in connection with such functions is discussed in later chapters.

3. DEFINITION OF JOB TERMS.   To avoid confusion of terms used in connection with work assignments, attention to definitions of jobs, positions, and occupations is in order. By a "job" is commonly meant an assignment of work calling for a set of duties, responsibilities, and conditions that are different from those of other work assignments. The foregoing elements determine job limits and not the tools, records, or location of a particular task. For example, two salesclerks who are performing work that involves similar duties and requires like training, experience, and personal characteristics would, according to the foregoing definition, be said to hold the same kind of job. Yet these two clerks may be working in widely separated stations in the store. On the other hand, two other salesclerks who do not have the same range of duties would be said to be working on different jobs even though they happened to be located side by side.

The term "job" may be clarified further by comparing it with "position" and "occupation." The term "position" is sometimes used as a synonym for "job," although in better practice a distinction is made between the two. Thus, when several persons are doing similar work, each one is said to have the same job, but different positions. The latter term is restricted to mean the tasks performed by a person without indicating whether or not the work differs from that of work assignments of other individuals. The term "stations" is somewhat similar in meaning to that of "positions." There invariably are more positions or stations in a company than jobs.

The term "occupation" refers to a group of jobs with common characteristics. Although selling, for example, may be divisible into a number of jobs, depending upon what is being sold, a group of closely related selling jobs may be considered as an occupation. "Job families" is another term used to cover the idea of groupings of similar jobs.

Within a particular job, two or more "grades" may also be recognized. Such a distinction is desirable when the work assignments on a given job can be graded according to difficulty or quality of workmanship. For example, a wide range of work may be performed in the case of a single-spindle drill press operation. Some of the work might involve intricate drilling, and other batches might be more or less simple. Hence it would be desirable to distinguish between operators on this machine according to whether they were, let us say, Class I, Class II, or Class III operators, meaning that they were highly skilled, semiskilled, and learners, respectively.

A PROGRAM OF SPECIFYING JOB REQUIREMENTS

Since labor is hired to carry out specific jobs, it would seem axiomatic that knowledge of work assignments is a basic prerequisite for performing the procurement function. This information may be gathered either after vacancies occur or in expectancy of vacancies. Under the former practice, the job of hiring is delayed somewhat as compared to the practice of gathering job data before vacancies actually occur. A survey of practice in this respect would undoubtedly show that the former is more commonly followed, although there seems to be an increased tendency to prepare job data in advance of need. It must be noted, however, that specifications of job content are not nearly so common—to go into another aspect of industry—as are material specifications. Perhaps the difficulty in prescribing job content and personal qualifications (this is to be taken up in the next chapter) seems to explain why specifications, at least any worthy of the name, are not very common.

When hiring is performed by line executives themselves, job specifications are of questionable value. However, when turnover of such executives is high, use of specifications is recommended because job information will not vanish when line executives are transferred, promoted, or leave the company. The use of job specifications is particularly desirable when a personnel department is assigned the task of hiring. In such cases, the efforts of the expert in procurement will be more effective if he possesses an accurate statement of the need to be filled. And as an organization grows, such information becomes indispensable.

The task of developing such information may be conveniently discussed under the following headings:

1. Information to be gathered
2. Responsibility for collecting information
3. Methods of gathering information
4. Writing up the job descriptions

INFORMATION TO BE GATHERED

The first step in a well-rounded program of job specifications is to prepare a list of all jobs in the company and where they are located. Too frequently, a well-devised and meaningful system of job titles does not exist. In addition, job titles are often too general to be distinctive. Frequently, similar jobs are called by different names or different jobs

FIGURE 12. Personnel and Job Inventory

I Job Symbol	II Personnel Number	III Job Title and Employee Name	IV Veteran's Status	V Occupational Dictionary Code	VI Clock Number	VII Worker Skills	VIII Minimum Training Time (Months)	IX Male-Female Jobs Suitable for Women	X Total Workers on Job	XI Number in Training or to Be Upgraded	XII To Be Upgraded or Transferred from (Personnel Number)	XIII Additional Needs to Meet Production Schedule	XIV Experience—Same—Related—Vocational Trainees Inexperience	XV Date Seniority Begins
A		FOREMEN	0	5-92.768			48		2	1		0		
	1	John Smith			940	ABC		M						6/1/18
	2	Bill Brown			975	BCA		M			3			7/1/36
B		TOOLMAKERS		4.76.210			36	S	3	1		0		
	3	Bill White			1296	BCA		M			6			1/2/33
	4	Harry Doe			1285	BCY		M						2/8/26
	5	Tim Black	11		1273	CB		M						3/4/44
C		MACHINISTS		4-75.010			24	S	3	2		0		
	6	Sam Roe			1476	CDB		M			10			2/6/33
	7	Russell Jones			1481	CDF		M			9			9/1/36
	8	Emmet Smith			1461	CDE		M						8/1/28
D		TURRET-LATHE OPERATORS		4-78.021			6	S	5	2		0		
	9	Dave White			1423	CDR		M			14			7/2/41
	10	Al Brown			1424	DEFGC		M			15			12/1/41

FIGURE 12.—Continued

PERSONNEL AND JOB INVENTORY

A Personnel and Job Inventory is a systematic but flexible plan for obtaining and recording information about the jobs and personnel in a plant for the purpose of analyzing and solving various personnel problems.

INSTRUCTIONS FOR PREPARATION

Col. I. Jobs throughout the plant should each be identified by their own symbol. Assign only one symbol to a job even though it appears in more than one department in the plant.

Col. II. Personnel should be numbered consecutively for the entire plant, as the names are entered on the form.

Col. III. All jobs should be listed in descending order of skill by department. For example: 1. Foreman; 2. Assistant Foreman; 3. Job Setter; 4. Turret Lathe Operator.

The personnel employed on each job should be listed under that job, by name.

Col. IV. Indicate after the worker's name in Column IV whether he or she is a veteran. If World War II, use II, if other, use 0.

Col. V. The code number assigned to the job definition, in the Dictionary of Occupational Titles, Part I, which most nearly fits the plant job may be inserted in this column. The local office of the USES will render assistance in coding, if needed, or plant coding system may be used.

Col. VI. Employee's clock number or identification number should be inserted in this column.

Col. VII. Each worker should be interviewed to obtain a record of his training and experience, if these records are not already available. From this record, all plant jobs in which he is skilled, should be indicated in Column VII by inserting the symbol of the jobs in which he is skilled. The symbols of the jobs for which the employee is qualified should be recorded with the highest skill to the left and then the next highest skills in their respective order. For example: Sam Roe has the Job symbol C-D-B listed in Column VII: turning to these symbols we find that C is a Machinist, D, a Turret Lathe Operator and B is a Toolmaker. This would indicate that Sam Roe's highest skill is a Machinist, his second highest skill is a Turret Lathe Operator and he has had some experience as a Toolmaker.

Col. VIII. Enter estimate of shortest possible time in months, absolutely necessary to train an experienced worker. This should be listed opposite each job title.

Col. IX. For each job on which women are at present employed, and for those which are considered suitable for women workers even tho they are not on them at present, the letter "S" should be inserted in Column IX opposite the job title. Opposite the name of each employee, enter in Column IX, the letter "M" for each male employee and the letter "F" for each female employe.

Col. X. The total workers employed on each job should be listed in Column X, opposite the job title.

Col. XI. The number of persons already employed being trained for upgrading into a specific job should be inserted in Column XI, opposite the title of the job to which they will be transferred.

Col. XII. For each person included in the figures of Column XI an identifying personnel number will be shown in Column XII. The personnel number of new and inexperienced employees (learners) being trained for specific jobs, will be listed in this column with a circle around the personnel number. Those being transferred or upgraded from other jobs will be included in this same space without a circle. Thus the number of inexperienced workers (learners) (the number enclosed in the circle) plus the number to be upgraded or transferred (the number not encircled) will equal the total number of people being trained for or upgraded to a specific job. For each addition in personnel anticipated on a job, the personnel number of the incoming employee should be inserted in Column XII opposite the job number and title, to which transfer is being made. For each replacement in personnel anticipated on a job, the personnel number of the incoming employee who is to replace the employee now on the job, should be inserted in Column XII opposite the name of the employee to be replaced. Thus when a personnel number is found in Column XII opposite the name of the employee working on the job, it means the anticipated replacement of that person on that job. When numbers are entered in Column XII, opposite the job title, these indicate additions rather than replacements.

Col. XIII. After exhausting all possibilities of upgrading, training and transferring from within the plant, the number of additional new workers needed on each job should be inserted in this column opposite job title.

Col. XIV. When additional new workers are needed to meet production schedules, the employer should indicate the minimum experience requirements necessary for new employees to do the job. The letter "S" may be used to indicate "same experience," the letter "R" for "related experience," "V" for "vocational trainees" and "I" for "inexperienced workers." Insofar as possible, additional demands should be for inexperienced workers.

Col. XV. Record day, month and year worker's seniority began.

by the same names. Such undesirable conditions can be cleared up quickly by the use of job lists and title descriptions.

The preparation of job titles is a step in the process known as "job analysis," which will be discussed more fully later in this chapter. It may be noted here, however, that information on job titles is best derived by using a number of sources in order to obtain a cross-check. These sources include, first, payroll records; second, organization chart titles; third, reports from supervisors, foremen, and managers; fourth, interviews with or questionnaires from employees; and, fifth, the *Dictionary of Occupational Titles*. The latter is a publication of the federal government which serves as an excellent source of information and as a basis of industry-wide comparison. The result of such studies will be a list such as that illustrated in Figure 12 (pp. 80 and 81). This shows the job titles, where jobs are located, and miscellaneous information about the various jobs.

Such lists of jobs and job titles are, of course, merely a start, although an indispensable beginning, in the process of gathering information for use in the procurement function. The next step is to gather detailed information about each job. To what extent we should go in gathering information of this character depends upon the various other purposes—training, compensation, organization development, etc.—to which job data will be put. In general, however, the information sought usually includes the following:

1. Identifying terms and locations of job
2. Duties performed
3. Responsibilities involved
4. Conditions and factors of work
5. Personal characteristics and traits apparently required to—
    a) Fulfill the foregoing duties and responsibilities, and
    b) Work under particular conditions and with factors specified

More specifically the following information would be sought for each job:

1. Job titles, including trade nicknames
2. Number of employees on the job and their organizational location
3. Names of immediate supervisors
4. Materials, tools, and equipment used or worked with
5. Work or instructions received from and to whom delivered
6. Salary or wage levels and hours of work
7. Conditions of work
8. Complete listing of duties, separated according to daily, weekly, monthly, and casual, and estimated according to time spent on each
9. Educational and experience requirements

10. Skills, aptitudes, and abilities required
11. Promotional and transfer lines from and to the job
12. Miscellaneous information and comments

Examples of such information are shown in Figures 13 and 14 (pp. 84–88). The latter example illustrates how the information was gathered by means of the questionnaires in the retail field; and the former shows a simple, yet reasonably clear, description of a band saw operator in the production field. These examples merit close study because they illustrate the form in which information may be gathered, the classes of information that are prepared, and the manner in which job information is written up.

Job information is particularly useful in connection with the selection and placement of special groups of workers. For example, disabled or otherwise handicapped war veterans may not be able to do general-run factory or office work, but they are capable of holding jobs successfully that require only a part of a person's physical capacities or attention. Hence, it is desirable to gather job data with a view to learning exactly what the requirements of each job are. The capabilities of the individual can then be compared with the requirements of jobs until a match is found. How this may be done is illustrated in the next chapter in Figures 17, 18, and 19. Another example of this sort is found in the case of women workers, who also are limited in the types of jobs which they can effectively, and sometimes legally, hold. Here, too, it is necessary to study all jobs in order to determine which can be filled with female employees.

RESPONSIBILITY FOR COLLECTING INFORMATION

Having described the kinds of job information that are useful, it is now appropriate to consider by whom such information is collected, how it is collected, and in what form it is presented. These matters fall within the province of a program of job analysis which may be defined as: A study of jobs to determine what duties are performed, what responsibilities and organizational relationships are involved, and what human traits and characteristics are apparently required. In addition to the pertinence of such information to the function of personnel procurement of interest at the present moment, it is also useful in connection with topics of interest later in this text, such as employee placement, training, and collective bargaining.

1. ORGANIZATION STRUCTURE OF JOB ANALYSIS. At a very early stage in establishing a job analysis program, its place in the organization structure of the company must be determined. Sponsorship of such

FIGURE 13. Band Saw Operator Job Description

BAND SAW OPERATOR

JOB DESCRIPTION

(For Use in Making Manning Tables)

1. COMPANY NAME: X. Y. Z. Co.   2. PAGE NO. __1A__ LINE NO. __5__
   (Part I of Manning Table)

3. PLANT NAME: _____   4. DEPARTMENT: Production Lathe

5. JOB TITLE: __BAND-SAW OPERATOR__
   *(List first most common title used in plant and any additional titles –
   separate by semi-colons)*

6. MINIMUM TIME NOW REQUIRED TO TRAIN A REPLACEMENT: __200 hours__

7. SPECIAL PHYSICAL REQUIREMENTS: __NONE__
   *(State unusual requirements of job – eyesight, strength
   or other, and what portion of the job requires this trait.)*

8. SUPERVISION: __Receives work assignments from Foreman, completing them
   according to prescribed standards.__
   (Indicate type of supervision received or given)

9. DESCRIPTION OF WORK PERFORMED:
   SUMMARY *(Give overall picture of job in one or two sentences.)* Cuts sheet metal
   blanks to specified dimensions using a power-driven band saw.

Steps performed in the job	Percent of Time	Exactly How Performed (Include special skills, machinery, tools, judgments, decisions)
a. Marks sheet * for entry, according to specifications	13%	Lays out lines to be cut using T square, compass, triangle and chalk or scriber.
b. Clamps marked sheet to work table	5%	Uses clamps to fasten workpiece to table.
c. Directs lubricating fluid against cutting edge	2%	
d. Cuts blank from sheet **	80%	Starts saw and turns handwheel or engages power-driven feed to move stock against blade of saw.

10. COMMENTS: (Use this space to enter additional information explaining items on this form; to give additional facts about this job; to indicate where job fits into industrial process; to explain difference between this and similar jobs; to define any special terms peculiar to the job; or any other pertinent information.)

Worker must exercise care to avoid amputating fingers.

Indicate most essential skill with •
Indicate next most essential skill with ••

FIGURE 14*

QUESTIONNAIRE FOR JOB ANALYSIS

Your Name   Jane White   Date   2-9-44

Title or Designation of Your Job   Inspector-wrapper

Regular or Extra   Regular

Your Department   Coat and Gown Room

To Whom Do You Report Directly (Name and Title):   Miss Nancy Brown

floor supervisor.

The purpose of this questionnaire is to ask each person here to write down exactly what his or her job is and also to write down the duties and the responsibilities of that job. This information will be of great assistance in carrying out the store's employment, training, and promotion program.

In the space below, please write a brief description of your work under the eight main headings indicated. To do this successfully, reflect for a few minutes on your activities, making a few notes of the things you do daily, periodically, and occasionally; any supervision of others which you may do; your contacts with other individuals and departments; any business contacts outside the Company, and whether personally, by telephone, or by correspondence; finally a notation of the equipment and material you use. Endeavor to put the essential things first and in order of their performance, then the lesser items.

Next, write four or five sentences covering that portion of your work falling under each of the headings. Do any revising necessary to make the statements more concise. Whenever possible, begin each statement with word denoting action. For example: "open mail, type forms," etc. (Omit "I"). Finally, copy this below in legible print or longhand (on typewriter if convenient).

Use additional paper if necessary and attach securely.

1. **Description of Work**

   A—DAILY DUTIES: Describe in detail the work you perform regularly each day. In case of selling, include the lines of merchandise sold and the price range. Where there are several steps involved in your job, show each separately and in order of performance.

---

* Jucius, Maynard, and Shartle, *Job Analysis for Retail Stores*, Bureau of Business Research, Ohio State University, pp. 15-17.

FIGURE 14.—Continued

1. *Check and put away supplies received from supply department.*

2. *Straighten and clean wrapping desk including washing paste jar, filling tape machine with water and tape.*

3. *Complete wrapping of after-four merchandise.*

4. *Receive sales check and merchandise from salesperson to be wrapped for takewith or delivery giving precedence to takewiths.*

5. *Open tube carriers for authorized saleschecks and check same against merchandise, noting quantity, price and condition of merchandise.*

6. *If salescheck is unauthorized, notify section manager. If there is change to be returned to customer, count and call sales-person.*

7. *Select correct size box, line with tissue, fold merchandise and prepare box for takewith or delivery, according to routines learned in training period.*

8. *Paste customer's address docket on packages and pin triplicate of salescheck on packages to be delivered in town or out of town and make record of shipments.*

9. *Bag layaways, fold sales chack and place in slot of layaway tag and place on hook of the hanger.*

10. *Keep stubs for stock record purposes.*

11. *Answer phone calls for section managers and salespeople.*

12. *Check supplies and make requisition for needed items.*

13. *Count dockets of merchandise wrapped the previous day.*

14. *Make out desk report if there is more than one person in the desk.*

B—PERIODICAL DUTIES: Describe in detail the work you perform regularly at stated periods, as, for instance, each week, each month, etc. If none, so state.

None.

C—OCCASIONAL DUTIES: Describe those duties you are called upon to perform at irregular intervals, that is, duties which are special or fill-in work.

None.

2. **Job Knowledge Requirements**

A—STORE PROCEDURE AND METHODS:

1. *Handling of sales transactions and authorizations according to store procedure.*

2. *Handling of wrapping according to store procedure.*

3. *Handling of inspector-wrapper reports according to store procedure.*

4. *Handling of delivery record of coat department.*

5. *Type and quantity of supplies needed.*

FIGURE 14.—Continued

B—MERCHANDISE:

1. Check mechandise for defects.

3. **What Equipment Do You Use?**

Inspector stamp, tape machine, paste bottle, scissors.

4. **What Materials Do You Work with or Sell?**

Wrapping paper, tissue paper, boxes, tape, twine and miscellaneous forms.

5. **If You Supervise the Work of Others, State How Many and What Their Jobs Are (for example: Two file clerks).**

None.

6. **What Persons in Other Jobs Do You Contact Regularly in Your Work?**

A—WITHIN THE COMPANY

Section manager	Assistant buyer
Salesperson	Floor supervisor
Buyer	Head supervisor

B—OUTSIDE OF THE COMPANY

Answer customers' phone calls to salespeople and questions of customers at desk.

7. **To What Job Would You Normally Expect to Be Promoted?**

Stock record clerk, Credit Department clerk, Adjustment office clerk, Shopping Service, Salesperson.

8. **From What Job Were You Transferred to Your Present Job?**

Hired for job—no previous retail experience.

programs, particularly in the initiating stages or when they are to be used for job evaluation purposes, should be by the top executives. When a major committee is established with the president or senior vice-president as chairman, it has been found that the "doubting Thomases," who are found in every organization, are more readily convinced that top management is really "sold" on the permanent value of the evaluation program. The committee would not carry out the job analysis work; but, in addition to the needed prestige it lends in the initial stages, it can periodically review the progress which has been made and lend its judgment to major problems that invariably will present themselves.

As to the specific unit that should make the job studies, there is some difference of opinion, although the majority of companies assign this task to the personnel division. Before personnel departments were as common as at present, this work—if done at all—was assigned to an operating executive, who then appointed staff specialists to handle the routine details. Since most firms now have personnel units, job analysis is often assigned to them. This is logical because personnel is commonly responsible for selection, training, and salary administration—all of which are helped by job analysis. In many instances, job analysis is assigned to the time study or engineering departments because of the interest of these units in the physical aspects of the jobs.

2. STAFFING THE JOB ANALYSIS UNIT. Coming to questions of how the unit that is to carry on the job analysis is to be staffed, two alternatives are available. Either trained help may be brought in from the outside, or members on the staff who seem to have abilities along these lines may be given special training in job analysis methods. The advantage of the former choice is that competent specialists are secured at once, but its disadvantage is that outsiders must learn the "personality" of the company and its special problems. The latter choice reverses the advantages and disadvantages. Most companies, however, select job analysts from their own ranks because it seems easier to train such specialists than to find them in the labor market.

Whichever choice is made in staffing the job analysis unit, a certain amount of preliminary training is called for, notwithstanding. For one thing, analysts must be trained in company policies and organization, or in job analysis techniques, depending upon whether they were selected from the outside or inside. They will also have to be trained on ways and means of co-operating with line personnel. It is particularly important to impress upon analysts the service nature of their work. Unless the co-operation of divisional managers, foremen, and supervisors is obtained, job analysts may do more harm than good to a personnel program. Of course, line personnel should be called together, also, for informative conferences regarding the purposes, methods, and expected results of job analysis. This is essential, in order, first, to convince line personnel that the purpose of the program is helpful to them and, second, to break down their natural reluctance to permit "anyone from personnel" to mix in their affairs. Moreover, when unions are involved, it may be desirable to consult with union representatives regarding the nature and purposes of such job studies.

METHODS OF GATHERING DATA

Information for job studies is obtained in either of two ways—questionnaires or personal interviews.

In the questionnaire method, a standard form is prepared by the job analysts and sent either to each worker or to the supervisors. Some companies prefer to gather job data from the workers, believing that they obtain more detailed information thereby, whereas others feel that the supervisor is a better judge of what should be included for each job. After the completed questionnaires are returned, the job analysts group them by jobs and then examine the findings, job by job. As may be expected, it is possible to survey all the jobs and positions in a company much more quickly by this method than by the interviewing method.

Under the interview method, the job analyst obtains information by personal conference with the workers or supervisors, and sometimes both. If he is well trained for his work, the job analyst can gather more relevant information by interviewing than is possible with questionnaires. Moreover, he carries away with him a personal impression of the job, which contributes greatly to the accuracy of the studies. Usually, personal interviews are more costly and time-consuming than questionnaires. Which should be used depends upon the value received and required as compared to the costs and time involved.

Whichever method of gathering information is used, a few words of warning are in order. The job analyst should know how to work with supervisors and employees to maintain smooth and understanding relationships. In order to help analysts maintain such relationships, analysts are sometimes supplied with written instructions such as the following example:

A. Procedure to be followed during the initial interview and discussion with Section Manager

    1. Analyst must adjust the technique of the interview to the Section Manager with whom working. If necessary he must be prepared to give an explanation of the program.

        a) Go over Selling Supervisor's list of job titles.

        b) Examine and discuss work sheet of sections' job titles, individual job responsibilities and duties, and organization structure. Make rough organizational chart.

        c) Be familiar with various job descriptions in order to refer to specific details immediately.

        d) Correct any faults discovered by making additions to the information on hand, or leave blanks for new descriptions. If the latter is necessary, make a definite date to pick up new descriptions.

    2. Results to be achieved from the initial discussion with Section Manager and Divisional Service Manager—

        a) Complete and accurate job descriptions of all jobs in section.

        b) Correct definitions of all job responsibilities, job duties, and organizational lines.

It is also essential to continue to caution whoever gathers job information that the analysis is concerned with jobs and not with particular employees now holding them. There is danger, otherwise, that resulting job descriptions will be colored by the personality or special skill exhibited by a given employee. Hence, when several employees are performing the same type of work, it is good practice to make analyses of two or three employees, in order to have comparative information that will serve to minimize the danger of personal bias.

On the other hand, jobs that seem to be identical on the surface should not be accepted as such without at least routine checks. For example, it would be a serious mistake to conclude that all floor sales personnel in a department store perform the same kind of work and call for the same grades of skills. Hence, in making job analyses by this method, it is safer to err on the side of too many than too few job studies. Should the results then indicate that some jobs considered to be different were actually similar, it is easy to cut down on the superfluous studies. Furthermore, by following the practice of making sufficient job studies, there is less danger of overlooking important details that have been incorporated in some jobs but not in others, particularly when innovations in procedures are introduced.

WRITING THE JOB DESCRIPTION

After the questionnaires or work sheets and other items of specific information have been checked over, tentative job descriptions should be written. The tentative statements must be submitted to various interested executives for review, change, and final approval. After this is done, the accepted descriptions are prepared. These statements are intended to provide in usable and well-thought-out fashion a clear and concise summary of the information collected by the job analyses. The job descriptions are catalogued by an appropriate system of symbols, permitting ready reference to field descriptions and better office control over job studies in process as well as those completed.

In writing job descriptions, a number of requirements must be met in their preparation. On the one hand, there are "language" problems that must be avoided. It must be remembered that the written word, unless carefully chosen, will not convey to the reader what the writer intended. Trade terms are particularly elusive and often colloquial; hence, when used, they should be defined in nontechnical terms if possible. Along similar lines, words should be used in the same sense and not with a changing connotation. On the other hand, it is essential to avoid overestimating the requirements of jobs. The job descriptions should define the minimum acceptable standards for employment and performance on the job. Exceptional functions, only occasionally per-

FIGURE 15. Job Analysis Schedule*

1. Job Title *POLISHER*	2. Schedule No.
3. Number Employed *30 (25-60)*	4. Establishment No.
6. Title of Verified Job *0*	5. Date *November 17, 1946*
8. Alternate Titles *JEWELRY POLISHER*	Number of Pages *6*
(see VIII)	7. Industry *Jewelry*
10. Dictionary Title *BUFFER I*	9. Branch *Costume*
11. Code *6-77.020*	12. Department *Polishing*
13. Analysis Prepared by *J. O. B. Analyzer*	14. Field Office *Watucca*

15. JOB SUMMARY

Holds pieces of costume jewelry and manipulates them against the surface of laminated muslin, flannel, and wire polishing wheels which are power-rotated, to produce polished surfaces of various types on them before they are plated and painted.

MINIMUM QUALIFICATIONS FOR EMPLOYMENT

16. Sex   *M*   Age   *18 to 60*

17. Necessary Physical Requirements (including height and weight): *Strong, dextrous hands to hold small objects while they are polished.*

18. Education: *S R W* English: Other: *0*

19. Experience: *6 months in the same job, served within the past five years. (See VIII).*

20. RELATION TO OTHER JOBS

May be promoted from *WASH BOY; JIGGER (See VIII).*
May be promoted to *FOREMAN (Polishing Room).*

21. Supervision Received: General   Medium *X*   Close   By (Title) *FOREMAN (Polishing Room)*

22. Supervision Given: None *X*   No. Supervised   Titles

23. Seasonality: Industry Peak: *August to December.* Trough: *May to July* Job: *Same as Industry*

Supplementary sheets should include the following items: I. WORK PERFORMED; II. EQUIPMENT; III. MATERIAL; IV. SURROUNDINGS; V. HAZARDS; VI. SPECIAL INFORMATION; VII. DEFINITION OF TERMS; VIII. COMMENTS.

* For instructions regarding how each of these items is to be compiled, see Appendix A.

FIGURE 15.—Continued

Supplementary Sheet

Schedule Number _____

Date _____ 11/17/46 _____

Sheet 2 of 6 Sheets

Job Title _____ *POLISHER* _____		
	Per Cent of Time	Degree of Skill

I. *WORK PERFORMED*

    Note: The polishing work done here falls into six groups: (1) *oiling* (2) *gloss* (3) *cut and gloss* (4) *mat* (5) *satin* (6) *clean wheel.* By using different *polishing* wheels and *polishing compounds* varied results are obtained. Each POLISHER is expected to and at times does perform all of the six polishing operations but the POLISHING FOREMAN confines them as much as possible to one of the groups. The work in each case is essentially the same and is covered by the following description.

1. Prepares for polishing: Mounts a polishing wheel on the horizontal arbor of a *Polishing Lathe* and locks it in position with a washer and a nut; dresses the wheel to make its sections even and somewhat softer by starting the Lathe and holding a small hand *rake* and then an *emery stone* against the rapidly revolving wheel; holds a stick of compound against the wheel to make it more abrasive and smooths this off by holding a pad (usually a used wheel) against it to remove excess; repeats the dressing operation whenever the wheel wears unevenly; applies compound frequently.   10   2

    Strong hands are required to dress the wheel and knowledge, gained through experience, is required to recognize when the wheel is satisfactorily dressed.

2. Polishes metal jewelry: Receives trays of jewelry from the POLISHING FOREMAN with oral instructions regarding the surfaces to be polished; holds a piece of jewelry against the rotating polishing wheel by hand, with pliers, or with the aid of a *hook*; develops a polishing routine for the job and follows it for each piece, skillfully turning and shifting the piece to produce an evenly polished surface; makes a rapid visual inspection and, finding the finish satisfactory, lays the piece in the tray, using layers of paper to prevent scratching the pieces; carries the tray of completed work to the PAY ROLL CLERK.   85   3

FIGURE 15.—*Continued*

Supplementary Sheet

Schedule Number
_____

Date   11/17/46
_____

Sheet 3 of 6 Sheets
_____

Job Title POLISHER	Per Cent of Time	Degree of Skill
I. *WORK PERFORMED* (Continued)		
Strong and dextrous fingers, hands and arms and well-coordinated use of hands are required to hold the pieces of jewelry against the wheel; good vision is necessary to recognize spots requiring further polishing.		
3. Makes simple *forms* from wood and nails to facilitate holding particular pieces of jewelry while polishing, using hammer, saw, and knife.	5	1

II. *EQUIPMENT*

Pliers; hammer; saw; and knife are supplied by worker.

Polishing wheels: Usually laminated muslin wheels having the circles of muslin sewed together near the center but with the outer edges loose. A hole through the center of the wheel is provided for mounting it on the arbor of a Polishing Lathe. Muslin is used for oiling and cut and gloss operations. Other wheels are (1) felt, for a coarser finish called mat (2) wire wheel for a coarser finish called satin (3) special bristle brushes usually used for oiling operations.

Polishing compounds of varying abrasiveness: Abrasive compounds which (in the order of their abrasiveness) are known as lea, tripoli, white diamond, and crocus are available in the form of sticks about 6 to 10 inches long and 2 inches in diameter. Lea is used to produce mat finishes. Tripoli is used for oiling (a cutting operation in which much oil is used.) White Diamond is used for light cutting and is advantageous because it is less oily than tripoli and the articles need not be cleaned after polishing. Crocus, which is a very fine abrasive, is used for polishing to a high gloss.

Polishing Lathe: (Polishing Lathe, Bench Model, ¾ H.P., 3600 R.P.M., manufactured by the Diamond Machine Company, Providence, Rhode Island). A variable speed electric motor having an arbor extending from one side

FIGURE 15.—*Continued*

Supplementary Sheet

Schedule Number _____

Date ____11/17/46____

Sheet 4 of 6 Sheets

Job Title   *POLISHER*

II. *EQUIPMENT* (Continued)

on which interchangeable polishing wheels can be mounted. Different speeds are required for different polishing operations; 1700 R.P.M. being desirable for coarser finishes like mat and satin, and speeds as high as 3600 R.P.M. being used for the gloss finishes.

Rake: A simple tool made by driving many nails through a short length of wood so that their points project; this is used to dress the polishing wheels.

Emery stone: A piece of broken emery wheel used to dress the polishing wheels.

Hook: A steel wire hook with a wooden handle; by hooking this into a piece of jewelry, especially initials, it is possible to hold a piece that would otherwise be pulled out of hand by the polishing wheel.

Forms: Simple wooden jigs made by the worker to facilitate holding of the pieces of jewelry; some are made to hold several pieces at one time.

III. *MATERIAL*

None.

IV. *SURROUNDINGS*

There is a constant, noisy hum from the many Polishing Lathes and the exhaust system in the workroom. Each Polishing Lathe is hooded and is locally exhausted to draw off dust from the wheels. Despite these provisions the surroundings are quite dirty. The worker's hands and clothing are soiled by the compounds used.

V. *HAZARDS*

There is danger of injuring the hands when the article being polished catches in the revolving wheel and is pulled from the worker's hands. Slight burns from the heated articles of jewelry may be incurred.

FIGURE 15.—*Continued*

Supplementary Sheet

Schedule Number _____

Date   11/17/46

Sheet 5 of 6 Sheets

Job Title   *POLISHER*

VI. *REGISTRATION AND PLACEMENT AIDS*

Basic Requirements: Some polishing experience is required, in which the worker has learned the "feel of the wheel" sufficiently to be able to control the pressure against the wheel to produce the desired surfaces.

A knowledge of polishing compounds and the polishing operations for which they are appropriate is required.

Must be able to distinguish between shades of color or luster to produce evenly polished surfaces.

Variable Requirements: Determine:

What kinds of metal worker will polish.
(Brass, silver, gold, aluminum and plated articles are polished.)

What kind of articles worker will polish.
(Slightly different skill is required to polish costume jewelry, rings, chains, cases, and bracelets.)

What polishing operations worker will do.
(Some workers specialize on such operations as cut and gloss, oil, mat, satin, or gloss finish; while others are able to do all.)

VII. *DEFINITION OF TERMS*

Oiling: The act of cutting through the surface of metal using an oily compound which must be washed off.

Gloss: A high luster finish produced by polishing with a fine abrasive; also a term applied to the operation of producing such a finish.

Cut and Gloss: The procedure of smoothing metal surfaces with a fairly abrasive compound which requires little oil and the immediate polishing to high luster on another wheel with a fine abrasive. The operations are combined when the cutting can be done with a compound which need not be washed off before glossing.

FIGURE 15.—*Continued*

Supplementary Sheet

Schedule Number _____

Date   *11/17/46*

Sheet 6 of 6 Sheets

Job Title   *POLISHER*

VII. *DEFINITION OF TERMS* (Continued)

  Mat: A dull finish produced by polishing with a coarse abrasive; also the act of producing such a finish.

  Satin: A soft finish produced with a wire brush wheel.

  Clean Wheel: A light polishing operation in which no compound is used on the polishing wheel.

VIII. *COMMENTS*

Job Title and Alternate Title: There is some justification for using the alternate title JEWELRY POLISHER in these items because there are POLISHERS in other industries who while using somewhat different techniques, are capable of being confused with this job.

Relation to Other Jobs: Experienced POLISHERS are usually hired, but occasionally WASH BOYS or male JIGGERS may be promoted to the job.

formed, should not be permitted to color the over-all description. Finally, it is essential to include information on how a given job ties in with other jobs, in terms of both work and procedures and organization structure. This insures against the writing of needless descriptions and assures that approved descriptions fit into an integrated pattern.

Further useful information regarding the preparation of job descriptions and specifications may be obtained by studying actual practice in these matters. For examples, see Figures 13, 14, and 15, above. These materials merit close study because they illustrate the care that must go into the development of good job specifications.

To those who examine such materials as these for the first time, the procedures involved may appear unduly complex, but with practice they become less formidable. Indeed, after practice along such lines, one wonders how any useful information was obtained previously.

QUESTIONS AND PROBLEMS

1. What are the major operative functions of personnel management? Show how they are interrelated.

2. Why is a specification of job content fundamental to the procurement function? Need these specifications be in written form?

3. Distinguish between the following terms: job, position, occupation, and station of work.

4. What major steps would you take in following a program of job specifications? Why is it desirable to start with a good system of job titles?

5. What is the *Dictionary of Occupational Titles?* How can it be used in a program of job specification?

6. Of what use is the various information that is listed in this chapter as illustrative of what is sought in building job specifications? Take several of the items listed and show how they might be used in selecting, placing, and training employees.

7. Explain how job specifications are particularly useful in connection with such special classes of workers as female employees, apprentices, and handicapped workers.

8. If you know of a company that does not use job specifications, try to interview someone who can tell you why they do not use them. What is your opinion of their reasons?

9. While gathering information for a job specification, you find that the supervisor's opinion of the duties on a given job are much lower than those of the operator. How would you, as a representative of the personnel department, go about handling this difference of opinion?

10. What factors or forces exist that suggest the advisability of periodic revisions of job specifications?

11. Define the term "job analysis." Distinguish between job analysis, job specification, and time and motion study.

12. Where in the organization structure would you place responsibility for job analysis studies? Why?

13. How should the unit made responsible for job analyses be staffed? What factors determine the choice to be made?

14. What are the advantages, disadvantages, and conditions of most favorable usage of the questionnaire and interview methods of studying jobs?

15. Whichever method of job analysis is used, what preparatory steps should be taken and what safeguards erected?

16. Select a job or occupation in which you are interested, or one regarding which you can readily obtain information, and write a job description for it following the form outlined in this chapter. (Serviceman, streetcar conductor, gas-station attendant, housewife, fraternity cook, etc., make interesting case studies.) Be sure to follow the suggested instructions concerning information gathered, style of writing used, and presentation of findings.

17. Why is it important to define the minimum acceptable standards for employment on a job specification rather than the average or maximum?

18. After a specification is written by a job analyst, by whom should it be approved?

19. What advantages would accrue from having a job specification read by employees and supervisors before receiving final approval? What are the possible disadvantages?

20. What has the purpose for which a job specification is to be used to do with how it is constructed? Do you see any reason why a given job specification could not be used for job evaluation purposes as well as for selection and training purposes? Would a multipurpose specification be too costly and too cumbersome?

6 | Manpower Requirements

LABOR REQUIREMENTS

After the nature of jobs is determined, it is then appropriate to ascertain the characteristics which labor must have to fill the jobs in question. This phase of procurement involves two large determinations: first, the number of employees that must be procured and, second, the qualifications that applicants must possess to qualify for vacancies.

ESTIMATING QUANTITIES OF LABOR

STEPS IN ESTIMATING

In many companies, advance preparations are not made to ascertain how much labor of various kinds will be needed. Only after vacancies occur or their occurrence is a certainty are steps taken to find replacements. For example, when a supervisor concludes that an employee who has been absent for several days is not going to report back to work, or the supervisor is so informed by an unexpected telephone call, he begins more or less urgently—depending upon the pressure of work —to look for new help, or he asks the employment section to find a replacement. Although this method of ascertaining the quantity of labor needed is simple to follow, it possesses little else to commend it. On the contrary, its use aggravates interruptions to production; tends to result in hurried and hence poorly considered selections; and is wasteful of executive time. Therefore, its continued use can probably be condoned only when the replacements that have to be made are few and far between.

The effectiveness of hiring can be raised by forecasting labor requirements. While such forecasts are not simple to make, the results are well worth the effort. During World War II, for example, many companies found it desirable to work out schedules of replacements that would have to be made because of draft calls by Selective Service Boards. By compiling lists of employees, classified according to sex, age, dependency, and importance to the industry, it was possible to determine how many employees were likely to be drafted by the armed forces. In turn, plans could be laid for seeking or training replacements.

On the other hand, variations in labor requirements due to fluctuations in the volume of production are more difficult to foresee. Random fluctuations within the broad swings of the business cycles are particularly troublesome in this regard. Although forecasts in such instances are likely to be more or less in error, nevertheless the fact that the forecasts were made places the hiring officers in a better position to cope with the actual conditions. The major steps in estimating labor requirements are as follows:

1. Forecast sales
2. Estimate master production schedule
3. Establish departmental production schedules
4. Convert production estimates into labor requirements
5. Tabulate present working force
6. Estimate number of employees to be separated from payroll
7. Deduct Item 6 from Item 5, to determine net working force
8. Deduct Item 7 from Item 4, to determine replacements to be made or employees to be released

To illustrate these steps, an example is taken from the field of production, although the same procedures would be applicable to employees in sales or office work.

THE SALES FORECAST

The sales forecast is the foundation upon which the estimate of labor requirements is built. Until sales for a definite period in the future are estimated, it is impossible to follow a logical sequence leading to a predetermination of labor needs. This may be seen by working back from labor requirements. Thus, how much labor is needed in a given department depends upon factory schedules, which, in turn, depend upon sales forecasts and storage policies. Of course, the initial step of making a sales estimate depends upon an interpretation of future possibilities, a matter which invariably includes a margin of error. Such margins result in smaller losses than those which accrue when labor estimates are left to hit-or-miss methods. Moreover, since most companies make sales forecasts for other purposes, e.g., in preparing financial budgets, there is little reason why the sales forecast should not be used for estimating labor requirements.

Sales forecasts are made and set up in a number of ways. Table 2 (p. 102) is illustrative of the data contained in such a forecast. In this instance the forecast is made by weeks for the next three months, then on a monthly basis for the following three months, and finally upon a quarterly basis. A detailed picture is obtained for the immediate future, while general estimates are sufficient for any action that need be taken regarding the later periods. Such forecasts are usually revised weekly or monthly, as conditions in a particular case demand.

TABLE 2

THE PRODUCTION OPERATING COMPANY REPORT OF SALES FORECAST
July 1, 19——, to June 30, 19——

		Product A	Product B	Product C
Week ending:	July 6........	10,100	102,000	60,010
	13........	12,250	101,800	59,200
	20........	13,700	100,300	58,050
	27........	16,100	99,800	59,300
	Aug. 3........	18,720	96,300	55,700
	10........	22,200	95,700	55,200
	17........	26,000	94,600	53,600
	24........	26,200	92,100	53,300
	31........	25,800	90,000	56,800
	Sept. 7........	24,200	86,500	52,950
	14........	23,800	81,900	55,900
	21........	21,100	72,200	53,600
	28........	21,050	66,350	54,120
October......................		75,500	280,000	248,000
November....................		68,500	321,500	242,000
December....................		62,000	383,300	263,000
January–February–March.........		150,000	1,250,000	990,000
April–May–June................		120,000	1,575,000	1,110,000

In making the forecasts, recourse may be had to a number of sources of information:

1. Past sales, set up in statistical or graphical terms, may be used to devise a pattern for the future. This method presupposes that cyclical and seasonal fluctuations in the past are likely to be projected into the future.
2. Estimates of sales may be obtained from local sales units or salesmen. These estimates are then summated by areas and products to obtain the total figures. This method presupposes that personnel in local units are best able to determine how sales are likely to go in their areas and that a summary of such estimates is an excellent forecast of future events.
3. Estimates of purchasing power are used in some cases to derive sales forecasts. This method is based on the assumption that if one can determine

how much customers have to spend, it will be possible to figure out what one's own sales are likely to be.

4. Interpretations of local or national trends in the business and political world are also used to calculate what future sales are likely to be. This method presupposes that such things as tax and labor legislation or general business conditions have an important effect up individual sales possibilities.

Ordinarily, a combination of these methods is employed. By starting with local estimates, comparing with past sales, adjusting for purchasing power, and then adjusting for possible economic and political changes, it is possible to derive very accurate estimates. All of this is time-consuming and expensive, but these are necessary costs of scientific management.

PRODUCTION SCHEDULES

Inasmuch as sales ordinarily fluctuate more than is desired for purposes of production, most companies do not produce strictly to the sales forecast. Instead, a production schedule is worked out which levels out the peaks and valleys of the sales estimate. The degree to which the production schedule is stabilized in comparison with the sales schedule

TABLE 3

THE PRODUCTION OPERATING COMPANY PRODUCTION SCHEDULE
July–September, 19——

Week Ending	Product A	Product B	Product C
July 6	15,000	95,000	60,000
13	15,000	95,000	59,000
20	15,000	95,000	58,000
27	15,000	95,000	58,000
Aug. 3	15,000	90,000	57,000
10	15,000	90,000	56,000
17	15,000	90,000	55,000
24	15,000	90,000	54,000
31	15,000	90,000	53,000
Sept. 7	15,000	86,000	54,000
14	15,000	86,000	54,000
21	15,000	86,000	54,000
28	15,000	86,000	54,000

is largely dependent upon the storability of the products in question and and their nonsusceptibility to the style factor. It is uneconomical to build up inventories of locomotives, for example, during slack periods, because the cost of storage (in the fullest sense) would offset economies of stabilized production. On the other hand, leveling out of production is practicable in cases of low unit value and easily storable products, such as soaps. But where style obsolescence is important, production schedules must be worked out closely with the sales curves. Usually some stabilization of production schedules is feasible, an example of which may be seen in Table 3 (p. 103); it was derived from the sales forecast in Table 2.

DEPARTMENTAL SCHEDULES

After factory schedules are computed, departmental work loads can be established. These will be easy or difficult to establish, depending upon the variety of work performed within a department. In cases where

TABLE 4

THE RELATION BETWEEN FACTORY AND DEPARTMENTAL SCHEDULES

Date	Product X Factory Schedule	Part X Department A Schedule
March 4	....	5,000
5	....	4,000
6	....	4,400
7	....	4,800
8	....	6,000
11	2,000	6,000
12	2,000	6,200
13	2,200	6,600
14	2,400	7,000
15	3,000	7,000
18	3,000	....
19	3,100	....
20	3,300	....
21	3,500	....
22	3,500	....

a department works upon one or a few operations or parts, the load of work can quickly be derived from the factory schedule. Thus, if the department in question must finish two units of a given part for each unit of finished product five working days before final production is completed, the departmental schedule can be obtained by multiplying the quantities on the factory schedule by 2 and then advancing the individual dates on the factory schedule by the number of days that it takes for units of work to travel from the department in question to the end of the production line. The data shown in Table 4 are based upon the foregoing information.

DETERMINING LABOR NEEDS

The departmental production schedules or estimates provide the basis for determining total labor needs. Information must also be ob-

TABLE 5

ESTIMATED LABOR REQUIREMENTS

Department A

KINDS OF LABOR	UNIT REQUIRE- MENTS	WEEK ENDING MARCH 8		WEEK ENDING MARCH 15	
		Production Schedule	Man- Hours	Production Schedule	Man- Hours
		24,200		32,800	
Supervisory....................	Variable		80		80
Clerical.......................	Variable		120		140
Set-up men.....................	Variable		80		90
Drill press operators:					
Grade 1......................	0.02		484		656
Grade 2......................	0.01		242		328
Grade 3......................	0.005		121		164
Bench hands:					
Grade 1......................	0.008		194		262
Grade 2......................	0.006		145		197

tained in regard to how much labor of various kinds is needed for each unit of output. It is then a simple process to multiply these unit quan-

FIGURE 16. Productivity versus Personnel for Varying Number of Man-Hours*

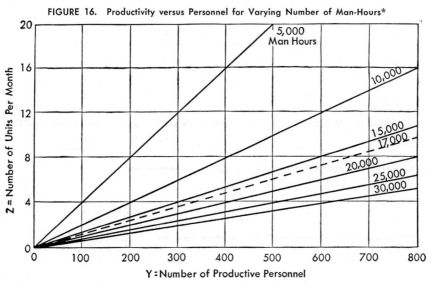

Relationships between the number of productive personnel, working one 8-hour shift a day, 25 days a month, and the number of units to be completed a month are shown in this graph. Graph shows relationships where the total of man-hours needed to complete each unit varies from 5,000 to 30,000. As an illustration of how to use the graph, assume that 4 units per month of a product which requires 17,000 man-hours to complete, are needed. By following the 17,000 man-hour line to point where it intersects the 4 co-ordinate, it is found that 340 productive workers will be needed.

*Source: Mark H. Smith, "Graphs Aid in Visualizing New Production Programs," *Factory Management and Maintenance*, April, 1946, p. 93.

tities by the estimated production. In Table 5 (p. 105), for example, the first column shows the kinds of labor needed in Department A to manufacture Part X; the second column shows the amounts of labor needed per unit of production; and in succeeding columns are shown alternately the production schedule for each week and the man-hours needed to complete the schedules. Inasmuch as the amount of labor of particular kinds needed does not always vary proportionately with production, it is necessary to work out tables or graphs to show the variations in labor as output changes. Figure 16 (p. 105) illustrates the use of charts to provide such answers. Some companies prefer to tie in labor estimates with their budget programs, in which case labor requirements would be stated in financial as well as hourly terms, as illustrated in Table 6.

AVAILABLE LABOR AND PAYROLL CHANGES

After the foregoing pictures of labor requirements are determined, it is then necessary to ascertain how much labor of various kinds is available to produce the output for the period of time in question. These two classes of information can be compared to compute labor to be added. In equation form, this problem resolves itself as follows:

Total labor requirements *less* Available labor *equals* Labor to be added to (or removed from) the payroll.

The computation of available labor begins with a listing of the present labor force. From this is subtracted the estimated number of employees who will leave the payroll for various reasons. This task of estimation

TABLE 6

ESTIMATED LABOR REQUIREMENTS

Department A

KINDS OF LABOR	WEEK ENDING MARCH 8		WEEK ENDING MARCH 15	
	Man-Hours	Dollars	Man-Hours	Dollars
Supervisory	80	112.00	80	112.00
Clerical	120	102.00	140	119.00
Setup men	80	100.00	90	112.50
Drill press operator:				
Grade 1	484	435.60	656	590.40
Grade 2	242	204.70	328	278.80
Grade 3	121	96.80	164	131.20
Bench hands:				
Grade 1	194	150.50	262	196.50
Grade 2	145	101.50	197	137.90

is seldom easy. However, from a careful study of cyclical and seasonal trends, turnover data, the ages of present employees, marriage rates, and absenteeism records, it is possible to establish reliable estimates. Figure 83 (see p. 618) illustrates a case study of absenteeisms, a record

TABLE 7

DEPARTMENTAL SEPARATIONS

Machine Department A

Week Ending September 28, 19——

Drill Press Operator

Number on payroll	30
Quits	1
Transfers and promotions	2
Estimated discharges	1
On leave	1
Pensioned	0
Average absenteeism	1
Miscellaneous (loaned to tool room)	1
Total separations	7
Number available	23

of which is essential in determining how much of an allowance must be made for the fact that all on the payroll will not show up for work.

A simple estimate of separations from a departmental payroll is illustrated in Table 7.

TABLE 8

ESTIMATES OF LABOR MOVEMENT

Week Ending September 28, 19——

	DEPARTMENT		
	A	B	C
Labor needs	28	32	36
Available	23	36	35
Shortage	5	..	1
Overage	..	4	..
Handled by—			
Transfer:			
In	1	..	1
Out	..	2	..
Promoted:			
In	1	..	..
Out	..	..	..
On leave:			
Returning	..	..	..
Going	..	1	..
Layoffs	..	1	..
Hirings	3	..	..

The figure of net available labor is then subtracted from total labor needs, to determine how much labor must be added to (or subtracted from) the payroll of each department. Such computations can be set up in table form, as shown in Table 8 (p. 107), to indicate overages and shortages by departments and how the differences are to be handled. Thus, in the example cited, in Department A, which is short five employees, the shortage is expected to be made up by one transfer, one promotion, and three hirings. In Department B, the overage is to be handled by two transfers, one on leave, and one layoff.

LABOR TURNOVER

1. SIGNIFICANCE. One of the oldest devices of estimating labor requirements is through labor turnover calculations. Inasmuch as vacancies are created by employees leaving the company, it is only wise to estimate statistically how many are likely to leave. Thus it may be possible to learn about the number of job vacancies, even though who specifically is to leave cannot be ascertained. Such estimates are best made in terms of past turnover. Knowing trends of turnover is an excellent means of appraising how many vacancies are likely to occur in the future.

2. NATURE OF TURNOVER. "Labor turnover" refers to the influx and efflux of the working force. It may be measured in terms of accessions to, separations from, or replacements on the payroll and may be classified as avoidable or unavoidable. The results obtained from measurements of any one of these evidences of turnover are subject to criticism; yet all are useful in greater or lesser degree. The important point to remember is that turnover measurements are most useful when compared upon some basis, such as time or area, and when the causes thereof are eliminated and not disregarded. How this may be done is shown in the following notes on measures of labor turnover.

3. MEASUREMENT. Labor turnover may be measured simply by relating accessions or separations during a given period to the average payroll for that period. For purposes of consistency and comparability, the month is the period commonly used. For example, if a company had an average payroll during a given month of 600 (585 at the beginning, plus 615 at the end, divided by 2), had taken on 50 employees and 20 had been separated from the payroll, then—

1. Based upon accession figures, turnover is calculated as follows:

$$\frac{50}{600} \times 100 = 8.33 \text{ per cent.}$$

2. Based upon separation figures, turnover is calculated as follows:

$$\frac{20}{600} \times 100 = 3.33 \text{ per cent.}$$

The important questions in either case would be: (1) How do these figures compare with those of previous periods and other plants? (2) What caused variations? Of course, neither would be useful measures during wide cyclical and seasonal swings. Thus, during periods of prosperity the separation formula would show no turnover; and during periods of depression the accession formula would show no turnover.

As a means of minimizing cyclical effects upon turnover calculations, some companies average the accession and separation figures and then divide by the average working force. Based upon both accessions and separations, turnover is calculated as follows:

$$\frac{\dfrac{50 + 20}{2}}{600} \times 100 = 5.83 \text{ per cent.}$$

It should be noted that when monthly turnover percentages are converted to an annual basis by multiplying by 12, the resulting percentages are often unbelievable. Some companies have been known to have a turnover of their working force of over 100 per cent. In other words, their working force is, on the average, replaced within the period of a year.

Although the foregoing formulae are simple and do provide indicators of trends, they fail to distinguish the costly aspect of turnover, that is, the replacements of separations necessary to carry on production. Accessions to the payroll are not necessary evidence of unsatisfactory conditions. On the contrary, they may be a sign of a highly profitable situation. And separations, when not replaced, may be a sign of inescapable reduction of labor force. But when a company fails to hold some of its employees, it must go to the expense of hiring and training replacements merely to maintain production. A formula based upon replacement figures will serve to detect when such failures are tending toward undesirable levels.

The most commonly used formula for calculating replacements is that of net labor turnover, which the Bureau of Labor Statistics of the United States Department of Labor uses to measure turnover on a national basis by lines of manufacturing and by types of industries. Data for these reports are collected by means of the form illustrated in Appendix B (p. 642–44).

4. DETAILED COMPARISONS. Over-all measures of labor turnover are generally useful only as trend indicators. It is necessary to make de-

tailed measures of comparisons. Thus separation should be classified by departments, to get behind over-all figures; and causes of separations should be detailed under such headings as the following:

1. Death
2. Pensioned or superannuated
3. Accidents and illness
4. Marriage
5. Discharges because of unsatisfactory work, insubordination, and other disciplinary measures
6. Short-time layoffs because of seasonal recesses
7. Long-time layoffs because of cyclical recesses
8. Voluntary quits for such reasons as returning to school, better jobs, or moving to new location

The more detailed the analysis, the more accurate will be the answers that management will derive to its turnover problems. To get this detail, it is necessary to establish a procedure whereby all who leave the employment of the company, in so far as possible, go through an exit interview in the personnel department before final payroll vouchers are approved.

MAN SPECIFICATIONS

GENERAL APPROACH

The foregoing has served to provide an answer to the quantitative question of how much labor, of various kinds, is required by a given company. Another major task, and one far more difficult, is that of specifying the personal characteristics that labor must possess if given workers are to perform assigned tasks capably.

A number of approaches may be followed in drawing up personal or "man" specifications. The line of least resistance is simply to use the job specification, which describes the duties to be performed on given jobs. For example, the specification of duties for a drill press operator, let us say, would indicate that such a worker must know how to set up a drill press, to drill holes, and to check the accuracy of his work. This at first glance might seem to be of use to those who are to do the hiring.

Such a mere enumeration of duties, however, would soon be found to be of little use. It says nothing, in the first place, about how fast or how accurately the operator is expected to work. In the second place, it gives no clues by which one can look at a candidate and determine whether or not he might become a good drill press operator.

Although many companies apparently rely upon such job specifications to measure candidates, the trend is toward a conversion of job duties to man characteristics called for by the job duties. Such conversions may be made simply in the minds of those who do the hiring, or they may be formal statements, examples of which are noted in the following paragraphs. Where such conversions are made, personal characteristics tend to be grouped as physical, mental, and emotional and social characteristics.

PHYSICAL SPECIFICATIONS

Undoubtedly, the easiest approach to the task of writing man specifications is to list the physical qualifications which are called for on given jobs. This has reference to the obvious fact that various kinds and degrees of physical capacities are required on different jobs. Thus, a "stock chaser" has to do a lot of walking, whereas a drill press operator does almost all of his work sitting or standing. And an assembler of parts in the tail section of an airplane should be small in stature, whereas a warehouseman should possess a large and strong physique.

A simple yet effective plan for recording and utilizing physical specifications is shown in Figures 17, 18, and 19. Although this plan has been developed for use in connection with the placement of disabled workers, it is useful in normal placements. The form shown in Figure

FIGURE 17. Job Requirements Card*

An Analysis of Job Requirements
FOR PLACING DISABLED WORKERS

DOES THE JOB REQUIRE ?

JOB TITLE OR NUMBER	1 100% Standing	2 Partial Standing	3 100% Walking	4 Any Walking	5 Talking	6 Any Kneeling	7 Any Stooping	8 Any Climbing	9 Pulling	10 Pushing	11 Nimble Use of Fingers	12 Use of Both Hands	13 Use of Right Hand and Partial Use of Left	14 Use of Left Hand and Partial Use of Right	15 Use of Right Hand Only	16 Use of Left Hand Only	17 Raising Right Arm above Shoulder	18 Raising Left Arm above Shoulder	19 Lifting from 10-25 lbs	20 Lifting over 25 lbs
1 Drill Press Operator		✓		✓									✓				✓			
2 Bench Assembler											✓	✓								
3 Stock Chaser	✓		✓		✓		✓	✓	✓	✓										
4																				
5																				

VISION? HEARING?

JOB TITLE OR NUMBER	21 Good (Vision)	22 Fair (Vision)	23 Poor Acceptable (Vision)	24 Good (Hearing)	25 Fair (Hearing)	26 Poor Acceptable (Hearing)
1 Drill Press Operator		✓				✓
2 Bench Assembler	✓					✓
3 Stock Chaser		✓				✓
4						
5						

WORKING CONDITIONS ?

JOB TITLE OR NUMBER	27 Hot	28 Cold	29 Wet	30 Humid	31 Slipping or Tripping Conditions	32 Dusty	33 Fumes	34 Noisy	35 Outdoors	36 Seldom Outdoors	37 Are Possible Skin Irritants Used
1 Drill Press Operator								✓			✓
2 Bench Assembler											✓
3 Stock Chaser								✓		✓	
4											
5											

IMPOSSIBLE FOR THE JOB TO BE DONE BY ?

JOB TITLE OR NUMBER	38 Worker with Poor Coordination	39 Worker with Nervous Instability	40 Worker Who Has Fainting or Dizzy Spells	41 A Deaf-Mute	42 One Legged Worker	43 One Armed Worker	44 A Blind Worker
1 Drill Press Operator							✓
2 Bench Assembler	✓					✓	
3 Stock Chaser			✓		✓		✓
4							
5							

NOTE: IF THE JOB'S DEMANDS DO NOT MATCH THE APPLICANT'S PHYSICAL CAPABILITIES, HIS PLACEMENT REQUIRES A CONFERENCE BETWEEN THE PHYSICIAN AND PLACEMENT OFFICER

* Source: *The Physically Impaired* (Association of Casualty and Surety Executives, 1945), p. 9.

FIGURE 18. Physical Capabilities Analysis Card*

NOTE: PLACE A CHECK (✓) IN EACH BOX DESCRIBING AN ACTIVITY THE EMPLOYEE IS NOT CAPABLE OF DOING UNDER NORMAL, HEAVY WORK CONDITIONS

Group	No.	Item	✓
IS APPLICANT INCAPABLE OF?	1	100% STANDING	
	2	PARTIAL STANDING	
	3	100% WALKING	
	4	MUCH WALKING	
	5	MUCH TALKING	
	6	ANY KNEELING	
	7	ANY STOOPING	
	8	ANY CLIMBING	
	9	MUCH PULLING	
	10	MUCH PUSHING	
	11	NIMBLE USE OF FINGERS	✓
	12	USE OF BOTH HANDS	✓
	13	USE OF RIGHT HAND AND PARTIAL USE OF LEFT	✓
	14	USE OF LEFT HAND AND PARTIAL USE OF RIGHT	✓
	15	USE OF RIGHT HAND	
	16	USE OF LEFT HAND	✓
	17	RAISING RIGHT ARM ABOVE SHOULDER	
	18	RAISING LEFT ARM ABOVE SHOULDER	✓
	19	LIFTING FROM 10–25 LBS	✓
	20	LIFTING OVER 25 LBS	✓
VISION CORRECTED?	21	GOOD (20/40 & 14/28)	✓
	22	FAIR (20/60 & 14/42)	
	23	POOR	
HEARING?	24	GOOD (20/10)	✓
	25	FAIR (20/5)	
	26	POOR	
IS THE APPLICANT INCAPABLE OF WORKING UNDER THESE CONDITIONS?	27	HOT	
	28	COLD	
	29	WET	
	30	HUMID	
	31	SLIPPING OR TRIPPING CONDITIONS	
	32	DUSTY	
	33	FUMES	
	34	NOISY	
	35	OUTDOORS	
	36	SELDOM OUTDOORS	
	37	ANY SKIN IRRITANTS	
DOES THE APPLICANT HAVE?	38	POOR COORDINATION	
	39	NERVOUS INSTABILITY	✓
	40	FAINTING OR DIZZY SPELLS	
	41	IS HE A DEAF-MUTE	
	42	IS HE ONE LEGGED	
	43	IS HE ONE ARMED	
	44	IS HE BLIND	

COMMENTS: *Applicant had severe injury to left arm and shoulder. Although he retains use of the member and it is advisable for him to use it in light exercise, he should not be given heavy work or jobs demanding that he raise the arm above shoulder level.*

NAME *X. Y. SMITH* PLANT REG. NO. *39401* EXAMINING PHYSICIAN *A.B. Brown* M.D.

PHYSICAL CAPABILITIES ANALYSIS

* *Ibid.*

FIGURE 19. Matching Job Requirements and Personal Capabilities*

An Analysis of Job Requirements FOR PLACING DISABLED WORKERS

JOB TITLE OR NUMBER: 1 DRILL PRESS OPERATOR; 2 BENCH ASSEMBLER; 3 STOCK CHASER

Group	No.	Requirement	1 Drill Press Operator	2 Bench Assembler	3 Stock Chaser
DOES THE JOB REQUIRE?	1	100% STANDING			✓
	2	PARTIAL STANDING	✓		
	3	100% WALKING			✓
	4	ANY WALKING	✓		
	5	TALKING			✓
	6	ANY KNEELING			
	7	ANY STOOPING			✓
	8	ANY CLIMBING			✓
	9	PULLING			✓
	10	PUSHING			✓
	11	NIMBLE USE OF FINGERS		✓	
	12	USE OF BOTH HANDS		✓	
	13	USE OF RIGHT HAND AND PARTIAL USE OF LEFT	✓		
	14	USE OF LEFT HAND AND PARTIAL USE OF RIGHT			
	15	USE OF RIGHT HAND ONLY			
	16	USE OF LEFT HAND ONLY			
	17	RAISING RIGHT ARM ABOVE SHOULDER	✓		
	18	RAISING LEFT ARM ABOVE SHOULDER			
	19	LIFTING FROM 10–25 LBS			
	20	LIFTING OVER 25 LBS			
VISION?	21	GOOD		✓	
	22	FAIR	✓		✓
	23	POOR ACCEPTABLE			
HEARING?	24	GOOD			
	25	FAIR			
	26	POOR ACCEPTABLE	✓	✓	✓
WORKING CONDITIONS?	27	HOT			
	28	COLD			
	29	WET			
	30	HUMID			
	31	SLIPPING OR TRIPPING CONDITIONS			
	32	DUSTY			
	33	FUMES			
	34	NOISY	✓		✓
	35	OUTDOORS			
	36	SELDOM OUTDOORS			✓
	37	ARE POSSIBLE SKIN IRRITANTS USED	✓	✓	
IMPOSSIBLE FOR THE JOB TO BE DONE BY?	38	WORKER WITH POOR COORDINATION		✓	
	39	WORKER WITH NERVOUS INSTABILITY			
	40	WORKER WHO HAS FAINTING OR DIZZY SPELLS			✓
	41	A DEAF-MUTE			
	42	ONE LEGGED WORKER			✓
	43	ONE ARMED WORKER		✓	
	44	A BLIND WORKER	✓		✓

NOTE: PLACE A CHECK (✓) IN EACH BOX DESCRIBING AN ACTIVITY THE EMPLOYEE IS NOT CAPABLE OF DOING UNDER NORMAL, HEAVY WORK CONDITIONS

Checked: 11, 12, 13, 14, 16, 18, 19, 20, 21, 24, 39

IS APPLICANT INCAPABLE OF? VISION CORRECTED? HEARING? IS THE APPLICANT INCAPABLE OF WORKING UNDER THESE CONDITIONS? DOES THE APPLICANT HAVE?

COMMENTS: *Applicant had severe injury to left arm and shoulder. Although he retains use of the member and it is advisable for him to use it in light exercise, he should not be given heavy work or jobs demanding that he raise the arm above shoulder level.*

NAME *X. Y. SMITH* PLANT REG. NO. *39401* EXAMINING PHYSICIAN *A.B. Brown* M.D.

PHYSICAL CAPABILITIES ANALYSIS

* *Ibid.*, p. 22.

17 is used to record the physical requirements of various jobs, which are listed in the left-hand column. At the top of the form, all capabilities that might be required are listed. Then, upon the basis of a job analysis, a check mark is placed under each capability that the job in question calls for. Thus the job of drill press operator has checks under the following headings: partial standing, walking, use of right hand and partial use of left, raising right arm above shoulder, fair vision, poor hearing acceptable, noisy working conditions, possibility of skin irritations, and impossible for a blind worker.

Figure 18 shows a form used to record the physical capabilities possessed by an individual applicant. The same headings of physical capacities, listed in the same order as in Figure 17, are employed. After interviews and examinations, the headings are checked to indicate which cannot be done by the person in question. With this information available, it is then possible to match the two forms, as shown in Figure 19, by sliding the first along the second until the check marks match. The job or jobs for which an applicant may be hired, or to which transfers or promotions may be made, is thus quickly determinable for a given individual.

MENTAL SPECIFICATIONS

In regard to mental specifications, this has reference to the various mental processes called for on particular jobs. It is ordinarily of little use to specify for a given job that the duties call for an ability to solve problems, to think, or to concentrate. Such specifications do not help in appraising a candidate. However, where a general approach to mental processes seems desirable, it is better done by specifying for a given job the required schooling or experience. In this way, a given educational level, let us say four years of high school in the case of a stenographer, may be used as an indirect measure of the mental processes required on the particular job.

Even better, however, is the attempt to specify particular types and degrees of mental characteristics. The following list is illustrative of characteristics that might be considered under this heading:

General intelligence	Ability to plan
Memory of names and places	Arithmetical abilities
Memory for abstract ideas	Reading abilities
Memory for oral directions	Scientific abilities
Memory for written directions	Judgment
Memory for spatial relations	Ability to concentrate
Ability to estimate quantities	Ability to handle variable factors
Ability to estimate qualities	

To obtain a measure of the degree to which the foregoing characteristics are required, some arbitrary method of grading is needed. Under some plans, each of the mental characteristics for each job is followed by a notation indicating whether it is required to a high, average, or low degree, or not at all. Because such measures are indefinite and do not mean the same thing to all concerned, some companies have followed the plan of using explanatory sentences to measure differences of degree. An example of such keyed sentences is as follows:

1. A high degree of this characteristic is required on
   a) All elements of the job
   b) The major elements of this job
   c) The minor elements of this job

2. An above-average degree of this characteristic is required on
   a) All elements of the job
   b) The major elements of this job
   c) The minor elements of this job

3. An average degree of this characteristic is required on
   a) All elements of the job
   b) The major elements of this job
   c) The minor elements of the job

4. A low degree of this characteristic is required on
   a) All elements of the job
   b) The major elements of this job
   c) The minor elements of the job

5. This characteristic is not required on
   a) Any of the elements of this job
   b) The major elements of the job
   c) The minor elements of the job

Thus the symbol "*2b*" written in after the characteristic "memory for oral directions" would indicate that it is required to the degree "above average" only for the major elements of the job in question.

Numerical scores may also be used in connection with degrees of differences for the mental characteristics. These may be entirely arbitrary, for example, 90 to 100 representing very high requirements, 80 to 89 high, etc. Or they may be based upon some recognized system of numerical scoring, such as those used in connection with the measurement of general intelligence, i.e., the intelligence quotient.

EMOTIONAL AND SOCIAL SPECIFICATIONS

Although the trend is by no means widespread, nevertheless there is a growing realization that perhaps the most important aspects of man requirements are those pertaining to emotional and social characteristics. Various studies have shown that the technical requirements of most factory and sales jobs are not too difficult to meet. Moreover, other studies have shown that most of our labor troubles stem from poor emotional or social adjustment of employees. Since the human requirements seem to be a greater cause of trouble than the technical, a trend toward consideration of this factor has developed.

Specifying required emotional and social characteristics is, however, a very difficult task. At present, it seems to be beyond the possibility of accomplishment by the average personnel department. When help from proficient psychologists, psychiatrists, or sociologists is available, constructive progress in this direction may be expected.

In most instances, however, about the best that can be done along these lines is to rely upon the interpretative judgment of executives who are aware of the significance of personality and social factors. For example, in one company the supervisors have been given short courses in elementary and applied psychology. They have been advised to note the personal problems that employees encounter in their respective departments. They have also been instructed to observe the social and group relationships that have developed in their respective areas. With such observations in mind, the supervisors are then asked to check candidates for vacancies in their departments. By this means, at least a rough form of personal and social specifications has been developed in the minds of the supervisors. Such specifications are far from precise, but they are also far better than nothing at all.

In this matter of personal and social adjustments, a few companies are also giving serious consideration to how the attitude of the wife of an employee will affect his success in the job. The practice here is to interview the wives as well as the husbands when the latter apply for jobs. In these cases, too, the "specifications" are not formally stated. But, again, in terms of what executives know about their company, employees, and community, they attempt to determine how well a newcomer is likely to fit in successfully. Most persons are personally acquainted with cases in which a wife has become so dissatisfied with her husband's company or its community that this condition has affected adversely the husband's effectiveness.

Although this trend of interviewing wives, as just noted, has not been widely adopted, it seems to have much merit. Someone may jocularly ask: Why not interview his children too? And the serious answer is that, if we are convinced that emotional and social adjustments are very important on job success in a given case and if we are convinced that the attitude of children is significant in the case of a given candidate, then such interviews are not beyond the realm of plausibility. Either that, or wait until the specific individual fails. Then the losses of turnover will far outweigh the costs of what might have seemed to be a naïve practice. And costs and losses are not respecters of ages.

EXAMPLE OF MAN SPECIFICATIONS

An excellent example of materials from which man specifications may be derived is provided by the tabulation below (pp. 116–20), which contains excerpts from a job analysis form used by a large retail establishment in connection with its job evaluation program. For each job that is studied, a decision is reached regarding the level or degree to which the following major factors are required:

1. Knowledge and experience
2. Skills and abilities
3. Responsibilities
4. Working conditions

Close scrutiny of this form will show how useful is the variety of information that is derived from it. Of special note is the fact that the form is built, not along lines of prosaic tradition, but along lines that would seek to solve the practical problems that must be met and solved. Certainly the section on social characteristics is a realistic recognition that such skills as well as technical skills have an important impact upon job success.

JOB FACTORS

I. KNOWLEDGE AND EXPERIENCE REQUIRED BY THE JOB

   A. Amount of formal and/or specialized business or trade education or its mental equivalent required by the job

   1. Less than eight years—Some grammar school, simple arithmetic
   2. Eight to ten years—Some high school, business school
   3. Ten to twelve years—High-school graduate, or some high school and and some specialized education
   4. Twelve to fourteen years—Some college or university education
   5. Fourteen to sixteen years—College or university education
   6. Over sixteen years—College or technical school graduate

   B. Length of preparatory experience that the job requires

   1. Less than one week
   2. One week to four weeks
   3. One month to one year—Part outside and part company experience

4. One year to five years—Several different jobs or trade apprenticeship
5. Over five years—Trade experience
6. Over five years—Important supervisory work requiring wide experience

C. Assuming that the formal or specialized education and previous experience requirements are met, length of time required to learn to perform job duties with minimum proficiency (quantity and quality)

1. Less than one week
2. One week to four weeks
3. One month to three months
4. Three months to twelve months
5. One year or more

II. SKILLS AND ABILITIES REQUIRED BY THE JOB

A. Variety of machines or special hand tools operated

1. One simple machine or hand tool
2. Several simple machines and hand tools common to semiskilled occupations
3. Highly technical machine and/or hand tools
4. Several different highly technical machines and/or hand tools

B. Strength and endurance required by the job

1. Lifting and/or carrying up to 30 lbs. not sustained, or up to 5 lbs. sustained
2. Lifting and/or carrying up to 100 lbs. not sustained, or up to 30 lbs. sustained
3. Lifting and/or carrying up to 200 lbs. not sustained, or up to 100 lbs. sustained
4. Lifting and/or carrying up to 200 lbs. sustained

C. Dexterity, precision, and/or acuity of senses required by the job

1. Definitions.
   a) Dexterity—Ability to manipulate objects by deft, quick co-ordinated movements of fingers, hands, arms, feet, and/or legs
   b) Precision—Degree of accuracy required
   c) Acuity of senses—Keenness in: perceiving form, space, color, speed of moving objects; estimating weight, resistance, and tension of objects by use of the muscular sense
2. Work requires some manipulation within wide limits of precision, and/or normal sense perception
3. Work requires some manipulation with high degree of precision, and/or acuity of all senses, or special acuity of one
4. Work requires exceptionally high degree of dexterity, but only average precision, and/or exceptionally acute sense perception of highly developed specialized senses
5. Work requires a very high or exceptional degree of dexterity and precision

  D. Verbal expression, both oral and written, required by the job

    1. Work requires very little to normal degree of verbal fluency

    2. Work requires specialized written expression in correspondence, reports, or specialized oral expression

    3. Work requires extremely diversified verbal ability, oral and written, delivered under pressure

  E. Initiative, ingenuity, and/or judgment (considering degree of supervision received) required by the job

    1. Work requires very little judgment, initiative, or ingenuity. Decision followed or applied under close supervision. Routine work, outlined and started by supervisor. Standard policies and practices

    2. Work requires some judgment, initiative, and/or ingenuity. Decisions of average nature made by precedents or standards with close supervision. Must follow suggestions and instructions but with some planning as to course of action and order of work required

    3. Work requires above-average amount of judgment, initiative, and/or ingenuity. Decisions of average nature made by precedents or standards without close supervision. Considerable imagination and shrewdness required in using new ideas followed by persistent development, and in planning and mapping course of action and order of work

    4. Work requires employee to make difficult decisions with few or no precedents or standards. Important to be quick and accurate without close supervision. Great ingenuity required in devising, planning, and developing course of action and order of work

III. RESPONSIBILITIES REQUIRED BY THE JOB

  A. Direction or group leadership and executive supervision required by the job

    1. Leading one to ten persons on routine work

    2. Directing ten to twenty-five persons on variety of work

    3. Directing through other supervisors and including some responsibility for methods used and interpretation of policy

    4. Executive direction in organizing efforts of others by selecting, developing, training, disciplining, and supervising employees

  B. Probability of equipment, cash, and/or material losses through diverted attention

    1. $ 5–$100 per month

    2. $100–$300 per month

    3. $300–$500 per month

    4. Over $500 per month

  C. Responsibility for directly influencing store sales position

    1. Little responsibility for directly affecting store sales position by means of related and/or suggestive selling to a clientele

    2. Responsibility for directly affecting store sales position by suggestive selling of moderately priced related items to a developed clientele

    3. Responsibility for directly affecting store sales position by suggestive,

promotional, and/or related selling of exclusive items. Must be constantly developing and maintaining clientele

4. Major responsibility is to directly affect store sales position by promotional, suggestive and/or related selling of all types of merchandise. Must constantly develop and maintain clientele

D. Responsibility for maintaining methods and operations affecting major cost factor (affecting profit) in the business

1. Methods and operations followed are not a major cost influence and require average degree of accuracy
2. Costly but highly routinized methods and operations followed. Constant check by supervisors prevents final errors
3. Follows costly but well-defined methods and operations with high accuracy requirements with close supervision
4. Follows costly but well-defined methods and operations with high accuracy requirements without close supervision
5. Interprets and uses very costly methods and operations with great accuracy requirements with very little supervision

E. Responsibility for safety of others

1. Small chance of injury
2. Considerable care required to prevent injury
3. Extreme care required to prevent injury
4. Responsible for equipment, methods, or personnel involving severe health or accident hazards

IV. WORKING CONDITIONS

A. Physical and/or nervous strain due to degree of physical effort required, method of regulating amount of work, or the need for concentration and perseverance in the midst of distraction

1. Normal physical and mental effort—not sustained
2. Considerable sustained physical or mental effort
3. Frequent excessive physical and/or nervous strain
4. Sustained excessive physical and nervous strain

B. Undesirability of working conditions due to accident or health hazard, extra cost to employee of special clothing or tools, or disagreeable surroundings

1. Generally satisfactory surroundings, little hazard, and no extra expense for clothing or tools
2. Surroundings cause discomfort and strain, and/or some accident hazards present, or considerable expense in clothing or tools
3. Disagreeable or hazardous working conditions
4. Very disagreeable and dangerous conditions

V. SOCIAL CHARACTERISTICS OF THE JOB (Contacts)

A. Requirements for social adaptability in human relationships

1. Limited social relationships in situations of minor importance
2. Limited simple social relationships of major importance

    3. Frequent social relationships; must deal repeatedly with unpleasant attitudes and situations of minor importance with immediate adjustment

    4. Constant delicate social emergencies of major importance

B. Relationship that exists between this job and store reputation

    1. None to very little. Little opportunity for work results to affect opinion

    2. Close relationship between manner of doing job and outside opinion of store efficiency, etc.

    3. Constant major effect of work results on public and/or employee opinion of store

    4. Major responsibility is to mold and influence the reputation of the store in the minds of public and/or employees

C. Personal appearance, including dress, posture, poise, features, and voice required by the job

    1. Social relationships and type of work require only average personal appearance

    2. Social relationships require above-average personal appearance

    3. Outstanding personal appearance required as part of the job

QUESTIONS AND PROBLEMS

1. By what methods may estimates of quantitative requirements for labor be made? What are the advantages and disadvantages of each?

2. In making forecasts of labor requirements, regarding what types of business fluctuations must estimates be made? Distinguish between seasonal, cyclical, secular, and episodic fluctuations. Are there instances in which forecasts might have to be made on a daily or weekly basis? Illustrate.

3. What are the major steps in estimating labor requirements? Indicate why each is significant.

4. To what factors and conditions would you turn attention in making a sales forecast?

5. To what extent should the sales division be permitted to establish sales programs? What do policies have to do with this question?

6. What factors determine whether a company will produce to a sales curve or attempt to smooth out the production curve?

7. How much weight would you give to personnel policies of guaranteed income plans or guaranteed employment plans in connection with stabilization of production schedules?

8. Where would information regarding unit labor time be obtained? How would the calculations to determine how much labor is required differ when a given department produced a wide range of products from a department that produced only one product?

9. What are the reasons for expressing labor requirements in dollar values and in man-hour units?

10. Why has labor turnover been of such long-standing use in business and industry? Of what use are such data? What pitfalls should be avoided in using turnover data?

11. Under what condition would you use the accessions rate to measure turnover? The separations rate? Both together?

12. Why are such measures of turnover as those provided by the Bureau of Labor Statistics of particular usefulness?

13. Why are emotional and social characteristics perhaps more important than technical characteristics on some jobs?

14. What is your opinion of the importance of what a man's wife may or may not think about his job, company, or place of work?

15. If emotional or social characteristics cannot be expressed quantitatively, what can be done to keep qualitative expressions from becoming vague and meaningless?

16. By what means can man specifications be kept up to date?

17. A given executive stated that he didn't need man specifications because he knew exactly the type of people he wanted for his jobs. Comment upon his comment.

18. What is the difference between a job specification and a man specification? Which is easier to establish? Does this explain why the man specification is not as common as the job specification?

19. Distinguish between job duties, standards of job duties, and employee aptitudes. Illustrate in terms of a specific instance.

20. Using the forms illustrated in the text, select a job which you are acquainted with or can obtain information on, and determine its man specification. Against this, check your own capabilities. How might you use the results disclosed by the comparison?

CHAPTER

7 | Sources of Labor Supply

VARIABILITY OF LABOR SUPPLY SOURCES

The hiring or placement procedure cannot be put into operation until suitable candidates are attracted. To do this effectively requires a knowledge of available sources of supply and how they may be tapped as occasion demands. These matters constitute the major interest of this chapter.

Ordinarily, the various sources of supply to be discussed here would neither be available nor necessarily of interest to all companies. Moreover, each source does not remain at a constant degree of usefulness but is affected by the general state of the labor market. The moral of these statements was illustrated very strikingly during World War II, when, on the one hand, sources such as over-age workers were utilized contrary to normal practice and, on the other hand, sources that previously had been satisfactory in many cases dried up, such as the casual floating supply of labor. Hence a study of sources of supply in a particular company must give consideration to state-wide and national conditions as well as to local factors. All that can be done here is to survey various sources of supply, noting their advantages, disadvantages, and conditions of most favorable usage.

TYPES OF LABOR SOURCES

Although a common and useful classification of sources of labor supply is that of internal as opposed to external sources, it is not easy to establish border lines between them. Strictly speaking, internal sources refer to the present working force of a company. In the event of a vacancy, someone already on the payroll is upgraded, transferred, promoted, or sometimes demoted. Occasionally, the definition is expanded (and for understandable reason) to include the following:

1. Those not on the payroll of a particular company but in the employment of affiliated or subsidiary companies
2. Those who were once on the payroll of a particular company but who

122

plan to return or whom the company would like to rehire, for example, those on leave of absence, those who quit voluntarily, or those on production layoffs

3. Anyone who has not been on the payroll of the company but who is well known and vouched for by a present employee (essentially an external source)

All sources not included within the internal supply area, such as advertising, employment services, schools, and floating labor, are external sources.

THE INTERNAL SOURCE

1. ADVANTAGES. The internal source is often credited with being better than the external. This contention is based upon a number of reasons. In the first place, it is argued that by cultivating the internal source the morale of employees in general is raised, because workers are thereby given concrete evidence that they are preferred over outsiders when good vacancies occur. On the surface, this argument does not prove that the internal source is a good source but rather that its use does have a healthy effect upon present workers. On the other hand, in so far as this policy of filling vacancies induces present workers to prepare themselves for transfers or promotions so that they are better than those who might have been hired from the outside, it is commendable. Moreover, so long as opportunities for present workers are made available in this manner, there may also be an indirect effect, in that outsiders soon learn that the company in question is a good place to work, with the result that a better quality of external applicant will be attracted.

Another and cogent argument in favor of the internal source is that the employer is in a better position to evaluate those who work for him, or who have worked for him, than the candidates who present themselves from the outside. Inasmuch as a work test concededly is the best test, and if the company maintains a satisfactory record of the progress, experience, and service of its present and past employees, then the validity of this argument is granted. However, it is essential that transfers and promotions be based upon measured merit, else the internal source will degenerate into a political monopoly for those on the payroll or into undeserved favoritism to those who once were with the company. Care must also be exercised in writing seniority policies or clauses in union contracts if the danger of unwarranted use of the internal source of supply is to be averted.

2. DISADVANTAGES. The chief weaknesses of the internal source are twofold: danger of "inbreeding" and possible inadequacy of supply.

The first of these weaknesses arises out of the fact that the learner seldom has ideas or notions that differ widely from those of his teacher. As a consequence, he seldom contributes any startling innovations or makes suggestions, which are so important in our competitive economy. His company, therefore, is not likely to be known for its progressiveness and, indeed, may be left behind in the parade. On jobs in which originality counts heavily, such as advertising, style designing, and certain types of selling, a practice of always filling vacancies from within is seldom followed. However, on jobs in which these qualities are of minor significance, the danger of "inbreeding" and "dry rot" is negligible.

The policy of using internal sources of supply also breaks down in periods when large numbers of vacancies occur or are created. Obviously, it would have been ridiculous to argue that this was the best source during the war years, for instance. So long as the number of vacancies does not outrun the number who can be transferred or promoted, the adequacy of this source is not in question. But when one vacancy calls for a number of replacements because the employee who fills the vacancy must be replaced by another employee and so on to the point at which an outsider must be hired, or when large numbers of vacancies occur at the same time, the source is neither adequate nor desirable.

3. Conditions of Favorable Use. For most favorable use of the internal source of supply, then, conditions must be right. The number of vacancies to be filled must be within practicable limits, adequate employee records must be maintained, jobs calling for originality should not be assigned to present employees in blind adherence to seniority rules, and opportunities should be provided in advance for employees to prepare themselves for promotion. Much good will come, too, if publicity about well-merited transfers or promotions is carried in the company and local papers.

THE EXTERNAL SOURCE

Ultimately, of course, all vacancies must be filled from the outside. Even the company that prides itself upon its policy of filling vacancies exclusively from within must go to the outside to fill vacancies at the bottom of the promotional ladder. Hence every company must be acquainted in some degree with the kinds of varieties of external sources. The major groups of external sources are employment agencies, advertising, floating labor, recommended labor, miscellaneous sources, and unions.

1. PUBLIC EMPLOYMENT AGENCIES. The employment agencies, particularly the public agencies, have grown in importance in the field of employment in recent years. The public agencies are discussed here first, and then attention is directed to private agencies.

The public agencies are represented by the several state employment services and the United States Employment Service, commonly known as "USES." Although the work of these groups has been closely intertwined in recent years, the state agencies are separate entities. During World War II, the state agencies were absorbed by USES but were returned to their independent status on November 15, 1946. The discussion here will deal first with the USES and then with the services of a state employment unit.

a) Development of Public Agencies. Although the public agencies now have an enviable position in the labor market, this reputation has been earned within the past several years. USES, for example, once possessed an unsavory, if not laughable, reputation as a source of labor supply. Indeed, employers had recourse to it only for the most casual and unskilled labor. Its history goes back to 1918, when its existence as an independent unit was authorized within the Department of Labor and separate from the Bureau of Immigration, in which employment activities had been undertaken in 1907.

During World War I, the federal employment service was named the sole recruiting agency for civilian workers in war industries. After the war, the service helped the returning veterans to get back to their old positions or to find new ones. With this work completed, the employment service fell upon lean years. Impetus was given the USES during the depression years with the passage of the Wagner-Peyser Act in 1933, which provided for financial benefits to states accepting the provisions of the act regarding a national system of employment offices under the direction of the USES.

b) Recent Growth of Employment Services. The heyday for the public agencies came with the passage of the Social Security Act and later with the advent of World War II. One of the major provisions of this act, it will be recalled, has to do with unemployment compensation, the purpose of which is to tide unemployed workers over relatively short periods until they can find new jobs. To be eligible for such compensation, displaced workers must, among other things, register with the employment services. This meant that the state employment services in 1938 were, theoretically at least, provided with a roster of all who were unemployed and desired to work. Moreover, the state agencies were given grants-in-aid beginning in 1937 if their employment compensation methods conformed with federal standards. Among the federal requirements was that the services should seek to find, if possible, jobs that were satisfactory for the registered unemployed who were seeking to qualify for compensation. Some agencies, to carry out this stipulation, went so far in getting information about available jobs, on the one hand, that they sent emissaries to various plants to learn more about their individual problems and requirements; and, on the other hand, they sometimes offered the facilities of trade, aptitude, and psychological tests to the unemployed in order to get a better picture of them to supply to potential employers.

Thus the employment services not only were given the legal right to build up a roster of the unemployed but also were alert to the opportunity of improving their own procedures, thereby making themselves better servants of employers. As a consequence, when World War II began, the employment services had attained an accepted position in the labor market.

The greatest stimulus to the growth of the public services and, in particular, USES came with the advent of World War II. On January 1, 1942, by presidential request, the state employment services were merged into USES. As time went on, USES was given various powers over hiring and employment matters that eventually gave it a practical monopoly in certain instances. To begin with, USES became a factor in the draft by being given a voice in determining which jobs were essential and which nonessential. Employers, in order to protect their key employees, were more than willing to open their files to this agency. As a consequence, it became even more expert on jobs and job requirements. Later, the War Manpower Commission laid down hiring rules in which USES played a large role. Thus employees could not, without good and specified reasons, quit their jobs or be rehired by anyone else without a certificate of availability and a referral card from USES. Finally, for a time, USES was given the right to establish ceilings on employment and priorities for individual companies. Obviously, under these conditions, it is not surprising that in large measure USES became the employment agency of American industry. In August, 1949, the USES was transferred to the Department of Labor, under whose jurisdiction it now operates.

c) Services of State Employment Agencies. The state employment units are the agencies which operate directly in the employment field. What they do is exemplified by the work of the Ohio State Employment Service. Its basic job is to serve both worker and employer—and indirectly the community—by acting as a clearinghouse for jobs and job information. Its program includes a number of activities which serve to carry out this fundamental task.

The Ohio State Employment Service supports a full plan of employment counseling. The aim is to assist the applicant to make a suitable job choice based on facts about himself and the labor market. To do this, an analysis is made of the applicant's experience, training, education, interests, abilities, aptitudes, and physical capacities. His school record, tests, and physical capacity ratings are reviewed in a personal interview. He is then given a picture of the labor market; of the kind and number of suitable opportunities; and of working conditions, salaries, required training, and promotional prospects in various jobs or establishments. And then he is helped to make a job choice or adjustment to labor market conditions, with actual referral to a job or employer. The counseling service gives special attention to young and inexperienced workers, in recognition of the critical point at which these applicants find themselves in their working lives.

The Service has also interested itself in the use of psychological tests. Proficiency tests, such as typing, dictation, and spelling, are given to applicants for jobs requiring these skills. Aptitude tests—measuring potentiality to acquire skills—are available for over 200 jobs, including such as machine shop trainees, drafting trainees, clerical occupations, punch press operators, grocery checkers, and sewing-machine operators. And a general aptitude test battery is available to give an applicant a better idea of his potential ability to do various types of work. This is particularly useful in counseling applicants who are unable to find jobs for which they may be prepared.

The state service operates in close touch with other state units affiliated with the USES. Thus 1,800 employment offices located throughout the United States and its territories are at the service of applicants and employees through their local office. Thus local employers may be helped to find qualified workers outside the immediate area, and workers may be given reliable information about out-of-town jobs and employment conditions.

Another service along somewhat similar lines is the labor market information gathered by the state services. Summarized from the reports of local offices is such information as number of men and women seeking jobs in each community, which industries are hiring and which laying off, wage rates in each community, surplus and scarce occupations, and kinds of workers needed.

The Service also offers a selective placement service for handicapped workers. In this regard, an analysis is made to ascertain the physical capacities possessed by a handicapped applicant. Analyses are made of jobs to ascertain physical demands. And the capacities of these applicants are matched with the physical needs of jobs. Help is also offered to employees to smooth the induction of handicapped workers into industry.

The Service also seeks to promote employment of minority-group workers at their highest skills. It attempts to broaden acceptance of minority groups by employers, labor unions, and community groups. And it provides technical information and advice on the orderly introduction, use, and integration of minority-group workers into a company.

Special help is also available to war veterans. In this connection the employment service secures and maintains current information as to various types of available employment; interests employers in hiring veterans; maintains regular contacts with employer and veteran organizations; and promotes the employment of veterans.

The Service has interested itself in the employment problems of college graduates. Although the registration procedure for college graduates and other applicants is the same, the Service has taken steps to help college students in additional ways. Representatives of the Service arrange meetings on college campuses. Interested students can schedule interviews for the purpose of asking questions about employment matters and to seek guidance on their possibilities for placement or on need for adjustment. The employment service can also give useful advice on working toward promotions and on possibilities of promotions.

The Service is also responsible for being prepared to carry out the aims and objectives of Defense Manpower Mobilization. In peacetime it serves to expand defense production, relieve labor shortages, and increase the fullest possible use of available labor in critical areas. In wartime, as noted earlier, the employment service becomes a paramount agency in the labor market.

2. PRIVATE EMPLOYMENT AGENCIES.   Private employment agencies have also grown apace with other sources during the recent years of labor shortages. These groups have tended to serve employees either in the technical and professional areas or in the relatively unskilled fields. In the former case, private employment services usually specialize according to such groups as office and clerical help, accountants and statisticians, engineers, salesmen, and dietitians. As a result of such specialization, they presumably are in a position to interpret effectively the needs of their clients, to build up a list of technicians upon whom they can readily draw as needed, and to develop proficiency in recognizing the aptitudes and abilities of specialized personnel. When an employ-

ment agency does develop a reputation in connection with a particular class of employees, it undoubtedly proves to be a good source of supply. Since most employers do not have to hire various types of specialized help frequently, they are not in a position to develop an adequate source of supply for themselves and must turn to others for help. The ability of such agencies to be of service is also increased when local agencies organize into national associations through which interregional information and needs can be exchanged.

Some private employment agencies have, as noted above, restricted their clientele to the lower levels of worker skills. In such instances, they serve to attract applicants in numbers that the employer himself could not. This is particularly true of companies that have seasonal problems or are located away from the larger labor markets. Thus a company that has a seasonal logging operation, for example, may need quickly, but temporarily, a large, but miscellaneous, crew, including such workers as cooks and carpenters as well as lumberjacks. By turning to the employment agencies in larger cities, the employer can gather and ship out a group of floating workers that could scarcely be recruited in any other way. Employment agencies, by providing a more or less stable source of information about jobs, develop a classified clientele from which the employer can draw the particular skills he needs.

In essence, then, the private agencies are brokers, bringing employers and employees together. For this service, they are compensated by fees charged against the employee or, more rarely, against the employer. The fee is usually computed as a percentage of a week's, two weeks', or a month's pay.

Charging for this service is, of course, legitimate, but the practice has led to abuses which, for a time, cast suspicion upon almost all private employment agencies. It was not an uncommon practice for some employment agencies to collude with employers, whereby applicants were kept on the payroll long enough for the agency to collect its fee which was then split with the employer. A new employee was then "hired," and he too soon lost his job. Such unscruplous practices led to state and local control being exercised over private agencies. Many of the employment agencies themselves led in the fight to remove unscrupulous operators.

For a time after USES had strengthened its position in the labor market, some felt that the day of the private agency had ended. Perhaps some of the weaker units were forced out, but the remaining ones certainly seem far from finished. Indeed, the competition has served as a tonic because the services of the private agencies have improved in the past several years. Some private agencies are no longer content merely to bring employer and employee together but are utilizing testing devices to classify and evaluate applicants, are adopting scientific counseling services to interpret the abilities of their clientele, and are employing advanced techniques of vocational guidance to increase the probabilities of correct placements. These advances have made private agencies even more attractive to employees who prefer their more personal and selective characteristics.

3. ADVERTISING FOR LABOR. Advertising in various media is also a widely used method of attracting labor. How much advertising is done usually depends upon the urgency of the demand for labor. In recent years the classified sections of metropolitan newspapers have been well filled with such advertisements. On the other hand, this source is scarcely used when other channels supply sufficient candidates. The main shortcomings of this source are its uncertainty and the range of candidates that are attracted. Perhaps some of this is due to poor copy work because most ads are uninspired, uninteresting, and not clear. Even when an advertisement is properly written and timed, the employer cannot be sure that it will "pull" the desired number of applicants. Moreover, he finds that he must cull the lot very carefully, since a good proportion of those who do present themselves are unqualified. And advertising copy must be written with even greater care when the media of radio and television are used, as is not uncommon at the present time.

On the other hand, such advertisements should not be expected to do more than any advertisement can do—that is, attract attention and create a desire, which must be followed up by other appeals and selective methods. That many employers are aware of this is seen in the fact that they continued to use newspaper advertising during the war years, even when all hiring had to come through USES. In these instances, the advertising was intended to create a desire upon the part of available workers such that they would ask USES to refer them to a particular company. When the medium of advertising is chosen carefully, the attention of desirable applicants can be attracted with a high degree of selectivity. For example, advertisements placed in trade journals or professional magazines can be directed so that only specific groups will be reached.

4. CASUAL LABOR SOURCES. Most companies rely to some extent upon the casual labor which daily applies at the employment office or gate. Here, again, the source is uncertain, and the candidates cover a wide range of abilities. Although it cannot be relied upon and does call for very careful screening, few companies care to shut off this source. In

the first place, it is an inexpensive source; the applicant comes to the door of the employer of his own accord. Second, there always is an occasional "good find" that makes up for the expense of culling. And, third, some companies believe it is good public relations—those in consumer-goods industries particularly (bakeries, food products, public utilities, etc.)—to receive cordially all who come to the company premises, whether or not jobs are or will be available.

When it is desired to rely upon this source of supply, the physical facilities of employment should be made attractive and convenient. More will be said in this regard later in this chapter, but it is worth noting that an inviting waiting room, conveniently located to a main street and easily reached, is necessary. Sometimes one wonders whether employers are trying to discourage applicants when one sees the untidy waiting rooms provided for casual applicants. In some cases, applicants must wait outdoors, even during unfavorable weather.

5. RECOMMENDED LABOR. "Recommended labor" refers to all applicants who come to the employer upon the direct suggestion of a present employee or other employers. Some employers cultivate this source, feeling that it provides a preselected class of applicants. When an employee recommends a friend for a job, it is likely that he does this with some degree of care. On the one hand, he knows that to recommend someone who is unsatisfactory will reflect upon his own good judgment; and, on the other hand, he recognizes that his friend will not appreciate a lead that does not materialize in a good job. In his position of knowing something about the company and the friend, he can determine whether or not the two are likely to be a good match.

In addition, emphasizing this source of supply is likely to develop a high degree of loyalty among employees. It is stimulating to work for a company that encourages its employees to make worth-while suggestions along lines that are not strictly confined to one's immediate job. And one is proud when an employee that he has recommended does turn out to be a very acceptable addition to the company family. These manifestations of pride in work, fellow workers, and the company are results of recommended hiring that are well worth cultivating.

6. RECRUITMENT PRACTICES. During periods of general labor scarcity or in connection with scarcity of applicants for specific occupations, positive steps of seeking employees must be taken. What may be done is discussed in terms of usual factory or office jobs, highly skilled jobs, and technical and professional positions.

a) General-Run Jobs. Industry has taken a particularly active role in seeking employees not only in war years but also during the tight labor market of recent years. For example, during a concentrated program of inducing people to enter war work, in the relatively small city of New Britain, Connecticut, a total of 2,341 housewives were recruited in forty days. A complete campaign was worked out that included newspaper advertisements, posters, movie-trailers, and shop-window displays. But of unique interest was a house-to-house canvass by women actually at war work.

A plant at Asheville, North Carolina, recruited blind workers for such jobs as sorting rough pieces of mica. The blind by touch alone were able to do as well as, or better than, those with normal vision who used a micrometer. Such discoveries of new uses in industry for the special skills of handicapped workers have been made through increased research in the field.

A unique way of tapping a labor supply was to inaugurate part-time, short-hour, "victory" shifts. A company in South Boston advertised for such help and got 2,000 applicants. The applicants held full-time regular jobs and came into the war plant from 6:00 to 11:00 P.M. for five days a week. Another company in Bridgeport, Connecticut, used such a "white-collar" shift to good advantage.

Along somewhat similar lines was the recruiting of "rush-job," temporary workers. When a peak load had to be handled, appeals were made for regularly employed workers to come in for part-time work. One company in Utica, New York, based its advertisements on the "Minute Man" and "Paul Revere" idea, with telling effect.

In some areas intercompany and community exchanges of labor supply were carried out. By pooling information regarding projected hiring and discharges, it was found in some communities that labor could be exchanged in a mutually satisfactory manner. Thus, when a given company determined that a certain number of employees with particular skills had to be laid off, this was called to the attention of other companies that were expanding and in need of such skills. Good workers were thus assured of relatively steady employment, and the industries of the community helped themselves by keeping good workers from migrating.

b) Highly Skilled Workers. The foregoing cases also serve to illustrate methods of recruiting highly skilled workers. Also noteworthy is the plan of dividing complicated jobs into relatively simple operations, although not a source of labor in itself, as a means of taking advantage of available or trainable sources. During the early years of the war when the shortage of skilled toolmakers became dangerously acute, many companies found it desirable to divide this work into its components.

Then trainees were assigned to the simple aspects of the toolmaker's job, while the craftsman retained the complicated operations himself. Thus his specialized talents were utilized to the highest possible degree and spread over the largest number of jobs possible. This plan has the desirable characteristic of making it possible to use lower levels of skilled and semiskilled employees, which are numerically larger than the highly skilled.

c) Technical and Professional Positions. Many companies have turned to the schools to look for desirable applicants for such positions. They send representatives to college campuses to seek the cream of the graduating classes. In a few cases the practice has been to offer summer employment to outstanding juniors and even sophomores with a view to permanent employment later. This practice enables the employer to try out the students and thus be in a better position to evaluate their potentialities. And the students not only gain useful work experience but also can better judge the desirability of making a permanent connection. Some college-recruitment programs have been extended to the point that companies are willing to pay for postgraduate training of students in particularly scarce, specialized job areas. In all cases of college recruitment, it is highly desirable to be very careful in screening candidates. A useful suggestion in this connection is the interviewing procedure illustrated in Figure 20 (p. 134).[1]

7. UNIONS. Unions have played, and are likely to play, an increasing role in the matter of sources of labor supply. In some industries, such as the building trades, unions have carried the responsibility of supplying the employer with skilled employees in adequate numbers. This not only has been of real service to employers but has also removed from their shoulders the obligation of how to allocate limited amounts of work during slack periods. The union has determined the order in which available workers are assigned to employers.

When unions have completely taken over the hiring function, as in the case of the "hiring halls" of the maritime industry, this practice has been restricted by the Taft-Hartley Act. Such "halls" must not discriminate against nonunion members. Many believe that the "hiring hall" is perhaps the best way of handling the hiring problem in certain industries.

Where unions do not actively engage in providing employment information or service to their members, they invariably take an interest in seeing that members laid off are given preference in rehiring. Most

---

[1] Richard S. Uhrbrock, "Recruiting the College Graduate," *American Management Association Bulletin,* 1953, p. 11.

union contracts contain some reference to the responsibility of the employer to rehire former employees, and usually in some order of seniority. It is more than probable that such clauses will become more detailed and specific, particularly when contracts are rewritten during periods of economic recession.

FIGURE 20

COLLEGE RECRUITING INTERVIEWING PROCEDURE

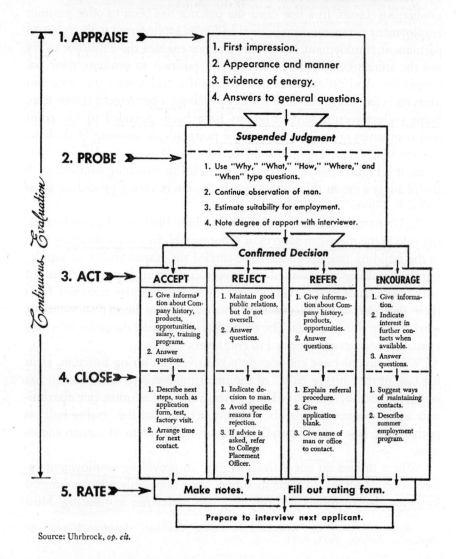

Source: Uhrbrock, *op. cit.*

While the participation of unions in the supply of labor has not been widespread or along lines of complete service, there is no reason to believe that such a trend is not likely to gain strength. As demands for better wages and hours find more resistance, the unions are undoubtedly going to move in the direction of serving their members in various ways. One of these is likely to be that of uncovering employment vacancies and counseling members as to how the vacancies may best be filled.

EFFECT OF LOCATION OF PLANT

Another tack which is worth taking is that of locating the enterprise at a location or locations in which the sources of labor supply are satisfactory. An interesting example of this is found in the plan of Henry Ford to decentralize some of his operations. One of the purposes of this plan is to locate operations in small towns where it is possible to take advantage of small, but nevertheless excellent, supplies of labor. Another example is found in the plan of Sylvania Electric Products, Inc., to decentralize its operations in relatively small- and medium-sized towns and cities so that it could, among other things, gain the advantage of such labor markets. This company began in 1935 to set its policies upon the principle of decentralization so that it was in an excellent position to expand along planned lines when World War II broke out. Among the advantages found in such operations are the following:

1. Small-town operations enable the company to tap new sources of labor supply.
2. Citizens of small communities show greater interest in their work, and hence do better work.
3. With this kind of help, fewer rejects are found among parts going into final assemblies.
4. Industrial harmony is best when the plant manager knows each worker by his first name, and vice versa.
5. Small-town workers are less inclined to absent themselves without cause.
6. Small plants offer greater incentives to maturing workers; hence the company is able to develop a more effective executive personnel.
7. It proved easier, under wartime operating conditions, to transport truckloads of partially finished products from feeder plants to main plants than to move trainloads of workers from home towns to distant plants.[2]

EVALUATION OF ALTERNATIVE SOURCES

A knowledge of available sources of supply should be augmented by an evaluation of their relative merits. Some plan should be devised by which it is possible to measure how good, or how poor, various sources

---

[2] L. K. Urquhart, "A Case Study in Decentralization," *Factory Management and Maintenance*, October, 1945, p. 106.

have proved to be. Some reference has been made in the foregoing discussion regarding the advantages and disadvantages of various sources, but such generalized conclusions should in particular cases be checked by objective measurements whenever possible. Of course, in every company some one person will aways have opinions on the relative value of particular sources, but such opinions are not always reliable nor available.

Perhaps the most accurate way, though by no means indisputable, of evaluating the effectiveness of sources of labor supply is to run statistical correlations. In this manner, it is possible to relate the factor of success on the job with the factor of particular sources of supply. A simple illus-

TABLE 9

SOURCE OF HIRING

	Gate Hiring		Referred by Present Employees		Rehiring of Layoffs		Total	
	No.	%	No.	%	No.	%	No.	%
January	27	71	5	13	6	16	38	100
February	15	60	4	16	6	24	25	100
March	12	70	2	12	3	18	17	100

TABLE 10

PERSONNEL RECRUITMENT PRACTICES OF 325 SELECTED COMPANIES, 1947*

	Yes		No		No Answer	
	No.	%	No.	%	No.	%
1. Are any new employees furnished by an outside source?	180	55.5	129	39.7	16	4.8
2. Do you make a general practice of securing applicants through the United States Employment Service (State Employment Service)?	182	56.0	132	40.6	11	3.4
a) Do you use this service exclusively?	2	0.6	256	78.8	67	20.6
b) Do you use this service occasionally?	270	83.0	9	2.8	46	14.2
c) Do you avoid this service?	16	4.8	237	73.0	72	22.2
3. Do you make a general practice of securing applicants through schools and colleges?	186	57.2	124	38.2	15	4.6
a) Do you use these sources occasionally?	265	81.6	15	4.6	45	13.8
b) Do you avoid these sources?	0	0.0	229	70.5	96	29.5
4. Do you make a general practice of securing applicants through private (fee) employment agencies?	92	28.3	220	67.7	13	4.0
a) Do you use these sources occasionally?	221	68.0	41	12.6	63	19.4
b) Do you avoid these agencies?	38	11.7	136	41.8	151	46.5
5. Do you make a general practice of securing new employees through labor unions?	30	9.3	285	87.6	10	3.1
a) Do you use this source occasionally?	68	20.8	137	42.2	120	37.0
b) Do you avoid this source?	94	28.9	94	28.9	137	42.2
6. Do you make a general practice of securing applicants through your foremen, employees, friends, and other miscellaneous sources?	253	77.9	64	19.6	8	2.5

* Source: W. R. Spriegel and R. F. Wallace, "Recent Trends in Personnel Selection and Induction," *Personnel,* September, 1948, p. 79.

tration of how this is done is shown by the study made in one company which, among other things, wanted to know how well people from various parts of the city in which it was located succeeded on the job. The map of the community in question was divided into parts that had somewhat common characteristics, for example, purchasing power, nationalities, and schools. The records of employees selected from these areas were then correlated with the degree of job success as measured by the plan of employee rating operated by the company. It was found that the employees who came from certain areas rated higher than those that came from other areas. As a consequence, it was decided to restrict hirings to those candidates who came from the areas from which the better employees had come in the past. It was recognized that, as a result of this policy, a few good employees from the restricted areas would be passed up, but it was felt that this loss would be less than that which would be incurred by hiring from the low-rated areas.

A simpler plan of evaluating alternative sources of supply is to use such measures as turnover, grievances, and disciplinary action. For example, by classifying turnover data according to the original sources

TABLE 11

SURVEY OF OPINIONS REGARDING AGENCIES OF EMPLOYMENT*

Question 1: *How did you get your present job?*

	Private	Public	Company
All workers questioned:			
City A, 1946 (N = 284)...............	18%	7%	75%
City A, 1948 (N = 393)...............	19	3	72
City D, 1948 (N = 299)...............	16	8	76
Workers using all three agencies:			
City A, 1946 (N = 106)...............	28	10	62
City A, 1948 (N = 109)...............	40	6	52
City D, 1948 (N = 98)..............	25	6	69

Question 2: *In your opinion, which offers the best opportunity for getting work, the private employment agency, the public employment office, or the employment department of companies which hire their own workers?*

	Private	Public	Company	No Opinion
All workers questioned:				
City A, 1946 (N = 261)............	24%	7%	58%	11%
City A, 1948 (N = 394)............	19	7	55	19
City D, 1948 (N = 299)............	22	7	61	10
Workers using all three agencies:				
City A, 1946 (N = 102)............	34	8	52	6
City A, 1948 (N = 104)............	34	3	57	6
City D, 1948 (N = 98)............	39	6	55	0

* Source: I. G. Nudell and D. G. Patterson, "Attitudes of Clerical Workers toward Three Types of Employment Agencies," *Personnel*, 1950, p. 331.

from which employees came, it is possible to contrast the relative merits of sources of supply. The same result may be obtained by tabulating

FIGURE 21. Employment Office of a Small Plant

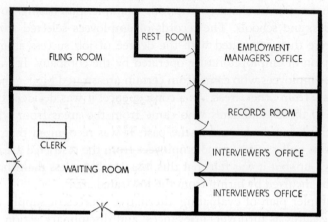

grievances and disciplinary action according to classes of hiring sources. Table 9 (p. 136) provides an illustration of such a tabulation. Such studies are not conclusive, but they do throw light upon a subject that otherwise is beclouded by personal opinions and even prejudices.

Of interest in the matter of evaluating sources of supply are general studies made of recruitment practices and toward selected employment agencies. In Table 10 (p. 136) are shown the results of the recruitment practices of 325 companies. Examination of this table shows that public agencies, private agencies, schools, and recommendations are most frequently used to attract candidates. Unions, in this study, were least commonly used. On the other hand, in particular geographical areas and for some jobs, union sources outweigh all others.

FIGURE 22. Personnel Layout of a Medium-Sized Company*

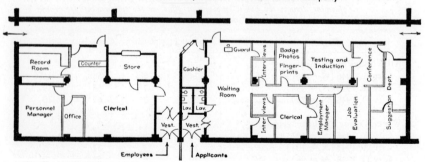

* Source: Cyril T. Tucker, "Three Ways to Lay Out a Personnel Department," *Factory Management and Maintenance*, September, 1943, pp. 154–55.

FIGURE 23. Personnel Layout of a Large Company*

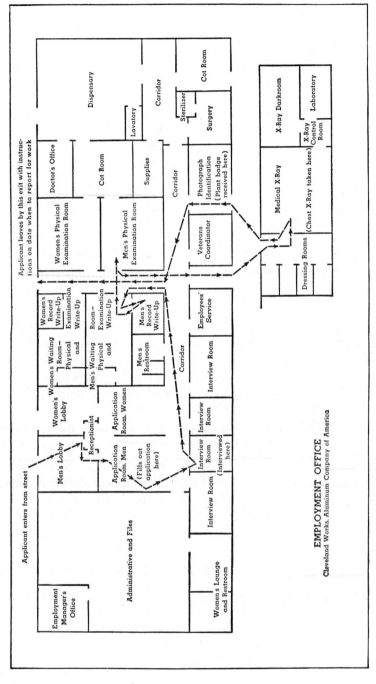

EMPLOYMENT OFFICE
Cleveland Works, Aluminum Company of America

* Source: Stanley R. Kuhns, "Making Job Applicants Feel They Belong," *Factory Management and Maintenance*, October, 1945, pp. 98–99.

Another example of an evaluation study is shown in Table 11 (p. 137). This summarizes the study of public employment agencies, private employment agencies, and company employment departments. In this sample, seekers of employment had better results from company employment departments than from public or private agencies.

LAYOUT AND LOCATION OF EMPLOYMENT OFFICE

The physical layout and location of the employment office has an indirect, though nonetheless important, effect upon the attraction of suitable candidates. An office with comfortable furnishings and a pleasing appearance leaves a favorable impression upon applicants and adds to the efficiency of the employing staff. Also, one that is conveniently located is more likely to attract candidates than one that is not so easily reached. Indeed, this matter of location has become so important during recent years that some unique experiments have been conducted to make employment offices more accessible. For example, during World War II, the Bell Aircraft Corporation established branch employment offices in downtown locations, from which applicants found suitable were taken to the plant by station wagon. Other organizations have also employed auto trailers as added means of reaching and attracting labor. When the labor market is exceedingly tight, recourse to such methods is justifiable, though it might prove too expensive as a regular practice.

The layout and appointments of the employment office require careful consideration. The main problem here is that the volume of hirings varied so widely that it is difficult to arrive at a satisfactory compromise as to size. Usually, the employment office is too large or too small. Some examples of office layouts are shown in Figures 21, 22, and 23 (pp. 138 and 139). It will be noted that all of the plans are designed to facilitate an efficient flow of applicants through the hiring process. The plan of the Aluminum Company of America is particularly to the point.

QUESTIONS AND PROBLEMS

1. What are the arguments, pro and con, regarding the "hiring hall"?
2. Under what conditions is the contention true that "a work test is the best test" for candidates for employment? In a rapidly expanding company, would you rely upon this principle? Explain.
3. What are the chief weaknesses of the internal source of supply? Do these weaknesses apply generally, or only to specific classes of jobs?
4. What conditions must be met for favorable usage of the internal source of supply?

5. How would you go about determining whether or not a policy of promoting from within had had a favorable effect upon employee morale?

6. What are the major external sources of labor supply? How would their effectiveness vary as business conditions change?

7. Explain the growing importance of the federal and state employment services. Do you believe that these agencies will maintain their important positions as a source of labor? Explain.

8. Private employment agencies have in recent years grown in prestige. How would you explain this trend?

9. Examine the classified advertising section of a newspaper carrying a representative number of labor want ads. Write a report describing good and poor practices of advertising for labor. Illustrate your report with examples.

10. How would you determine the value, or lack of it, of casual applicants as a source of labor supply? Under what conditions would reliance upon it be justified?

11. Justify the favor in which many employers hold recommendations of present employees as a source of labor supply.

12. Describe the plan of intercompany and community exchanges of labor supply. Indicate some of the problems that must be solved and policies that must be agreed upon before these plans can be adopted effectively.

13. If you were asked to establish a plan for a house-to-house canvass of labor candidates, what instructions would you specify for canvassers? How and where would you select your canvassers?

14. If women were used so widely in industry during the war years, why do not such sources as housewives constitute a relatively cheap source of labor supply at present?

15. Make a list of types of handicapped workers who could provide an acceptable source of labor supply. Is the hiring of such candidates a matter of charity or of sound business? Give examples.

16. How can the plan of dividing technical jobs into components of varying degrees of complexity help solve the problem of locating candidates for employment?

17. Draw up a table comparing the small, medium-sized, and large city as sources of labor supply. Indicate the shortcomings as well as advantages of each.

18. How can the relative merits of alternative sources of labor supply be measured objectively? Need such measurements always consist of involved mathematical analyses? Explain.

19. What values can a good physical location and layout of an employment office contribute to the matter of sources of labor supply?

20. Visit a company and draw a floor plan of their employment office. Indicate how the applicants "flow through" the hiring procedure. Also, note the location of the office with reference to the factory, general office, or sales activities of the company in question. Support your plan with a critical analysis.

CHAPTER

8 | The Selection Procedure

MAJOR STAGES

The "selection procedure" is the sequence of functions adopted in a given case for the purpose of ascertaining whether or not candidates possess the qualifications called for by a specific job. In some cases the qualifications of a progression of jobs are considered when promotional possibilities are of importance. As noted in earlier chapters, the selection or "hiring" procedure cannot be effectively placed in operation until three major steps have been taken—

1. Requirements of the job to be filled have been specified.
2. Qualifications workers must possess have been specified.
3. Candidates for screening have been recruited.

After the foregoing steps have been taken, it is then the purpose of selection to match the qualifications of candidates with the requirements of the job. Undesirable candidates are "screened" out and the qualified retained.

Selection (also termed "screening" or "hiring") processes of companies differ widely. Some companies are content with a cursory personal interview and a simple physical examination. At the other extreme, elaborate series of tests, examinations, interviews, and appraisals are employed. The order of arrangement of functions also differs—some companies give physical examinations, for example, early in the procedure, whereas others place this step toward the end of the procedure.

Although there are numerous differences in how this task is performed, all selection procedures have common features. The following broad steps are generally taken:

1. Initiation of the selection process
2. Gathering pertinent information about candidates
3. Interpreting findings and comparing with job requirements
4. Making decisions and recording results
5. Induction or placement of employee

INITIATION OF SELECTION PROCEDURE

The selection process is placed in operation by means of a release of authority to fill an existing or expected vacancy. How such authority is released, by whom, and to whom differs from company to company. In its simplest form, where the company is small and the line form of organization structure is in use, each executive decides for himself when vacancies should be filled. Such instances represent informal and personalized management, which is beyond the possibility of study here.

As an organization grows, release of authority is clothed in formalized records and systems. Very common in such instances is the use of a form called the "hiring requisition," issued to the employment office by the executive in need of help. Regarding the question of who may issue such requisitions, practice differs. Some companies permit first-line foremen and supervisors to issue them for any vacancies that occur. Other companies grant this right to supervisors in regard to direct help, such as machine operators, but require higher approval in the case of indirect or so-called "nonproductive" help, such as truckers, messengers, and clerks. Still other companies require all requisitions made out by foremen and supervisors to carry the signatures of higher executives. The purpose of such requirements is to control more closely the number of hirings and thus reduce the possibility of needless employment.

Hiring or labor requisitions differ in the kind and amount of information which they carry. The form shown in Figure 24 is illustrative

FIGURE 24. An Employment Requisition

EMPLOYMENT REQUISITION

(FOREMAN KEEP DUPLICATE – COLORED COPY)

NUMBER

TO EMPLOYMENT MANAGER:— DATE.............................194...

PLEASE EMPLOY FOR.......................................DEPARTMENT THE FOLLOWING:

	NO. MALE	NO. FEMALE	OCCUPATION	RATE	ADDITION TO FORCE	☐ TO REPLACE (NAME OF EX-EMPLOYEE) ☐ FOREMAN'S RECOMMENDATION	DATE WANTED	TEMPORARY (DATE TO END)
1								
2								
3								
4								

SIGNED...FOREMAN APPROVED...SUPERINTENDENT

TO BE FILLED OUT BY EMPLOYMENT MANAGER

	EMPLOYED (NAME)	CLOCK No.	STATUS (SEE NOTE BELOW)	DATE HIRED
1				
2				
3				
4				

* NOTE—USE THESE DESCRIPTIONS: REPLACEMENT, ADDITION, TEMPORARY, PART TIME, SEASONAL, STUDENT (MINOR), APPRENTICE, EXTRA OR CASUAL

RECEIVED BY...EMPLOYMENT MANAGER

HIRED { ______MEN ______WOMEN

DATE..............................194.......

FORM FF-180

of a simple means of informing the employment section that a vacancy exists. Under conditions in which the employment office is personally acquainted with the job in question and the needs of the various departments, as is true in smaller companies, such a form serves the purpose of initiating the selection process. In cases where such information is not personally known by the employment officer or his assistants, which would be true in large organizations, a more detailed statement is needed on the labor requisition, as illustrated in Figure 25. Here the

FIGURE 25.   An Employment Requisition

EMPLOYMENT REQUISITION					
NUMBER REQUIRED				DATE OF REQUEST	
DEPARTMENT		POSITION			
DUTIES AND RESPONSIBILITIES					
ADDITION TO PRESENT FORCE	PERMANENT	TEMPORARY		IF TEMPORARY, HOW LONG?	
REASONS FOR ADDITION					
REPLACEMENT	PERMANENT	TEMPORARY		IF TEMPORARY, HOW LONG?	
IF REPLACEMENT, GIVE NAMES OF EMPLOYEES REPLACED					
RATE OF PAY	PER HOUR	PER WEEK	IS APPLICATION FOR BOND REQUIRED?	YES	NO
MALE	FEMALE	WHITE	COLORED	AGE LIMIT - MINIMUM	MAXIMUM
EDUCATION REQUIRED					
ELEMENTARY SCHOOL	HIGH SCHOOL		COLLEGE OR UNIVERSITY		
SPECIAL TRAINING					
OTHER REQUIREMENTS					
EXPERIENCE					
KIND	YEARS DESIRED		KIND		YEARS DESIRED
TECHNICAL			CLERICAL		
TYPING			MECHANICAL		
STENOGRAPHIC			SPECIAL		
REPORT TO (SUPERVISOR)		LOCATION	DATE	TIME	A. M. P. M.
REQUESTED BY			DEPARTMENT		
APPROVED BY			DEPARTMENT		
REMARKS					

(NOTE· TYPE IN DUPLICATE. ORIGINAL TO PERSONNEL DEPT. DUPLICATE FOR YOUR FILE.)

PLEASE ANTICIPATE YOUR WANTS AS FAR IN ADVANCE AS IS POSSIBLE AND GIVE SUFFICIENT DETAILS SO THAT THE PERSONNEL DEPARTMENT CAN MAKE AN INTELLIGENT SELECTION OF APPLICANTS.

TELEPHONE REQUESTS MUST BE COVERED BY A WRITTEN REQUISITION WITHOUT DELAY.

specifications are stated in coded as well as descriptive terms, so that reference may be made quickly to more complete specifications of job and personnel requirements.

As requisitions are received, they may be recorded in a labor journal or register, so that the status of unfilled requisitions may readily be ascertained and controlled. Employment requisitions are then assigned to employment assistants, who acquaint themselves with job and labor specifications and thus prepare themselves to check on available candidates.

GATHERING INFORMATION ABOUT CANDIDATES

1. INFORMATION SOUGHT. A variety of information may be gathered from and about candidates for vacancies. The efforts exerted in gathering such information may be studied in terms of (1) the information which is sought and (2) the means of deriving desired information. In the first of these divisions, the general classes of information include the following:

1. Training, experience, and general background
2. Mental ability and level of intelligence
3. Physical condition, aptitudes, and skills
4. Moral and emotional characteristics and skills

Under the second of these divisions, the general groups of means of gathering information include the following:

1. Interviews
2. Tests and examinations
3. Personal observation
4. Application blanks, references, and similar reports
5. Union sources

In the present section, the discussion will be restricted to application blanks, references, personal observation, and union sources, inasmuch as the use of tests, examinations, and interviews for collecting desired information is treated more thoroughly in the next few chapters.

a) *The Application Blank.* The application blank is undoubtedly one of the most common tools of selection. It invariably occupies a leading role because information gathered in this manner provides a clue to the need of and a basis for other selective processes. Its design differs widely from company to company, but the following general classes of information are sought in practically all cases:

1. Identifying information, such as name, address, telephone number, and social security number
2. Personal information, such as marital status, dependents, age, place of birth, birthplace of parents, number of sisters and brothers, etc.

3. Physical characteristics, such as height, weight, health, defects
4. Education
5. Experience, usually through the last three or four employers only
6. References, personal and business
7. Miscellaneous remarks and comments, such as hobbies, memberships in organizations, financial status, and insurance programs

Details included under the foregoing headings may be noted by a study of the form illustrated in Figure 31 (p. 155).

In determining what information is to be asked for on an application blank, it is invariably necessary to reach a compromise between what is wanted and needful and what can be obtained effectively on such a form. Applicants are not always willing to give answers (particularly when they are not sure of being hired) to such questions as financial status or details of personal history. Moreover, detailed application blanks may drive applicants away, particularly during conditions of a tight labor supply.

As a consequence, it is necessary to decide how much information can reasonably be asked for on the applicant blank. A particularly useful test in this connection is: How needful is the information to the company? When this question is answered squarely, it will be found that some information sought on application blanks is used so infrequently that it does not merit a place on the application blank. When information is needed only in isolated cases, it is well to seek it by other means, such as the interview or by references.

There is good reason to doubt the wisdom of placing too much confidence in the application blank as an unsupported source of hiring decisions. For example, what does it really prove to find out from an applicant that he graduated from high school? How standards differ from school to school, how a student applies himself to school work, the value of various extracurricular activities, and motivational factors during school life are not disclosed by the application blank. Similar questions could be raised about other "information" on the blank, such as work experiences, hobbies, family obligations, and living-quarters arrangements. If the bare record will not serve to rank or grade applicants, weighting the information on the blank—as some have suggested—cannot add something to nothing. The real usefulness of the blank must come elsewhere; it can provide the basis for reference checking, good interviewing, and correlation with testing data. In and of itself, the application blank has little discriminating value as between various candidates.

Another aspect to which attention must be directed in this connection is the design and form of the application blank. On the one hand, it must be considered from the viewpoint of the applicant. It should be designed to provide needed information easily and quickly. In this connection the use of such devices as the following have been found helpful: grouping similar questions in adjacent blocks of space; using "yes" and "no" questions, as well as questions that can be checked, whenever possible; and using legible print. On the other hand, it must be designed with the company's purpose in mind. It should be relatively easy to handle in the employment office. This calls for consideration of such matters as ease of filing, durability throughout frequent handling, and prominence of most pertinent information. In addition, it may be desirable to adopt two or more types of blanks so that they will fit the various classes of personnel to be selected, for example, general factory employees, general office employees, and executive and technical employees.

b) Use of References. The use of references is also common to most selection procedures. This practice places reliance upon the evaluation of former employers, friends, and professional acquaintances. Inasmuch as most people are reluctant to make reports that may hinder the chances of others, their opinions are not likely to result in accurate appraisals unless carefully controlled. For example, when a personnel officer seeking information knows and has the confidence of another personnel officer whose company has been given as a former employer; then reliance can be placed upon the reference. In localities in which associations of personnel executives have been formed, bringing those executives into a position of closer acquaintanceship, it has been found that the degree of reliance that can be placed tends to go up sharply. Or if a reference form, such as that shown in Figure 26 (p. 148), is used, which requires definite appraisals, the chances of getting unbiased references are increased. Moreover, the number of returns is increased; in the case of the cited form, it is reported that 88 per cent of the inquiries made by this method were returned, most of them promptly.

The usefulness of references is also dependent upon the speed with which they can be checked. During times when the need of labor is great, decisions may have to be made about candidates very quickly. In urgent cases, the telephone and the telegraph are employed.

c) Personal Observation. Despite the increased use of various types of formal tests and despite the high probabilities of error due to personal prejudice or ineffectiveness, personal observation is undoubtedly widely used and weighs heavily in reaching decisions in the selection process. There is no reason why this method of gathering information should not be employed so long as it is practiced with due consideration for its possible weaknesses and is supplemented by other aids. Certainly, interviewing, which essentially is a form of personal observation, has been credited with a higher role in selection since its operations have been studied more scientifically in recent years.

Indeed, interviewing is proving such a useful tool that its principles are worthy of description, which is the subject of a later chapter. In any event, much useful information can be obtained by talking to and sizing

FIGURE 26.   A Sample Reference Form*

_____, Social Security No._____, has applied to us for a position as_____. Applicant claims to have been in your employ from_____to_____. Having had an opportunity to observe above applicant as an employee, your frank answers to the questions on the reverse side of this card will be valuable to us, and would be greatly appreciated. *We assure you that your replies will not be revealed to the applicant, or anyone else, under any circumstances.*

(Reverse)

1. When was he in your employ? From_____to_____.
2. What position did he hold?_____
3. Was his attendance regular? Yes_____No_____. If not, what was the cause of his absences?_____
4. Was he liked by his co-workers (well-liked, acceptable, sometimes criticized)? _____
5. Was his rate of progress slow, average, above average?_____
6. Was he asked to resign, or did he resign voluntarily?_____
7. Would you re-employ for a similar position? Yes_____No_____ If not, why?_____
8. In view of your knowledge of his character, ability, and dependability, how would you rate him as an employee? Below average_____Average_____ Above average_____
9. If you prefer, we will call you on telephone No._____.

---

* Source: C. W. Brooks, "Checking Applicants' References," *Management Review*, September, 1948, p. 465.

up candidates; hence it would be unwise to forego its inclusion in the selection process simply because it can be easily misused. After all, any tool can be mishandled; the moral is that users should be properly trained to use such tools.

   d) Union Sources. Information may also be obtained from local union offices regarding the preference to be given candidates. Indeed, in some instances, as noted earlier, the "union hall" would be the first and perhaps the only source of supply of labor. In such cases the union would pretty largely sift out the candidates for employment. And it seems probable that, as time goes on, the union office is likely to take a greater interest in who among their members is hired, in their competency to hold jobs, and in the company's tests of selection. As this trend builds strength, the company may find it desirable to work out agreements on standards of employment which go beyond technical questions of seniority or order of rehiring.

2. INTERPRETING FINDINGS. The next major step in the selection process is to interpret findings and make decisions. Of course, this is a phase of selection that takes place at all stages of the process. Inasmuch as the selection process is also a rejection process, some candidates will fall by the wayside after each step. Some candidates may be rejected before they are even permitted to fill out an application blank, others will be rejected because of information received on the application blank, and still others will not fail until a final survey of all evidence is made.

This task of separating acceptable from nonacceptable candidates is very difficult, particularly in "twilight" cases and in cases where the candidates succeed in passing the preliminary hurdles. Let us assume that on a test used in connection with a particular job, the minimum passing grade is 75, and that on it a candidate gets 74. What should be done if his personal qualities are satisfactory and so are his training, experience, and references? The tendency is to accept the candidate in such instances in spite of the test score. But what if the test score is 73 or 72 or 71 or 70? When does the weight of the test outbalance the other factors? Most companies leave this to the personal judgment of the employment officer or to his superior in important cases. Some companies are attempting to place this on an objective basis by using a report form on which the various findings are summarized and scored.

REPORTS AND RECORDS

1. REJECTIONS. As decisions are reached regarding applicants, it is necessary to make out reports and records. These records may be classified according to whether the candidates are rejected, are not hired but would be desirable employees if vacancies were available, or are hired.

Keeping records of candidates not hired may seem a useless gesture, but it is not necessarily so. In the first place, if considerable study has been made of a candidate and he is found unsuitable, records of the case will prevent a restudy if the applicant should later present himself again, as sometimes happens.

For example, an applicant was refused a job in one company because his educational background indicated that he was unsuited for the job. The applicant returned a few days later and gave a new set of educational data, having deduced from the interview that the educational factor had stood in his way. Only the fact that the interviewer happened to remember the case (no file of unsuccessful candidates was maintained) prevented the man from being hired. Since microfilming has come into use, such records can be kept in a minimum of space. Figure 27 illustrates a record of rejected candidates.

In the second place, a record of reasons for rejection is highly desirable in cases in which a company might be accused of unfair labor practices. This factor grows in importance as rules governing fair employ-

FIGURE 27. Acceptance or Rejection Form

NOTICE OF ACCEPTANCE or REJECTION OF APPLICATION FOR EMPLOYMENT

TO SAMUEL MARKUM DEPT. HEAD PAUL SMITH DATE 10-1 1946

THIS IS TO ADVISE YOU THAT THE APPLICATION OF:

NAME JOHN DOE ADDRESS 1754 South Sixth St. PHONE Wa. 2046

HAS BEEN ACCEPTED / XXXXXXX FOR XXXXXXXX / PERMANENT EMPLOYMENT. (IF ACCEPTED - DATE STARTS TO WORK 10-5-46

IF REJECTED - GIVE REASONS FOR REJECTION ____________________

THIS GOES TO FOREMAN AT TIME OF INTERVIEW AND MUST BE COMPLETED AND RETURNED TO SUPERINTENDENT'S DESK FOR REVIEW.
(THIS FORM TO BE SIGNED AND RETURNED DIRECT TO SUPERINTENDENT'S DESK) ____________ FOREMAN

ment practices become formalized in state laws, as is true in the state of New York.

Practically all companies maintain a file of information on candidates who would make desirable employees if vacancies existed. This is a desirable practice, inasmuch as such people, having undergone some investigation, constitute a possible source of labor supply. The usefulness of such a file depends upon the economic position of the industrial and business community. During the war, for example, applications filed by candidates were usually found to be useless as a source of supply unless followed up within a day or two. There were too many jobs available for people to wait for one with a particular company. On the other hand, during depression years, applications were found useful even after months had passed.

UNISORT PERSONNEL RECORD - STD. FORM Y11 - CHARLES B. HADLEY CO., PATHFINDERS

(1) NAME: (LAST) (FIRST) (MIDDLE)

ADDRESS: STREET AND NUMBER CITY

TELEPHONE NO.

RESIDENCE ZONE NO.

(1) EMPLOYEE NUMBER
SOCIAL SECURITY NUMBER

(1) EMPLOYEE NAME OR NUMBER

PLACE OF BIRTH

CITY
STATE OR COUNTRY

(2) DATE OF BIRTH
MONTH DAY YEAR

(3) CITIZEN OF:

DESCENT:

(4) RACE:

HEIGHT: FT. IN. WEIGHT: LBS.

HAIR: EYES:

MALE FEMALE

(9) HANDICAPS: (DESCRIBE)

IDENTIFYING MARKS:

(10) OWNS HOME?

OWNS CAR?

SPOUSE WORKING?

(11) UNION: (IF ANY)

LOCAL NO.

(5) MARITAL STATUS

SGL.
MARRIED
WID.
SEP.
DIV.

(6) BIRTHDATES OF CHILDREN UNDER 18
NO. MONTH DAY YEAR
1
2
3
4
5

(7) ADULTS OVER 18 LEGALLY DEPENDENT ON EMPLOYEE
NO. RELATIONSHIP
1
2
3
4
5

DRAFT ORDER NO.

LOCAL BOARD NO.

DRAFT CLASSIFICATION RECORD

LOCAL BOARD ADDRESS

STREET AND NO.
CITY

COUNTY
STATE

(12) CLASS (13) EXPIRES

DATE

EMPLOYMENT RECORD — ORIGIN?

(14) DATE (15) DEPARTMENT JOB TITLE

(16) CLASSIFICATION NO.

RATE

(17) SHIFT

(18) TERMINATED O.K. REHIRE

REMARKS

DATE EMPLOYED
MONTH YEAR UNITS TENS

DEPARTMENT
UNITS TENS

OFFICE

(3) ALIEN
(4) WHITE
(5) MARRIED
(6) CHILDREN UNDER 18
(7) OTHER DEPENDENTS
(8) FEMALE
(9) HANDICAPPED
(10) OWNS HOME
(11) UNION MEMBER
(12) DRAFT CLASS
(13) REPLACEMENT MONTH
(14) YEAR
(15) DEPARTMENT
(16) JOB CLASSIFICATION
(17) SHIFT
(18) TERMINATED
(19) RE-HIRED
(21) EDUCATION
GRADE HIGH GRAD. COLL. DEGREE
(22) OTHER SPEC. SKILL

(Over)

* Unisort Personnel Record. Reproduced with permission of Charles R. Hadley Company, Los Angeles.

FIGURE 28.—Continued

PERFORMANCE RECORD

DATE	RATING	BY

(21) EDUCATION

NAME OF SCHOOL	NO. OF YEARS, HRS. OR LESSONS	GRADE	MAJORED IN OR COURSE	DEGREE	DATE COMP.

(22) OTHER JOB EXPERIENCES OR SKILLS

JOB TITLE	CLASSIFICATION NO.	HOW LONG	WHERE PERFORMED	RATE EARNED

HOBBIES AND INTERESTS

REMARKS

CLEARANCES

DATE	DESCRIPTION	BY
	AVAILABILITY CERT.	
	UNION	
	PHYSICAL EXAM.	
	CITIZENSHIP	
	PHOTOGRAPH	
	FINGERPRINTS	
	BADGE	
	SURETY BOND	
	COMPANY RULES	

IN EMERGENCY NOTIFY:

ADDRESS:

RELATIONSHIP   TELEPHONE

OTHER SKILL (22)   EDUCATION (21)
HI.Gen. COLL. Degree SPEC.
17   18   19   20   21

FIGURE 29

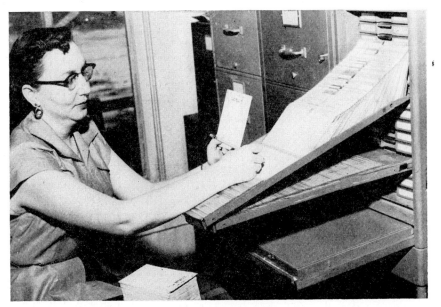

Kardex equipment makes personnel records available quickly at point of use*

Supporting papers are kept in insulated files for reference when needed

* Source: Robert D. Johnson, "Personnel Files," *Systems*, July–August, 1954, p. 8. Reproduced by permission. Courtesy of Remington Rand.

FIGURE 30. Tabulating Card, Manual Sorting

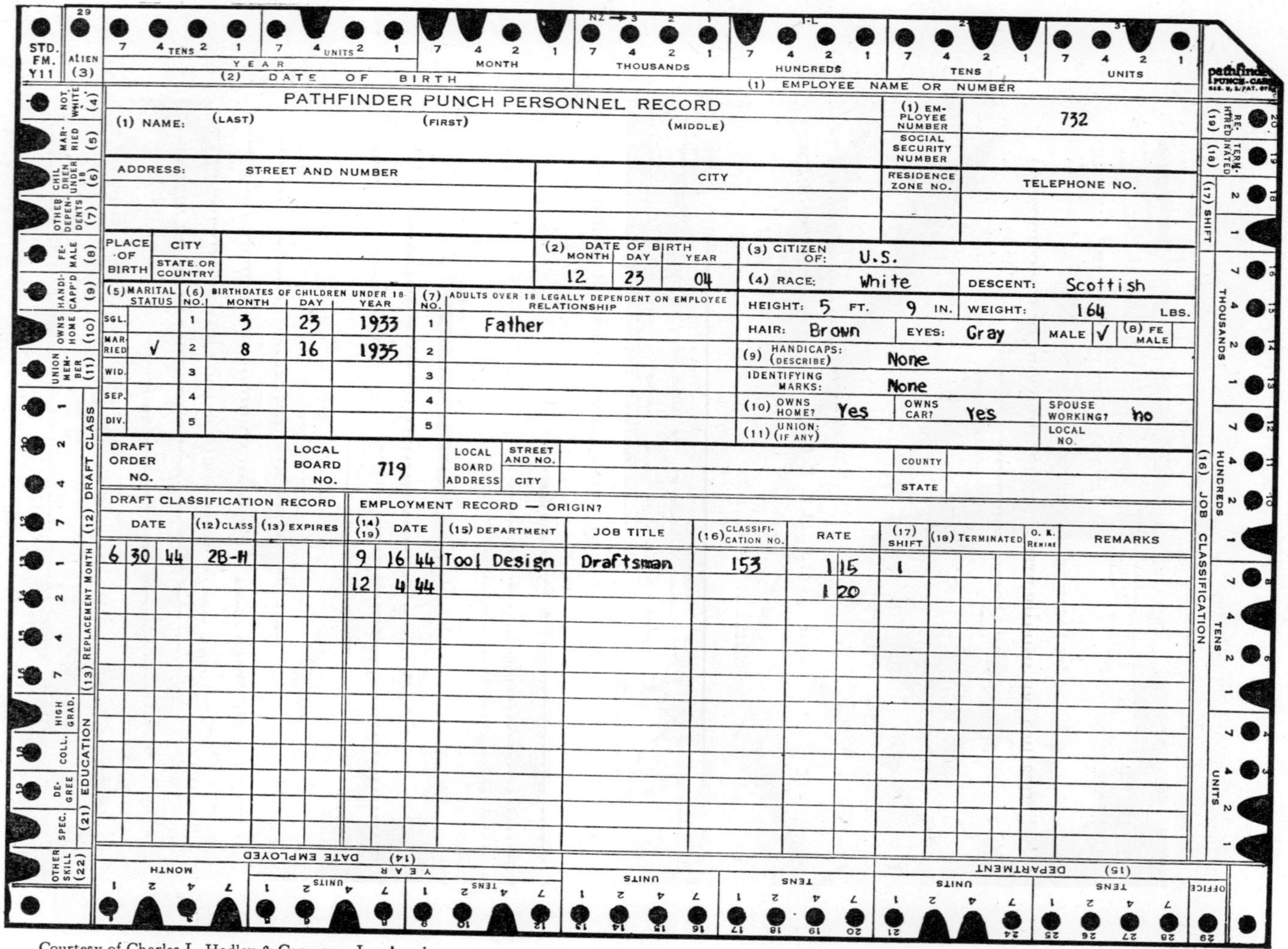

PATHFINDER PUNCH PERSONNEL RECORD

(1) EMPLOYEE NAME OR NUMBER: THOUSANDS / HUNDREDS / TENS / UNITS

(2) DATE OF BIRTH: YEAR (TENS, UNITS) / MONTH

STD. FM. Y11 | ALIEN (3) | NOT WHITE (4) | MARRIED (5) | CHILDREN UNDER 18 (6) | OTHER DEPENDENTS (7) | FEMALE (8) | HANDICAPP'D (9) | OWNS HOME (10) | UNION MEMBER (11) | (12) DRAFT CLASS 1 2 4 7 | (13) REPLACEMENT MONTH 1 2 4 7 | (21) EDUCATION: HIGH GRAD., COLL., DEGREE, SPEC. | OTHER SKILL (22)

(19) RE-HIRED | (18) TERMINATED | (17) SHIFT 2 1 | (16) JOB CLASSIFICATION: THOUSANDS / HUNDREDS / TENS / UNITS

(1) NAME: (LAST) (FIRST) (MIDDLE)

(1) EMPLOYEE NUMBER: 732

SOCIAL SECURITY NUMBER

ADDRESS: STREET AND NUMBER | CITY | RESIDENCE ZONE NO. | TELEPHONE NO.

PLACE OF BIRTH: CITY / STATE OR COUNTRY

(2) DATE OF BIRTH: MONTH 12 DAY 23 YEAR 04

(3) CITIZEN OF: U.S.

(4) RACE: White DESCENT: Scottish

HEIGHT: 5 FT. 9 IN. WEIGHT: 164 LBS.

HAIR: Brown EYES: Gray MALE ✓ (8) FEMALE

(9) HANDICAPS: (DESCRIBE) None

IDENTIFYING MARKS: None

(10) OWNS HOME? Yes OWNS CAR? Yes SPOUSE WORKING? no

(11) UNION: (IF ANY) LOCAL NO.

(5) MARITAL STATUS		(6) NO.	BIRTHDATES OF CHILDREN UNDER 18 MONTH	DAY	YEAR	(7) NO.	ADULTS OVER 18 LEGALLY DEPENDENT ON EMPLOYEE RELATIONSHIP
SGL.		1	3	23	1933	1	Father
MARRIED	✓	2	8	16	1935	2	
WID.		3				3	
SEP.		4				4	
DIV.		5				5	

DRAFT ORDER NO. | LOCAL BOARD NO. 719 | LOCAL BOARD ADDRESS: STREET AND NO., CITY, COUNTY, STATE

DRAFT CLASSIFICATION RECORD

DATE	(12) CLASS	(13) EXPIRES
6 30 44	2B-H	

EMPLOYMENT RECORD — ORIGIN?

(14) (19) DATE	(15) DEPARTMENT	JOB TITLE	(16) CLASSIFICATION NO.	RATE	(17) SHIFT	(18) TERMINATED	O. K. REHIRE	REMARKS
9 16 44	Tool Design	Draftsman	153	1 15	1			
12 4 44				1 20				

(14) DATE EMPLOYED: MONTH / YEAR (UNITS, TENS) | (15) DEPARTMENT: UNITS / TENS | OFFICE

Courtesy of Charles L Hadley & Company, Los Angeles.

2. RECORDS OF HIRED EMPLOYEES. As to candidates who are hired, the systems of recording fall into two major groups. On the one hand, some companies establish a folder for each employee and place in it all hiring information. Into it is filed all additional data, such as service or merit ratings, job and rate changes, grievances and disciplinary cases, and any added educational accomplishments. The folders are filed alphabetically (but usually first by major divisions of the company).

On the other hand, some companies compile, in addition to the folder, a card recapitulating important information in the folder. The card is filed separately from the folder and becomes the working source of information about employees. Figure 28 (pp. 151 and 152) illustrates such a card. This system of duplicating information makes available in ready and handy form pertinent data about employees. In addition, the folder with its valuable information need not be disturbed

FIGURE 31. A Personnel Tabulating Card*

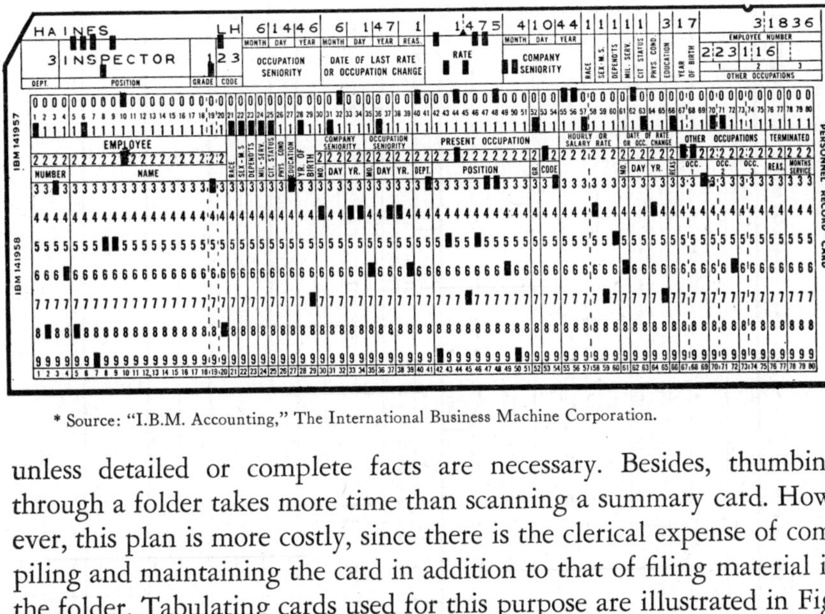

* Source: "I.B.M. Accounting," The International Business Machine Corporation.

unless detailed or complete facts are necessary. Besides, thumbing through a folder takes more time than scanning a summary card. However, this plan is more costly, since there is the clerical expense of compiling and maintaining the card in addition to that of filing material in the folder. Tabulating cards used for this purpose are illustrated in Figures 30 and 31. The former are sorted manually and the latter by machine.

Whether the form of tabulating card system should be used depends upon the value of the extra service received from it as compared to the cost. Such records are commonly called "personnel service records" or "personal history cards."

Careful planning of personnel records will make it possible to maintain them at minimum expense. It is reported, for example, that in one

FIGURE 32. A Multi-Purpose Personnel Form*

EMPLOYMENT APPLICATION

DATE:

FILL IN BOTH SIDES COMPLETELY

NAME: ___ (Last) ___ (First) ___ (Initial.)

SOCIAL SECURITY NO.:	SEX:	HEIGHT	WEIGHT

ADDRESS: ___

			TELEPHONE NO.	DATE OF BIRTH:

U.S. CITIZEN: YES ( ) NO ( )   MARRIED ( ) SINGLE ( )   SEPARATED ( ) DIVORCED ( )   WIDOW(ER) ( )

NO OF DEPENDENTS CLAIMED FOR INCOME TAX EXEMPTIONS: CHILDREN ( ) PARENTS ( ) OTHERS ( )   AGES OF CHILDREN:

IF FEMALE AND MARRIED STATE MAIDEN NAME

IF YOU HAVE NO TELEPHONE, THROUGH (Give name WHOM CAN YOU BE LOCATED? & Tel. No.)   DO YOU OWN YOUR OWN HOME?   YES ( ) NO ( )

DESCRIBE PHYSICAL DEFECTS, IF ANY:

DO YOU HAVE ANY INCOME OTHER THAN WHAT YOU GET FROM WORKING?   YES ( ) NO ( ) IF YES, WHAT?

MILITARY EXPERIENCE: FROM ___ TO ___   BRANCH OF SERVICE

HIGHEST RANK OBTAINED   HONORABLE DISCHARGE: YES ( ) NO ( )   IF IN RESERVES: ACTIVE ( ) INACTIVE ( )

ARE YOU A FORMER EMPLOYEE?   WHEN?   WHY DID YOU LEAVE?

NAMES AND RELATIONSHIP OF RELATIVES WORKING HERE:

MACHINES YOU CAN OPERATE:

POSITION DESIRED: SHIFT DESIRED: WAGES EXPECTED: WHEN CAN YOU BEGIN WORK?

RECORD OF EDUCATION

	No. of Years	NAME OF SCHOOL	DID YOU GRADUATE?	DATE YOU LEFT	AVERAGE GRADE	COURSE	DESCRIBE COLLEGE OR OTHER TRAINING—
GRAMMAR							
HIGH							
TRADE							

RECORD OF PREVIOUS EMPLOYMENT — SHOW PRESENT OR LAST POSITION FIRST

STARTING DATE	NAME AND ADDRESS OF COMPANY:	NAME OF SUPERVISOR	WAGES RECEIVED
LEAVING DATE	TYPE OF WORK DONE:	REASON FOR LEAVING:	
STARTING DATE	NAME AND ADDRESS OF COMPANY:	NAME OF SUPERVISOR	WAGES RECEIVED
LEAVING DATE	TYPE OF WORK DONE:	REASON FOR LEAVING:	
STARTING DATE	NAME AND ADDRESS OF COMPANY:	NAME OF SUPERVISOR	WAGES RECEIVED
LEAVING DATE	TYPE OF WORK DONE:	REASON FOR LEAVING:	

(Page 1)

* Source: J. S. Kornreich, "Personnel Records for a Small Company," *Personnel*, March, 1953, pp. 431–36.

FIGURE 32.—Continued

FAMILY INFORMATION (HUSBAND, WIFE, FATHER, MOTHER, BROTHERS AND SISTERS)

RELATIONSHIP TO YOU	PRESENT OR LAST OCCUPATION	CITY WHERE NOW LIVING	RELATIONSHIP TO YOU	PRESENT OR LAST OCCUPATION	CITY WHERE NOW LIVING

HOW LONG HAVE YOU LIVED AT YOUR PRESENT ADDRESS?

IF LESS THAN ONE YEAR, GIVE PREVIOUS ADDRESS:

WHAT TRANSPORTATION WILL YOU USE TO GET TO WORK?

☐ I DO NOT OWN AN AUTO   IF YOU OWN AUTO, STATE MAKE AND YEAR: ☐ I DO

REFERENCES GIVE THREE REFERENCES WHO KNOW YOU WELL. DO NOT GIVE RELATIVES OR FORMER EMPLOYERS.

1. _____ (NAME)   _____ (OCCUPATION)   _____ (ADDRESS)

2. _____ (NAME)   _____ (OCCUPATION)   _____ (ADDRESS)

3. _____ (NAME)   _____ (OCCUPATION)   _____ (ADDRESS)

GIVE NAMES OF PEOPLE WORKING HERE WHO KNOW YOU VERY WELL:

Additional Remarks and Information
(DESCRIBE OTHER EXPERIENCE, RELATED HOBBIES OR SPECIAL QUALIFICATIONS)

I UNDERSTAND THAT IF EMPLOYED, FALSE STATEMENTS ON THIS APPLICATION SHALL BE CONSIDERED SUFFICIENT CAUSE FOR DISMISSAL.

_____ (Applicant's Signature)

READ CAREFULLY →

SIGN HERE ↓

APPLICANT — DO NOT WRITE BELOW THIS LINE

(Page 2)

FIGURE 32.—*Continued*

INVESTIGATION

DATES	DATES	DATES
ATTENDANCE	ATTENDANCE	ATTENDANCE
WORK RECORD	WORK RECORD	WORK RECORD
REASON FOR LEAVING	REASON FOR LEAVING	REASON FOR LEAVING
REHIRE	REHIRE	REHIRE

TEST SCORES AND INTERPRETATION

PHYSICAL EXAMINATION	DATE	RESULTS:—
BY DR.		

INTERVIEWED BY	DATE	GENERAL COMMENT	
1.			WORK ATT.:
2.			ALERTNESS:
3.			APPEARANCE:

STARTING DATE:	STARTING POSITION:	DEPT.:	SHIFT OR WORK HOURS:
STARTING WAGE:	AUTOMATIC INCREASE: PROMISED? YES ( ) NO ( ) AMOUNT?	DATE?	APPROVED BY

(*Page 3*)

FIGURE 32.—Continued

MEDICAL EXAMINATION

PERSONNEL RECORD (Attendance, Salary or Job Changes, Efficiency Rating, Awards, etc.)

GENERAL APPEARANCE:

DATE   HT.   WT.

EYES: (R.

        (L.

EARS: HEARS WATCH   (R.

                    (L.

NOSE | THROAT

TONGUE | TEETH

NECK | CHEST CONTOUR

HEART

PULSE | BLOOD PRESSURE

LUNGS

ABDOMEN

EXTREM. (U.   (L.

ING. REG.   PAST MEDICAL HISTORY

G. U.

URINE

SPINE

SKIN

NOTES:

SIGNED: DR.

DATE	ACTION	EXPLANATION	DATE	ACTION	EXPLANATION

(Page 4)

case the personnel records of nine hundred employees are kept by one clerk.[1] Another interesting example of a personnel record for a smaller company is the multipurpose form illustrated in Figure 32 (pp. 156–59).[2] It may be used in the following ways:

1. Application blank (pp. 1 and 2)
2. Interview rating, test record, and reference check-up (p. 3)
3. Basic payroll record (pp. 3 and 4)
4. Medical examination form (p. 4)
5. Record of other personnel data, such as attendance, salary or job changes, and efficiency rating (p. 4)

INDUCTION OF NEW EMPLOYEE

The final step in the selection process is that of inducting the new employee into his new surroundings and placing him on his new job. In many companies this stage of an employee's tenure is handled very superficially. But there is a strong movement in the direction of handling this stage with great care because the first days on a job are recognized as being critical in the employment life. This conviction stems from the realization that a new employee is uncertain, critical, and insecure; hence he is much more aware of his surroundings. Impressions are consequently made that will remain for a long time if the employee stays. Or the impressions may cause him to quit. And it is generally true that turnover among new employees is higher than among workers with greater seniority.

The stage of induction should take into account two major aspects: (1) acquainting the new employee with his new surroundings and its rules and regulations, and (2) indoctrinating him in the "philosophy" of the company and its reasons for existence. More companies build their programs around the first of these aspects than the second. Nevertheless, an appreciation for the importance of indoctrination is growing.

1. GETTING ACQUAINTED. In acquainting the new employee with his new surroundings and company regulations, practice tends toward giving introductory materials and instructions away from the working center. Either a "classroom" lecture, a movie, or a group conference is used by a member of the personnel department. In any event, such subjects as the following are covered:

1. Company history, products, and major operations

2. General company policies and regulations

---

[1] R. D. McMillen, "Personnel Records," *Factory Management and Maintenance,* June, 1947, p. 109.

[2] J. S. Kornreich, "Personnel Records for the Small Company," *Personnel,* March, 1953, pp. 431–36.

3. Relation of foremen and personnel department

4. Rules and regulations regarding

   a) Wages and wage payment
   b) Hours of work and overtime
   c) Safety and accidents
   d) Holidays and vacations
   e) Methods of reporting tardiness and absences
   f) Discipline and grievances
   g) Uniforms and clothing
   h) Parking
   i) Badges and parcels

5. Economic and recreational services available

   a) Insurance plans available
   b) Pensions
   c) Athletic and social activities

6. Opportunities

   a) Promotion and transfer
   b) Job stabilization
   c) Suggestion systems

It is ordinarily not expected that much of the foregoing will "stick" in the minds of the inductee, but this preliminary step does serve to prove that the company is taking a sincere interest in getting him off to a good start. Moreover, a permanent record of the materials seen and heard is provided by supplying him with a booklet of rules and regulations and other materials illustrating company history, products, etc. Then, too, such off-the-job sessions may be continued occasionally after the new employee does settle down on his job. In this way, the theory of repetition is brought into play.

After preliminary sessions in the personnel department, the new employee is conducted to his working center. At one time, the employee was given oral instructions and left to find his way himself, and some companies still use this system. Better practice, however, is to have either a representative of the personnel department act as a guide or someone from the operating department come over and take the new employee in hand.

Upon arriving at the assigned department, the inductee is introduced to his foreman and fellow workers. Some foremen turn over the new employee to a "lead" man, "gang boss," or departmental trainer. This individual instructs the employee on such matters as to how to "ring" in and out, where the lockers are, departmental rules, and how his job is to be done. He also follows up on the employee from time to time to see whether a satisfactory adjustment is being made and whether or not the employee has any questions or problems.

There is a growing trend, however, to have the foreman or supervisor handle this stage of induction. The trend is based on the recognition that, if management is to gain the loyalty of employees, it must take the time to work with employees. Time and again, employees have been hired without more than a cursory acquaintance with the foreman. Little wonder that they turn to union stewards who make a concerted effort to prove they are the real friends of the employee. When the foreman takes the necessary effort to handle induction, he proves at a critical time his desire to build a friendly and co-operative relationship.

After an employee has been "placed" on his job, good induction practice also involves periodic follow-up. Either by reports or, better, by personal visits from the supervisor or representative of the personnel department, the status of the new employee is ascertained after a period of thirty or sixty days, and thereafter for another equivalent period or two. In this way, it is possible to check to see whether the employee has been properly placed, whether the promises the company made to him have been kept, and whether any problems have arisen that require solution.

2. INDOCTRINATION. The induction stage provides an excellent opportunity to develop attitudes of new employees toward their new employment and surroundings. The mind of the new employee is more open to suggestion and change than it perhaps will be again during his tenure with the company. Hence more and more companies are taking advantage of this opportunity to sell their "philosophies," the whys and wherefores of the private-enterprise system and capitalism, the need for productivity, and the reasons why they operate as they do.

Since modern employees are no longer satisfied with just a job but want to know why things are as they are, this phase of induction is both needed and commendable. It is useless for a company to complain that its employees "really don't know its problems," if it does nothing to discuss, explain, and talk about them. The opportunity to present its views to new employees should therefore not be overlooked. The inductee wants to know "what all the shooting is about." Of course, if the company presents a distorted or selfish picture, such action is not condoned and is bound to boomerang. But, with a good story honestly told, the company has much to gain and nothing to lose.

Such indoctrination is a job for the personnel department and the supervisor. In the very first sessions conducted by the personnel department, discussions of technical rules and practices should be sprinkled with explanations of company activities and suggestions on the role the company plays in our economic, political, and social system. Such indoctrination should also be included in any printed or visual-audio materials that are used.

When the employee reaches his new department, the supervisor or "lead" man should continue the indoctrination program. To do this, the supervisor himself will have to be thoroughly grounded in company philosophy and theory. Special lectures or conferences should be provided for this purpose, so that the supervisor can better explain what the company is trying to do and why.

Perhaps the essence of indoctrination is to convince the employee that, in the last analysis, what is good for the company and our economic system is best for the employee. This may seem to appeal to selfish self-interest; but, if it is true, then there is no reason for condemnation. If the system is serving only the best interests of the employer, then the indoctrination is built on sand. But it is abundantly evident that such indoctrination does have the advantage of advancing the best interests of both employer and employee. Hence it seems the better part of wisdom that the employer indoctrinate when he inducts new employees.

Moreover, such indoctrination has a large element in it of good public relations. If an employee is convinced that he is working for a good company and a good cause and has the arguments to prove his convictions, he is one of the best channels by which the public is also convinced of the merit of the company and the cause. There is little doubt that good public relations begins in the factory and office; and there the best beginning is indoctrination of new employees.

SUMMARY

By way of summary, some suggestions are in order regarding the characteristics that must be built into a selection procedure. Of course, the essential feature of a selection procedure is that it produces results effectively and economically. To do this, each step in the selection sequence must be assigned a place so that it may contribute its fullest share to the final result. Moreover, each step or phase of the selection procedure must be equipped and manned to a degree commensurate with its importance. For each step, too, it is necessary to establish, first, standards of performance and, then, means of allocating and determining responsibility for results. In designing the procedure, care should be taken to make it reasonably flexible, on the one hand, so that it can manage effectively temporary changes in volume and, on the other hand, to make it sufficiently stable so that it is not subject to whimsical changes. The selection process should have definitely established starting and finishing points, so that unauthorized or dangling procedures will not be in operation. And, finally, each step should give due consideration to cost, time taken, tradition, and legal requirements. These suggestions, in general form, apply to any procedure and hence possess a universal usefulness.

QUESTIONS AND PROBLEMS

1. Define the term "selection procedure." How does this differ from selection functions?
2. What tests would you apply in order to determine whether or not a specific selection procedure is a good one? Visit a local employment office and find out what their hiring procedure is. Afterward, apply your tests to the procedure in question.
3. Compare the selection procedure of small, medium-sized, and large companies. What are the essential differences between the procedures of these classes?
4. Why is the physical examination usually placed toward the end of the selection procedure?
5. As an employer, why might you ask the following questions on an application blank: How much salary do you expect? What are your hobbies?
6. What classes of information are ordinarily sought from candidates for employment? By what methods is the information sought?
7. List the major classes of information usually asked for on an application blank. Justify the types of questions asked.
8. What characteristics should be sought in designing the form of an application blank?
9. How much confidence can be placed in the average reference letter? What practices can be followed in order to increase the usefulness of references?
10. Why is personal observation a widely used method of gathering information about candidates? Does the reliability of this method justify its wide use?
11. Write a brief report on the advantages, disadvantages, and conditions of most favorable use of microfilming.
12. What effect do fair employment practice laws have upon the design of hiring records and forms?
13. What factors determine how long application blanks of candidates who are not immediately hired should be kept on file?
14. What systems are commonly in use for recording and filing information on candidates who are hired? Under what conditions would you recommend the use of each?
15. Why is the induction of new employees such an important function? Note some of the reasons why new employees are "critical."

16. What are the advantages and disadvantages of using movies in the induction process?
17. Upon whom, and why, would you place the greatest burden for the induction of new employees?
18. Of what value, and why, are tours through the factory and office as an induction device?
19. Of what value are postinduction interviews?
20. What relation should exist between line departments and the personnel department in the selection procedure?

CHAPTER

9 | Interviewing and Counseling

THE ROLE OF INTERVIEWING AND COUNSELING

The interview is one of the most commonly used methods of seeking to derive information from job applicants. It is a face-to-face, question-and-answer, observational, and personal appraisal method of evaluating the applicant. Usually, it is more than a means of getting information. It also involves, first, giving information that will help the applicant make up his mind about the company and, second, giving advice or suggestions that may serve to change the attitude, mental or emotional, of the interviewee. Hence there usually is an element of counseling in interviewing, although there is a tendency to try to keep the purposes of the two somewhat separate and distinct.

The subjects of interviewing and counseling are taken up at this point because they are of significance in the procedure of hiring. However, these techniques are also of significant importance in handling grievances, taking disciplinary action, vocational guidance, handling employees being separated from the payroll, assisting employees with personal problems, handling transfers and promotions, and training sessions. Hence, the discussion here is intended to serve not only the needs of the employment procedure but also those of the activities just noted. And the examples and practices taken up here may be related to employment, but the basic principles are also pertinent to other uses of interviewing, counseling, and guidance.

These tools are more involved than many believe. Indeed, interviewing was for a long time considered to be an unreliable tool for employment purposes. This conclusion was reached after various studies had been made of selected executives who were asked to interview and then rate groups of candidates. Insignificant correlations were found when work success or failure was compared with the ratings. But later studies showed that the apparent ineffectiveness of interviewing was really the fault of the interviewers; they may have been good executives, but their interviewing techniques were hit or miss and almost entirely the "by-ear" type. Later studies have shown that careful interviewing and counseling can be a most effective tool.

To be effective, close attention must be paid to the development of techniques based upon good principles and applied by skilled personnel. What these principles and skills are may be seen by examining interviewing under the following headings:

1. Methods of interviewing and counseling
2. Rules of good interviewing
3. Recording results of interviewing and counseling
4. Evaluating results of interviewing and counseling
5. Selection and training of interviewers

METHODS OF INTERVIEWING AND COUNSELING

In actual practice there are undoubtedly as many methods of interviewing as there are interviewers. By and large, most interviewing has been unplanned and unskilled. In such cases, the interviewer may have some notion of the information he desires or the purpose he hopes to accomplish. Beyond that he relies upon "spur-of-the-moment" questions or insight to guide the actual interview. As might be expected, such practices are not very successful; nor do they serve to contribute to a student's understanding of good principles and practices of interviewing. Much more can be learned from study of the following methods:

1. The planned interview
2. The patterned interview
3. The nondirective interview

1. PLANNED INTERVIEWS. Without going to the extent of the patterned interview, which is discussed next, many interviewers have improved themselves by following definite plans of action. Before entering into the actual interview, they work out in their minds, if not on paper, what they hope to accomplish, what kinds of information they are to seek or give, how they will conduct the interview, and how much time they will allot to it. During the interview, deviations from the plan may be made; but, when the interviewer deviates, he does so with the knowledge of what he is doing and how far off he is from his intended track. Although there is some formality about such plans, flexibility is one of its major advantages.

Such interviews are within the capacities of almost any executive or personnel staff member. They are based upon the simple proposition that it is well to give some thought to how he will conduct himself before actually talking to a candidate or an employee. When this is done, the actual task of getting or giving information can proceed with a minimum of wasted time, embarrassing interruptions, or failure to obtain or communicate pertinent facts.

2. THE PATTERNED INTERVIEW. The patterned interview is a planned interview, but one preplanned to a high degree of exactitude. It is based on the assumption that, to be effective, every pertinent detail of interviewing must be worked out carefully in advance. And, equally important, the interviewer must be skilled in its operation; he need not be a trained psychologist, but he must have the uncommon faculty of common sense and interpretative ability.

The starting point in the use of the patterned interview is to have detailed job and man specifications. This provides the interviewer with one basis for arriving at the questions he expects to ask. Another basis is a careful study of application forms and references that candidates have submitted. From such sources a number of questions may be formulated. And those derived for one interview will be found to be pertinent to others. Hence most practitioners of the patterned interview develop a formal list, such as the excerpt illustrated in Figure 33.

It should be noted that such a formal list does not limit the interview but, rather, acts as a guide to points that may be followed up as the conditions of a particular interview may seem advisable to him. For example, in the excerpt cited, the question relating to recreation is really intended to disclose something about the maturity of the candidate. Hence the interviewer, should he decide that the hobbies of a given candidate seem of significance, may ask several questions extemporaneously about the hobbies in order to get at the underlying purpose of the simple question on recreation as listed.

Thus the formal list of questions is but a device to aid the memory of the interviewer. He follows through his check list and devises additional questions to amplify his knowledge of the candidate wherever needed. This is the point at which the psychological skill of the interviewer comes into play. As he gathers information from the candidate, he must interpret it in the light of his understanding of normal standards of human behavior and attainments. Should he find from his questions on recreation habits, for example, that a given candidate seems immature for the job in question, the interviewer will be more vigilant when other classes of questions are asked, in order to ascertain whether or not the clue on immaturity is substantiated.

In carrying out the patterned interview, it is, of course, necessary for the interviewer to be competent. He must know the rules of interviewing and how to elicit information. He must be well trained

FIGURE 33. Excerpt from Patterned Interview Form*

DOMESTIC AND SOCIAL SITUATION

Married   Single   Widowed   Divorced   Separated   Date of marriage
Are he and his wife compatible?

Living with wife?   Yes   No   (If no) Specify   Dependents: Number

Ages _____ What plans do you have for your children?
Do dependents provide adequate motivation?

What difficulties or serious arguments have you had with your wife?   Financial?   Social?   Personal?

Have you been married previously?   Yes   No   (If yes) How many times?

When and what was the reason for end of marriage or marriages?   Death   Divorce

Separation _____ (Unless death) What were the reasons?
Do his domestic difficulties indicate immaturity?

Of what lodges and clubs are you a member?   Officer?   Does he show leadership?

What do you do for recreation?   What hobbies do you have?   Will his hobbies help his work?
Does his recreation show maturity?

To what extent do you and your wife entertain?   Does he seem socially well-adjusted?

When did you last drink intoxicating liquor?   To what extent?   (Doesn't drink)
Is this sensible drinking?

What types of people, racial or religious groups or nationalities do you actively dislike?
Is he biased?

* Source: Robert N. McMurray, "Validating the Patterned Interview," *Personnel*, June, 1947, p. 266.

in measuring the behavior of people—whether this training is formal or self-acquired is not of importance. He himself must be emotionally, socially, and mentally well adjusted. And he must be aware of his organizational relationship to the candidate and those he serves through his interviews.

3. THE NONDIRECTIVE INTERVIEW. In recent years much interest has been shown in the nondirective interview. As its name implies, the applicant in such an interview is not directed by questions or comments as to what he should talk about. While the "interviewer" may intersperse brief phrases, these should be noncommittal, so that the candidate determines the trend of conversation.

The theory of such interviews is that a candidate is thus more likely to reveal his true self than when he answers set questions. In the latter case there is a much higher probability that the candidate will tend to give answers which he thinks the interviewer wants or answers that will get him the job, whether they are true or not. But in the nondirective approach, the candidate obviously does not know how to "slant" his replies or commentary. It has also been found that a candidate not only is more likely to talk about things he thinks are important but also will relate things that are important to the interviewer. Indeed, what a candidate doesn't say may be as revealing about his competency, abilities, and interests as what he does say.

Of course, the nondirective approach requires a much higher type of interviewer and of preplanning. In one respect, it is easier—the fact that questions are not asked makes it easier for the interviewee to relax because he doesn't tense as he does when questions are fired at him. In other respects, the task of interviewing is more complicated. As in the case of the patterned interview, a major preliminary step of the nondirective interview is to study the requirements of the job to be filled and then to learn as much about the candidate as possible from such sources as the application blanks, tests, and references. From such studies, the interviewer ascertains what he must listen for when the candidate is interviewed.

Perhaps the most difficult part of this technique is carrying on the actual interview to the point or extent that the interviewer is sure that he can determine whether or not the candidate will be a success on the job in question. Starting such interviews is usually accomplished by putting the candidate at ease by the usual introductions, courtesies, and idle talk. Then the candidate is requested by an appropriate statement or opening question to talk about his personal history. After the candidate starts talking, the interviewer must keep the candidate talking. Suggested aids to do this are as follows:

1. Give your entire attention to the applicant.
2. Listen attentively and resist the temptation to talk.
3. Never argue.
4. Do not interrupt or change the subject abruptly.
5. Use questions sparingly, but for purposes of keeping the candidate talking, filling a gap in the story, obtaining more specific information, and checking conclusions.
6. Allow pauses in the conversation, but interject some nondirective comment if the pause becomes uncomfortable.
7. Phrase responses briefly.
8. Keep conversation at level suited to applicant.
9. Try to appreciate the applicant's underlying feelings.
10. Diplomatically and carefully talk to applicants who seem to be withholding information.[1]

As in the case of the patterned interview, the task of the nondirective interview is to determine what kind of person the candidate really is. This means that the interviewer must be exceptionally skilled in measuring the story the candidate tells against the normal standards of human behavior, attitudes, and attainments. In terms of how the candidate conducts himself, from his disclosures of training and experience, and from his statements on recreational and social activities, the interviewer must appraise the candidate's qualifications to fill the job in question.

1. INTERVIEWING TOOLS. Some interesting experiments are being carried on in the use of various tools as aids in interviewing. Some companies are recording important interviews so that the discussion may be reviewed with greater care in a more leisurely atmosphere. Another example of mechanical aids is the use of a so-called "interaction chronograph" developed by Professor Eliot B. Chapple of Harvard University. The device is operated by pressing different keys during an interview. In this way measurements are obtained of the length of time each person talks, intervals between questions and answers, and tendencies to carry the discussion. The trained analyst then deduces from these measurements such personality traits as inclinations to dominate or submit and to argue or agree. Results reported from its use indicate that this "mechanical interviewer" has increased the success in screening applicants.[2]

RULES OF INTERVIEWING

A number of principles of interviewing have been developed by trial and error and by study of actual interviewing practices. Their adoption

---

[1] N. A. Moyer, "Non-directive Employment Interviewing," *Personnel*, March, 1948, pp. 383–87.

[2] Lester Smith in the *Wall Street Journal*, Monday, February 16, 1948.

does not provide an unfailing high road to successful interviewing but serves to increase the probability of a useful exchange of information or views. Nor does a mere listing provide anyone with automatic tools; they must be practiced in order to gain proficiency.

1. Perhaps the basic rule of interviewing is to respect the interests and individuality of the interviewee. Unless one conveys a sympathetic understanding of the other fellow's point of view and desires, it is difficult to develop a feeling of confidence, which is essential to getting or giving information. For example, an employment interviewer can easily antagonize applicants, merely because he "occupies the driver's seat," whereas the applicants are somewhat in the position of supplicants. Should this attitude manifest itself, the applicants tend to "freeze up" in giving information. Or, in interviews connected with handling of grievances or disciplinary action, a superior must beware of implying that he is "smarter" than his subordinates. To underestimate the intelligence of employees in regard to their economic interests is foolish, and to display an attitude of superiority is certain to nullify any possible good of an interview. The use of trick questions is also to be deplored, unless, as in the case of stress-type interviews, they serve a real purpose.

2. Also of high importance in interviewing is to pre-establish clearly the objectives to be gained or purposes to be served by interviews. Until this is done, it is impossible either to plan an interview effectively or to act convincingly during one. A practical difficulty, however, is that many interviews must be conducted on the spur of the moment. The pressure of other jobs may make it impossible to schedule interviews so that allowances may be made for preplanning time. This excuse should seldom be used in employment interviewing, but lack of time often affects the interviewing that takes place between executives at various levels and their subordinates.

3. There is no principle of interviewing that has been more frequently stated—and deservedly so—than that of making the interviewee feel at ease. To this end, the interviewer must act and be relaxed and at ease himself. Any failure in this respect, particularly where grievances or disciplinary action are concerned, results in an atmosphere of tension and belligerence unconducive to a free exchange of ideas. In the employment interview, too, the feeling of newness that obstructs the interview must be reduced by placing the interviewee at ease. As good a way as any to attain a relaxed discussion is to start slowly with some topic known to both parties. No matter how busy the interviewer is, he must give the impression at the outset that sufficient time for an unhurried discussion is available. When time is short, it is preferable to postpone the interview.

4. Another principle of good interviewing is to allow, indeed, to encourage, the interviewee to talk copiously. In the case of grievances, for example, this practice serves not only to draw out the whole complaint but also to "cool off" the aggrieved party. Only by encouraging a full discussion, is it possible to lead the interviewee to unburden himself to the point that nothing important or relevant is left unsaid. Hence ample opportunity for expression should be permitted. As a prerequisite for encouraging discussion, the interviewer should refrain from talking too much and from asking leading questions. Some carry this principle to the point of contending that in certain types of interviews, e.g., those concerned with problem employees, the interview should be "unguided," that is, the interviewer should say no more than the absolute minimum needed to keep the interviewee from stopping talking, no matter what he talks about. It is felt that in this way the employee will eventually divulge what is really bothering him.

5. An important suggestion to the interviewer is that he be a close student of the meaning of words, i.e., of the field of semantics. He must be sure that he knows what meaning an applicant gives to such words as "capitalism," "profits," "rights," and "merit." He must guard against using words that might arouse unnecessary antagonism or reservations, such as "low intelligence," "boss," "governmental interference," or "psychoneurosis." And, although very difficult to do, he must try to ascertain how words used by a particular individual may be colored by past working experiences or charged with emotionalism of personal experiences.

6. The interviewer should keep his views and opinions to himself unless they are of significance to the interviewee or until the latter has had sufficient opportunity to express himself. Even though keeping quiet is difficult, he must develop this virtue. Moreover, should he make up his mind as to what is to be done, he should not end the interview abruptly but close it diplomatically, so that the interviewee feels satisfied that a full hearing has been accorded him. In the case of a job refusal, for example, the applicant may otherwise feel that the decision was hasty or based upon an incomplete picture of the facts. Or in the case of a grievance, the interviewee may gain the impression that the company was prejudiced from the start.

7. In regard to concluding an interview, the interviewer should know how to draw it to a close and should be prepared to state his views or decisions clearly and concisely, and, if possible, conclusively. A final and positive answer need not be made; but, if such an answer is possible, so much the better. If an answer cannot be given with finality, it is a good rule to indicate what other steps are to be taken

and why. In addition, a definite time schedule for a decision or another meeting should be set. In this way, the interviewee is more likely to feel that the interviewer is capably and reasonably seeking a fair solution.

8. Physical conditions and layout should be selected that are suitable to the purposes of the interview. In so far as practicable, quiet and secluded (out-of-hearing, if not out-of-sight) surroundings should be available. Few interviewees, whether looking for a job, airing a grievance, or being rebuked, want to be overheard by others. Most of us like to have others hold the opinion that we are accepted members of the group; an open interview may give evidence to the contrary. An unobtrusive location also makes it possible for the interview to proceed without interruption and with a minimum of distracting influences.

9. It is well to note that the use of interviews is justified only when other means are not as effective, economical, courteous, or confidential in exchanging information. For example, such a question as the following is sometimes found on application blanks: "What financial obligations do you have?" The matter raised is of such a personal nature, however, that it is likely to prove less embarrassing to a candidate if it is asked during an interview when the reason for asking it can be given. Some go so far as to say that interviews should be used to gather personal and qualitative information, whereas other devices, such as application blanks and tests, should be used to secure quantitative information. This suggestion has some merit, although it is often difficult to draw a clear boundary line between qualitative and quantitative information. Perhaps a more practical rule to follow is to gather as much factual and biographical data as possible on the application blank and then follow up in the interview with detailed questions on those subjects which appear, in a particular case, to have potentialities for adding useful clues. Thus, in nine cases out of ten, there may be no reason for following up the answers that applicants give regarding hobbies, let us say; but occasionally the listing may provide a basis for further personal questioning of a person's hobbies, habits, and personal inclinations.

RECORDING RESULTS OF INTERVIEWING AND COUNSELING

Information obtained during an interview will soon be forgotten or become distorted unless recorded. While a few companies use sound recordings for this purpose, by far the greater number employ the printed and written word to preserve pertinent data and findings. An excellent example is contained in Figure 34 (pp. 175–76). This form succinctly records (1) the areas of information that are to be consid-

FIGURE 34. Interview Form*

(First Page)

FORM 69 (9-1-44)

INTERVIEWER'S EVALUATION OF APPLICANT

DATE 6-27 1944

NAME OF APPLICANT Helen Frances Davis

LOCATION 1631 Arch St. Phila.

JOB CONSIDERED FOR Telephone Operator

INTERVIEWER Stella Burns

AREAS TO CONSIDER	FINDINGS	INTERPRETATION OF FINDINGS
I VOICE, MANNER & APPEARANCE 1. VOICE AND SPEECH (PLEASANT, CLEAR, DISTINCT, NO ACCENT) 2. MANNER (COURTESY, SPEECH, GESTURES, FACIAL EXPRESSIONS) 3. APPEARANCE (POISE, DRESS, CLEANLINESS, FEATURES) 4. PHYSIQUE (WEIGHT, HEIGHT, REACH, STRENGTH, HANDEDNESS) 5. VISION AND HEARING 6. PERSONAL CHARACTERISTICS (COOPERATIVENESS, FRIENDLINESS, ADAPTABILITY, TEMPERAMENT, AGGRESSIVENESS, NERVOUSNESS)	Voice clear, tone pleasing, enunciation good Manner courteous, responsive, and composed Well groomed and dressed in good taste Slender, average height, no noticeable defects of sight or hearing.	Meets voice requirement for operating Conversational ability and attitude should result in satisfactory customer contacts Size satisfactory
II WORK HISTORY 1. KIND OF JOB OR HOME DUTIES (APTITUDES, SKILLS AND COOPERATION REQ'D) 2. WORKING CONDITIONS (HOURS, HAZARDS, SURROUNDINGS, SUPERVISION) 3. REASON FOR LEAVING JOB (INCOMPETENCE, INSTABILITY, TEMPERAMENT, FRICTION WITH SUPERVISION, LAY OFF) 4. ATTENDANCE RECORD 5. MILITARY EXPERIENCE (DATES OF SERVICE, BRANCH, STARTING AND FINAL RANK, DUTIES AND RESPONSIBILITIES, KIND OF DISCHARGE) 6. EMPLOYER REFERENCES (DATES OF EMPLOYMENT, TYPE OF WORK, PAY, WOULD HE RE-EMPLOY)	One month in insurance office, filing forms and correspondence Hours 8:30 to 5:00. Saturday 8:30 to 12:30 Supervision close, helpful and considerate; co-workers congenial. Temporary job, during school vacation only	Filing experience not significant for operating, but might help in CA's Work less confining, better hours, used to close supervision Apparently, got along well with supervisors and co-workers. May be co-operative Employee left job to return to school
III SCHOOLING 1. FORMAL SCHOOLING (AMOUNT AND KIND, DATES) 2. SPECIALIZED TRAINING OR ON-JOB TRAINING 3. MILITARY TRAINING 4. BEST AND LEAST LIKED SUBJECTS (IN SCHOOL) 5. REASON FOR LEAVING SCHOOL 6. ATHLETIC AND SOCIAL ACTIVITIES, SPECIAL INTERESTS (IN SCHOOL) 7. SCHOOL REFERENCE REPORT (STANDARD TESTS, CLASS STANDING, ATTENDANCE, PERSONAL RATING)	Two years high school. Liked English, Math., History, Latin, reading assignment and book reviews. Favorite subject, English. Left school to aid family financially. Honor student, elected to student council Engaged in gym, soft ball, tennis. Never late — attendance good.	Meets educational requirements. Liking for English and reading should insure good usage of English in customer contacts. Financial need may assure motivation and permanence Intelligence probably adequate. Physically active, healthy. Co-operative. Probably dependable
IV SPARE TIME ACTIVITIES 1. HOBBIES 2. CHURCH ACTIVITIES 3. COMMUNITY ACTIVITIES 4. TYPES OF READING 5. SOCIAL ADJUSTMENT FACTOR (GREGARIOUSNESS, SECLUSIVENESS, PARTIES, SOCIAL HABITS)	Knits for Red Cross; sells War Bonds and Stamps two nights a week at neighborhood movie Sings in church choir Reads biography and fiction	Interest in helping others Likes contact work. Co-operative. Conduct wholesome. May indicate desire for self-improvement.

* Source: N. A. Moyer, "Non-directive Employment Interviewing," *Personnel*, March, 1948, pp. 391–92.

ered, (2) the interviewer's findings by areas, (3) his interpretations of findings by areas, and (4) his total detailed evaluations.

EVALUATING RESULTS OF INTERVIEWING AND COUNSELING

The final test of interviewing and counseling is, of course, whether or not they achieve established goals satisfactorily. As noted earlier,

FIGURE 34.—Continued

(Reverse Side)

AREAS TO CONSIDER	FINDINGS	INTERPRETATION OF FINDINGS
V HOME & FAMILY BACKGROUND		
1. CHILDHOOD AND ADULT FAMILY LIFE (CONDITIONS EXPOSED TO AND ADJUSTMENTS MADE)	*Five other children; one in Navy, four in school.*	*Co-operative attitude required.*
2. FINANCIAL STATUS (APPLICANT'S STANDING, INDEBTEDNESS, SOURCE OF INCOME)	*Father, claim adjuster for many years.*	
3. FAMILY'S ATTITUDE TOWARD TELEPHONE COMPANY AND JOB	*Good home and religious training.*	*Good conduct and integrity likely.*
4. HOME VISIT REPORT (FAMILY CONSISTS OF, ATTITUDE OF FAMILY TOWARD JOB AND COMPANY, ADJUSTMENT OF APPLICANT IN THE HOME, OTHER INFORMATION)	*Parents favorable to Company.*	*Parents will help insure permanency and effort*
5. CREDIT INVESTIGATION REPORT		
VI HEALTH		
1. HEALTH AS A CHILD AND PRESENT STATE OF HEALTH	*Childhood diseases: measles, mumps, and whooping cough.*	*Health satisfactory.*
2. WIFE OR HUSBAND'S AND CHILDREN'S HEALTH (IF MARRIED)	*Family insured good health habits.*	
3. OPERATIONS, SERIOUS ILLNESSES, OR ACCIDENTS (IF ANY)		
4. HEALTH AS INDICATED BY DRAFT STATUS OR MILITARY DISCHARGE (IF DISCHARGED FOR MEDICAL REASON)	*Family healthy.*	

EVALUATION OF FINDINGS*

JOB QUALIFICATIONS	JOB SPEC.	I	II	III	IV	V	VI	JOB QUALIFICATIONS	JOB SPEC.	I	II	III	IV	V	VI
COMMON QUALIFICATIONS (ALL JOBS)								EDUCATION, KNOWLEDGE, AND PROFICIENCIES:							
AGE (SATISFACTORY)	✓	CHECK FROM APPLICATION BLANK						A. MINIMUM FORMAL EDUCATION OR EQUIV. (IN SCHOOL 8 YEARS)	✓		✓				
GOOD HEALTH AND APPEARANCE	✓							B. MATHEMATICS	✓		✓				
COOPERATIVENESS	✓		✓	✓	✓			C. PHYSICS							
PERMANENCY (DESIRE FOR)	✓			✓				D. PRINCIPLES OF ELECTRICITY							
GOOD CONDUCT	✓				✓	✓		E. HANDWRITING AND PRINTING (NEAT)	✓	LOOK AT APPLICATION BLANK					
INDUSTRY	✓							F. TYPING							
DEPENDABILITY	✓		✓					G. STENOGRAPHY							
INTEGRITY	✓			✓		✓		H. MECHANICAL DRAWING							
MOTIVATION	✓			✓											
								APTITUDES:							
SPECIAL QUALIFICATIONS								A. INTELLIGENCE				✓			
PHYSICAL:								B. PLANNING							
A APPEARANCE (PLEASING)								C ANALYSIS							
B. STRENGTH								D. OVER-ALL PHYSICAL COORDINATION				✓			
C. SIZE (WITHIN NORMAL LIMITS)															
D. VOICE (PLEASING, NO DEFECTS, ETC.)	✓	✓						PERSONAL CHARACTERISTICS:							
E. HEARING (NORMAL)	✓	✓						A. EASE AND QUALITY OF CONVERSATION		✓					
F VISION (NORMAL ACUITY)	✓	✓						B. EMOTIONAL STABILITY OR TEMPERAM'T		✓	✓				
G. RIGHT HANDED								C ADAPTABILITY		✓			✓	✓	
H. ARM REACH (SATISFACTORY)	✓	✓						D TACT					✓	✓	
								E. INTERESTS (STATE):					✓	✓	
WORK EXPERIENCE (STATE):															

*UNDER "JOB SPEC" INSERT A CHECK MARK (✓) FOR EACH REQUIREMENT LISTED ON THE JOB SPECIFICATION UNDER "EVALUATION" INSERT, WHEREVER THE FINDINGS INDICATE IT: A CHECK (✓) TO INDICATE "QUALIFIED" A CROSS (X) TO INDICATE "NOT QUALIFIED"	INTERVIEWER'S RECOMMENDATIONS

INTERVIEWER'S RECOMMENDATIONS: *Appears to meet all requirements of job. Unable to verify school history at moment because schools are closed.*

CHECK OVER-ALL CLASS. FOR SPECIFIC JOB:
1. WELL QUALIFIED ☑
2. INTERMEDIATE ☐
3. POORLY QUALIFIED ☐

interviewing was once considered to be an unreliable tool of selection; and, to this day, it remains so when performed in an unplanned and unregulated manner by unskilled executives.

However, in those instances in which interviews have been carefully planned by skilled personnel, the results have been highly suc-

TABLE 12

COMPARISON OF INITIAL INTERVIEW SCORE WITH SUCCESS RATING*

(Men and Women Combined)

FOREMEN'S SUCCESS-ON-THE-JOB RATING	INTERVIEWERS' RATINGS			
	1	2	3	4
Outstanding..................	6 (35.3%)	8 (47.1%)	3 (17.6%)	
Above average...............	2 (1.2%)	88 (53.0%)	75 (45.2%)	1 (.6%)
Below average................	....	13 (6.6%)	175 (88.8%)	8 (4.6%)
Very poor....................	....	....	4 (14.8%)	23 (85.2%)

* Source: Robert N. McMurray, "Validating the Patterned Interview," *Personnel*, June, 1947, p. 270.

TABLE 13

COMPARISON OF DRIVER INTERVIEW RATINGS WITH
"PASS-FAIL" CRITERION*

	INTERVIEWERS' RATINGS			
	1	2	3	4
Still in service (successful).......	6 (75.0%)	15 (38.5%)	12 (26.1%)	2 (13.3%)
Left service any reason (failures)	2 (25.0%)	24 (61.5%)	34 (73.9%)	13 (86.7%)
Total number originally interviewed.................	8 (100%)	39 (100%)	46 (100%)	15 (100%)

* Source: Robert N. McMurray, "Validating the Patterned Interview," *Personnel*, June, 1947, p. 270.

cessful. Results of studies made by McMurray are rather conclusive in this respect. For example, as may be noted in Table 12, interviewers' ratings of prospective employees correlated very closely to the employees' ultimate success on the job as measured by foremen's ratings. In another study of truck drivers (selected excerpts of findings are tabulated in Table 13), he again finds a good correlation between interview ratings with "pass-fail" criterion. And in selecting salespeople by use of the chronograph, it was reported that in one company no one now sells less than 65 per cent of standard, as compared with a low figure of 35 per cent before the new technique of interviewing was used.

In connection with nondirective interviewing, the following results are claimed in one case:

1. The percentage of turnover cases which could be ascribed in whole or in part to faulty selection, while the labor market was growing tighter, has declined steadily.
2. The department supervisors say they are getting people better fitted for the work. Follow-up studies bear this out.
3. Interviewers who have used both the questionnaire and the nondirective method say the latter enables them to make more effective appraisals.
4. Applicants frequently tell interviewers they liked the interview because it did not seem like an interview. They had expected to be asked a lot of questions; instead, they just had a pleasant chat.
5. Other companies in the Bell System that have adopted this method report similar results.[3]

These few studies could be supported by others indicative of similar results. They are sufficient to show the value of good interviewing practices. It is to be noted that such practices are not perfect; but they are far better than poor practices.

SELECTING AND TRAINING INTERVIEWERS AND COUNSELORS

It has already been noted that an important element in interviewing is the skill of the interviewer. This suggests the need for careful selection and training of interviewers.

In selecting interviewers, practice varies considerably. Some companies select for such work only those who are college trained in psychology and psychiatry. Others place emphasis upon mature experience in the type of work for which people are going to be interviewed. But, allowing for variations, a list of qualifications would include the following:

1. A suitable background of experience similar to that of those who are to be interviewed
2. Maturity of action and viewpoint, so that others unconsciously tend to assume an attitude of confidence and co-operation
3. Experience and training in "sizing up" people from their behavior and actions (as opposed to mere physical build or appearance)
4. A combination of an objective viewpoint and an appreciation of human feelings and attitude
5. Good judgment, so that the "chaff may be separated from the wheat" during the interview and so that the proper weight is assigned to information obtained from the interview in relation to other sources of information
6. An ability to work through organizational channels with supervisors and other executives

---

[3] Moyer, *op. cit.,* p. 396.

7. An ability to plan the work of interviewing and to see the total as well as individual implications

Individuals with such capacities or potentials for their development are not too difficult to find in most companies. Usually the main thing to be done is to train available talent properly. A review of such training programs is therefore in order.

The practices of training interviewers and counselors is varied.[4] The conference method is used for training counselors at the Warner and Swasey Company. After such training, the counselor is given to understand that his job is as big as he wants to make it. He is also given the opportunity to continue evening courses at local colleges at company expense. The Bell Aircraft Corporation uses instruction sheets that cover the following points: (1) factors common to all interviews, (2) subjects to be covered during introductory interviews, (3) how to conduct follow-up interviews, and (4) how to conduct counseling interviews. The Briggs Manufacturing Company emphasizes plant visits and study of departmental policies in its training program. In the Servel, Inc., program, training revolves largely about the duties, problems, and responsibilities of the foreman and the work at his level.

At the Bell Telephone Company at Philadelphia, the basic training given interviewers consists of ten lessons:

1. Establish tentative job qualifications
2. Review application for employment
3. Preparation for conducting practice interviews
4. Conducting practice interviews
5. Recording the findings
6. Interpretation of the findings
7. Introduction of job specifications
8. Evaluation of findings
9. Closing the interview
10. Practicing the complete interview[5]

In addition, trainees conduct practice interviews, study plant operating departments, and write job specifications. Later, follow-up training is given interviewers as specific cases require.

Another good training device is a check list, which is used by the interviewer to review his own methods. One such list includes the following suggestions:[6]

---

[4] *The Employee Counsellor in Industry* (New York: Policyholders Service Bureau, Metropolitan Life Insurance Co.), pp. 21–22.

[5] Moyer, *op. cit.,* p. 395.

[6] An excerpt from training materials of the Ohio Employment Service.

   a) Take the interviewee's point of view
   b) Examine and discount your own prejudices
   c) Help the interviewee to be at ease
   d) Deserve and gain the interviewee's confidence
   e) Listen
   f) Allow time enough without dawdling
   g) Take pains to phrase questions so that they are easily understood
   h) Avoid implying answers
   i) Avoid impertinence and embarrassment on the part of the interviewee
   j) Encourage the interviewee to qualify or explain answers
   k) Achieve something definite
   l) Make subsequent interviews easy
   m) At the close of the interview, watch for casual leads
   n) Separate facts from inferences
   o) Record all data at once

SAMPLE OF INTERVIEWING INSTRUCTIONS

An excellent review of the uses, content, and rules of interviewing may be obtained from the following excerpt of instructions contained in a pamphlet on personal counseling:

I. The responsibilities which constitute the major part of a counselor's work may be explained as follows:

A. *Counseling employees as part of an orientation program*

Employees with immediate need for housing, financial, or other aid are sent to employee counselors for aid if the first interviewer is not prepared to take care of such cases. The counselor should have up-to-date information as to rooms available and should help find a place by telephone so that the employee's anxiety on this score may be allayed. If funds are needed, the employees should be directed to some local agency through which a loan can be obtained, with arrangements for repayment on the first or second pay day.

The person who conducts the first brief interview will arrange for the employee to go to the counselor for his entrance interview sometime during the first week. If this is not practical, employees may at some time in the induction process be sent to the counselor either to have the full interview or to make an appointment to see the counselor sometime during his first week.

This interview usually takes from 20 to 45 minutes. If possible, the personal history of the employee should be obtained beforehand and entered on the counseling interview blank.

The employee is urged to raise questions about personal needs and employment. The counselor acquaints the employee with facilities and resources which will contribute to his well-being and a more ready adaptation to the job. Everything possible should be done to make the employee's first experience with the counseling program satisfying and helpful, so that he will wish to return if the need arises. In many installations, the counselor may be the ideal person to introduce the employee to the supervisor. These informal contacts also help to promote good relationships between supervisors and counselors.

In an adequately-staffed counseling service, time can be taken for a regular follow-up interview with each employee within a month of his induction. This is a part of the orientation process in that its purpose is to check on job and personal adjustment after a reasonable period at work and to arrange for further assistance as needed.

B. *Counseling employees on a voluntary or referral basis*

 a) General counseling interviews which are not a part of the orientation or exit interview program are sometimes classified for research purposes and in monthly summaries as follows:

 (1) Initial interview, which applies to the first interview with employees already on the job when the counseling program is established. This breakdown is useful in showing the degree to which older employees accept the counseling service.

 (2) Renewal interview, which includes all counseling interviews with an employee after the first, excepting only the exit interview.

 b) Many kinds of questions and difficulties are presented in these interviews because they grow naturally out of the needs and reactions of employees. The counselor will have to draw on all his knowledge and use all his skill and common sense in order to meet them adequately.

 c) Studies show that among Federal employees in large cities, counseling interviews deal most frequently with these subjects:

 (1) Housing
 (2) Budgeting and finances
 (3) Adjustment to job
 (4) Adjustment to community
 (5) Health
 (6) Family problems
 (7) Emotional and mental disturbances
 (8) Legal aid and insurance

 d) The elements which will go into meeting any one problem are defined in the several sections of this statement on counseling. The fusing of these elements into an instrument which will operate to help the employee solve his problem is a matter for the individual counselor to work out according to his particular abilities and the resources available to him.

 e) While the person-to-person talk is the fundamental method used in counseling, the counselor who is thoroughly trained in the administration and interpretation of tests, case history investigations, and other special procedures may wish to use them occasionally.

C. *Counseling employees in exit interviews*

While the aid of the supervisor in routing employees to the counselor is important to the success of an exit interview program, it is even more important that the counselor have the confidence of employees to the extent that they will seek his aid when circumstances arise which make them wish to leave the service.

D. *Working with supervisors and others to bring about necessary adjustments*

1. In many ways the counselor is a co-ordinator of all the activities and services of the plant as they converge upon the individual employee when he has a particular problem. In that role it becomes necessary for the counselor to gather related information from supervisors, health and safety, placement, classification and wage administration staff and others and to suggest to them or with their help work out ways for meeting the employee's need.

2. Counselors utilize meetings with small groups of supervisors for promoting understanding of employee relations functions and for an exchange of information pertaining to employee adjustment.

3. It may seem that by conferring with other people about employees the principle of confidential relationship will be violated. The counselor should always have the permission of the employee before divulging anything confidential.

E. *Conferring with management officials concerning personnel policies and working conditions*

1. Through day-to-day contacts with individual employees, who speak freely because they know he has no direct administrative authority over them, the counselor has an unparalleled opportunity to gain insight into employee reactions to the policies and practices of management and to working conditions within the plant.

2. Usually, such information is collected and made up into a report which is transmitted through the proper channels to responsible officials who will be in a position to revise and modify policies and procedures.

II. *Interviewing*

A. The method most commonly used by the counselor is the interview, or to express it more simply, a talk with the employee. Sometimes this takes place informally at the employee's desk or workbench or wherever the two may meet. More often, because of the comparative rigidity of shift and work hours, and the necessity for having counselors available at a definite place part of the time, the employee goes to the counselor. The spirit and general atmosphere should be kept as friendly and informal as possible under these circumstances.

B. Skill in managing the exchanges of the interview is acquired gradually and with experience. Interviews dealing with purely informational material are usually easy to manage. Those involving personal matters are more difficult and are likely to take up too much time unless they are carefully directed. The suggestions given here have grown out of the experience of successful interviewers.

C. Counselors will follow all or some of the following procedures according to the circumstances and the problem presented:

1. Offer the individual opportunity to tell freely what is on his mind. This relieves tension, tends to clarify his problem for him, and gives the interviewer insight into the way the employee is thinking and feeling.

2. Ask an occasional question to clarify a statement. In this way the counselor may gain more information about the area of difficulty, the length of time the problem has existed, and the methods already used in dealing with it.

3. Give encouragement to think through the problem; suggest or get him to discover for himself a solution or next step to take. If the employee works out a way for himself, he is much more likely to pursue it than if he is told what to do. Avoid giving advice or prescribing a course of action unless the circumstances make it absolutely necessary.

4. Show consideration for the person to be interviewed, for example, in adjusting your time to his convenience, taking note of his good qualities, reassuring him, and offering him a choice whenever choice is possible.

5. Ask for advice or suggestions. This approach is often successful in winning co-operation and building self-confidence.

D. There is only one basic rule for counselors to follow in talking to employees, take a sincere interest in what the person is saying and try to understand and meet his need. It is especially important to keep a friendly attitude and to avoid dealing with matters in an overly-analytical way.[7]

INTERVIEWING IN CONNECTION WITH TESTING PROGRAMS

A particularly difficult area of interviewing is that concerned with counseling those who have taken psychological tests. An excellent example of suggestions which executives should follow in such cases is seen in the following excerpt from a test interpolation manual prepared for each personnel manager of branch plants and divisional units of a large company:[8]

Introduction

Most persons who have been tested are intensely curious about their results. At the same time they are frequently apprehensive. They may come to the in-

---

[7] *Personnel Counseling* (Civilian Personnel Pamphlet No. 1) (Washington, D.C.: War Department, 1943).

[8] Hubert Clay, "Experiences in Testing Foremen," *Personnel*, May, 1952, pp. 466–70.

terview somewhat tense and nervous, and everything possible should be done to put them at ease.

The test profiles are arranged so that the interest patterns are discussed first, ability and aptitude second, and personality characteristics last. This sequence is followed because it is believed to be most conducive to free discussion.

The interview should be held where interruptions will not occur. Plenty of time should be allowed so that the interview need not be terminated if the interviewee wishes to talk. He may get into a mood for discussion which will never occur again, and an unusual opportunity is lost if he is hurried away. If interruption or too-early termination is positively unavoidable, another appointment should be suggested.

Nothing at this time, not even skilled test interpretation, is so important as a genuine human interest in the individual. This implies an understanding, noncritical attitude which encourages talk. Avoid cross-examinations in regard to test findings and do not use test results as a basis for criticism of job performance. If *he* wants to discuss any problems which the tests bring out, let *him* take the initiative.

Interest Patterns

The discussion of interests provides an easy opening to the interview because nothing threatening to the individual is involved. His scores in an interest area can be either high or low and he is not upset. By the time he has gone through his interest scores and agreed or disagreed with them he is usually relaxed and far better able to accept anything unfavorable which may come up later in the interview. The interviewer, too, has a chance to "size up" the individual and his reactions during this warm-up period and thereby handle the balance of the interview more smoothly.

Ability and Aptitude

The discussion of ability and aptitude has to be carefully handled, especially in the case of an individual whose scores are below the average. This is particularly true of low general ability scores. Avoid using the terms "intelligence" and "IQ." It can be pointed out to the individual that one reason for reporting the results in letter grades is that some persons get too concerned over differences in numerical scores, even when the differences are too small to be significant.

It may be advisable to stress to the interviewee the research nature of the project and to say quite frankly that we do not know yet how much a given score means as far as supervisory success in our company is concerned. It should be emphasized particularly that the best men do not necessarily get the highest scores.

An important aspect of ability testing is the fact that while we can measure a man's ability we cannot measure his willingness to use that ability. Many men of high ability fail to succeed at a high level because of a lack of persistence, initiative, and other hard-to-measure qualities.

Personality

The discussion of personality is left until last because it often results in the individual "opening up" or unburdening himself of some problem or problems. It is a great advantage to be able to continue such talk, as mentioned earlier.

It should be remembered that scores on a personality questionnaire depend upon the individual's willingness and ability to rate himself frankly and honestly. Some persons merely answer the questions the way they think they should be answered rather than the way they actually feel. It is always well to inquire whether the scores agree with the individual's estimate of himself. For example: "Do you believe that you have more energy than the average man, as this score indicates?" or "This score suggests that you tend to be oversensitive and rather easily hurt. Is that an accurate picture of you?"

Certain personality traits cannot always be accepted literally. The individual's behavior actually may be a cover-up for the opposite tendencies. Aggressiveness, for example, may be an artificial role which a man assumes to cover up feelings of inadequacy and insecurity. This kind of aggressiveness is quite different from a wholesome aggressiveness expressed by a really confident person. Personality scores should always be compared, if possible, with observations of the individual in his everyday living. Scores should never be presented as final and conclusive evidence. Rather, they should be thought of as guideposts which may help a person to gain insight into himself and his relations with others.

QUESTIONS AND PROBLEMS

1. A given executive in conducting interviews follows the plan of making no advance preparations on the grounds that he thereby undertakes the interview without any preconceived or prejudicial notions. Comment upon this plan of interviewing.

2. Under what conditions would you use interviewing to give and get information, and under what conditions would you use other tools, such as application blanks, tests, and reference letters?

3. What is the difference between qualitative and quantitative information? Cite examples of each.

4. Prepare a set of "patterned interview" type of questions for hiring a stenographer. Try out the list with a fellow student, and report on how the original list of questions could be improved.

5. Try out a nondirective interview before the class on a student who is tardy, in order to try to determine why he came in late. Do your difficulties give a clue to the kinds of problems for which this type of interviewing can and cannot be used? Explain.

6. Do you expect the nondirective method to be used widely in industry? Why or why not?

7. If recording instruments are available, try out an exit interview. What lessons are learned from the playback that might otherwise not be learned?

8. Can most executives become good interviewers? If they can, how should this objective be sought? If they cannot, what are your recommendations?

9. Make some notes indicating what the interviewer must do in order for him to keep an "unguided" interview from being guided and from coming to an inconclusive halt.

10. Produce a sample interview in which one student, acting as an employment manager, interviews another student who acts as a candidate. Have a third

student act as an observer and make notes on the interview. The observer should then suggest improvements in the interview. The students should then rotate roles. If recording devices are available, record the interview and play back the recording for class discussion. Do not look for faults except to improve the method of interviewing.

11. If you were to interview a candidate for employment, what preparations would you make and with what types of information would you first acquaint yourself?

12. Assume that an employee comes to you, his supervisor, with a grievance. Assume further that he is decidedly upset. Suggest ways and means to put him at ease.

13. It is said that allowing interviewees to talk freely is a desirable way to settle many problems. How can the average executive find time to give employees unhurried discussions?

14. Suggest ways in which an interviewer may draw an interview to a close, gracefully, yet conclusively.

15. What is the objection to the practice of taking notes during an interview? How else may the interviewer be sure of remembering exactly what he should remember? In what types of interviews may note taking be desirable and permissible?

16. Suggest ways in which appropriate physical arrangements for interviewing may be provided for supervisory interviews in the shop.

17. What is meant by counseling? In the industrial enterprise, whose job is it to counsel? Why is counseling a task of industry at all?

18. An employee who was dissatisfied with his progress went to the personnel manager to complain. The personnel manager advised the employee to seek work elsewhere. Suggest possible reasons why such advice was given.

19. It has been said that, in the final analysis, each person must make his own decision regarding a choice of vocations. If this is so, why do people so often seek advice from others regarding the relative merits of alternative occupations, companies, and localities of work? Discuss the term "vocational guidance." Note to what extent guidance is interpretative and to what extent it is actually directive.

20. In interviewing a candidate for employment whom you believe possesses aptitudes that fit him for advancement, what questions would you ask him in order to check on his future possibilities?

CHAPTER

10 | Tests

POPULARITY OF TESTS

Perhaps no subject in the field of selection has received as much study and attention as that of testing. Since World War I, when psychological tests were adopted by the U.S. Army as a means of aiding in the placement of army personnel, much has been written about tests, their development, application, and usefulness. But even as late as 1940, usage did not come up to the volume of writings. In that year, one student found only eight companies which to his knowledge were making systematic and extensive use of tests in the selection of employees. Obviously, after a period of over twenty years, this was not an admirable record. Although data are not available, it appears that many companies adopted testing programs during and after World War II. Estimates based upon recent sample surveys would put current usage somewhere around ten thousand.

The limited usage is not, however, a serious reflection upon the desirability and feasibility of testing. Nor is the fact that numbers of companies have discontinued the use of tests a sign of the inherent weaknesses of tests. Limited usage or discontinuance of programs may be due to a number of reasons. Some companies do not care to invest the time and money needed to build a successful testing program. Others became discouraged because tests did not "solve" their hiring problems, a conclusion they should have reached before seeking a cure-all. And others think that their selection problems are susceptible to more understandable solutions.

As experimentation continues, refinements are bound to lift testing above such arguments. Tests will sooner or later become a generally accepted tool of personnel management. The use of tests requires much study and skill, however, and for these reasons it has perhaps lagged in adoptions. And, for similar reasons, the complexity of the subject will permit no more than a generalized discussion of testing here. This discussion is taken up under the following headings:

1. Basic concepts and assumptions of testing
2. Purposes for which tests may be used
3. Types of tests
4. Operating a testing program
5. Rules in testing

BASIC FUNDAMENTALS

It is desirable to understand at the outset that a test—any test—is a process of measurement. By such measurement it is hoped to determine how well a person has done something or may do something in the future. The measurement may be in intangible or quantitative terms. When we "size up" a person, for example, we are selecting a sample of the person's activities and reaching a qualitative conclusion about him. Thus, upon being introduced to someone, we decide immediately or soon after that our new acquaintance is a "right guy" or perhaps someone who should not be trusted. Our judgment is qualitative, since we do not specify how "right" or how untrustworthy he is. Nevertheless, in our own fashion, we have given a test and reached a conclusion regarding his future performance.

On the other hand, our conclusions may be expressed quantitatively. As a result of a formal intelligence test, a definite score would be obtained for each person, e.g., intelligence quotient of 102. Of course, a quantitative score is better in the sense that it can be communicated to others more readily, yet it is not necessarily any more accurate than qualitative scores or verbal descriptions.

To note another fundamental characteristic, tests are samples. Although the most accurate basis for measuring a person's value to a concern is his performance, obviously this is not possible in the case of job applicants, for example. It is impractical to hire all applicants and then retain only those who prove satisfactory. Instead, applicants may be asked to work on a sample of actual operations or on factors that are of importance in actual operations. In the case of typists, for example, candidates may be requested to transcribe or copy a set of material. Their efforts in terms of such measures as speed of typing, neatness of work, and number of errors would then be established. Or tests might be given in regard to such elements as finger dexterity, visual acuity, and word memory on the assumption that these are basic factors in typing success. That a test is a sample need not destroy one's confidence in them. So long as steps are taken to see that given samples are truly representative of the areas of which they presumably are samples, their usefulness is not questionable on that score.

Another fundamental assumption regarding tests is that they are relatively accurate measures of past efforts or predictors of future events. This assumption or characteristic of tests must be clearly understood, else an inevitable avenue to failure will be followed. On the one hand, the score of a test, which is intended to disclose how much experience, training, or ability along given lines one has acquired, does not disclose unerringly what may happen in the future. The very characteristic that a sample is a sample precludes unequivocal forecasts. But the test score is a better predictor, when used in combination with other methods of evaluating people, than intuition and observational appraisals.

On the other hand, tests which seek to predict future events, although useful, are as yet more accurate in their negative implications than in their positive significance. For example, if Candidate A receives a high score on a battery of tests and B receives a low score, the reasonable deduction here is that B is not likely to succeed if hired and hence should not, other things considered, be hired. As for A, it is plausible to expect him not to fail, but the contention at the present stage in the development of tests is not that he will succeed in proportion as his grade is high.

And, finally, even the most enthusiastic supporters of tests do not insist that decisions regarding applicants or employees be reached solely on the basis of test scores. This technique should be viewed as a contributor to the process of hiring, for example. It should add to the sum of information gathered from application blanks, references, observation, and interviews. Its measurements should be given a place in the general scheme of interpretation and not be permitted to usurp or minimize the contributors of other tools. Perhaps the chief reason for dissatisfaction with tests has arisen out of the fact that, when reliance has been placed upon them as the major source of information, they have proved unreliable. Hence, at the outset, it is imperative to remember that, although the discussion here is concerned with tests, they are to be viewed as contributory and not the only source of information.

In the various tasks related to selecting, developing, maintaining, and utilizing labor, innumerable decisions must, of course, be reached. What is the best basis or bases upon which to build decisions? To proponents of tests, these devices constitute an indispensable and increasingly accurate tool. As one writer has put it, "The most important results of our six years' experience [with tests] is to enable me to say without hesitation that it is beyond anyone's power to do as good a job of employment without tests as can be done with their careful use."[1]

---

[1] Edward N. Hay, *Inaugurating a Test Program* (Personnel Series No. 43) (New York: American Management Association, 1940), p. 26.

Yet this same writer is not blinded by his enthusiasm but adds the following words of caution: "Don't expect too much from tests. Remember that they give information which must be used with judgment and experience in conjunction with other facts about the applicant or employee. Test scores alone cannot be depended upon to give the answers."[2]

PURPOSES OF TESTS

The purposes for which tests may be used do not preclude the use of other techniques at the same time for the same purposes. The purposes of testing discussed now are those related to employment, placement, and training.

1. OPERATIVE EMPLOYMENT. Evidence is plentiful that tests have proved helpful in screening applicants for employment. An example of successful testing is found in a company that compared 88 hirings with testing and 45 without testing during a five-month period.[3] Percentages of those who subsequently failed on the job was 7.8 for those tested and 49 for those not tested. Based on a minimum cost of $55 to train a replacement, $990 was lost by not testing the 45. This figure was computed on the assumption that testing the 45 would have eliminated the unfit from this group as successfully as it did with the 88. In that event, only 4 would have had to be replaced, instead of 22, as was the case. The saving in 18 replacements at $55 would have amounted to $990. On the other hand, if the 88 had been hired without testing and if 49 per cent had failed—as was true of the nontested group—the loss would have been $2,035 ($55 × 37).

An example of how effective a single test can be is shown by an analysis of the production record of workers whose vision differed. It was found that average hourly earnings of employees who met visual standards were $0.827 as compared with $0.69 for those who did not.[4] Thus the former earned about 20 per cent more than the latter. Moreover, the quality of workmanship of the former was found to have increased about 8–15 per cent.

2. EXECUTIVE SELECTION. Although the surface has been little more than scratched, much study has been given to the adoption of tests for screening executives, particularly at the supervisory level. Here, more than in the case of operative levels, it is necessary to combine

---

[2] *Ibid.,* p. 33.

[3] A. R. Michael, "Tests Help Cut Turnover Rate 74% in Five Months," *Factory Management and Maintenance,* Vol. CIX, No. 5, pp. 78–80.

[4] N. Frank Stump, "Vision Tests Predict Worker Capability," *Factory Management and Maintenance,* February, 1946, pp. 121–24.

ratings and interviews with selected batteries of tests, to be able to screen potentially good from inferior supervisors. Thus to results of tests on such factors as interests, emotional stability, general intelligence, and personality must be added opinions on such factors as training, experience, social responsibilities and relationships, productive record, and hobbies.

In this connection, the conclusion reached in one company that has had success with such a program is of particular interest and value: "The chief value of such a plan is negative in nature. That is, the absence of the necessary training, experience, mentality, and interests to do a given job is an excellent indication that a person cannot do the job, but the presence of these traits is no guarantee that a man will do the job. (Because of the importance of attitude, domestic relations, lack of motivation or incentive, etc.)"[5]

Another company installed a selection procedure heavily weighted with psychological testing, interviewing, and performance analysis.[6] It reported that, before installation, 1 out of every 2 foremen failed, on the average. In the first year after installation, one of its factory units had 33 successes out of 35 promotions to the supervisory level.

3. SELECTION OF SALES ENGINEERS. Merely to provide one more example to illustrate the fact that the most technical jobs are not being overlooked by students of testing, brief reference is made to experience with sales engineers. One company has employed tests of vocational interest, mental maturity, personality, and mechanical aptitude with other selection devices. It feels that its selection and placement of its sales engineers may be improved by 10–20 per cent by the use of psychological tests.[7] This conservative estimate contains an important moral: A selection device should not be judged by whether it provides perfect results but rather by its capacity to make a reasonably significant improvement in results.

4. TESTS IN PLACEMENT. A report in connection with the selection of apprentices is of interest, in that it shows that tests have been used in connection with other than strictly production jobs with satisfactory success.[8] In this case twenty-four applicants for an apprentice course were given tests, and the results thereof were then compared

[5] Lee Lockford, "Selection of Supervisory Personnel," *Personnel,* November, 1947, p. 199.

[6] Matthew Radom, "Picking Better Foremen," *Factory Management and Maintenance,* Vol. CVIII, No. 10, pp. 119–22.

[7] James Onarheim, "Scientific Sales Engineers," *Personnel,* July, 1947, p. 34.

[8] C. A. Drake, "Aptitude Tests Help You Hire," *Factory Management and Maintenance,* June, 1937, p. 92.

TABLE 14

A RECORD OF TEST AND RANKING SCORES*

Name Symbol	Table I — Scores on Three Pencil-and-Paper Tests			Table II — Scores on Three Performance Tests			Table III — Combined Ranks, 24 Apprentice Applicants Compared with Standing of 5 Apprentices Now in Training	
	Otis S.A. I.Q. (Points)	Stenquist II (Points)	Minn. Paper Form Board (Points)	Wiggly Block (Minutes)	Spatial Relations (Minutes)	Mechanical Assembly (Points)	Rank	Present Apprentice
Noy	129	69	50	2.11	3.63	70	1	
Syw	101	66	53	2.41	3.65	80	2	
Nal	89	71	45	1.32	4.58	87	3	
Gew	113	66	41	3.10	4.92	84	4	
Tor	113	58	54	2.66	5.17	50	5	
Der	101	62	43	1.29	5.50	73	6	
Hic	110	62	45	4.06	4.90	73	7	
Das	102	63	56	4.88	4.85	60	8	
Zir	91	67	39	2.66	5.75	61	9	
Raz	106	66	27	6.71	4.50	68	10	
Coh	95	57	26	2.72	5.67	86	11	
Nac	109	39	38	4.50	4.55	52	12	A
Zeg	98	48	48	4.48	6.08	59	13	B
Maj	91		43		5.50	53	14	C
Tid	101	60	32	3.01	5.53	39	15	
Dim	93	54	36	5.59	4.83	60	16	
Vac	108	58	39	2.78	8.58	33	17	
Nok	87	50	35	4.19	6.25	45	18	
Zaj	76	38	26	2.86	4.83	40	19	
Rig	99	38	25	4.43	6.17	52	20	D
Tac	95	50	30	4.36	6.50	30	21	
Nes	106	40	24	4.80	5.33	25	22	
Ner	77	50	31	7.42	6.15	45	23	
Tai	91	32	14	5.46	8.93	67	24	E

* Source: C. A. Drake, "Aptitude Tests Help You Hire," *Factory Management and Maintenance*, June, 1937, p. 57.

with test scores of present apprentices who had been hired without tests. The data in Table 14 disclose rather strikingly how ineptly the selection process had functioned in the past. The first eleven apprentice-applicants outranked all the present apprentices. This shows strikingly not only that hit-or-miss methods of selection are expensive for the company but that they are unfair to applicants who are mis-hired and misplaced.

5. TESTS IN TRAINING. Tests have also been useful in strengthening training programs. An interesting example of this is reported in using tests to determine who should be trained, where training should begin, and whether training has been adequate. It was found that the learning cost of employees who had scored lowest on a finger-dexterity test, as measured by a simple peg board, averaged $59.00 before they earned the minimum hourly rate on a piecework basis. On the other hand, those with the highest finger dexterity incurred a learning cost of $36.40 before

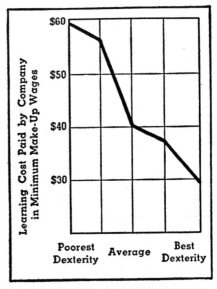

FIGURE 35.   Relationship between Scores on a Finger-Dexterity Test and Average Learning Cost to the Plant in Minimum Make-up Pay*

* Source: C. H. Lawshe and Joseph Tiffin, "How Tests Can Strengthen the Training Program," *Factory Management and Maintenance*, March, 1944, pp. 119–21.

making the rate. Figure 35 illustrates these relationships. Obviously, savings in training costs would more than offset the cost of such selection tests.

This report also showed that tests can save training costs by determining where training should begin. On a simple measurement question asked about an illustration showing some blocks adjacent to a scale, it was found that 70 per cent of 650 applicants were unable to read to $\frac{1}{32}$ inch. Obviously, training would be wasted in these cases unless the training were started at a level low enough to teach measuring fundamentals.

The question of whether training has been adequate is also of significance. Figure 36 illustrates the relation between scores on an electrical information test and hours of instruction. By pre-establishing a measure to indicate when a person has sufficient knowledge to handle a particular job, it is possible to determine how many hours of training are ordinarily required to attain the desired score. Thus, if it is decided that anyone who has a grade of 80 may be turned loose on a job, then, by the use of such a chart as that in Figure 36, it may be noted that training would be needed for about 200 hours. Obviously, any figure above or below this would be wasteful either by overtraining or by poor production due to under-training.

FIGURE 36. Relationship between Length of Training Period and Scores on an Electrical Information Test*

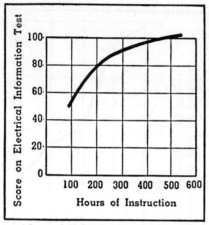

Hours of Instruction

* Source: C. H. Lawshe and Joseph Tiffin, "How Tests Can Strengthen the Training Program," *Factory Management and Maintenance*, March, 1944, pp. 119–21.

In brief, the foregoing has shown that tests have been used successfully in selection, placement, and training. Although most work with tests in these fields has been done largely with repetitive jobs in the factory or office, there is a growing tendency to expand the area of usage to include various highly skilled and professional fields. Much has been done recently with tests in the sales field, for example. It should be remembered that this discussion of why tests are used has made little reference to where they may be used, because there seems to be no field in which they cannot be applied with some degree of success.

TYPES OF TESTS

Having seen the uses to which tests have been put, it would now be desirable to review and describe various kinds of tests. Time and space preclude this because estimates show that tens of thousands of tests have been developed. No one single classification of tests is sufficiently descriptive of all types; hence in the following presentation consideration is given to:

1. The human characteristics being tested
2. Individual versus test batteries
3. Mechanical construction of tests
4. Illustrations of common tests

Perhaps the most common classification of human characteristics for testing purposes is intelligence, skills, interests, and personality. Among the earliest tests, and still of great prominence, are those relating to native intelligence. Perhaps next in order are those relating to skills; i.e., the ability to do things. These may refer to: aptitude—the potential to develop skills—or proficiency or achievement—the skill which one has acquired. Interest tests seek to ascertain the preferences one has for alternative choices of occupations, professions, or avocations. And personality tests measure poise, personal adjustment, temperament, emotional and social balance, extroversion versus introversion, etc.

Another way of classifying human characteristics is suggested in the following grouping:

1. TESTS TO MEASURE THE ABILITY TO UNDERSTAND AND TO USE IDEAS (AND ANALYSIS OF IDEAS). These ideas include: the material out of which are made all abstract and general thinking; all chemical formulas, legal decisions, and scientific principles; all the higher forms of thinking that differentiate the human from the animal; all plans, programs, values, and logical thinking such as similar and dissimilar, profit and loss, cause and effect, and right and wrong. The ability to understand and to manage ideas and their symbols is spoken of as common sense, verbal intelligence, ingenuity, practicability, and educability.

2. TESTS TO MEASURE CLERICAL AND MECHANICAL APTITUDES AND ABILITIES. These refer to such aspects as the ability to understand and to manage things and mechanisms: the motor control essential for skilled handwork; the mechanical imagination essential for the creating and for using complicated blueprints; co-ordination of hand and eye essential for running a machine whether it be a typewriter, a printing press, a bicycle, or an airplane.

3. TESTS TO MEASURE OCCUPATIONAL INTERESTS AND ABILITIES. Reference here is to such aspects as vocational interests, personality inventories, supervisory insight into human relations, and supervisory appraisals.[9]

Another interesting bases for classifying tests arises out of the use of a group or "battery" of tests instead of a single test. A battery of tests is considered to give much better results. This does not mean that a candidate must receive high grades on all the tests given. On the contrary, some of the tests included in a battery may be given with a view to finding what things a candidate is not equipped to do or interested in doing. This tends to strengthen conclusions reached on the "positive" tests included in the battery. Some examples of test batteries include the following:

[9] W. D. Scott, R. C. Clothier, and W. R. Spriegel, *Personnel Management* (New York: McGraw-Hill Book Co., Inc., 1954), pp. 255, 268, and 285.

1. In order to derive a picture of a person's general aptitudes or interests, tests have been given for the following characteristics:[10]
   a) Finger dexterity, or manipulative skill
   b) Accounting aptitude—clerical aptitude
   c) Ability to visualize structure
   d) Tweezer dexterity
   e) Inductive reasoning
   f) Creative imagination
   g) Visual memory
   h) Observation
   i) Personality
   j) Tonal memory

2. In one experiment, inspectors were given the following battery of tests:[11]
   a) The Minnesota Rate of Manipulation Test to measure hand and finger dexterity
   b) The Purdue Hand Precision Test to check co-ordination between hand and eye
   c) Tests of reaction time and strength of grip
   d) Stereoscopical vision tests
   e) Measures of height, weight, and age were also recorded

3. In checking the usefulness of tests for time study men, the following battery of tests was employed:[12]
   a) Otis Employment Test (general mental ability)
   b) Bennett Mechanical Comprehension (in mechanical comprehension)
   c) Moore Arithmetic Reasoning (in quantitative thinking)
   d) Minnesota Paper Board Form (in visualizing bidimensional objects in relation to space)
   e) Guilford-Martin (working with and getting along with others; objectivity, agreeableness, co-operativeness)
   f) Kuder-Preference (in major interests; mechanical, computational, scientific, persuasive, artistic, literary, music, social service, clerical)

4. A battery of tests given to supervisors included the following:[13]
   a) Strong Vocational Interest Blank for Men
   b) Kuder-Preference Record
   c) Wonderlic Personnel Test
   d) Classification Test for Industrial and Office Personnel
   e) How Supervise
   f) General Clerical Test
   g) Test of Mechanical Comprehension
   h) Guilford-Zimmerman Temperament Survey

---

[10] Johnson O'Connor, *Making Fullest Use of Present Personnel* (Office Management Series No. 79) (New York: American Management Association, 1937), pp. 4–16.

[11] Joseph Tiffin and H. B. Rogers, "The Selection and Training of Inspectors," *Personnel,* July, 1941, pp. 14–31.

[12] Charles A. Thomas, "Special Report on a Test Analysis of a Group of Time Study Men," *Advanced Management,* August, 1953, pp. 13–14.

[13] Hubert Clay, "Experiences in Testing Foremen," *Personnel,* May, 1952, pp. 466–70.

5. A battery of tests used in a selection procedure for salesmen included the following:[14]
   a) P.R.I. Classification Test
   b) Purdue Adaptability
   c) Minnesota Paper Board Form
   d) Cardall Test of Practical Judgment
   e) Sales Selector
   f) Allport-Vernon Study of Values
   g) Guilford-Zimmerman Temperament Survey
   h) Strong Vocational Interest Test

Another interesting view of tests may be taken by noting briefly the way in which testing materials are presented. In the fields of intelligence or mental ability, for example, a variety of methods has been used. During World War I, the U.S. Army employed nonverbal (the beta test) and verbal (the alpha test) means for this purpose. Since then, the experiments have been innumerable. Test materials include such forms as the following: multiple-choice word sentences, arithmetical expressions, pictures, and figures; disarranged sentences or displays; matching and nonmatching words or numbers; similarities and opposites of various kinds; and incomplete sentences that must be completed.

It is well to note that students of the subject are aware that intelligence is not a simple characteristic. Rather, it is perhaps irrevocably mixed up with other phases of human characteristics, such as learning, experience, background, personality, mechanical ability, executive talent, sales ability, and interest. Hence, in testing intelligence, a pure score is never obtained but is tainted by the other characteristics.

Perhaps a good view of types of tests may be obtained by briefly describing some common tests and what they are testing:[15]

1. Tweezer dexterity tests are used to determine whether a candidate possesses sufficient finger performance and control to handle small parts efficiently and without undue fatigue.
2. A test of mechanical ability may be obtained by checking the speed with which a candidate can assemble oddly shaped jigsaw blocks.
3. Another test used to determine mechanical ability is the spatial relations test. This serves as a measure of a candidate's ability to visualize the shape of physical objects.
4. Tests of machine skill have been designed in which the operator is checked, first, for speed and accuracy in controlling two cranks turned at different speeds and in different directions, and, second, for hand-eye

[14] Erwin K. Taylor and Edwin C. Nevis, "The Validity of Using Psychological Selection Procedures," *Personnel*, November, 1953, pp. 187–89.

[15] R. S. Uhrbrock, "The Expressed Interests of Employed Men," *American Journal of Psychology*, July, 1944, pp. 317–70; October, 1944, pp. 537–54.

co-ordination in turning a crank while following with the eyes a line drawn on a revolving drum.

5. A test used to screen candidates for fine assembly work has been based upon dexterity in handling small parts.

6. Inspection tests are usually made up of sample jobs which check visual acuity and finger dexterity.

7. Technical intelligence has been measured by the use of pictorial multiple-choice questions, as have mechanical comprehension to understand various types of physical relationships.

8. A classification and placement test designed to measure individual performance in twelve basic skills of seeing is incorporated in a testing instrument called the "Ortho-rate."

9. In checking the interests of people, the samples following are illustrative of the types of tests which have been employed.

    a) Below are names and accomplishments of persons who have attained fame. If the life and work of a man interest you, circle the L before his name; if you are indifferent to his accomplishments, encircle the I; if you dislike the type of activity he stands for, encircle the D.

        L   I   D   1. Johann Gutenberg—movable type for printing presses
        L   I   D   2. Harvey Allen—author of *Anthony Adverse*
        L   I   D   3. George Corliss—valve gear for steam engines
        L   I   D   4. Thomas Edison—incandescent lamp

    b) Below are listed several paired occupations. Suppose that each occupation pays the same salary, carries the same social standing, and offers the same future advancement. Place a check ($\sqrt{}$) in front of the one occupation of each pair which you would prefer as a life work. BE SURE TO MARK ONE OF EACH PAIR.

1. Research chemist Factory superintendent	6. Sales manager Advertising manager
2. Budget director Sales manager	7. Research chemist Personnel director
3. Office manager Construction engineer	8. Factory superintendent Office manager
4. Research chemist Sales manager	9. Design engineer Sales manager
5. Personnel director Office manager	10. Budget director Design engineer

OPERATING A TESTING PROGRAM

Since it has been impractical to analyze even a part of all tests in use, some useful suggestions regarding any tests may be provided by commenting upon: (1) staffing and organizing a testing program, (2) recording and interpreting test results, and (3) measuring the accuracy of tests.

1. STAFFING AND ORGANIZING. Undoubtedly a most important requirement of a good testing program is that of assigning it to competent personnel. Immediately there comes to mind the psychologist,

trained in the theory of tests, their construction, their uses, and their meaning. When possible, such a person should be given responsibility for operating the testing program. However, it is not always possible to utilize the services of a psychologist. In such instances, there is no reason why it is not possible to assign some individual with the required potential and have him study in this field himself. Many a case is on record of executives who have become interested in testing and, after years of study and experimentation, have performed very creditably in constructing and giving tests and interpreting tests results.

From an organizational point of view a number of suggestions is in order. To begin with, the top executives must be convinced of the desirability of testing. Until and unless they are "sold," the battle with the lower levels of an organization will be eventually lost or hard-won. Hence it is good practice, first, to convince top management of the value of testing; second, to bring it actively into the developmental stages of the program; and, third, to keep it informed of progress by means of reports illustrating the success of the testing program.

Those on lower levels of an organization will also have to be convinced of the usefulness of testing. Unless one wants a forced acceptance—and consequently an unstable position—it is best in these levels to go slowly. Usually only a department or two should be selected as the area of installation. Results here should then be so self-apparent that the program will expand of its own accord. The following statement illustrates convincingly how this actually works out:

By the third year we had developed enough confidence in one or two department heads so that they were willing to allow us to test some of their employees. After a time one of these department heads sent us, gradually, most of the 200 employees in his department, and subsequently he never made a promotion or transfer without consulting me and inquiring about test indications.

One of the best ways to commence testing employees is to appeal to them for assistance in helping to develop standards for selection of new workers in the same occupation. If tactfully done and if the support of the supervisors affected has been secured, no trouble should ordinarily result.

The influence of tests on selection and promotion was thus being extended and gave us an increasing number of opportunities to "sell" supervisors and employees on the value of tests. This job of selling is never finished. By now we are not merely tolerated; our testing program is taken for granted in most departments, and in some it is regarded as an essential aid to the supervisor. There are departments, nevertheless, where, even yet, testing employees is impossible. Such departments challenge us to further effort in establishing clearly the value of psychological methods, including testing.

After about three years we reached the point where employees began to come and ask to be tested, and several department heads asked us to test all their clerks. Sometimes this was to gain a better understanding of their own strong and weak points; sometimes it seemed to be merely an attitude of approval. We are now constantly being asked to recommend men for promotion and encouraged to test them to help our decision.[16]

This need to "sell" testing should not be considered satisfied, once the program is accepted. A continuous and unending program of selling must be followed to maintain it at its highest possible stage of development.

Organizationally speaking, there is no reason why unions, too, cannot be consulted in connection with the use of tests. Although unions have not displayed much interest in this subject, there are cases in which management has worked with unions in applying tests in cases of selections, transfers, and rehirings. Tests are used as an aid in connection with other devices to decide on such matters as employee placement, with union consultation and consent.

2. RECORDING TEST RESULTS. Another operational aspect worthy of consideration is that of recording test results. Such records can be expressed simply in arithmetical or verbal terms, or they may be displayed graphically. Arithmetical or verbal terms have simplicity and ease of recording in their favor, but they lack the desirable characteristic of visualization. For example, Figure 37 illustrates the graphical method of displaying test results in regard to visual measurements. The "profile," or line connecting various test scores, quickly and clearly reveals to the reader the co-ordination of given operators as compared to desirable limits.

On a broader scale, the value of profile recording may be seen in Figure 38. Here test scores on nine tests are recorded. The tests were as follows: (1) pin board, (2) right-right turning, (3) special inspection, (4) case sorting, (5) visual perception, (6) controlled turning, (7) right-left turning, (8) hand-foot co-ordination, (9) rhythm. The profiles of the four candidates shown in Figure 38 make it possible to draw conclusions much more quickly than if the scores had merely been expressed arithmetically.

3. MEASURES OF ACCURACY OF TESTS. Tests are usually measured in terms of their "validity" and "reliability." On the one hand, tests are obviously developed and designed to test something, e.g., intelligence, temperament, finger dexterity, or reading ability. The degree to which a given test does this is a measure of its validity and is commonly expressed by means of the statistical device of coefficient of correlation. Simply, this refers to a measure of the degree to which

---

[16] Hay, *op. cit.*, p. 27.

those who have high, average, and low scores also have high, average, and low production records, for example. On the other hand, a test which is supposed to measure something should yield approximately the same answer for the same person at different times (allowing for the memory factor and improvement on the job because of experience). The degree to which a given test does yield consistently the same scores

FIGURE 37. Visual Patterns Desirable for Electric Soldering Operations, and the Actual Score Made by One of the Employees in the Highest Hourly Rating Group. Scores in the Darkened Area Are Undesirable*

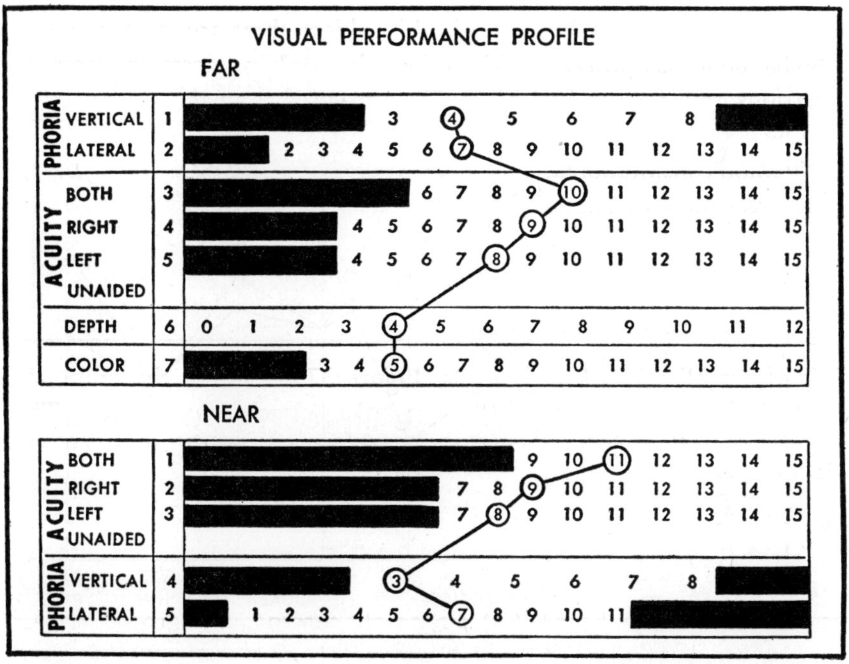

* Source: N. Frank Stump, "Vision Tests Predict Worker Capacity," *Factory Management and Maintenance,* February, 1946, pp. 121–22.

is a measure of its reliability and is also commonly expressed as a co-efficient of correlation.

An example of a simple determination of validity is provided by the following case of selection of office employees:

After administering five different tests we found two which predicted success to a fairly high degree. The critical score on each test is such that, of the 20 best operators, 15 made good scores; and of the 20 poorest, only 5 made good scores; or, in other words, if we had discharged all the operators with scores below the critical point of either test, we would have lost 25 per cent of our best operators, but no less than 75 per cent of our poorest.

This is not as high a degree of correlation between test scores and performance as is often obtained; we believe we can improve it by further experimentation with other tests.

The correlation indicates, however, the probability of a very substantial degree of success in selecting operators who will subsequently prove satisfactory. As a matter of fact, of 5 operators employed in the last three years as beginners, that is, without experience, 4 are now among the 20 best girls and only 1 is in the lower group. That one is well up in the lower 20 and, we think, will move higher after a little more experience.[17]

FIGURE 38. Inspection Test Profile*

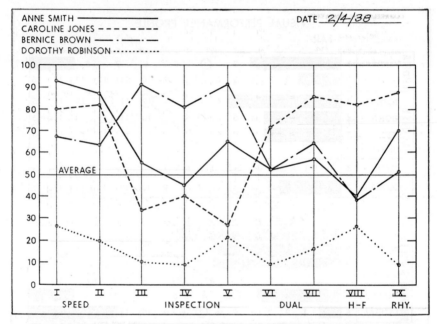

* Source: C. A. Drake and H. D. Oleen, "The Technique of Testing," *Factory Management and Maintenance,* March, 1938, pp. 77–78.

An example of a simple determination of reliability is provided by the following case in which pupils who had been given a test in blueprint reading were later retested:

Months later, people were retested at random, the same test being used. There was an improvement in the scores, but not more than 7 points. Seven points out of 100 is a negligible figure which could be charged to remembrance or practice. Theoretically, we could say that each person hit his own level again on a retest, and that the test was reliable. Or, in other words, that each time it was used one could depend on getting accurate results. The reliability of a test can be bettered by lengthening it. This should not be done to extremes because the element of

[17] Hay, *op. cit.,* p. 32.

writing fatigue may void any good results. Employment tests should not run more than 30 minutes to be practical.[18]

A graphical illustration of the accuracy of tests is shown in Figure 39. Here the relationship between test scores for inspectors and measures of their success are summarized in table form. By drawing lines to denote areas of good relationship, it was found that 95 per cent of

FIGURE 39. Correlation of Ratings and Test Scores*

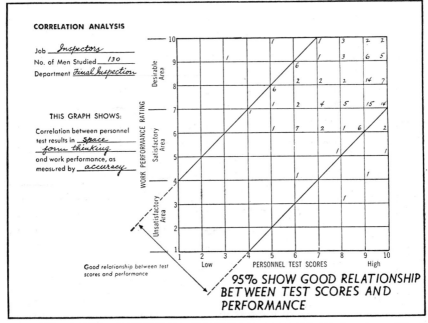

* Source: Robert E. Kline, "We Know Our Employment Tests Match Man and Job," *Factory Management and Maintenance*, September, 1949, p. 122.

employees who received acceptable test scores turned out to be acceptable inspectors.

RULES OF USING TESTS

Perhaps this discussion of testing can be best summarized by reviewing some rules of good testing practice.

From an operational point of view, several suggestions are in order. First, it is highly desirable to make careful job and position studies as a basis for building tests. Job analysis is essential in order to determine the skills, aptitudes, or other characteristics for which tests must be de-

[18] R. W. Gillette, "Tests Help You Hire Right," *Factory Management and Maintenance*, October, 1941, p. 80.

signed. Until this information is obtained, the selection or development of tests can only be based upon guesswork.

Next, it is generally agreed that tests should be selected or developed with a view to particular jobs in a particular company. Although there are tests which may have general reliability, such as the general intelligence test, specific adaptations are invariably called for. Local conditions, variations in jobs (even with the same title), and differences in company policies and operation methods are sufficient reason for making individual adaptations.

Another operational principle is that reliance should not be placed solely upon tests in reaching decisions. Tests are most useful when they are given a part in the task of selection, placement, or training of employees. Other devices such as application blanks, interviews, and rating scores should be given a prominent role. There is a danger that one's initial enthusiasm for tests may tend unwarrantedly to relegate these other instruments to a small role. When this first flush has passed, there is equal danger that tests may be discarded for failing to provide "all the answers."

Other principles of test usage also deserve mention. Thus, it is well to establish upper limits of test scores beyond which a person's acceptability is in question. There is as much possibility of hiring a person who will become dissatisfied if he is too intelligent or proficient, as of hiring one who is too dull. Also, the nature of the significance of test scores and of all aspects of testing is so involved that it is not desirable to expose test methods or scores to those who do not understand them. The personnel department should be the keeper and interpreter of tests. Others certainly have an interest in them, but that is an interest of use and not of operation. Hence the expert should be recognized as the authority of operation, respected for it, and able to explain its ramifications and to answer all pertinent questions. "Self-medication" should be avoided.

It is also important to use correlation figures with care. A high validity rating does not mean that the given test can be used with impunity. For example, an individual may score low on a test of high validity. Yet through high personal motivation he may more than make up for, let us say, a minimum of technical skill. On the other hand, a test with a low validity rating may nevertheless give a valuable clue to a particular applicant's strength or weakness. These warnings are in addition to that already given to the effect that tests are best used in connection with other instruments of selection, placement, or promotion.

An essential principle of installing testing is that the program be supported sufficiently and be given ample time to be worked out. A good program will, at the minimum, take a few years to put in operation. Unless adequate time is allowed and resources provided, the results will not be as satisfactory as desired. Yet this plea for time and resources does not mean that the outlay will be expensive. Most companies that have gone into such a program do not have to spend more than several dollars (at the most) for each employee tested. The improvement in selection, training, and placement results is more than adequate to offset such expenditures.

In the final analysis, tests must be judged in terms of their contribution to the solution of problems of selection, placement, and training. Such judgments might not be too difficult to arrive at, were it always possible to try out various tests by comparing test scores with the production records of employees. But unlimited resources are seldom provided for such research. As a consequence, most tests must be devised and evaluated within time limits and budget expenditures that do not allow all the latitude that might be desired.

QUESTIONS AND PROBLEMS

1. If testing is, among other things, a sampling process, how does one know when one has an adequate and representative sample?

2. How would you explain the rather infrequent use of tests in industry?

3. Why does a "profile" increase the effectiveness of testing programs?

4. What are the fundamental assumptions that underlie the use of psychological tests in employment?

5. Look up the meaning of the words "diagnostic" and "prognostic." What relation do these terms have to the possible use of tests?

6. How do you explain the fact that, relatively speaking, tests do not enjoy wide usage although much has been written about them during the past thirty years?

7. Assume that an applicant for a job receives a score of, let us say, 69 on a battery of tests for which the passing grade is 70. What would your decision be in this case, and why?

8. Explain the difference between tests designed to measure acquired skills and those designed to measure aptitude.

9. Discuss the usefulness of a general intelligence test as opposed to a "specific characteristic of intelligence" test.

10. What would you conclude about a candidate who made high grades on some and low grades on other parts of a battery of tests?

11. What relationship is there between organization structure and the develop-

ment and use of tests? How does this relationship change as a company grows from small to very large size with decentralized factory operations?

12. Some companies have experienced strong objections from line supervisors when attempting to introduce a testing program, and others have gained immediate co-operation. How would you explain the difference in acceptance by supervisors?

13. Visit a few companies that are using tests, and write a report covering the following points: How long did it take them to get their program of testing to work with reasonably good results? What were the major obstacles they had to overcome? What pitfalls do they suggest must be watched for? Specifically what tangible proof do they have of the effectiveness of testing?

14. Why is it desirable to establish upper as well as lower test scores as limits of hiring?

15. What is the relation of testing to job analysis?

16. What qualifications should a person have in order to be permitted to use test scores? To interpret test scores? To develop tests?

17. Indicate what is meant by "validity" and "reliability" of tests. Describe how measures of validity and reliability may be obtained.

18. Assume that a given test is revealed to possess only fair validity and reliability. Indicate what factors, other than the test itself, may be at fault.

19. In order to minimize misuse of tests, what advice would you underline in preparing a report to a company that is proceeding to install a new program?

20. Why are psychological tests, properly used, examples of scientific management?

| Transfers and Promotions

SCOPE OF TRANSFERS AND PROMOTIONS

Many vacancies are filled by internal movements of present employees. These movements are termed "transfers" and "promotions." The former term refers to changes in which the pay, privileges, and status of the new position are approximately the same as of the old. In the case of promotions, the new position commands higher pay, privileges, or status as compared with the old. The simplicity of these definitions belies the many difficulties that stand in the way of a good program of position changes and the undesirable results that flow from a poor program. Hence it is important to know the purposes of such programs, their operational aspects, their practical limitations, and the requirements of a good procedure of transfers and positions. Inasmuch as transfers and promotions have much in common, they will be considered here together. Since these subjects are also influenced by the factor of seniority, attention to this is also directed in this chapter.

PURPOSES

The primary purpose of a transfer or promotion is to increase the effectiveness of the organization in attaining its service and profit objectives. When an employee is placed in a position in which he can be most productive, chances for successful results of the organization for which he works are consequently increased. It should be the aim, therefore, of any company to change positions of employees as soon as their capacities increase and vacancies warrant. Unfortunately, this is not always done for reasons which will be noted later in this chapter. It is of interest to note here that failure to utilize the highest skills of employees sometimes becomes a matter of concern outside the company. During World War II, when such failures occurred, permission was granted employees to leave their jobs and secure employment where their highest skills would be utilized.

Another significant purpose of transfers and promotions is of a personal nature. Job changes provide an opportunity for present employees to move into jobs that provide greater personal satisfaction and prestige. Being transferred to a new job may open up new avenues of advancement or add the spice of variety to daily routines. Often, too, prestige is a factor, in that the person transferred is publicly recognized for his accomplishments. Of course, not all employees want to be transferred or promoted. Many like the assurance of a settled security, but most of them like to feel that opportunities for transfer or promotion are available.

OPERATIONAL ASPECTS

Transfer and promotion systems are either informal or formal. Under the informal plan decisions as to who should be transferred or promoted usually await the occurrence of a vacancy. Moreover, the bases upon which decisions are made vary from vacancy to vacancy and from time to time. As a consequence, no one knows what his status is or is likely to be under this system. However, it is simple, in that nothing is done about vacancies until they occur. Owing to this apparent simplicity, informal plans are undoubtedly used more frequently.

The informal plan gives way, as the losses in morale flowing from it become evident, to some formal statement of program and policy. The plan may simply be based upon seniority as the test for determining who shall be transferred or promoted; or it may involve a complete system of job analysis, merit rating, and filing of records. In this section, attention will be directed to the details of a more or less complete formal plan, and then seniority plans will be discussed.

As already suggested, a plan of transfers and promotions which pretends to be complete must contain the following:

1. A plan of job relationships
2. A plan and policy for selecting appropriate employees
3. A plan of records and reports

PLAN OF JOB RELATIONSHIPS

The basic step in building a plan of transfer and promotion is that of determining the horizontal and vertical relations between jobs. Thus for each job a schedule must be provided, first, of the jobs to which transfers may be made and, second, to which promotions may be made.

Job analysis is an indispensable tool for securing the information upon which such determinations can be made. It provides information on the skill, experience, training, responsibility, and environmental factors involved in each job. When such information has been obtained,

FIGURE 40

JOB SPECIFICATION

Job Title: <u>MOLDING MACHINE OPERATOR</u>   Department: <u>MAKE-UP</u>

EMPLOYEE QUALIFICATIONS

MALE: <u>X</u>   FEMALE: <u>   </u>   ENGLISH S: <u>X</u>   R: <u>X</u>   W: <u>X</u>   Race: <u>W</u>

EDUCATION: Public<u>   </u>   High<u>   X   </u>   or Baker's<u>   </u>

EXPERIENCE: 2 months Pan Greaser and Molding Machine Helper.

PHYSICAL REQUIREMENTS: No contagious or venereal disease; pass physical examination of food handler; normal eyesight.

MISCELLANEOUS: Worker must be careful, honest, co-operative, dependable, and alert. Must have fine sense of touch and good memory. Must have ability to move hands rapidly and skillfully to twist pieces of dough.

CONDITION OF WORK

Machine<u>   X   </u>   Hand<u>   </u>   Heavy<u>   </u>   Light<u>   </u>   Medium<u>   X   </u>

Stand<u>   X   </u>   Sitting<u>   </u>   Stooping<u>   </u>   Hazard<u>   X   </u>

Rough<u>   X   </u>   Accurate<u>   </u>   Inside<u>   X   </u>   Outside<u>   </u>

Dusty<u>   X   </u>   Hot<u>   X   </u>   Cold<u>   </u>   Dirty<u>   </u>   Greasy<u>   </u>

Quick<u>   X   </u>   Slow<u>   </u>   Humid<u>   </u>   Sticky<u>   X   </u>

Miscellaneous:

EMPLOYEE INFORMATION

RATE OF PAY: 70c hr.; time and ½ for overtime.
HOURS OF WORK: 8-hr. day, 48-hr. week, Sunday to Friday; longer hours overtime.
WORK SHIFT: 1 P.M. to 9 P.M.
VACATION: One year, one week; five years, two weeks.
PROMOTIONS: May be promoted to Divider Man.
    May be promoted from Pan Greaser and Molding Machine Helper.
    May be transferred to Cake Baker apprentice or Wrapping Machine Helper.
PERSONAL EFFECTS REQUIRED: White uniform, hat, and apron.

DUTIES

1. Under general supervision of Divider Man to properly mold all bread into cylindrical form.
2. To uniformly twist pieces of dough together.
3. To put into pans twisted pieces of dough.
4. Supervise Pan Greaser and Molding Machine Helper to see that proper types and amount of pans are greased prior to beginning of run and to see that panned bread is properly racked.

study of jobs can be undertaken to determine which jobs are related horizontally and vertically. How this task is made easy by job analysis is illustrated by the job specification shown in Figure 40 (p. 209). Based upon job analyses, this specification of a selected job in a mechanized bakery shows immediately, among other things, that a molding machine operator may be promoted to a divider man. Furthermore, the lines of promotion to the operator's job are also noted. On the other hand, when it comes to transfers, the operator may be moved to a cake-baker helper or wrapping machine helper.

FIGURE 41.   A Progression Chart*

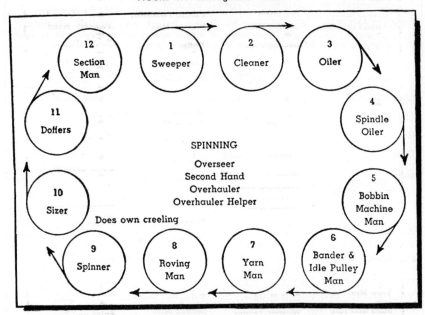

* Source: "Training New Employees Quickly," *Textile World*, July, 1943, p. 60.

It should be noted that such job studies do not imply that the lines of transfer and promotion are unbending. If it happens that a particular person filling a given job has the qualifications, as often happens, to jump into another line of transfer or promotion, this should be permitted. However, this is a matter of personal qualifications and does not destroy the validity of natural job relationships.

When job relationships have been fully explored in this manner, it is desirable to construct a promotion chart and sometimes a transfer chart. Samples of charts of related jobs are shown in Figures 41, 42, and 43. Such diagrams may appear to be complicated, but study of them quickly provides an answer regarding the jobs to which promotions or transfers can be made. Moreover, such charts are superior to the unde-fined images of job relationships that exist merely in the minds of executives, on the one hand, and subordinates, on the other. There can

FIGURE 42. Upgrading Sequence Chart for Job Classifications
in a Cotton Textile Plant*

Carding:			Weaving:
Section Hand			Loom Fixer
↑			↑
Card Grinder	Upgrading sequence		Weaver
↑	chart for job classifications in		↑
Card Tender	a cotton textile plant.		Tying-on Warps
↑			↑
Card Stopper			Laying-up Warps
Slubber Hand and Fly Frame Tender	Spooling:	Filling Twisting:	↑
	Section Man	Section Man	Pick-out Hand
↑	↑	↑	↑
Can Turner	Section Man Helper	Doffer	Smash Hand
↑	↑	↑	↑
Transfer Hand	Spooler Hand	Creeler	Battery Hand
	↑	↑	↑
Draw Frame Tender	Yarn Man	Filling Helper	Taking-off Cloth
	↑		↑
Oiler	Piece Rocker		Filling Hauler
	↑	Slashing:	↑
	Yarn Cleaner	Section Man	Oiler
	↑	↑	↑
	Tailing Machine Hand	Slasher Tender	Cloth Hauler
		↑	↑
		Size Man	Loom Blower
	Warp Twisting, Warping and Winding:	↑	↑
Spinning:		Slasher Helper	Loom Cleaner
Fixer and Section Man	Section Man	↑	↑
	↑	Beam Man	Overhead Cleaner
Doffer	Twister Tender		Baling, Trading, Burling:
↑	↑	Beaming:	Folder Hand
Sizer	Twister Creeler	Beamer Tender	↑
↑	↑	↑	Brander and Sewer
Spinner	Twister Doffer	Beamer Helper	↑
↑	↑		Press Booker
Roving Man	Oiler		↑
↑	↑	Drawing-in and Tying-in:	Head Pressman
Yarn Man	Reel Hand	Section Man	↑
↑	↑	↑	Press Helper
Band and Idle Pul. Man	Warper Tender	Drawing-in Hand	↑
↑	↑	↑	Baler and Sewer
Spindle Oiler	Warper Helper	Drawing-in Helper	↑
↑	↑	↑	Grader
Oiler	Warper Creeler	Tying-in Operator	↑
↑	Winder Tender	↑	Remnant Hand
Cleaner	↑	Tying-in Helper	↑
	Winder Holper		Calender Hand
			↑
			Burler

* Source: "Training New Employees Quickly," *Textile World,* July, 1943, p. 60.

be much room for disagreement in the latter system of establishing job relationships.

SELECTING CANDIDATES FOR PROMOTION

The next important step in building a transfer and promotion plan is that of determining which employees are worthy of consideration when vacancies occur. The significance of this step, at least to the employees, simply cannot be overestimated. After all, in their eyes, this is the crucial test of the company's transfer and promotion plan. Hence every care should be exercised to select the best-qualified employees and to be prepared to justify the selections should any questions be raised. Where a union is involved, some agreement will usually be reached regarding

FIGURE 43. Upgrading and Transfer Chart for Machine Shop and Tool Department

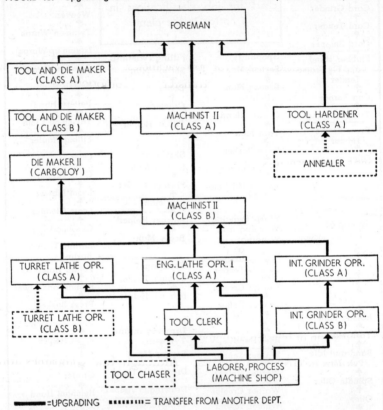

━━━━=UPGRADING ▪▪▪▪▪▪▪▪= TRANSFER FROM ANOTHER DEPT.

the relative weight to be given to merit and to seniority; this subject is discussed later in this chapter.

Perhaps the best plan in this connection is to have a good, over-all procedure of employee evaluations. The quantity and quality of various aspects of each employee's performance should be measured periodically. This evaluation should pertain not only to the output of work but also to intangible aspects of performance. For example, such factors as co-operation, ease of supervision, willingness to accept responsibility, ability to get along with others, and degree of initiative should be determined. This, of course, calls for some plan of merit rating, which subject is discussed in the next chapter.

The plan of employee evaluation should include an arrangement for consultation and perhaps vocational guidance. By discussing a person's strong points and weak points before vacancies occur, a two-edged weapon is employed. Those who are ambitious can get suggestions as to how they should seek to improve themselves. On the other hand, a record of such discussions can be cited to those who did not get a desired transfer and who failed to follow suggestions. In other words, by using the device of consultation, it is possible to forestall serious grievances by impressing upon the minds of employees what steps they must take to merit consideration for job vacancies. When discussions with employees take place only after transfers or promotions have not been received, it is difficult to convince the disgruntled employees that they were fairly treated. This is an illustration of the principle that, to be acceptable, standards should be discussed before as well as after use.

RECORDS AND REPORTS

A third important step in building a transfer and promotion plan is that of designing adequate records and reports. Unless procedures are available for keeping and relating information discussed in the first two steps, the equity and effectiveness of the plan will suffer. The system should include the following:

1. Forecasts of job vacancies
2. Central reporting of vacancies
3. Locating qualified employees
4. Notification of all parties concerned
5. Follow-up of transfers and promotions

1. FORECASTING VACANCIES. Although few companies follow the practice, it is highly useful to determine how many vacancies are likely to occur during coming periods on various jobs. When such forecasts are available, advance preparations can be made to find appropriate employees to fill them. As a consequence, the stability of the organization can be maintained. Moreover, a good picture of the number of possible vacancies will minimize the danger of "overselling" present employees on the possibilities of advancement. It is indeed destructive of morale when employees are led, consciously or unconsciously, to expect job changes that do not materialize.

Such forecasts are not too difficult to make, provided that records of turnover and expected plant operations are maintained. As noted in the chapter on "Manpower Requirements," it is then possible to estimate with a high degree of accuracy how many vacancies will have to be filled. For example, in a factory that has forty supervisors at present, turnover of supervisors has been 10 per cent annually and increases in production are expected to increase the supervisory force by 5 per cent; hence six vacancies will have to be filled in the supervisory ranks during the coming year. When information on vacancies is established in this manner, steps can be taken in advance to develop the needed number of replacements. Moreover, there will be a minimum error in the direction of overhiring at the lower levels. In other words, hiring at the lower levels should seek a proper proportion, but no more than needed, of promotable candidates.

Another effective way of forecasting vacancies is to show ages of executives on the organization chart. This can be done graphically by using different colors for different age groups; e.g., red for the ages 50 and over, orange for 40–49, blue for 30–39, green for 20–29, and brown for 19 and under. Such an organization chart will immediately show the general areas which may be out of balance in terms of age groups and in which steps should be taken to provide for transfers or promotions. In what areas training of executives for transfer and promotion should be undertaken may also be disclosed.

2. REPORTING VACANCIES.   Central reporting of vacancies is an indispensable essential of a transfer and promotion procedure. Unless a specifically designated unit is informed of all vacancies, the inevitable will happen—vacancies will be filled from the outside rather than the inside. When this occurs, the confidence of employees in the promises of the company is destroyed. The procedure which suggests itself here is, first, to have all hiring done on a requisition basis and, second, for all requisitions to pass through the hands of a transfer and promotion section in the employment office. In this way, requisitions can be reviewed with an eye to filling vacancies from within before outside sources of supply are explored. This may result in some delay during rush periods, but it is a cost well worth paying when contrasted with the increased morale and decreased grievances which are brought about thereby.

3. LOCATING CANDIDATES.   Perhaps the type of record that is hardest to maintain in this connection is that of employees qualified and worthy of transfer or promotion. It is scarcely practical to operate a record of an indefinite number of qualifications. Hence the better plan is to keep a personal history record of each employee and then to devise some means of searching through the records to find the best candidates for particular vacancies when they occur. This is a formidable

task unless simplified methods of filing are employed. As an example, qualifications of each employee may be transcribed onto cards, which may be sorted mechanically or manually. Punched cards may be sorted

FIGURE 44. Employee Information Card

EMPLOYEE INFORMATION CARD

EMPLOYEE NO._____

NAME_____ ADDRESS_____ TOWN_____

DEPT _____ CODE ____ POSITION _____ CODE ____ EMP DATE _____

SEX = MALE ☐[1] FEMALE ☐[2] | COLOR = WHITE ☐[1] BLACK ☐[2] OTHER ☐[3] | DATE OF BIRTH_____

EMP STATUS = REG ☐[1] TEMP ☐[2] PART TIME ☐[3] CO·OP ☐[4] | RELIGION = PROT ☐[1] CATH ☐[2] OTHER ☐[3]

MARITAL STATUS = MARRIED ☐[1] SINGLE ☐[2] DIVORCED ☐[3] SEPARATED ☐[4] WIDOWED ☐[5]

NO DEP CHILDREN ☐[1] ☐[2] ☐[3] ☐[4] ☐[5] | RELATIVES IN CO = YES ☐[1] NO ☐[2] WHO_____

MILITARY SERVICE = WORLD WAR ONE ☐[1] WORLD WAR TWO ☐[1] BOTH ☐[1] OTHER ☐[1] RESERVE = YES ☐[1] NO ☐[2]

UNION = C.I.O. ☐[1] A.F.L. ☐[1] OTHER ☐[1] EMP·CLUBS = GASCO ☐[1] THREE STAR ☐[1] OTHER ☐[1] VETERANS ☐[1]

EXPERIENCES OR SKILLS = CLERICAL ☐[1] MECHANICAL ☐[1] SALES ☐[1] SUPERVISORY ☐[1] OTHER ☐[1]

SPECIAL TRAINING = DEPARTMENTAL ☐[1] J.R.T. ☐[1] J.I.T. ☐[1] J.M.T ☐[1] OTHER ☐[1]

ACCIDENTS = LOST TIME ☐[1] ☐[2] ☐[3] ☐[4] ☐[5] AUTO ☐[1] ☐[2] ☐[3] ☐[4] ☐[5] OTHER ☐[1] ☐[2] ☐[3] ☐[4] ☐[5] ☐[6] ☐[7] ☐[8]

COMPANY INSURANCE = YES ☐[1] NO ☐[2] HOSPITALIZATION = YES ☐[1] NO ☐[2] CREDIT UNION MEMBER = YES ☐[1] NO ☐[2]

ABSENTEEISM = DAYS = ☐[001] ☐[002] ☐[003] ☐[004] ☐[005] ☐[006] ☐[007] ☐[008] ☐[009] ☐[010] ☐[011] ☐[012] ANY NO._____

PUNCH CARD OPERATIONS COMPLETED DATE _____ OPERATOR _____

SEPARATION INFORMATION

RESIGNED		IN GENERAL	YES[1]	DOUBTFUL[2]	NO[3]
DISLIKED OUTSIDE WORK	0	WAS HIS WORK SATISFACTORY? ... .68			
DISLIKED INSIDE WORK	1	WOULD YOU REHIRE HIM? ... .69			
DISLIKED SUPERVISOR	2	DID HE WORK OUT TWO WKS NOTICE? ... 70			
DISLIKED FELLOW EMPLOYEE	3	DOES MAN AGREE WITH THE REASONS			
DISLIKED RATE OF PAY	4	REPORTED AS TO HIS SEPARATION? ... 71			
DISLIKED WORKING CONDITIONS	5	COULD THIS SEPARATION HAVE BEEN AVOIDED? 72			
DISLIKED TYPE OF WORK	6	DID HE LEAVE OUR COMPANY			
DISLIKED PROMOTIONAL OPPORTUNITIES	7	FOR ANOTHER JOB? ... 73			
BECAUSE OF LACK OF PROPER TOOLS	8	WAS HIS ATTITUDE TOWARD THE			
OTHER REASONS WHAT? ____		COMPANY GOOD WHEN HE LEFT? ... 74			
____	9	WOULD YOU RECOMMEND HIM TO			

RELEASED		ANOTHER COMPANY? ... 75			
LACK OF WORK	00	IF NOT WHY?____			
DISHONEST	01	____			
INTOXICATION	02	____			
LOAF OR SLEEP ON JOB	03	____			
INADAPTABILITY	04	GENERAL COMMENTS____			
DESTRUCTION TO COMPANY PROPERTY	05	____			
DISLOYAL TO COMPANY	06	____			
LOST INTEREST IN JOB	07	____			
UNSAFE PRACTICES	08	____			
WOULD NOT FOLLOW INSTRUCTIONS	09	____			
WOULD NOT ACCEPT RESPONSIBILITIES	10	____			
OUTSIDE DISTRACTIONS	11	____			
OTHER REASON = EXPLAIN ____					
____	12				

mechanically by means of tabulating equipment, or through manual methods as illustrated in Figures 29 and 30 (pp. 153 and 154). Figure 44 illustrates one that may be sorted manually. By such means, it is possible to determine quickly whether any employees with the necessary qualifications are available to meet the specifications called for by specific job vacancies.

Of course, a record should also be maintained of employees who specifically request or are recommended by their superiors for transfer or promotion.

Another method of locating candidates is that of "job posting." Under this method, notice of vacancies is posted on bulletin boards and on the time clock or is announced through the company newspaper or some other form of communication. Such posting may be limited to the department or division in which the vacancy occurs, or it may be posted on a company-wide basis. The notice may be posted for some limited time; e.g., a week or ten days, or it may remain posted until the job is filled, no matter how much time is needed. This practice of posting has grown out of union desires that present employees be given an opportunity to bid on good jobs before outsiders are given a chance at them.

4. AUTHORIZATIONS AND NOTIFICATIONS. Another important aspect of a procedure of transfers and promotions is that of proper authorizations and notifications. On the one hand, the central unit responsible for locating qualified workers should not be permitted to initiate transfers of its own accord. It should request superiors of qualified employees to authorize a recommendation or approval of transfer. This may require some "selling" on the part of the personnel department, but it is effort well worth while. Then, too, the personnel department should be ready to suggest replacements to the superior involved. If these things are done, there usually will be little difficulty in operating such a plan after its initial stages. After all, those who lose good men will also gain others.

On the other hand, a system of notifying all those interested should be provided. The employee selected is usually best informed by his own superior. In that way, line authority is not divided. In addition, subordinates are impressed favorably by executives who show signs of looking after the interests of employees. The new superior under whom the employee is to work should be notified by the personnel department, so that his approval may be obtained. In this way, the staff position of the personnel department does not intrude upon the authority of the department served. And, finally, notices of the change should go to the payroll department, personal history section of the personnel department, and any other sections that keep records of employees.

5. FOLLOW-UP. The final step of a good transfer and promotion plan is that of follow-up. It is well to determine how well the job

change has taken effect. Are the employee and the superior satisfied with the change? By means of a regular follow-up, say a month or two after the change, a brief interview with both parties would suffice to determine whether all is going well or whether some form of corrective action is in order. This form of follow-up is similar to that which is recommended for new employees. After all, the transferred employee is a new employee in his new job, even though he is an old employee to the company. Hence it is desirable to determine the correctness of the job placement in these cases, too. Some companies allow the follow-up to come from the employee himself in the form of a grievance or complaint. This practice assumes that all employees will complain if they are not satisfied, which is not always true. Moreover, it places upon the employee the responsibility for a function that is largely managerial; and management should not shirk its responsibilities.

REQUIREMENTS OF A GOOD PLAN

From what has been said thus far, it can be seen that there are a number of tests which can be applied to determine whether or not a transfer and promotion plan is a good one. In the first place, the purposes of the plan should be definitely understood. It should, on the one hand, contribute to the attainment of the company's service objectives; and, on the other hand, it should make possible for ambitious and qualified employees the attainment of personal goals for advancement in pay, prestige, and privileges, or placement in desired working conditions. This twofold set of objectives should be recognized and their attainment encouraged.

In the second place, the procedures and organization structure by which the objectives of the plan are to be attained should be carefully worked out. This should begin with a careful estimate of future vacancies in various jobs; then there must be a study of jobs to determine the relationships which exist between jobs. Also, a plan for selecting appropriate employees should be established, which usually means some form of merit rating. Then, too, records and reports, upon which the information of transfers and promotions may be kept, should be designed. Finally, responsibility for the execution of the plan should be placed definitely upon some organization unit, preferably the personnel department.

In the third place—and this has only been hinted at thus far—a plan can be called good only if it has the co-operation of the superiors in giving up employees qualified for transfer and promotion. After all, it takes real understanding for a superior to agree to the loss of an employee who is doing an excellent job in his unit. The effectiveness of his own organization unit is bound to decrease, for the time being, because it is scarcely possible that the replacement will be as effective as the displaced employee. And when work is at a high-pressure stage, the reluctance to give up proved employees can readily be understood.

Hence such reluctance must be overcome. The only lasting solution is to prove to those who lose good employees that they will gain by the loss. Two types of arguments are available. First, arguing negatively, an executive who stands in the way of transfers or promotions will soon become notorious for it, and the best employees will, if at all possible, keep clear of his department. As a consequence, the effectiveness of his department is bound to suffer. Second, arguing positively, a department that gains a reputation for good transfers and promotions attracts the better workers and hence has, by that factor, a higher effectiveness. Or, put in other words, a test of an executive is the quality of his subordinates; and this in turn depends in part upon the opportunities in his department.

Finally, a test of any plan is the confidence which employees have in its fairness and equity. If the promises of transfers and promotions are greater than the fulfillments or if the most deserving employees are not selected, confidence of employees in it will not be gained. Without this ingredient, the objectives of the plan cannot be obtained, because the reward of job betterment is not available to motivate employees. Hence great care should be exercised to see that promises are met and the best workers rewarded. Moreover, interviews backed with facts should be had with any employees who feel that they were not dealt with fairly in particular transfers or promotions. If these precautions are heeded, there should be no reason for employees to lose faith in the plan.

LIMITATIONS

Whether or not, and to what extent, a transfer and promotion plan can be put into operation depends upon a number of factors. Obviously, there must be sufficient vacancies to warrant investments in an involved plan. That is why a small company or one in which turnover is very low would be foolish to waste time and resources on a formal plan. The objectives to be gained would not be worth the effort.

If there is danger of "inbreeding," a plan of filling the better positions from within should not be adopted. In organizations where new ideas, initiative, and originality rate a premium, outside hirings are to be preferred. Otherwise, replacements are bound to be made with employees who know little more, if any, than those whom they replaced. The result is bound to be unsatisfactory in a highly competitive situation.

Again, a plan of transfers and promotions should be circumscribed if satisfactory horizontal and vertical job relationships cannot be readily established. Thus, where jobs in a factory or office differ radically, it may not be possible to establish job sequences which make it possible for a candidate to progress readily from one job to another. In such cases, a plan of training must be established so that those who deserve transfers or promotions can be prepared for job changes.

Perhaps the most serious limitation upon transfer and promotion plans arises out of the difficulty of measuring the over-all qualifications of employees. When such factors as quantity and quality of output, cooperation, acceptance of responsibility, and aptitude to progress must be measured and weighed together, the task is time-consuming and difficult. Moreover, those who are affected by the results of such measurements many not be able to understand the methods of measurement. As a result, many companies, when not forced by outside pressures, have themselves sought a plan which, though not as accurate, is simpler, quicker, and more readily understood by their employees. The choice is usually some measure of length of service, which is discussed more fully later in this chapter.

Another limitation comes from the objection of some unions to the use of plans other than seniority in determining priorities of transfers and promotions and, for that matter, demotions and layoffs. Anticipating later discussion, the position taken by some unions in favor of seniority is readily understandable. For one thing, one can scarcely argue about such a definite matter as the date on which an employee started to work with the company. On the other hand, merit ratings and interpretations of the relative abilities of employees to advance are subject to some debate, even when the best of systems is employed. So the unions cannot be blamed for refusing to embroil itself in such arguments. For another thing, though less justifiable, there are the traditional arguments, which some unions still uphold, that all employees in a given occupation or unit of work are to be treated alike. If individual differences were recognized, this would lead to arguments within the union itself. This internal debate would weaken the solidarity of the union's bargaining power with the company. Hence it is more sensible for the union to forego theoretical accuracy in order to enhance membership solidarity.

SENIORITY

Inasmuch as length of service is a governing factor in matters of transfers and promotions in many companies, its discussion here is appropriate. However, it is also of significance in collective bargaining, relations with returned veterans, and such matters as vacations and wages, in which connection it will be mentioned later. Hence it is pertinent to examine its meaning, methods, and policies of application and usage, as well as its advantages and disadvantages.

Seniority may be defined as the practice of basing employment privileges upon length of service. This simple definition belies many points that must be clarified if the seniority principle is to be employed with a minimum of trouble. First, it is important to indicate the conditions under which seniority is accumulated. Provisions must be incorporated covering the effect of absences, layoffs, leaves of absence, and other temporary breaks in service. Second, it is necessary to define the extent to which seniority will govern employment privileges. Rarely is seniority given complete control in such matters. Hence its weight as compared with merit and ability to perform work should be specified. Third, the employment privileges affected by seniority should be specifically defined. As noted in the foregoing paragraph, there may be several of these. And, fourth, it is highly significant to define the area of a company within which seniority of a given employee is effective. Thus for some factors it may be company-wide, and for others it may be restricted to departmental borders. These matters will be expanded in the following pages.

1. APPLICATION AND USAGE. The method of calculating length of service is an important part of a seniority plan. It should provide for the following factors: first, when seniority starts to accumulate; second, effect of various interruptions to employment; and, third, the effect of transfers and promotions upon seniority calculation.

a) Accumulating Seniority. When there are no outside factors involved, seniority begins to accumulate as soon as an employee is hired. This should be specifically stated, particularly when a company undertakes collective bargaining. Otherwise, there is a possibility that the seniority of employees hired before a contract goes into effect may be dated from the date of the contract. Also in the case of union contracts, it is important to note whether or not new employees have seniority rights during their period of probation and whether or not the probationary period will be included in the calculation of seniority. Again, where large numbers of employees are hired on the same date, a question of seniority may arise unless a basis for priority is established. In such instances, priority may be established upon such an arbitrary basis as order of clock numbers assigned or upon an agreement between union and management officials.

b) Interruptions to Service. After seniority begins to accumulate, there are a number of interruptions to service for which provision should be made. Ordinarily, interruptions that are due to the company's actions or are relatively short are customarily not deducted in calculating seniority. For example, time off for short personal absences, layoffs, and sick leaves are included in seniority accumulations. However, extended leaves of absence, layoffs beyond designated periods of time, and extended sick leaves are often deducted in computing seniority. These aspects of calculating seniority will not cause difficulty so long as they are recognized and provided for.

c) Job Changes and Seniority. More difficult to handle is the effect of transfers and promotions upon seniority calculations. Unless these matters are taken into account, some serious problems will be encountered. For example, workers may be unwilling to accept or may even refuse transfers if the change means a loss of seniority. Or workers who have been promoted to a supervisory position and later demoted have sometimes found themselves at the bottom of a seniority list. Except in a few industries, such as the building trades, where the seniority of foremen is protected, the seniority status of supervisors and transferees is not protected traditionally unless specifically stated by company policy or union agreement. Hence it is desirable, when questions of this type are likely to arise, to specify what the seniority privileges will be. Perhaps the fairest provision is to allow demoted supervisors the seniority they had before the promotion took place. In the case of transferees, it would seem fair to allow them to retain their seniority if they return to their old jobs and to have some measure of adjusted seniority if they remain on their new jobs. Otherwise, only the most adventuresome will be willing to transfer.

Exemptions from seniority rules may also be desirable for technical and professional employees and for trainees. In order to avoid discriminatory practices in connection with such groups, unions sometimes require that the number of exempted employees must be limited to some percentage of nonexempted groups. In any event, to prove its fairness to all employees, it is well for management to define specifically exempt jobs and positions and restrict the conditions under which the exemptions shall apply.

2. MERIT VERSUS SENIORITY. A second important part of any seniority plan is the matter of balancing seniority in relation to merit. This will occasion much debate unless carefully defined. It might seem

that a statement such as the following would be clear and fair: "As between two employees with equal ability, the one with the greater seniority will be given preference." Unfortunately, in the event of disagreement, the employer or executive involved may permit his opinion of ability to outweigh seniority, whereas the employee or his union representative may stress the seniority far above ability. Although the element of personal opinion will always be of significance, it is nevertheless important to specify whether ability and seniority will have equal weight or whether one or the other will be given greater weight. Usually, in smaller companies, the merit factor will weigh more heavily; but, in the larger companies, particularly where unions have a strong voice, seniority is given greater weight.

The extent to which a company can logically work out a plan balancing merit and seniority will depend upon a number of factors. First, a set of job and man specifications should be carefully prepared so that claimants for jobs can be shown that requirements are objective and not capricious. Second, a complete and thoroughly understood transfer and promotion plan should be promulgated. Third, a good system of employee merit rating should be installed. This system is best developed with the approval of the union, and ratings under it should be subject to some set plan of review. Fourth, performance standards should be set as objectively as possible so that measurements of employee productivity and co-operation may be more readily acceptable by all. And, lastly, a well-thought-out grievance procedure should be established which is acceptable to employees and to the union if employees are so represented. These requirements are not easily met; until they are, there is little use in arguing for merit in place of seniority. Merit must be measurable, or its proponents have built their house of arguments upon sand.

EMPLOYMENT PRIVILEGES AFFECTED

The relative weight that seniority will have upon various classes of employment privileges also should be carefully defined. For example, it may be completely controlling in such matters as length of vacations and choice of vacation periods; or it may be controlling in choice of work periods, shifts, or runs in the case of transportation services. On the other hand, it may be only partly controlling in such matters as transfers and promotions. Similarly, in the matter of discharges and layoffs, seniority may be given part or total weight. In any event, the effect upon these employment aspects should be considered individually if disagreements are to be minimized.

Moreover, how seniority shall apply in each class must also be determined. For example, limitations must be placed on senior employees who replace or "bump" junior employees. Senior employees may be required within a given period of time to demonstrate that they can competently perform the jobs of employees they bump, or junior employees may be protected if they hold special types of jobs or if they have been with the company after a specified number of years.

On "recall" of employees after a production layoff, seniority rules vary. In some companies no "new" employees may be hired until all "available" laid-off employees are recalled. In other cases the company may have some discretion in hiring new employees as compared to lay-offs. In addition, the sequence of recalling seniority employees should be carefully indicated in terms of area of work to which their seniority applies and in terms of its importance relative to merit.

On all other aspects of employment privileges, the foregoing examples will suggest the need for specifying the influence of seniority.

AREA OF APPLICATION

Finally, the application of the seniority principle should give consideration to the area to which it applies. For example, it is unwise to give seniority company-wide application in such matters as transfers. The result, otherwise, will be that workers unqualified for vacancies will nevertheless apply for them if they have company-wide seniority. Hence it is important to select carefully the area over which, or the occupations within which, seniority of given classes of employees will apply.

The usual areas of application are the department, the occupation (the "family" classification), or company-wide. No one of these of itself is without disadvantages. As noted above, the company-wide plan unduly favors the senior employee who wants to bump more qualified employees in departments outside the immediate experience of the senior employee. In the case of departmental plans, very capable and key employees may be lost because they cannot replace less qualified employees with less service in other departments. And the occupational plan may be affected by the disadvantages of the departmental or company-wide plan, depending upon how narrow or wide the "job family" in a given occupation happens to be.

To minimize disadvantages arising out of seniority areas, it may be desirable to establish restrictive rules. For example, company-wide seniority may be applied to all unskilled and semiskilled jobs; departmental seniority may be applied to skilled jobs; and occupational seniority may be applied to certain highly specialized classifications. Another restrictive rule, of course, is that of applying merit qualifications to such seniority areas.

SUMMARY

In summary, the seniority plan of determining employment changes has the advantage of apparent simplicity in its favor. However, as may be deduced from the foregoing discussion, extreme care must be exercised in writing the seniority clauses; otherwise troubles will arise that may be more bothersome than those that had been hoped to be avoided. The major disadvantage of the seniority plan is that merit and ability tend to receive a minor place in reaching employment decisions. As a consequence, this places another hindrance in developing better workmanship. This is particularly true of the younger worker, who finds it useless to exert himself because only time will push him up the ladder of privilege and position. Unless more definite and acceptable methods of calculating ability and merit are applied, however, seniority may be expected to retain, if not to gain, a higher place as a tool for measuring employment preferences.

QUESTIONS AND PROBLEMS

1. How do you think an organization chart showing the age range of executives would be received by the executives? If they objected, what would your course of action be if you thought such a chart was desirable to point out future personnel needs at the upper levels?
2. What plan can you suggest to keep "job postings" from becoming out of date? From being overlooked? From being posted too long?
3. If any company in your community is using "job posting," ask one of their executives how the plan is working out. If a union is involved, try to get their opinions, too. How do the two sets of opinions agree?
4. When an employee is transferred or promoted to a new job, how long would you give him to prove himself? Check your estimates with industry practices in your community.
5. What must be done to distinguish between actual skills that employees possess and their propensity to overvalue their abilities?
6. What are the relative merits of formal as compared with informal plans of transfer and promotion?
7. What values are contributed by a promotional chart to a plan of transfers and promotions?
8. Why is a good plan of employee evaluation so important in operating a transfer and promotion plan? Are employees likely to be more trustful of executives when a rating plan is in use?

9. Why is it desirable to adopt a program of counseling and vocational guidance in connection with a rating plan?

10. An employee is dissatisfied because he has not received a transfer that he considers should have been made. How would you go about convincing him that the right decision had been made?

11. Under what conditions would you advise against transfers and promotions as means for filling job vacancies?

12. Assume that a given supervisor is opposed to recommending transfers or promotions of his employees because he contends that he would thereby be faced with the task of replacing skilled workers with unskilled workers. What arguments would you give in rebuttal?

13. Who should initiate transfers and promotions? Why?

14. What tests would you use to determine the effectiveness of a program of transfers and promotions?

15. Why is there a tendency for unions to favor seniority over merit rating as a basis for determining who shall be given transfers or promotions?

16. Develop a plan for calculating length of service. To what factors must consideration be given in making such calculations?

17. Assume that an employee is promoted to a supervisory position. What recommendations would you make regarding the computation of seniority so that the individual in question would be protected if he later must be demoted?

18. Indicate the extent to which seniority should be weighted as compared to merit in relation to such matters as transfers, promotions, demotions, choice of vacation periods, and choice of working shifts.

19. Discuss the merits of seniority plans that are job-wide or apply to the "family of occupation" as opposed to those that are company-wide. What problems arise in each case?

20. What would be the merits, if any, of using merit rating for upward advancements and seniority for demotions, layoffs, and discharges?

12 | Merit Rating

RATING PROGRAMS

As noted in the preceding chapter, employment privileges are often dependent upon the merit of employees. It is appropriate, therefore, to examine plans of measuring merit. It should be noted that merit rating has other uses too, e.g., in counseling, training, compensation, and handling grievances and disciplinary matters.

Rating of employees is one of the oldest and most universal practices of management. There never was a time when executives and supervisors did not estimate the relative worth of employees, one to another. But it is only within recent years that rating has progressed from a highly personalized, indefinite, and esoteric status to a level of uniform, consistent, and studied practices. Such formalized plans, nonetheless, cannot be adopted without careful planning. Some managements have given up—or have been forced to give up—merit rating plans, in favor of the alternative, seniority programs, because merit rating fell into disrepute with the employees. Some defect in the plans, or in their use, led to their being discarded. The moral is that formal merit rating plans will not, in and of themselves, operate effectively. Hence, while it may be argued that formalized programs are superior to indefinite, personalized ratings, this argument assumes that the former are carefully designed and controlled.

In approaching this question of rating, a decision must be reached as to who is to be rated. Most companies at the outset rate only operative employees and exclude executive, professional, and technical groups. The need is greater among the former, while rating of the latter is also much more difficult. However, a good rating program should eventually encompass all employees of a company. The discussion in this chapter will give consideration to suggestions which are useful for all levels and categories of employees, but it will be devoted primarily to practices concerned with operative employees.

Rating programs are called by a variety of names. Most popular has been that of "merit rating." Some object to this term on the grounds that it smacks too much of school grading or that there is no connotation of progressiveness or constructiveness. Hence, such terms as "service rating," "progress rating," or "development rating" are preferred. Important as a good title may be for this program, much more significant, of course, are the uses to which such ratings are put and how they are made.

In this description of rating practices, the subject will be discussed under the following headings:

1. Objectives
2. Fundamental issues of rating
3. Design of rating forms
4. Rules of rating
5. Accuracy of ratings

OBJECTIVES OF RATING

Any of a number of objectives may be sought by means of rating programs. First and foremost is the simple objective of determining more accurately which employees should receive pay increases, which should be given transfers or promotions, and which should be given preferred status. Obviously, vacancies, for example, can be and are being filled in many companies without planned rating programs. The result invariably is unnecessary grievances, whether or not they are recognized by the company. Second, when disputes arise over such matters, the availability of a series of ratings (particularly if they have been discussed with the employees concerned) provides management with information that will help to satisfy the aggrieved persons. Third, from the viewpoint of management, supervisors and executives who know that they will be expected periodically to fill out rating forms (and be prepared to justify their estimates) will tend to be more observant of their subordinates and hence tend to become better day-to-day supervisors. Such improvements in supervision, in the fourth place, are more significant as companies attain a size which makes it impossible for the "head man" to know all the employees. Unless supervisors follow uniform rules of rating, the treatment received by all employees and the opportunities opened to them will not be consistent throughout the organization. And, lastly, a rating program recognizes the existence of individual differences and serves both the employees and the company by helping to place each employee in the job he is best suited for.

The practical application of these objectives may be seen in the list of purposes compiled by the National Industrial Conference Board in a survey of ninety-four companies:

1. To help in deciding who should be promoted, demoted, or given a raise in pay
2. To discover workers' weaknesses as a basis for planning training
3. To uncover exceptional talents
4. To furnish a basis for discharge of totally unfit employees
5. To help top supervisors learn how each person is appraised by his foreman
6. To help top supervisors judge the fairness, severity, or leniency with which supervisors judge their people
7. To help in assigning work in accordance with workers' ability
8. To serve as a check on employment procedures generally and interviews and tests specifically
9. To stimulate people to improve
10. To develop people's morale through stimulating confidence in management's fairness[1]

A rating plan need not encompass all these objectives. Indeed, by union agreement, it may be decided that merit shall have little or nothing to do with choosing candidates for transfer or promotion, let us say. Yet merit rating could serve as a basis for counseling employees about their strengths and weaknesses or in improving supervisory-employee relations. Thus employment of merit rating is justifiable, even though union agreements preclude its use for some purposes.

This discussion of objectives would be incomplete without the admonition that merit rating must not be used for purposes beyond its capacities. To be specific, some plans have been wrecked by using merit rating to grant general wage increases that really stemmed from labor market conditions and not relative individual merit. For example, a supervisor may know that a key employee is thinking of quitting to get more money elsewhere. The supervisor does not want to lose the employee. So he rates him much higher than he deserves in order to get him a wage increase. The "news" gets around, and soon others demand the same treatment. And the merit rating plan becomes a "used" rather than a useful tool. If general increases are called for, that is a matter of wage and salary policies. Misusing the merit rating plan for this purpose makes everyone a participant in a "crooked" game which leads to distrust of management and of other personnel policies.

---

[1] Reign Bittner, "Developing an Employee Merit Rating Procedure," *Personnel,* Vol. XXV, No. 4 (January, 1949), p. 277.

FUNDAMENTAL ISSUES OF RATING

Perhaps the best place to begin a description of merit rating is with the fundamental issues raised by rating. These include, first, the basic theory of rating; second, the bases of comparison involved in rating; and, third, the basic question of whether or not ratings should be discussed with employees.

1. BASIC THEORY OF RATING. As already indicated, rating is the act of estimating the relative worth of employees in order to determine the rewards, privileges, or advantages that should be given or withheld from each. One measure of relative worth is the contribution made by each employee. In simple form, this may be diagrammed as follows:

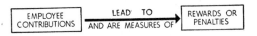

However, it is not always possible to measure employee contributions. Or, when it can be done, it nevertheless may be desirable to advise employees how their contributions may be increased. In such instances, it is necessary to ask: What is there about the individual that caused the contribution? For example, individual characteristics, instead of contributions, may be used as the basis of rewards and penalties, as shown in the following diagram:

Let us assume that Employees A and B receive 90 cents an hour on a given job and are being considered for raises. Their respective contributions to service objectives should be weighed because the contributions that anyone makes to the ultimate customers of a company are the justification for compensation. But if, in the first place, it is impossible to measure such contributions because an individual's work is intermixed with those of others, ratings may be made of the characteristics that caused the contributions. Or, second, if it is desired to tell each employee why his contributions are as they are, then a rating should be made of employee characteristics as the basis for such suggestions. Thus ratings may be made of employee contributions, such as quantity and quality of work, supervision required, responsibilities assumed, and influence upon the work of fellow employees. Or ratings may be made of employee characteristics, such as appearance, initiative, dependability, perseverance, and loyalty.

This distinction of what is measured is important. If it is not recognized, the mistake will be made, as many companies have, of including both characteristics and contributions on the same rating scale. On the other hand, if recognized, such duplication may be used to good purpose. The performance of employees may be compared with their personal qualities to determine whether or not performance is up to personal possibilities as indicated by the rating.

2. BASIS OF COMPARISON.   Another fundamental issue of rating concerns the bases of comparing personal characteristics or contributions. When it is said, for example, that Employee A is better than Employee B, is the comparison based upon—

1. The two employees relative to each other,
2. A and B as compared to other workers,
3. A and B as compared to an ideal worker, or
4. Arbitrary yardsticks of various factors?

Perhaps there is no more common method than that of comparing two or more people in a given situation. To be sure, this practice suffers from the lack of a common and unvarying standard, but it is simple. Hence some of the earliest attempts to rate employees were based upon a simple ranking of employees. The names of all employees were placed on cards, and the cards were sorted in order, from highest to lowest. While this method does not indicate the relative differences in employees and the rating depends upon who is on the payroll at a given time, it nevertheless is a step forward. At least the rater has put himself on record and is, therefore, likely to be more careful in his estimates.

However, this plan may be easily improved. Accuracy of ratings may be advanced by comparing all employees with selected employees who are considered to be representative of the best, above average, average, below average, and the poorest. In this way, an employee who rated "above average," for example, could be given a better impression of his relative worth than when he is told that he was twelfth, let us say, in a list of forty employees. This form of man-to-man rating may be improved in two ways. First, this may be done by using several factors of rating man to man. For example, an employee may be compared to a five-man standard in terms of such factors as initiative, co-operation, and dependability. These factor ratings are then arranged to establish an over-all grade. Second, instead of using actual employees as standards for best, above average, and so forth, ideal descriptions may be developed. This avoids changes in standards that occur when employees who have been used as models leave the department or company.

While some companies use refined systems of man-to-man rating plans, the trend has been toward plans in which measuring sticks of factors common to all employees are used. The measuring sticks may be descriptive or quantitative. Descriptive measuring sticks are those in which words are used to describe varying degrees of personal factors or contributions of employees. For example, Figure 45 (pp. 232–33), illustrates a form in which raters evaluate workers by checking appropriate items among the choices available. Quantitative measuring sticks may be arithmetical or graphical. In the arithmetical plan (Fig. 45), various factors to be rated are listed. Opposite each, the rater is required to write in a number or letter grade indicating the degree to which the employee being rated possesses it. In the graphical plan (Fig. 46, p. 234), lines, divided into various lengths to indicate degrees of contribution or personal characteristics, are used to aid the rater in making his decisions. The graphical method has gained in favor over other methods because qualitative differences are easier to visualize.

3. CONSULTATIONS WITH EMPLOYEES. Another important question is whether or not results of ratings should be discussed with employees. The decision not to do so may be reached for two reasons. First, some companies feel that rating discussions lead to needless controversy and recrimination. And, second, in connection with the forced-choice plan of rating, to be described later, it is necessary that the method of scoring the rater's evaluation be kept secret. On the other hand, most companies discuss ratings with employees as a regular practice or upon the request of employees. This policy is based upon the principle that interchange of information between employer and employee is the best way of uncovering and removing sources of irritation.

Although there may be occasions when ratings should be withheld from employees, it seems better to work toward a relationship of frank discussion between employer and employee. If grievances exist or if employees have shortcomings, they cannot be reduced or removed simply by waiting. Sooner or later the matters must be discussed. The question is one of timing: When is it most appropriate to open discussions? Of course, after a rating program has been installed, the first ratings will raise what appears to be a hornet's nest of controversy. Once these are cleared up, subsequent ratings will result in fewer controversies.

The periodicity of rating which most companies follow is indicative of the fact that ratings tend to reduce rather than increase disagreements. It is rather common to rate new employees more frequently than old. Thus in one company, new employees are rated after one month, three

FIGURE 45

FORM 6 850-3 e e D

EMPLOYEE PROGRESS REPORT

DISTRIBUTION-PLANT

Code No. **1-1-45**

Name of Employee __John Doe__   Position Title __Serviceman A__   Date _____   Report by __Frank Doe__

INSTRUCTIONS FOR RATING

Column No. 1 POST OPPOSITE each item, applicable weights determined on basis of following classification.

FOR ITEMS OF:

PRIMARY	importance to this position		3
SECONDARY	"	" "	2
MINOR	"	" "	1

Column No. 2 After weights have been posted in column No. 1, use scale "A" to determine how employee rates with respect to each item in Part I and post in column 2. Use scale "B" on reverse side for rating Work Performed by the employee in Part II after consideration to aids and handicaps to performance.

Column No. 3 Multiply weights in column No. 1 by scale ratings in column No. 2 and post resultant point ratings in column No. 3.

(Show totals of items "1" to "4", "5" to "8" and "9" "13" in spaces indicated)

PART I

PERSONAL QUALIFICATIONS

	SCALE "A"					RATING COLUMNS		
	1	2	3	4	5	1	2	3
	Does not meet requirements of this position	Partially meets requirements of this position	Meets requirements of this position	Exceeds requirements of this position	Far exceeds requirements of this position	Weight this position	Scale A rating	Point rating (Weight X Scale rating)
1. APPEARANCE	Consider Physical Appearance, Carriage, Dress.					3	3	9
2. MANNERS & DISPOSITION	Consider Courtesy; Tact; Adherence to Business and Social Customs; Poise; Self Control; Temperament (Pleasant, Even, Surly).					3	4	12

Item			
3. CHARACTER — Consider Dependability; Sense of Social and Moral Responsibility; Sincerity; Courage of Conviction.	3	3	9
4. INFLUENCE ON OTHERS — Consider Degree of Animation; Enthusiasm; Power of Expression (Speech · Writing); Sales Ability.	3	3	9
I-A PERSONALITY (Total of items 1 to 4) - - - - - - - - - -	12		39
5. IMAGINATION — Consider Powers of Mental Visualization; Inventiveness.	2	3	6
6. CONCENTRATION — Consider Thinking Power; Ability to Focus and Apply Full Mental Power Effectively.	3	3	9
7. COMPREHENSION AND JUDGEMENT — Consider Ability to Grasp and Understand Principles, Ideas, Facts; Consider Mental Alertness, Speed of Reactions; Power of Analysis; Ability to Reason and Reach Logical Conclusions.	3	3	9
8. MENTAL FLEXIBILITY — Consider Adaptability to Changes, New Problems, New Ideas; Open Mindedness; Receptivity to Suggestions and Ideas.	3	2	6
I-B INTELLIGENCE (Total of items 5 to 8) - - - - - - - - -	11		30
9. INITIATIVE AND ORGANIZING ABILITY — Consider Self Starting Energy; Ability to Plan and Carry Out Work Systematically.	3	3	9
10. COORDINATIVE ABILITY — Consider Ability to Understand, Analyse and Define Objectives; To Work Towards a Common End in Harmony with Others. Attitude Toward Other Employees, Work and Company Policies.	3	3	9
11. ACCEPTANCE OF RESPONSIBILITY — Consider Ability to Understand Assignments Clearly and Perform Them At Once.	3	3	9
12. QUALITY OF WORK — Consider Quality of Work Performed.	3	3	9
13. QUANTITY OF WORK — Consider Quantity of Work Performed.	3	3	9
APPLICATION ON JOB (Total of items 9 to 13) - - - - - - -	15		45

FIGURE 46

EMPLOYEE PROGRESS RATING

NAME OF EMPLOYEE _____

POSITION TITLE AND LINE NO. _____

REPORT BY _____ Date _____

DEPARTMENT _____

LENGTH OF SERVICE: 1. ON THIS JOB _____   2. WITH COMPANY _____

PREVIOUS RATING _____

GRADING SCALE

Factor	40	50	60	70	80	90	
1. QUANTITY OF EMPLOYEE'S OWN WORK — How much work does this employee complete as compared with other employees who are doing or have done similar work?	More than 33% under average output. Cannot or does not keep up to acceptable minimums of output. New on job	From 10 to 33% under average output. Works slowly or in short spurts, but produces enough to get by. New on job	Actual output equals output expected after normal training and experience.	From 10 to 33% above average output. Does more than his share. Works rapidly and consistently.	Over 33% above average output. Recognized as top worker. Consistently top performance.		□ × □ = □ Rating Weight Factor Score
2. QUALITY OF EMPLOYEE'S OWN WORK — How well is work performed? Consider here the degree of completeness or the number of errors, mistakes and rejection.	More than 33% under quality average. Workmanship very poor. Output has an excess of unacceptable units. New on job	From 10 to 33% under average quality. Quality is occasionally poor and unacceptable. New on job	Quality of work equals that expected after normal training and experience.	From 10 to 33% fewer errors than average. Covers almost all details of work thoroughly.	Over 33% better quality than average. Does a complete and thorough job in all respects.		□ × □ = □ Rating Weight Factor Score
3. INFLUENCE UPON THE WORK OF FELLOW-WORKERS — How does this employee affect directly the output of fellow-workers?	Reduces output of others very much. Is surly or inconsiderate, upsets morale, and makes trouble. Can't seem to cooperate.	Reduces output of others somewhat. Visits or gossips excessively. Plays practical jokes. Or just fails to click with others.	Neither improves nor harms output of others. Fits in without hindrance Co-operates as requested.	Works helpfully and pleasantly with others. Tones up work. Cooperates on own initiative.	Brings out the best in others. Helps and teaches others willingly. A strong force for good morale.		□ × □ = □ Rating Weight Factor Score
4. INFLUENCE UPON THE ATTITUDE OF OUTSIDERS — How does this employee affect directly the attitude which customers or other outsiders have toward the company?	Often antagonizes others. Personal appearance, manners, habits, or language are annoying. Often complained about. New on job	Occasionally antagonizes others. Lacks tact or a desire to be helpful. Occasionally complained about.	Does work impersonally and meets people with unimpressive politeness. Rarely criticized or complimented by outsiders.	Has sincere interest in others and shows it. Usually makes them feel at ease and satisfied.	Invariably impresses others with work, manners, and attitude of helpfulness. Very often complimented		□ × □ = □ Rating Weight Factor Score
5. TECHNICAL SUPERVISION REQUIRED — How much instruction does this employee require? How often must this employee be checked on the technicalities of his work?	Must be instructed and followed-up often. Very easily confused. Slow in grasping the obvious. New on job	Understands only simplest routines, must be checked on others. Sometimes confused. Overly cautious. New on job	Handles routine jobs without training or supervision. Needs help on more difficult tasks.	Handles routine jobs and some difficult jobs on his own. Needs help on some difficult jobs.	Very skilled and resourceful. Can work on all jobs without supervision. Very keen and quick to understand.		□ × □ = □ Rating Weight Factor Score
6. HUMAN SUPERVISION REQUIRED — How much supervisory attention does this employee require • personal point of view?	A problem employee. Has groundless grievances. Disciplined frequently. Supervised more or less constantly.	Must be prodded at times. Stays in a rut. Resents suggestions. Has little enthusiasm.	Cooperates as instructed. Neither dull nor overly reliant. Makes no trouble. Seldom complains or disciplined	Needs very little attention. Can be stimulated easily. Makes no trouble. Accepts personal advice and suggestions.	Very loyal and reliable. Works harmoniously with supervisor. Never nags or causes any trouble. Self starter.		□ × □ = □ Rating Weight Factor Score
7. USE OF COMPANY RESOURCES AND PROPERTIES — How efficiently and carefully does this employee utilize safe-guard machines, tools, materials, supplies, or other properties?	Consistently misuses materials, tools and machines, extremely careless and inefficient. New on job	Occasionally misuses materials, tools, and other properties. Sometimes careless. New on job	Care in use equals that expected after normal training and experience. Neither noticeably careful nor careless	Seldom wastes or misuses materials or tools. Obviously careful with supplies and equipment.	Does work with a minimum of waste or damage. Handles tools and materials with craftsman's ability		□ × □ = □ Rating Weight Factor Score
8. FUTURE POSSIBILITIES OF THIS EMPLOYEE — Does this employee have potentialities for future growth? What skills, or aptitudes that can be utilized in the future?	Lacks interest, ambition, or training. Has no particular skills or experience. Little chance of improvement. New on job	Lacks interest and initiative, otherwise has good skill and education. Never makes suggestions. Not apt to do better New on job	Interested in work and has aptitude which must be developed by training or experience Occasionally makes suggestions	Displays interest in self-improvement. Taking additional training. Very alert Notices ways of improving methods.	An exceptional prospect for technical or leadership position. Has excellent record of suggestions. Superior to requirements of present job. Capable of filling better job.		□ × □ = □ Rating Weight Factor Score
							□ × □ = □ Rating Weight Total Factor Weights
							Sum of Factor Scores + Total Factor Weights = □ Final Score

months, six months, and a year. Thereafter they are rated annually. This practice recognizes that newer employees are more likely to be sources of trouble than older employees who have had advice on their progress or lack of progress. Some companies that have started rating plans, placed them on a quarterly basis. It was decided later that semiannual or annual ratings would suffice. This, too, recognizes that after years of unplanned attack upon sources of trouble, many grievances and problems will have piled up that, for a time, will require extra attention.

DESIGNS OF RATING FORMS

The term "theory" has been used several times in connection with rating, for the reason that there is no one way of rating that has been proved completely superior to all others. In the following discussion of rating designs, more attention will be paid to the graphical method because up to the present it has been the most widely used. However, the forced-choice method seems to possess very strong advantages; and, although limited in use at present, it seems to have a good future.

1. DESIGN OF GRAPHICAL FORMS. The use of rating forms can lead to excellent results, provided that practical rules of design are adopted. In the following are listed and described some of the more significant rules:

1. Perhaps the most important step, at least initially, in the design of rating forms is to determine precisely the objectives of the program. As noted earlier, there are two major uses of ratings: first, as the basis for rewards and penalties and, second, as the basis for explaining to employees why they are making or not making progress. If the first of these objectives is sought, the rating form should include factors that measure as closely as possible employee contributions. Figure 46 is an example of such selections, in that, except for the last item, all factors relate to production or efficiency in production. Figure 45 (pp. 232–33) illustrates a rating form in which personal characteristics predominate. If it is desired to attempt to accomplish both purposes, factors of each type must be included in the form.

2. Having determined the type of factors to be rated, the next step is to determine which factors, and how many, should be selected. This problem is not too difficult when ratings are made of productivity. For example, the factors in Figure 46 are very inclusive, covering all aspects of a given individual's work; yet the number of factors to be rated is not unduly large.

Rating forms that delve into personal characteristics present a more difficult problem. To begin with, even a brief review of the following list of personal characteristics reveals differences in specificness and problems of overlapping:

Personality	Honesty	Persistence
Character	Initiative	Imagination
Dependability	Industriousness	Enthusiasm
Attitude	Leadership	Aggressiveness
Adaptability	Judgment	Loyalty
Appearance	Co-operativeness	Creativeness
Manner	Impression on others	

In selecting the factors to be rated, it has been found that not more than nine to twelve traits should be used. Some investigations have shown that as few as three or four traits are sufficient to give good results. However, until various groups of executives are taught to give up their belief that there is a safety in numbers, it is easier to get their co-operation when a higher than a lower number of traits is used.

As to the traits to be selected, a better choice can be made if the following rules are watched:

a) Select traits that are specific rather than general; e.g., honesty is more definite than character.

b) Select traits that can be defined in terms understandable in the same way by all raters.

c) Select traits that are common to as many people as possible.

d) Select traits that raters can observe or be taught to observe in the day-to-day performance of employees.

3. Since all factors usually do not have equal weight in all jobs, it is also necessary to determine how much importance should be accorded to each one. This can be accomplished by conference with interested line executives. Some companies provide space for the weights on the form itself, whereas others contend that it is better to omit the weights in order to avoid confusing the raters. In the latter case, the weighting is done by the personnel department.

4. In the physical design of rating forms, an important question is that of how to arrange the factors and the spaces for rating. This involves, first, order of arranging factors and, second, the particulars of rating. There is no general rule that is followed in arranging factors; some arrange them from specific to general, and others reverse this; some like to list factors easy to rate and then go on to the more difficult; and still others adopt a considered disorder.

In the matter of particulars of rating, there is a diversity of practice, much of which is mere whim. When the graphical plan of rating is to be used, adoption of the following suggestions may be desirable:

a) Do not number all scales in the same direction from high to low or low to high. To do this, encourages the tendency of raters to evaluate all factors as they do the first, irrespective of warranted differences.

b) Use of scales of varying length, as shown in the following design, also serves to reduce the influence of the rating of earlier or subsequent factors:

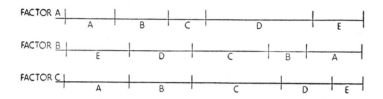

c) Use descriptions to indicate varying degrees of each trait instead of grades and numbers, and omit division points along the scales. As a consequence, the tendency of raters to fit each employee to the scale rather than to concentrate on the employee will be avoided. For example, some raters tend to check the following scale in the center or edge of each grade, depending upon their personal bias:

The following type of scale tends, however, to take the mind of the rater off of the scale and make him concentrate on the employee:

FACTOR A |HIGH OUTPUT   AVERAGE   BELOW AVERAGE   POOR |

5. The description of factors and degrees of factors, already mentioned, deserves special attention. Some of the hypothetical illustrations used in the foregoing would, if adopted, be weak because descriptions are not given. To use such terms as "excellent," "above average," "average," and so forth, to describe varying degrees of factors is undesirable because each rater must make up his own mind as to their meaning. As a result, varying standards are used to rate employees. Much to be preferred is the practice illustrated in Figure 47 (pp. 238–39) of providing raters with detailed descriptions.

6. It is also good practice to provide space under each factor wherein raters can enter comments or significant incidents. This adds a check on the rating and makes the rater more careful in appraising employees. Indeed, some students of rating believe that the comments are the most valuable aspect of rating forms. A form in which comments are stressed is illustrated in Figure 48 (pp. 240–41).

FIGURE 47.   Rating Form for Use of Oral Examiners*

PLACE_____

DATE_____

BOARD NUMBER_____

1. APPEARANCE.   What sort of first impression does he make?   Does he look like a well-set-up, healthy, energetic person? Has he bodily or facial characteristics which might seriously hamper him? Is he well-groomed or slovenly? Erect or slouchy?   Attractive or unattractive in appearance?

2. VOICE AND SPEECH.   Is the applicant's voice irritating, or pleasant?   Can you easily hear what he says? Does he mumble, or talk with an accent which offends or baffles the listener? Or is his speech clear and distinct, so that it would be a valuable asset in this position?

3. POISE AND BEARING.   How well poised is he emotionally?   Is he sensitive to criticism? How does he react to close questioning? Is he easily upset or does he control himself? Does he show shyness or is he self-confident? Does he adapt himself to the situation without very much effort?

4. TACT AND FRIENDLINESS.   Is he a likeable person? Will his fellow workers and subordinates be drawn to him, or kept at a distance? Does he command personal loyalty and devotion? Is he cooperative? How will he get along with others? Will he command the respect of his associates?

5. ALERTNESS.   How readily does he grasp the meaning of a question? Is he slow to apprehend even the more obvious points, or does he understand quickly even though the idea is new, involved or difficult?

6. ABILITY TO PRESENT IDEAS.   Does he speak logically and convincingly? Or does he tend to be vague, confused or illogical? Does he have good command of language? Does he express himself clearly and to the point?

7. JUDGMENT.   Does he impress you as a person whose judgment would be dependable even under stress? Or is he hasty, erratic, biased, swayed by his feelings? Is he self-critical? Does he weigh situations or act impulsively?

8. PERSONAL FITNESS FOR THE POSITION.   In the light of all the evidence regarding this person's characteristics (whether mentioned above or not) how do you rate his personal suitability for work such as he is considering? Recalling that it is not in his best interest to recommend him for such a position if he is better suited for something else, would you urge him to undertake this work? Do you endorse his application?

Fuller instructions and space for comments on applicant's behavior will be found on the back of this sheet.

* Source: The State Civil Service Commission of Ohio.

7. And, finally, consideration should be given to general rules of form design. That is, size of type, color and weight of paper, size of form, and so forth, should be chosen to conform with such matters as who is to use the form, how long the forms are to be kept, where and

FIGURE 47.—Continued

IDENTIFICATION NUMBER_____

POSITION APPLIED FOR_____

EXAMINATION NUMBER_____

| Unsuitable Unimpressive | Creates rather unfavorable impression | Suitable Acceptable | Creates distinctly favorable impression | Impressive. Commands admiration |

| Irritating or indistinct | Understandable but rather unpleasant | Neither conspicuously pleasant nor unpleasant | Definitely pleasant and distinct | Exceptionally clear and pleasing |

| Lacking in balance and restraint. Very timid and awkward | Self-conscious, easily disconcerted | Fairly at ease, no tension, good poise | Self-assured, calm. Very good self control | Exceptional poise. Dominates situation. Adjusts easily |

| Keeps people at a distance. Too aggressive, ill-mannered | Does not easily attract people. Manner somewhat abrupt | Approachable, likeable, polite | Draws people to him. Considerate of others | An inspirer of loyalty. Outstanding qualities of leadership |

| Slow in grasping the obvious. Often misunderstands meaning of questions | Slow to understand subtle points. Requires explanation | Nearly always grasps intent of interviewer's questions | Rather quick in grasping questions and new ideas | Exceptionally keen and quick to understand |

| Confused, illogical. Ungrammatical | Tends to scatter or to become involved. Has to be drawn out | Usually gets his ideas across well | Shows superior ability to express himself | Unusually logical clear and convincing. Excellent vocabulary |

| Uncritical. Does not evaluate situations | Shows some tendency to react impulsively and without restraint | Acts judiciously in ordinary circumstances. Might be hasty in emergencies | Gives reassuring evidences of habit of considered judgment | Inspires unusual confidence in probable soundness of judgment |

| Unsuited for this work. Not endorsed | Might do. Endorsed with hesitance | Endorsed | Endorsed with confidence | Endorsed with enthusiasm |

SIGNATURE OF RATER

_____

how forms are to be filed, and whether or not information is to be transferred to other records. Unless these matters are also kept in mind, rating forms will be designed, as many have, that are difficult to handle at various stages of the rating procedure.

8. These recommendations, it is important to note, need not be fol-

FIGURE 48*

EMPLOYEE PROGRESS REPORT

NAME __John Richards__ AGE __29__ DATE __August 20, 1945__	

JOB CLASSIFICATION __Draftsman__ DEPT. __Engineering__

DATE EMPLOYED __September 4, 1938__ HOW LONG HAVE YOU KNOWN HIM? __7 years__

HOW LONG HAS HE WORKED FOR YOU? __3 years__ IN PRESENT CLASSIFICATION? __June 4, 1942__

CHANGE SINCE LAST REPORT, OR SINCE HE HAS WORKED FOR YOU. (CHECK A, B, C, D & E)

IMPORTANT—BE SURE YOU CONSIDER ONLY ONE CHARACTERISTIC AT A TIME, REGARDLESS OF HOW GOOD OR POOR HE MAY BE IN THE OTHERS. IT IS ESSENTIAL THAT EVERY QUESTION BE ANSWERED. IF MORE SPACE IS NEEDED TO ANSWER ANY ITEM, PLEASE WRITE ON PLAIN PAPER AND ATTACH TO THIS FORM.

Column headings: HAS GONE BACK | LITTLE OR NO CHANGE | HAS IMPROVED | CONT'D GOOD PERFORMANCE

A. KNOWLEDGE OF PRESENT JOB CHECK WHICH→ [✓ HAS IMPROVED]

(1) WHAT EXPERIENCE ON HIS PRESENT JOB DOES HE LACK OR WHAT TRAINING DOES HE NEED IN ORDER TO DO BETTER WORK?

Knowledge of accounts and office routine

(2) WHAT INFORMATION ABOUT RELATED JOBS DOES HE NEED TO IMPROVE HIS EFFICIENCY?

Knowledge of outside plant distribution records and methods

B. QUALITY OF WORK CHECK WHICH→ [✓ LITTLE OR NO CHANGE]

(1) WHAT SHOULD HE DO IN ORDER TO IMPROVE THE QUALITY OF HIS WORK? *Take more pains with lettering; otherwise quality is good.*

(2) TO WHAT EXTENT CAN HE BE DEPENDED UPON TO DO AN ASSIGNED JOB THOROUGHLY AND COMPLETELY WITHOUT SUPERVISION OR CHECKING? *Requires only normal supervision*

(3) HOW DOES THE QUALITY OF HIS WORK COMPARE WITH WHAT YOU EXPECT OF HIM? *Very satisfactory in every respect except as mentioned above*

C. QUANTITY OF WORK CHECK WHICH→ [✓ CONT'D GOOD PERFORMANCE]

(1) HOW DOES THE QUANTITY OF HIS WORK COMPARE WITH WHAT YOU EXPECT OF HIM? *Very favorably-- gets his work completed on time*

(2) DOES HE HAVE INITIATIVE (SELF-STARTER)? *Yes-- doesn't have to be told when he notices a job to be done*

(3) IS HE PERSISTENT (STICK-TO-ITIVENESS)? *Very much so.*

D. ABILITY TO PLAN AND UNDERSTAND WORK CHECK WHICH→ [✓ HAS IMPROVED]

(1) IN ORDER TO WORK EFFECTIVELY AN EMPLOYEE SHOULD: (A) ANALYZE A PROBLEM, (B) PLAN THE JOB ROUTINE SO THERE WILL BE A MINIMUM OF LOST MOTION, (C) EXECUTE THE PLAN, (D) CHECK THE RESULTS AND (E) PROFIT BY MISTAKES. ON WHICH OF THESE STEPS DOES THIS EMPLOYEE NEED TO IMPROVE IN ORDER TO DO BETTER WORK? *(A) and (B)*

(2) DOES HE THINK OUT BETTER WAYS OF DOING THINGS (RECOGNIZE SHORT CUTS)? *not especially; follows normal pattern well however*

(3) DOES HE THOROUGHLY UNDERSTAND INSTRUCTIONS QUICKLY? *Yes-- he listens attentively and makes sure he understands, too.*

IF PERFORMANCE OF ANY OF ABOVE IS BELOW EXPECTATIONS, WHAT SHOULD BE DONE TO BRING ABOUT IMPROVEMENT? *Plan the work so there will be a minimum of repetition of views on the drawing.*

*Source: A. R. Laney, "Getting Results from Merit Rating," *Personnel*, November, 1945, pp. 173–74.

lowed to the letter in every case. Indeed, it is often unwise to insist upon some of these rules, when such insistence would lead to objections from executives who must finally approve the program, but who are as yet not sufficiently educated to appreciate the finer details of design. In one case, for example, the personnel director had to violate rules of which he was aware because he knew that to insist upon his views might jeopardize the whole rating program. Wisely, he calculated how far he

FIGURE 48.—Continued

	HGB	LNC	HI	CGP

E. **PERSONAL QUALITIES** CHECK WHICH→ ✓ (CGP)

(1) IS HE RECEPTIVE TO SUGGESTIONS? *Is always willing to accept suggestions.*

(2) IS HE WILLING TO HELP OTHERS? *Yes.*

(3) HOW DOES HE GET ALONG WITH HIS FELLOW EMPLOYEES? *Works well with others.*

(4) DOES HE LOSE MUCH TIME? *Has a good attendance record.*

(5) DOES HE HAVE A GOOD SAFETY RECORD? *Yes -- has never had a lost-time accident.*

(6) IS HE AS NEAT IN APPEARANCE AS HIS JOB REQUIRES? *Very much so.*

(7) IN WHAT PERSONAL QUALITIES COULD HE IMPROVE? *none.*

LIST ANY GOOD TRAITS OR WEAKNESSES NOT COVERED ELSEWHERE IN THIS REPORT:
He is an exceptionally conscientious and loyal worker.

DO YOU THINK THAT HE IS BETTER QUALIFIED TO DO SOME OTHER TYPE OF WORK (SQUARE PEG IN A ROUND HOLE)?
Well qualified for his present assignment

REMARKS:

PREPARED BY *E. J. Williams* DATE *August 22, 1945*

*REVIEWED BY *Dale Harrison* DATE *August 24, 1945*

* THIS REPORT SHOULD BE REVIEWED WITH YOUR SUPERVISOR BEFORE DISCUSSING IT WITH THE EMPLOYEE.

RECORD OF INTERVIEW

THIS REPORT WAS DISCUSSED WITH THE EMPLOYEE ON *9/4/45* (DATE). DISCUSSION REVEALED THAT *John was pleased to know he was doing a good job. Said he liked his work and would try to improve his knowledge of accounts and office routine, his lettering, and his planning. I promised to arrange for him to spend one day a month at the plant for a while in order that he may become acquainted with records and methods.*

SIGNED: *E. J. Williams* SUPERVISOR

could go in designing a good system and yet get it approved. He did not confuse top executives with technical details, because he knew that, once the program began to show results, he could get the changes that were desirable. Knowing how fast to push the extension of various personnel programs is an absolute requirement if a personnel director expects to be successful, personally, as well as professionally.

2. DESIGN OF THE FORCED-CHOICE METHOD. The forced-choice method of rating has been developed in an attempt to improve the ac-

curacy of ratings by reducing the biases, intentional or not, of raters. Under the graphical method, for example, a rater may "give" a particular person high ratings because he wants the person to receive a raise. Under the forced-choice method, the rater, when making his choices cannot tell how the final rating is going to turn out.

How this is done may be seen in the following excerpt from such a plan, as described by Bittner:

> A number of groups of four statements descriptive of supervisors were set up, like the following:
>   1. Avoids responsibility
>   2. Inspires pride in the organization
>   3. Lacks sense of humor
>   4. Offers suggestions
>
> The rater was then asked to choose from each group of four statements the one that was most descriptive of the person to be rated and the one that was least descriptive.
>
> Now two of the statements are favorable to the person and two of them unfavorable. The two favorable statements look equally attractive to the rater, and the two unfavorable look equally unattractive. At least they would if they had been paired on the basis of research. The important point is that only one of the favorable statements counts for the person and only one of the unfavorable ones counts against him. But the rater does not know which these are because the scoring key is not revealed to him. So he is forced to decide solely on the basis of how *he* describes the man. If he is biased, he cannot mark the one that will reflect his bias because he does not know which one that is. He does not have to wrestle with trait names or the problem of how many points to give because he is merely asked to choose which of four rather dissimilar statements best or least describes the person.
>
> The trick, of course, is to set up these groups of four statements, and much research must go over the dam before this is achieved. I shall not attempt to go into this in detail but shall merely sketch the steps involved. They are the following:
>   1. Gather actual words and phrases used in describing supervisors.
>   2. Cull them for observability and universality.
>   3. Scale them for their degree of attractiveness or unattractiveness.
>   4. Determine how well each discriminates between good and poor supervisors.
>   5. Determine the score that each gets in adding up the total score.
>   6. Verify the scoring system set up by check experiments.[2]

This method was developed by the army during World War II, but it has excellent possibilities for industry. An interesting example of the forced-choice technique in industry is reported by Eileen Ahern of the American Management Association. She notes that the United Parcel Service has used this technique in evaluating executives and supervisors.

---

[2] *Ibid.*, p. 290.

Emphasis here in rating is upon performance reports, with a separate form being used for rating. An example of the type of choices provided follows:

Most	*Least*	
A	A	Would be very difficult to replace.
B	B	Lets difficulties get him down.
C	C	Alert to new opportunities for the company.
D	D	Tries to run things his own way.
E	E	Tends to delegate things which will not reflect credit on him.

Most	*Least*	
A	A	Not willing to make decisions unless he has very complete information.
B	B	Makes snap judgments about people.
C	C	Has not demonstrated up to now that he has the ability to progress further.
D	D	Very valuable in a new operation.
E	E	Good for routine supervisory job.

As may be seen from the foregoing, however, this is not a simple plan to develop. However, its accuracy is high because the biases of raters and their misinterpretations of trait terms are reduced measurably. The rater can scarcely bias his answers, except through ignorance, because he does not know the significance attached to each block of choices: some are neutral, some have zero weights, and others have positive or negative weights. Since methods of scoring must be kept secret, however, it is not an easy plan to sell to employees or unions.

RULES OF RATING

Forms of rating are merely means that must be used properly if desired ends are to be attained. Hence instruction in the proper use of rating forms is also an essential of a good rating program. In this regard, a number of rules have been evolved which, if followed, will increase the value of ratings.

First of all, it is important to determine who is to do the rating. In some companies, two raters, usually the immediate supervisor and his superior, rate each employee. The purposes of the double rating are to derive a check on ratings and to induce higher executives to keep in touch with lower levels of the organization. It is debatable, however, whether or not rating should be made in this way. The purposes are admirable, but it is unwise to ask an executive to make estimates about employees with whom he seldom comes into contact or when he cannot do so practically without neglecting his regular duties. Ordinarily, it is better practice to place the burden of rating on the person best able to assume it—the immediate supervisor. He not only can do the best job but also will improve himself in his daily supervision by becoming more observant of his employees in order to be in a better position to rate them.

Second, raters should be thoroughly instructed in the purposes and values of the program. Most supervisors are suspicious of new methods because they seem to reflect upon their own ambitions. A rating program, particularly, can easily give this impression unless it is properly introduced. Hence it is desirable to hold conferences in which the reasons for the program, the part that supervisors are to play, and the advantages to all concerned are carefully explained. Such conferences also can increase the prestige of the supervisor and his own feeling of worth-whileness by showing him how important he is to the success of the program.

Third, all factors, degrees of factors, and terms should be meticulously explained to raters. Both verbal and printed explanations are worth using. In most instances, explanations are printed on the rating form, but this usually is not enough. It is invariably essential to hold conferences in which explanations are amplified, opportunity is provided for questions, and even demonstrations of filling in rating forms are given. In this way, there is greater assurance that all raters will interpret all terms in the same way and hence produce ratings that are based upon the same standards.

Fourth, several suggestions can be made that will improve the accuracy of ratings. To begin with, raters should be impressed with the need for observing workers in terms of the factors in which they are to be rated. In this way, the task of rating will not be a chore or a matter of guesswork. Raters should also be advised to guard against allowing recent events or isolated cases to influence unduly their decisions. In this connection, the practice of recollecting examples of individual performance and traits is desirable. Then, too, raters should be advised to allow enough time and find a relatively quiet office for the rating job. Interruptions tend to reduce the accuracy of ratings. It has also been found advisable to rate all employees one factor at a time because the consistency of rating is thereby increased. And, finally, it should be suggested to raters that, by taking an attitude of helpfulness rather than vindictiveness, they will make the ratings more accurate and acceptable.

CHECKING ACCURACY OF RATINGS

Unless the accuracy of ratings is checked, they will be unacceptable to those rated and useless to the company. Hence an investment in a rating program should allocate part of the time and resources to a check of ratings. There are a number of plans of evaluating the accuracy of ratings, some simple and some complex, but all are intended to do one or the other of two things. Some check the validity of ratings or the accuracy with which ratings really measure the factors that they set out to rate. Thus, if a rating plan purports to measure, among other things, "initiative," it is valid if this trait is accurately appraised. Other tests check the reliability of ratings or the consistency with which ratings are made. Thus, if a rater gives an employee the grade of "very good," let us say, on two successive ratings of "dependability," and the employee actually has attained that level both times, the ratings are reliable. And, finally, the accuracy of one rater as compared to another may be ascertained.

1. VALIDITY OF RATINGS. Measuring the validity of ratings is not easy because standards are seldom available against which to compare ratings. When an employee is rated for such a factor as "personality," for example, the very fact that he is being rated for it is usually an indication that a better method of estimating it is not available. Yet, by comparing ratings with various aspects of an employee's employment records and performance, adequate checks of validity can be obtained.

Perhaps the simplest over-all check of validity is to compare ratings with the performance of employees. For example, when ratings of personal traits compare favorably with ratings of performance, a smooth progression should be obtained when the data for all values are arranged from high to low. Somewhat similar in nature is a comparison between ratings and other measures of employees, such as psychological tests. Of course, the latter are not precise measures of validity because the psychological tests invariably have an error of validity. The existence of the "halo effect" is also a sign of low validity of ratings. This can be determined by examining ratings to note whether there is a tendency for raters to rate all other factors the same as some one factor about an employee with which they were particularly impressed, favorably or unfavorably.

A check upon validity can also be obtained by comparing estimates of two or more raters on the same employees. For example, if two raters, A and B, rated a given employee as shown in Figure 49 (p. 246), the validity of one or the other, or both, is in error. The lines connecting the scores for each factor by each rater are called "profiles" and are commonly used because they aid the eye in interpreting the ratings. Such differences in estimates are common because most raters tend to be somewhat easy or harsh. Hence the tendency of each rater must be discovered and either corrected by instruction or allowed for if given raters are too set in their ways.

2. RELIABILITY OF RATINGS. The reliability of ratings is ordinarily checked by comparing the ratings of given raters from period to period. If an employee has improved in certain aspects or remained the

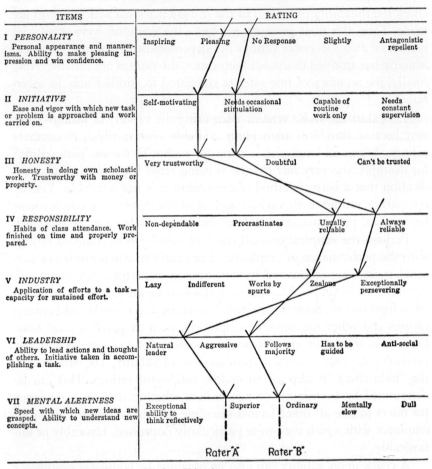

FIGURE 49. Comparison of Profiles*

ITEMS	RATING				
I PERSONALITY Personal appearance and mannerisms. Ability to make pleasing impression and win confidence.	Inspiring	Pleasing	No Response	Slightly	Antagonistic repellent
II INITIATIVE Ease and vigor with which new task or problem is approached and work carried on.	Self-motivating	Needs occasional stimulation		Capable of routine work only	Needs constant supervision
III HONESTY Honesty in doing own scholastic work. Trustworthy with money or property.	Very trustworthy		Doubtful		Can't be trusted
IV RESPONSIBILITY Habits of class attendance. Work finished on time and properly prepared.	Non-dependable	Procrastinates		Usually reliable	Always reliable
V INDUSTRY Application of efforts to a task — capacity for sustained effort.	Lazy	Indifferent	Works by spurts	Zealous	Exceptionally persevering
VI LEADERSHIP Ability to lead actions and thoughts of others. Initiative taken in accomplishing a task.	Natural leader	Aggressive	Follows majority	Has to be guided	Anti-social
VII MENTAL ALERTNESS Speed with which new ideas are grasped. Ability to understand new concepts.	Exceptional ability to think reflectively	Superior	Ordinary	Mentally slow	Dull

Rater "A"   Rater "B"

* Excerpt from a form used at Ohio State University.

same, the ratings should have increased in value or remained the same, as the case may be. When such comparisons are made for the first time, it will invariably be found that most raters have not made necessary adjustments in their estimates. Discussions with supervisors at this time will serve to clear up mistakes in using the rating form and in interpreting the various terms and descriptions. It is unwise to rely too heavily upon such comparisons as a check on the validity of ratings because employees are bound to change from period to period. Hence checks should be made also with other measures which indicate the relative changes in employees from period to period. For example, records that show how an employee's performance has changed can be used to determine whether or not sufficient allowances have been made in the ratings from period to period. Some companies also compare the estimates of a number of raters for the same ratees as a check on their validity. There is some question whether this is a test of validity or reliability, or both. In any event, its use is advisable for the good it will do in calling attention to variances in raters.

3. ACCURACY OF RATERS. It is also desirable to determine, first, which raters are more lenient than others and, second, which have a tendency toward the "halo effect." Leniency of raters can simply be determined by averaging the ratings of each and then getting an average of the averages. Any rater whose average is significantly off of the average should be checked for leniency or undue strictness, as the case may be. Another check on leniency can be obtained if two or more raters rate the same employees. Significant deviations can be readily checked.

In the case of "halo" effect, as noted earlier, ratings are influenced by a particularly impressive characteristic of an employee. For example, a given supervisor may be impressed by the neatness of a particular employee. Unconsciously or consciously, the supervisor proceeds to over-rate the worker on matters of dependability, initiative, co-operation, etc. Sometimes this tendency can be discovered by a simple examination of ratings. At other times interviews will be necessary to ascertain the degree to which given supervisors are susceptible to such errors.

The foregoing checks of validity and reliability may be made by simple observation or by means of statistical correlations. As noted earlier, for example, a simple diagram of the estimates of two raters is sufficient to bring out the need for corrective measures. On the other hand, more complex measures can be derived by correlating statistically various aspects of ratings.

QUESTIONS AND PROBLEMS

1. Since merit rating is essentially a process of expressing opinions, as one executive has put it, what must be done to gain the confidence of employees in such opinions?

2. Which employees in an organization should be rated? Can all be rated with equal ease? Explain.

3. What is the difference between rating employee contributions and employee characteristics? If employee contributions could always be measured accurately, would there be any need to measure employee characteristics? Explain.

4. In designing a merit rating form, why is it essential to state as precisely as possible the objectives that are to be sought in the use of the plan?

5. How is it possible to secure a good rating of an employee when only three or four factors are used? Is there not safety in numbers?

6. Design a form of merit rating for rating students. Select the factors that you think are appropriate, arrange them, establish the weights for the various factors, and prepare the physical rating form.

7. By what methods is it possible to minimize the "halo effect" and the tendency of raters to grade the rating form rather than the employee?

8. Why is it undesirable to use merely the names of factors or the simple grades of "above average," "average," "superior," etc.?

9. Some rating forms provide space wherein the rater provides specific examples to illustrate the grading he has made on particular factors. What advantage is there in this practice?

10. What is the theory behind the forced-choice method of rating? Is this not an indictment of executives? Explain.

11. Since the key to the forced-choice questions is unknown to the rater, can this method be used to counsel with employees as can the other rating methods? Explain.

12. Attempt to work up a list of forced-choice questions that might be used to rate your instructor. What difficulties do you encounter in this task?

13. Why is it desirable that ratings be both valid and reliable? Which, in your opinion, is more difficult to achieve? Why?

14. In the case of operative employees, who should do the rating? Is it desirable for the superintendent as well as the supervisor to rate each employee?

15. Is it desirable to ask subordinates to rate their superiors? Explain.

16. Why is it invariably necessary to overcome the suspicions of most executives regarding merit rating when it is first introduced? How may this be done?

17. What are the relative merits of showing and not showing the results of ratings to employees?

18. After ratings have been obtained for each employee, how far would you go in relating such ratings to wages to be paid? To need for training? To need of counseling?

19. The following excerpt (see top of page 249) has been taken from an employee rating form. What is your critical opinion of the form as illustrated by the selected excerpt?

Leadership:

Rate this executive's ability
   to gain co-operation and
   to direct others.

Superior	Above Average	Average	Fair	Poor

Appearance:

Rate his personal neatness,
   dress, and attractiveness.

Superior	Above Average	Average	Fair	Poor

20. List the factors that can be expressed in quantitative terms (units or percentages) that might be used to measure the accomplishments of a supervisor or the department for which he is responsible.

CHAPTER

13 | Training Operative Employees

TRAINING AND EDUCATION

This and the next chapter are devoted to a study of training in industry, and the two chapters following these are concerned with education. The term "training" is used here to indicate any process by which the aptitudes, skills, and abilities of employees to perform specific jobs are increased. This task may be contrasted with that of increasing the knowledge, understanding, or attitude of employees so that they are better adjusted to their working environment. The term "education" is used here to denote the latter task.

To clarify these terms, the example of a trainee on a drill press may be considered. Teaching him how to operate the drill press is called "training," whereas giving him a course in economics is called "education." The two may go hand in hand, as in the case of a supervisor who, while showing an operator how to seal a package, also talks about the sales policies of the company and their importance to each factory employee.

Although education in attitudes is often undertaken at the same time as training, and wisely so, it is better for discussional purposes here to take up the two phases of learning separately. The principles and practices of acquiring skills can be viewed, thereby, apart from the process of education or "attitude training," as some prefer to call it.

In the present chapter, training of operative employees is taken up under the following major headings:

1. Justification and scope of training
2. Courses and programs of training
3. Factors in a training program
4. Evaluation of training programs

JUSTIFICATION AND SCOPE

One of the first questions that must be answered regarding training is whether or not the cost is justifiable. The simplest argument in favor of a formal training program is that a company pays for a training program whether it has one or not. Some executives conclude that they do not have any training costs because they do not have a training program. That is far from the truth. A few minutes of thought will suffice to show how wrong they are. Let us take the case of a company that has no program. Are all their employees hired with skills and abilities and aptitudes equal to the jobs to be done? Do their employees learn nothing while they are working? Whose machines, materials, and space are employees using while they are "learning" by themselves? Do they never make mistakes that could have been avoided? Do they never scrap usable materials? Are they fully acquainted with company policies, practices, and procedures when they come on the payroll? The answers will show that the employees are conducting a costly educational program, for which the company is unwittingly footing the bill.

Viewed positively, the values of training, it can be shown, are not far to seek. First, training brings about an improvement in employee skill, which in turn increases the quantity and quality of output. Second, this increase in primary objectives will find a reflection in increased returns to employees; personal rewards are affected by individual productivity. Third, the relative amount of equipment and material required to produce a unit of output is decreased. Fourth, executive effort will tend to shift from the disagreeable necessity of correcting mistakes to the more pleasant task of planning the work of and encouraging expert workers. And, last, the general tenor of relations between employees, as well as their individual morale, will tend to be more wholesome, resulting in more pleasant and satisfactory working conditions. All these objectives, it is worth repeating, may be sought without adding to company budgets. The money is being spent, so it may as well be spent wisely.

Although all employees should undergo training, all need not be trained in the same amount, and seldom can all be trained at the same time. Company facilities for training are seldom sufficient to undertake such a broad program. Hence the guiding principle should be that of attacking training problems where the needs are the greatest. After urgent training needs are taken care of, those with lower priority should be served.

As yet, standards as to the amount of training that should be provided on various types of jobs are practically nonexistent. Even in the field of apprentice training, practice differs considerably. In some trades the apprentice period is two years, and in others it is as high as seven years. But compared to this, other types of training are variable beyond mention. Hence each company must work out time standards of training for itself, changing them as their experience warrants. Standards should be set for the following:

1. Over-all length of course in calendar or working days
2. Total hours of training time
3. Hours of training by days and weeks
4. Proportion of day assigned to various classes of training

COURSES OF TRAINING

Many approaches to training are being used in industry. To describe and examine them all is beyond the scope of this chapter. However, the

FIGURE 50. Graphic Presentation of the Approach to Nonsupervisory Training Programs in the Automotive Industry*

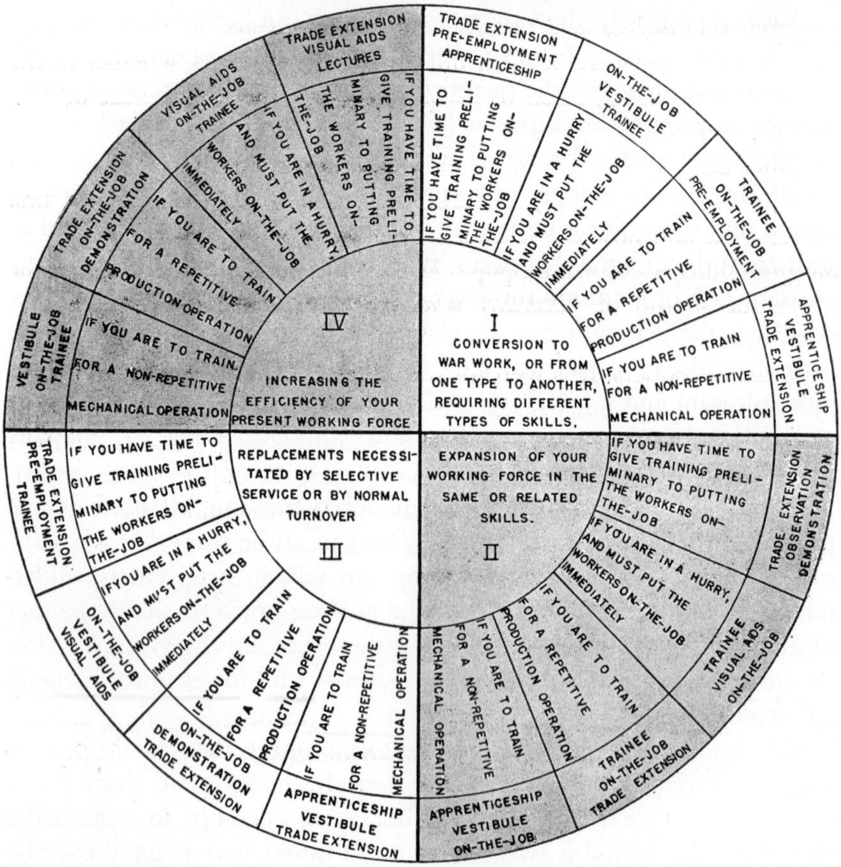

In the center circle are listed the problems generally faced; in the second circle, the different situations involved; and in the outer circle, the methods recommended to meet the specific problem.

* Source: *Training and Upgrading* (report of Automotive Council for War Production) (Detroit), p. 6.

more common methods of training operative employees are taken up now. The types of training are not mutually exclusive but invariably overlap and employ many of the same techniques. For example, Figure 50 illustrates graphically the types and methods of training that may be used to serve various purposes under various conditions. Which is best for a given need deserves careful study.

ON-THE-JOB TRAINING

Undoubtedly, training is most commonly done on the job. It requires no special school, the student is being trained at a point where no "changeover" will be required, and his output adds to the total of his department. Favorable though the situation may be, most training on the job is not economical. Ordinarily, no course of progressive and correlated materials of instruction is prepared; the instructors are ill prepared themselves and usually not very interested in their students because of the pressure of other duties; and the students, whether in the office or in the shop, often feel lost and ill at ease in the maze of production routine.

Since on-the-job training is commonly used and is likely to continue to be, the requisites of a good program are now described. In the first place, what and how the learner is to be taught should be determined and preferably set down on paper, at least in major outline. Second, the instructor should be carefully selected and trained. Such courses as "Job Instructor Training," to be discussed in the next chapter, should be given to trainers. It is well for the supervisor to do the training himself if time will permit, because it will give him a favorable opportunity to get acquainted with the new worker and to "sell" himself and the company to him. When time does not permit the supervisor to do this work, the next best practice is to have a departmental trainer. When this is not practical, a seasoned and understanding worker should be appointed to teach the new worker. But it is well to pay such part-time instructors a bonus for each learner trained, so that they will not hurry this responsibility in order to return to their own duties on which incentive payments may otherwise be lost. And, third, a definite follow-up schedule should be provided, so that the results of the training and the progress of the learner can be established. In this way all instructors will be more likely to do their work effectively.

VESTIBULE TRAINING

In "vestibule" training, employees are taken through a short course under working conditions that approximate actual shop or office conditions. It gets its name from the resemblance of the school to a vestibule through which one passes before entering the main rooms of a house. Such a course usually takes from a few days to a few weeks at the most and is used where the acquisition of a few skills is the goal. Thus training may be given to newly hired shop clerks on how to fill out various shop papers, such as time reports and departmental inventory cards. Or lessons may be given to clerks who have been hired to operate, let us say, comptometers. As a result, they will be able to do the work required of them when they step into the departments for which they were hired.

Vestibule training has the advantage of training relatively large numbers of people in a short period of time without disturbing the flow of shop or office routines. Moreover, the employees can be adjusted to actual conditions under guided direction and gradually speeded up as they gain confidence in themselves. In addition, misfits or poor practices can be eliminated before actual production conditions are encountered.

Vestibule training, however, requires the duplication of shop or office facilities in a school area. Consequently, it must be limited to types of instruction in which the machinery used is not too expensive to install in a school or which can be used, on and off, as employment demands, without excessive overhead cost. Moreover, all types of machines in actual use can seldom be practically placed in a vestibule school; so it is limited in application to those jobs in which there is a high turnover or a continually increasing demand for workers.

APPRENTICESHIP TRAINING

Apprenticeship training pertains to training in which the course of work varies from a minimum of two years in some trades to six or seven in other fields. It is used in trades, crafts, and technical fields in which proficiency can be acquired only after a relatively long period of time in direct association with the work and under the direct supervision of experts. A partial list of trades in which apprentice training is practiced includes the following:

Barbers	Draftsmen	Lens grinders	Printers
Boilermakers	Drop forgers	Machinists	Shipfitters
Bricklayers	Electricians	Mechanics	Stone masons
Carpenters	Engravers	Millwrights	Toolmakers
Coppersmiths	Furriers	Molders	
Coremakers	Horseshoers	Painters	
Die sinkers	Jewelers	Plumbers	

Inasmuch as a number of groups, in addition to business itself, are interested in apprenticeship training, those who carry on such training should be aware of these groups. First, the federal government is interested in apprentices, for one thing, because of the Wages and Hours and Walsh-Healey Acts. If an employer desires to pay apprentices less than amounts regularly prescribed by these laws, apprenticeship agreements must be covered in writing and submitted to the administrators of these acts in order to obtain a certificate of exemption. The agreement must describe the term of apprenticeship and probation, the major processes in which the apprentice is to receive instruction and experience, the graduated scale of wages to be paid, the amount of time spent at work and in school, and any special provisions.

More recently, the federal government became directly interested in apprentice courses through the allowances granted to such learners under the G.I. Bill of Rights and the Vocational Rehabilitation Program. Thus, in the case of World War II veterans and post-Korean veterans who are apprentices and whose courses of study and work are approved by the Veterans' Administration, their pay from their employers will be augmented in varying amounts according to dependents and service-incurred disabilities, if any.

The federal government, through its Federal Committee on Apprenticeship, has also co-operated with state apprenticeship councils to standardize the apprenticeship practices. More than half the states have such councils. In each of these states, provisions are suggested regarding amount of training, wages, and standards of work. Another aim is to protect the apprentice who accepts lower remuneration for relatively long periods of time. Otherwise, some employers might use apprenticeship to secure low-cost labor.

Unions, too, have interested themselves in apprenticeship programs. On the one hand, they are interested in establishing apprentice quotas in order to prevent displacement of fully trained workers by apprentices. Second, they are interested because the apprenticeship program can be used to restrict entry into a trade or industry. As a consequence, such courses may well be the subject for collective bargaining.

INTERNSHIP TRAINING

Internship training refers to a joint program of training in which schools and business co-operate. Selected students carry on regular school studies for periods ranging from three to nine months and then work in some factory or office for a designated period of time, alternating in this fashion until the course is completed and the student is ready to accept permanent employment. The training is usually conducted in connection with highly skilled or professional types of training. Trade and high schools often co-operate with industry in this way to train various vocational help. And it has been employed by industry and colleges for training for management and engineering positions.

By such training, it is hoped to gain a good balance between theory and practice. In addition, students may gain a better understanding of the "school books" by having the practical background against which to visualize classroom principles. Moreover, the students who have a definite vocation or profession in mind are likely to be better students because they can see the practical side of their objectives being achieved. From the company's side, the gain is in a better-balanced employee and one who has already been interned to its practices.

Internship has its disadvantages. It is such a slow process as to try the patience of the student as well as the instructor or supervisor. It takes so long that one or both of the parties involved may become discouraged. It suffers when business depressions call for layoffs; and, under it, present employees feel that the interns are being favored at their expense. However, within limits, it is a desirable plan to follow as part of a complete program in which other employees, as well as the selected classes of prospective employees, are given consideration.

LEARNER TRAINING

During periods of heavy demand for and short supplies of semi-skilled labor, industry is faced with the task of training "green" hands or "learners." The learners usually receive a program of education and training. This is necessary because the learners come into industry without the rudiments of industrial knowledge. In one case, for example, it was found desirable to send learners to public vocational schools for a period of several weeks for the study of arithmetic, simple shop mathematics, shop science, reading and using gauges, reading simple blueprints, and operation of shop machines. After this training and education they were assigned to regular production jobs.

OUTSIDE COURSES

A number of agencies and groups have co-operated with industry in the solution of its training problems. Vocational, correspondence, trade, and evening schools have been a constant source of supply of semi-skilled, skilled, and technical workers. The usefulness of these schools can be seen in the figures from one community in which 1,200 out of 8,000 workers were attending night school. Of course, their training, except when internship arrangements have been worked out, must be of a sufficiently general nature to qualify graduates for any one of a number of employers. Some communities have organized committees to point such training toward the needs of particular employers. For example, in Cleveland various programs for solving the wartime shortage of skilled workers were worked out through the joint effort of the Cleveland Personnel Association, Cleveland Chamber of Commerce, Cleveland Board of Education, and the federal agencies of Works Progress Administration and the National Youth Administration.[1] On a broader scale local community plans of employment and training have been organized upon the recommendation of a committee to study employment. In each community there is an unpaid committee on which serve representatives from such groups as organized labor, the school board, the American Legion, the employment service, and industry.

The federal government, through a number of agencies, has assisted industry in its training work. Vocational training is given particular support by providing for contribution of federal funds to match contributions by the states. The Smith-Hughes Act of 1917 apportioned seven million dollars annually for such programs. Subsequent amendments in 1934 (the George-Ellsey Act) and in 1936 (the George-Deen Act) increased the federal contribution. Federal support is also given to vocational training of the handicapped and veterans.

The federal government also gives assistance in apprentice training through its Apprentice Training Service established in 1937 as a section of the Division of Labor Standards, the United States Department of Labor. Agencies interested in such vocational education are illustrated in Figure 51 (p. 258). A brief outline of its cost-free services is as follows:

1. *Training Apprentices.* Assistance is given in improving or inaugurating apprenticeship programs and providing suggestions on methods and techniques relating to the operation of such programs.
2. *Training Advancing Workers.* Advisory assistance is provided regarding the training of advancing workers. These are workers being trained for skills beneath the journeyman level but which require a fairly high degree of skill. The period of training for such workers is shorter than for apprentices, but the problems of training are comparable.
3. *Labor Relations Affecting Training.* Assistance is provided in dealing with labor problems encountered with the operation of on-the-job training programs. Typical problems applying to training include: seniority rights, wages, number to be trained, hours of work, establishment of training schedules and breakdown of operations, establishment of shifts, standards of selection, and supervision of trainees.
4. *Supplementary Labor Agreements.* In plants where employees are organized, assistance is provided in preparing supplements to established bar-

---

[1] J. W. Vanden Bosch, "Training People for Factory Work," *Factory Management and Maintenance*, September, 1940, pp. 54–60.

gaining agreements where the existing agreement is not sufficiently flexible to cover such situations as war training and employment.

5. *General.* In many instances assistance is also provided with regard to employment requirements of federal or state laws and problems of production as they relate to training.

During the war, the federal government also performed yeoman service through its efforts in advanced training and education. Its work in connection with the Training within Industry and the Engineering,

FIGURE 51. Federal-State-Local Relations in Vocational Education*

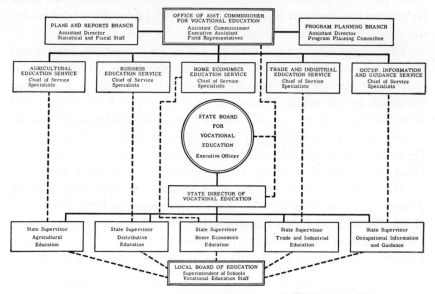

* Source: Federal Security Agency, Office of Education, Division of Vocational Education.

Science, Management, and War Training Programs will be discussed in the next chapter.

RETRAINING AND UPGRADING

When demands for semiskilled and skilled labor exceed the supply, industry must undertake programs to retrain and upgrade unskilled and semiskilled employees. For example, war conditions create a need for such training because most companies have to change from civilian pursuits to war work and have to increase their output at the same time. Hence, on the one hand, employees who had skills for making automobiles, let us say, have to be retrained to make tanks. And, on the other hand, many who are performing semiskilled jobs must be given additional training so that they may be upgraded to skilled jobs. Their jobs are filled by upgraded unskilled workers, and these in turn are replaced by learners, many of whom may be women with no industrial experience whatsoever.

Courses in upgrading and retraining are much the same as other training methods discussed thus far. Their unique feature lies in the fact that otherwise experienced workers are given additional training to handle new and more difficult assignments. The problem is to pick and choose course material so that trainees can take on their new jobs relatively quickly. For example, one company that took forty-eight months on its toolmakers' apprentice course, selected parts from it so that operators could be taught to perform a few skilled jobs in from six to eighteen months. Such intensive training in which students spent approximately 25 per cent of their time in class and 75 per cent on machine operations built up a working force that could meet war production demands on time.

FACTORS IN A TRAINING PROGRAM

The operation of a successful program requires that due consideration be given to a number of factors. These include (1) the organization of a training program, (2) planning the program, (3) selection of trainees and instructors, and (4) adherence to rules or principles of learning.

ORGANIZATIONAL ASPECTS

A training program has a much better chance of being effective if it is well organized. To begin with, one person or unit in the organization should be made responsible for training. In a small company, this means that a line executive will have to be given this responsibility. In larger organizations, the personnel manager or a training director should be assigned the task of planning, organizing, and evaluating the program. Such division of responsibility should be made with the clear recognition that the foremen, supervisors, and other executives assisted by the designated teaching officers possess ultimate authority over and responsibility for training within their respective units. As an example of this, Figure 52 (p. 260) shows the various types of training for which a training co-ordinator in one company was made responsible for planning and co-ordination. Fig. 53 (p. 261) shows how the execution of some of the training work was actually assigned to the shop departments.

Second, a training program must be "sold" to the top level of the organization to be most effective. Unless the interest and prestige of the administrative levels are behind it, a training program will be accepted with reluctance by the lower levels. As a consequence, some companies follow the practice of starting various training programs, in synopsis form if not in complete outline, at interested top levels and

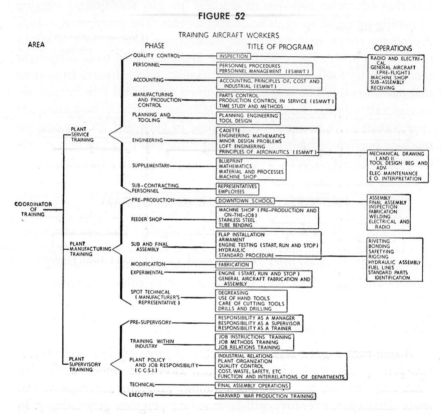

FIGURE 52

gradually working the instruction down through the organization to the group for whom the instruction was originally planned.

And, third, it is well to consider the role of the union in the organization for training. This may involve such matters as courses of training to be installed, responsibility for selecting or restricting candidates, and evaluation of training work. These matters may be handled informally, through collective bargaining or through joint committees established for the purpose. In any event, it is probable that, with the passing years, union interest in training is likely to grow rather than diminish. Therefore, it is only good judgment to try to determine how best to work with unions in developing and operating a training program.

FIGURE 53. Training Organization Chart

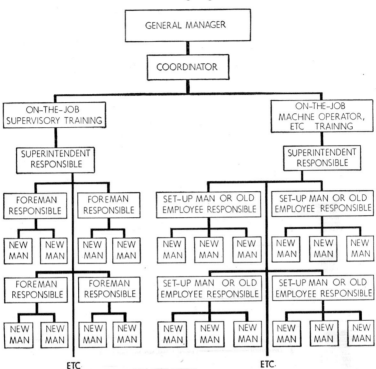

PLANNING THE PROGRAM

Along with a good organization, careful planning is a most important prerequisite of training. When such aspects as where, who, how, what, and when are preplanned in a training program, the result will be fewer mistakes and better trainees when the program gets under way. An excellent example of this is seen in Figure 54, which illustrates the results obtained from a careful study that led to the building of an effective training program. The lower curve in this chart shows how much progress might be expected in a year from "normal efficiency growth," meaning the happenstance methods of learning in most offices. By developing a "procedure of training," employees attained in three months results which ordinarily took a year. And when to this training was added instruction aimed at improving the attitude of the employee towards his work and his fellow workers, the relative efficiency attained by employees within a year was more than double. Anything which can double efficiency with the relative inexpensiveness of planned training, such as this program has, certainly proves its value.

Another aspect of planning is that of building training programs on a good foundation of, first, job and man specifications and, second, measurements of what employees actually know. This follows from the proposition that a training program should be based on the following formula: what should be known *less* what one knows *equals* what must be learned. Thus job and man specifications serve to disclose the kind and degrees of skills, abilities, and aptitudes required on various jobs, whereas checking of employees through records of past experience and

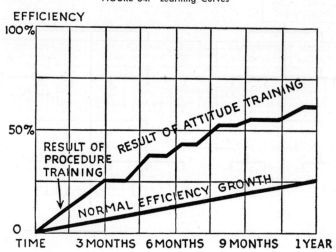

FIGURE 54.   Learning Curves*

* Source: E. F. Wonderlic, *Procedure and Attitude Training* (Personnel Series No. 47) (New York: American Management Association, 1941), p. 50.

education, interviewing, testing, and surveys of difficulties encountered on the job reveal their current status. The differences shown by these two broad investigations should provide an answer to the question of how much training must be allowed for in the program of a company.

SELECTION OF TRAINEES AND INSTRUCTORS

Another basic factor in training is to select trainable employees. Inasmuch as training costs money, expenditures are warranted only for those from whom the greatest returns will be received. Thus higher production results are obtained sooner at a lower training cost. Employees may also be preselected for various types of training by having detailed knowledge of their past experience and training. An example of a form which has been used to obtain this information is illustrated in Figure 55. In this connection, testing programs are highly worth while. As

FIGURE 55.   Experience Record*

EXPERIENCE RECORD

NAME:_____   CLOCK NO._____

ADDRESS:_____   S.S. NO._____

For the purpose of determining the qualifications and experience of the employees as to their mechanical experience for defense work, the questions below are submitted:

1. Grade completed in school_____

2. Have you completed a school course in:
   (1) Arithmetic _____   (4) Trigonometry _____
   (2) Algebra _____   (5) Shop (Mach.) _____
   (3) Geometry _____

3. Have you served an apprenticeship as:
   (1) Machinist_____ (2) Toolmaker_____   (3) Diemaker_____ (4) Any other_____

4. Can you read blueprints?_____

5. Can you read micrometers?_____

6. Can you read a Vernier?_____

7. Have you had experience operating the following machine tools?:

	Prod.	Tool-room	Specify Type		Prod.	Tool-room	Specify Type
(1) Lathe	___	___	___	(10) Diamond Boring Mach.	___	___	___
(2) Multiple Turning Machine (Bullard, etc.)	___	___	___	(11) Auto. Screw Mach.	___	___	___
				(12) Hand Screw Mach.	___	___	___
(3) Milling Machine	___	___	___	(13) Chucking Machine (New Britain, Cleveland, etc.)	___	___	___
(4) Drill Press	___	___	___				
(5) Drill Press (Multi)	___	___	___	(14) Gear Cutter	___	___	___
(6) Grinder External	___	___	___	(15) Broaching Mach.	___	___	___
(7) Grinder Internal	___	___	___	(16) Semi-Automatic Lathe	___	___	___
(8) Planer	___	___	___	(17) Any other	___	___	___
(9) Shaper	___	___	___				

8. Have you had any training in mechanical drawing or design? _____

                  School   Practical

9. Have you had experience as·
   (1) Mach. shop foreman _____   (7) Cutter grinder _____   (14) Instructor-Machine Shop _____
   (2) Mach. shop inspector _____   (8) Tool hardener _____   (15) Indicate experience, if any, on manufacture of ordnance parts; if so, what parts _____
   (3) Toolmaker _____   (9) Machine repairman _____
   (4) Diemaker _____   (10) Welder _____
   (5) Machinist _____   (11) Boring mill (toolroom) _____
   (6) Tool and gage grinder _____   (12) Layout (bench) _____ (Surface Plate) _____   (16) Any other (use reverse side if necessary)_____
                   (13) Patternmaker _____

10. Please indicate any other mechanical qualifications (use reverse side if necessary)_____

---

11 Indicate class of work you prefer_____

12 Indicate class of work best qualified for_____

Your answers will be supplemented by further practical examination and demonstration

---

* *Factory Management and Maintenance,* October, 1943, p. 117.

noted in an earlier chapter, employees selected by tests learn faster and better than nontested employees.

The selection and training of instructors also is significant. Here is an excellent opportunity for supervisors. The supervisor who becomes skilled in training methods can show the employees his interest in their welfare better than all the words in the world. By working with them to help them better themselves, he will gain their loyalty and their confidence. If "lead" men or "gang bosses" are used as trainees, these, too, deserve careful preparation, if training time and effort are not to be wasted. In the case of regular full-time instructors, special care should be exercised to see that such individuals not only know the rudiments of instruction but also like to teach and have an interest in the student.

RULES AND PRINCIPLES OF LEARNING

Although the subject can be little more than scratched, it is desirable here to note some rules and principles that should be followed if a training program is to be effective. To begin with, in planning a program, it is wise to determine how frequently instruction should be given, and the effect of recency, types of materials, and visual and audio devices upon the learning process. The conditions and atmosphere of instruction are also items to be considered.

More specifically, industrial training is more effective, too, when shop instruction is correlated with classroom instruction. This follows, not only because the learner can see the improvement he is making in actual production, but also because of the principle that the more specific and concrete the material of instruction, the better the learning. All of this suggests, too, that it is imperative to select trainers who can stimulate the learners to exert themselves. An otherwise admirable plan of training will almost inevitably fail to achieve desired results if this principle of instruction is violated.

Of interest, too, is the fact that in teaching it is sometimes best to start describing the middle steps of an operation rather than the first or last, as is usually done. Students who are pushed at the most rapid rate of which they are capable do better than when a more leisurely pace is maintained. It is also well to alternate lectures, demonstrations, and actual shop practice at carefully worked-out time intervals to get the best results. And to cite one more principle of this nature, the instructor should stand beside the student when demonstrating so that the student will not have to reverse the images he receives, as is true when the instructor stands in front of him.

Another category of rules pertains to the media and mechanics of instruction. These are so numerous that only a few suggestions can be mentioned here.

1. Use graphical, illustrative, and sample materials freely and frequently. Such matter as charts, drawings, and models increase the effectiveness of teaching and learning.

2. Use good classroom facilities and select the best possible shop areas for instruction purposes.

3. Determine the best time for classroom work. Lectures ordinarily should not be longer than fifty to sixty minutes; discussion periods can be longer, provided that intermissions of about ten minutes are provided after forty-five minutes.

4. Examinations or tests should be scheduled at appropriate intervals in order to check the student and provide him with a sense of progress.

5. Groups in training together should seldom be larger than thirty if discussion is to be encouraged and if instructors are not to be overworked.

6. Questions should emphasize 'how" and "why" rather than "yes" or "no."

7. The use of pictures, whether shown by movies, slides, strip slides, or other methods, cannot be overstressed. It has been discovered that thereby—
   a) Interest of students may be increased up to 40 per cent
   b) Their range of immediate understanding increased up to 25 per cent
   c) Their time for completing a course decreased up to 25 per cent
   d) Their retention of information increased up to 35 per cent

EVALUATION OF TRAINING PROGRAMS

Although it is contended here that training programs are well worth their cost, it is nevertheless argued that the activities of training should be evaluated. This will not only result in getting more for the training dollar but also make it possible to improve training techniques and practices. In the final analysis, the savings and improvements resulting from training must be set off against the cost of training, to determine the extent of positive advantage. Such comparisons must be made on a month-to-month, company-to-company, or interdepartmental basis, to establish worth-while conclusions.

The types of evidence which may be gathered to show savings and improvements include the following:

1. Production factors
   a) Increase in output
   b) Decrease in scrap
   c) Decrease in unit times and unit cost of production
   d) Reduction in space or machine requirements

2. Labor factors
   a) Decrease in labor turnover
   b) Decrease in absenteeism
   c) Decrease in number and severity of accidents
   d) Betterment of employee morale
   e) Decrease in grievances and disciplinary action
   f) Reduction in time to earn piece rates
   g) Decrease in number of discharges or quits

When such information is gathered, the value of training will seldom be taken for granted or questioned. Yet it is not an onerous task to gather such data. In gathering them, care should be used to bring out the results of training by comparing the records of trainees with those of employees who were not trained. How this may be done is illustrated in Figure 56. This is a striking contrast between the efficiency of

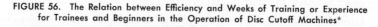

FIGURE 56. The Relation between Efficiency and Weeks of Training or Experience for Trainees and Beginners in the Operation of Disc Cutoff Machines*

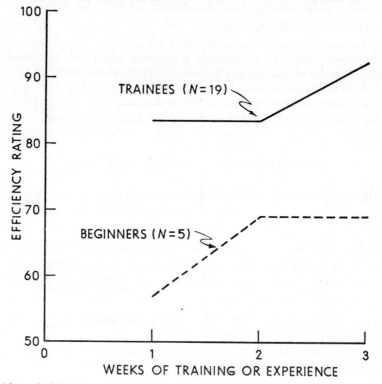

* Source: L. G. Lindahl, "Training Operations by Activity Analysis," *Personnel*, January, 1948, p. 304.

trainees and those who learned on the job. Such data establish strongly the desirability of planned training.

Another way of evaluating training programs is that illustrated in Figure 57. Here is shown the progress made by two trainees, one who is "too good" for the job and one who is just right. Certainly, when it is possible to ascertain the future prospects of employees so early in their employment tenure, the tool which helps is deserving of favorable support.

A few words on evaluation also are in order from a legal and professional point of view. Some training programs may have to be measured in terms of legal requirements. For example, a company that desires to qualify war veterans under an approved learner or apprentice course must meet minimum standards on such matters as quantity and quality of instruction. In cases in which a company seeks exemptions under the Wages and Hours and Walsh-Healey Acts, such information must be available. Even when not mandatory, establishing such standards is desirable in order to keep the planning of courses on a definite schedule and to stipulate times for evaluating training results.

FIGURE 57. Learning Curves*

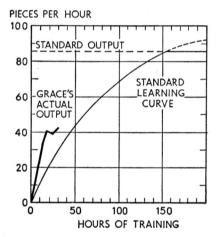
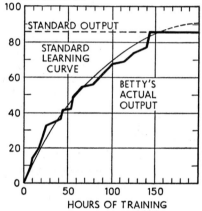

GRACE WAS TOO GOOD

Too good, that is, for this particular job. From the start, her progress (*heavy line*) was far better than standard. She'd worked before on repetitive jobs, and was glad to be transferred to the machine shop.

BETTY? JUST RIGHT

It paid to train her. Her learning curve (*heavy line*) practically coincides with the standard curve. She reached full production on the twenty-first day; consistently met standard without difficulty.

* Source: A. R. Knowles and L. F. Bell, "Training Curves," *Factory Management and Maintenance*, June, 1950, p. 115.

If the quantity of training is relatively unstandardized, its quality is even less so. To be sure, where federal or state agencies supervise vocational, learner, apprentice, and rehabilitation training, some review of the quality of courses and instructors is made, but this is as yet largely personal and variable. There is little doubt, however, that the quality of training has improved in the last few years. A favorable sign is the formation of the National Association of Training Directors and local associations of training directors, with raising standards of industrial training one of their major purposes.

QUESTIONS AND PROBLEMS

1. Is it desirable to separate training and education in actual practice? Explain.
2. Assume that a union in a given company desired to operate a school for learners for that company. Comment upon this plan in terms of (*a*) the company in question and (*b*) the learners.
3. Of two employees who are acquainted with each other and who have been hired at the same time for the same type of work, one can be placed on the job with very little training but the other requires extensive training. Need anything be done to keep either from developing a feeling of discrimination? What?
4. Although on-the-job training is used more widely than any other plan, does this mean that it is the best plan of training operative employees? Explain.
5. How would you justify the cost of a formal training program for an industrial plant?
6. Why is it unreasonable for business to assume that the school system should provide it with trained personnel?
7. What basic questions must be answered in establishing a training program for operative employees, in the shop, office, or salesroom?
8. Why is it undesirable as well as unnecessary to give all employees doing the same amount of work the same kind and amount of training?
9. What contributions can be made to training by job analysis, psychological testing, and merit rating?
10. By what methods may the effectiveness of part-time instructors be increased?
11. What is meant by "vestibule training"? When would its use be advisable? When not?
12. Why do such varied groups as unions and governmental agencies concern themselves with apprenticeship training?
13. What are the merits and demerits of the internship plan of industrial training?
14. How should training plans be established in order to serve the needs caused by (*a*) rapid, but short-run, expansion and contraction of business and (*b*) long-run changes in volume and technology?
15. If training is more effective under actual shop conditions, why not scrap the educational system and train everybody right from the start under practical working conditions?
16. Write a report on the following experiment. Select some simple operation such as tying a particular type of knot or solving a mechanical puzzle. Select one which is unknown to your prospective students. Then select three "students." Explain the operation to each, starting with the first student at the beginning of the operation, starting in the middle of the operation and then going back to the beginning with the second, and starting at the end of the operation with the third student and then coming back to the first steps of the operation. Let each student try out the operation. Which method seems to work best?

17. Discuss why the principles of good physical conditions of instruction are necessary. Are there any which might be dispensed with?
18. Draw an organization chart of an actual company showing the place assigned to training. Is the location right, or too high or too low?
19. How would you proceed to evaluate the effectiveness of a training program?
20. Someone has said that most industrial jobs can be performed by workers of relatively low mental ability. If that is so, is emphasis upon a training program misplaced? Why?

CHAPTER

14 | Training of Executives

SIGNIFICANCE OF EXECUTIVE TRAINING

One of the most encouraging developments of training activities during recent years is the recognition given executive training. Earlier, few companies either considered such training necessary or gave it any thought whatsoever. Too commonly it was felt that anyone who was appointed to the management ranks at the supervisory levels or those who were moved up the executive levels either possessed leadership aptitudes and know-how or could acquire the required qualifications themselves.

But anyone who has been given supervisory responsibilities without instruction and training knows how false such assumptions are. Indeed, appointees to supervisory positions are usually uniquely unfitted for their new positions. Almost without exception, the practice in most companies has been to select for supervisory positions those who have exhibited the most proficiency in technical work. Thus the fastest worker, the most skilled mechanic, or the most proficient technician is made the supervisor of his respective department when a vacancy occurs. Yet the qualifications which led to his selection are usually of no value, and, indeed, often a hindrance, in his new position. If he is to become successful, it usually requires a more or less extended period of stumbling and disagreeable self-education.

Nor do those who move up the managerial ladder have a happier experience when they must educate themselves. It is one thing to supervise operative employees and another to supervise supervisors. The task of planning, organizing, and controlling major decisions of a company calls for skills and aptitudes that differ from those a minor operative executive must possess. And those who must solve the broad problems of and set policies for the company need experience and talents above those of the administrators of plans and policies. Yet the acquisition of needed knowledge, principles, and skills in these areas, too, has been left invariably to individual effort and the laws of chance.

However, many companies have seen and are seeing the light. Training at all executive levels, from supervisory through middle management levels to the top side, is receiving increased attention. And the results of formal training programs at these levels are as one would expect. In such companies, executive leadership is improving, operational activities are carried out more economically and effectively, managers look upon their jobs as a challenge and not as a chore, and the morale of well-directed employees is improved.

To show how these results are attained, the material in this chapter is divided into the following parts:

1. Types of courses developed for executive training at various levels
2. Content of training materials
3. Follow-up and evaluation of training results

TYPES OF EXECUTIVE TRAINING PROGRAMS

Experience with executive training programs is as yet too limited to warrant any positive conclusions regarding which types are best under various conditions. However, it is possible to suggest some of the more widely used practices and their conditions of application. A good summary of plans of executive training and the purposes to which they may be put is provided in the diagram in Figure 58 (p. 272), which displays the approach to supervisory training programs in the automotive industry. A description of various courses follows.

ON-THE-JOB TRAINING

Most commonly, executive training is done on the job. With or without formal guidance, most executives must eventually learn how to do their work while working. The advantages of this type of training are strong. The trainee learns the job under actual fire. He can size up his subordinates and, in turn, be appraised by them, without artificial support or backing. He can demonstrate independently his latent leadership aptitudes. Some have argued that the best executives will naturally rise to their opportunities without the support of formal training. And it is also claimed that this "normal" progress up the executive ladder does not build up artificial hopes of understudies or destroy the initiative of those not specifically being groomed for promotion.

However, undirected on-the-job training has many serious disadvantages. One no longer expects chemists, engineers, accountants, or designers to learn on their own. Yet the profession of management, where requirements are just as technical, is expected by many to be acquired "by ear." Hence companies whose practices are advanced are supplementing unguided on-the-job training with recognition of formal training in management. Moreover, on-the-job training is too costly, time-

FIGURE 58.   Graphic Presentation of the Approach to Supervisory Training Programs in the Automotive Industry*

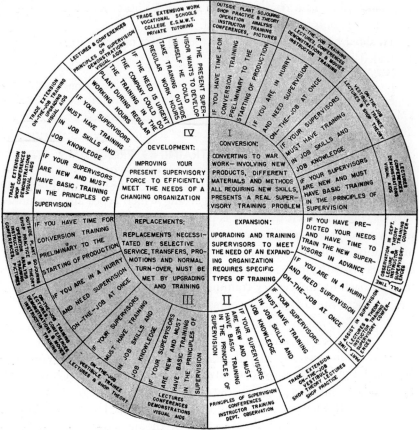

    In the center circle are listed the problems generally faced; in the second circle, the different situations involved; and in the outer circle, the method recommended to meet the specific problem.

    * Source: *Training and Upgrading* (report of Automotive Council of War Production) (Detroit), p. 6.

consuming, and ineffective in developing capable executives. Of course, geniuses may rise to the top by their own efforts, but there are more executive jobs than geniuses to fill them. Hence more realistic methods of developing executives must be sought. And, finally, on-the-job training is wasteful, in that the lessons learned by one "generation" are not transmitted efficiently to succeeding generations.

Although it has not generally been recognized until recently, the shift away from unguided on-the-job training is becoming more noticeable. Its use is defensible only in small companies which cannot afford to develop, or do not have available in the community, any form of training program. Or in periods of very rapid expansion, the expedient recourse may be more or less unguided on-the-job training. However, as a general proposition, its continuance represents a failure to take advantage of better methods of training executives, some of which are now discussed.

UNDERSTUDY PLANS

Executive training by means of understudies also has its proponents. Under this plan each executive is assigned an understudy who, in addition to his regular duties, is expected to acquire some familiarity with the tasks and practices of his superior. The understudy is thus expected to be prepared to take over his supervisor's work while he is away from the office. Moreover, he is groomed to replace the executive when a vacancy occurs.

Whether the replacement is temporary or permanent, the understudy plan of preparation does seem to operate under favorable conditions. The trainee presumably is schooled in the atmosphere and position in which he will be expected to perform. As a consequence, he should become well acquainted with his responsibilities and the manner in which they are executed.

The understudy system suffers from several disadvantages which may well outweigh its advantages. First, aspirants for promotion other than the selected understudy may feel that their chances are so remote that it is useless to exert themselves. Second, understudies themselves who have to wait for long periods for vacancies may become discouraged, particularly when they see some other learners whose apprenticeship is shorter fortuitously have vacancies open quickly. In addition, some executives, jealous of their positions, may feel unwilling to open their store of knowledge to potential replacements. Because of such real and practical personal complications, many companies prefer to place the race for promotions upon an open and unpreselected basis.

ROLE PLAYING

A method that has in recent years received much favorable attention is that of "role playing," which was first introduced as the psychodrama or sociodrama. Under this method, a group of supervisors meet in conference, and two are selected to act out some situation which is commonly encountered or is causing trouble. For example, the situation might be that of an employee who is seeking a transfer. Then one of the supervisors is assigned the role of the employee, and the second becomes the supervisor. A few pertinent facts are decided upon, and then the two, without rehearsal, act out how the supervisor and employee would react.

As the two act, the members of the conference observe, make mental notes, and evaluate the performance. After the drama is completed, others may be selected to act out the same situation, or a general discussion of the acting thus far may be reviewed. Often a recording is made so that the "actors" can review their own performances.

The desirable features of this method may be seen in the following advantages which have been ascribed to role playing:

1. The learner learns by doing, and puts what he has learned into immediate practice. This means a maximum of acceptance and utilization on the part of the trainee.

2. The trainee assists in training himself. He is in front of a group of his colleagues when he is playing a part, and he knows what he says is being recorded. He is under pride's pressure and is anxious to turn in a good performance. Because of this he puts the same intensity of effort into his role-playing that he would in dealing with an employee in the shop. He can observe, sometimes for the first time, his own actions in a critical way.

3. Sound recording encourages self-development; hearing his own voice seems to have a powerful effect on a person. Much discussion is eliminated, of course, by playing back the supervisor's part in the human relations skit, thus giving him an opportunity to point out many of his own mistakes. Strangely enough, it was discovered that supervisors often became so absorbed in the role they handled that they lost sight of the use of the principles and techniques. Again, the recording gave them an opportunity to make a critical analysis, and thus evaluate their performance and the performance of a colleague.

4. There is a high degree of learning by observation and listening. The competitive instinct makes each man do his best to excel.

5. When a supervisor takes an employee's part in a skit, it gives him a real approach to the employee's position in a difficult situation.

6. The whole procedure does an excellent job of improving the supervisor's ability to speak effectively and secure acceptance of his ideas. Recording and playing back the speeches is almost identical to the procedure used in training in public speaking. The real plus value of role-playing is that the case situations require the supervisor continually to seek acceptance of his ideas just as his job normally requires this in the shop.

7. It enables management to separate those who talk a good job in training sessions from those who perform a good job in the plant. In certain in-

stances, we have noted a terrific drop in the performance of some persons, and on tracing it back have learned that there seems to be a direct correlation between good performance in role-playing and good performance in the factory.[1]

TRAINING WITHIN INDUSTRY

An outstanding contribution to training of supervisors was made during World War II by the Training within Industry section of the War Manpower Commission. Its work was so outstanding that the methods which it refined and developed have much of permanent value to commend them. This group, made up of representatives from industry, labor, and government, after much study and trial and error, came to the conclusion that supervisors require specific knowledge and skills if they are to do their jobs properly. The statement of TWI (as it is commonly known) on the subject of the needs of the supervisor is:

EVERY SUPERVISOR HAS FIVE NEEDS

1. *Knowledge of the Work.* Materials, tools, processes, operations, products and how they are made and used.
2. *Knowledge of Responsibilities.* Policies, agreements, rules, regulations, schedules, interdepartmental relationships.

   These two knowledge needs must be met currently and locally by each plant or company.

   Such knowledge must be provided if each supervisor is to know his job and is to have a clear understanding of his authority and responsibilities as a part of management.
3. *Skill in Instructing.* Increasing production by helping supervisors to develop a well-trained work force which will get into production quicker; have less scrap, rework and rejects, fewer accidents, and less tool and equipment damage.
4. *Skill in Improving Methods.* Utilizing materials, machines, and manpower more effectively by having supervisors study each operation in order to eliminate, combine, rearrange, and simplify details of the jobs.
5. *Skill in Leading.* Increasing production by helping supervisors to improve their understanding of individuals, their ability to size up situations, and their ways of working with people.

   These three skills must be acquired individually. Practice and experience in using them enable both new and experienced supervisors to recognize and solve daily problems promptly.[2]

The Training within Industry Service assisted companies in giving their supervisors a start in acquiring these skills through four ten-hour

---

[1] Allan H. Tyler, "A Case Study of Role Playing," *Personnel,* September, 1948, p. 138.

[2] *The Training within Industry Report* (Washington, D.C.: War Manpower Commission, 1945). This report contains an excellent description of the development, operation, and results of this program.

programs: job instruction, job methods, job relations, and program development training—

  I. Job instruction training
     A. How to get ready to instruct
       1. Have a time table.
       2. Break down the job.
       3. Have everything ready.
       4. Have the work place properly arranged.
     B. How to instruct
       1. Prepare the worker.
       2. Present the operation.
       3. Try out performance.
       4. Follow up.
  II. Job methods training
     A. Break down the job.
     B. Question every detail.
     C. Develop the new method.
     D. Apply the new method.
  III. Job relations training
     A. Get the facts.
     B. Weigh and decide.
     C. Take action.
     D. Check results.
  IV. Program development training
     A. Spot a production problem.
     B. Develop a specific plan.
     C. Get plan into action.
     D. Check results.

Each of the foregoing programs was written up in "package form" so that they could be given almost identically anywhere by qualified instructors. The instructors originally were few in number, but, by following the practice of the learners becoming instructors to other groups, and so on, eventually over 23,000 TWI trainees had instructed 1,750,650 in these courses.

These courses have been described because they have so much to offer to those who desire to build short courses for supervisors. Obviously, in thirty or forty hours it is impossible to train supervisors in these matters completely. But, in such time, supervisors can be instructed to an extent that will give them more confidence in themselves and more satisfaction from their work.

Although the federal government no longer offers its help in connection with these war-born courses, some of the original founders of these courses have organized a private nonprofit association to continue these useful programs of training.

OTHER SUPERVISORY PROGRAMS

TWI provided but one plan of supervisory training. A few other plans are now mentioned out of the long list of attempts to train this particular level of the executive group. Since many supervisors start out as group leaders with the primary responsibility of training and some simple supervision, an example of training for this initial stage of leadership is desirable. In one instance, a program has been developed in which trainees are given a three-month course under the guidance of trained instructors and under shop conditions. The trainees are given work that is intended to provide working knowledge along technical lines in the application of leadership qualities to improve production, in the workings of various line and staff departments, and in principles of supervision.

In another program, emphasis is laid upon the development of better relations between supervisors and the upper levels of management. This is accomplished by bringing small groups of foremen into a series of full-day meetings, lectures, and conferences with top management. By means of a carefully planned schedule and topical outline, various aspects of company and supervisory problems are explained to and discussed with the supervisors. In this way, the policies of the company can be instilled, and the association of top and supervisory officials leads to more friendly relations. After the foremen return to their jobs, a series of meetings is conducted with their immediate superiors and leaders of associate departments. Thus, from the top levels to his own department, the supervisor gets a feeling of working relationships that is most helpful to him and to the "family" for which he works.

Another supervisory program is based upon guided reading of published literature. Books, bulletins, and magazine articles dealing with good foremanship are distributed to the supervisors. At intervals, conferences are held to discuss particular views, and tests are given to determine how much has been read and how well.

POSITION ROTATION PLAN

Another plan of training which has had some acceptance in industry, perhaps influenced by assignment shifts in military organizations, is that of rotating key and promising executives and subordinates. The assumptions of such plans are threefold: first, that, by job rotation, executives will tend to think in terms of managerial principles rather than the technical aspects of particular functional fields; second, that rotating will permit good executives to determine the functional fields in which they would prefer to manage; and, third, by gaining a broad view of interdivisional problems, the top positions in the company can be filled by better-qualified appointees. Against these values must be cited the disadvantages of the disturbances caused in inaugurating the plan and in the periodic changes of leadership in various departments and divisions.

The "merry-go-round" plan of the Consolidated Edison Company of New York is an example of this type of executive training. The plan operates at both supervisory and "middle management" levels. Assignments of supervisors to the rotation plan are made by a committee of department heads, subject to the approval of the executive vice-president. Assignments of department heads are made by the senior vice-president and his committee of vice-presidents. The progress of appointees is evaluated by the respective committees. The appointees are removed from the plan, reassigned, or kept on their jobs as the committees decide. Moving days come twice a year, on the first of April and the first of October. In order to prevent disruption of operations in the units to which trainees have been moved, the policy is followed of not moving too many executives out of any one unit at the same time. In this way, the experienced men help to stabilize operations while the new appointee is getting his feet on the ground.

Some of the more important advantages which this company has derived from this plan have been stated as follows:

a) Provides a well-rounded training and background of experience for the individual, familiarizing him with many other phases of the Company's operations. The individual so trained considers his problems and makes his decision more intelligently in the light of their effect on the operations of the organization as a whole.

b) Streamlines the organization through periodic introduction of a new managerial viewpoint. Eliminates situations or operations which may have been carried down unnecessarily over a period of years. Prevents over-manning and "dry rot" in the organization.

c) Stimulates the development of the individual because of the element of competition introduced.

d) Eliminates the assumption by an individual of any "vested right" in a particular job. Explodes a man out of a job, "inherited" through favor which may or may not have been justified.

e) Tests the individuals. The executive ability and versatility demonstrated in the progressive assignments provide an indication as to which men are most suitable as material from which Top Flight executives can ultimately be drawn. Any lack of executive ability is also demonstrated and the "Merry-go-round" provides a means of placing an individual in a job for which he is best qualified.

f) Will improve and should in most instances eliminate any situation where the efficiency of the organization is being impaired by lack of co-operation between individuals. The periodic changing from one job to another and from one set of associations to another would tend to minimize friction caused by personality clashes or personal feuds, and would tend to expose any chronic sources of such friction to suitable corrective action.

g) Widens the trainee's circle of acquaintance among Company executives. In one year's assignment he will probably meet and work with some two hundred new acquaintances.[3]

MULTIPLE MANAGEMENT

An interesting development in the training of the group of executives in between the supervisory and top level of an organization is that inaugurated in 1932 by McCormick & Company of Baltimore. Under this plan, known as "multiple management," three boards supplement the senior board of directors. These boards are the factory executive board, the salesboard, and the junior executive board. Interest here is in the latter of these.

The theory of the plan is that by working on managerial problems in much the manner that a board of directors does, the executives on the junior board will gain useful education. To make the plan practical and realistic, the board works on such problems as those pertaining to bonuses, wages, working conditions, company plans and policies, etc., submitted to it by employees. In carrying on its discussions and in reaching its decisions, the board has access to all company records. The solutions and suggestions adopted by the board, if approved by the senior board or the president of the company, are made company rules and regulations.

The organization of the junior board provides for rotation of members and stresses the advancement of promising executives. Membership on the thirteen-man board is by elections held every six months, at which time at least three of the current members must be replaced. Each member in turn sponsors an apprentice for two months. The thought here is to guide, encourage, and indoctrinate employees who have been hired within the preceding two years and who seem to possess executive ability. And the junior board members by their own work are aware that their activities may lead ultimately to selection for the senior board,

---

[3] D. S. Sargent, "Appraising Executive Performance," *Supervision,* November, 1945, pp. 6–7.

membership in which is dependent, for one thing, upon service on one of the boards mentioned earlier.

This plan has much to commend it. Executives in the middle group are given the opportunity to tackle significant company problems, to discuss them freely and openly, to exhibit their judgment and originality, and to meet with senior officers on matters of significance to them. They can develop a sense of worth-while contribution to the solution of over-all problems of the company. Above all, to themselves personally, they know that opportunities for promotion are available and that their chances depend upon their own performances, open to the view of their colleagues as well as superior officers.

CONFERENCE TRAINING

Although not a particular type of training, conference training is so widely used in so many types of executive training that a description of it is warranted here. In conference training, the essential feature is the provision for guided discussion in a small group of conferees. To be most effective the plan calls for the following:

1. A competent conference leader, who can carry out the principles of good conferences
2. A preplanned outline of what the conference is to cover and how it is to be conducted
3. A satisfactory and well-equipped conference room
4. A limit to the number of conferees, preferably not over fifteen
5. An interesting beginning, spirited and pointed discussions, and a good summarization

MISCELLANEOUS TYPES OF COURSES

A number of other types of training programs are also worth mentioning. For example, growing in popularity in some fields is the short intensive school program. Executives are brought together for periods of a week to two weeks of training on well-defined topics. These short schools, or "workshops" as they are also known, are conducted by companies themselves or by various universities from time to time. They are usually restricted to qualified executives and professional staff. Their purpose is to provide refresher courses and training in new developments and techniques. Work in counseling, testing, job analysis and evaluation, managerial principles, and various aspects of industrial relations are examples of training received in such schools. In addition to the value of the courses themselves, the opportunity for discussion by small groups of executives with common interests and problems is an advantage of this form of training. A possible shortcoming of such schools, which can be minimized by scheduling them during seasonal lulls, is that they take executives away from their desks for a relatively extended period of time.

Many companies follow the practice of sending executives to conventions, association meetings of industries, educational institutes, and conferences which last at most up to three or four days. This is more of an educational than a training program, although some sessions of these meetings are very technical and practical in nature. Such training gives executives an opportunity to become acquainted with others in their industries, to gain suggestions about latest developments, and to learn of practices and sources of materials which can be followed up later by correspondence or personal visits.

Correspondence courses are also underwritten by some companies. This practice is particularly advisable in companies in which the cost of developing individualized programs is prohibitive or personally conducted courses of good caliber are not available in the community. Careful investigation is desirable in order to be sure of the reliability of the school and quality of instructional material supplied. Executives and supervisors can then be assured of receiving instruction, direct guidance, and evaluation which would not otherwise be available.

An unusual combination of operative and executive training is provided by the "career man in industry" concept of building a strong organization. The principle behind this training is that carefully selected employees should be given training and opportunity for promotion. Then, as vacancies occur, well-prepared aspirants to positions will be available. In addition, the employees themselves will recognize the fact that opportunities are presented to worth-while candidates. The training program for new employees, using the sales field as an example, is made up of the following four parts:

1. A week of orientation in which the general make-up, policies, and practices are presented by various executives. The aim here is twofold: to draw an over-all picture of the company and to sell the company to the new employee.

2. An eight-month training in the essentials of salesmanship. This is a combination course of classroom work, study of various departments, and practice selling.

3. Sales work in the field, under strict supervision, is then provided. This consists of a month of retail selling, then an intensive review period at the home office, and finally a month in a field office doing sales promotion work.

4. Every two years, a week of "postgraduate" training is provided. This provides an opportunity for refresher work, learning of new products and merchandising methods firsthand, and strengthening personal contacts with the company.

CONTENT OF TRAINING

The foregoing has covered the most important types of executive training programs and has also noted various techniques and tools used in connection therewith. It is now pertinent to examine the subject matter which is covered in such courses. This might seem a relatively easy aspect, but actually it is most difficult for the simple reason that so little is known about what makes for successful leadership. And this is, of course, the essence of management. Some executive training programs seek to improve and develop leadership capacities and some satisfy themselves with the various problems that a manager, executive, or supervisor is likely to encounter. Attention is given first to the latter type of content, and then leadership qualities are examined.

Perhaps the obvious and simplest approach to the matter of content is to take up tasks which the executive is most likely to encounter. Of interest is the fact that most executive training programs, from this angle, take up various subjects connected with handling people—the so-called "human relations" problem. Such subjects as the following are discussed:

1. Present-day labor-management philosophy and policies
2. Working with others through organizational channels
3. Communicating up and down organizational channels
4. Employment policies and practices
5. Training and education policies and practices
6. Discipline, grievances, and rules and regulations
7. Employee services and recreation
8. Transfers, promotion, merit, and seniority policies
9. The union contract; its meaning and implications
10. Community agencies and institutions

On the other hand, a more basic approach is to try to develop content, which has reference to the basic characteristics that a leader should possess, irrespective of the specific tasks performed. Unfortunately, there is as yet no agreement as to what these characteristics are. Fortunately, however, much study is being devoted to this problem, and it is likely that agreement among students will consequently develop. To illustrate the characteristics that have been included in executive training programs, the following list is of interest:

1. Ability to think
2. Ability to organize
3. Ability to handle people
4. Ability to plan
5. Ability to lead
6. Ability to get and interpret facts
7. Loyalty
8. Decisiveness
9. Teaching ability
10. Ability to solve problems
11. Courage
12. Self-motivation
13. Desire for achievement and prestige
14. Social balance and understanding
15. Sense of responsibility
16. Emotional balance and poise
17. Ability to influence people, individually and in groups
18. Attitudes toward subordinates and associates
19. Attitude toward community associations
20. Attitude toward economic and political systems

This list is by no means complete, but it does illustrate the wide range of subjects that have been considered basic leadership traits.

An interesting illustration of the characteristics desirable in leaders may be found in Figure 59. This depicts the fundamental responsibili-

FIGURE 59.   Executive Characteristics*

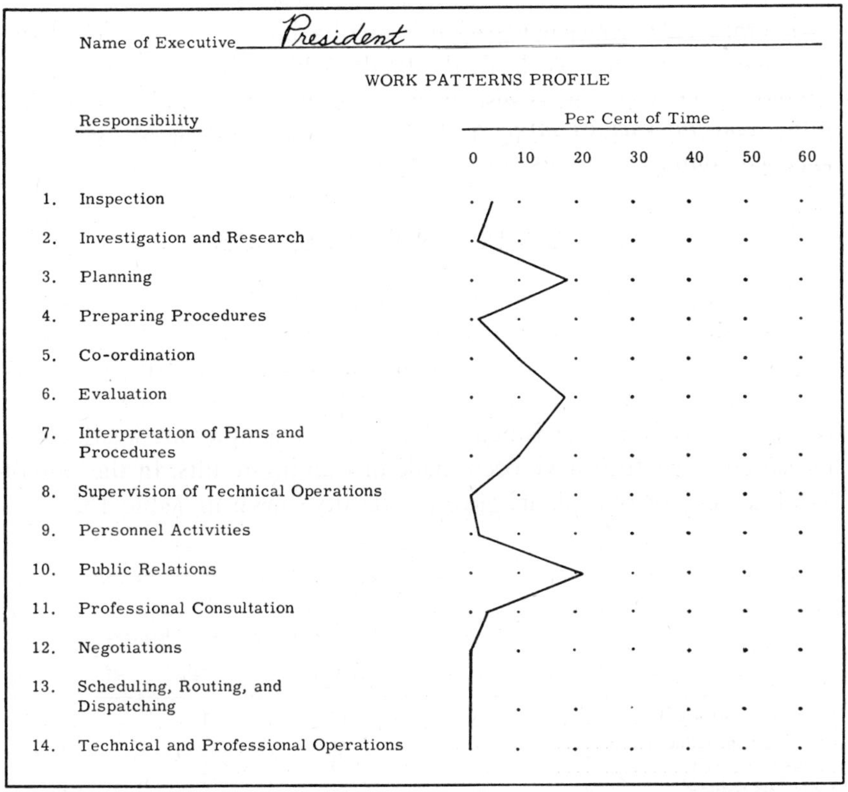

* Source: C. L. Shartle, "Leadership and Executive Performance," *Personnel*, March, 1949, p. 371.

ties of executives and, in the case cited, the approximate percentage of time spent in performing the duties. Certainly, if the content of a job can be so determined, the next step of appropriate training is more easily taken.

Since there is so much variation in executive training content, the best practice for any company in establishing its own program is to give consideration to outside practices but to build its program in terms of its own needs. This can be done by taking the following steps:

1. Determine as precisely as possible the major objectives or tasks that the company faces
2. Inventory present executive capacities
3. Compute the shortages of executive capacities as compared to major needs
4. Establish content of training required by individual executives to bring them up to desired standards

By tailoring content to suit individual needs, it is possible to arrive at a program which will invariably prove valuable. Moreover, such an approach usually achieves better executive co-operation in the training program because the executives themselves must help in developing the program. And where participation is involved, there is a greater desire to make the program work. In the final analysis, this in itself helps to develop a better leader because an executive who seeks to improve himself possesses a sound feeling of service to others—a desirable quality of true leadership.

FOLLOW-UP AND EVALUATION

Follow-up and evaluation of executive training programs are particularly difficult because it is almost impossible to determine which results of executive efforts are attributable to training and which to other causes. Nevertheless, it is desirable to make an attempt in this direction because a partial answer is better than none. Examples are available of measurements which have been made of training results. In the case of TWI, a study of 600 plants gave the results shown in Table 15.

TABLE 15

TRAINING RESULTS

KIND OF RESULT	PERCENTAGE OF PLANTS REPORTING RESULTS			
	Under 25%	25–49%	50–74%	75% and Over
Production increased...........	63	16	1	20
Training time reduced..........	52	25	7	16
Manpower saved..............	89	9	1	1
Scrap loss reduced............	89	5	5	1

FIGURE 60*

TWI OUTSTANDING "RESULT OF THE WEEK" IN DALLAS DISTRICT

Result was noted and reported to us on (Date) *May 3, 1945*

Result of: J.I.   *x*   J.M.   *x*   J.R.   *x*   P.D.

1. Kind of establishment (name of product or service)   *Shipbuilding*

2. Name and location of plant   *"X" Company*

   May we use company name?   Yes   *x*   No

3. Number of employees in plant   *18,749*

4. Number of employees affected   *15,000*

5. Just what happened in "before and after" terms:
   (State evidence in facts, figures, man hours, etc.)

   During the past 4 years four different types of vessels have been built. When the yard opened only 2% of the workers had previous shipbuilding experience. About 50% had no previous experience in any related industry.
   The average employment during this 4 years has been 18,000. The number of certificates issued in the three TWI "J" programs are:

   > J.I. 2850
   > J.M. 800
   > J.R. 540

   Mr. Newell Hogan, Training Director, and Mr. James D. McClellan, Production Manager, reported the following beneficial results from TWI programs:

   > Increase in production. 45%
   > Reduction in training time. 78%
   > Reduction in scrap. 69%
   > Reduction in tool breakage. 75%
   > Saving of manpower. 45%
   > Reduction of accidents. 70%

   These results were arrived at by comparison of production department records, based on the construction of the first 50 destroyer escorts as compared with the last 50. The credit for these beneficial results is largely attributed to the successful continuous use of TWI programs.

   All levels of supervision in both the yard and the office have been processed in one or more of the "J" programs. This accounts for the large number of employees affected.

---

* Source: *The Training within Industry Report* (Washington, D.C.: War Manpower Commission, 1945), p. 94.

Interesting results in individual plants are shown in the reports illustrated in Figures 60 and 61.

FIGURE 61*

TWI OUTSTANDING "RESULT OF THE WEEK" IN DENVER DISTRICT

Result was noted and reported to us on (Date) *April 16, 1945*

Result of: J.I. *x*   J.M. *x*   J.R. *x*   P.D.

1. Kind of establishment (name of product or service) *Rubber products*

2. Name and location of plant *"X" Company*

   May we use company name?   Yes *x*   No

3. Number of employees in plant   *5,000*

4. Number of employees affected   *40*

5. Just what happened in "before and after" terms:
      (State evidence in facts, figures, man hours, etc.)

   Before "J" Programs:
      In one clerical department, where 46 were employed, 375,000 units were produced in one year.

   After "J" Programs:
      By applying the three "J" methods conscientiously and continuously, 450,000 units were produced by 40 workers.
      This is an increase of 20%, or 75,000 units, in output by a work force reduced by 13%, or 6 workers.

   The quality of the work was also greatly improved.

   Note: Most credit is given to J.I. and J.R., as the work force has always been method-improvement minded.

---

* Source: *The Training within Industry Report* (Washington, D.C.: War Manpower Commission, 1945), p. 93.

An interesting summary of the results that should flow from a good executive training program is contained in the following listing (certainly it is a broad gauge test of this subject, as well it should be):

1. Increased executive management skills
2. Development in each executive of a broad background and appreciation of the company's over-all operations and objectives
3. Greater delegation of authority because executives down the line are better qualified and better able to assume increased responsibilities
4. Creation of a reserve of qualified personnel to replace present incumbents and to staff new positions
5. Improved selection for promotion
6. Minimum delay in staffing new positions and minimum disruption of operations during replacements of incumbents

7. Provision for the best combination of youth, vigor, and experience in top management and increased span of productive life in high-level positions
8. Improved executive morale
9. Attraction to the company of ambitious men who wish to move ahead as rapidly as their abilities permit
10. Increased effectiveness and reduced costs, resulting in greater assurance of continued profitability[4]

EVALUATION OF TRAINEES

Another approach to evaluation is that of determining how well executive trainees have learned. On the one hand, they may be tested and rated after their courses of training. Thus, in some of the plans mentioned in the foregoing, supervisors, and higher executives as well, are rated as to their promise for further training. In addition, regular examinations are scheduled to ascertain how well various phases of technical and descriptive materials have been absorbed. Such tests should be given with care in order to avoid the development of a feeling on the part of trainees that a "school" is being operated; most executives like to feel that the "little red school house" is a part of their past.

More informal plans of follow-up include conferences and discussions by superiors with those who have taken training work. In this way, the supervisors can obtain some measure of the value of the training received, and the trainees can prepare themselves more carefully, knowing that such talks are to take place. An added value of such informal talks is that they bring various levels of leadership together more frequently, giving each the opportunity to get better acquainted with the other.

An inversion of follow-up which has desirable points is that in which trainees are asked to express themselves on the quality or results of training. In one company, for example, executives are asked to sign and comment upon the quality and usefulness of each conference they attend. This acts as a double-edged weapon: first, the conference leader and training school are alert to build and conduct better sessions; and, second, the conferees must be more attentive in order to be able to express pertinent interpretations and criticisms. In another company, executives who take various forms of training are required to fill out weekly reports indicating progress in various aspects of their work. All that is required is a simple check (without quantitative estimates) opposite any of the following items: reduction of indirect labor, indirect

---

[4] E. W. Reilley and B. J. Nuller-Thym, "Executive Development," *Personnel,* May, 1948, p. 412.

cost, daywork operations, materials or supplies; and increase or improvement in processes, quality, personnel relations, or suggestions. Here again knowledge that the training is expected to produce results will keep the trainees alert to see how training material can be applied in various phases of their work.

QUESTIONS AND PROBLEMS

1. Why is the training and experience that one receives while working as an operator of relatively little value when one becomes a supervisor?

2. If previous experience is usually valueless, how do most people who are appointed to supervisory positions get by on their new jobs?

3. If you were asked to prepare a supervisory training program, what use would you make of job analysis in this connection?

4. Indicate what differences in training programs might be found in the case of lower levels of executives, middle groups, top executives, and staff executives.

5. Assume conditions of role playing with another student and pretend to handle an employee who has a habit of coming in late. What difficulties do you encounter in this practice session, and what must be done to overcome them?

6. Assume conditions of role playing, and pretend that a supervisor is being told by the general manager that his departmental expenditures are 10 per cent over budgeted figures. What lessons do you learn from this practice? Can executives use role playing to learn how to handle situations that concern only them? Explain.

7. Do you think that role playing will ever be widely used? Why or why not?

8. If you were to compile a list of abilities that an executive should possess, would you not come out with one that would set up an impossible task of training? Explain.

9. If supervisory and executive training is so valuable during war years, why is it not also valuable during peacetimes? Explain.

10. Assume that, in a company following the understudy plan of executive development, you, contrary to your expectations, are not made the understudy of a particular executive. Would you consider the door of opportunity closed in your face? Would this not tend to lower your morale and your desire to work hard?

11. Explain the general principles of the TWI plan of supervisory development. What are its strong and weak points?

12. Under what conditions is the statement true that: "If the worker hasn't learned, the instructor hasn't taught"?

13. In the job relations training program, "get the facts" is one of the essential steps. Assume that an employee asks you about the profits of the company and, upon asking your superiors, they inform you that such information is not being made available to the lower levels of the organization. What

happens then if you have based your hopes in handling grievances on the job relations training program?

14. How can you be sure that as an executive you have all the facts necessary to handle a job relations problem?

15. A number of organizations have used the job rotation plan of executive development to good effect. Why would this plan have good results? What are its shortcomings?

16. It has been said that the groups of executives between the top and bottom levels of the organization are usually the poorest trained. How may this be accounted for?

17. Some have contended that conferences serve merely to waste time, avoid decisions, and increase organization politics. How may these pitfalls be avoided?

18. Some companies follow the plan of encouraging their executives to attend conventions in order to broaden their views. How can the effectiveness of such plans be increased?

19. Write a report on the merits of visual education methods in executive training.

20. By what methods may executive training methods be evaluated? What are the major difficulties in making such measurements?

CHAPTER

15 | Basic Aspects of Education

SCOPE OF EDUCATION

As noted earlier, "education" is used here to refer to the general increase in ability to adjust to one's environment. Businesswise this contrasts with learning how to perform specific tasks, which is the province of training. While a person may be skilled in doing (trained to do) a particular job, his performance may nonetheless be mediocre because his understanding of (education in regard to) it is of a low order. The lack of (or mis-)understanding may be in regard to the particular job itself, to the policies regarding the job, to the desires of superiors, or to the actions of subordinates (if any).

Poor adjustment may be found as often among executives as among employees. When executives fail to understand and provide for the social, economic, and political aspects of business, they will lead their company to unsatisfactory results. When they fail to understand their subordinates and employees, they bring about or accentuate labor-management disputes. On the other hand, when employees fail to adjust— through their own fault or that of others—they become parties to unnecessary grievances, create disturbing labor problems, lead frustrating lives, and are poor producers.

The ultimate goals of education are to increase productivity, to safeguard the success of the company, and to increase the personal satisfactions of the individuals themselves. These goals are sought through education's effect upon understanding, perspective, and attitude. Labor, for example, works more effectively when it understands what management is doing, when it feels management's objectives are significant, and when it agrees that management's methods are justifiable. And executives, in turn, can lead a more effective team when they understand the motives, needs, and thinking of labor. Through such understanding comes, first, appreciation for one another's interests and problems; second, adjustments in their thinking and action; and, third, fair compromises in their plans and actions.

290

This discussion of education, therefore, is as much concerned with the education of executives as with workers. In actual practice the education of both is so intertwined that it is difficult, if not impossible, to separate the two even for purposes of discussion. It is felt, however, that if management is to educate labor effectively, it must first know what labor knows or needs to know. Hence this chapter is devoted to principles and practices of developing an upward flow of information by which management may learn about the thinking of lower levels of the organization. In the next chapter, attention will be directed to downward and horizontal flows of information. Thus is established the two-way flow of communications which is the blood stream of an educational program for management and for employees.

In regard to the upward phases of educational communications, the following aspects are discussed in this chapter:

1. Basic considerations in employee education
2. Nature and role of employee morale
3. Knowledge of employees
4. Measuring attitudes and understanding
5. Encouraging employee expressions

BASIC CONSIDERATIONS IN EMPLOYEE EDUCATION

NEED OF A PROGRAM

Broadly speaking, any worker's effectiveness, in terms of himself, depends upon his "know-how" and "know-why." It is with the latter that we are now concerned. "Know-why" has a number of facets. It underlies the understanding that a given employee has to such questions as these:

1. Why is this job important?
2. How does this job tie in with the work of fellow employees?
3. What is there in this job for me?
4. What is the company getting out of it?
5. Is there a fair division between us?
6. Will I benefit in the long run from "putting out" on it?
7. Does my boss really appreciate how I'm doing here?
8. Why are they always talking about competitive conditions?
9. Why is my job less important than Bill's?

All these questions have an impact upon motivation. Answers to them will determine the degree of exertion which an employee puts forth. His co-operation with superiors; his loyalty to the company; his willingness to work really hard; and his use of company properties all are closely affected by his answers. And these questions are being answered every minute of every day, whether or not a company has an educational program. From newspapers, radio, and television; from the informal actions of supervisors; from the communications of unions; from governmental channels; and from his fellow workers, he is getting information, ideas, and impressions. Unless management formally participates in the educational program too, its views will not be communicated correctly or completely. So the first point that needs to be made on education is that management must take a forceful, constructive role in such a program.

FACTORS OF EDUCATION

A little thought about the questions asked in the foregoing section will disclose two broad aspects of any employee's education:

1. What he really knows, or doesn't know
2. What he feels or senses

Of course, the two are related—our thinking is affected by our emotions and vice versa. Were employees guided solely by logical, mental, and rational processes, the educational process would be somewhat simplified. The impact of emotional and nonrational factors on the decisions of all of us (management as well as labor) cannot be denied. Hence the lesson for management is obvious, both emotions and logic must be affected by an educational program.

DYNAMIC ASPECTS OF EDUCATION

It must also be recognized that education is a continuing, repetitive, and dynamic process. At a particular moment, employees may be convinced of the fairness of management. But new employees are hired and the old forget, so the lessons must be repeated. Or new processes or such changes as automation arouse fears in employees; so education is called for to reassure them. And as employees acquire new ideas, management must be alert to learn about them, transmit new information to employees, note the reactions of employees to the educational efforts, and proceed to repeat or add to the educational process, as the case may be. Whether we like it or not, the need of a permanent program must be accepted as an important fact about education.

MEASURING EDUCATIONAL NEEDS

Among these introductory remarks, one more should be made—that resources of education will be utilized most effectively when educational needs are measured. To minimize waste, it is essential to determine how much employees know and what their attitudes are. From this base, the program can be designed more intelligently regarding how much education is to be aimed for in succeeding periods. At the end of each period, measurements can again be taken to ascertain how much progress has been made. Thus the effectiveness of the program will be evaluated; and also the basis for the next phase of the program will be laid.

In using the term "measurement," it is recognized that absolute yardsticks of educational matters are not available. Nevertheless, there are arbitrary, relative, and useful measures of what employees know, their opinions and attitudes. These will be noted later in this chapter. The absence of perfect measuring sticks is no reason to discard others from which partial, yet practical, estimates of progress and programs may be derived.

MORALE

SCOPE

With the foregoing suggestions about education in mind, it is now pertinent to note the relation of education to employee productivity. Worker productivity or effectiveness depends upon technological resources, managerial skill, employee skills and aptitudes, and employee willingness to co-operate. And such willingness more and more seems to be a major factor in labor-management relations. It seems to be determined in any given case by, first, the understanding which an employee has of company practices and, second, his attitude toward his company and its management. Education's task is to improve such understanding and attitudes. Before this task can be undertaken effectively, management must have a clear picture of existing understanding and attitudes. Hence the subject of understanding is discussed in the next section, and attitudes in the present section.

Attitudes toward a company or its management essentially find expression in terms of a spirit of zeal, confidence, and loyalty—or lack thereof. This intangible attitude, this "esprit de corps," this mental set, is generally known as "morale." It is so influential in its impact that it is well to devote attention now to (1) the theory of its development, (2) important considerations in its development, and (3) steps or stages of development.

THEORY OF MORALE DEVELOPMENT

Since morale is a mental attitude, it must have its source in some causal factors. Close inspection of situations in which good morale exists reveals an understanding on the part of employees (and executives, too) that high output, low costs, good profits, and, of course, superior service to the customer are indispensable to high wages, good working conditions, and superior opportunities for personal advancement.

Because of such understanding, they are willing to subordinate themselves to the good of the company. And, not unlike the Biblical injunction that to gain life one must lose it, the act of subordination results eventually in personal enhancements. In short, employees who advance the interests of the company thereby advance their own. In such instances, the interests of company and employee have been satisfactorily integrated to the benefit of each, and with a resulting effective mental attitude or morale.

Such a process of integration of interests will have desirable morale effects. Employees will follow orders willingly, adhere faithfully to company rules, carry on in spite of difficulties, co-operate voluntarily, and exhibit pride in their company and its products. They are willing, and with initiative and personal pride, to follow their leaders to achieve established objectives. They are, on the other hand, ready to repel attacks on the reputation of their working environment.

These favorable aspects of morale do not arise spontaneously. Management must recognize the various relationships and cultivate the forces that yield the desired effects. In cases in which management has failed to promote morale or actually prevented the process, the results have eventually been most unsatisfactory. Those who avariciously have lined their own pockets at the expense of labor have brought forth increased labor trouble, burdensome legislation, and the opposition of the general public. And those who ignored the need of instructing employees in an appreciation of the important relation of company objectives in the attainment of personal objectives have also helped to bring forth undesirable results. After all, employees ignorant of the process of integration of interests can obstruct the development of good relations just as much as those aggrieved by injustices.

To summarize, morale is an attitude of mind. It is developed out of the process of integrating interests. And its effects are combined in a total willingness to apply skills and aptitudes with efficiency and economy. It is, therefore, indispensable to the attainment of the goals that the company deems worth while.

IMPORTANT CONSIDERATIONS IN MORALE DEVELOPMENT

Of significance in morale development are, first, the responsibilities of management; second, factors of development; and, third, need of continuous vigilance.

1. Management's Responsibilities. Perhaps the foremost requirement for morale development and maintenance is the realization that these are high responsibilities of management. It would indeed be fine were labor to come to work with good morale and to assume responsibility for its maintenance. Unfortunately, this is not true. Hence, if management is to protect and enhance its desired prerogatives of leadership, it will do well to take the time and effort to improve the morale of its supposed followers. If and when management does not, neither it nor anyone else should be surprised when the allegiance of employees attaches to outside groups rather than internal management. And even though management may take the financial risks of operating a business, that in itself does not convince labor that its loyalty should be on management's side.

2. Factors of Morale. Another significant requirement is the recognition that the number of factors which may cause morale to be raised or lowered is infinite. Every factor in a business—its objectives, ideals, leadership, functions, faculties, environmental aspects, organization structure, procedures, and controls—and how it is planned, organized, and controlled, affects the morale of employees. For that reason, every executive in the organization should be made conscious of the possible effect that any of his acts may have upon the morale of employees.

This is an excellent reason why someone with a knowledge of personnel relationships and effects should be high in the administrative councils to interpret all matters that may be discussed from a personnel viewpoint. If it is significant to have sales, production, and financial representation upon executive committees, present-day conditions in labor relations are such that the representation of the specialist in personnel management is no less important. Indeed, one may find that one reason why personnel departments have not succeeded in developing better labor relations is that, until very recently, few companies have assigned them a sufficiently high place in the organization. As a consequence, their efforts are stifled at the point at which it is imperative that they gain backing and recognition—the top administrative level.

3. Maintaining Morale. It must also be recognized that even though morale is slow to develop and difficult to maintain, it can be lost overnight. It seems to be a human trait to remember the bad and to forget the good, to believe the rumors and to shy away from logic and facts, and to pursue heroes one day and to cast stones upon them the next. The occasions on which such things have happened in labor relations should have been sufficiently frequent to show business leaders

the fragile threads that tie employee and employer together. Illogical though it may be, it is at once pathetic and humorous to see employees criticize employers for bad practices of years ago as reason for not trusting them in the present. For example, not long ago during an arbitration hearing, a representative of labor claimed that piece-rate data could not be trusted because the company had cut some rates in 1932. Although the company representative contended and the labor representative agreed that no cuts had been made since that time, labor was still skeptical. Such evidences are striking in the lesson they teach: Eternal vigilance is the price of good morale.

STEPS IN DEVELOPING MORALE

In broad outline a program to develop morale would consist of the following:

1. Divide and locate responsibilities for morale upon—
   a) Line and staff executives
   b) Administrative and operative executives
2. Determine the relationships that exist between—
   a) Company objectives and personal objectives
   b) The factors which cause good morale and the results which flow from it
3. Determine the extent to which good morale exists in terms of—
   a) Effectiveness of the organization in attaining its objectives
   b) The attitudes of employees toward various phases of the company
4. Develop and install plans for—
   a) Counteracting the forces leading to poor morale
   b) Strengthening the forces leading to good morale
5. Follow up and evaluate morale-building programs—
   a) By periodic audits of specific programs
   b) By periodic audits of all personnel activities

This outline is not expanded here because in essence it is the outline of the entire text. The factor of morale has been important in everything that has been said thus far and, if possible, will be of increasing significance in the topics to be discussed soon. A momentary pause to summarize the concepts of morale building has been deemed advisable, because of their relation to an understanding of the important factor of employee attitudes.

KNOWLEDGE OF EMPLOYEES

SCOPE OF SUBJECT MATTER

The willingness of employees to co-operate is also affected by the knowledge they possess about various company practices and policies.

Anything or anybody connected with or related to the company may come into an employee's sphere of fact or opinion. Hence there are no subjects which can be said to be "none of his business." Since they affect his thinking—and thus his willingness to co-operate—an employee's reactions to anything or anybody must be made company business. At least this is true in terms of determining what may be included as subject matter in an educational program.

When it is said that nothing is outside the realm of education, there is danger that something important may be left out. Hence it is desirable at least to list the major categories with which an educational program is to deal. These may include such headings as the following:

1. Objectives
   a) Of the company in relation to customers, profits, stockholders, employees, and the community
   b) Of a nonfinancial as well as a financial nature for employees and management at all levels
   c) Of a short-run and a long-run nature
2. Policies
   a) In relation to production, sales, financing, prices, and wages
   b) In relation to personnel matters, such as selection, training, wages, and promotions
   c) In relation to handling grievances and disciplinary action
3. Organizational relationships
   a) Of management levels down through to the ranks
   b) Employee channels of communication upward
   c) Relationships to staff departments
   d) Authority and responsibility limits
4. Extracompany relationships
   a) Role of the economic system
   b) Role of the political system
   c) Social and community factors
   d) Problems of national welfare and security

INCLUSIVENESS OF PROGRAMS

More specific examples of the foregoing will be cited in later discussions. The breadth and variety of topics of interest to the employee are apparent. But is the company to educate all employees in all of these? Won't it spend all of its time in education? The job is big, but the stakes are great. Either management spends time on them, or it will lose in the battle of reaching the minds of its employees. Not all subjects need be discussed at one time—the load may be staggered as to subjects and as to different groups of workers. But over the long pull such a coverage must be a part of everyday business practice.

Education need not be conducted on some high plane and in distinctive quarters. Indeed, in the industrial world, education may be effectively carried on in conjunction with training or day-to-day supervisor-employee relations. For example, no more striking lesson in capitalism and the free-enterprise system can be given than the explanation that could accompany a supervisor's discussion with an employee concerning some parts or materials which the latter, let us say, has spoiled. Or in taking up a request for a raise, the supervisor has an excellent opportunity to relate the case to how our profit system operates. Or in writing up an accident report, the employee is in a favorable mood to appreciate the social implications of his actions, and how the company is doing its utmost to accept its social responsibilities. Education can be built into day-to-day industrial relations and not established as a frill or process apart from current realities.

MEASURING ATTITUDES AND UNDERSTANDING

Having seen the importance of attitudes and knowledge of employees, it is now appropriate to see what can be done about their measurement. This task is discussed under the following headings:

1. Need of measurement
2. Information sought
3. Methods of gathering information
4. Reporting findings
5. Rules of measuring attitudes

NEED OF MEASUREMENT

Most executives, to a greater or lesser degree, like to think that they are good judges of what is on the minds of their subordinates. If they were as good as they think they are, the task of measuring employee attitudes would require little more than passing attention here. But the evidence is to the contrary; the minds of employees are far from an open book to most executives, although much can be learned if the organization is taught how to "stop and read."

How far wrong management can be in its interpretations of what workers think may be deduced from a survey in which foremen and employees were asked to rank various morale factors. The results are summarized in Table 16. Here we see that the employers' emphasis upon fair pay, job security, interesting work, and promotion, to mention but a few factors, is not shared in equal degree by the employees. The latter, surprisingly enough, placed promotion, working conditions, and job security at the bottom of the list. When management's sights are so far off the mark, something should be done to correct its aim.

The answer seems to favor some form of formal measurement of employee attitudes. This should not be taken as a peremptory dismissal of more informal interpretations, such as those which supervisors should be making constantly in their daily associations with employees. On the contrary, the supervisor-subordinate contact should be developed into the most commonly used method of measuring attitudes. It is contended here, however, that a study of the techniques and principles of formal methods is useful not only to those who wish to make quantitative measurements but also to those who wish to improve their understanding of employee attitudes.

TABLE 16

RANK ASSIGNED VARIOUS FACTORS BY FOREMEN AND EMPLOYEES*

Job Goal	*Ranked by Workers*	*Ranked by Foremen*
Full appreciation of work done...........	1st	8th
Feeling "in" on things....................	2d	10th
Sympathetic help on personal problems......	3d	9th
Job security.............................	4th	2d
Good wages..............................	5th	1st
"Work that keeps you interested"...........	6th	5th
Promotion and growth in company..........	7th	3d
Personal loyalty to workers................	8th	6th
Good working conditions..................	9th	4th
Tactful disciplining.......................	10th	7th

* From *Foreman Facts* (Newark, N.J.: Labor Relations Institute), Vol. IX, No. 21; reproduced in *Management Review*, June, 1954, p. 362.

INFORMATION SOUGHT

In general, attitude surveys cover all kinds and types of topics for the single reason that action on the part of an employee may be caused by thoughts extraneous to the business as well as those arising out of company practices. A simple outline of classes of information follows:

1. Information about the individual
   a) Relating to his position in the company
   b) Relating to personal matters
2. Information about the company
   a) Degree of participation in various types of company activities
   b) Degree of understanding of company policies and practices
   c) Likes and dislikes
   d) Feelings of fairness and unfairness
3. Information about extracompany matters
   a) Relating to the community
   b) Relating to economic and political affairs

1. THE INDIVIDUAL. The purposes of the first category of information are to allow for individual differences in appraising answers in the

other categories and to interpret the nature of the individual himself. For example, when interpreting the answers on whether or not employees like their supervisors, it is desirable to be able to classify the answers according to such factors about the individuals as the departments in which they work, their age, how long it has been since their last promotion, and the amount of earnings. Again, when such individual characteristics as health, home conditions, affiliations, and temperament are known, it is possible to appraise more intelligently the answers to questions pertaining to the company for which he works.

2. THE COMPANY. The second category of questions is, of course, the heart of such a survey. Here is sought information about what the employee thinks of his company. Using the outline suggested above, unless employees, in the first place, understand company policies and practices, there can be little hope of gaining their confidence, of building morale, and of building an effective working force. To get information on this subject, such questions as the following have been asked:

1. Do you understand how the bonus system works?
2. Did you find the last copy of the Annual Report to Employees interesting and easily understandable?
3. Do you have any questions about the Employee Handbook?
4. Are you getting the kind of company information you want?
5. Have your training courses been useful to you?
6. Has your supervisor explained company policies to your satisfaction?

Questions about the degree of participation in various company activities and programs have three purposes: first, to determine how extensively employees use various facilities; second, to gain an indirect measure of whether or not they like them; and, third, to detect which programs presumably need changes and improvements. Following are examples of questions in this category:

1. Do you take part in company-sponsored athletic or social programs?
2. Do you like the type of music played on the public address system?
3. What features do you like in the company newspaper? (A list of the features is then given.)
4. How often, on the average, do you eat in the cafeteria during the week?
5. Do you read the bulletin boards as a regular practice?

Though the likes and dislikes of employees and their opinions of fairness and unfairness may be illogical, irrational, and emotional, nevertheless these, more than anything else perhaps, are the key to the morale of employees. Consequently, it is essential to determine as accurately as possible the opinions of employees along these lines if proper corrective action is to be taken toward factors producing undesirable attitudes. Following are examples of questions that seek information in these categories:

1. Do you think the principle of our incentive pay plan is fair?
2. Do you find that your fellow workers are friendly?
3. Do you think that promotions are based upon pull?
4. If you had your choice of working hours, which would you choose?
5. Do you hope to stay with the company permanently?

The foregoing description of types of information is not intended to be exhaustive or critical. How much detail should be sought must be a matter of individual cases, and how and in what form questions should be asked are matters that will be dealt with more fully in considering methods and principles of making surveys.

3. EXTRACOMPANY MATTERS. The purposes of the third category are to ascertain how the company compares with standards in the community and to determine what trends are developing in the community or nation which may have intracompany effects. Information along these lines has been sought by individual companies and by various outside groups such as trade magazines. Examples of questions that have been asked are as follows:

1. What do you consider to be a fair rate of return on invested capital?
2. Do you feel that unions should be subject to governmental control?
3. Do you believe that unions have helped the rank and file of workers?
4. Is management doing all it can for employees?
5. Are you in favor of strike legislation?
6. Should the Taft-Hartley Act be amended?

METHODS OF GATHERING INFORMATION

A number of methods have been employed to learn what employees are thinking. All are as yet in more or less experimental stages. At least, students in this field have up to the present not tended to favor any one. Hence all that can be done here is to describe the more common methods and indicate their strong and weak points. Measurements may be based upon the following:

1. Direct observation of results and behavior
2. Employee-initiated methods
3. Employer-directed methods
4. Experimental methods

1. DIRECT OBSERVATION. Direct observation of results and behavior is the most common method of ascertaining employee opinions and attitudes. It may consist of a simple observation by a foreman of the

daily output records or of how his workers appear to be acting, e.g., more or less friendly than on previous days. Or it may consist of detailed statistical analyses of trends, indexes, and correlations of data on such results as absenteeism, grievances, disciplinary action, turnover, incentive earnings, man-hours per unit of output, output, quality, strikes, and accidents. Or, again, carefully prepared reports may be compiled to show such things as how employees are behaving, labor unions are growing, legislation is developing, and social conditions are changing.

The theory of this method is that of working from effect back to cause. If one keeps a close eye on results and particularly on changes in trends, it should be possible to follow the trail back and reach conclusions as to how employees are thinking. Certainly, in the event of such disturbances as strikes or slowdowns, the conclusions are obvious that employees are dissatisfied. When supervisors, personnel counselors, or representatives in union meetings report that employees are becoming more demanding, somewhat sullen, less co-operative, and more radical, it can also be concluded that their attitudes are unfavorable. Thus the advantage of this method lies in its obviousness; the existence of unfavorable or favorable attitudes is apparent to anyone who keeps his eyes and ears open. Casual and cursory observation is often enough, although more detailed analysis is invariably worth while to show how the "winds are blowing."

Direct observation suffers from two major disadvantages. First, it is backward- rather than forward-looking. The tenor of employee thinking is not determined until the damage has been done. Hence the method is negative in effect; it is curative rather than preventive. Second, it is study by deduction. Although the observed results may be described accurately, their causes may at best be only indirectly and not directly observed. Hence corrective programs may be aimed at the wrong aspects of employee thinking and attitudes.

When the advantages and disadvantages of direct observation are weighed together, the net result seems to favor its use under two conditions. First, observational methods can add balance to methods that seek more directly to measure attitudes. And, second, usually much information can be derived so easily by direct observation that it would be wasteful indeed to disregard its contributions.

The methods of measurement to be discussed now are based upon the principle that trouble can be avoided or minimized if steps are taken to detect and correct the attitudes which bring on unfavorable action. In this sense, they are forward-looking. They lay stress upon the principle of prevention rather than cure.

2. EMPLOYEE-INITIATED PLANS. Employee-initiated methods are those by which the employees themselves present their thinking and ideas to management. Employees are expected to express their opinions voluntarily, although management may provide some facilitation or encouragement. How this is done may be shown by describing the more common types of plans coming under this heading.

The "open-door" policy is an example often encountered. Under it, executives claim that their doors are open at all times to anyone who wishes to present a grievance. The mere statement on the part of executives that the door is open is considered enough to insure that employees will avail themselves of the privilege. Suggestion and question boxes are also commonly used as means whereby employees can feel free to express themselves. Under more advanced plans, boxes are strategically placed, their use is explained in various ways, and the identity of users is protected. And, finally, some companies establish procedures whereby employees may unburden themselves to counselors in the personnel department or to labor relations experts not connected with the departments for which they work. Here again, better plans provide for trained interviewers who are patient and understanding and who do not have prejudices and axes to grind. The interviewers and counselors do not take the initiative but await visits from any employees who may wish to call upon them.

The advantage of this method lies in the willingness of a company to allow employees freely to present their views. Rather than searching into their views and attitudes, it places the opportunity for initiating action in the hands of the employees. Presumably, any sign of pressure from management is thereby removed.

Beyond this, the employee-initiated method has serious drawbacks. Most employees are reluctant for one reason or another, unless their grievances are very serious, to talk to their supervisors about their troubles. The superiors themselves, for all of their apparent availability, inhibit rather than induce employee discussion. The "open-door" policy, for example, when examined is found to have few, and in many cases no, footprints of employees in the doorway. Second, employees are aware of their language limitations. Hence the majority do not want to undertake the task of writing out suggestions, asking questions, or telling their stories. Of the small minority who do express themselves, a large part is made up of chronic complainers or "back-slappers" who distort the impression which management receives. And, third, even the well-intentioned employee who does take advantage of this opportunity, invariably does not know what really is his trouble. He may complain about wages when the source of irritation is his supervisor. Hence, to rely upon his expressions may lead to the creation of another problem—maladjustment of wages—rather than the correction of the real trouble.

3. EMPLOYER-INITIATED PLANS. Employer-initiated plans of measuring employee attitudes are of two kinds: the interview and the questionnaire. The first is a person-to-person discussional method, and the second is an impersonal broadside approach. Each has a number of variations, the more important of which will be described here.

a) *Interviews.* Interviews may be guided or unguided. In the guided interview, conversation is subtly directed to bring out the salient features for which purpose the interview has been arranged. Usually a definite outline or pattern of questions is memorized by the interviewer. In that way, he keeps the interview from rambling unduly, makes sure that all points are covered, and can make a better formal record of the interview. In the unguided interview, the worker is encouraged to talk about anything on his mind. The encouragement is done with a minimum of talk and, preferably, with no guidance, except to get the employee to talk. The theory is that in this way the talk will almost inevitably gravitate toward his problems and troubles.

The personal contact upon which it invariably depends provides the chief advantage of the interview. Its informality makes for flexibility; it can be adjusted to meet the needs of individual cases; and all employees are not cast in the same mold. Moreover, personal discussion affords some emotional release, which other methods do not. These advantages are even stronger in the unguided interview because the employee is led to volunteer his own ideas and feelings as they occur to him.

The chief disadvantages of the interview method are cost and time of operation. In the first place, interviewing takes more time than other methods of getting at information. The interviewer must establish rapport, he must avoid the feeling of rushing, and he must allow the interviewee to express himself in his own words. When all employees are interviewed, a considerable amount of time is lost from regular operations. In the second place, well-trained and skilled interviewers must be used, or interviews may be worse than useless. Hence this is a costly feature. The unguided interview, particularly, calls for exceedingly skilled interviewers and time-consuming discussions so that employees can get things "off their chest," in their own way.

Balancing the advantages and disadvantages leads to the conclusion that the interview is best used when the problems on the minds of the employees and the troubles besetting employee relations are sufficiently serious to outweigh the cost and time of interviewing. Besides, it is a desirable tool when used in combination with the other methods. Thus it would be well to use interviewing in departments or with groups of employees from which other methods of attitude testing have brought trouble reports. But in any event, the warning is pertinent that interviewing should not be used unless skilled interviewers are available.

b) Questionnaires. Questionnaires, requiring written response to printed questions, are being increasingly used to measure attitudes. They may be sent to the employee's home to be filled out there, or may be given on company time. They may ask questions that can be answered: first, in yes-or-no and true-or-false fashion; second, by choosing from a group of several possible responses; and, third, by ranking lists of items of varying degrees of favorableness. They may be limited to a few subjects or cover practically all phases of employee relations.

Results from the questionnaire method can be obtained relatively cheaply and quickly. Questionnaires can be given to large groups of people within a short period of time by inexperienced help. Responses can be secured which are highly specific, are easily marked for tabulation, and yield satisfactory measures of attitudes.

The chief disadvantages of this method are the same that apply to any questionnaire. Are the questions constructed so that they really ask what the inquirer wants to know? Will the one who answers the questions interpret them as intended? Will he give his real thoughts? Are there leading questions? Is the questionnaire too long and complicated? Is it useful for present purposes, even though it is impersonal?

Thus the scale is balanced in favor of the questionnaire method when the attitudes of large numbers of employees are to be measured in relatively short periods of time. It is assumed, of course, that questionnaires are skillfully constructed, administered, and evaluated, else the results are of no value. Some, although their extreme criticism seems unjustifiable, even go so far as to argue that questionnaires rarely provide useful measures.

REPORTING FINDINGS

After information is gathered, it must be summarized. For example, a simple way of reporting results is to give the number of employees who expressed various views on a variety of subjects. Figure 62 (p. 306) is an example of this method. Another way is to show the percentages of employees who held particular views on the questions asked. Figures 63, 64, and 65 (pp. 307 and 308) are examples of this method.

FIGURE 62

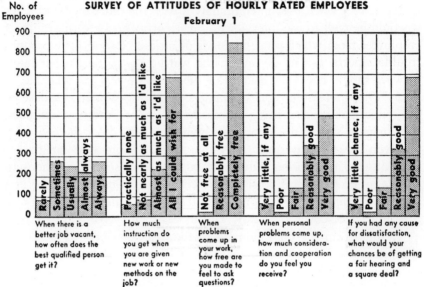

THE BLANK COMPANY
SURVEY OF ATTITUDES OF HOURLY RATED EMPLOYEES
February 1

These figures also illustrate the use of cartoons and descriptive material in bringing out the meaning of the answers.

More complicated systems have been devised in which numerical measures of morale for an employee, department, or the company are obtained. This is done in the following way:

1. Numerical values are arbitrarily assigned to all possible responses on various questions. For example, the responses for the following question are given the following values: "Do you get a fair answer from your supervisor when you ask about wages?"

   Always.. 8
   Usually... 6
   Sometimes... 4
   Seldom.. 2
   Never... 0

2. The numerical values of all answers are weighted. Thus the question just cited is given a weight of 3 as compared to a weight of 1 given to the following question: "Do you read the descriptions of company products in the company newspaper?"

3. The values on the answers are thus arranged to give an over-all expression of morale. For example, the morale of a given employee may be 4.5, of his department 6.3, and for the company as a whole 3.8.

Such measures, though arbitrary, have the desirable feature of making various comparisons possible. Departments may be compared, or a

FIGURE 63

FIGURE 65

THE survey disclosed that employee thinking with respect to individual recognition extends to an appraisal of steps taken by the company to provide for the comfort and convenience of the working force in addition to facilities directly connected with the job.

Cafeteria facilities, food quality and prices meet with general employee approval. Here is how employees rate cafeteria services:

26% say "Consistently good"

34% say "Good most of the time"

32% say "Satisfactory"

8% say "Unsatisfactory"

78% say "Prices are reasonable"

22% say "Prices are excessive"

given department may be compared with the company averages, or trends may be compared. Of course, such measures are arbitrarily constructed; they should be used carefully and their limitations understood.

RULES OF MEASURING ATTITUDES

Although a number of suggestions have been made in the preceding discussion, several more are worth noting if the results of attitude measurement are to be valid and reliable. In the first place, attitude measurement should not be viewed as a single-process program. No company contemplates taking just one inventory of materials; nor should it be satisfied with a single inventory of attitudes. Such a program should provide for continuous measurements at definite times. This will provide significant indications of trends as well as information of use at particular times.

In the second place, employees must feel completely assured that none of their statements is used to their disadvantage. When questionnaires are used, every precaution should be taken to preserve anonymity. This is not possible in the interview, hence it is important for the interviewer to convince the employee that his confidences will in no way be violated. Along similar lines, the results of attitude testing should not be used to establish rules which will work to the detriment of the employees. If any such association should develop in the minds of the employees, it will be improbable that they will ever express their opinions.

In the third place, it is necessary to be aware of errors that should be avoided. First, it is essential to accept with reservation the views that employees express, since people are reluctant to reveal, and often hold back unknowingly, their true feelings. Second, it is essential to know the time, place, and conditions under which answers were given because these and the effect of recent events color replies. Third, it is essential to avoid simple and generalized conclusions, since people are complex beings with varying degrees of satisfactions and dissatisfactions that cannot easily be disassociated.

And, finally, the organization structure, which is established for the purpose, has much to do with the success enjoyed by a program for testing employee attitudes. Hence it should be planned with care, and its scope and place carefully explained to all concerned. If the company in question is too small to warrant assigning this work to its own staff, an outside consultant may be called in to make the survey. This practice is sometimes suggested in large companies. When it is deemed necessary to remove any appearance of company dictation or when company executives may be suspect, outside sources should be secured. Otherwise, this activity should be handled by permanent members of the organization.

The personnel department is the organization unit in which this work logically belongs. These activities may be assigned to existing units in personnel, such as the employee service or employee relations sections, or new units may be created for the assignment. In any event, it is highly desirable to appoint someone who has a sound background in psychology and psychological methods, whether acquired through formal education or through personal effort. An untrained person can do infinite damage here.

ENCOURAGING EMPLOYEE EXPRESSIONS

Throughout the foregoing discussion of the upward flow of information, there has been a concern with "truth." Are we finding out what employees really are thinking? Do we know what they really feel and believe? Are we getting a true picture of their attitudes? These questions are warranted. Unless the real facts are disclosed, managerial action will be ineffective, if not actually dangerous, since it stems from inaccurate appraisals.

How well employees reveal their true feelings and attitudes is largely determined by the confidence which they have in the essential fairness of management. Management's actions are therefore a major causal factor in getting or not getting the "truth" from employees. In everything that management does—from top executive to first-line supervisor—the attitude of employees is being conditioned. Top management's plans and policies determine the whole course and personality of a company. But it is the supervisor or foreman who influences the employee day in and day out, no matter what top levels may be thinking. Hence the policies of the supervisor become the policies of the company to the employee. If top management wants its policies carried out, it is imperative that supervisors be directed and controlled along desired lines. Only then will there be consistency in management's efforts to affect the attitudes and actions of employees.

When the philosophy and actions of management all along the line are right, techniques and procedures for encouraging employee expressions will be more fruitful. Everything from suggestion systems to grievance machinery, from counseling of employees to attitude surveys, and from interviews to observation can be utilized with greater confidence. But always the use of techniques must be buttressed by vigilance in convincing employees that every member of management governs all his actions by the test of fairness to all, and with prejudice to none.

QUESTIONS AND PROBLEMS

1. Distinguish between the terms "training," "education," and "communications." How would "indoctrination," "induction," and "propaganda" fit into your differentiations?

2. What are the various goals of education? Do any of them seem overly idealistic to you?

3. Distinguish between "know-how" and "know-why." What is their relation to motivation?

4. To what extent is education a logical process? An appeal to emotionalism?

5. What arguments favor basic, broad, and general education for operative employees as well as executives? Why should industry concern itself with such education?

6. Define the term "morale." What are the factors affecting morale? What are the effects of good morale?

7. How would you proceed in a given case to show how employee willingness to co-operate is changing from month to month?

8. What is meant by the "process of morale development"? What steps are included in this process?

9. Analyze critically the term "prerogatives of management." Are the interests of labor identical, opposed, or partly both? Explain.

10. Discuss the advantages and disadvantages of interviewing as a method of learning employee attitudes.

11. How may the relationships between company objectives and personal objectives be described or disclosed to employees?

12. In a given company prevailing base wage rates are maintained at least 5 per cent above community levels, yet employee morale is rather low. What reasons may be offered in explanation of this?

13. Why do most people think that they are good judges of people? What evidence can you offer in support of the argument that most people are wrong in this belief?

14. In conducting an employee attitude survey, what difficulties must be circumvented—among employees, among executives, and among the survey staff?

15. Conduct a survey on some subject as: "What do you think of unions?" or "Should management prerogatives be upheld by law?" Use two different population samples; e.g., students who have worked in industry and those who haven't. What difference can be ascribed to background differences? What is the moral?

16. Regarding the interchange of information and views between executives and employees, in your opinion where should the interchange start and where should it stop? Explain.

17. If you found that a given employee—only 1 out of 1,000—held the wrong ideas about company profits, would you or would you not do anything about "sharing information" with him? If 999 out of 1,000 had misconceptions, what would you do?

18. What right has a company to delve into an employee's opinions about himself or about his economic, social, or political attitudes?

19. Many companies have found that their employees often hold a conglomeration of correct and incorrect impressions. What would you conclude about the suggestion that it is as important to find out why they hold correct impressions as to find out why they believe the incorrect points?

20. How would you determine whether or not in a given case the "open-door" policy of determining the existence of grievances is effective?

16 | The Educational Program

After the successive managerial levels have learned the attitudes and opinions of employees, the educational process can then be reversed in direction. Upward have come ideas, comments, reactions, attitudes, and reports through all levels from the very lowest. Now downward must flow clarifications, interpretations, orders, instructions, and policies.

This two-way flow of communications completes the circle of a well-rounded educational process. Each direction of flow should stimulate and be stimulated by the other. In fact, several exchanges, up and down, may be needed to complete the education on some subjects. For this reason, the phrase "sharing information" is perhaps a clearer term of best practice. Certainly, the downward flow is apt to be better designed and much more effective when it is based upon a clear understanding of what employees are thinking (or not thinking) about various subjects.

What is said in this chapter should constantly be viewed, therefore, in terms of what was said about the upward flow in the preceding chapter. The downward flow of education presupposes an effective upward stream of communications. In this discussion of the downward flow, the subject will be taken up under the following headings:

1. Education of the several managerial levels
2. Content and conveyors of education and communications
3. Rules of education and communication
4. Organizing the educational program

EDUCATION OF THE SEVERAL MANAGERIAL LEVELS

If the education of the employee is to proceed satisfactorily, the leadership of ideas must stem from the top of the organization down through the intervening managerial levels. Hence it is advisable to review educational practices for (1) top management, (2) middle management groups, and (3) supervisory levels.

1. Top Management Groups.   One of the most significant movements in the past ten years has been that concerned with top-level executive development. This is a most encouraging trend, and one for which management deserves the utmost credit. It takes real courage for any executive to concede that he needs to learn more about his job. Particularly is this true of those who have reached the top. After all, hasn't the top-level group reached those heights because of ability and skill? Although this is true, there has nonetheless been a widespread acceptance of the idea of continuing education for higher executives.

Emphasis in such education has to do mainly with managerial concepts and organizational subject matter. This tends to insure the employment of the best possible administrative techniques. Inasmuch as the executive levels must operate through others to accomplish the objectives of the enterprise, such emphasis is warranted. Thus education inquires into questions of whether or not correct designs of planning, organizing, and controlling are being used at top as well as lower levels in the company, and also whether or not top-level executives act in their realms in a constructive manner.

When subject matter of a managerial character has been reviewed, technical subjects may then be well considered by top executives. Here a variety of topics suggest themselves. Until top management educates itself about such questions as the following, it can scarcely expect lower levels of management to know how to communicate with workers:

1. What are the social responsibilities of management?
2. How do these responsibilities change with time?
3. To what extent is business liable for the various risks which endanger employees?
4. To what extent are profits reasonable and justifiable?
5. Can workers be loyal to both the company and the union?
6. What are realistic policies toward political activities on the part of the company?
7. What are just wage levels, and how can they be proved?
8. What are the real roles of management, capital, workers, and unions?
9. To what extent, and how, should employees participate in managerial decisions of importance to them?

These are significant questions. Anyone who assumes that he alone is gifted to answer them or has derived final answers to them is riding for a fall. So the movement of top executives to take counsel on them represents a most wholesome advance in labor-management relations.

2. MIDDLE MANAGEMENT GROUPS.   The task of education of middle groups of management tends to include the following three major areas:

1. To learn precisely the educational plans of top management
2. To co-ordinate the educational responsibilities horizontally of various line and staff units
3. To transmit specific educational plans to lower supervisory levels and ultimately to employees

The nature of these educational responsibilities is readily apparent, so that brief comments concerning them will suffice here. If it is significant for top levels to continue acquiring an education, it is equally, if not more, so for those who are as yet moving up the line. Moreover, since the middle groups stand between the top and the bottom, they occupy a strategic position affecting labor-management relations. They must be adequately prepared to transmit accurately, and to control constructively, the plans, policies, and ideas of the top levels.

The middle management groups determine also the degree of consistency and uniformity with which employees in the various divisions of a company will be educated. Hence co-ordinating educational sessions are particularly needful here, so that production and personnel units, let us say, take the same views on how the ideas of top management are to be carried out. When such units operate at cross-purposes, even though with the best of intentions, the destructive effect upon employees is beyond measure.

This crosswise interchange of ideas leads some to conclude that organizational communications are essentially three- rather than two-dimensional: up, down, and across. The evidence favors such a conclusion. Even though the main flows may be up and down, crosswise co-ordination is increasingly important as a company grows. The various functional and staff units must be brought into a common plan of thought, if the top and the bottom are to work together effectively and harmoniously.

3. SUPERVISORY LEVELS.   In the thinking of many, the education of supervisory levels of management is the key factor in employee education. Without doubt, day in and day out the supervisor is in closer contact with workers than any other management level or unit. In the formal organization structure, it is the foremen and supervisors who are "management" to the workers. And, even informally, workers tend to feel that the supervisors determine how well they will or will not be treated as individuals. And when channels of communication are followed, it is through the supervisors that most information will be chan-

neled downward and upward. Indeed, they may be bottlenecks, mis-interpreters, and deceivers—or the reverse, depending upon the kind of education to which they are exposed by upper managerial levels.

Granting the truth of these contentions, any neglect of supervisory education is to be condemned. Moreover, such education is greatly needed because few, if any, supervisors learn anything about the educational phases of their jobs before they become supervisors. They step into their managerial responsibilities with practically no knowledge of what is expected of them or how their obligations are to be performed. So, added to the fact that they are asked to carry out certain tasks, there is the fact that supervisors generally don't know how to carry them out. Therefore, it is manifest that this group must be educated not only in the various subject matter which top management considers important but also in how to get such subject matter across to the worker. No wonder that some feel that one of the biggest jobs of a supervisor is to learn how to be a good teacher.

COMMUNICATION CONTENT AND CONVEYORS

The key point of communications is, of course, the message. Through the message, the executive hopes to educate the employee. And thereby are to be changed the attitudes, opinions, the information, and—ultimately—the behavior of the employee. The content of such messages is therefore important. But since messages must be transmitted through some agent (human or mechanical), it is important to give consideration to this aspect of communications. Hence the content and the conveyor are discussed together here, because they are so closely related.

In the space of this section only excerpts and selected illustrations of communication content and conveyors can be given. It is not possible to examine the extent to which such content should be developed or the pros and cons of usage of various conveyors. It is hoped that the examples will serve to disclose typical content and usages. The materials in this section will be grouped under the following headings of typical subject matter, while examples of conveyors from the classification that follows will be incorporated in the discussion of communication topics:

1. Major topics included in communication programs
   a) Company history, objectives, and services
   b) Company organization, finances, and operations
   c) Personnel objectives, policies, and practices
   d) Economics and the American system
   e) Political and community relations
2. Major groups of communication conveyors
   a) Individualized, personal contacts

    b) Group personal contacts
    c) Written media
    d) Demonstrations and displays
    e) Radio, television, films, and recordings

1. COMPANY HISTORY, OBJECTIVES, AND SERVICES. The significance which an employee feels is in part due to the importance which he and his associates attach to the company. If he knows nothing of a company's history, objectives, and services, he can take little pride in his company. An avoidable loss in significance is taking place. It is wise, therefore, to give him such information. A number of plans may be cited in this connection.

The induction program for new employees is a common way of communicating the message of company history, objectives, and services. Part of the personal conferences of new employees with staff members of the personnel department and with their respective supervisors may be devoted to such subjects. At this time, too, some companies have used films to highlight the story of how the company was founded, by whom, and some of the early trials and tribulations. The story can be brought up to date to show the present position of the company in the industry.

Booklets are often used to cover these subjects. They are relatively inexpensive for presenting the story of a company's origin and growth. Moreover, they have a degree of permanence which films, for example, do not have, as far as ready reference to them is concerned. But to induce workers to read them is a problem. In this connection, well-designed, excellently illustrated, and carefully worded copy are helpful. An interesting case of stimulation is provided by one company which developed a quiz game, based upon plant publications and meetings, to be played during the lunch hour.[1] Winners were given free lunches for answering correctly questions about the company's history, products, and personalities.

Plant publications are also used to provide materials about the background of a company. The Reed and Barton Company of Massachusetts prepared a special issue of its *The Silver Lining* on its 125th anniversary. After an opening statement by the chairman of the board on the lessons of this extended period of growth, the publication covered such subjects as how management had sought to provide job security, the influence of quality production, the importance of various specialists,

---

[1] For some of the illustrations cited here, the author is indebted to the *Case Book of Employee Communications in Action,* published under the sponsorship of the National Association of Manufacturers, 1950.

and a review of various company operations. Somewhat similarly, the Studebaker Corporation used a yearly "special edition" of its bi-weekly *Forging Ahead* to review company history and to describe and explain operations, organizational matters, and personal benefits.

Product display boards are used by the AC Spark Plug Division of General Motors Corporation to help employees visualize their contributions to the final product. Cutaway models serve to show each part of the product, its name, and its purpose. Plant tours are also used to give employees a better understanding of these matters. Some companies show displays of competitive products, so that employees will understand the task facing the company in maintaining its position in the industry and in meeting competition.

2. COMPANY ORGANIZATION, FINANCES, AND OPERATIONS. This area of subject matter receives a great deal of attention from many companies. The reason is that it is necessary to help an employee see how he fits into the structure and operations of the company. Group meetings have been widely used to explain current problems of the company to employees. One company holds regular monthly meetings in which various executives take turns in explaining the cost and profit position of the company. Supervisors are briefed before the meetings so that they will be in a better position to carry on with the explanations in their own departments.

Television has also been employed for this purpose. The Detroit Edison Company used a seven-minute film in which the president and the board chairman were televised highlighting the company's operations.[2] To insure a wide audience, advance notices of the time and channel station were given to employees, stockholders, and customers. The program also was used to commend employees for their contributions to the company's success and for their safety record.

The comic-book format has been used by the American Type Founders in presenting its annual report to employees. This presentation serves in a graphic and interesting way to describe its many operations, as well as to bring out the workings and benefits of the American economic system.[3]

At the San Diego plant of Consolidated Vultee Aircraft Company the public address system is used once a week during a ten-minute rest period to tell employees about new orders or cancellations, about training courses, and about other interesting news items. Every two weeks,

---

[2] *Management Review*, May, 1952, p. 283.

[3] "How Industry Is Using Comics," *Factory Management and Maintenance*, Vol. CVIII, No. 10, p. 82.

some member of management expresses some of his ideas of pertinence to employees and management, criticisms, or appreciation for operational results.

A very interesting program for discussing company operations is that of the Elgin National Watch Company. It illustrates the care and the co-operative attitude taken in designing communications. Each month a member of management is selected to discuss with employees some phase of management. To prepare himself, the executive selected meets:

1. With an advisory group consisting of
   a) 5 foremen
   b) 4 members of the Job Masters Association
   c) 7 members of the Watch Workers Union (Independent)
   d) 4 members of the International Association of Machinists (Independent)
   e) 4 employees representing office personnel
2. With an advisory group of 25 rank-and-file workers selected
   a) By shop stewards for union workers
   b) By supervisors of nonunion workers

After discussions with these groups regarding matters they deem important and the content which the executive deems of significance, a presentation is prepared that has been exposed to a wide range of constructive suggestions and criticisms.

3. PERSONNEL OBJECTIVES, POLICIES, AND PRACTICES. Of immediate interest to employees is, of course, their financial and nonfinancial returns and possibilities. It is understandable, therefore, why many companies concern themselves with communications in this area. Practically all companies do some explaining of wages, hours, and employment conditions during the induction process. But it would be foolhardy to stop there, because interest in these subjects continues throughout an employee's tenure with a company.

Every conceivable conveyor has been used for communications in these areas. Undoubtedly the best here is the supervisor. He should be trained so that he can clearly and with conviction explain personnel policies and practices to his team of workers. The personal contact permits the supervisor to observe how well his messages are getting across, to shift his arguments and explanations to meet the individual needs of particular employees, and to tie his explanations into day-to-day working situations. He can give the personal attention which practically everybody prefers to impersonal or mass media of communication. And when the competency of the supervisor in this regard is upgraded, this serves to make him a more confident leader, with a reward not only to himself but also to the members of his group. When the area of human relations and personal interests is being considered, therefore, the supervisor deserves the greatest possible support.

Personal interviews are often employed in this area. Again this approach provides the personal touch. At the Procter and Gamble Company, for example, each supervisor reviews with each of his workers his personal situation with respect to wages, desirable benefit plans, profit sharing, pensions, vacations, and holiday arrangements. The Budd Company uses such man-to-man interviews to discuss safety practices on specific jobs. Interviews are used by the American Machine and Foundry Company to be sure that employees know what their jobs are, how they are getting along on them, what the future has in store, and whether or not they are using all the help their supervisors can give them.

Even though the supervisor is well qualified to communicate in this area, the use of other media is also desirable. Indeed, this subject matter is of such vital importance that enough could never be done in explaining and interpreting personnel policies and practices. So, in addition to supervisory channels, booklets, for example, have been used by the Bristol Myers Company to answer questions frequently asked about its retirement income plan and by the Schenley Distillers Corporation to explain its pension plan. The Republic Steel Corporation incorporates a "letter" in its monthly employee magazine for such purposes.

Group meetings have also been used in this area of communications. At the Kimberly Clark Corporation, the plant manager and personnel manager have a weekly discussion meeting with a group of 20 to 25 plant employees. Each employee is included at least once a year. Employee forums—of large as well as small groups—are sponsored by the Western Electric Company at which subjects of interest are covered by company or outside speakers. The Thompson Products Company uses informal dinner meetings at which written questions are answered by a panel of management "experts."

Interesting examples of communications may also be cited in connection with questions of job security and union-management relations. Many companies have taken pains to show how job security is tied in with competitive leadership and high productivity. From the positive side, employees are told such things as "the success of a company depends greatly on you"; "job security and job opportunity depend on satisfying the customer"; "the security of your job is wrapped up in improvements of quality, reliability, and reputation." And when layoffs are likely, it is well to advise employees on prospects for re-employment in terms of—

a) The company situation, so that damaging rumors among employees are minimized

b) What is being done to reduce the numbers of layoffs

c) The order of layoffs, should they come

d) The probable length of layoffs

e) What employees laid off should do to keep the company informed of their availability for recall

As to union-management relations, much is being done to improve mutual understanding. For example, union and company officials have taken joint tours of their own plants as well as those of competitors to promote a better understanding of their own positions and problems. A booklet has been used by the Pittsburg-Plate Glass Company on a *Charter of Labor Relations for Foremen and Stewards,* so that the company position can be made known to employees, supervisors, and union representatives. Other companies are using columns of their periodicals to give union news, views on union relations, and explanations of contract clauses. Many companies also use conferences and meetings with supervisors to gain their views and to clarify their understanding of labor-management problems. Thereby the ability of supervisors to transmit the messages to employees is improved.

4. Economics and the American System. One of the most interesting phases of education has been along lines of increasing economic understanding. The movement has gained strength particularly in the last several years because of the belief that an employee who does not comprehend how our economic system works cannot feel confident about the fairness of his wages, the reasonableness of profits, or the significance of the capitalistic system. Hence industry itself and various public and private institutions have interested themselves in disseminating economic knowledge. Interesting as are these efforts, space here permits only the citation of a few examples of various types of efforts along these lines.

A number of devices and approaches have been used to advance economic education among workers. For example, the Inland Steel Company and the Borg-Warner Corporation developed a series of four films which attempted to show the following:[4]

1. How We Got What We Have
2. What We Have
3. How to Lose What We Have
4. How to Keep What We Have

---

[4] These films have since been taken over by the American Economic Foundation for purposes of general distribution.

After each of the films is shown, a discussion period is devoted to an examination in detail of the particular subjects.[5]

The Du Pont Company developed a conference method program with a board-type of presentation in this connection. This conference concerns itself with the features of the American economic system, its accomplishments, the place of competition, the place of individual freedoms in the system, and the place of the company in our system. A trained conference leader first conducts an appreciation session over the whole subject matter. Then he leads three one and one-half hour discussion sessions, based on a broad presentation. He also trains others to conduct conferences on the program. The technical aspects of the program have since been made available for general distribution through the National Association of Manufacturers.

The Republic Steel Corporation also uses a conference program, but on a more extensive basis. Its program contains fifteen sessions and in the first year was restricted to supervisors. The conferences are built around lectures, discussions, and visual aids. This program is now available for general distribution through the University of Chicago, and has as its objectives the following:

1. Raising the level of knowledge and understanding about the economic system and how the corporation fits into it
2. Providing a framework for analyzing and appraising economic proposals and problems
3. Developing in individuals an appreciation of the role to him of the corporation and the economic system
4. Developing confidence in the corporation and the system
5. Encouraging desirable changes in attitudes and behavior both on and off the job

5. POLITICAL AND COMMUNITY RELATIONS. In addition, some industries have worked closely with various community agencies and groups to make education a community project. An example of such cooperation is illustrated in Figure 66 (p. 322). The instruction in such instances has been intended to support the following propositions and procedures:

1. Every citizen benefits from industry's growth.
2. You are entitled to the facts.
3. Collective bargaining is the one practical means to assure fair wages, reasonable hours, satisfactory working conditions.
4. All employees, as well as management, benefit by improving productive efficiency.

---

[5] A very useful survey of various programs similar to this may be found in Dillard E. Bird's *Survey of Economic Education* (Dayton: Foremanship Foundation, 1951).

FIGURE 66. Organization Chart of Community Groups*

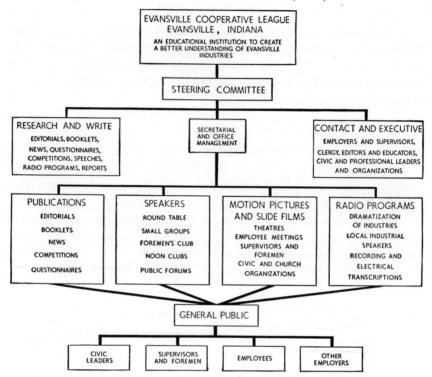

* Source: Thomas J. Morton, "Public Relations Job," *Factory Management and Maintenance*, December, 1938, p. 40.

5. Citizens should be protected in their right to work.
6. The American system of industry is best for everybody.
7. Management and wage earners have mutual interests, need close personal relations.
8. Management is obligated to give a square deal to every employee in the shop.
9. Adherence to the letter and spirit of the law avoids strikes except after all means of peaceful adjustment have been exhausted.
10. Demands for recognition as sole bargaining agency only after an impartial election proves more than 50 per cent of employees have chosen the agency.
11. No coercion or intimidation in choosing a bargaining agency.
12. After the bargaining agency is chosen, bargaining to proceed.
13. Any differences irreconcilable by collective bargaining to be mediated by a board—one chosen by management, one by workers, the two to choose the third.
14. Strike to be called only after mediation has failed to bring agreement, and after strike authorized by secret ballot of more than 50 per cent of all properly qualified employees.

RULES OF EDUCATION AND COMMUNICATIONS

In operating a program of education and communication, it is desirable to base plans upon sound principles. A complete set of such principles is not available as yet and perhaps never will be. At the present state of knowledge, however, the following summary offers perhaps the best suggestions along these lines:[6]

1. GENERAL PRINCIPLES.—

    1. No one communication technique will meet all needs. A communication program uses many techniques, methods, and channels.
    2. Confidence is a basic principle of communication. An employee who suspects that he is being sold a bill of goods will resent the communicator's intrusion and will not be receptive to his message.
    3. Action speaks louder than words in communication.
    4. Each communication program needs to be tailored to fit the needs and wants of the individual human organization.
    5. Planning with regard to any major managerial decision should include planning for communicating it to those who will carry it out and those who will be affected by it.
    6. Generalized or "canned" communications cannot form the core of a communication program. Communications which are directed to everyone will probably fail to meet the specific need of anyone. "Canned" communication should be used only when it is complementary to the central theme.
    7. Establish good daily communication. If employers communicate solely as a defense against attack, then employees may turn elsewhere for information. Or even worse, they may create in their own imagination answers which will be worse than the truth.
    8. A person's ability to communicate tends to vary directly with his own understanding of the subject to be communicated.
    9. Management's effectiveness with communication tends to vary directly with its belief in the importance and value of adequate communication.
    10. Respect for downward communication channels tends to be in direct proportion to the extent to which the supervisor receives and transmits information before the subordinate gets it elsewhere.
    11. Development of good communication relationships takes time. They cannot be built in a day—or a year—but they can be improved regularly.

2. PREPARING THE COMMUNICATION.—

    1. Communicate within a context. Each communication problem presents a different situation. Each problem can be best solved in terms

---

[6] John F. Mee (ed.), *Personnel Handbook* (New York: Ronald Press, 1951), pp. 833–34. These have been prepared by Professor Keith Davis.

of that situation. Both the communicator and the receiver gain more insight to the problem by dealing with it in context.

2. Communicate in terms of the receiver's background. For example, economic concepts should be related to matters of practical economics familiar to the worker in everyday life.

3. Communicate in terms of the receiver's self-interest. Communications, if they are to be welcomed, must be in terms of the receiver's interests and attitudes. One does not send television impulses to a telegraph receiver.

4. Talking down to the receiver produces a negative response. Management may be superior to the worker in the organizational hierarchy, but as individuals both stand equal. Talking to the worker through the organizational hierarchy is different from talking down to him as an inferior individual.

5. A communication will be better accepted and understood if it gives acceptable reasons for the particular viewpoint or fact that is being presented.

6. Disclose the communicator's self-interest in communications. For example, why is management sharing this information? Unless the employee can see the self-interest of management in a communication and its relation to his own self-interest, he will suspect management's sincerity and motives.

7. Variety of communication methods and themes will help secure the receiver's attention. For example, poster locations may be varied. New voices may be used over the plant broadcasting system. Or the idea of "increased productivity" may be treated from different angles.

3. TRANSMITTING THE COMMUNICATION.—

1. Communicate in small doses. People maintain interest in, and absorb, only a small amount of information at a time.

2. Information to be retained for long periods should be repeated periodically. People forget easily, and the same facts need to be represented now and then.

3. The flow concept of communication requires that information and viewpoint flow both ways between management and employees.

4. By-passing any level within the organizational hierarchy from president to worker will weaken the effectiveness of a communication program. It is especially important that the immediate supervisor be a central figure in the program.

ORGANIZING THE EDUCATIONAL PROGRAM

In concluding these remarks about education it is worth commenting upon three aspects of organizing the educational program; first, what organizational elements are involved in the program; second, where responsibility for educational programming should lie; and, third, how far the organization should carry its educational program.

From what has already been said, it should be apparent that in answer to the first point every level and segment must concern itself with education. In the formal structure, from supervisors to top management and crosswise between line and staff executives, there must be acceptance of the educational obligation. But it would be unwise to overlook the flow of communications which takes place through informal channels. The "natural" lines of communication should be "used," but with subtle care so that they do not go "underground" because of fear or misunderstanding. Also, the extra-formal structures of union channels should be employed to communicate information upward and downward.

But when "everyone" is responsible, turning now to the second point, there is grave danger that no one will be responsible. Hence specific delegation of authority for leadership of an educational program is desirable. The personnel division is a natural choice here. It should provide leadership of ideas, but always submit program proposals to the appropriate line executives for suggestions and approval. The latter with line authority would then spearhead the execution of approved plans using the help of trained leaders supplied by the personnel division. Moreover, the personnel division can seek out help on educational matters from management consultants, educational institutions, professional societies, and business and trade associations. Such an organizational setup would serve to insure proper design of programs, minimum conflict between organization units, a strengthening of the work and support of line executives, and advantageous use of all sources of educational resources and opportunities.

In answer to the third point, it must be remembered that education has a utilitarian and selfish purpose. Communications with employees are intended to raise ultimately the productivity of the workers. Presumably, their efforts will be more effective because they are better adjusted to their working environment.

So long as employee development proceeds along such lines, the educational program has substantial justification. But what if employee development is intended to change or clarify his basic economic, social, or political ideas? For example, a program may be undertaken to convince him that private enterprise is better than any form of government ownership; that a system of private investment is better than socialism; that the profit system is superior to national planning; that union membership will bring no lasting benefits; and that management leadership is fairer and more democratic than union or political administration of industry. Such phases of education may be termed "indoctrination." To some this may mean propaganda or possibly unfair twisting of the truth.

Such opinions or criticisms are based, not upon the type of education, but upon its fairness, accuracy, and validity. And those who voice them may themselves indoctrinate or propagandize but see nothing wrong in it because they believe that the content of their programs is right and just.

Hence the right to indoctrinate or propagandize is not the issue. Since capitalists ("management" is too often used incorrectly as a synonym for this term) have so much at stake in a business enterprise, they should have the right to protect their investments by all legal and ethical means. This would include their right to instruct their managements to carry on programs of indoctrination and propaganda in such matters as the principles and the desirability of capitalism. But to go beyond the borders of fairness in such efforts by employing high-pressure tactics and partial truths is at issue. The question, however, of what is fair, ethical, and accurate is one that is difficult to answer in many cases. Nevertheless, this should not be a reason to remove the rights of management (or, for that matter, of unions, political groups, or other agencies) to indoctrinate.

To sum up, whether the education is intended to provide information or change the attitudes of employees (even to the extent of indoctrination or propagandizement), the efforts of management are justified. But the premise of fairness, honesty, and ethical standards is assumed and must be protected. Without this, counterforce will be built up that will result in loss of faith, confidence, and loyalty.

QUESTIONS AND PROBLEMS

1. What is the relation between upward communication and downward communication? Which takes place first?
2. How would you explain the fact that formal executive education for top-level groups is such a recent development?
3. With what subject matter is top management education primarily concerned?
4. Are there absolute answers to questions which top management poses for itself in its own educational programs? If not, isn't the future of labor-management relations to be viewed with pessimism?
5. What is the task of education for the middle management group of executives?
6. Why is such significance generally attached to the role of the supervisor in labor-management relations? Do you think that, actually, the supervisor has as high a position in business as some would have us believe? Why, or why not?

7. What is the key factor in communications downward? What is it supposed to accomplish?

8. What are the major topics included in communication programs? What are the major groups of conveyors used to transmit messages downward?

9. Can you give examples of how knowledge of a company's history, objectives, or services has been of significance to a given employee? Was this knowledge used by himself or in relation to fellow workers, his family, or his friends?

10. How would you proceed to tell employees about the finances and financing of a company? Are these matters really any of their business?

11. Why is the "comic-book" type of conveyor of communications so effective? Does this necessarily imply anything about the mentality of the average worker?

12. Some companies employ committees of workers to advise and counsel management about content and conveyors of communications. What is your considered judgment of this practice?

13. Why is there so much interest in such communications as those concerned with economics and the American system? Why doesn't industry concentrate on the task of producing and distributing goods and services and leave such education to the schools?

14. If you were to co-operate with community groups in developing and operating an educational program for employees, to what agencies or groups might you turn? What subjects would you desire to have in such a co-operative educational program?

15. What principles would be useful in organizing and conducting a program of communications?

16. What organizational units would usually be involved in a program of education and communications?

17. For what reasons is it desirable to assign the leadership of an educational program to the personnel department? How must this responsibility be assigned to the personnel division so that it doesn't usurp "line" authority?

18. How far should a company go in its educational program? Couldn't it overdo the education, thereby diverting executive time and effort which should be used in enhancing the company's efficiency and competitive position?

19. What is the fundamental justification for an educational program? What is the fundamental basis upon which it should be built?

20. To what extent, if any, should the co-operation of a union be sought in developing and operating a program of education and communications?

| Remuneration Policies

THE PROBLEM OF WAGES

Scarcely any factor is as important in affecting labor relations as wages. Certainly, most of labor's openly expressed grievances are about wages. In part, this may stem from the fact that if his work is irritating, the worker sometimes expresses his discontent by complaining about wages. Then, too, labor sometimes complains because it feels that management is establishing unfair wage rates. Moreover, labor is continually reminded of wages by the race between expenditures and the next payday. And each worker's standard of living is significantly affected by how much he earns, and, consequently, how he feels about his wages is also affected by what his neighbors think about his spending power. Thus labor's consciousness of its wages is constantly resharpened by the effect of its exertions, the rapidity with which the pay check is spent, and the evaluations placed upon it by friends and neighbors.

AVAILABILITY OF MEASURING DEVICES

Such sensitivity to wage levels is not necessarily undesirable. Indeed, all economic groups are sensitive about their economic affairs. The trouble, so far as wages are concerned, lies elsewhere. There does not exist a method of measuring wages that is above question. All existing methods have some elements of arbitrary calculation. In other words, we do not have a measuring device that will tell us exactly what any man is worth.

In part, the explanation for the belief that wages can be set accurately derives from false deductions relative to the use of time-study methods. In this connection, one often hears the phrase that such methods lead to the determination of a "fair day's pay for a fair day's work." Time-study methods are useful only in regard to the latter half of this phrase; they can be used to determine standards of output with a high degree of accuracy. But having established, for example, that on a given job a well-selected, trained, and experienced worker should be able to produce 800 units a day, all that can be expected from time-study methods has been derived. What the wage value of the 800 units is cannot be determined by time-study methods. To be sure, time-study analysts proceed from there to set value rates, but they are using other yardsticks or techniques in doing so, not time study. Since the time-study man does the rate setting, many incorrectly conclude that his slide rule also is capable of deriving economic values.

The use of time-study methods is not criticized here but rather their misuse. To claim for them results that they cannot yield is a serious error, which is cited here as evidence of the belief held by many that unimpeachable wages can be set. If management is to make intelligent progress in its wage policies, it must convince others of its understanding of the complexity of the subject by refusing to take an unbending or narrow attitude toward it. Certainly, unions in many cases have become vigorous opponents of time-study methods because of misuse in setting rates.

There are some reasonably accurate methods, but all have aspects that are subject to controversy. Hence, even granting that all employers are unimpeachably fair (obviously, a far-fetched assumption, so long as employers are human beings), labor will be in a position to debate wage issues until the day when a "thermometer of wages" is developed that has the same degree of general acceptability as a precision thermometer for measuring temperature.

This somewhat gloomy prospect is stated at the outset because it is highly desirable to recognize fundamental limitations in a subject of such significant consequences. There then is less likelihood of rushing glibly and unknowingly ahead with a wage program that can only lead to disaster. Many employers who have done this still cannot understand why their employees are dissatisfied with their well-intentioned wage policies. If they had really recognized the fact that it is impossible precisely to calculate a "fair day's pay," the first step toward the development of a realistic wage policy would have been taken. For until this is openly admitted, so that employees can be convinced of the fundamental honesty of management, mutual self-respect and confidence, which are the foundation of a sound wage policy, cannot be laid.

The absence of unassailable accuracy is admitted, not necessarily as a sign of weakness, but rather as a recognition of realistic limitations. As a result, the student will not be embroiled in useless and unending controversies. He can concentrate his attention upon the practical question of how available tools and principles can be made to work better to the greater satisfaction of all concerned.

THE CONFLICT OF INTERESTS

Another source of trouble, which could be eliminated if measuring devices were accurate, arises from the somewhat conflicting interests of various groups who are affected by wages. Labor and management, to be sure, want as much as they can get out of their common and individual endeavors. They must, however, recognize the interests of consumers, competing industries, and governmental agencies.

Enough evidence has been made available since World War II, without digging into earlier history, of the tugging between various groups as a result of wage matters. For example, when employees in one industry receive increases as a result of a strike for higher wages, other employees follow suit to keep in the parade and costs go up to consumers in general. As a consequence, labor, which is the largest member of the consumer group, sees its living costs go up and demands further wage increases; management resists, and the government steps in, trying to reconcile differences and to affect compensation, and so on in a never-ending vicious circle.

Although all groups are members of the same economic and political systems and all sink or rise together, too often each acts as though its life alone were at stake. Here again the removal of a source of trouble awaits the time when all groups are able and willing to recognize, first, the interdependence of the members in the system and, second, the legitimate and reasonable interests of each other.

SCOPE OF DISCUSSION

The purpose of the next four chapters is to describe various aspects of the problem of remuneration. It is divided into the following parts:

1. General wage issues and principles
2. Job evaluation and wage classification systems
3. Specific wage payment plans
4. Job and wage stabilization plans

The present chapter is devoted to a discussion of general wage issues and principles. It is divided into the following parts:

1. Significant basic issues
2. General theories of wages
3. Legislative aspects and regulations
4. Effect of union activities
5. Wage measurement and policies

BASIC ISSUES

Before a plan of remuneration can be successfully developed, it is essential to understand clearly why employees are paid and the effect of long-time and short-time forces on wages.

1. FACTORS OF REMUNERATION. Employees are remunerated because of the contributions which they make to their companies. By helping to produce goods and services that are sold to customers and patrons of the business, the wherewithal is received to compensate workers, as well as other co-operators in the business enterprise. But what happens when employees help to produce goods and services that cannot be sold profitably, or perhaps not at all? They nevertheless receive their wages and salaries, by legal priority above other creditors, if the business fails as a result of mistaken judgments regarding what and how much should be produced.

Thus, to begin with, employees are paid for their efforts irrespective of their ultimate value or usefulness. Continuing to produce unsalable goods would, of course, lead to ultimate loss of pay opportunities through failure of the company. It is well to point out that this preference is not an inherent and irrevocable right of labor, but one which has been evolved through the years. What may be customary in years and ages to come is conjectural. The forces of custom, tradition, and change should be recognized, however, as important in setting wage patterns.

More particularly, what are the efforts for which labor is paid? The following seem to be basic:

1. Time spent at work
2. Energy—physical, mental, and emotional
3. Willingness to co-operate

It might seem on the surface that time and exertion are the only factors in determining wages. Obviously, time is a factor, since productive results take time. And results depend, too, upon application of various types of energy. But anyone who has worked or watched people work soon realizes that very often willingness to expend energy is perhaps the most important factor for which people are paid wages.

2. IMPORTANCE OF WILLINGNESS TO CO-OPERATE. The proof of this is immediately seen in cases of method changes. Let us assume that energy can be expressed in units and that management improves job methods with the following results:

	Old Method	New Method
Output per hour.................	100	200
Energy expended by labor.........	30	20

If the principle of cause and effect were invoked to support its claim, management presumably should be given credit for the increase in production. Indeed, to follow the argument to its logical end, wages should be decreased because labor is spending less energy in working and taking no more time.

But, in all likelihood, wages will have to be raised! And this despite the claim that management might make that it caused the increased output by devising the improved method. Labor would look, not at who caused the result, but at the result. Having noted that output has now been doubled, it would simply conclude that it should share in the increase and just as simply refuse to co-operate, were a share not forthcoming.

The control that labor exercises in withholding its services reaches an extreme in the case of strikes, but "soldiering" on the job is often as destructive a form of unwillingness to expand energy. And yet the expenditures called for may actually be smaller, because of improved methods of doing the work!

In short, willingness of workers to co-operate, as well as their time and energy, must be compensated. How to measure willingness is a difficult matter and is largely left to rule-of-thumb methods. For example, many time-study people follow the precept of Frederick Taylor that wages should be increased from 15 to 30 per cent when output is increased—even when it is doubled or tripled. The reason Taylor chose this figure is that he believed that larger increases at any one time spoil workers rather than stimulate them to greater effort.

ABILITY TO PAY

Another basic issue about which there is a great deal of confusion is the effect of long-time and short-time forces on wages. A pointed example is the controversy that often arises about the ability of industry to pay or not to pay wage increases demanded by labor. Many on the management side claim that ability to pay has nothing to do with wages. Apparently they are blind to the fact that productivity and wages practically run parallel in American industrial history. Yet some companies are giving recognition to productivity by granting wage increases based on an "annual improvement" factor, which presumably measures the amount by which output per employee on the average has increased during each year.

But those on labor's side who claim all for ability to pay fail to explain why concerns that are losing money or actually failing do not pay their workers relatively less than their more prosperous fellows.

1. SHORT-RUN FORCES. The answer to the riddle is simple. It lies in an understanding of short- and long-run influences on wages. In the short run, the economic influence on wages of ability to pay is practically nil. All employers, irrespective of their profits or losses, must pay no less than their competitors and need pay no more if they wish to attract and keep workers. For example, if those who are operating unprofitably cut wages because of losses, they would soon find that their employees were leaving them, provided that other jobs were available.

2. LONG-RUN FORCES. In the long run, productivity is of vital influence. When industry in general is able to pay high wages, individual producers who wish to take advantage of the tide of prosperity have to bid for labor to help carry on profitable operations. And the limit to their bidding, which, of course, they hope is not approached too closely, is their increased ability to pay. Conversely, when productivity falls generally, wages must be cut because funds are not available to do otherwise.

3. THE INDIVIDUAL PRODUCER. The key to the difference between short-run and long-run influences is found mainly in the position of an individual producer as compared to that of industry in general. For example, when industry in general is prosperous, an employer who is losing money would soon lose his employees if he attempted to cut his wage rates. He cannot influence a downward trend in wages because his competitors are forcing wages upward. Conversely, when business is generally poor, an isolated producer who is making excessive profits would rarely raise wages because prevailing wage rates are sufficient to attract all the labor that he can use. His ability to pay has absolutely no influence on his wage rates. Of course, when most employers become more prosperous, they will begin to bid wages up. And they will do so, first, because they have to if they want to keep up in the parade and, second, because of their increased ability to pay.

To sum up, a personnel manager must properly evaluate short-run influences and long-run influences if he is to help his company reach correct wage decisions. Moreover, companies which foolishly raise arguments that apply in the short run but not in the long run, or vice versa, merely weaken themselves in the eyes of their employees when the truth is known. When economic forces are against him, the employer should be the first to admit it and not confuse the issue. This does not mean that he should not seek to protect his interests by legitimate means, but to do so by ignorant claims is folly. The employees' confidence in the judgment of the employer is thereby lost.

COST OF LIVING

The relation of cost of living to wages is another basic question in establishing remuneration policies. Its significance has increased in the past several years because many companies have agreed to tie in wage increases (and decreases, too, in some instances) with changes in cost of living as reflected in cost-of-living indexes such as that compiled by the Bureau of Labor Statistics. For example, adjustments in wages are made monthly or quarterly as the index changes. How much of a wage adjustment will be made depends upon the agreement between labor and management as to percentage of wage changes that is to be made for each percentage change in the cost-of-living index.

Such practices seem to have a logical appeal. Yet analysis will show that cost of living has an indirect, not a direct, bearing upon wages. The reasonableness of cost-of-living "escalator clauses," as they are sometimes called, lies in the fact that wages and cost of living tend to go up and down at the same time. For example, in the rising phase of a business cycle all prices tend to rise. Thus the items which labor buys go up in price. And wages of labor do, too. In the case of labor, its requests for increases are then met for the very simple reason that the supply of labor is relatively less than the demand for labor. The supply-demand relationship also favors increases in the goods that labor buys in its standard of living.

Similarly on the down side of a business swing, the supply of labor tends to exceed the demand. Workers compete against one another for available jobs. The net result is a lowering of prices (wages for) of labor.

The cost of living tends to go down likewise during the down side of a business swing. So any way one looks at it, the cost of living and wages seem to be related directly. And it is easy to conclude that one causes the other, particularly when one works for wages which are used to buy one's "cost of living." The relation is not, however, causal; each goes up or down because of general market and competitive conditions. It is like a cloud and a sail boat moving in the same direction. No one would say the cloud was pushing the sail boat. Rather the wind would be recognized as the causal factor in the case of cloud and boat. Similarly with wages and cost of living, the "wind" is the force of supply and demand.

Since cost of living and wages tend to move together, it may be practical to use the former as a measure of the latter. But this should be done with a clear statement that the cost-of-living indexes are an expedient, not the real measure of wages. Otherwise, confusion and endless debates will result.

But even when used as expedients, the practice of tying wages to cost-of-living indexes eventually runs into one or more difficulties. In the first place, the tie between wages and living costs is usually made during periods of rising prices when employers are not reluctant to grant wage increases. But during deflationary periods, employees are irritated by the periodic (even though small) readjustments of wages that are made as living costs go down. Second, arguments eventually are raised as to how cost-of-living indexes should be computed. Also, there is much room for disagreement, as evidenced not long ago when the claims of various groups differed as much as 100 per cent in regard to how much costs had risen. Finally, a vicious circle would be induced if all employers followed this practice. Thus a price rise would call for a wage increase, which would increase costs, which would lead to an increase in prices, which would mean another wage adjustment, and so on.

GENERAL THEORIES OF WAGES

ECONOMIC ASPECTS

In a world in which various groups have recourse so often to the use of force in gaining desired goals, the effect of economic principles often seems negligible. But sooner or later the millstones of economics grind out their truths to the disadvantage of those who did, as well as those who did not, obey its precepts. Hence the personnel manager should possess an understanding of the subject of economics so that he can explain the courses it dictates to management as well as labor. Although this is not the place to delve into detailed aspects of economic wage principles, some of the more important ones will be touched upon.

1. WAGES AS A PRICE. Without forgetting the human aspects of labor, it is nevertheless necessary at the outset to recognize that the term "wage" is a particular kind of price, that is, the price of labor. As such, it is subject to the same type of analysis as any other price. Assuming, for the moment, the absence of political regulations and pressure groups (either managerial or labor), wages are set at the point where the demand curve for labor crosses the supply curve of labor.[1] Hence, to act

---

[1] This oversimplified statement has the merit of making it possible to discuss, in a limited space, a topic that otherwise would have to be left untouched here.

rationally in setting wage policies, it is necessary to determine the curves for demand for and supply of labor.

Although this is extremely difficult, if not impossible in most cases, nevertheless an understanding of the theory of demand-and-supply determination is very useful. At least, the personnel manager who studies the forces behind demand and supply can make more intelligent suggestions to management than one who relies upon intuition or guesswork.

2. DEMAND CURVE. The demand for labor (to begin with this factor) has two major aspects. First, each company has a demand for labor, that is, the quantities of labor that it is willing to hire at varying prices. Ordinarily, these quantities go downward, as indicated in Figure 67. The downward trend is due to the decrease in productivity of any

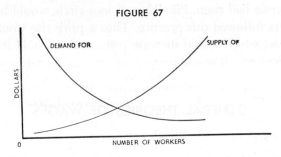

FIGURE 67

group of workers, as explained by the general principle of diminishing productivity. Every company should be able to produce a reasonably accurate chart of its labor requirements, or demand curve, at any given time. Second, for every company there usually is a community or industry demand curve, depending upon the number and type of competitors for labor in the area in which a company is operating. This type of demand curve is difficult to produce exactly, but it, too, has a downward trend, as depicted in Figure 67. A simple way of doing this is to estimate the types and quantities of labor that all users of labor require at different rates of output.

3. SUPPLY CURVE. The supply curve, on the other hand, has an upward trend, as indicated in Figure 67. This is a recognition of the fact that, ordinarily, it takes increasing quantities of dollars to lure larger numbers of labor into the working market. Here, again, there are company and area supply curves. Most companies have a supply of labor that is loyal to it irrespective of general wages or competition. And then there is a general supply curve representing quantities that can be drawn upon or lost by a particular company, depending upon the wages it is

willing to pay. Supply curves are difficult to draw, although here, too, more or less accurate estimates can be made by counting the population by sex and age groups and by getting estimates of types of skills available in the community. Much work of this nature was done by the War Manpower Commission during World War II in discharging its responsibilities of channeling labor to high-priority industries.

4. FORCES AFFECTING DEMAND AND SUPPLY. Besides having a good picture of the demand-and-supply curves at any particular time, it is essential to determine and weigh as accurately at possible the forces at work that may change the existing demand-and-supply curves. In brief, the following are forces for which signs should be watched:

1. Demand factors
   a) Short-run
      (1) Changes in company production schedules
      (2) Changes in competitors' production schedules
      (3) Seasonal production changes
      (4) Changes in consumer demands
   b) Long-run
      (1) Changes in fundamental processes of production
      (2) Changes in demands of competitors for labor
      (3) Changes in fundamental productivity of labor
      (4) Growth or decline of industry
      (5) Profitability of the industry

2. Supply factors
   a) Short-run
      (1) Mobility of labor in or out of the community
      (2) Seasonal changes in working habits
      (3) Union demands
   b) Long-run
      (1) Cyclical depressions or periods of prosperity
      (2) Influx of new industries or departure of old
      (3) Changes in family size and other population characteristics
      (4) Changes in costs and standards of living
      (5) Trends in union strength and governmental regulation

Close study of such factors as the foregoing will enable any employer to draw more accurate conclusions about the demand and supply of labor. With such information, he can determine what changes, if any, he should be prepared to make in wages. He will certainly not make the mistake of foolishly agreeing to wage changes in direct proportion to such things as changes in cost of living. Instead, he will attempt to interpret their effect upon the supply of labor and in turn its relation to his price curve. Also, he will recognize that his demand for labor is a derived demand based, in the final analysis, upon the demand for his product. When his sales curve is falling (or rising), changes will have to be made in the labor payroll, but not necessarily in the same proportion. Hence he should be prepared to calculate what changes in his demand curve (wages) should be made as a result of changes in production schedules, in production processes and productivity, and in the profitability of the business.

LEGISLATIVE REGULATIONS

Economic forces rarely have an opportunity to work themselves out free from the influence of the foregoing factors. For example, in recent years there has been a growing tendency for governmental regulation of wages. Of significance in this respect are the following:

1. Minimum wage controls
2. Wage and salary stabilization rules of war and postwar years
3. Collective bargaining regulations

MINIMUM WAGE CONTROLS

Minimum wage controls are enforced by federal and, in some cases, state regulations. The state regulations follow federal plans, so the latter only are discussed here. The Fair Labor Standards Act, the Walsh-Healey Act, and the Bacon-Davis Act are the federal controls.

THE FAIR LABOR STANDARDS ACT

The Wages and Hours Law was enacted in 1938 and amended in 1949 for the dual purpose of helping to spread employment and to outlaw unsatisfactory wage rates. The latter purpose is accomplished by establishing a minimum pay level of 75 cents an hour. The former purpose is achieved by penalizing employers who work their employees beyond 40 hours a week by requiring them to pay 50 per cent more for the excess hours. This is where the term "time and one-half for overtime" is derived, the actual overtime being paid for at the rate of one and one-half times the regular base rate. For example, an employee who works 48 hours in a given week in an industry subject to the F.L.S.A. and whose base rate is $1.00 per hour would be paid $12.00 for the extra 8 hours of work, or a total for the week of $52.00. This may be computed by two methods, as follows:

Let:

Regular work week of 40 hours	$= R$
Overtime hours	$= O$
Total hours worked	$= T$
Base rate	$= B$
Wages	$= W$

Then, according to the first method:

$$(T \times B) + (O \times B) \; \tfrac{1}{2} = W$$

or

$$(48 \times \$1) + (8 \times \$1) \; \tfrac{1}{2} = \$52.$$

According to the second method:

$$(R \times B) + (O \times B) \; 1\tfrac{1}{2} = W$$

or

$$(40 \times \$1) + (8 \times \$1) \; 1\tfrac{1}{2} = \$52.$$

Some companies prefer the first of these methods because it shows the total hours worked and the overtime hours, whereas others prefer the second because it shows the extra amount paid for overtime and hence the need for keeping it at a minimum.

1. COVERAGE OF THE ACT. The F.L.S.A. covers all businesses and employees, with stated exceptions to be noted later, who engage in interstate commerce or who produce goods that enter interstate commerce. While the Act defines "interstate commerce" in broad terms, in test cases the courts have defined it so stringently that any business which is not strictly intrastate should be prepared to follow its provisions. Thus companies that ship only a small percentage of their goods across state lines have been judged to be affected by the law. If only a small percentage of one's business is interstate, let us say anywhere up to 10 per cent, it is highly desirable, if possible, to segregate employees working on interstate business, since the others may then be legally excluded from the provisions of the law.

2. EXCLUSIONS UNDER THE ACT. There are three classes of exclusions under the Act. First, completely exempt are the following:

1. Strictly intrastate activities
2. Retail or service activities which are at least 75 per cent retail or service and at least 50 per cent intrastate
3. Transportation employees (covered by another federal law)
4. Agricultural and fishing employees
5. Executive, administrative, and professional employees

Second, exempt from overtime requirements for specific periods are the following:

1. The first processing of various agricultural and livestock products for the first fourteen weeks of a seasonal period
2. Any seasonal industry, if specified as such by the administrator of the act, and then for fourteen weeks only
3. Employees under certain types of work guarantees and as specified in a union contract

Third, exempt for limited periods from the minimum wage provisions are apprentices, learners, handicapped workers, and messengers.

3. EMPLOYEE EXEMPTIONS. It is important under this Act, and the Walsh-Healey Act, too, that the coverage of the term "employee" be clearly understood. Generally speaking, an employee is one who is subject to the directions of an employer or his managerial representatives regarding what is to be done and how. Having the right to discharge also serves to separate employers from employees. More specifically, owners, executives, and independent contractors are examples of those considered to be employers. Of particular interest here are the tests by which it is determined whether or not particular employees may be included in the following exempt groups: executives, administrative employees, professional employees, certain sales employees, and a miscellaneous group.

a) Executive Exemptions. In general, the nature of the work and the salary received determine executive exemptions. More specifically, an executive is considered to be one whose primary duty consists of managing an establishment or a recognized department or subdivision thereof. He must also customarily direct the work of others (at least two subordinates), have authority to fire or recommend discharge or promotions, and exercise discretionary powers. He must devote not more than 20 per cent of his hours worked to performance of duties not related to managerial duties. And he must be compensated (exclusive of board, lodging, or other facilities) at a rate of not less than $55 a week.

If the executive in question receives at least $100 a week and meets all other requirements except the 20 per cent rule, he shall also be deemed to be an exempt executive.

b) Administrative Exemptions. Administrative exemptions are also related to nature of work and salary received. Exemptions are granted to those who perform office or nonmanual work that is concerned with management policies or general business operations. The work must require exercise of discretion and independent judgment, be of a specialized or technical nature, and be performed only under general supervision. Not more than 20 per cent of the time must be spent on tasks not related to administrative work as defined. And the salary received (exclusive of board, lodging, etc.) must not be less than $75 a week.

If the administrative employee receives at least $100 a week and meets all other requirements except the 20 per cent rule, he shall also be deemed to be an exempt employee.

c) Professional Exemptions. The professional tests are similar to those of the administrative employee in respect to the $75 minimum salary under a 20 per cent rule, or $100 a week without this rule. Definitions of duties are, of course, different. A professional employee is one who performs intellectual and varied duties as opposed to routine, manual, or physical work. He must exercise discretion and judgment. His education must have been in a field of science of learning customarily acquired by a prolonged course in specialized and intellectual study, as distinguished from general academic training, apprenticeships, or trade courses. Or the work may be in a recognized artistic endeavor dependent upon invention, imagination, or talent as opposed again to work calling for general, manual, or broad training and ability.

d) Sales Exemptions. In addition to retail exemptions noted earlier, "outside" salesmen may also be exempted. Such salesmen must, to begin with, make personal calls at the customer's place of business. Mail or telephone sales are not exempt unless they are an adjunct of the personal call. And not more than 20 per cent of the time must be spent on such activities as clerical work, attending sales conferences, making incidental deliveries or collections, and traveling.

e) Miscellaneous Groups. As noted earlier, apprentices, learners, handicapped workers, and messengers are the principal classes eligible for exemption from minimum wage provisions.

For apprentices to be exempted, their training agreement must be in writing and it must cover the following points:

1. Provide for not less than 4,000 hours of reasonably continuous employment
2. Provide for participation in an approved schedule of work and at least 144 hours per year of related supplemental instruction
3. Set forth the proportion between the number of apprentices and the number of experienced workmen in a given job classification
4. Specify the relation of apprentice rates at various periods to the rates paid experienced workers
5. Be approved by the State Apprenticeship Council or other established state authority, if state authority exists

In the case of handicapped workers, learners, and messengers, subminimum wage rates may also be paid. This cannot be done, however, until certificates of exemption noting the specific reductions permissible are obtained from the federal agencies.

4. CONTRACTUAL EXEMPTIONS. Under certain types of collective bargaining agreements, exemptions are permitted. Under the Belo-type contract—named after the case in which this clause was legalized—the

employer need not comply with overtime requirements. However, he must guarantee a certain sum each week, no matter how many hours worked.

Such agreements have further conditions. No employee shall be employed more than 1,040 hours during any consecutive 26-week period, or more than 2,080 hours in 52 weeks. In any event, hours over 12 a day, or 56 a week, are entitled to the overtime pay provisions.

5. COMPUTING OVERTIME. The next major problem in connection with this Act is that of computing overtime. In order to describe various phases of this problem, the following are now discussed:

a) Computing time and rates
b) Overtime calculations for hourly employees
c) Overtime calculations for nonhourly employees
d) Effect of bonuses
e) Time-off plans
f) Overtime on overtime

a) *Computing Time and Rates.* In computing how many hours an employee has worked, the general rule is that compensable time is that during which an employee works or remains on duty, and which is directly related to his major activity.[2] By custom, tradition, or contractual agreement, other activities related to normal work duties may also be included.

Having computed the hours worked during a given week, the next step is to determine the rate to be used for overtime purposes. Normally included are, first, all regular earnings and, second, any bonuses or incentive pay directly geared to services rendered. Normally excluded are, first, pay for periods not worked, such as holidays and vacations, and, second, extra pay for periods outside of regular hourly work or bonuses not directly related to individual work effort.

b) *Overtime Calculations for Hourly Employees.* Overtime calculations for hourly employees vary. For those on an hourly basis completely, the calculations are simple. Thus an employee who worked 50 hours in a given week and is paid $1.00 an hour would have his pay figured as follows: 50 hours × $1.00 = $50.00, plus ½ of $1.00 × 10 hours overtime $5.00, or a total of $55.00.

For pieceworkers the calculation would differ. Suppose an employee receives $0.10 for each unit produced. During a given week of 50 hours, he produces 600 units. His base rate would be (600 × $0.10) ÷ 50 hours, or $1.20. To his piecework earnings of $60.00 would be added

---

[2] This has been clearly established under the provisions of the Portal-to-Portal Pay Act of 1947, as incorporated in the 1949 revisions of the F.L.S.A.

$1.20 × 10 hours × ½, or $6.00, making a total of $66.00 for the week.

An employee who works on hourly rates and piece rates during a given week would have his pay calculated differently. Assume that an employee worked 50 hours in a given week. Of these, 20 hours were paid on an hourly basis of $1.00, and during 30 hours he was on piece-work. The piece-rate earnings came to $40.00. His regular earnings therefore amount to $60.00. This amount when divided by 50 hours gives his base rate of $1.20. For the 10 overtime hours, he would therefore receive 10 × $1.20 × ½, or $6.00, which when added to his regular earnings yields a total of $66.00 for the week in question.

c) *Calculations for Nonhourly Employees.* For employees on weekly, semimonthly, or annual bases, the overtime calculations are made in weekly rates. Hence the nonweekly rates must first be converted to a weekly basis. This is done by converting to an annual base first, then dividing by 52.

When such employees are paid a flat salary for a regular number of hours each week, the fixed hours must be divided into the weekly salary to get the base rate. All overtime hours must then be paid at one and one-half times that rate. Any other forms of compensation, such as bonuses or commissions, must first be added to the weekly salary before it is divided by the fixed number of hours.

For employees paid a fixed salary regardless of the number of hours worked in the week, the base rate is obtained by dividing the fixed weekly salary by the number of hours actually worked in the week. Then all overtime hours are paid at one and one-half times the calculated base rate. Again, any extra bonuses which depend upon service rendered must be first added to the fixed weekly salary before calculating the base rate.

d) *Effect of Bonuses.* Of interest also are bonuses dependent upon production but not paid until some period subsequent to that in which it is earned. In such cases, original overtime payments must be based on earnings exclusive of the bonus. Then when the bonus is distributed, additional overtime must be paid by recomputing for the earlier period the effect which the bonus would have had upon the base rate.

Where employees are paid either a salary plus commissions or straight commissions, all commission earnings must be counted in computing overtime pay.

e) *Time-Off Plans.* Of further interest is the time-off plan of compensating employees for overtime. In such instances, employees must be given an hour and a half off for each hour of overtime. However, the employee must be guaranteed a fixed sum for a definite number of hours and must work a regular number of hours to earn that salary. And the amount due the employee for overtime earned in one week within a pay period must be compensated by being given time off in another week of the same pay period.

f) Overtime on Overtime. Because the Wages and Hours Law as originally passed was not clear on the matter, some employees whose union contracts called for time and one-half or double time on Saturdays, Sundays, and holidays, irrespective of previous hours worked during the week, claimed that double-time earnings should be averaged in with regular earnings to ascertain the base rate for overtime purposes. This would result in "overtime on overtime," and an affirmative decision was reached in the Bay Ridge Stevedoring Case in 1948. But the ruling had many unfavorable effects, so an amendment to the Wages and Hours Law was passed in 1949. This provides, first, that an employer may pay premium rates for work done outside of regular hours without adding the premium to regular rates to arrive at the overtime base rate. Moreover, the law provides that the premium rates may be credited toward overtime compensation due under the Wages and Hours Act. Thus an employee who receives double time for Sunday work would have the overtime requirements satisfied if he worked 48 hours in a given week in which 8 hours were worked on Sunday.

6. RECORDS. Although the F.L.S.A. does not require that specific forms of records be kept, rulings of the Administrator indicate that certain types of information should be recorded. First, for each employee such personal data should be kept as name, address, date of birth if under nineteen, and occupation. Second, time records should be kept regarding the standard work week, hours worked each day and each week, and absences. Third, payroll records should cover dates of payment, pay periods, daily and weekly earnings, basis on which payment is made, bonuses earned, and any deductions from wages paid. And, fourth, if the company hires employees who work at home, detailed records should be kept on the foregoing, as well as the amount of work distributed to and collected from each such worker.

7. PENALTIES. Employers who violate this Act may be punished in a variety of ways. By injunction, an employer may be forbidden to ship goods interstate, to pay less than minimum wages, or to keep inadequate records. By criminal prosecution, if an employer is convicted of having willfully violated the Act, he can be fined up to $10,000 or imprisoned for a term of not more than six months, or both. And if an employee has not been paid his due under the law, he may sue to recover the wages

due plus double the sum as liquidated damages plus attorney fees and litigation costs. It is not necessary that the employer's failure to pay be willful.

THE WALSH-HEALEY ACT

The Walsh-Healey Act differs from the F.L.S.A. in two important respects. First, the overtime provisions are set on a daily basis, beginning after eight hours of work. Second, the minimum wages are based upon prevailing community rates, as determined by the Secretary of Labor after public hearings.

1. COVERAGE UNDER THE ACT. The matter of coverage is also important under this Act. In general terms, it covers those parts of an employer's business which come into contact with federal contracts of $10,000 or more. For example, the following firms would be covered—

1. Those dealing with any federal agency
2. Those that supply or manufacture contracted articles
3. Those that accept subcontracts from the prime contractor with a federal agency, or work with him in the execution of a contract
4. Those that ship goods on behalf of a regular dealer

The more important exemptions include the following:

1. Various transportation and communication facilities
2. Construction contracts
3. Personal service contracts
4. Perishable commodities
5. Stock on hand

The definitions of employees under this Act are much like those of the F.L.S.A. The following are the principal exemptions:

1. Employees not engaged in work directly connected with the manufacturing, fabrication, assembling, handling, or shipment of articles, supplies, and equipment
2. Office, custodial, and maintenance employees
3. Executive, administrative, and professional employees

2. METHODS OF COMPUTATION. Methods of computing time and pay for overtime are much the same for the Walsh-Healey Act as for the F.L.S.A., except that the day instead of the week must be used in computing overtime. The basic work period is eight hours, and the minimum rate used in computing overtime must be at least the prevailing rates in the community for comparable types of work.

Whereas an employee who worked 36 hours during a given week, but did so in 3 days of 12 hours each, would receive no overtime under the F.L.S.A., he would under the Walsh-Healey Act. If his rate were $1.00 an hour, his pay for each day would be $14.00, calculated as follows:

8 hours at $1.00	$ 8.00
4 hours at $1.50	6.00
Total	$14.00

If he were on piecework or a bonus plan, the extra earnings would have to be included when determining the rate to be used for overtime purposes.

3. REQUIRED RECORDS. The records required by this Act are much the same as by the F.L.S.A. The Walsh-Healey regulations require the same personal data as the Wages and Hours Law plus these two additional items:

1. The sex of each employee
2. The number of each contract each employee works on, and the dates when the work is performed

Except for the overtime column, payroll records under both the Wages and Hours and the Walsh-Healey Acts may be identical. The reason for the exception is that the Wages and Hours Law requires overtime pay only for hours worked over forty per week, whereas the Walsh-Healey Act requires overtime pay for hours worked over eight per day or forty per week, whichever is greater.

Beginning May 1, 1943, firms covered by the Walsh-Healey Act had to keep a record of the "injury frequency rate" in their establishment on a quarterly basis. This information was to be tabulated on January 1, April 1, July 1, and October 1 of every year. The injury frequency rate is calculated by multiplying the total number of "disabling injuries" which occur during each three-month period by one million and dividing that sum by the total number of man-hours actually worked within the same quarterly period.

A "disabling injury" is one which prevents an employee from continuing to work beyond the day or shift on which the injury occurred. All employees in an establishment must be counted in figuring the total number of man-hours worked, even though they may not be subject to the Walsh-Healey Act.

4. PENALTIES FOR VIOLATIONS. The penalties for violations of this Act may be very severe. They are as follows:

1. Money damages for child or prison labor
2. Wage restitutions
3. Concellation of contract
4. Blacklisting

Perhaps the most effective method of enforcing the Walsh-Healey Act is that which provides for the assessment of money damages against the contractor.

If the contractor violates the minimum wage or overtime stipulations, he has to pay the wages due, equal to the amount of any unlawful deductions, rebates, refunds, or underpayments.

Failure to comply with the stipulations of the Walsh-Healey Act, which are a part of the contract, constitutes breach of contract by the contractor. As in other instances of breach of contract, the penalty is cancellation of the contract. In addition, he can be made to pay any increased costs if the government gets someone else to complete the contract.

The Comptroller General is required to distribute a "blacklist" to all government agencies. The persons or firms whose names appear on this list cannot be awarded any government contract for a period of three years following the date upon which the Secretary of Labor determines that a breach occurred, unless the Secretary recommends otherwise. Obviously, to be placed upon this list would be a serious penalty in many cases.

THE BACON-DAVIS ACT

The Bacon-Davis Act is similar to the Walsh-Healey Act, since it, too, regulates minimum wages on governmental contracts. It relates to contracts in excess of $2,000 for the construction, alteration, and repair of public works. All mechanics and laborers must be paid at least the prevailing rate as established by the Secretary of Labor.

If contractors pay more than prevailing rates, they do so at their own risks, since such additional costs are not reimbursable. If contractors pay less, they are subject to any of the following penalties:

1. The Secretary of Labor may withhold accrued payments due to the contractor from the federal government.
2. The contracts held by the contractor may be canceled outright by the government.
3. The contractor's name may be placed upon the Comptroller General's ineligibility list for further contracts.

COLLECTIVE BARGAINING EFFECTS

The collective bargaining regulations of the federal government are also of serious consequences in the matter of wages because they affect the weight which employers and employees can bring to bear in the bargaining processes. Since this subject is discussed in detail in later chapters, it is merely cited here as an important factor in wage determination. Certainly, in many ways the Taft-Hartley Act and its predecessor, the National Labor Relations Act, have in recent years been the most important factor, the influences of World War II excepted, in wage disputes.

EFFECTS OF UNION ACTIVITIES

The strength and principles which labor unions have brought to the labor market are also of significance in determining wages and wage policies. Anyone who has bargained with labor individually and then collectively, through its representative, is soon made aware of the difference in bargaining practices and theories. Indeed, the force and direction of union demands are so new and novel to many, that unions have been viewed by some, not as an economic institution, but rather as a political mechanism. Certainly, the efforts of some labor leaders to perpetuate themselves in office, to retain disproved economic theories because of their apparent appeal to workers, and to participate actively in the election of governmental officials, lend support to those views.

1. LEARNING ORGANIZED LABOR'S VIEWS. From the standpoint of good personnel management, however, it is foolish to call names or condemn practices regarding which contrary opinions are held. But it is wise to know the views of labor (as it does those of management), to ascertain the policies of labor, to learn the strength and direction of its activities, and to interpret its aims so that management can react intelligently and fairly thereto. For example, the desire of some employers to break unions may be commendable in theory for them, but it is unrealistic in practice. Instead of fighting them, it would be far better to exert their energies in disseminating facts and information, which in the long run would be more effective in combating undesirable practices and in building a better relationship between labor and management.

2. THE LUMP-OF-WORK THEORY. The wage policies of unions are, of course, many and varied. The purpose here is merely to describe briefly some of the more important of them. To begin with, some of its wage policies are obviously unsound, but they have been retained so long in some instances that their effect may take years to disappear. First, there is the principle that workers should take it easy on their jobs because to do otherwise will result in working themselves out of their jobs. This is the lump-of-work theory, which is false, yet has an apparent and occasional accuracy, as anyone will agree who has seen

the well of orders dry up, and jobs with it. Yet "soldiering" and practiced restriction of output as a means of keeping up wages, as a general proposition, can lead to one result—decreased employment because of higher labor costs and a consequent decrease in sales.

3. THE EQUALITY OF WORKERS THEORY. There is encountered occasionally the principle that all workers are economically equal on given types of jobs (presumably because they are born politically equal). A common application of this principle is that of paying all workers on a given class of work the same rate, irrespective of individual merit. Its application is desirable for the union because it eliminates the troublesome controversies between workers of varying ability as to the rates they should receive. The union can then concentrate its attention upon other matters than that of reconciling intra-union differences. Such supposed equality is the basis of seniority rules for granting wage increases which otherwise have little validity.

4. UNION STRATEGIES. Other attitudes of unions toward wage matters are more realistic. For example, wage demands are used as an effective tool of bargaining. It is important to recognize that union strategy may call for asking for more money than they expect to get, by putting out a wage demand in order to get something else, or by placing wages last on a list of demands so that management in its eagerness to get to wage questions may be more lenient on other demands. Of course, management may counter with proposals that tend to offset the strategy of labor, but to do this, it must be aware of the extent to which labor is using wages as a bargaining tool. When labor in a given case asks for a 30 per cent increase in wages, what does it really want? Until an answer is attempted, management cannot intelligently set its counterproposals at the most advantageous point.

Wages are used by unions to control or affect their internal affairs as well as relations with employers. For example, wage rates have been bargained for that will retard the flow of learners into a trade. In addition, levels of wages between different grades of work are often closely watched so that members do not quarrel among themselves over relative wages. In some instances, wage adjustments have been sought to offset the introduction of laborsaving equipment. And most unions nowadays estimate closely the possible effect upon employment of the levels of wage increases they seek.

The foregoing is sufficient for present purposes to illustrate the various ways in which unions use wages in collective bargaining and with which management must be prepared to deal. It should not be concluded that management and labor are inevitably doomed to warfare because of past and present conflicts over wages. Of course, many "battles" will continue to be fought. But when management can anticipate the demands, and reasons therefor, of unions, it can prepare facts to buttress its counterproposals and arguments. Through information, and not name calling, will progress toward better relations evolve because only bigots can close their eyes to the truth. And there is good reason to believe that both management and labor have in their ranks leaders who more and more are seeking facts to fight their battles and less and less are desirous of relying upon shows of brute strength.

SUMMARY REMARKS

In the light of the various forces at work in the field of wages, what should be management's policy toward wage determination? To begin with, it should be perfectly obvious that anyone who is convinced that he has a perfect answer to wage problems and can correctly set wages is merely deluding himself. There is, as yet, no method of such perfection available. To believe so merely establishes a block in the road that otherwise leads to intelligent compromise.

Next, management's wage policies should be based upon a full account of all factors—economic, legal, union, and social—that have some effect on wages. To do this, it is absolutely essential to determine as precisely as possible how these factors exert their influence. Such factors as cost-of-living indexes, union demands, changes in population structure, competition, and federal regulations all have their place in the wage structure. However, some work directly and others indirectly, some work slowly and others rapidly, and some are positive in wage determinations and others negative. Unless the direction and force of the composite of factors is determined, grievous errors will be committed in establishing wage policies.

Finally, and perhaps most important of all, wage policies should be viewed as an integral part of the structure of a personnel program. Wages are undoubtedly the keystone to the arch of this structure, but not the structure itself, as some employers seem to believe. Indeed, some have been so preoccupied with wages that unions have taken advantage of this bias to gain unwarranted and ill-advised concessions on working conditions and rules. The ill-advised seniority rules accepted by some companies, which they must follow thereafter to their regret, are a case in point.

When wages are given their proper place in the personnel program, they are neither overemphasized nor underemphasized. Wages alone cannot bring about higher production, better morale, and better relations with employees. Nonfinancial incentives, proper handling of grievances, good working conditions, availability of various services, and development of confidence in workers are examples of other matters that can add to or detract from the efficiency of the wage program itself.

QUESTIONS AND PROBLEMS

1. An employee working for a company operating under the Walsh-Healey Act is scheduled to work on a given day from 8:00 A.M. to 4:45 P.M., with a half hour off for lunch. He works the scheduled time, except that he comes in two minutes late, for which tardiness he is penalized a standard fifteen minutes. His hourly rate is $1.60. How much should he be paid for the day in question?

2. If an employee received a production bonus at the end of the year, covering work done during the entire past year, would it be necessary to go back through each week of the year and recompute overtime earnings? Doesn't this place a heavy burden upon the businessman? What is the justification for this?

3. What do you think of the proposition of paying people according to their contributions plus their needs? According to physical units of production as a measure of dollar wages? Explain.

4. Can wages be measured precisely? If they cannot, what hope is there of ever minimizing wage disputes?

5. Assume that two manufacturers in the same line of business, of the same size, in the same community, and employing the same kinds of labor in the same amounts report the following data:

	Results for Current Year	Prospects for Next Year
Company A	$1,500,000 (profit)	$ 250,000 (loss)
Company B	500,000 (loss)	1,000,000 (profit)

What effect should these data have upon wages in the individual companies?

6. Upon what theory are such employees as supervisors and professional employees exempted from the provisions of the F.L.S.A.?

7. Does your state have a state wages and hours law? If so, how do its provisions differ, if at all, from those of the federal acts? Why may state laws be necessary in addition to the federal laws?

8. Illustrate the ways in which overtime pay would be computed for an office employee who had worked the following hours, and whose weekly rate for a forty-hour week is $48.00:

```
1st week ............................................. 43
2d week .............................................. 47
3d week .............................................. 32
4th week ............................................. 36
```

9. What is the relation of ability to pay to wage rates?

10. Should wages be adjusted directly as cost of living changes? Why or why not?

11. If a company wishes to make wage adjustments in line with changes in cost of living, what suggestions would you make to it and against what pitfalls would you provide safeguards?

12. What is the purpose of minimum wage laws? What are their presumed benefits? In what ways are they likely to be harmful to labor?

13. In what respect does the Walsh-Healey Act differ from the F.L.S.A. in regard to minimum wages?

14. Would you ascribe the strength of unions in wage matters to their convincing explanation of economics, to their political power, or to their bargaining power in the industrial field? If you select their political or bargaining power as the explanation, is it not true that these bases of power are short run rather than fundamental?

15. What can time-study methods contribute to the determination of wages? What should not be expected of such methods?

16. What is meant by "absolute wages," and what by "relative wages"? Why must both be given consideration in setting wages?

17. What is the difference between "money wages" and "real wages"? Show how each may be measured.

18. What is meant by "take home" wages? With what may these be compared?

19. Some companies have established the rule that employees are not to discuss wages or wage rates with each other. Explain why you do or do not believe the policy is good.

20. A wage earner in a company operating in interstate commerce has a basic wage rate of $1.10 an hour. On a particular day his time ticket reads as follows:

Hours	Job	Rate	Units Produced
8:00–10:00	Piecework	$0.03	84
10:00–10:30	Daywork		
10:30–12:30	Piecework	0.07	31
Lunch			
12:45– 3:00	Daywork		
3:00– 5:00	Piecework	0.10	24

How much is his wage for the day in question?

CHAPTER

18

Job Evaluation

and Wage Classification

INTRODUCTION

As noted earlier, relative wages perhaps even more than absolute wages are of significance in affecting employee morale and effort. It is surprising to see the change in an employee who, seemingly satisfied with his wage, learns of the higher earnings of a fellow worker whom he considers his inferior. His whole attitude reflects his dissatisfaction with the unfairness of a company that permits such inequities. Hence it is imperative, if a company wishes to minimize such occurrences, to determine what each job is worth and, if a range is allowed on each job, what each individual is worth. Determining job values comes under the heading of "job evaluation and wage classification" (which is the subject of the present chapter); and determining the value of employees (which has been discussed in Chapter 12) is known by a variety of names, such as "merit rating," "employee rating," and "service rating."

Job evaluation is essentially a process of measurement. Factors considered of importance in determining the value of jobs are measured by the use of arbitrarily designed yardsticks. The quantities for the factors are summed up for each job, and the totals are converted into dollar values. Thus each job is assigned a monetary value that has a definite relation to other jobs, since all have been measured by the same yardsticks.

Various methods have been designed to make such measurements. In major outline, all follow the same general pattern, which includes the following major steps:

1. Establishing organizational responsibility
2. Determining jobs to be evaluated
3. Making the job analysis
4. Evaluating the jobs
5. Preparing wage and salary classifications

ORGANIZATIONAL ASPECTS

Almost without exception, those who have had experience with job evaluation programs have concluded that such programs should have the approval and sponsorship of top executive levels. Particularly in the initial stages, a major committee, of which the president or executive vice-president is chairman, should guide the development of job evaluation. This is desirable in order to convince any "doubting Thomas" that top management is convinced of the permanent value of the program. After the program is well under way, periodic conferences should be scheduled with top executives so that they may be kept informed of results and may have the opportunity to offer constructive criticisms.

1. ORGANIZATION RESPONSIBILITY. Responsibility for job evaluation is usually assigned to the industrial engineering section, a wage unit of the personnel department, or to some interested operating executive. There is much sense to its assignment to industrial engineering because of the professional interest, competency, and activity in this area. Its placement in the personnel division has much to commend it, too, particularly since a total wage and salary administration program is often its responsibility. The "interested executive" assignment is usually made in smaller companies or when it is wise to avoid jurisdictional disputes over its placement in personnel or industrial engineering.

2. STAFFING THE UNIT. Wherever in the organization the job evaluation program is assigned, provision must be made for staffing it with competent help. In some companies, trained and experienced help is hired from the outside. In others, members of the staff are given special training. By the former method, competent help is secured at once, but it takes some time for the outsiders to become acquainted with the characteristics and policies of the company and its employees. Under the latter method, the staff selected for the job is acquainted with the company, its executives, and its employees, but it must acquire skill in carrying out job evaluation. Both plans have been used successfully, so the choice in any particular case depends upon which can be installed most economically and effectively. In any event, the staff should be a permanent one, with opportunity provided for continuing study and experience in order to improve its competence.

3. APPROVAL OF EVALUATION PLANS. Where authority rests in approving and using job evaluation, data should also be specified if all organizational aspects of the program are to be properly considered. Since the personnel department is a staff department, obviously it cannot

enforce the program, the development of which has been assigned to it. Hence approval of the plan must be in the hands of some top-line executive. Even when this is provided for, the personnel department must solve the problem of securing full co-operation of unions and using departments. More and more, job evaluation has become subject to collective bargaining. Hence close co-operation with unions at all stages of development and use seems desirable. Moreover, building satisfactory relations with foremen and supervisors is an essential part of the organizational problem. Even though top management approves a job evaluation program, the supervisors can delay or even sabotage its development if they withhold their co-operation or give it grudgingly.

SELECTION OF JOBS TO BE EVALUATED

Few companies have included all jobs and positions in their evaluation programs. Ordinarily, the program is limited in most companies to shop jobs or office work. In some instances, sales and executive positions have been evaluated, too. It might seem at first glance that all types and levels of jobs should be included. Usually there are practical difficulties in the way of an all-inclusive study. It would take too long, and, at the outset, the staff is usually not sufficiently sure of itself to tackle the nonroutine jobs. Moreover, such jobs are not the ones ordinarily from which the cries of discontent arise. Executive, professional, and technical jobs are usually excluded, at least in the beginning. The line of demarcation has been conveniently set in some instances by excluding all jobs receiving more than a set amount a year in salary—in some cases as low as $4,000 and in others up to $15,000. Or a particular level in the organization chart is used; all jobs below the first line of supervision have been selected in one case.

Such exclusions should not, however, be made permanent. When time and conditions permit, all jobs should be brought into the plan. Otherwise, there will be groups of discontented employees because of salary discrepancies between evaluated and nonevaluated jobs. When selling jobs are separated from nonselling jobs, or clerical from shop jobs, for example, in order to get an evaluation job done, the grievances of employees whose jobs have not been studied remain unsettled, even though these grievances may be more easily satisfied than those in the studied jobs. Indeed, the excluded group may become more vociferous when they see the changes being made in the studied jobs. After all, though it is easy to separate jobs into those that will and will not be evaluated, they are economically related despite exterior differences and cannot, for wage and salary purposes, be considered apart.

Moreover, when companies try to include heretofore excluded jobs in the program, they find that the new jobs can seldom be fitted into the existing scheme. The alternatives were to have two evaluation programs, which did not quite match, or to start all over and re-evaluate the old jobs under an over-all program. Either course is unsatisfactory and could have been avoided, had the evaluation plan been developed with a view to including ultimately all jobs, though at the outset only particular groups of jobs were to be evaluated.

MAKING THE JOB ANALYSIS

The basic material of job evaluation is provided by job analysis. Since the nature and scope of job analysis have been described in an earlier chapter, it is necessary here merely to note the information which is secured by job analysis and which is essential to subsequent steps of job evaluation. The following information is usually collected:

1. Job title or titles, including trade nicknames
2. Number of employees on the job and their organizational and geographical locations
3. Names of immediate supervisors
4. Materials, tools, and equipment used or worked with
5. Work received from and delivered to whom
6. Hours of work and wage levels
7. Conditions of work
8. Complete listing of duties, with an estimate of time spent on each group and classified according to daily, weekly, monthly, and occasional
9. Educational and experience requirements
10. Skills, aptitudes, and abilities required
11. Promotional and transfer lines from and to the job
12. Miscellaneous information and comments

JOB EVALUATION

After the foregoing preparations have been made, measurement of jobs in nonfinancial terms may then be undertaken. This step, to repeat, is based on the assumption that to develop correct financial relationships between jobs it is first necessary to develop quantitative relationships based upon arbitrarily constructed yardsticks. In simple terms this means that if it is found that Job A is worth 2 units on a predetermined scale and that Job B is worth 4 units on the same scale, then whatever A is worth in dollars, B should be worth twice as much. How the jobs are quantitatively related to each other depends upon the system employed. The following systems of evaluation are described here:

1. The simple ranking plan
2. The job classification method

3. The point system
4. The factor comparison method

1. THE SIMPLE RANKING PLAN. Under the simple ranking plan of evaluation, jobs are arranged in order of increasing value in accordance with the judgment of the arrangers. This is first done on a departmental level by a committee of job analysts and supervisors, and then on interdepartmental levels by a committee which also includes higher line executives. In all cases of ranking, the committee members read the job descriptions or, if descriptions are not available, examine their mental pictures of the jobs and grade the jobs in terms of their individual interpretations of the relative amounts of such elements as the following:

1. Difficulty and volume of work
2. Responsibilities involved
3. Supervision given and received
4. Training and experience requirements
5. Working conditions

After all jobs have been ranked, they are grouped into a small number of classes, usually from six to ten. Wage and salary rates are established for each of the classes, either arbitrarily or by job rating methods to be defined later. All jobs are then paid within the dollar range established for each class.

This plan is obviously simple, can be done quickly, and does not require a large staff; but it has many disadvantages. The reasons why jobs have been ranked as they are, are locked in the minds of the rankers whose scales of value vary from one time to another and whose individual concepts of jobs differ. The rankers are ordinarily inexperienced in such work, so that their decisions are uncertain and largely a series of compromises. When it comes to interdepartmental ranking of jobs, their inexperience is even more apparent because few raters are acquainted with all jobs. Under the circumstances, the job ranking plan should be used when time or resources to employ a better method are not available or as a check on the accuracy of other methods.

2. THE JOB CLASSIFICATION METHOD. The job classification method is a refinement of the ranking method. Under it, major job classes or grades are first established, and then the various jobs are assigned by rankers to these grades. Figure 68 (p. 358) illustrates a gradation of five classes, designated by a title label and increasing in value. The raters read the job descriptions and, depending upon their personal interpretations of relative difficulty of tasks, responsibilities in-

volved, and knowledge and experience required, decide in which of the classes each job should be placed.

This method, too, is relatively simple to operate and to understand, does not take a great deal of time, and does not require technical help. Although it represents an advance in accuracy over the ranking method, it still leaves much to be desired, because personal evaluations by executives unskilled in such work establish the major classes and determine

FIGURE 68

DESCRIPTION OF JOB CLASSIFICATION

Third Class Clerk:	Pure routine concentration, speed and accuracy. Works under supervision. May or may not be held responsible for results.
Second Class Clerk:	No supervision of others; especially skilled for the job by having exhaustive knowledge of the details. Person: close application, exceptional accuracy and speed.
First Class Clerk:	Must have characteristics of 2nd class clerk. Assume more responsibility.
Senior Clerk:	Technical, varied work, occasionally independent thinking and action due to difficult work, which requires exceptional clerical ability and extensive knowledge of principles and fundamentals of business of his department. Not charged with supervision of others to any extent, work subject to only limited check. Person: dependable, trustworthy, resourceful—able to make decision.
Interpretive Clerk:	Those handling or capable of doing a major division of the work. Complicated work requiring much independent thinking, able to consider details outside control of supervision or routine.

into which class each job shall be placed. In this case, as in job ranking, it is difficult to know how much of a job's rank is influenced by the man on the job. Although the job and not the man should be evaluated, the foregoing methods provide practically no safeguards against this form of error. The job classification method should be used when an organization is small, when jobs are not too complex or numerous, or when time and resources to use another method are not available. It will produce better results than the ranking method without great increase in time or cost.

3. THE POINT SYSTEM.   The point system of job evaluation is the most widely used and, according to its proponents, yields accurate results without undue expense or effort. In simple outline, it values jobs by means of yardsticks, one for each factor that is considered to be common to all jobs. By summing up the readings of the several yardsticks a quantitative expression is derived for each job. These sums are point values, which must then be converted to dollar values.

In applying the point system, the following steps are taken:

1. Establish and define a list of factors common to all jobs that are being covered
2. Construct a measuring yardstick for each factor
3. From the job description, prepare a schedule showing qualitatively to what degree each job possesses the various factors enumerated above
4. Apply the yardstick to convert the qualitative descriptions to quantitative units
5. Sum up for each job the readings obtained for the individual factors
6. Rank the jobs in accordance with the scores obtained in the foregoing steps
7. Determine the dollar value to be assigned to relative positions in the job ranking

a) Job Factors.   Job factors are characteristics that are common to all jobs to be covered in the program. They can be readily determined by making a survey of representative jobs. Ordinarily, no more than six to nine major factors with appropriate subheadings should be used; otherwise, the ratings will be subject to useless controversy.

The factors and subfactors that are found most commonly in job evaluation programs are responsibility, skill, effort, education, working conditions, and experience required. The factors of the widely used plan of the National Metal Trades Association are shown in Table 17 (p. 360), and those in a plan devised by the National Office Managers Association are shown in Table 18 (p. 360).

b) Measuring Yardsticks.   After the factors to be used are determined, yardsticks must be established by which increasing importance in each of the factors may be measured. This is usually done in two stages. First, the total points that any factor or major subheading of a factor may have are established. Such assignments of points determine the relative value of the various factors. For example, in the N.M.T.A. plan, "skill" has a maximum of 250 points and "responsibility" 100, and in the N.O.M.A. plan, "skill" has a maximum of 500 points and "responsibility" 200, so in both cases the ratio between the two factors is 2½ to 1. Second, varying degrees of each major factor are then as-

TABLE 17

POINTS ASSIGNED TO FACTORS OF NATIONAL METAL TRADES ASSOCIATION PLAN

Factor		2d Degree	3d Degree	4th Degree	5th Degree
SKILL					
1. Education	14	28	42	56	70
2. Experience	22	44	66	88	110
3. Initiative and ingenuity	14	28	42	56	70
EFFORT					
4. Physical demand	10	20	30	40	50
5. Mental or visual demand	5	10	15	20	25
RESPONSIBILITY					
6. Equipment or process	5	10	15	20	25
7. Material or product	5	10	15	20	25
8. Safety of others	5	10	15	20	25
9. Work of others	5	10	15	20	25
JOB CONDITIONS					
10. Working conditions	10	20	30	40	50
11. Unavoidable hazards	5	10	15	20	25

TABLE 18

POINTS ASSIGNED TO FACTORS OF NATIONAL OFFICE
MANAGERS ASSOCIATION PLAN*

1. Elemental—250 points

2. Skill—500 points

    a) General or special education 160
    b) Training time on job 40
    c) Memory 40
    d) Analytical 95
    e) Personal contact 35
    f) Dexterity 80
    g) Accuracy 50

3. Responsibility—200 points

    a) For company property 25
    b) For procedure 125
    c) Supervision 50

4. Effort—physical factors—50 points

    a) Place of work 5
    b) Cleanliness of work 5
    c) Position 10
    d) Continuity of work 15
    e) Physical or mental strain 15

* Source: *Clerical Job Evaluation* (Bulletin No. 1) (New York: National Office Managers Association, 1946).

signed an increasing number of points within the total established for it. For example, in the N.O.M.A. plan, 160 of the 500 points for "skill" are allotted to general or special education, which is divided into three levels, each receiving a share of the 160 points. Thus a job that requires the maximum education would receive 160 points, one that required high-school training would receive 92 points, and one that required grammar-school training would be given 40 points.

These determinations are arrived at through the pooled opinions of line and staff executives. Cross checks of various kinds can be employed to compare the accuracy of major divisions and point assignments within divisions. The N.M.T.A. plan, for example, has been adopted in numerous companies, so that its allocations have weathered the most difficult of tests. In any event, after the points have been allocated, they, along with verbal descriptions of major classes and grades within classes, should be formally written up so that all may use and interpret the system similarly. The N.O.M.A. plan cited here is an example of how this may be done in simple yet relatively clear terms.

Although yardsticks are arbitrarily determined and vary in "value" from company to company, this does not impair their accuracy. So long as the yardsticks in each company are carefully designed and adhered to in measuring jobs, the relative values of all jobs can be established with accuracy. For example, if Company A and Company B have a maximum total of 300 points and 450 points, respectively, for "responsibility," then, on a similar job, if A gives it 100 points, B should give it 150 points. And if the total points received by the job are 400 by Company A and 600 by Company B, this does not mean that the job is worth 50 per cent more in Company B, but it means that the yardsticks in Company B are 50 per cent longer. In each company, similar jobs will be in relatively the same position, as may be seen in the following table:

	Company A (Points)	Company B (Points)	Ratio
Job X.................	400	600	150.0
Job Y.................	550	825	150.0

Some companies use as few as 400 points as the maximum, and others go into the thousands. What figure to use is not so important as accuracy in the allocation of the points among the factors and grades in the factors.

c) Rating Jobs. After the job factors and measuring sticks have been established, the task of evaluating individual jobs can begin. The first step is to translate the job descriptions for each job into a written statement of the various job factors contained in each job. Thus, if the first factor to be measured is "education," the amount of education required should be listed on a work sheet for each job. The next step is to apply the "education" yardstick against the amount of education specified on each job. For example, if a given job calls for four years of high school and the points assigned to that level of education are 92, then this amount is written on the work sheet for the job in question.

And so on, in order, each factor of each job is measured until points have been assigned to all. The points for each job are then totaled to get its point rating. Obviously, these steps of rating are largely routine. The big tasks are preparing acceptable job descriptions and yardsticks. When these have been done, the function of applying the yardsticks to each job is relatively easy.

d) Monetary Conversions. The point values assigned to jobs at this juncture are, to repeat, stated in point values which are nonmonetary units. Through such measurements, it has been determined how jobs rate relative to each other. To be of practical use, the relative positions

TABLE 19

Selected Jobs	Point Values	Average Company Salary per Week	Average Community Salary per Week
A....................	400	$24.00	$25.00
B....................	420	25.50	25.00
C....................	460	27.50	27.00
D....................	500	30.50	30.00
E....................	540	33.00	33.50
F....................	560	34.50	35.00
G....................	600	37.00	38.00
H....................	660	43.50	45.00

accorded jobs by the point system must be expressed in monetary terms. To accomplish this, two major steps are usually taken. First, a plan is established for determining how nonmonetary units are to be converted into dollar units. And, second, a decision is reached as to how jobs of increasing importance are to be grouped into wage classes.

The task of conversion is usually based upon a comparison of present company salary rates with those being paid in the community for comparable jobs. By making a check with other employers in the community, the data for such a comparison are derived. The comparison need not be made for all jobs; a limited number of selected jobs that are representative of several points on the job list is sufficient. Let us assume, for example, that data on community and company rates, as shown in Table 19 are collected for selected jobs.

Study of such figures would indicate that company rates in this case are well in line with community rates. Hence a conversion of point values to dollar values could be undertaken. If company and community rates were not in line, decisions would have to be made as to how rates out of line would be reconciled with community rates.

Careful analysis of these two sets of weekly rates (particularly if charts were prepared) would indicate that company salaries increase in an arithmetical progression, whereas those in the community follow a percentage increase. This provides a clue to two possible bases of conversion—the arithmetical and the percentage bases. In the foregoing case, the company salary increase is approximately $1.50 for each 20-point increase, whereas the community increase is about 5 per cent for each 20-point increase. The arithmetic plan results in a straight line when point values are set off against dollar units on a chart. The percentage plan results in a line that curves upward.

The arithmetic plan has simplicity in its favor, but economic principles favor the percentage plan. It has been found, for example, that most companies without a considered wage plan tend to overpay the lower jobs and underpay the higher jobs. Yet the supply of labor available to fill the lower jobs is invariably relatively more plentiful than that to fill the higher jobs. Hence, in developing a salary curve, it is preferable to select the percentage plan of increase. In this way, jobs in the higher point ranges will be accorded a wider dollar range than those in the lower point ranges.

e) Job Classes and Rate Ranges. In most job evaluation plans, it is felt undesirable to establish a salary curve in which separate dollar values are assigned to each unitary increase in point values. Instead, a number of job classes are established, increasing in point values, with all jobs in each class being paid the same salary base. It might be decided, for example, that all jobs would be grouped and paid as follows:

Point-Value Range	Salary Base	Fixed Range ($5.00)	Percentage Range (20%)
400–439	$25.20	$22.70–$27.70	$22.70–$27.70
440–479	27.25	24.75– 29.75	24.50– 30.00
480–519	30.00	27.50– 32.50	27.00– 33.00
520–559	33.00	30.50– 35.50	29.70– 36.30

As may be noted in the foregoing illustration, the brackets of one class overlap somewhat those in the ones below and above it. Indeed, the top rate for the 400 to 439 class, for example, is above that of the lowest rate for the 480 to 519 class. Such overlapping is a recognition of the fact that each class includes a number of jobs of varying point values. Moreover, it provides an opportunity for employees within a given class to obtain base-rate increases if their work and length of service merit them.

The range within each class depends, in part, upon arbitrary decision and, in part, upon the number of classes. The ranges in the case cited above were based upon a fixed rate of $5.00 and of a 20 per cent difference, respectively. The arithmetic base might have been set at more or less than $5.00, and the percentage might have been set at some figure other than 20 per cent. The range in each class is usually set somewhere between 20 per cent and 50 per cent of the minimum figure, or the percentage is divided by 2, and the range for each class is established by adding and subtracting the percentage amount from the average salary rate for each job class. On the other hand, the class range depends upon the number of classes. Thus the more classes there are in a given plan, the narrower is the bracket for each class. An example of a wage chart is shown in Figure 69.

FIGURE 69

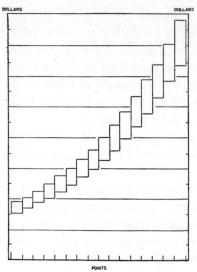

* For this chart and much of the material in this chapter, the author is indebted to Jucius, Maynard, and Shartle's *Job Analysis for Retail Stores* (Columbus, Ohio: Bureau of Business Research, Ohio State University, 1945).

After the wage brackets are established and jobs assigned to their respective classes, comparisons will ordinarily show that actual salaries in some cases exceed the maximum for their job class and others fall below the class minimum. In such instances, the usual practice is to raise, gradually, the underpaid jobs and to allow time to take care of the overpaid employees. The latter will eventually leave the payroll or be promoted to higher job classes commensurate with the salaries they are already receiving.

4. THE FACTOR COMPARISON SYSTEM. The factor comparison system is also widely used. It is similar to the point system in that jobs are evaluated by means of standard yardsticks of value. It differs from the latter by using key jobs as the basic yardsticks. Otherwise, the same steps are taken in making preliminary job descriptions and in bringing together the expert opinion of trained specialists and line executives.

The major steps in the program consist of the following:

1. Determine key jobs
2. Rank the key jobs
3. Value the factors into which key jobs are divided
4. Compare all jobs with key job ratings
5. Establish the dollar value of all jobs

The first step in this plan is to determine the key jobs. For this purpose, jobs are selected that cover the range from low- to high-paid jobs. Moreover, the jobs must be ones over which job analysts and executives do not disagree on the amount of pay. The jobs, too, must be definable in accurate and clear terms. Usually, from ten to thirty jobs are picked at this stage.

Next, the key jobs are ranked. This is first done on an over-all basis. Then the jobs are ranked, factor by factor, somewhat similarly to the point system. Here, too, salient factors must be selected, such as mental requirements, skill requirements, etc. An example of how this may be done is shown in Table 20. The five key jobs are ranked in the follow-

TABLE 20

TABLE OF KEY JOBS

Rankings and Factor Values

JOB	TOTAL BASE RATE	MENTAL REQUIREMENTS		SKILL REQUIREMENTS		PHYSICAL REQUIREMENTS		RESPONSI- BILITIES		WORKING CONDITIONS	
		Rank- ing	Rate	Rank- ing	Rate	Rank- ing	Rate	Rank- ing	Rate	Rank- ing	Rate
No. 1.....	$1.47	1	$0.37	1	$0.50	5	$0.25	2	$0.25	5	$0.10
No. 20....	1.39	3	0.25	2	0.40	3	0.33	1	0.30	4	0.11
No. 35....	1.31	2	0.31	3	0.33	4	0.30	3	0.22	2	0.15
No. 75....	1.23	4	0.24	4	0.31	2	0.40	5	0.15	3	0.13
No. 120...	1.15	5	0.16	5	0.22	1	0.43	4	0.18	1	0.16

ing order for "mental requirements": Job No. 1 is first, Job No. 35 is second, Job No. 20 is third, Job No. 75 is fourth, and Job No. 120 is fifth. On "physical requirements," however, the ranking is almost reversed.

After the key jobs are ranked factor by factor, the base pay for each job is allocated to each factor. As may be seen in Table 20, the base pay of Job No. 35, for example, is divided in the following way:

Mental requirements............................ 0.31
Skill requirements............................... 0.33
Physical requirements.......................... 0.30
Responsibility................................... 0.22
Working conditions............................. 0.15

Next, all jobs, one at a time, are compared with the table of key job values as just established. This is done by determining for each job the key job to which it is most similar, factor by factor. Assume, for example, that Job No. 27 is being checked against Table 20. Assume further that it is found to have the following characteristics:

Similar to	*For*
Job No. 1	Mental requirements
Job No. 20	Skill requirements
Job No. 35	Physical requirements
Job No. 35	Responsibilities
Job No. 20	Working conditions

The final step of dollar evaluation can now be taken. The individual jobs are then given the factor values, factor by factor, of the jobs to which they are similar. In the instance just cited, the rate would be $1.40 an hour, which is the sum of the factor values of $0.37 for mental requirements, $0.40 for skill requirements, $0.30 for physical requirements, $0.22 for responsibility, and $0.11 for working conditions.

In carrying out the comparison plan, the various steps included are much more detailed than outlined above. For example, after the key jobs are selected, ranked, and rated, it is usually found desirable to include other jobs, in order to establish a comparison table against which all jobs are to be checked. Thus, to the dozen or two jobs that constitute the master list, there are added up to 50 or 100 supplementary jobs, so that enough detail will be available to fit, without argument, all the other jobs into the table. Moreover, as the rating of jobs progresses, it may be found desirable to make some changes in the master key jobs because some are found, for one reason or another, to be out of line with other jobs. These changes obviously take more time than anticipated at the outset, but they do reduce errors in the plan.

5. INTERNAL AND EXTERNAL CONSISTENCY. This plan calls for a great deal of work because it is essential to develop consistency not only in the rankings of the key jobs but also in the allocations of the base rates of the key jobs to the various factors. This two-way check, in the eyes of the proponents of the factor comparison system, makes it superior to the point plan. They admit that their system involves more time and effort but insist that the internal consistency of rates is increased by the methods of checking and cross-checking which they employ.

The external consistency of this plan is obtained in the same fashion as in the case of the point rating plan. As noted in connection with the latter, it is necessary to compare company rates with community or industry rates for comparable jobs. Through such a comparison, a smooth progression of rates, from key job to key job, can be obtained. In the case of the comparison method, company rates are related to outside rates before the final selection of key jobs is made, whereas in the point plan the company rates are usually related to outside rates after the point values have been established.

SUMMARY

In summary, the point plan and the factor comparison plan make possible job evaluations of relatively high accuracy. The plans do not eliminate all wage controversies. It is possible to debate such issues as why Job X received 87 points and not 89, but the debates over relative and even absolute wages will eventually dwindle in number and intensity. The personnel manager who can support his discussions of wage matters with the evidence of a job evaluation plan will have serious complaints, but they will be more infrequent and less disturbing than those of the one who must rely solely upon his powers of persuasion.

Whatever plan is adopted, if a union is involved, it is desirable to work with it at every stage. If the union is informed after a plan is adopted, there is a natural objection because it wasn't "in on the development." When its co-operation is sought from the start, there may be disagreements, but the final product becomes a "baby" that will be protected as much by the union as by management.

QUESTIONS AND PROBLEMS

1. In a given job evaluation program, employees whose jobs fall within the point range of 400–419 receive anywhere from $1.40 to $1.65 an hour; those within the range from 420 to 439, receive from $1.60 to $1.90. A given employee whose job is rated 419 points has now reached the maximum in his bracket. He comes to you and argues that his job is worth at least one point more for experience or training, or even skill. Do you think you could convince him of his "error"? Explain how you would go about this problem.

2. If you had to develop a job evaluation program for a company in which employees were generally disgruntled about wages and working conditions, what plan of action would you pursue?

3. How far would you go in bringing the union into the development and operation of a job evaluation program? Be specific.

4. A given company pays all employees who come within the same point range the same rate; e.g., all those who come within the established range of 675–715 receive $1.18 an hour. What is the reason for this? What is your opinion of this plan?

5. What are some of the problems encountered in staffing the job evaluation department? How may they be solved?

6. In undertaking a program of job evaluation, what jobs should be included? Why do some companies leave out positions in the higher-paid levels?

7. When all jobs are not evaluated at the same time, what policy should be followed in developing the job evaluation program?

8. What role should supervisors and employees play in a program of job evaluation?

9. In what respects is the job classification method of job evaluation an improvement over the simple ranking plan?

10. How are yardsticks established for arriving at measurements of the job factors? Inasmuch as all companies that use the point system do not employ job yardsticks of the same length, is their accuracy doubtful? Explain.

11. Can job evaluation be called an exact process of measurement? Is there not a great deal of approximation or estimation in the construction of yardsticks and in applying them to particular jobs? In view of such estimates, why should job evaluation be deserving of use and confidence?

12. The use of yardsticks results in determining how many points are to be assigned to each job. What do these points mean? How may they be converted to monetary values?

13. What difficulties are likely to be encountered in making community wage surveys? What suggestions can you offer to reduce or circumvent the difficulties?

14. What are the relative merits of the arithmetic base and the percentage base in calculating wages for jobs with low point values? With high point values?

15. What policies seem most reasonable in dealing with the wage rates of jobs that are found to be above or below the rates indicated by the wage curve established by wage classification?

16. What are the advantages of providing a wage bracket for each wage class over that of using a single-rate plan? What effect is the single-rate plan likely to have upon individual initiative? Why is it used?

17. What is the factor comparison system of job evaluation? Why do its proponents claim it to be the most accurate of available evaluation plans? What are its disadvantages?

18. What is meant by the terms "internal consistency" and "external consistency" when used in connection with evaluation plans?

19. Interview a number of companies using evaluation programs, and find out how long it took and how much it cost to install them.

20. If a job evaluation program is used, does this eliminate the need of a wage incentive plan? Explain.

19 | Plans of Remuneration

INTRODUCTION

In addition to determining how much employees are to be paid, it is necessary to select a method for calculating wages. Two companies may have approximately the same wage and salary schedule, yet each may apply different methods by which wages are computed. Thus one company may employ the piecework plan and the other a timesaving bonus plan. Or one company may pay its salesmen on a straight commission plan, and another may use a combination plan of drawing account and commissions. The result in salaries may be approximately the same. Yet in both of these cases, the individual companies may be highly pleased with their selections and would not consider changing to the plan of the other. And each may be justified in concluding that a change would be undesirable.

A wage payment method cannot be selected wisely unless the management knows the workings, advantages and disadvantages, and conditions of best usage of available plans. It is the purpose of this chapter to describe and examine the more common types of wage and salary plans for production employees, clerical and sales employees, and executive groups. The plan that should be adopted in a specific case may then be better determined.

The discussion here is taken up under the following headings:

1. Basic kinds of plans
2. Tests of a wage plan
3. Specific wage plans
4. Remuneration of salesmen
5. Executive compensation

BASIC KINDS OF PLANS

There are two major kinds of wage and salary payment plans. In the first category are plans under which remuneration does not vary with output or quality of output. Instead, they are computed in terms of some time unit. Since it once was common to pay workers by the day, time plans of shopworkers are referred to as "daywork," even though the hour is now the standard time unit of calculation. In the case of office and executive employees, the time unit may be the week, half-month, month, or occasionally the year. Such plans are called "non-incentive" plans because the methods of calculation will not result in greater earnings irrespective of how hard employees exert themselves during given time intervals. An example of this category is illustrated by Curve *I* in Figure 70.

The second category is composed of incentive plans, or those in which remuneration depends upon output or factors related to output. The

FIGURE 70

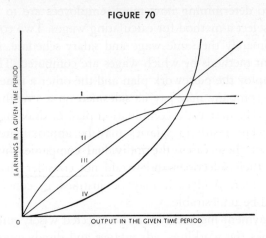

relation between remuneration and output may take any of three directions. Thus, as output during a particular time period increases, pay may be increased (*a*) at a decreasing rate, (*b*) proportionately, and (*c*) at an increasing rate. These plans are illustrated in Figure 70 by Curves *II, III,* and *IV,* respectively.

All wage plans are based upon one or a combination of the foregoing plans. Those that are derived from Curve *I* have in themselves no power to stimulate production. Plans based upon Curve *III* possess stimulating power, presumably, of equal intensity at all levels of production because earnings increase proportionately as output. However, this does not follow because more effort is required of an operator to produce, let us say, the one-thousandth unit in a day than the one-hundredth. Yet each unit increases his earnings by the same amount. Allowance for this is provided in plans based upon Curve *IV.* The earnings increase faster than output, rising very rapidly at higher levels of production when the greatest force must be applied to obtain desired results. However, on some jobs, as will be noted later, it is not desirable to stimulate output beyond a certain point; hence a plan in which stimulating power falls off rapidly would be preferable. Such plans may be based upon Curve *II* in which earnings increase as output does, but at a decreasing rate, finally tapering off to an insignificant increase.

This brief description of fundamental curves of wage progression serves to show that each type has conditions of favorable use. There is no one plan that is best under all circumstances. A plan (or plans in some cases) must be selected to do the job that has to be done. Before describing and evaluating in more detail the more common types of wage plans, it is desirable, therefore, to outline the tests by which the feasibility of particular plans may be ascertained.

TESTS OF WAGE PLANS

The apparent purpose of a wage plan is to remunerate employees for the work they perform. This is only one side of the story because it gives the impression that output is a function of wages alone. Wage plans do more than this; the nature of the plan itself may or may not appeal to workers. Hence it is important to know what characteristics of wage plans appeal to employees so that they will bestir themselves to greater efforts. The following are desirable qualities in a wage plan:

1. Easily understood
2. Easily computed
3. Earnings related to effort
4. Incentive earnings paid soon after being earned
5. Relatively stable and unvarying

1. UNDERSTANDABILITY OF WAGE PLANS. The reasons for these qualities may be quickly explained. To begin with, all employees like to know how their wage plan works. If they do not, they become fearful that they are not getting what is justly due them. This is simply a specific application of the general rule that we fear or distrust that which we do not understand. Hence it is desirable to select a simple wage plan; or, if a complicated one is chosen, all employees should be shown how it works. The plan need not be a simple one, but it must be understood. Mere acceptance of a plan by the employees does not mean that it is understood. For example, a supervisor in one company was asked to explain to a group of foremen his company's wage plan. He took about fifteen minutes in his attempt, but succeeded only in confusing everyone. Obviously, if a supervisor cannot describe the basic outlines of a plan in fifteen minutes, it is scarcely conceivable that any of the employees understand how it works.

2. EASE OF COMPUTATION. Somewhat similar to the characteristics of understanding is that of ease of computation. Most employees like to be able, first, to compute daily, from time to time, what they are making and, second, to check the accuracy of their pay envelopes. If they can do neither without help or taking too much time, they will lose confidence in the plan. The effect upon their output will be adverse. Thus a wage payment plan should be sufficiently simple to permit quick calculation, or arithmetical tables should be supplied by reference to which employees can quickly determine or check their earnings.

3. EFFECTIVE MOTIVATION. A pay plan should also provide for incentive within the work range of a particular job. To begin with, standards should be set so that they are attainable by competent workers. Obviously, if par is beyond the capacity of employees, they will not try. However, a par standard attained without trying is equally poor. Again, if quality of workmanship is significant in particular cases, a wage payment plan should not be selected that will stimulate output and affect quality adversely. Or, if it is desired to stress output, a wage plan should be selected that pays a high premium at the upper levels and penalizes—or at least does not overcompensate—low production. And, finally, if quantity and quality are to be stressed at the same time, a plan should be selected that will not unduly influence the worker to overspeed or to become careless of quality.

4. RELATION BETWEEN EFFORT AND PAYDAY. Incentive wage plans, if adopted, should provide for remuneration to employees as soon after effort is exerted as possible. In this way, the reward or penalty is fixed in the minds of the employees in connection with the work they did. Payment at the end of each day would be best from this point of view, were it not for the undue cost of distributing a daily payroll. A weekly period is customary and serves this purpose, provided that the payday is not too distant from the work to which it applies. An interval of three or four days, at most, should be sufficient to calculate and distribute the payroll.

5. STABILITY OF WAGE PLANS. Finally, a wage plan should be relatively stable and unvarying. Frequent tinkering with wage plans gives the impression that the management is seeking to defraud the employees. Hence it is imperative thoroughly to consider available plans, so that need for subsequent changes or tinkering is eliminated. But incentive plans, particularly, though stable in appearance, may be made variable or given the appearance of variability by rate cutting, changes in time standards, or changes in the value of money. As will be noted later, rate cutting has been an evil that has made the piecework plan suspect in many quarters.

TYPES OF WAGE PAYMENT PLANS

A large number of wage plans have been devised, but relatively few have been used to any significant degree. Various surveys have disclosed that daywork and piecework are used to pay about 90 per cent of all industrial workers. The other 10 per cent or so are paid under a miscellany of plans, with the Halsey Plan of timesaving, or some variant, predominating. Hence only the following plans, which include the more widely used and are representative of various types, are discussed here:

1. Daywork	6. 100% Plan
2. Measured daywork	7. Bedaux Plan
3. Piecework	8. Gantt Plan
4. Taylor Plan	9. Rowan Plan
5. Halsey Plan	10. Emerson Plan

In the formula of the wage plans the following symbols are used:

W = Wages earned
H = Hours actually worked
S = Standard time
P = Percentage
R = Rate per hour in dollars
U = Rate per unit in dollars
N = Number of units produced

1. DAYWORK. Daywork is not only the oldest but the most common way of remunerating employees. It refers to all time payment plans used in paying workers, although the hour is the time unit most commonly employed. Wages are computed under it by multiplying the number of hours worked by the rate per hour, as follows:

$$H \times R = W.$$

For an employee who works overtime and is paid extra for the overtime, either of the following formulae may be used; assuming H to be the total hours worked, H_n the nonovertime hours, and H_o the overtime hours:

$$(H \times R) + (H_o \times R) \ 50\% = W,$$
$$(H_n \times R) + (H_o \times R) \ 150\% = W.$$

If an employee had worked 52 hours in a given week and his basic rate were $1.10 an hour and he received overtime allowance over 40 hours, using the latter formula his pay would be calculated as follows:

$$(40 \times \$1.10) + (12 \times \$1.10) \ 150\% =$$
$$44.00 + 19.80 = \$63.80.$$

The daywork plan has been widely adopted for several reasons. It is simplicity itself to compute and to understand. Also, it is unnecessary to set standards as the basis for computing wages. Hence it can be used whenever it is possible to calculate the amount of time workers put in on their jobs. It is also strongly supported by many unions because the plan does not stimulate "speed-ups" or penalize the average or less-than-average worker. And under it quality is not sacrificed because it does not stimulate workers to concentrate on production alone. On the other side, the major disadvantage of daywork is its lack of motivation, which is very serious if high production is desired. It is also undesirable from the point of view of cost accounting because unit costs are more difficult to compute than under such plans as piecework.

The adoption of daywork is generally advisable under the following conditions:

1. Standards of output cannot be readily or accurately set.
2. Output is mainly made up of odd-lot jobs differing one from another.
3. Quality, material and machine costs, and workmanship are more important than quantity.
4. Output can be controlled by management or conveyors and is not subject to individual influence.
5. Employees insist upon its use.

Daywork should not be used when the reverse of the foregoing holds true. In addition, where cost calculations are significant, some other plan may be more desirable or a system of standard costs should be installed.

2. MEASURED DAYWORK. The advantages of daywork may be gained and the disadvantages minimized by the system known as "measured daywork." Under this plan, employees are paid under the daywork system, but hourly rates are revised periodically in accordance with measures of their over-all qualifications. The following steps are taken under this plan:

1. The base rate for each job is carefully established by means of job evaluation.
2. A table of values is prepared to show the percentage to be added to the base rate on each job because of varying degrees of personal performance in regard to productivity, quality, dependability, and versatility.
3. Each worker is rated periodically (practice varies the period from three to six months) on his productivity, quality, dependability, and versatility.
4. Each worker is then paid during the next work period at the base rate plus the percentage as determined by his rating and the table of values.

For example, in a given installation it has been decided to allow up to 30 per cent above base rate for superior personal performance in productivity, quality, dependability, and versatility. A table of values is established so that ratings of 70 per cent or less earn the base rate, whereas higher ratings earn an addition to the base rate for the coming period. For example, employees who rate 80 per cent are allowed an additional 10 per cent; those who rate 90 per cent are allowed 20 per cent; and those who rate 100 per cent are allowed 30 per cent.

The advantage of this plan is that wages may be easily computed, yet employees are provided with a motive for improving their performance. Moreover, earnings are not dependent upon one factor, such as output, but are affected by quality of output, dependability, and versatility. In addition, this plan provides supervisors with an opportunity to point out to employees specifically which aspects of their jobs can be improved. Management thereby assumes a job which is often shifted to the workers themselves by other plans.

The major disadvantages of this plan are twofold. First, it is not easy for employees to understand why various factors have been assigned particular weights or why the base rate and why the maximum amount that may be added to the base rate is, let us say, 30 per cent, as in the case just cited. Unless employees have confidence in the fairness of a company, these matters may be questioned. Second, the incentive value of the plan is not particularly strong from day to day because rate changes are made at relatively infrequent periods. Hence, on any given day, the employee may let down and feel no remorse because the effect on the rate for the next period is somewhat remote.

The conditions under which this plan would be most plausible include the following:

1. Over-all performance is important in measuring employee worth.
2. Specific output standards cannot be accurately set, yet some incentive for better production is desirable.
3. Gradual and stable improvement in workers is desired rather than variable day-to-day performance.
4. Supervisors are to be impressed with the need of more careful observation of employees and the need for better guidance, training, and improvement.

3. PIECEWORK.   The most widely used incentive plan is piecework. As its name denotes, wages are determined by the number of pieces or units of work that are completed. Each piece is given a prescribed value, which is known as the "piece rate." Rates are commonly set by time study, although in the past and in some companies in the present, rates have been set by using past experience on similar jobs or even mere

guesswork. The formula for wage computations under this plan is as follows:

$$N \times U = W.$$

Thus, if on a particular day an employee produced 1,080 units on a given job, the rate for which was $0.01 a unit, his earnings would be

$$1,080 \times \$0.01 = \$10.80.$$

His earnings at different rates of production would take the direction shown in Figure 71. When employees are working on small lots,

FIGURE 71

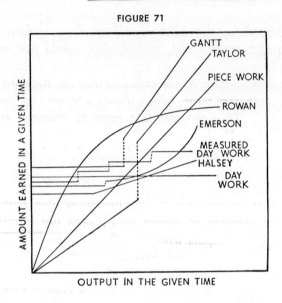

OUTPUT IN THE GIVEN TIME

making more than their hourly rate on some and less on others, it is the usual practice to add the piecework earnings together for a particular period, sometimes for a day but in no case for more than a week, to determine whether total piecework earnings exceed daywork. If they do not, it is customary to pay the day rate. Under this practice, piecework is called "guaranteed piecework." In most cases, too, output is inspected to determine how many parts have been spoiled, because these are not included in calculating the operator's earnings.

Its incentive value, simplicity in calculation, and understandability are its most commanding advantages. While there may be misunderstandings about the content of a piecework system, the form of it never gives trouble. Piecework is also favorable from a cost accounting point of view because the labor cost of each unit of output is the same, irrespective of output.

The major disadvantage of the plan derives from its misuse. Over the years, many employers either selfishly or to correct mistakes in setting rates have cut rates time and time again. To the employee who is at the receiving end of such cuts, it looks like a scheme to get more production at his expense. For example, if an employee has become accustomed to earning $8.00 a day on a job on which the rate is $0.04 a unit, he would attempt to keep to that amount if the rate were adjusted to $0.03½, then to $0.03, and maybe if it were cut to $0.02. This means that his output, which was 200 a day under the first rate, would have to be increased to 229, 267, and 400, respectively. After this happened to him or his fellow workers, a resistance movement would develop along the following lines: first, workers would loaf while being time-studied and, second, they would not earn over an amount which would encourage the management to cut rates.

Another disadvantage of piecework is that the standard for a job is expressed in monetary terms which makes it subject to changes in the value of money. Thus the standard must be changed as the dollar changes in value. During a period of increasing prosperity, for example, piece rates have to be revised upward (and downward during depressions), although the time taken to do the job still remains the same. Such changes tend to weaken the confidence of the employee in the fairness of the system. Finally, the piecework plan, with its uniform progression of earnings as output varies, does not provide sufficient incentive at higher outputs when the effort required is greater.

4. TAYLOR DIFFERENTIAL PIECEWORK PLAN. To provide additional incentive to reach higher levels of production, Frederick Taylor developed the piecework plan with two piece rates, a high and a low. Thus an employee who produced less than a prescribed rate an hour was paid at the low rate, whereas his earnings were computed at the high rate if his output equaled or surpassed the prescribed rate. This plan is illustrated graphically in Figure 71. Assuming that the low and high rates on a job were $0.02 and $0.03, respectively, and the breaking point 25 units, an operator's earnings would be:

24 × $0.02 = $0.48 if he produced below the breaking point, and
25 × $0.03 = $0.75 if he produced above the breaking point

Thus there is a strong incentive to produce at least 25 units an hour in this instance.

The major advantage of this plan is its high incentive value. The high labor cost may seem to be a disadvantage to the employer, but it is not because high production reduces the overhead costs per unit by an amount greater than the added labor costs. The disadvantage of this plan lies in the losses to the employer and to employees if the breaking point is incorrectly set. Care must be taken in setting it high enough so that it represents a real challenge to workers, yet not so high that it can be attained only infrequently, or so low that it can be reached without exertion. Since most employers have not been willing to spend the necessary time and money in setting rates with such precision, its adoption has been infrequent. Yet under appropriate conditions, it has attractive features.

5. HALSEY PLAN. One of the oldest wage incentive plans is the Halsey Premium Plan under which employees are paid a bonus based upon a percentage of the time saved under the standard time set for the jobs on which they work. Under this plan the following formula is used:

$$(H \times R) + [(S - H) R] P = W.$$

Thus, if a worker whose rate was $0.90 an hour took 8 hours on a job on which the standard time was 12 hours, and the percentage was 66⅔ per cent, his earnings would be:

$$(8 \times \$0.90) + [(12 - 8) \$0.90] \ 66\tfrac{2}{3}\% = \$9.60.$$

When the plan was first developed, time standards were loosely set. Hence the percentage of time saved which went to the employees was rather low, usually 33⅓ per cent. As standards have been set with greater accuracy, the percentage allotted to the workers has steadily gone up, so that in some installments of this plan employees are receiving as much as 100 per cent of time saved. The increase in the percentage does not necessarily mean that workers earn more than before. The effect of the increased percentage may be offset by the decreased time allowed in the time standard. For example, in the following, the earnings are the same, although the time standards and percentage allowed vary:

$$(8 \times \$1.20) + [(16 - 8) \$1.20] \quad 33\tfrac{1}{3}\% = \$12.80,$$
$$(8 \times \$1.20) + [(13\tfrac{1}{3} - 8) \$1.20] \ 50\% \quad = \$12.80,$$
$$(8 \times \$1.20) + [(12 - 8) \$1.20] \quad 66\tfrac{2}{3}\% = \$12.80.$$

The Halsey Plan has two major advantages. First, since the standard upon which earnings are based is expressed in time units, it is not subject to the random fluctuations of the dollar. If adjustments must be made in earnings, the hourly rate can be changed, leaving the time standard unaffected. Thus the employees are not inclined to lose faith in job standards. Second, since the bonus is based upon time saved, the attitude of employees is conditioned by the positive factor of gaining through saving. This has a better psychological effect than that produced by the pressure of piece rates, for example.

6. THE 100 PER CENT TIME-SAVING PLAN. These advantages have been recognized by the users of the 100 Per Cent Time-Saving Plan and the Bedaux Plan, which are variations of the Halsey Plan. The 100 Per Cent Plan gives the same results as piecework; yet the emphasis of the former leaves a better impression with the worker. As shown in the following example, piecework and the 100 Per Cent Plan yield the same "take-home" results. If a piece rate of $0.03 a unit is established on a given job, to a worker whose base rate is $0.90 an hour that is the same as saying the time allowed to do each piece is 2 minutes. If he produced 270, 300, and 360 during 8 hours each on 3 successive days, his earnings under piecework would be:

$$270 \times \$0.03 = \$\ 8.10,$$
$$300 \times \$0.03 = \$\ 9.00,$$
$$360 \times \$0.03 = \$10.80.$$

If his earnings had been computed under the 100 Per Cent Plan, the pay would have been the same. In that event, the jobs on which he worked would have been allowed the following times:

First day, 270 units × 2 min. = 540 min. or 9 hr.,
Second day, 300 units × 2 min. = 600 min. or 10 hr.,
Third day, 360 units × 2 min. = 720 min. or 12 hr.

The remuneration in each case would have been calculated as follows:

$$(8 \times \$0.90) + [(\ 9 - 8)\ \$0.90]\ 100\% = \$\ 8.10,$$
$$(8 \times \$0.90) + [(10 - 8)\ \$0.90]\ 100\% = \$\ 9.00,$$
$$(8 \times \$0.90) + [(12 - 8)\ \$0.90]\ 100\% = \$10.80.$$

7. THE BEDAUX PLAN. The Bedaux Plan is a copyrighted plan which may be used only upon authorized permission. It follows the Halsey Plan in being a timesaving plan. In the Bedaux Plan, time standards, instead of being expressed in hours, are expressed in minutes, which are known as "B's." Moreover, the percentage of the saving allowed to workers is usually 75 per cent, with the other 25 per cent usually going to supervisors and helpers instead of being retained by management. This sharing with assisting workers is intended to spur their co-operation in making direct workers more effective. If the

worker cited in the previous paragraph had been given 75 per cent of time saved as a bonus, his earnings, on the third day for instance, under the Halsey Plan and under the Bedaux Plan, respectively, would have been as follows:

$$(8 \times \$0.90) + [(12 - 8) \$0.90] \ 75\% = \$9.90,$$
$$(480 \times \$0.015) + [(720 - 480) \$0.015] \ 75\% = \$9.90.$$

The Halsey Plan and timesaving plans derived from it are more complicated than piecework, and hence are not used as frequently. Moreover, the varying cost per unit makes it less desirable from a cost accounting point of view. However, were the 100 per cent feature adopted with standards set accurately, this type of plan would have a better appeal than piecework, despite the simplicity of the latter.

8. THE GANTT PLAN.   The Gantt Plan is another one of those designed around the turn of the century by a member of the group that became disciples of Taylor and extenders of his school of scientific management. This plan, like Taylor's differential piecework plan, was based upon careful study to set time standards. It departed from Taylor's plan in that it is a timesaving bonus plan. But, unlike the Halsey Plan, it pays a very high bonus for attaining or surpassing the time standard. The formula for this plan is divided into two parts, as follows:

1. For those who do not equal standard time, wages are paid at the hourly rate for the time expended, thus—

$$H \times R = W.$$

2. For those who exceed the standard, the wages for the time expended are computed as follows:

$$(S \times R) \ 120\% = W.$$

Thus, on a job for which the standard was set at 10 hours of two workers whose hourly rate was $0.90, one who took 10 hours and 1 minute would be paid $9.02, and one who took 10 hours would be paid $10.80, computed as follows:

First worker: $(10 + 1/60) \times \$0.90 = \$9.015,$
Second worker: $(10 \times \$0.90) \ 120\% = \$10.80.$

Obviously, the pressure to equal the standard is great because the difference in wages is striking. And the pressure to exceed standard continues because the time saved can also be applied to other jobs, thus increasing the pay even more.

The advantage of the Gantt Plan lies in the strength of its motivation. Establishing fair standards for it is not easy, nor is it easy to compute or understand. Its use, therefore, should be restricted to the following conditions: first, when overhead costs are high and workers must be stimulated to achieve high production in order to lower unit overhead costs; second, when standards can be set accurately; and, third, when workers can be taught to have confidence in the fairness of the standards.

9. THE ROWAN PLAN. One of the oldest wage incentive plans is that devised by Rowan during days when standards were not set accurately and consequently there was high probability of employees "running away" with the rate—that is, earning wages that are excessively high. Under it, wages increase, but at a decreasing rate as output increases, as shown in Figure 71. Hence, an employee, no matter how hard he worked, could not make more than twice his hourly rate. The formula for this plan is as follows:

$$(H \times R) + \left(\frac{S - H}{S}\right) HR = W.$$

Thus an employee whose hourly rate is $0.90 and who did a job in 8 hours that was supposed to take 12 hours would be paid $9.60, computed as follows:

$$(8 \times \$0.90) + \left(\frac{12 - 8}{12}\right) 8 \times \$0.90 = \$9.60.$$

The curve which earnings take as output increases is its major advantage. Since it is fruitless to overexert oneself, of course there should be no need to cut rates because employees will not "run away" with the rates. In addition, this makes the plan useful when it is desirable to stimulate production to some extent but not to the point that quality is endangered. And since the highest increases in wages are obtainable at lower rates of production, its use is advisable in the case of learners who need encouragement within the narrow limits of their capacity. The major and critical disadvantage that has limited its use to a very few cases is the obvious complication involved in calculating it and understanding the theory of its operation.

10. THE EMERSON PLAN. A plan which illustrates another type of wage computation is the Emerson Efficiency Plan. Under it, the relative efficiency of employees is computed each week and a bonus paid of varying degree, depending upon the efficiency attained. Thus the plan calls,

first of all, for establishing a table of values for increasing degrees of efficiency. Selected values taken from one plant in which bonuses start at 66 per cent efficiency follow:

Efficiency	Per Cent Added to Basic Earnings
66	1
70	4
75	5
80	8
85	11
90	15
95	20
100	25

For each job, a standard time allowance is established, by time study or reference to records of similar jobs completed in the past. At the end of each week, each worker's efficiency is derived by dividing the time allowed on various jobs by the time taken. To his base wage is then added a percentage for his relative efficiency. For example, a worker who took 40 hours to complete jobs on which the allowance was 36 hours would be paid $41.40, computed as follows:

$$(H \times R) + (H \times R) \text{ selected } \% = W,$$
$$(40 \times \$0.90) + (40 \times \$0.90) \, 15\% = \$41.40.$$

The major advantage of this plan lies in its emphasis upon efficiency. Comparisons can readily be made from week to week or between employees; thus personal efficiency tends to rise because of the competitive factor. The plan has two disadvantages: first, the plan is expressed in terms which are not readily understandable, and, second, employees tend to complain about the standards that they must surpass in order to earn a bonus.

The plan has the most favorable conditions of use when it is desired to educate workers in the need of efficiency and to bestir them to compete in raising their relative efficiency.

GROUP PLANS

The foregoing plans have been discussed on the assumption that each individual is remunerated in terms of his own efforts. In addition to such individual or "straight" calculations, plans may be placed upon a group basis. Earnings of individuals are thus computed by prorating the bonus or premium produced by the group. For example, the following table shows how the individuals in a group would share a bonus of $32.50 which they had earned as a unit:

Employee	Hours Worked	Rate per Hour	Basic Wage	Pro Rata Share	Bonus	Total Wage
A................	40	$0.90	$36.00	$ 36.00/ 133.32	$8.78	$44.78
B................	36	1.00	36.00	36.00/ 133.32	8.78	44.78
C................	38	0.94	35.72	35.72/ 133.32	8.69	44.41
D................	32	0.80	25.60	25.60/ 133.32	6.25	31.85
			$133.32			

In summary, there are numerous plans from which it is possible to select one or more that will fit one's requirements. Significant, in any event, is the importance of calculating basic standards fairly and equitably. But perhaps most important of all is the need for determining how much remuneration should be provided to attain varying degrees of employee efficiency. To this aspect of wage plans, there is no simple answer except the advice that intense study is indispensable.

Whether or not incentive plans should be used is not examined here, for the simple reason that, unless unions or conditions prevent, incentive plans are ordinarily superior to nonincentive plans, not only for the employee but also the employer. It is scarcely conceivable, for example, how the record of production displayed in Figure 72 (p. 384) could have been attained, had not the company in question used an incentive plan. Of course, they are not easy to install in intermittent and nonstandardized types of work, but even here successful plans may be found. Maintenance jobs, for example, once thought of as daywork jobs, are increasingly being paid on some plan of incentive. The key in all of these instances is careful determination of standards of production and careful establishment of a unit of output.

REMUNERATION OF SALESMEN

Remuneration of salesman may be by straight salary or some form of incentive compensation. Since the salesman's job is usually more variable than the average factory job, the problem of establishing a stable and satisfactory unit of output is much more difficult; some even conclude that it is impossible. Nevertheless, various incentive plans have been devised that have had varying degrees of success. Although details vary, all plans can be grouped under one or more of the following headings:

1. Straight salary
2. A commission based upon units sold
3. A commission based upon factors affecting sales other than units sold

1. STRAIGHT SALARY PLANS.   Straight salary plans include those in which salesmen are paid strictly in accordance with the time they spend on their jobs. The week is the common time unit. This plan finds favor with those who contend, first, that the salesman in the particular case has little or no control over how much he sells and, second, that the

FIGURE 72.   Total Annual Compensation per Employee, Lincoln Electric Company and Six Selected Major Corporations,* 1934–50, and Sales Value per Employee, Lincoln Electric Company and Electrical Manufacturing Industry, 1934–49†

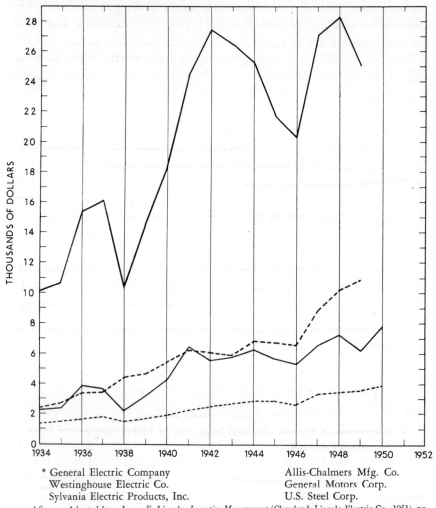

    * General Electric Company   Allis-Chalmers Mfg. Co.
      Westinghouse Electric Co.   General Motors Corp.
      Sylvania Electric Products, Inc.   U.S. Steel Corp.
      † Source: Adapted from James F. Lincoln, *Incentive Management* (Cleveland: Lincoln Electric Co., 1951), pp. 258–63.

number of factors which are important in affecting sales is so large that it is impossible to give due consideration to all of them in any incentive plan. Some also favor straight salary because they have seen commission plans misused to the point that no one retains confidence in them. Where the foregoing conditions prevail, the use of commission plans is obviously questionable.

2. UNIT COMMISSION PLANS. Straight salary plans, in and of themselves, contain no incentive value. Hence, when the amount of sales depends largely upon the calls that are made and supervision itself cannot spur salesmen to take the necessary initiative, commission plans are desirable. Under these plans, salesmen are paid a set commission for each unit sold, a commission that varies as output increases, or a commission that begins only after a set quota has been sold. The bases for commissions are so numerous that space does not permit full descriptions. However, two opposing theories are worth citing. In some companies the rate of commission decreases as sales increase; and in others, the rate increases. In the former case, the belief is that salesmen who make too much will lose their zest for work. In the latter case, it is recognized that large volumes are harder to make, yet add greatly to the profit of the company. Hence it is concluded that increasing commissions are needed to attain the high volumes. Which theory should be followed depends, among other things, upon the nature of the sales problem, the type of salesmen required, and the type of sales executives directing the sales. But in any event, the existence of such opposed theories illustrates the need for care in selecting an appropriate plan.

3. GENERAL COMMISSION PLANS. Because selling often involves much more than repeated calls to get more business, some incentive plans are based upon other factors as well as volume of sales. For example, bonuses may be computed in terms of such factors as the following:

1. The quantity of various products sold, graded by their profitability to the company
2. New business obtained
3. Service calls made
4. Repeat orders obtained
5. Sales expenses reduced
6. Cash business obtained relative to credit accounts
7. Percentage of bonuses obtained from new or highly competitive areas
8. Complaints received on old customers' list

Such plans call for important decisions regarding the weights that the various factors will have and how they are to be measured. This is very difficult; yet if the factors are of importance and the salesmen's attention should be called to them, the work necessary to the development of standards will have to be taken.

4. CHARACTERISTICS OF A GOOD COMPENSATION PLAN. Of interest in this connection are the findings of the Dartnell Corporation, which surveyed 1,800 plans. It was concluded that successful compensation plans allowed for the following payments to salesmen:

1. Security money, in the form of a basic salary or drawing account against commissions
2. Incentive money, over and above base pay, earned by putting forth extra effort
3. Opportunity money, earned through promotion to more profitable territories or branch managerships
4. Loyalty money, which allows in the base salary for length of service or special contributions to the welfare of the business
5. Practice money, to encourage testing of new sales ideas which might otherwise adversely affect regular income sources.[1]

EXECUTIVE COMPENSATION PLANS

The compensation of executives, although paid to a relatively small number of employees, nevertheless affects many, many more. For example, all employees are more or less interested in what the "boss" gets. If the earnings are out of line with their standards, however arrived at, they become disgruntled, and then the undesirable results of industrial unrest become apparent. In addition, if executive salaries are exorbitant, they may cut into the share that employees receive. This is usually a negligible amount, however. One company illustrates the relation of executive salaries to employee wages by stating that, were all salaries of top executives distributed to employees, the latter would gain the equivalent of a package of cigarettes a week.

And executive compensation is, of course, of interest to the executives themselves, who, like the employees, are desirous of receiving as much as possible for their services. The question is raised, then, and as yet is unanswered, as to how much should be paid to executives in order to obtain their services. It is easy to say that they should be paid what they are worth, but some violent controversies have raged as to whether or not any executive is worth a million dollars a year, as some have been paid. One side argues that, without the leadership of the executive who received such a salary, the company would not have been so successful as it was, nor could it have employed as many workers at the wages that it did. The other side retorts that the same results could have been at-

---

[1] "Trends in Salesmens' Compensation," *Management Review,* November, 1953, pp. 663–64.

tained without such munificent compensation to the executive in question, since a lesser amount and the prestige of the position would have been sufficient compensation. Executive talents are not so scarce, add the opponents, that a few isolated individuals possess a monopoly.

All of this leads to the conclusion that great care must be used to set compensations for executives, since such decisions affect the attitudes of others in addition to the efficiency of the executives. It is desirable to describe executive compensation methods so that the relative merits of available plans may be noted. This is done here under two headings: first, major executives and, second, minor executives.

1. MAJOR EXECUTIVES. Straight salary, bonuses, and stock purchase plans are used to compensate major executives. Straight salary is undoubtedly the most common method. It is often adopted because the task of managing is made up of many variables and imponderables, the direct measurement of which would be a Herculean task. Hence, as is true of any job whose units of work cannot be readily defined or measured, the only alternative is the daywork or time interval principle. With top-level executives, the month or the year is commonly used.

However, many companies hold the opinion that the full measure of executive effort cannot be obtained unless some stimulant is applied. In such cases, indirect measures of accomplishment are used to determine how much effort executives have exerted beyond that which is normal for the job and which is compensated for on a salary basis. The most common measures are profits, sales, and expenses. Using these as a base, bonuses are paid in addition to the salary. Thus one company pays its top executive a percentage of the profits the company earns. Another establishes a quota of profits which must be earned before executives share in profits. And a third establishes a sliding scale of percentages related to sales (a fourth ties this to expenditures) by which the base salary will be increased.

Another plan of compensating executives is that in which stock is offered to them at a nominal figure or at a figure that leaves ample room for speculative profit. The executives are thus given a stake in the business, which can redound to their benefit if their efforts are skillfully applied to its operation. Usually, these plans make handsome rewards possible. For example, an executive who took charge of an ailing business was given the option to buy 100,000 shares at $12 a share. Within a year the stock rose in value to $16, yielding the executive a paper profit of $400,000. Had the stock not risen in price, however, his efforts would have been rewarded only by a small salary. Hence the probability of small earnings as well as of high profits makes such plans highly stimulating. Indeed, the plan is criticized by some on the grounds that executives become so conscious of the market price of the stock and the short-run factors that affect prices that they do not pay attention to the fundamentals that make for long-run stable growth of a business.

The theory in these cases is that profits are correlated to executive efforts and thus an accurate measure of executive contributions.[2] The theory is weak because profits are sometimes made no matter how unwisely executives act and losses are incurred despite the best possible judgment. Prosperity periods and depressions leave in their wakes results for which no individual should take credit or be penalized. This condition should be recognized in any plan in which executive compensation is based upon results, else executives will from time to time be overpaid and underpaid. That the theory is weak is not offered as a reason for not using incentives for executives. It is mentioned so that a plan is not idly adopted, thus inviting the chance of yielding undesirable consequences to all concerned.

All the foregoing methods of compensating executives result in taxable income. Since tax rates take a large part of such increases, there is a trend for the company to pay for a variety of expenses incurred by executives. The range of such payments or "fringe benefits" to executives includes the following:

1. Medical care
2. Counsel and accountants to assist in legal, tax, and financial problems
3. Facilities for entertaining customers and for dining
4. Company recreational areas—golf course, swimming pool, and gymnasium
5. Membership fees in clubs and business associations
6. Costs of education and development of executives; scholarships for children of employees; and business magazines and books.[3]

Such benefits are tax-free to the recipient. Were he to pay for them himself out of salary, his income would have to be increased a minimum of 30 per cent for lower-income executives and much higher for executives in the upper tax brackets. Obviously, this is a form of executive compensation that merits favorable consideration.

2. MINOR EXECUTIVES. Most minor executives are paid on a salary basis, although incentive plans of one form or another are used in a minority of cases. The proponents of the salary plan expound the usual

---

[2] The favorable incidence of capital gains tax as opposed to the higher personal income tax is also important.

[3] *Business Week,* June 20, 1953, pp. 183–84.

claims for it and make the usual charges against incentive plans, which need not be repeated here. The discussion will be limited to a description of typical plans for incentive compensation of minor executives.

Perhaps the oldest form of compensating supervisors and foremen upon a basis other than straight salary is that of paying them a bonus, depending upon the incentive earnings of their subordinates. For example, under the Gantt Plan (one of the early plans), provision was originally made for paying supervisors a bonus which increased as the number of subordinates who earned a bonus increased. And under some adoptions of the Halsey Plan, the supervisor shared in part of the time saved by his subordinates. Thus the employee received 66⅔ per cent of the time saved, and the supervisor, an indirect worker in the department, received the remaining 33⅓ per cent. In some installations of the Bedaux Plan, the supervisor receives 25 per cent of the B's saved. Such practices are commendable because they stress the fundamental responsibility of the supervisor—to help make the efforts of his workers more effective and economical.

Another type of incentive plan is based directly upon departmental productivity or cost reductions. Under such plans, it is necessary to take the following steps:

1. Define in quantitative terms the factors to be included in the plan
2. Establish standards by which to measure varying degrees of success
3. Establish a sliding scale of bonus percentages for increasing degrees of accomplishing the factors specified in the plan

For example, in simple outline, the plan of one company is based upon attainment of production schedules. This plan requires careful review of production standards, machine methods, and sales requirements, so that extraneous factors will not affect the supervisors unfairly or too leniently. Then the schedule for each job during a particular period is set. Actual completion dates are then compared with scheduled dates, to arrive at a percentage of success. Supervisors receive a bonus depending upon their effectiveness in meeting schedules. This company stresses meeting of schedules because delivery to customers is a prim factor in its success.

In another plan, reduction in expenditures is the key to supervisory bonuses. A flexible budget is established for each department, depending upon its expected rates of output. If actual expenses of a department are less than budgeted figures, the supervision receives a bonus varying with the percentage of saving. The emphasis upon cost reduction makes this plan appealing to the company.

Other plans of supervisory bonus payments are more complicated. For example, one company weighs the following factors in:

1. Attainment of budgets
2. Scrap reductions
3. Direct laborsaving
4. Efficiency in output
5. Savings in materials used
6. Savings in maintenance costs

Under this plan, standards are established for each of the foregoing factors, their relative importance is determined, and a scale of values for over-all achievement is established. The value of all this work, it must be noted, goes beyond the effect upon supervisory efficiency; it has the added value which careful planning brings forth. Although such plans may require a great deal of preliminary thought, the calculations a supervisor must make to compute his earnings can be simplified by preparing statistical tables from which foremen can, at a glance, determine the bonus they have earned.

RECORDS

A significant problem in all wage plans is the effect they have upon record keeping. It has been noted from time to time that some plans aid the work of cost accounting, for example, whereas others are not so simple to handle. The same holds true for payroll computations. Hence plans should be weighed in terms of the effect they are likely to have upon the work of payroll computations. Of course, the whole problem of payroll calculation has been complicated by the extra records required by the Social Security Act, the Wages and Hours Law, and various deductions, such as "pay-as-you-go" federal income taxes and bond purchase plans. As a consequence, it is desirable to design forms that will make this work as speedy and economical as possible. Illustrative of practices that employ mechanical devices is the growing use of tabulating card equipment.

QUESTIONS AND PROBLEMS

1. Differentiate between a wage plan, a wage incentive plan, and a job evaluation plan.
2. Although the proposition that each operator should be permitted to earn as much as his capacities and abilities permit seems palpably apparent, much opposition may be found to wage incentive plans. Why?
3. When a company uses a wage incentive plan, is there any need for nonfinancial incentives? Explain.
4. What is the theory of wage plans in which wages increase at a ratio faster than output?

5. Prepare a table of comparison of wage plans by listing wage plans in the left-hand column and by listing the desirable characteristics at the top of successive columns. Then for each plan, opposite the characteristics, write in the words "yes" or "no" to indicate whether or not the plan possesses the characteristic. What plan or plans are the best?

6. Why is it desirable to compensate employees soon after they have earned a bonus?

7. If a complicated wage plan is in use, why do employees not have confidence that the company is nevertheless being fair?

8. During times when the purchasing power of the dollar is varying, how is it possible to build stability in a wage payment plan?

9. In the case of operations in which the output of employees is largely controlled by machines or conveyors, what system of wage incentive, if any, would be desirable?

10. With the advantages of the piecework plan so numerous, why is it viewed so often in such a poor light?

11. If an increased percentage were used in calculating the portion of time saved for which an employee is to be paid, would it necessarily mean that the employee would earn more? Explain.

12. In what respects is the Bedaux Plan similar to the Halsey Plan?

13. Since the 100 Per Cent Time-Saving Plan and the piecework plan give the same results to the employees, how would you determine which one to use in a given case?

14. Assume that in a company operating in interstate commerce, a group of five employees earned a bonus of $74.40 during a given week. How much would each receive as his share, assuming the following facts?

Employee	Hours Worked	Rate per Hour
Smith	33	$1.20
Jones	48	0.90
Brown	42	0.95
Roe	40	1.03
White	44	0.96

15. What is the essential factor that serves to explain why incentive plans are more difficult to establish in the case of such employees as salesmen and maintenance workers than production employees?

16. For what factors, other than sales output, may a salesman be compensated?

17. Are executive earnings of interest solely to the executives themselves? Are employees fair in being inquisitive about such matters?

18. How would you determine what a fair salary is for the president of a company? Indicate the factors to which you would give consideration.

19. If profit-sharing plans and stock purchase plans find favorable usage among executives, why are they not equally good for operative employees?

20. What voice should employees have in regard to the establishment of wage payment plans?

Related Wage

Problems

INTRODUCTION

A number of matters related to remuneration have thus far been ignored which may now be given attention. These may be illustrated in
terms of the following questions, to which some answers are now
sought in this chapter:

1. How is time related to wage and salary determination?
2. What are the possibilities of guaranteeing wages?
3. What contribution can sharing of revenues with employees contribute to
   the wage problem?

TIME PROBLEMS

VARIABLES

How long should an employee work? This simple question involves
numerous problems that are not easy to solve. For example, within the
memory of many who are still working, the average workweek has decreased from around seventy hours to forty hours. Some contend that a
decrease to thirty-five, or even thirty hours, is justifiable. And the working day has decreased from one of dawn to dusk to an average of eight
hours, with some companies on a six-hour day. Then, too, such practices as the five-day week, vacations with pay, rest periods during the
working day, and reduced hours for female and child labor are relatively
recent innovations that have not necessarily been standardized beyond
change.

As already suggested, the question of the work period resolves itself
into a series of questions depending upon the particular time periods
under consideration. The day, the week, and the year are major time
periods, and each in turn raises problems. In the day interval, decisions
must be reached regarding total hours to be worked, starting and stopping time, lunch hours, rest periods, and over-all time calculations.
Within the week interval, there are matters of working days, shift

changes, and paydays to be considered. And during the year, weeks to be worked, vacation periods, and holidays must be determined.

How these matters should be resolved can easily be stated in principle. The length of working periods should be such that the maximum productivity is derived, at the least cost, with due regard to the health and welfare of the employees. Its application is something else again. As will be seen as particular time intervals are described, various interested groups are sometimes in violent disagreement among themselves as well as with each other about the standards that should be adopted. Management, unions, employees, governmental agencies, and other groups have disputed and continue to dispute these matters vehemently from time to time. And it may be well to point out at the outset that no final solution is likely because the problems are affected, on the one hand, by social and political as well as economic conditions and, on the other, by the conflicting views which various groups bring to bear upon their solutions.

DAILY TIME PROBLEMS

At the present time, the eight-hour day is rather general throughout the United States. A number of companies exceed this figure, but only a small percentage work fewer hours. Ordinarily, when a day of less than eight hours is worked, it is usually due to the fact that no time out is taken for lunch—the employees eat while working. Thus a seven-and-one-half-hour day is found occasionally. A few companies have tried a six-hour day, usually in cases in which around-the-clock operations are desirable or necessary. This practice makes it possible for four shifts to be employed, each shift working six hours without a break for lunch. As the productivity of industry increases, there is no reason why the length of the working day may not be decreased to or below six hours, just as in the past it has been decreased from the fourteen-hour day once worked.

1. STARTING AND STOPPING TIME. Although the length of the working day for particular classes of workers is usually the same in particular communities, considerable variation is found in other aspects of daily hours. For example, starting time in some companies is as early as 6:30 A.M. and in others as late as 9:30 A.M. Stopping times differ in like manner. These variations may be explained as follows:

1. Some trades, such as service industries, must start earlier to be ready to meet the needs of other industries.
2. Employee preference; in one company that asked its employees to note their wishes, a starting time of 7:00 A.M. was selected.

3. Staggered starting times are encouraged to permit transportation and restaurant services to handle loads without burdensome peaks.

4. Tradition or growth without plan.

Even within the same company starting and stopping times may differ for shop and office workers and sometimes between divisions of shop workers. This is done to prevent overlapping of various facilities and services or as a form of perquisite of office workers. Of course, maintenance workers usually have to arrive early to get the plant ready for operation.

2. LUNCH PERIODS. Lunch periods constitute another problem of daily working hours. Practice here is varied. As in the preceding instance, office workers often have a longer lunch period than shop workers. In their case, periods up to one and one-quarter hours are occasionally found, while an hour is the maximum for shop workers. Usually office workers are given forty-five or sixty minutes and shop workers thirty to forty-five minutes. In some plants lunch hours are staggered so that restaurant facilities need not be too large. While employees seem to prefer a shorter lunch period because their over-all working day is decreased, there is danger that sufficient time may not be available for getting back to work on time. Employees will then tend to "jump the gun" in starting their lunch period. In the event that this happens, supervision must be more alert, or the lunch period must be lengthened. A short lunch period may also result in the harmful practice of eating too hurriedly.

3. REST PERIODS. Whether or not rest periods should be provided constitutes another problem of daily working hours. Almost without exception, this practice has been found to have favorable effects— fatigue, loitering, visiting, accidents, and spoilage are reduced, and productive efficiency is increased. Breaks of eight to twelve minutes in the morning and again in the afternoon are found to be effective. Except where the nature of operations prevents, the only obstacle to the universal adoption of this practice is the reluctance of employers to try it. They do not like to break with traditional practice, or they fear that employees will demand a shorter day instead of the rest periods.

4. OVER-ALL WORKING DAY. And, finally, what constitutes the over-all working period must be defined for pay purposes. Ordinarily, the stated hours of starting and stopping constitute the limits of the working day. This must be understood by the employees, particularly where time clocks are used and employees must stamp their time cards on the clocks. In such instances, the cards will be punched before the starting time and after the stated stopping time by employees who are

on time and do not quit early. The times as thus recorded are not used to calculate hours worked but to check an employee's on-time arrival and departure. For example, in the following case, the employee would be paid for eight hours of work and not for eight hours and twenty-one minutes:

	STATED TIME		TIME CARD PUNCHED	
	Starting	Stopping	In	Out
Morning...........	8:00	12:00	7:52	12:01
Afternoon.........	12:45	4:45	12:40	4:47

WEEKLY TIME PROBLEMS

1. TOTAL HOURS A WEEK. The weekly time interval also raises a number of problems. First, there is the question of the total hours to be worked. During normal times the workweek in most companies is about forty hours. Of course, during peak periods the workweek is extended. For example, War Manpower Commission directives required a forty-eight-hour workweek in many areas during World War II, although many companies exceeded this standard. Indeed, in one company, at their own request, employees worked from seventy to eighty hours weekly. But before the war and after, the forty-hour week has been growing in favor. By following it, a five-day week, also growing in favor, can be adopted, and no overtime need be paid.

During normal times, the overtime pay provisions of the Wages and Hours Law militate against a workweek of over forty hours. Obviously, a 50 per cent increase in labor costs will not be assumed unless offsetting reductions or customer demands warrant. During the war, on the other hand, it was a question of how long the workweek should be extended. The experience of the British seemed to indicate that a week of fifty-six to sixty hours was satisfactory, but that beyond this various losses outweighed the gains. However, in this country, a forty-eight-hour workweek seemed to be best. Very likely, it will always be hard to determine what a workweek should be because of the effect of what employees become accustomed to.

2. WORKING DAYS A WEEK. The number of days to be worked is also of importance in the weekly picture. The five-day week is gaining in popularity in the United States. Certainly, the evidence during World War II indicated that employees disliked the six-day week more than they did longer hours. Even the five-and-one-half-day week is disliked by those who once have the opportunity to try the five-day week. From the employer's point of view, the effectiveness of employees on

the half day is not always worth the cost. When the employer can be persuaded, therefore, that no significant loss of business will be incurred, he will close on Saturday.

3. SHIFT ARRANGEMENTS. Of course, when the nature of operations or rush of business demands, the workweek may have to be extended and extra shifts of workers employed. The matter of shifts has debatable alternatives. Beyond mentioning the alternatives, space here does not permit a statement of the advantages and disadvantages of each. The matter of shifts may be handled in the following ways:

1. Each group of employees is set permanently in a given shift position.
2. Each group rotates shift positions, at weekly, monthly, or other periods.

YEARLY TIME PROBLEMS

In the yearly interval, the major problems revolve about holidays and vacation periods. There is a discernible trend toward paying shop, as well as office, workers for holidays. Hence, what holidays will be recognized should be specifically stated. Even when pay for holidays is not granted, holidays may be important because many companies pay time and one-half or even double time to those who have to work on these days. To avoid possible arguments about premium days, therefore, these days should be established in advance. Since absenteeism after holidays by those who worked on and received double time for holidays is excessive, one company reduced this by providing that pay would be calculated at straight rather than double rates for holidays in the event of unexcused absences following them.

Vacation periods are also of growing importance since more and more companies are granting vacations with pay (because of collective bargaining in many instances) to shop as well as office workers. Two problems must be decided here: first, the length of vacations, and second, the time of taking vacations. Office workers generally get two and in a few instances three weeks, and shop workers get one or two (very rarely three) weeks, depending upon seniority. All vacations may be taken at the same time, which has the advantage of avoiding conflicts about vacation selection and the need of replacing key employees. Or they may be staggered, so that business can be conducted as usual right through the year. Which plan should be used may be determined by checking in a particular case the advantages and disadvantages in the list provided in Figure 73.

PORTAL-TO-PORTAL ISSUES

Reaching one's assigned station and departing from it have consumed enough time that the matter became a serious problem, leading to the passage of the Portal-to-Portal Act of 1947, the provisions of which have been incorporated in the revisions made in 1949 in the Wages and Hours Law. The events leading to the passage of this act are worth reciting before the important aspects of the Act are noted.

FIGURE 73. Comparing Vacations Plans*

MASS VACATIONS | **STAGGERED VACATIONS**

ADVANTAGES

☐ **Using the slack season** to close the plant for paid vacation period can help avoid the unpleasantness of seasonal layoffs. Especially useful for highly seasonal industries.

☐ **Capacity operation** is easier for 50 weeks of the year. Efficiency isn't cut by vacation absences.

☐ **Extensive repairs,** equipment installation, and inventory taking can be done during the vacation without slowing output or causing lay-offs.

☐ **It's easier to schedule work.** There's no more need to keep making allowance for employees away on vacation. So every department's output is easier to predict.

☐ **All workers are treated the same.** This simplifies the foreman's job of scheduling vacations, and the accounting department's job of issuing vacation pay. It also stops complaints that "Bill got his vacation in July, why must I take mine in May?"

☐ **Continuous deliveries** to regular customers, and all normal services, are possible the year around. Interruption might play into competitors' hands.

☐ **New orders can be accepted** at all times and completed on schedule. A maker of cardboard boxes could take a rush order any time, give it priority (or overtime) and complete it even with 20% of his force on vacation.

☐ **Rapid processing of perishable goods** on hand is assured. Continuous manufacturing would prevent spoilage of goods.

☐ **Employees have a wider choice** of vacation time. Those who want to take their time off during the hunting or fishing season—or in the winter —can be accommodated.

☐ **Good community relations** are preserved. The load on recreational and travel facilities is spread more evenly.

DISADVANTAGES

☐ **The expense of closing** the plant down and of reopening it two weeks later may be high.

☐ **Some maintenance operations and routine services** must be kept going even while the plant is closed. Don't forget their cost.

☐ **You might miss some business.** And some customers may be inconvenienced.

☐ **New employees not eligible** for vacations will lose income during the shutdown—unless you can find work for them in the plant.

☐ **Some employees may be eligible** for longer vacations than the shutdown period.

☐ **Vacation facilities may be overloaded** in the area if too many employees are off at once.

☐ **Employees may not like** to have vacation periods fixed for them. It's tougher to tie in with plans of relatives or friends—or with game seasons.

☐ **Production may slow down** because of operation with a reduced labor force.

☐ **Bottlenecks may be created** by the absence of even a few people—particularly in small plants or in departments with small staffs where the effect of absences is felt more strongly.

☐ **Poorer supervision** and short-range planning may result when an assistant takes over during the key man's vacation.

☐ **Work may pile up for specialists,** who will then have a heavier-than-ever load when they return.

☐ **Resentment and friction may arise** among employees if too many want off at the same time. Since it is impossible to satisfy all requests, management is forced to refuse some.

☐ **Costs can run high** for training temporary replacements and for overtime work made necessary by vacation cuts in the work force.

* Source: J. B. Bennet, "Vacations—Mass or Staggered," *Factory Management and Maintenance,* June, 1950, p. 128.

Several years ago the coal miners won an important concession from the coal operators when the latter agreed to pay miners for the time they spent traveling to and from work on the mine premises. Thus, from the time a miner entered the portal of a mine until he reached the coal vein—and the return later—was time-consuming. For this time, the miners now received compensation. Upon the conclusion of this union contract, unions in manufacturing industries set out to ascertain whether or not traveling time in their cases was a subject worthy of collective bargaining. And some wondered whether or not such traveling time should have been paid for under the Wages and Hours Law. A suit was instituted (which reached the Supreme Court and became the now famous Mt. Clemens Case) that ruled that walking time between the plant gate and time of certain make-ready activities must be included for purposes of computing overtime.

This ruling let loose suits to collect back pay and liquidated damages that amounted to five to six billions of dollars. Because the suits might have ruined many businesses that had honestly obeyed wages and hours regulations and because the wages and hours rules were uncertain regarding going to and from work, Congress passed the Portal-to-Portal Pay Act of 1947. This Act specifically outlawed the suits, except those in which portal-to-portal activities are covered by contracts or existing practice.

As for compensable activities, this Act specifically excludes the time an employee spends going to a workplace, starting his "principal activity," and returning from the workplace. Thus such activities as going to work, reaching one's station, checking in and out, washing, changing clothes, and getting one's pay check are not compensable. However, if any of the foregoing is not for the convenience of the worker but is really an integral part of one's job, they are compensable.

More specifically, activities compensable as part of an employee's principal activity include:

1. Waiting to begin or resume work for reasons beyond an employee's control—such as waiting for materials
2. Getting instructions before going on a shift, or getting materials
3. Remaining on call on the employer's premises, where the employee is not free to leave the plant (except for scheduled sleeping time)
4. Preparing reports required by the job
5. Getting medical attention during working hours
6. Eating meals where the employee must remain at his working post
7. Rest periods under twenty minutes
8. Time spent in handling grievances, under an established plan in effect in the company
9. Attending business conferences or schools in connection with work duties

STABILIZATION PROGRAMS

Employees are interested not only in fair wages but also in uninterrupted wage opportunities. Unfortunately, various seasonal and cyclical disturbances disrupt continued earning power. Many believe that nothing much can be done to secure employees against such risks. Yet a number of programs have been devised to provide some degree of protection against such losses of income.

This is not the place to debate the issue of income stabilization. All that can be done here is to note what has been done by industry and government in this respect. The programs fall into two major categories:

1. Job stabilization, which seeks to provide continuous work opportunities and thereby assures employees of steady earnings, and
2. Wage stabilization, which provides steady wage payments, whether or not employees are actually working.

JOB STABILIZATION

To all concerned, stabilization of jobs would be a real boon. The employer seeks job stability because it leads to production efficiency, which means, in turn, that excess capacity, with its high costs, can be reduced to a minimum. And to employees the assurance of steady employment is of real significance, dependent as they are on a steady source of income. Unfortunately, cyclical and seasonal fluctuations are formidable obstacles to these hopes. The effect of these fluctuations must be reduced or removed, if possible, if stabilization of jobs is to be attained. Attempts to do this may be classified as follows:

1. By individual companies
   a) By adoption of sales policies that stabilize production
   b) By adoption of production policies that stabilize production
   c) By adoption of personnel policies that stabilize production
2. By intercompany co-operation in regard to—
   a) Sales practices
   b) Production practices
   c) Personnel practices
3. By governmental regulation and assistance
   a) Unemployment compensation regulations
   b) Assistance of employment services
   c) Assistance of informational service

INDIVIDUAL PLANS

The basic question a company must answer when considering job stabilization is: Is the program worth the cost? Although it has been contended that such is the case, nevertheless any proposals offered by the personnel department should carry schedules of, first, losses due to job fluctuations; second, costs of programs aimed at reducing fluctuations; and, third, the gains to be derived therefrom. To make such estimates, it is first necessary to examine statistically the seasonal and cyclical fluctuations that have and are likely to beset the company. Only after this has been done, can the size of the stabilization job be appreciated and the desirability and flexibility of alternative plans for solving it be considered.

Most job stabilization programs start with sales policies, since anything which will stabilize sales will obviously stabilize production and hence jobs. Reappraisals of sales policies fall into two groups—those which correct unstabilizing company practices and those which seek to make customers purchase in a more consistent manner.

Much can be done by companies themselves to eliminate practices that tend to unstabilize sales. Unplanned sales programs and activities are cases in point. In many instances, salesmen receive no instructions regarding products to be pushed, types of sales to be avoided, or what promises may be given on shipping dates. As a consequence, production bulges are extended or opportunities to fill in production valleys are missed. All this suggests that a simple and early step toward job stabilization can be taken by developing and adhering to planned selective sales programs.

Further positive steps can be taken by devising sales policies that work on the customer so that he becomes a more "stabilized" buyer. On the one hand, sales practices should be established under which sporadic buying is discouraged. For example, pricing policies should be set so that fear of price changes will not induce overbuying or underbuying. During periods when prices are falling, buyers tend to hold off in order to take advantage of still lower prices and to avoid inventory losses. In such instances, a policy of guaranteeing buyers against price declines will tend to induce more consistent purchases. Another good example is that of using special sales at times when they will coincide with periods when production is expected to be at low levels. The urge to buy should be sharpened by keeping the number of such sales at a minimum.

On the other hand, customers should be induced to become more stable buyers. First, in the case of seasonal items, buyers may be encouraged to send in advance orders by allowing special discounts, guaranteeing against price declines, offering exclusive rights of distribution, offering exclusive selection of styles, and permitting purchase on consignment. Second, in the case of items that are being ordered in small lots, buyers may be induced by methods suggested above to place a large order, with deliveries to be made periodically. And, third, by inducing the ultimate consumer to use, the year around, items that he is using only at certain seasons, all the distributors back to the manufacturer will tend to become more stable buyers. Perhaps no better example of success in this regard can be found than that of sellers of soft drinks, who market almost as much of their product in winter as they do in summer months.

PRODUCTION POLICIES

Production practices and policies should also be studied with a view to stabilizing employment. One of the most useful practices in this respect is that of producing to stock during seasons of low sales. This is not a cure-all because it is not universally feasible. When the following conditions prevail, its use should be given favorable consideration:

1. Parts or products can be stored—
   a) With a minimum of loss due to deterioration or evaporation
   b) At a minimum cost of handling, storing, and financial investment
2. Minimum losses will be incurred because of—
   a) Style changes while goods are stored
   b) Declines in price during storage

Such products as locomotives and construction equipment fall outside this class because of the physical problems of storing and the cost of carrying the items. On the other hand, many consumer items, which are regularly purchased, can be stored within the foregoing requirements.

Another practice which has much to commend it is that of "dovetailing" or producing different items for different seasons. This is usually difficult from a production point of view because facilities that are economical for the production of one type of product are ordinarily uneconomical for others. However, diversification should be considered because it may provide a way to balance production. Ordinarily, the less specialized the equipment a company uses, the more feasible is dovetailing or diversification of product. The food and clothing industries have scored substantial successes in this regard.

A variety of other production practices has been devised with a view to stabilizing production. Production control methods, for example, have much to offer here. Available work may be routed and scheduled to provide a stable work load. Another practice that has desirable features in this connection is to defer work of certain kinds to slack periods. Maintenance work, construction jobs, and scrap handling are cases in point. Another useful idea is to design products so that various parts are interchangeable irrespective of exterior style or variations in size. In that way, sales of particular products may fluctuate, yet production can be stabilized by producing to stock, if need be, or by producing to a plan of production control that has, so far as the workers are concerned, removed some of the vagaries of size or style factors. And, finally, a close tie-in of production and sales efforts should be developed so that both are directed toward the same goals.

PERSONNEL PRACTICES

Job stabilization may also be favorably affected by planned personnel practices. More accurate analysis of labor requirements, development of versatility of employees, and planned placement of work loads are the major ways in which this may be done.

1. STABILIZING HIRING PRACTICES. Lack of information regarding labor needs and hiring is a major cause of instability. When such poor employment practices are permitted, foremen in departments in which work loads are increasing will hire extra labor to handle this, not knowing that the load is temporary and that layoffs will soon be in order. Even when it is known that work loads are temporary, some companies proceed to hire willy-nilly, not caring about the disturbing influence to the labor situation. If, then, job stability is a desirable goal, the first and easiest step that any company can take in attaining it is to forecast the labor requirements as accurately as possible and, on the basis of this, to lay down stabilizing rules of hiring. Indiscriminate, inconsistent, and temporary hirings may then be reduced to a minimum.

2. DEVELOPING VERSATILITY. The development of versatility in workers also has much to be said for it because varying work loads then can be handled by a smaller number of employees. The theory of this practice is that workers who are kept on the payroll can be shifted, with a minimum loss of effectiveness, from jobs on which output is falling to those on which output is increasing. This makes it unnecessary to hire one worker for the first job, lay him off, and then hire another specialist for the second job, who in turn would have to be laid off when work loads in that area decline. This solution may not help the total unemployment problem, but it does provide job security to employees who meet the versatility requirement.

Versatility may be attained in two major ways—selection and training. Most companies, in hiring, seek an employee to fill a particular vacancy. As a consequence, they tend to select the candidate who is best suited to do the required job but who has no other aptitudes or skills, instead of looking for a candidate who has all-around abilities. If the latter course is followed, the employee selected can be shifted to other jobs, as work loads require, thus adding a link to the chain of job security. Under the former plan, however, specialized workers must be laid off if the general efficiency and ultimately the ability of the company to hire anyone are to be maintained.

Training of workers is a highly desirable practice because it may lead to the development of versatility, to increase in present efficiency, and to the development of satisfaction of employees in their work. To be effective, the training program must be designed so that current employees are given opportunity to learn basic techniques and methods of allied jobs. Moreover, it must be started and continued far enough in advance of actual need to allow employees time to gain new and added skills. For best results, the objectives of job security should also be stressed throughout the various training courses.

3. LEVELING WORK LOADS. A third important way of stabilizing jobs by means of personnel practices is to level work loads. For example, hours of work may be adjusted so that available work is shared by all employees. Such flexibility of hours must be tied in with sales and production practices. On the one hand, customers may have to be willing to accept shipment delays; and, on the other, changes in production schedules to meet current conditions must not be unduly difficult to make.

If these things can readily be done, adjustment of hours is a possible means of job stabilization. Ordinarily, it will be practicable, on the downward side of the business cycle, so long as reductions in hours of work do not reach the point at which all workers are on "starvation" wages. When this point is reached (what it is, is a variable depending upon employee opinion and standards of living), employees with seniority lose their desire to share the work with the younger employees and insist that the latter be released. On the upward side, taking care of peak loads by means of overtime, without hiring extra workers who must before long be laid off, depends upon the willingness of employees to give up their leisure and upon their efficiency as the factor of fatigue takes effect. However, within the practicable limits, adjustment of hours is a simple way of stabilizing jobs.

A good system of transfers is also effective in this regard. If work loads of varying amount are scheduled in different departments at different times, transfer programs can be worked out so that employees may be shifted between departments without need for layoffs. This practice can be adopted, however, only if, in addition to the requirements of sales and production tie-ups suggested in the preceding paragraph, employees possess versatility.

INTERCOMPANY CO-OPERATION

In a competitive society, no one company can install practices, the cost of which will place it in an unfavorable position as compared to other firms. Job security is a goal, the attainment of which involves some practices that, if adopted, call for intercompany action to be successful. Great progress in this direction has been made by a number of groups. Favorable results have been achieved by such groups as local and state chambers of commerce acting in behalf of their areas, trade associations working for the benefit of particular industries, and national business associations such as the National Association of Manufacturers and the more loosely knit Committee of Economic Development, acting for the benefit of all businesses. Such diverse groups as the American Legion, church bodies, and unions have also interested themselves in ways and means of stabilizing jobs.

A variety of sales, production, and personnel practices have been developed on an intercompany basis. Perhaps the most important contribution in this respect is the collection and dissemination of various types of information. Certainly information on such subjects as inventory positions, buying potentials and trends in various markets, new developments of materials and machines, trends in employment, and price fluctuations is highly useful in keeping employers from making mistakes that lead to overemployment or underemployment and the inevitable layoffs. Intercompany co-operation in gathering such information may be obtained through their own bureaus of information or outside bureaus subsidized to carry on this work.

In addition to the contributions to the ability of individual companies to make better decisions which aid in stabilizing production, intercompany co-operation can lead to the elimination of unstabilizing practices. For example, fluctuation of output in the automobile industry has been reduced by changing the time of introducing new models from the spring to the fall of the year. And the agreement of various industries to avoid extravagant claims, excessive discounts, and high-pressure salesmanship has tended to reduce unsettling results in the market and, thus, in turn, to stabilize employment. More positive action has been taken by industries that have sought on a co-operative basis to educate customers in more stable buying and selling methods.

An intercompany practice which has been successful in stabilizing production is that of interchanging workers as slack periods develop in one company while a peak load must be carried by another. Of course, such interchanges are the responsibility of workers in most markets, but the results of individual search are not always satisfactory to the workers, nor do the companies always get back desirable workers. When companies in a community get together to discuss their work loads, however, employees may be shifted from company to company with a minimum of lost time and effort to the employees. Some interesting problems, such as effect upon seniority, must be worked out; but their solution seems to be a small price to pay compared to the losses that are avoided thereby.

GOVERNMENTAL INFLUENCES

Job stabilization has also been influenced by governmental regulation and assistance. Regulatory influences have come chiefly from the Wages and Hours Law and the unemployment compensation laws, while the work of such agencies as the employment service and the Departments of Commerce and Labor has been of an assisting nature.

1. THE WAGES AND HOURS LAW. As noted in earlier chapters, one of the fundamental purposes of the Fair Labor Standards Act is to encourage the sharing of available work by penalizing employers who work their employees more than forty hours a week. Obviously, an employer who has to increase his labor costs by 50 per cent for overtime will consider very seriously the advisability of hiring additional workers. If he does, then the objective of stabilizing employment in the over-all sense by reducing unemployment will be attained.

More direct encouragement of employment stabilization is also provided by the exemptions from overtime payments granted to companies that establish employment guarantees by collective agreement. Section 7 (*b*) of the Act provides as follows:

No employer shall be deemed to have violated subsection (a) by employing any employee for a work week in excess of that specified in such subsection without paying the compensation for overtime employment prescribed therein if such employee is so employed—

1. In pursuance of an agreement, made as a result of collective bargaining by representatives of employees certified as bona fide by the National Labor Relations Board, which provides that no employee shall be employed more than one thousand hours during any period of twenty-six consecutive weeks.
2. On an annual basis in pursuance of agreement with his employer, made as a result of collective bargaining by representatives of employees certified as bona fide by the National Labor Relations Board, which provides that the employee shall not be employed more than two thousand hours during any period of fifty-two consecutive weeks or
3. For a period or periods of not more than fourteen work weeks in the ag-

gregate in any calendar year in an industry found by the Administrator to be of a seasonal nature, and if such employee receives compensation for employment in excess of twelve hours in any workday, or for employment in excess of fifty-eight hours in any work week, as the case may be, at a rate not less than one and one-half times the regular rate at which he is employed.

Interpretations by the Administrator of the Act make some adjustments in these hours to 2,080 in the case of annual agreements.

2. THE SOCIAL SECURITY ACT.   Another encouragement to stabilized employment stems from the unemployment compensation provisions of the Social Security Act. Under Titles III and IX of this Act, employees of industry, in states that have approved plans, are compensated for periods up to twenty-six weeks, depending upon the legislation of the states in which they reside. The funds for compensation are obtained by taxes computed as a percentage of individual payrolls. Records are kept of the contributions of each company and of compensation paid out against the individual accounts. In most states adjustments are made in the taxation for particular companies if the withdrawals from the fund, because of a low record of layoffs, are at a minimum. The amount of the adjustments depends upon the system of "merit" or "experience" rating which particular states have adopted. Obviously, it is to the benefit of companies operating in states in which rating may lead to reduction in taxes to reduce fluctuations in employment whenever possible.

3. ASSISTANCE OF FEDERAL AGENCIES.   Other federal agencies have lent an assisting hand in reducing job instability. The Department of Commerce and the Department of Labor have collected a variety of data which is useful to employers in reaching more intelligent decisions regarding business problems, thereby reducing mistakes that lead to layoffs and employment fluctuations. Also, the United States Employment Service and the state employment services assist employers in the selection of workers who are better suited to their jobs; consequently, layoffs due to misplacements are reduced.

WAGE STABILIZATION

SCOPE OF PLANS

Programs of wage stabilization are based on the proposition that wages and salaries should be continued at a more or less constant rate when it is impossible to stabilize production. A variety of such plans have been developed. The key points of difference pertain to:

1. The employees covered by guarantees
2. Guarantee periods and amounts
3. Voluntary versus negotiated programs

These variables are discussed in this section. In addition, examples will be given of a number of stabilization programs, and then attention will be directed to governmental activities in this area.

EMPLOYEE COVERAGE

Most plans are limited to certain classes of workers. Length of service, type of work, and a calculated number of employees are used to establish limits. Length of service is undoubtedly the most popular method for determining the employees who are to participate in wage stabilization plans. It is, of course, easy to calculate and understand and, moreover, has the actual advantage of the test of time—since the company has been able to retain them for a length of time, probabilities are in favor of being able to continue their employment. The service requirements of some plans are as low as six months and as high as five years, with a period of one year being favored.

Job classes are also used by some companies because the retention of employees on certain key jobs is highly desirable. Technical, professional, supervisory, and maintenance employees are examples of those to whom guarantees are extended.

And, finally, some companies establish the number of employees to whom guarantees can be extended by calculating labor requirements for a future period of time. After this figure is determined, seniority by job classes is then employed to determine which of the employees will be included in the number of employees to whom the guarantee can be extended. This method has the advantage of protecting the company against excessive guarantees, but it has the disadvantage of making some key employees uncertain about income stability.

GUARANTEE PERIODS AND AMOUNTS

All plans establish a definite period of time during which guarantees apply or are calculated. In most instances, the year is the base period, although some plans limit the time to as low as three months. Obviously, if a plan is to give employees assurance of steady income, they should at least aim toward the annual basis. This does provide a sufficiently extended period so that employees are not disturbed by what is going to happen to their income in the near future. Of course, from the company's point of view, guarantees beyond a year's time are full of danger because economic conditions and prices beyond its control and its powers of foresight may lead to impossible financial burdens. However, most companies should be able to forecast within reasonable limits of accuracy the sales it will make during a year's time and, hence, be able to establish this period as a limit to its guarantees.

Although questions of who is to be covered for how long may be answered with relative ease, how much is to be guaranteed is a much more difficult question. The variations in this regard in actual practice show that differences of opinion are wide. Guarantees differ in terms of liability of payments and amount of payment.

With rare exceptions, most companies limit their guarantees or establish rules for counterbalancing overpayments or underpayments. A common way of doing this is to establish a basic workweek and a basic pay check for each week. If the actual earnings of employees are less than the basic check, the differences are recorded and must be made up in future weeks when overtime hours raise actual earnings above the basic check. The basic pay check may be based upon a standard work week of forty hours (or upon some lesser figure) if actual hours from week to week fluctuate around forty. If the period within which shortages must be made up is definitely stated, let us say a year, as some plans provide, then the liability of employers is minimized, yet the wage plan may be termed a "guaranteed wage plan."

Many companies limit their liability by agreeing to advance employees, for specified periods of time only, an amount sufficient to make up the difference between the amount earned and the guaranteed weekly pay check. These advances are continued only for a limited period of time or up to the pay for a given number of hours. Should these limits be reached, the make-ups are stopped. And, as noted earlier, the advances must be made up by the employee when work weeks exceed the basic week or some percentage of a basic week. To minimize the losses that may develop if long periods intervene before work periods are sufficient to warrant repayments by employees, these plans are usually restricted to employees of specified seniority.

NEGOTIATED PLANS

The foregoing plans have been voluntarily promoted by industry itself. There is a growing movement on the part of unions to drive for wage guarantees. The large national unions are forcing the issue in current negotiations. It is not improbable that gains will be made on a broad scale.

A number of contracts have already been signed incorporating such guarantees. Thus far they provide a given number of high-seniority employees—not all employees—with assurance of 40 hours of work for 50 weeks in a given year. In some instances, payment must be made, even though unemployment is caused by lack of materials brought on by a strike of employees of suppliers. The employees also have the right to respect—without a pay loss—picket lines of other unions. Nor is overtime counted against the hours guaranteed annually.

How far this movement wil go is conjectural. Guaranteed wages have an appeal, however, that is difficult to resist. And it must be granted that most companies never have laid off all their employees at any time. At least, guarantees of this amount could be feasible. So it is safe to conclude that negotiations for such guarantees are not likely to abate. How many employees will be covered and the extent of guarantees will depend upon economic conditions, type of industry, strength of union bargaining power, strategy of union drives, and the facts that management can marshall about its industrial situation.

EXAMPLES OF WAGE PLANS

A number of companies are widely recognized for their contributions to wage stabilization programs, and a brief description of their plans is in order.

Procter and Gamble, for example, has been a pioneer in this field. Their plan is essentially an employment guarantee plan. Permanent factory workers are guaranteed employment for at least forty-eight weeks of the year. To make this plan feasible, the company had, first, to redesign certain key manufacturing operations so that year-round instead of seasonal operations could be carried on and, second, to revamp their distribution methods so that retailers purchased on a periodic rather than a casual basis. The work guarantees are given to employees with two or more years of consecutive service. Workers also are subject to job changes as work loads of various divisions dictate.

The Nunn-Bush Company, noted for its plan of fifty-two checks a year, is another pioneer in wage stabilization. This company, too, has worked out very carefully the conditions under which wage guarantees can be made. It has found that the amount that can be paid to employees is about 20 per cent of the value of production. Hence, by forecasting sales for any year, it can determine what its payroll will be. Jobs throughout the company have been evaluated, and each employee included in the plan may draw one fifty-second of his annual rate each week. At the end of four-week periods, adjustments are made if actual earnings are above or below drawings. Only workers who are in an "A" group, consisting of those whose seniority and ability merit, are included in this weekly pay check plan; the other or "B" workers are paid on an hourly basis without any guarantees. The guarantees in this case are not a fixed amount but a fixed percentage of whatever business the company gets.

The Hormel Company of Austin, Minnesota, has also been in the vanguard of the movement for wage stabilization. Employees receive 52 pay checks a year, with a minimum of 38 hours at the hourly rate in any week. In weeks of over 40 hours, no overtime at premium rates is paid. Overages and underages are balanced at periodic intervals. At the end of the year employees earn bonuses based upon the earnings of the company and for production in excess of estimated quantities. Thus this plan includes a profit-sharing feature.

The elements of a few other companies that illustrate some variations in practice are also worth citing as follows:

The William Wrigley, Jr., Company pays a percentage of regular earnings to employees laid off. Payment is made to employees of six months' service, or more, and continues for four to thirty weeks, depending upon service.

The Armstrong Cork Company will make up the pay of employees up to forty-eight hours for any two weeks at its own expense and will prepay wages between 60 per cent of standard earnings and actual earnings, which difference must subsequently be repaid by the workers.

The Sears, Roebuck and Company plan pays its employees a regular weekly amount fifty-two weeks a year, requiring workers to work whatever number of hours, up to but not beyond reasonable limits, needed to get the work done. Earnings in excess of weekly guarantees during the year are paid to employees. Payments in excess of earnings are absorbed as a loss by the company.

CONDITIONS OF FEASIBLE USAGE

Wage stabilization requires favorable conditions. Desirable though it may be to employees and employers, it is not something that can be established or not, as the whim dictates. To begin with, wage stabilization is practically limited to periods of a year or less. Hence, as a stabilization of cyclical forces, it is an aid, not a cure-all. And even within the yearly or seasonal period, many companies are unable to do much about wage stabilization. For example, those whose swings of business are violent and unpredictable—the so-called "producer-goods industries" are a case in point—cannot undertake such programs.

On the other hand, those whose business is in the consumer-goods field and are more or less "depression-proof" (meaning more resistant than others) may adopt such plans. A review of the names of companies that have installed them soon indicates the predominance of consumer-type industries. And, finally, industries which can economically store parts or finished products are in a better position to stabilize wages than others. Thus anything that a company can do to reduce seasonal fluctuations, to increase storability of products, and to increase the versatility of employees makes wage stabilization more feasible.

The variations in these conditions explain why some companies can be more liberal in their guarantees than others. Whereas some can guarantee weekly pay checks of fixed amount without repayment features in the event of overpayments, others must restrict their guarantees to little more than wage advances that must sooner or later be repaid. In any event, the steps taken by any company in this direction serve to reduce one of the most serious threats to labor's security and peace of mind.

UNEMPLOYMENT COMPENSATION

The federal government, through the Social Security Act, has taken steps to stabilize income. Through the sections of this Act that pertain to unemployment, employees who reside in states with approved legislation and machinery may receive compensation of varying amounts. The amounts that eligible unemployed workers may receive varies from state to state. As an example of the factors covered by such laws, the following provisions in the state of Ohio are of interest:

1. The amount of compensation for totally unemployed is one-half of the normal, average weekly wage, but not to exceed $25.00 per week, up to 26 weeks in any 52-week period, after a waiting period of 3 weeks; and up to $5.00 for dependent children.
2. The amount for partially unemployed, provided that earnings fall below 60 per cent of normal earnings, is computed on a sliding scale of from 10 to 40 per cent of normal earnings.
3. To be eligible, unemployed must—
   a) Have worked in jobs not exempted from coverage
      (A few examples of exempted classes are—agricultural labor, employees of governmental agencies, domestic service, and "extra" workers.)
   b) Have worked in each of 20 weeks in the year before application is made for benefits, for an employer of 3 or more persons
   c) Have registered with the employment service
   d) Be able and willing to work
   e) Have earned at least $240 during the base period

Obviously, this program does not establish wage stabilization. It does provide a buffer while unemployed are looking for work. Moreover, it indicates the type of program that government may be asked to expand, as some already are demanding, if periods of unemployment should become severe.

PROGRAMS OF REVENUE PARTICIPATION

A final group of programs related to wages is characterized by some form of sharing in profits or revenues. These programs include, first, direct profit sharing; second, sharing through stock ownership; and, third, sharing through royalty provisions.

PROFIT SHARING

A reawakening of interest in sharing of profits took place during the years of World War II when some companies sought to use it as a means of granting wage increases that were otherwise prohibited by war controls. Also during the war there was considerable discussion of providing reduced rates of income tax for companies that had approved profit-sharing plans. Labor unions, too, in some cases have come out with demands that profits be shared with employees. And, of course, some employers have felt that profit sharing is a highly desirable means of solidifying relations with employees by making them conscious of their partnership stake in the success of the business.

1. COMPUTING AND ALLOCATING SHARES. Profit-sharing plans differ largely in terms of how shares going to labor and capital are to be computed and the method of administering the plan. Looking first at the division of profits, the simplest plan is to establish the set percentages that will go to capital and to labor and then to determine the basis upon which labor's share will be allocated among eligible workers. Ordinarily, the division is arrived at by a formula under which an amount for "fair return on investment" is first deducted from available profits and the remainder then divided upon a fixed basis or a sliding scale, varying with the amount of profits. Usually labor's share is far less than a fifty-fifty cut. Under sliding-scale arrangements, however, labor's share goes up rapidly as profits increase.

The division of labor's share among eligible workers is usually based upon seniority. For example, under one plan, employees with five or more years of service get full shares in labor's share of the profits, employees with three and up to five years' service get two-thirds of a share, and those with one and up to three years' service get one-third of a share. Under another plan, employees receive a share in profits based upon a percentage varying with years of service. Thus employees with one to two years' service receive 5 per cent, and the scale goes up so that those with fifteen or more years of service receive 10 per cent of their wages as their share of profits. In some cases, seniority is disregarded, except for a probationary period, after which all share alike in the division of profits.

2. DETAILS OF ADMINISTRATION. Details of administration differ considerably. How a plan is operated depends, in the first place, upon its purpose. If it is used as a means of stabilizing turnover and rewarding seniority, with payments deferred to some future time, the plan must be properly qualified under the regulations of the internal revenue department. Such deferred distribution plans are called "profit-sharing trusts" and, to qualify, must, among other conditions, establish a definite formula for contribution to the fund from profits and a formula for distribution among participants. If it is intended as a stimulant of production, methods of announcing, publicizing, and paying out employee shares should be developed carefully.

Second, administrative details differ because of the degree to which profit-sharing plans are tied in with other personnel programs. In most companies, profit sharing is intended to be another link of a chain of personnel practices; hence its administration is determined by what happens to other segments of the program. In other companies, it stands on its own legs and what is done in this respect is done with practically no regard for the administration of other personnel practices. One company, for example, may weave its profit-sharing plan in with pension, health, and stock purchase plans, whereas another may set up its plan entirely independently of the others, if any.

3. RELATIVE MERITS OF PROFIT-SHARING PLANS. Whether or not a company should install a profit-sharing plan, as noted earlier, is a debatable subject. A number of companies have tried it and have discarded it because the employees or employers were dissatisfied with results.[1] Yet other companies, with the years, have been more convinced that profit sharing is an indispensable tool of labor relations. This much can be said, however: A company must have a fairly stable history of profits, else the plan is bound to fail. Employees cannot be stimulated to greater effort or expected to increase their loyalty to a company when there are no profits to divide. Hence profit sharing as a device of labor relations should not be viewed with favor unless and until steps can be taken to stabilize profits.

[1] P. A. Knowlton, *Studies in Profit Sharing* (Long Island City: Profit Sharing Research Foundation, 1953). This contains an excellent analysis of discontinued (as well as successful) plans.

Moreover, plans that rely upon profit sharing to stimulate individual efficiency are proceeding against two fundamentals of wage incentive plans. First, remuneration is spaced too far from the effort of employees. A plan in which profits are shared in February will scarcely possess much stimulating power in July, let us say. Second, the connection between reward and effort is scarcely discernible. An employee may work very conscientiously and get no share in profits because there are none in some years. Or he may see a fellow worker loaf and get just as much as he does in prosperous years. Hence, profit sharing is no stimulant to production.

On the other hand, as a means of developing team spirit and for educating employees in the risks and interdependencies of business, profit sharing has much to be said for it. Some companies have noted such favorable trends as the following after experience with profit sharing: a sharp decline in labor turnover, a greater loyalty to the company, a better spirit of co-operation with fewer petty grievances, and a generally improved tone of relationships and understanding between employee and employer. And it is difficult for an employee to complain about excessive profits when he shares in them too.

Finally, profit-sharing plans will not succeed as a substitute for other personnel practices. The companies that have had the most success with their profit-sharing plans are those that stress their other personnel plans. Thus they note their high wages, savings plans, good supervision, recreational and educational facilities, and grievance-handling machinery as parallels of a successful profit-sharing plan. Satisfied with good wages, employees are then stimulated to higher efforts by the prospects of sharing also in profits. Profit sharing, to repeat, is an added element, not a replacement, in the general scheme of personnel management.

EMPLOYEE OWNERSHIP OF STOCKS

From time to time interest in employee ownership of stocks waxes strong as a means of improving employee and employer relations. The usual practice is to allow employees to purchase stock at prices more or less reduced from current market levels. The purchases must usually be made on a time basis, to encourage the thrift idea and to prevent employees from selling at higher prices. Also, the number of shares that an employee may buy is restricted by seniority or earning power clauses. If an employee leaves the company before stocks are paid for, most plans provide for the employee to receive the amount of the payments, plus interest usually computed above current rates.

Stock plans are preferred by some because employees are made partners of the business in name as well as in fact. It is felt that, since employees share in losses as well as profits, they become more conscious of the problems that beset their companies. As a consequence, they become more tolerant and loyal.

Unfortunately, the risks of stockownership sometimes result in large losses to employees. For example, it is obvious what will happen when a stock sold to employees at $30.00 goes up to $150.00 and then toboggans to $0.50. This has happened, with the result that employee morale for a time was not worth the proverbial "plugged nickel." As a consequence of such experiences, many have concluded that the risks of stockownership plans exceed the possible advantages. Moreover, employees can gain little feeling of self-assurance or of contribution when they watch stock prices go up and down for no obvious reasons whatsoever.

Seasoned thought on stockownership plans lead to the conclusion that their best area of usage is as a long-run savings plan. A certain amount of fluctuation adds to the zest of the program; but, if there is danger of rapid fluctuations of wide amplitude, it is a questionable plan to offer employees. If, however, employees do see prices of the shares of their company's stock going up, they may feel that they are being discriminated against unless they are given an opportunity to participate in these profits. But the plan, in such instances, should be restricted to prevent employees from becoming overly stock-market conscious, as has happened in some companies at certain periods during bullish markets.

ROYALTY PROVISIONS

Labor, in its organized endeavors, is seeking to gain a greater share of industry's earnings by "royalty" demands. These consist of payments, usually to a union organization of employees, based upon a levy for each unit of output. The funds thus collected are to be used for a variety of purposes—for example, to aid the unemployed, to supplement payments to those injured on the job, and to support various other welfare activities.

Among the first of these royalty arrangements was made by the American Federation of Musicians. It has arranged for the payment of royalties on radio and television transcriptions and phonograph records according to frequency of broadcast. The funds so collected are to be used for the relief of unemployed musicians. In 1946, John L. Lewis created a furor in the coal mining industry by demanding a royalty of ten cents on every ton of coal mined. He then gained a five-cent royalty, which has since been raised to forty cents in soft coal and fifty in anthracite. The proceeds are used by the union to compensate injured miners and their families. Other unions are also considering the advisability of seeking royalties, and it is almost certain that the demands in this direction are bound to take a sharp upturn.

As a personnel practice, management cannot be exceedingly happy over this development, for it represents a practice over which it has no control and from which it can seemingly derive no benefit. Perhaps the most significant lesson that management can learn from these demands is that it must anticipate the reasons for which royalty demands are likely to be made and to be prepared to rebut them. If labor can prove that royalties are needed to serve welfare needs which management could but does not carry, public sympathy will be on the side of labor. And management will have to pay for, but will lose control of, another "prerogative."

QUESTIONS AND PROBLEMS

1. From what risks can employees be secured? From which can they not? Distinguish between undesirable events and the costs thereof.

2. How may the shift problem in industry be handled? Discuss the advantages and disadvantages of the fixed- versus the swing-shift plan.

3. Make a survey among a number of companies to determine their hours of work each day and each week. Is there a tendency for acceptance of common standards?

4. What are the arguments for and against the provision of rest periods during the working day? What are the practices in your community?

5. What is an effective workweek? What do you expect the workweek to be five years from now? Why?

6. Assume that, in a debate, one person argued that employees most want economic security and another argued that they prefer a feeling of worth-while-ness. How would you go about determining which was valued more?

7. What types of economic fluctuations cause employment fluctuations? What is the probability of eliminating them? Of minimizing them?

8. Why is it that a single company acting alone can seldom do much about job stabilization? Is it not true, however, that some companies have scored singular successes in stabilizing jobs? What conditions are present in such cases?

9. If work is stabilized in some departments of a company but not in others, is this likely to lower morale in the latter departments? If so, would it be better to forego job stabilization until the entire company can be included in the plan? Explain.

10. Although training is likely to increase the versatility of employees, will not

training also increase unrest because employees will become dissatisfied if new opportunities are not opened to them?

11. Why is intercompany co-operation desirable in developing job stabilization plans? Is it possible that some types of intercompany co-operation might be construed as illegal? Which ones?

12. What is meant by merit and experience rating when used in connection with unemployment compensation?

13. Under what conditions is wage stabilization preferred to job stabilization as a means of providing economic security?

14. Is it possible to establish guaranteed wage programs for any extended periods of time? Why or why not?

15. In establishing wage stabilization programs, which classes of employees and how many should be covered?

16. Some have argued that wage stabilization should be nation-wide and cover all employees. What difficulties inhere in such proposals?

17. Many otherwise favorable to profit-sharing plans state that they would install such plans if employees were willing to share losses. What light do such statements throw on the feasibility of profit sharing?

18. Under what conditions has profit sharing an excellent chance of succeeding? To what interests of employees is profit sharing likely to appeal?

19. Evaluate stockownership plans for employees.

20. What is meant by royalty demands of labor unions? Do you expect such demands are likely to increase or decrease? Explain.

CHAPTER

21 | Union-Management Relationships

A relatively effective and satisfied labor force is a major objective of programs of personnel management. In general, success may be said to attend such programs in better companies. No matter how skillfully and fairly personnel practices are pursued, however, conflicts and disagreements of greater or lesser extent will arise to disturb relations between labor and management.

These situations of satisfactory relations as well as of conflict constitute the subject known as "labor relations." More specifically, the following relationships are included:

1. Grievances or occasions in which employees are significantly discontented with something related to the company (which topic is discussed in Chap. 22)
2. Disciplinary action, or occasions in which management is sufficiently displeased with employees to take some punitive steps (discussed in Chap. 23)
3. Positive motivation, or occasions in which management and labor are relatively satisfied with each other, and management seeks to continue this relationship (discussed in Chap. 24)

The concept "labor relations" encompasses also the organizations, forces, practices, and policies used to resolve disagreements, correct undesirable conditions, arrive at new agreements, or maintain good relationships.

Viewed strictly from the viewpoint of management, labor relations are a joint task of line and staff departments. In the final analysis, line executives must be responsible for developing good relations and for minimizing the undesirable. The labor relations department—the specialized staff personnel unit—should be prepared to develop plans, policies, and procedures that will be helpful to the line executives. What is said in these chapters on labor relations should be construed as applying with particular reference to line executives and not solely to the personnel department.

418

In recent years management has had to work increasingly with unions in the solution of labor relations problems. Establishing wages, hours, and working conditions; resolving grievances and disputes; and evolving plans and activities of mutual interest have more and more been done in concert with unions. Hence it has seemed desirable to discuss labor relations in terms of working with unions before taking up the specific subject matter which one finds in labor-management relations. This is done in the present chapter under the following headings:

1. General background of union-management relations
2. Concepts and nature of organized labor
3. The Labor Management Relations Act
4. Contractual aspects of labor relations

GENERAL BACKGROUND

OVER-ALL HISTORY

Although labor unions have been in existence in the United States since the Revolutionary period, they have not been a significant factor in labor relations generally until recently. Prior to the Civil War, a few sporadic efforts resulted successfully in the formation of labor unions. Small-scale manufacturing and legal hindrances prevented any expansion of such organizations. After the Civil War, from which time modern industrial growth may be considered to date, labor agitation became particularly violent. Of particular interest in this regard was the Noble Order of the Knights of Labor that flourished briefly but spectacularly during the two decades following the Civil War. Its programs and ambitions, however, were beyond its resources and the opposition which industry could muster. As a consequence, it sputtered into insignificance and then extinction during the late 1880's.

This decade is an important era, however, because it marks the formation of the American Federation of Labor (AFL) in 1886. This group has grown in strength and stature so that at present it is rivaled only by the Congress of Industrial Organizations (the CIO). The latter was formed in 1935 by a number of unions which were dissatisfied with the policies pursued by the AFL. The name chosen by the new group was the Committee of Industrial Organization, and it was changed in 1938 to its present name. Figure 74 (p. 420) shows the relative strength of unions in terms of the number of employees covered by collective bargaining agreements of various types at the beginning of 1945. Present estimates show union membership to total upward of 16,000,000.

The growth of unions was slow until 1933. Prior to that time, their fight for recognition was slowed by the legal strategies of industry. In

← 1933 the first place, industry by and large would not have anything to do with unions, even though labor had the right to organize and to bargain collectively. The legal right was a matter of mutual consent and not compulsion. Second, legal injunctions could easily be obtained by industry to halt a variety of labor activities such as strikes, boycotts, pick-

FIGURE 74. Employees Covered by Union Contracts, January, 1945*

TYPES OF COLLECTIVE BARGAINING AGREEMENTS

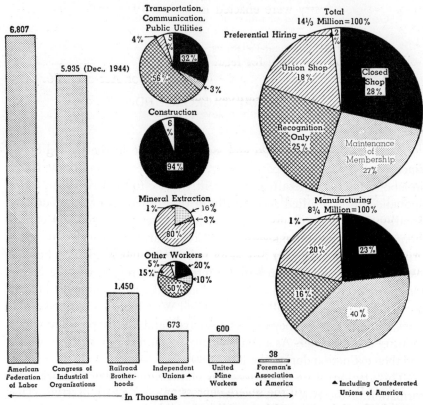

The above charts are based on National Industrial Conference Board figures, and are published in NICB's series, "Road Maps of Industry"

* Source: "Labor Union Membership," *Factory Management and Maintenance*, July, 1945, p. 93.

eting, and efforts to increase their membership. And, third, industry could insist upon making employees, as a condition of employment, agree not to join unions (the "yellow-dog" contract).

LEGAL CHANGES

Against the legal bulwarks and the relative strength of industry, labor organizations made small but nevertheless constant gains. Perhaps the first important legal victory for the union movement came in 1888, when the federal government passed the Act to Regulate Interstate Commerce and used this legislation as its right to settle disputes that arose between railway carriers and their employees. The Erdman Act of 1898 was more specific in its labor provision, first, by making it a crime for a railroad employer to discharge employees for belonging to a labor union and, second, by providing for mediation and conciliation when requested by both parties. Other refinements in labor relations in this industry were enacted in law in 1913 and 1916, during World War I years, and finally led to the Railway Labor Act of 1926, which was amended in 1934. It was not until 1930, however, that a solid foundation was made for legal progress, when the Supreme Court upheld the constitutionality of the Railway Labor Act of 1926.

In fields other than the railroad business, progress in amending or passing legislation to favor labor developed in the states and was gradually extended to the federal front. A large number of states had passed laws dealing with mediation and conciliation by 1900, although only those in New York, Massachusetts, and Pennsylvania are credited with constructive use in the adjustment of labor disputes. At the present time, a large majority of states have laws covering conciliation, mediation, and arbitration. State legislation is ineffective in these areas unless some form of federal legislation affords protection against employers who, when obstructed by the laws of a particular state, move on to another with more lenient laws or none at all.

Changes in the attitude of the federal government toward labor came with the depression starting in 1929. To be sure, labor organizations were construed as exempted from the federal provisions pertaining to conspiracy to combine in restraint of the Sherman Act of 1890 by the Clayton Act of 1914. And in 1913 the U.S. Conciliation Service was provided for, with the establishment of the United States Department of Labor. But not until the severe depression of the early thirties was it possible for labor to achieve political solidarity to an extent which moved legislative representatives to write laws that more nearly met labor's desires. The first important change came in 1932 with the passage of the Norris–La Guardia Act, which placed severe restrictions upon the use of court injunctions intended to curb or limit union activities, and outlawed the "yellow-dog" contracts, which required a worker to promise, as a condition of employment, that he would not join a union.

Of vital import was the enactment in 1933 of the National Industrial Recovery Act in which, for industry's right to set prices, labor was allowed to write in the famous Section 7 (a). This gave employees the right to organize and bargain collectively and prohibited employers from using the "yellow-dog" clause.

The President of the United States, in August, 1933, created a National Labor Board to handle labor disputes arising out of codes of fair competition or re-employment agreements established under the N.I.R.A. The Board was composed of representatives of labor and industry and established regional boards to carry on its business. More specifically, the Board was given authority to investigate labor controversies in cases of interstate commerce and to conduct elections among employees to determine their representatives for purposes of collective bargaining. But this Board ceased operation when the N.I.R.A. was declared unconstitutional—on May 27, 1935. Almost immediately Congress passed the National Labor Relations Act, which was signed by the President on June 27, 1935. This Act not only gave labor the right to organize but made it mandatory for employers to bargain collectively with representatives of labor if employees so desired. After the U.S. Supreme Court upheld this Act in April, 1937, growth of membership in unions surpassed the advances made during the code-making days of the N.R.A.

During World War II, as controls were established for various parts of the national economy, it was not surprising that rules were promulgated relating to labor-management relations. To begin with, President Franklin D. Roosevelt established the National Defense Mediation Board to settle disputes by peaceful means in order to permit uninterrupted production to meet the needs of the national defense program. This Board was finally wrecked by a dispute between the CIO and the Board over the question of union security. The CIO feared that settlement of disputes by the government would tend to protect the open-shop principle. It demanded, therefore, that the closed shop be granted to miners in the case of the "captive mines"—those owned by the steel companies. This the Board refused to do, and the CIO withdrew its members from the Board. It was replaced by the War Labor Board by executive order on January 12, 1942, which, with added war powers, heard and settled disputes; it was also given authority to administer wage and salary regulations established by the federal government as one part of its anti-inflationary policy.

In June, 1943, the War Labor Disputes Act (the Smith-Connally Act) was passed, giving the War Labor Board statutory existence. This Act also provided for government seizure of plants threatened by strikes or those notified of intent to strike. Only after a waiting period and a strike vote, could a strike be called by representatives of labor without incurring the penalties of the Act. These rules have been strengthened by the Labor Management Relations Act, discussed later in this chapter.

Since the end of World War II, the passage of the Labor Management Relations Act (Taft-Hartley) in 1947 has been the most important legislation in the area of labor relations. After an extensive series of hearings in both houses of Congress and after bitter acrimony, this law was passed over the President's veto. It provides for rights to employers and employees as individuals as well as members of unions. A large number of states have passed somewhat similar legislation, but space does not permit their consideration here.

This brief outline of the development of labor organizations has shown the trend from the time when management largely dictated labor relations to the present when labor's voice often predominates. Some see a possibility of greater governmental dictation of labor relations if labor and management cannot resolve their difficulties without recurring disastrous strikes. Although an examination of such developments is beyond the scope of this study, nevertheless personnel management has a serious burden to carry if it is to advise and counsel management so that its dealings with labor are to lead to reasonably satisfactory relations instead of more restrictive measures.

CONCEPTS OF UNION-MANAGEMENT RELATIONS

Before discussing various types of unions, it is desirable to define various terms used in connection with the settlement of labor disputes.

DEFINITION OF TERMS

"Collective bargaining" presumably is the key to the settlement of labor disputes by organized efforts. Its meaning has not been established in a single definition to the satisfaction of all concerned. It is difficult to define because the extent, degree, and kind of bargaining and of "collective" effort depend upon the time, place, and parties of the bargaining process. The subjects over which labor and management will bargain also affect the definitions, and the methods and organizations used in bargaining powers vary from case to case and from time to time. Thus, at one time, bargaining was what the employer wanted to make it. Nowadays, bargaining must result in a written contract if the representatives of labor desire. Furthermore, some unions and managements rely heavily upon facts and information to examine their differences, whereas others prefer to use emotional appeals or strong-arm tactics. In general terms, which is the only way in which collective bargaining can be defined, it refers to a process by which employers, on the one hand, and representatives of employees, on the other, attempt to arrive at agreements covering the conditions under which employees will contribute and be compensated for their services.

To those who deplore the use of the word "bargaining" as indicative of a struggle between employer and employee, the relationship would be better stated by calling the process "collective co-operation."

EMPLOYEE REPRESENTATION PLANS

As indicated, collective bargaining may be carried on through a variety of organizational forms. There are two general classes of forms —employee representation plans and unions. The representation plan, once viewed as a promising contribution to better labor relations, has been largely discarded as the result of the N.L.R.A. This Act made it an unfair labor practice for a company to interfere with or assist in the organization of employees for purposes of collective bargaining. Since representation plans are organizations founded for this purpose at the behest of management, they were viewed with suspicion under the N.L.R.A. Of course, if they are organized independently by employees and act independently of employers, such plans acquire the status of independent unions, which are permissible by law. But, as originally designed, representation plans are largely illegal because their formation was influenced by management.

Unless such plans can prove independence of organization and operation, their chances of survival are slim. Those that have retained their legal existence have done so by reorganizing as independent unions to remove any question of company domination. In such instances, their organization is based upon committees of the "joint" or "federal" types. Joint committees are composed of representatives of labor and management. The federal system employs labor committees that act as a congress to debate issues and to submit recommendations to the executive branch of the organization, the management, whose vetoes, if any, could not be overridden by the congress.

TYPES OF LABOR UNIONS

The "union" is the predominant form of organization of collective bargaining. The major types are the "craft" and the "industrial" unions, although important also are the miscellaneous, foremen's, and independent groups.

1. THE CRAFT UNION.   The craft union is one in which membership is restricted to employees for a particular trade or craft. The employees may or may not be employed by the same company. For example, carpenters in a given community, irrespective of who employs them, may belong to the same union. Or all the carpenters of a given company may form a craft union and restrict membership to carpenters of the given company.

The American Federation of Labor is essentially an association of craft unions. Each "local" or union of craftsmen is represented through a sequence of city, state, regional, and national craftsmen organizations, which, in turn, are affiliated with the AFL. The latter group acts as the agency that sets national policies for the craft unions and serves to protect the labor movement from influences beyond the control of local units. It is subject, however, to the regulation of the local units through the system of state and national representatives, elected by the locals to serve on the boards of the large organizational units.

2. THE INDUSTRIAL UNION.   Opposed to the form of structure of the craft union is the so-called "industrial" union, which includes all types of workers in its ranks. Thus all occupations would be eligible for membership in the same industrial union. Because of this policy of inclusion, it is sometimes referred to as the "vertical" type as opposed to the "horizontal" type of stratification employed by the craft union.

The CIO is the chief exponent of the industrial union. It came into existence largely because certain leaders in the AFL became dissatisfied with the alleged failure of the AFL to pursue vigorously the organization of the mass of workers in American industry who had no particular skills to qualify them as craftsmen. Contending that those workers, as much if not more than the craftsmen, needed the protection and services of unions, the dissatisfied leaders branched out in 1935 with the industrial union. In the span of a few years, its membership has risen to a point that leads the CIO to contend that its members equal in number those of the AFL.

3. MISCELLANEOUS GROUPS.   In addition to these two giants, a number of other unions are of interest. The railroad industry has long been a stronghold of the union movement. It is organized largely on a craft basis, with its various brotherhoods of trainmen, engineers, and other classes of railroad workers. The United Mine Workers, led by the militant John L. Lewis, are also deserving of separate mention. They returned to the fold of the AFL after playing a leading role in the formation of the CIO, but are now acting independently. This union, made

up of a miscellany of industrial workers as well as of miners, has been in the van of many drives to gain new and added emoluments for labor. And their leader has displayed cunning leadership in timing his drives and choosing his strategy so that success has attended his efforts much, much more than failure.

4. THE FOREMEN'S UNION.   A newcomer into the union field is the Foremen's Association of America. Starting in August, 1941, it grew to a point where it has been a decisive influence in several labor disputes, particularly in the Detroit area. It is of particular interest because its membership is limited to supervisory employees. Some unions of operative employees have for a long time admitted supervisory employees to membership, but the F.A.A. is strictly a supervisor's union intended to advance the interests of the supervisor as its sole task and not as a minor by-product. For a while the legal status of foremen's unions was in doubt, but the Supreme Court of the United States ruled that, for purposes of collective bargaining, foremen are employees under the terms of the National Labor Relations Act. Under the Labor Management Relations Act, however, supervisors are excluded from the group of employees for purposes of bargaining. As a consequence, the growth and significance of this union have been stymied.

5. INDEPENDENT UNIONS.   Finally, there is a group of unions that act independently and are not associated with any national group. For this reason, they are called "independent" unions. Ordinarily, they are formed by employees of a given company, exclusively from which members may be selected, for the purpose of dealing solely with the company in question. Sometimes they take members from a group of companies in a given locality. When an independent union is formed to bargain with a particular company, it may also be called a "company" union. This connotation must be distinguished from company-dominated independent unions, which are outlawed by the L.M.R.A.

COMPARISON OF CRAFT AND INDUSTRIAL UNIONS

The relative merits of the craft unions of the AFL, the industrial unions of the CIO, and the independent or company unions are worth considering for a moment. First, the question of craft versus industrial unions has favorable answers on both sides. The craft unions are older, more settled, and presumably more attentive to the particular problems, and needs of given classes of workers. The industrial unions contend, however, that the crafts cater only to the "elite" of labor, disregard the millions of workers who belong to no craft, and have grown stagnant and conservative, if not reactionary. Hence the industrial unions have had more militant leadership, even going to the extent of participating actively in political elections, contrary to the policies of the AFL, held since the day of the leadership of Samuel Gompers. The Political Action Committee (the PAC, as it is commonly referred to) is evidence of the policy of the CIO. The AFL has changed its basic policy to the extent of attempting to influence politics through its Labor's Educational and Political League.

Moreover, the industrial unions contend that modern industry, with its interdependent links of various classes, groups of workers, and vocations, cannot be served effectively by craft unions that maintain an artificial separation of labor that encourages rather than reduces jurisdictional disputes. That the arguments of the CIO are appealing can be seen in its striking growth; but that the merits of the craft unions are also strong may be seen in the high level of membership that the AFL has maintained. Obviously, both have a place in the organized labor movement in the United States.

COMPARISON OF AFFILIATED AND INDEPENDENT UNIONS

The controversy between the affiliated and independent unions is also far from settled. The former have undoubtedly given the labor movement a more active and professional leadership than has characterized independent unions. In the latter, the leadership often does not have the training or time to gain the competence and skill to deal effectively in labor disputes. These shortcomings are offset, according to the proponents of independent unions, by the less truculent attitude, better understanding of local problems, and greater interest in settling the issues of local importance which leaders of independent unions possess. Back comes the argument from the proponents of affiliated unions that the independents are company-dominated, weak, and shortsighted. And so the charges and countercharges fly back and forth. Undoubtedly, each side has evidence to support its arguments. It is easy to find cases of good and bad leadership in the independent and in the affiliated unions. The "racketeer" is, for example, embarrassing to the well-intentioned leader of affiliated unions. But without the militant leadership of our large unions, it is difficult to see how unions could have made the rapid progress which, at least in their eyes, they have made.

THE LABOR MANAGEMENT RELATIONS ACT

As already noted, the Labor Management Relations Act (L.M.R.A.), which amended the National Labor Relations Act.

(N.L.R.A.) of 1935, is the federal legislation currently significant in organized relations and collective bargaining. It is based upon the power of Congress to regulate interstate commerce and applies, therefore, only to businesses which enter into or affect interstate commerce. In particular, Congress seeks through this law to reduce interferences to the free flow of such commerce caused by labor-management disputes. To this end, labor is given rights of organizing and collective bargaining. If management transgresses these rights, it is guilty, by definition of the Act, of unfair labor practices and therefore subject to punitive measures. On the other hand, management is provided with certain protections against certain practices of labor organizations stated to be unfair.

How management should operate under this Act and build its labor relations to conform with prescribed rules will now be discussed under the following headings:

1. Rights of employees
2. Rights of employers
3. Rights of unions
4. Coverage of the Act
5. Procedural rules

RIGHTS OF EMPLOYEES

The L.M.R.A. or the Taft-Hartley Act, as it is commonly called, cites five major rights possessed by employees, which, if obstructed by employers, become unfair labor practices. Employees are protected against:

1. Interference, restraint, or coercion of employees in the exercise of their right freely to organize
2. Domination and interference with the formation or administration of a labor organization
3. Encouragement or discouragement of membership in a labor organization by discrimination in regard to hire or tenure
4. Discrimination because of filing charges or giving testimony under the Act
5. Refusal to bargain collectively with properly chosen representatives of the employees

On the other hand, the employee has certain protections from certain union actions or relationships. Among these are the following:

1. The "closed shop," in which all workers eligible to belong to the union must be members in good standing, and new workers must become, or be, union members at time of hiring, is outlawed.
2. The "union shop," in which all employees must join a union after hiring,

is permissible only if a majority of all eligible workers (not just union members) have voted the union power to try to negotiate such a clause.

3. Dues may be deducted from an employee's pay check and turned over to the union by the employer only when this (the so-called "check-off") is authorized in writing. Such authorizations are good only for one year.

4. Employees do not have to pay initiation fees which, upon complaint by a worker or a group of workers to the National Labor Relations Board, are found to be excessive.

5. An employee can take his grievances through the union up to management, or do it alone if he so desires. Any settlements reached individually must not undermine the union contract.

6. Nonpayment of initiation fees and dues in a "union shop" is the only reason why a union can ask for a member's dismissal.

7. Union members are now entitled to annual union financial reports and to know how the union operates and spends its money.

8. Employee welfare funds must be administered through a joint employer-union board.

RIGHTS OF EMPLOYERS

The employer now has protection from practices which might be unfair to him. Among his rights are the following:

1. He may express himself freely about labor matters so long as no threat or coercion to employees is implied.

2. He may discharge, without obligation to rehire, employees who engage in illegal strikes, such as those intended to force employers to refuse to handle the products of another producer (the secondary boycott).

3. He may ask the N.L.R.B. that a vote be taken to determine whether or not a union claiming to be recognized as the bargaining agent has a majority of employees signed up.

4. He must bargain in good faith, but can now insist that the union also do so.

5. He can sue unions in the federal courts as entities, whose agents by their acts can be held liable.

6. He can set in force a sixty-day "cooling-off" period, before a strike can be legally called, when a contract is due to terminate or be modified.

7. He is freed from "featherbedding," or rules requiring that pay be given for work not done.

8. He may refuse to deal with unions whose officers have not signed "anti-communist" affidavits.

9. He may refuse to bargain with unions representing supervisors.

RIGHTS OF UNIONS

The Taft-Hartley Act has undoubtedly imposed certain responsibilities upon unions, as to both management and workers. On the other hand, practically all the rights which unions gained under the Wagner Act are still retained. To begin with, employees retained all rights to organize and bargain collectively through representatives of their own choosing. Moreover the union has the right, under proper conditions, to:

1. Ask the N.L.R.B. for recognition elections
2. Ask the employer to bargain in good faith
3. Represent all employees who were eligible to vote
4. Maintain its status for one year without fear of jurisdictional disputes
5. Represent all employees who ask its assistance in processing grievances
6. File charges with the N.L.R.B. against unfair labor practices
7. Appeal to various government boards or the courts
8. Call strikes

COVERAGE OF THE ACT

Not all companies and employees are subject to the provisions of the Act; but of those that are, management must be certain that it commits none of the unfair practices defined therein. There are three major tests of coverage, relating to businesses, employers, and employees concerned.

As already noted, "interstate commerce" is the governing test for businesses that are included in the provisions of the Act. The Act does not specify which businesses are subject to it but includes all those "affecting" interstate commerce. The Supreme Court, in cases arising under the earlier N.L.R.A., has interpreted the coverage so broadly that practically all businesses, interstate and intrastate, are affected. So long as the operations affect interstate commerce, even in the slightest way, the business is subject to this Act. Moreover, the business itself may be very small as measured by value of business or number of employees and still be nonexempt. For example, the Act was applied to a small coal company, local in nature, which delivered coal to customers who did interstate commerce and who purchased only a small percentage of their coal from the local dealer.

In the case of distributive businesses, the N.L.R.B. has taken jurisdiction when there is interstate shipment before and after sale of the product or when there is integration with interstate commerce. However, purely local retail sales have thus far been construed as exempt.

In summary, so long as the interstate test is met, the Act has been used to cover such a range of businesses as transportation, communication, retailing, manufacturing, mining, public utilities, banks, brokers, and insurance.

1. DEFINITION OF EMPLOYER. The definition of "employer" is equally broad. It pertains not only to the general areas of management normally understood to be the employer group but also to any person acting as an agent of an employer, directly or indirectly. A few examples will be helpful. In one case, two subsidiary companies were held to be employers. One of the companies acted as personnel agent, while the

other company was involved in the affairs of a union dominated by the first. The second company could not escape a charge of an unfair labor practice because the Board decided that the two companies functioned as an integrated system and hence both were "employers" as far as the union was concerned.

In another case, the Board held subsidiary operating companies to be the employers where one of the companies admitted it was the employer but that the other paid the wages of the employees. They were both subject to the same management and control; their operations were interrelated and interdependent; and the labor policies of both were controlled by the parent company.

In addition, no employer may move his plant to a new locality and then transfer it to a new and purportedly independent corporation without remaining the employer. He is still responsible for the unfair labor practice of the "independent" corporation.

Moreover, the rules of agency apply, and an employer is liable for the acts of his agents. Acts of his ordinary employees or outsiders may bind him only if he has given them authority, actual or implied, or if he has subsequently ratified their acts. Thus corporate officials when they are acting in the interest of their corporation are employers.

Excluded from the Act are employees of the United States or any state or political subdivision thereof. This exemption of the government from the operation of the Act, however, does not extend to all enterprises in which the government is interested. Also, employers subject to the Railway Labor Act are excluded from the term "employer" in the Act.

2. DEFINITION OF EMPLOYEE. The coverage of "employees" must also be known because the benefits of the Act are limited to those who qualify legally. In general, the term applies to all who normally would be considered employees. Of great import is the status of striking workers. Those who strike against an unfair labor practice of an employer are "employees" protected by the law against discrimination or replacement. Also, those who participate in an economic strike (in which a sixty-day notice of intent to strike has been given and during which time the status quo has been maintained) are employees. But those who participate in illegal strikes, e.g., boycotts, sympathetic strikes, jurisdictional strikes, and those to gain "featherbedding" rules, lose the benefits of the Act or may be enjoined by the courts to desist from such practices.

3. EXCEPTIONS. Several exceptions and exclusions are worthy of mention. Independent contractors are exempt only if they actually are completely independent of an employer who does not use this form of

relationship as a subterfuge to escape the provisions of the Act. Similarly, intermittent workers are excluded only if they actually are casual employees. Seasonal and part-time workers are not generally construed to be "employees." Excluded also are agricultural labor, domestics in the service of a family or person at his home, and persons employed by a parent or spouse. Of particular interest is the exclusion of supervisors, the attempted unionization of whom under the N.L.R.A. was opposed by many employers.

OPERATIONS UNDER THE ACT

Although the operation of the N.L.R.A. was completely under the jurisdiction of the National Labor Relations Board, an important change has been established under the Labor Management Relations Act. Under the latter, the N.L.R.B., which consists of five members appointed by the President with the consent of the United States Senate, is established as a judicial body, a labor court, except for cases concerned with which unions shall be certified as the representative of the employees. The administrative functions of the Act are assigned to a General Counsel. This individual, appointed as are the Board members, is responsible for investigating charges of unfair labor practices, issuing complaints, and prosecution of unfair labor practices. It is estimated that he is able to settle a majority of cases in the field, on behalf of the Board. In a word, the administrative duties and the judicial functions have, under the L.M.R.A., been separated.

In cases in which the Board finds unfair practices, its orders, however, are ineffective in and of themselves. There are no fines or penalties for its violation. The Board may find very flagrant practices and require full remedial action to correct conditions brought about by the practices. But whatever the provisions of the order and however flagrant the conditions disclosed by the findings of fact, there are further necessary and important proceedings before the order has the slightest legal compulsion. These are set forth in Section 10 (e), which empowers the Board to petition any circuit court of appeals within the circuit wherein the unfair labor practice in question occurred or wherein the person proceeded against resides or transacts business, for the enforcement of the order. The jurisdiction of the court is exclusive, and its judgment and decree are final except upon review under the statutes governing writs of certiorari granted by the Supreme Court of the United States [Section 10 (e)].

Any person aggrieved by the order of the Board may likewise obtain a review of a Board order by petitioning the appropriate circuit court of appeals to have the order set aside. He files with the court the record certified by the Board. In all essentials the case then becomes a court proceeding like that resulting from a petition of the Board for enforcement. The court has the same power to enforce as well as set aside or modify and enforce as so modified [Section 10 (f)]. Only after court approval of the order does it carry legal compulsion. Violation of it then becomes contempt of court, with such fines or penalties as the court may consider appropriate.

CONTRACTUAL RELATIONSHIPS

THE UNION CONTRACT

The machinery of the Taft-Hartley Act has one purpose—to facilitate the process of collective bargaining. In other words, it does not prevent disputes or settle them. It serves to bring labor and management together so that they may resolve their difficulties and arrive at agreements as to how they shall work together. It requires all parties to bargain and confer in good faith.

This agreement—the union contract (it is as much a management contract)—for a specified period of time outlines the relations between the employer and the employee. Hence the employer should exercise every care (which many have not in the past, to their own sorrow) to arrive at an agreement that will be reasonably satisfactory. Perhaps the most serious failure of management has been caused by the following, in some instances:

1. Top management has attempted to carry on bargaining without aid from experts.
2. The personnel department has been incapable of supplying management with expert advice and service.
3. The suggestions and advice of line executives have not been sought or have been disregarded.
4. Preparations for negotiation were inadequate.
5. Interdependency of contract clauses has not been recognized.

For a number of years after the Wagner Act was passed, many top executives attempted to carry on the work of bargaining with unions. Although they recognized the need for experts in such fields as engineering, purchasing, sales, and production, they felt capable of handling personnel functions themselves. The results were as expected. The unions, with full-time specialists on their staffs, gained many concessions unnoticed by the top executives, who seemed to think that wages alone were of importance in union negotiations. The advantages gained by unions in regard to such matters as grievance machinery, seniority rules, and discharge rules are evidences of the ineptness displayed by some top executives.

Again, personnel departments in some companies were little more than employment clerks and record keepers, so that they were in no position to advise management in negotiations. Indeed, the personnel manager seemed to be the last one to consult in such instances. Although lawyers were often called in, the company personnel department was invariably ignored. Only in recent years has there been a growing tendency to develop a strong labor relations division in the personnel department and to make it responsible for handling contract negotiations.

Many companies have also failed to avail themselves of suggestions and advice of line executives, who must "live" with union contracts. Many supervisors first hear of a union contract by being told that one has been signed and that they are expected to adhere to it. Yet, were their suggestions sought, they could have told management what types of clauses to avoid and which to seek in order to make the task of working with employees more pleasant and efficient. Some companies have "seen the light" and discuss with line executives all phases of union contracts before and after they are signed.

In this connection, preparation for negotiation deserves special mention. Management simply cannot afford to assume that it can bluster its way through contract negotiations and renegotiations. It should begin its preparations by keeping careful records, day by day, of how it is getting along with its present contract. Such instances as grievances, unrest, disciplinary action, and other difficulties should be noted under the sections or clauses of the current contract to which they pertain. Then, too, those who "live with" the contract should be asked—well in advance of negotiation dates—what changes or additions they feel are needed. It is also imperative to compare one's contract or conditions with those in his own area or industry. Since the new contract will deal with the future, it is also necessary to forecast economic and political conditions for the forthcoming period. With all the foregoing information, it should then be possible, first, to prepare the case to be submitted to the union and, second, to anticipate with factual arguments the possible demands of the union. Preparation for negotiations would not be complete, however, unless avenues of information and executive counsel are provided for, to which quick recourse may be had as the actual negotiations are under way.

And, finally, many companies have failed to recognize the interdependency of contract clauses. In their anxiety to clear up wage matters, for example, other clauses have been accepted by management with apparently no review whatsoever. As a consequence, it is later found that more has been lost in the other clauses than could ever be gained from the wage negotiations. Moreover, once unions gain concessions on working conditions, for example, they seldom give them up, no matter how arbitrary or unsatisfactory they may be to management. To reduce the number of such cases, the total implications of specific clauses should be determined.

CONTRACT CLAUSES

The range of subjects covered in union contracts does not differ significantly. These usually include:

1. Management prerogatives	6. Seniority
2. Union recognition	7. Working conditions
3. Hours of work	8. Layoffs and rehirings
4. Wages	9. Arbitration and mediator
5. Vacations and holidays	10. Renewal clauses

The detail and treatment of these subjects differ so much that it is impractical even to begin to cite examples here. On the other hand, most of these subjects are discussed in preceding or succeeding chapters. In a sense, the union contract merely formalizes what should be good personnel practice on all these subjects. However, some comment is needed on management prerogatives, union recognition, renewal clauses, and intercompany co-operation.

1. MANAGEMENT PREROGATIVES. A clause of management prerogatives pertains to the rights, responsibilities, and areas of action which it retains, free from questioning or joint action by the union. It may be stated in general terms such as the following:

Except as otherwise in this agreement expressly provided, nothing in this agreement contained shall be deemed to limit the company in any way in the exercise of the regular and customary functions of management, including the making in connection therewith of such rules relating to operations as it shall deem advisable.

Or it may be more explicit, as in the following:

Nothing in this agreement shall limit the company in the exercise of its function of management, under which it shall have, among others, the right to hire new employees and to direct the working force; to discipline, suspend, discharge for cause; transfer or lay off employees because of lack of work; to require employees to observe company rules and regulations, not inconsistent with the provisions of this agreement; to decide the number and location of its plants, products to be manufactured, the methods and schedules of production, including the means and processes of manufacturing, provided that the company will not use these prerogatives for the purpose of discrimination. It is agreed that these enumerations of management prerogatives shall not be deemed to exclude other prerogatives not enumerated.

The former is preferred by some because it is general and all-inclusive. However, those who favor the latter argue that generalized clauses leave its meaning open to questioning by the union. But the latter is weak in the sense that what is not specifically reserved by management is presumably open to bargaining or union action. Some students also feel that all prerogative clauses are useless because labor will not countenance them if it feels its rights injured. Moreover, labor is moving in on so many areas that were once construed to be "out of bounds" that there are few, if any, subjects that have not come within the scope of bargaining in some company or another.[1]

2. RECOGNITION OF UNION CLAUSE. Whereas clauses of management's prerogatives are not written into all contracts, clauses covering union recognition and prerogatives are invariably included. The "recognition" clause is necessary to indicate specifically the bargaining agency and the unit covered. Although not universal practice, the rights of unions and permissible activities are also included. Examples of clauses in this category are the following:

1. The Company recognizes the Union as the sole representative of its hourly and piece rate employees, including employees in the retail store, but excluding executive supervisory employees, watchmen, office employees, and technical advisers, for the purpose of collective bargaining in respect to rates of pay, wages, hours of work, and other conditions of employment.
2. The Company recognizes the Union as the sole collective bargaining agency of the workers in those departments in which the Union has a majority of the workers.
3. Union activities may be conducted by employees on the Company property on the free time of such employees, but, except as provided herein under the subject of "Grievances," the Union shall not engage in any Union business, discussions, or activities during working hours, and shall not solicit memberships, collect dues, or conduct organizing activities on the Company property on the Company time. The Company will not permit any anti-Union activities or discussions during working hours.
4. The Union agrees that neither its officers, nor its members, nor persons employed directly or indirectly by the Union, will intimidate or coerce employees; nor will it solicit members on Company time.
5. The Company recognizes and will not interfere with the right of em-

---

[1] Worth watching in this connection is the movement toward "co-determination," in Germany, where labor representatives by law are given a place on the Board of Directors. The exclusive rights of management are in such an event completely diluted.

ployees to become members of the Union and will not discriminate against employees because of their Union affiliation. The Union agrees not to intimidate or coerce employees into membership. The Union also agrees not to solicit membership or dues during working hours.

3. RENEWAL CLAUSES. The term of the contract and arrangements for renewals are also included in union contracts. Two examples of such clauses are shown in the following:

1. This agreement shall remain in force for one year from the date hereof and shall automatically renew itself from year to year, unless written notice of desire to terminate or to modify any portion or any of the terms hereof, is given by either party to the other at least thirty days prior to the expiration of any such annual period.

   If notice of desire to terminate or to amend shall have been given, negotiations for a new or amended agreement shall begin not later than twenty days prior to the expiration of the current yearly period and shall continue until an agreement has been reached. During such negotiations, this agreement shall remain in full force and effect, provided however that, if negotiations continue beyond the termination of the annual period, either party may then terminate this agreement at any time upon thirty days' written notice to the other party.

2. This agreement becomes effective as of May 1, 19——, and shall remain in effect until May 1, 19——, and each year thereafter unless written notice of cancellation or changes desired is given sixty days prior to any yearly expiration date by any of the other parties of this agreement. If changes or amendments are desired, such written notice shall contain a complete list of the changes and amendments proposed. In that case, conferences shall be arranged to begin during the fifteen days immediately following the sixty days' notice date.

4. INTERCOMPANY CO-OPERATION. Although union-management relations are generally handled by each company on an individualized basis, there are instances in which bargaining and dispute settlements have been handled on an industry-wide or area basis. An example which comes to mind at once is the coal industry. Here the UMW has carried on bargaining with the coal operators through their southern, northern, and anthracite producers groups. Agreements must be approved, however, by the individual companies and local unions with whom contracts are signed. Another interesting approach is found in the Mountain States Employers Council. This group, composed largely of employers in Wyoming, New Mexico, and Colorado, provides such services as information on wages, personnel policies, and labor relations; a staff to assist on negotiations; holding management workshops and conferences; and publishing bulletins and surveys.[2] Some of the larger

[2] *Business Week*, December 12, 1953, pp. 164–66.

airlines have also experimented with group talks with a view to conducting mediation before troubles get far out of line and to negotiating upon an informal basis.

Also of significance are attempts in various cities to bring all interested parties together with a view to better labor-management relations. The Labor-Management Citizens Council of Toledo is an excellent case in point.[3] The Committee has been established by the City Council but acts on an independent basis through a committee of eighteen members. It discusses current industrial problems, formulates policies, and helps settle disputes through available mediation, conciliation, and arbitration services. By bringing community and civic interests to bear upon industrial problems, this plan has exercised a constructive influence on current problems. Variations of this program have been undertaken in a number of other cities, including Boston, San Francisco. St. Louis, Buffalo, Minneapolis, Newark, Pittsburgh, Tacoma, and South Bend.

CONCLUSION

No attempt has been made here to indicate how management should react to the labor movement. This involves broad matters of policy and forces whose analysis requires much more space than is available here. For example, it is imperative to assay correctly whether the leadership of a union with which one is dealing is motivated by economic or political objectives and whether it feels that its objectives can be best attained by peaceful means or only by more drastic, forceful pressures.

All that could be done here, therefore, has been to outline the minimum considerations and safeguards of which management must be aware. And it is also hoped that from this chapter (and from the three that follow) will be derived the conclusion that the basis for good union-management relations is essentially found in good personnel practices and human relations—union or no union!

QUESTIONS AND PROBLEMS

1. As you view the history of labor-management relations in this country, do you think progress is being made? Why or why not?
2. In your own philosophy of collective bargaining, do you lean toward optimism or pessimism as to the use of logic in settling disputes? Can you explain why you lean as you do? If you lean toward the feeling that "strong-arm" tactics are best, what courses of study should you pursue? If you feel otherwise, what courses should you pursue?
3. Define the term "collective bargaining." Examine your definition, to be cer-

[3] *Labor Law Journal,* October, 1952, Vol. III, No. 10, pp. 663–76.

tain that it does not contain ambiguities. How would you explain the contention of some students that collective bargaining cannot be defined when you have just finished defining it?

4. If collective bargaining is to bring out reasonably satisfactory agreements between labor and management, what attitudes and information must all parties bring to the bargaining table? Is it probable that such conditions can be approximated?

5. Distinguish between the terms "closed shop," "union shop," "preferential shop," and "open shop."

6. Why do you suppose some employers object so strenuously to the checkoff and maintenance of membership?

7. One of the objectives of the L.M.R.A. as specified by Congress is that it is intended to reduce interferences to interstate commerce arising out of labor disputes. If that is so, how do you explain the large number of strikes that grew out of the organization of labor and collective bargaining?

8. After the passage of the N.L.R.A., an employer concluded that, since he could not obstruct unionization, he would kill it in his plant by kindness and gifts. To what extent, if at all, were his intentions legal?

9. What constitutes a threat under the L.M.R.A.? If an employer says that he will go out of business if his employees organize, is that an unfair labor practice? If it is, does not a ruling to prevent him from going out of business constitute an interference with his own freedom of private property?

10. How would you as an employer protect yourself against possible charges that you demoted or promoted individuals to obstruct union organization?

11. A foreman, after working hours, in his own home and, unknown to his company, condemns unions before a group of his workers. Would he or would he not subject his company to possible prosecution? Why or why not?

12. Why have personnel managers sometimes proved useless to management when dealing with unions?

13. What can first-line executives, such as supervisors, contribute to collective bargaining? Suggest ways by which their help and counsel can be obtained without undue waste of time and innumerable conferences?

14. Show how such a clause as that pertaining to vacations is related to wage clauses. To seniority clauses. To management prerogative clauses.

15. What are management's prerogatives? Some people claim that management has no prerogatives, only responsibilities. What do you think?

16. Some claim that a union contract is also a management contract. Do you agree, or not?

17. It has been argued that eventually union contracts will become as long as a "big-city" telephone book. Why would such lengths be desirable? Undesirable?

18. Try your hand at writing a seniority clause by taking a case such as that of streetcar motormen. Indicate in your clause what happens in the event a motorman is promoted to supervisor, a supervisor is demoted to motorman, and interchanges take place between motormen and repairmen.

19. When union activities are performed by the members of the union upon a rotation basis rather than a permanent full-time basis, what advantages does that have for the company?

20. During a conference between the plant manager, personnel manager, and chief shop steward (union representative) of a given company in regard to a proposed pension plan, a number of disagreements became apparent. The plant manager stated that pension plans did no good so far as younger employees were concerned; the personnel manager stated that he was going to have one put in anyhow; and the chief steward insisted that the benefit payments as stated in the proposal be doubled. Discuss this case from the viewpoint of organizational and managerial principles.

CHAPTER

22

Handling Grievances[1]

Perhaps the most common impression of labor-management relations is that they are generally unsatisfactory. When it is seen that time lost through strikes—the most violent expression of employee dissatisfaction —averages less than 1 per cent of total man-hours of work, the common impression is subject to question. But what may be lost day in and day out by employees who are at work but who are not working to their full capacities because of dissatisfaction with some aspect of their working conditions has never been measured or estimated. The general opinion is, however, that such industrial unrest is one of the greatest causes of losses in productivity.

If this is so, then it behooves management to exert every effort to reduce employee dissatisfactions. Whether management proceeds on an individual basis or operates in conjunction with unions, it is argued here that the basic steps and principles of handling grievances—the particular subject of dissatisfactions discussed in this chapter—are much the same. Hence grievance handling is taken up here first without reference to union relations. Then note is made of some specific grievance procedures of interest when unions are involved. In either case, emphasis is to be placed upon the role of line executives and supervisors in grievance handling. While specialized staff personnel departments may assist through program development, policy planning, and procedural designs, the heart of good grievance procedures—as of all good labor relations methods—will be found in expert line management. Specifically, the subject of grievances is discussed here under the following broad headings:

1. Basic considerations of grievance handling
2. Steps in handling grievances

---

[1] The author is indebted to the Ohio Fuel Gas Company for some materials used in this chapter and the next two.

441

3. Principles of handling grievances
4. Union-management relations in grievance machinery

BASIC CONSIDERATIONS

MEANING OF GRIEVANCES

Although definitions are sometimes considered sophomoric, in few cases are definitions more useful than in the case of grievances. This is so because failure to recognize as grievances matters that are grievances is almost certain to result in troubles going unnoticed until they have become serious and difficult to handle. Although various experts disagree over the wording of the definition, the major factors of grievances are easily noted.

Perhaps the safest course to pursue is to give the broadest possible scope to the term "grievance." It means any discontent or dissatisfaction, whether expressed or not and whether valid or not, arising out of anything connected with the company that an employee thinks, believes, or even "feels," is unfair, unjust, or inequitable. This definition covers a lot of ground, but it serves to reduce the possibility of overlooking any grievances. When this course is pursued, there is real assurance that grievances will be minimized.

IMPLICATIONS OF THE DEFINITION

To understand the implications of this definition, it is desirable to analyze it. In the first place, when discussing grievances, stress may be laid upon the causes of trouble or upon the resulting trouble. For example, if an employee is disgruntled because he was not given a desired raise, some would call the unreceived raise the grievance, whereas others would call the disgruntled attitude the grievance. Obviously, the two must go together. Thus the mere fact that a raise was not granted is not a grievance unless the particular employee is dissatisfied about it. Furthermore, it must be assumed that the dissatisfaction is going to have some adverse effect upon the efforts of the employee.

In the second place, of particular interest to management are problems arising out of something connected with the company. This statement has two pertinent aspects. On the one hand, it recognizes that anything—activity, policy, supervision, etc.—in the company may be the source of grievances. Nothing, nor anyone, may be above being, at one time or another, and to some person or another, a cause of dissatisfaction. And, on the other hand, it limits sources of trouble to the boundary lines of the company. But, in addition, workers may be dissatisfied because of trouble at home, because they do not like the way the country is being run, or for dozens of other reasons. Such outside sources are beyond the control of the company and its executives, except in the sense that employees who insist upon bringing outside troubles into the company can be requested to leave them out or to seek employment elsewhere. Even in such cases the supervisor or personnel department may try to help an employee clear up his own troubles.

In the third place, the definition recognizes that discontent may be expressed or implied. It must be noted here, however, that some companies will recognize as grievances only those that are expressed in writing. This may serve to formalize the processes of the grievance procedure. But it would not be wise to assume that no discontent exists unless it is in writing. On the contrary, implied grievances are very dangerous because it is not known when they may "explode." Moreover, the damage which dissatisfied workers do to productivity goes on unimpaired. Hence effort should be exerted at such times to make certain that there are no smouldering materials of unrest.

And, finally, the definition recognizes that the injustice or unfairness may be a matter of emotional reaction or rational analysis. The point is that when a grievance is held by an employee, it will not be removed by concluding that "it's just the employee's opinion, and besides he is wrong." Indeed, the hardest grievances to handle are those based upon emotionalism, misconceptions, and lack of thinking.

MACHINERY FOR HANDLING GRIEVANCES

Although a technical matter, channels for handling grievances should be carefully developed and information thereof thoroughly disseminated. The labor relations department, various levels of executives, and the employees should know what relationships exist among them and how the various groups should work together. As noted earlier, it is assumed that grievances are handled by the company and the employees themselves, or through unions.

1. ROLE OF THE SUPERVISOR. It is, of course, imperative that employees know the channels that they may use in presenting grievances. Ordinarily, the supervisor should be accorded the first opportunity to handle grievances. Employees should be required to present their grievances to their supervisors, whether or not the grievances are finally disposed of by them. Unless this rule is established and enforced, supervisors will soon lose face with employees and become unimportant cogs in the organization. Allowing aggrieved employees to by-pass supervisors and to take their complaints to higher executives or to the labor

FIGURE 75. Chart of Grievance Machinery*

* Reprinted by courtesy of Thompson Products, Inc., Cleveland, Ohio.

relations department weakens unnecessarily a key factor of management.

2. INTERMEDIATE AGENCIES. All grievances cannot be handled by supervisors because many of them involve issues or policies beyond the limits of supervisory authority or capacity. Hence provision should be made for a second step in handling grievances. In some companies this is done by providing that employees with unsettled grievances are to be sent to the labor relations department. Other companies specify that employees are to be sent to the next supervisor or line executive, e.g., the shop superintendent or the office manager, as the case might be. This stage provides the facilities of additional knowledge and authority and will often be sufficient to resolve most of the difficulties that the first line of supervision cannot.

3. ADMINISTRATIVE LEVELS. Since the second level of appeal will be incapable of handling some of the grievances involving company-wide issues or many groups of employees, machinery should provide for ready access to the administrative levels of the organization. Either the top executive of the company, by himself or in committee with administrative line and staff executives, should be established as a final court of appeal. To be effective, this court must prove itself in action and not merely brag of its "open-door" policy.

4. UNION ASPECTS. And, finally, the union may play an important role in how grievances are channeled to and from company and union-organization levels. This phase of the subject will be discussed later in this chapter.

5. ILLUSTRATING THE CHANNELS. These channels of communication should be drawn up so that charts or pictures of them can be distributed to supervisors and employees. Figure 10 (p. 71) illustrates the use of a formal chart to serve this purpose. In Figure 75 is shown a descriptive cartoon-type chart used to acquaint employees with the steps which may be taken in seeking the settlement of grievances. It is an excellent example of a plan of disseminating information which attracts the eye, holds the attention, and clearly describes the steps involved.

STEPS IN HANDLING GRIEVANCES

Throughout all stages of handling grievances, there are a number of steps that should be taken if the probabilities of removing discontent are to be increased. These phases of the process will be little more than mechanical routine, however, unless the reasons why they are taken and the principles upon which they are based are thoroughly understood. Hence the materials in this section on steps of handling grievances and the materials in the next section on principles are related and interdependent, though for convenience of discussion they are taken up separately. In handling grievances, the following steps should be taken:

1. Define, describe, or express the nature of the grievance as clearly and as fully as possible
2. Gather all the facts that serve to explain when, how, where, to whom, and why the grievance occurred
3. Establish tentative solutions or answers to the grievance
4. Gather additional information to check the validity of the tentative solutions, and thus ascertain the best possible solution
5. Apply the solution
6. Follow up the case to see that it has been handled satisfactorily and the trouble eliminated[2]

1. Describing Grievances.   As stated, Step 1 assumes that the grievance has been expressed. However, this may not always be the case. When grievances are not expressed, there nevertheless may be discontent. In such cases, Step 1 should read: "Know or find out what employees are thinking that may affect their attitude toward the company." Attitude surveys, as noted in an earlier chapter, would be useful in this respect.

a) Determining the Correct Grievance.   Many grievances, after being "settled," turn up again to plague management. The trouble in such instances invariably is that the wrong grievance has been handled. This could have been avoided if care had been taken at the outset to describe as accurately as possible the issue at the heart of the employee's complaint. As it is, superficial aspects of grievances are adjusted while the fundamental cause of trouble remains untouched.

As a common case in point, employees often ask for raises when what really troubles them are such things as uncertainty about their jobs, a supervisor's failure to be polite, preference being given to a fellow worker, and an employee's dislike for the type of gloves the company is issuing. These matters are often difficult for the average employee to express in what he considers reasonable terms, yet they do irritate him. The irritation continues until he decides consciously or unconsciously to use wages as a basis for his complaint. And when the wage case is cleared, management is later surprised to find that something is still disturbing the "ungrateful" employee.

Another case will serve to illustrate the difficulty of being sure of the exact nature of a grievance. An employee in a war plant complained

---

[2] Contrast these steps with those included in the job relations training program discussed on pages 275–76.

to his grievance committee that his supervisor was picking on him. The committee heard the case, at which time the employee submitted a list of alleged discriminations, such as being assigned more than his share of tough jobs and being reprimanded excessively and without just cause. The supervisor had to admit that such jobs were assigned and that he had to reprimand the employee in question but contended that other employees were similarly treated without bias or prejudice. The committee suggested that the supervisor use greater consideration in dealing with the employee, but the aggrieved employee continued his complaints. A more thorough investigation into the employee's past history disclosed a highly developed personal feeling of insecurity. When this complex was cleared up and the baselessness of the fear disclosed, this employee stopped complaining.

The foregoing two cases are not intended to prove that employees do not have the courage to express their real grievances or do not really know the real nature of their complaints. On the contrary, employees in industry today are registering many thoughtful complaints, and they do "kick up their heels" over a wide variety of issues. The point is that if the diagnosis of a grievance is wrong or incorrectly stated, the prescription is almost bound to be useless, if, indeed, it does not lead to other trouble.

Whether or not a grievance, once determined, should be written up is an important element of the grievance and company policy. In order to encourage more careful consideration of grievances and to keep the record straight, better practice indicates the wisdom of putting grievances in writing. A good example of a form for this purpose and one that would be useful for recording the entire "history" of a case is shown in Figure 76 (p. 448). This form could also be used in disciplinary cases.

b) Unexpressed Grievances. The foregoing has assumed that an employee in one way or another makes known his grievances. There are cases, however, when individual grievances go unexpressed and unexposed for long periods of time. Were these discovered early, the intensity of feeling which is ultimately expressed would be largely minimized. Hence line executives should be encouraged to develop a "seventh" sense for incipient grievances. This does not mean that executives should go looking for trouble; but "little" troubles, discovered early, can be handled more easily than those that grow to dangerous proportions.

The techniques of attitude surveys and statistical interpretations are also invaluable in this connection. As noted in Chapter 15, the attitude survey is a very useful device for discovering grievances. Another

FIGURE 76

THE OHIO FUEL GAS COMPANY
INCIDENT REPORT

REPORTED BY _____

Name	Position	TO		Location
Name	Title		Name	Title

DETERMINE OBJECTIVE — What I am trying to accomplish —

1. GET THE FACTS
(Be sure you have the whole story)

2. WEIGH AND DECIDE
(Don't jump at conclusions)
(Possible actions)

3. ACTION I HAVE TAKEN

RECOMMENDED ACTION FOR MY SUPERVISOR
(Don't Pass the Buck)

4. CHECK RESULTS

Condition Found _____ Date _____

Condition Found _____ Date _____

HOW TO HANDLE A PROBLEM
DETERMINE OBJECTIVES

1.—GET THE FACTS.
  Review the record.
  Find out what rules and plant customs apply.
  Talk with individuals concerned.
  Get opinions and feelings.
  Be sure you have the whole story.

2.—WEIGH AND DECIDE.
  Fit the facts together.
  Consider their bearing on each other.
  What possible actions are there?
  Check practices and policies.
  Consider objective and effect on individual, group, and production.
  Don't jump at conclusions.

3.—TAKE ACTION.
  Are you going to handle this yourself?
  Do you need help in handling?
  Should you refer this to your supervisor?
  Watch the timing of your action.
  Don't pass the buck.

4.—CHECK RESULTS.
  How soon will you follow up?
  How often will you need to check?
  Watch for changes in output, attitudes, and relationships.
  Did your action help production?

DID YOUR ACTION, HELP TO SOLVE YOUR PROBLEM?

If you were the employee involved, would you be satisfied with the action taken?

CHECK RESULTS _____ DID YOUR ACTION SOLVE YOUR PROBLEM? _____ HAS THIS INCIDENT BEEN HANDLED TO THE SATISFACTION

OF THE EMPLOYEE? _____ FOREMAN? _____ SUPERINTENDENT? _____ MANAGEMENT? _____ HOW OFTEN HAS THIS CASE BEEN FOLLOWED UP

BY YOU? _____ DAYS, WEEKS? _____ HAVE YOU SEEN ANY CHANGES IN OUTPUT, ATTITUDE, RELATIONSHIPS?

BETTER OR WORSE? _____

APPROVED: _____

Could this problem be avoided through the use of the foundations?

example is the contest conducted by the General Motors Corporation on the subject of "Why I Like My Job." In this case, areas not mentioned in the tabulation of "likes" were construed to be indicative of possible or potential dislikes. And statistical summaries and trends of turnover, complaints, transfers, earnings, sources of suggestions and lack thereof, etc., can provide excellent clues regarding actual or probable grievances.

This task of anticipating grievances must be followed with extreme care. Only by exercising painstaking caution is it possible to discover what is bothering employees before they themselves are aware of grievances. Moreover, unless precautionary measures are taken, it is possible to make employees suspicious of the supervisor's efforts. Even though the ultimate purpose of looking for grievances is to relieve the minds of the employees, they may assume that spying for undesirable ends is going on. When employees distrust their supervisors, it is indeed difficult to remove the doubts.

The anticipatory method of discovering and defining otherwise unexpressed grievances must be based upon unobtrusive observation. The best method is to make a careful study of the behaviorisms, attitudes, expressions, and habits of each employee. This takes time, but the effort is decidedly worth the cost. When, after a long period of study, a supervisor has "sized up" a given employee, it will be easy to note significant changes.

For example, a certain employee who had always been noted for his neat appearance began to grow less tidy. In the rush of work, the supervisor in question did not notice this until it was later pointed out to him as a "sign" that he had failed to see. The change had occurred immediately after the employee in question was passed over in a promotion. He seemingly gave up trying, although he did not immediately turn into a complainer. Had the supervisor noticed the change, he might have deduced that the employee was discontented because of the failure to receive what he thought was a warranted advancement. His conclusion, although erroneous, should have been corrected immediately, and would have been corrected, had the supervisor in question been more observant. The labor relations department can be helpful by training supervisors to become proficient in observing employees.

2. GATHERING FACTS.   Having defined grievances as accurately as possible, the next step is to gather all relevant facts about the issue. It is important to know when the alleged grievance was first experienced, whether or not it has been repeated, how and where it took place, and the circumstances under which it transpired. This does not imply that

grievances should be handled like law cases. It does mean that if the confidence of the employee is to be gained and held, he must be thoroughly convinced that management is completely sincere in seeing that justice is done. Such fact gathering or sifting requires a knack in interviewing and listening to employees, the principles of which will be reviewed later.

a) Nature of Facts. Besides serving to convince the employee of the employer's sincerity, the step of gathering data is indispensable to a fair decision. But what are facts? That question is, in most cases, more easily asked than answered. Of course, if an employee complains that he did not get a promotion because his supervisor was unfair, it is possible to get some hard facts to bear on the case. It can often be shown that the successful candidate had more experience and more training, made more suggestions, been rated higher, etc. Yet there are times when it is impossible to prove positively that the facts on one side were "heavier." Unless the losing candidate then has confidence in the judgment of management, the grievance will not be cleared up.

Along these lines, in gathering the story from the employee, the facts must be separated from the opinions. Again, this is not easy. For example, some of his opinions about himself or management stem from their respective roles in the industrial social world. Such status evaluations are usually interchangeable only after long years of education and attitude molding. An employee may believe that he deserves a raise. That is his opinion, and it must either be proved to be an unwarranted opinion or be accepted as the truth, and the raise therefore recommended. And here is the test of a fact. Does it hold true or not? If a claim or statement cannot be substantiated to the satisfaction of a reasonable person, it is an opinion. If an employee can, however, prove a claim, the grievance is based on facts. As noted above, however, many things in the realm of dealing with people are yet and are likely to remain for a long time in the field of opinions. As a consequence, confidence in each other must be sought by both parties.

b) Importance of Records. Since fact gathering is not an easy task, after a grievance arises it is perhaps wise to develop a set of records and keep them up to date. For example, such records as merit rating, job rating, attendance records, educational and business records, and suggestions are particularly invaluable. They serve to show in advance, for example, who should get a promotion and to warn others why their chances of advancing are not good.

3. ESTABLISHING TENTATIVE SOLUTIONS. After getting a clear picture of the grievance, the next step in the procedure calls for the establishment of tentative solutions or answers. This step—to digress

for a moment—is indispensable to that of gathering information vital to arriving at a final solution. It is impossible to arrive at a final decision except by guessing or gathering facts. Ruling out the guessing method, it is useless to gather facts unless the purpose for which the facts are being gathered is known. The tentative solutions provide the basis for the fact gathering, which will in turn indicate the tentative solutions to be rejected and the one to be accepted.

The method suggested here is similar to that employed by a scientist in the laboratory. The chemist, for example, does not carry on experiments willy-nilly. Instead, he sets up a tentative solution and then runs an experiment to see whether he is right or wrong. If the experiment fails, he has to start with another tentative solution, and he proceeds this way until he finds the right answer. The significant point is that the experiments he runs are specifically set up to prove or disprove a tentative solution.

And so, too, in handling grievances, management must make a list of alternate solutions and later test them. In compiling possible solutions, management need not at the time make them known to the worker. It is usually better to reserve judgment until some opportunity is afforded to check them. Of course, if an immediate answer is required, the selection of the "right" answer will be dependent upon the experience, training, and good judgment of the executive involved.

But how are tentative solutions determined? In the first place, management has its own experience to fall back upon. Very likely it will have had similar cases in the past, and these should provide it with the perspective required to figure out solutions applicable to the present case. In addition, it should have observed how other companies have handled similar grievances. In the third place, alternative answers may be collected from technical and trade publications. And if all the foregoing fail, the best possible guesses will have to be made. The important point is that a thorough search, commensurate with the importance of the case, should be made for alternative solutions.

4. CHECKING TENTATIVE SOLUTIONS. Some of the work required here will already have been performed in earlier steps because in all of them much information will have been gathered. At this stage, it is necessary to take each bit of available information and opinions and to match it against the possible solutions. If sufficient information is not already available, a search for more will have to be made. This will involve such things as further conference with the aggrieved employee, looking through the employee's past record, and perhaps questioning of other employees and supervisors.

More specifically, it involves the practical step of proving or disproving the wisdom of suggested solutions by determining whether or not the employee's dissatisfaction would be made to disappear without loss to either interested party. Let us assume that an employee who has not received a desired transfer complains about it. After making certain that the grievance is accurately stated, let us assume further that management has tentatively concluded that the employee in question did not deserve the transfer. It should check its conclusion by going back over the various records. This survey, let us say, shows that a transfer had been warranted. In that case, the first conclusion is in error and another must be tested—the employee should be given a transfer. This in turn, let us say, proves not to be feasible at the moment. Then a third solution presents itself—the employee should be given a transfer at the earliest possible moment. This is tested by seeing whether other employees have been promised transfers and whether vacancies are likely to be opened. If the solution is favorable, the final conclusion is accepted for application.

In this step, then, the alternative solutions are checked by all available information. Sometimes, in the process, additional solutions may be suggested. The ones added should be thrown into the hopper and examined in their appropriate turn.

5. APPLYING SOLUTIONS.   Having reached a decision, it seems common sense that it should be applied. Yet it is not uncommon to find executives who shrink from making an unfavorable, although warranted, decision. Indeed, some avoid making decisions favorable to employees for fear of "spoiling" them or because it would signify that they were wrong in the first place. Yet there are few things that subordinates dislike more than supervisors who refuse to take a definite stand, one way or the other. To be sure, all of us like to receive favorable news, but that does not mean that employees will not accept unfavorable decisions. On the contrary, they will, particularly when they are certain that the decision is based upon a thorough study of the facts and is passed on to them, not vindictively, but in a matter-of-fact way. Moreover, they do not have respect for executives who pass out favorable decisions that are unfair to the company or to some employees, just to get on the "good side" of the employees in general.

The decision, having finally been reached, should then be passed along in clear unequivocal terms. After all, a grievance cannot be handled just by listening to an employee's complaint; something must be done about it. The ultimate decision is the tool of action.

6. FOLLOW-UP OF THE GRIEVANCE.   It is unsafe to conclude that a grievance has been well handled until a check is made to determine

whether the employee's attitude has been favorably changed. To assure themselves along these lines, executives concerned need a timetable and a method of follow-up.

So far as a timetable is concerned, too many executives rely upon their memories to check on how grievances have been handled. This way has its strong points; but, if there is any danger of forgetting, a written record should be made. These records are a bit more cumbersome, but avoiding serious loss is worth the added effort.

As for checking methods, several are available. Perhaps the most common is casual observation—just "see" how the employee is taking the decision, whether favorably or unfavorably. Next in order is to ask the employee whether or not the employee is satisfied with the decision. Somewhat similar in nature but more subtle is the practice of a general discussion with the employee with a view to deducing indirectly his attitude. A fourth method is to ask others about a given employee's reactions. This latter is dangerous because it smacks of spying or of "stool pigeoning." However, when used in the hands of an expert, it is desirable because it takes place away from the particular person involved.

PRINCIPLES OF HANDLING GRIEVANCES

A "principle" is a basic rule which, if followed, is likely to lead to desirable results or help avoid trouble. It is not an absolutely certain road to success or avoidance of failure, because "laws" of human behavior are nonexistent. However, principles do work most of the time, and that is why it is so helpful to discover principles and then rely upon them. In the field of handling grievances, a number of principles have been discovered by trial and error. There still are many, many gaps, but it is wise to take advantage of those that are available.

A grouping of principles of handling grievances is at best a makeshift. Hence the classification used here merely lumps available principles under the general headings of interviewing, attitudes toward employees, attitudes toward supervision, and long-run rules.

1. PRINCIPLES OF INTERVIEWING. In handling grievances, a considerable amount of time must be spent talking to employees, gathering information from them, and passing on various types of information. Such talks, to be most effective, should follow definite patterns and adhere to some well-tested rules. Interviewing has been discussed in an earlier chapter, but a brief review is in order here.

a) Place Employee at Ease. To begin with, every effort should be exerted to make the employee who has a grievance feel at ease during any conference, discussion, or talk. This means that speech, gestures, attitude—every element of the interview—should be geared to the purpose of relaxing the aggrieved employee. Any failure in this respect is bound to keep the employee tense or provoke an attitude of belligerence. As good a way as any to attain a relaxed discussion is to encourage and allow the employee to talk completely and fully about his trouble without any feeling of hurry. No matter how busy an executive is, if he allows that to interfere with a full, frank, and unhurried discussion, a mistake is made right at the start.

b) *Encourage Talk.* Another principle of good interviewing is to allow the worker to tell his story and retell it. In this way, the employee will not only get out the whole complaint but will tend to "cool off" in doing so. After all, one of the fundamental complaints of workers is that they do not have enough opportunities to talk things over with their supervisors. The mere opportunity to talk may be sufficient to clear up some grievances.

But where are executives to find time to hear all the complaints and to listen to long-winded discussions by employees who "really have no grievance anyhow"? The answer is that the executive's time must be weighed against the losses flowing from disgruntled employees. Besides, when management "opens its doors," it may be flooded for a while, but the flow of grievances will tend to fall off quickly. If line executives cannot take the needed time, aggrieved employees should be referred to experts in the personnel department. Obviously, if the grievances are there, refusing to listen to them will not reduce their number, intensity, or ill effects.

c) *Select a Favorable Location.* In addition, discussions or interviews should be held wherever possible under the best conditions possible for the worker. By this is meant a quiet and secluded spot where the conversation cannot be overheard. If possible, it should also be out of sight. Few workers in airing a grievance either want it to be overheard or want others even to guess that a complaint is being made. Hence, by providing facilities for such purposes, the interview can proceed without interruption and without others learning about it.

d) *Hear the Case Fully.* The interviewer should seek to keep his views and opinions entirely to himself until the story has been told and the time has come for some expression. He will, therefore, have to keep quiet (which is a hard thing for most anyone to do) except for leading the discussion on the right path. Even though he discovers or decides upon his solution or answer immediately, he should remain silent until the employee is fully heard. Otherwise, no matter how wise and equitable the ultimate decision, the employee may feel that it is a snap decision or one based upon an incomplete understanding of the facts. Moreover, by refraining from jumping in with his views and arguments, the supervisor offers no grounds on which the employee can base a feeling that he is prejudiced from the start.

  e) *Reach a Definite Closure.* When the interview is coming to its conclusion, the executive must be prepared to state his position clearly, accurately, and without any attitude of ill feeling or disregard for the employee. In stating his position, he need not be prepared to give a final and definite answer. If such an answer is possible, all well and good. If a final answer is not available, the aggrieved employee should be told specifically what other steps must be, and are going to be, taken and why. Moreover, a definite time for another meeting should be set. In this way, the employee will more likely feel that management is courageously, fairly, and capably seeking a solution. Indeed, by deferring final action, the employee may be led to feel that a snap judgment is being avoided.

MANAGEMENT'S ATTITUDE TOWARD EMPLOYEES

  During the interview and afterward and in other connections, the wise executive seeks to develop an attitude toward his employees that will result in gaining their confidence. Without this ingredient, grievances can never be handled with the highest degree of success.

  To gain such confidence, the executive must have and must show the right attitude toward those who have (and also those who do not have) grievances. In the first place, a supervisor, for example, should not take the attitude that his subordinates are more or less ignorant. Perhaps some are, but to take that attitude means that the supervisor will most certainly underestimate the strength of the aggrieved and sooner or later one of them will trip him. Moreover, no one, no matter how ignorant he is (and we all are, more or less, about different subjects), likes people to show by their attitude that they feel superior because of their allegedly greater wisdom. And, to gain their confidence, management must seek to understand why employees feel and think as they do. Getting across to the aggrieved the idea that management is really interested in their viewpoints is the high road to gaining the respect of labor.

  To develop confidence, it is also wise to take the attitude that employees are fair in presenting their grievances. This does not and will not mean that care should not be exercised to guard against unfair, prejudiced, and unwarranted demands. It does mean, however, that to convince others of management's fairness, it must make workers feel that it has confidence in their basic fairness unless and until proved otherwise.

And, finally, in handling grievances, management should display a sincere interest in the problems of the employee and a willingness to be of help. Although the supervisor, for example, is in large measure the representative of management to the employees, he is also a representative of employees to management. If he does not assume this responsibility, who will? The answer has been given in many cases to the decided disadvantage of management. Therefore, in acting as an "agent" of the employee, supervisors particularly must display a sincere interest in, and spirit of helpfulness toward, their problems. Should any executive, however, fail to develop and show this attitude, grievances at best will be handled in an unfriendly atmosphere and at times will lead to miniature wars.

MANAGEMENT'S RESPONSIBILITIES

In handling grievances, all executives must have confidence in themselves, be fully aware of their responsibilities, and be willing to carry them. Such an attitude of responsibility of executives toward their own jobs will be apparent to employees and help to gain their respect and confidence.

An executive who lacks confidence in himself soon finds that his employees are aware of this and tend to be wary of him. Employees do not like to come to such a supervisor with their grievances because they feel that their grievance is not in capable hands. They will tend to go around him or over his head. In either case, the prestige of the executive and the effectiveness of his efforts suffer. Each executive should recognize that he is human and does have weaknesses, but he should also recognize that, granted reasonable qualifications, he is capable of handling his job. To be a bluffer is bad, but to have an inferiority complex because of ordinary shortcomings from which all suffer is perhaps worse.

Likewise, an executive should recognize the serious responsibilities which he has undertaken. He has obligated himself in many ways for the success, happiness, and well-being of a number of fellow beings. Within his capacities and opportunities he must seek to carry out those responsibilities. In dealing with grievances he must give the impression of serious consideration. There must be no light-minded attitude or flippant remarks about the grievances of employees—they are no joking matter. They are important to the employee and an important part of the executive's job. By acting accordingly, the executive is much more likely to gain and hold the confidence of his employees when decisions have to be reached.

LONG-RUN PRINCIPLES

In handling grievances, it is important that consideration be given not only to effects in the present but also to long-run and sometimes far-distant implications. Thus a decision reached today has an immediate effect and also very likely will have an influence upon the future relationship between employees and management. As a consequence, grievances should be handled in terms of their total effect upon the organization and not solely upon their immediate or individual effect.

1. LONG-RUN EFFECTS. As an example, take the case of an employee who complains that he rather than someone else should have received a particular promotion. How this case is handled and what decision is reached will certainly have an effect upon the individual in question, but there will also be repercussions among other employees both now and later. Others too will watch the case; they will note the decision and reach conclusions. And conclusions are guides to behavior. If other employees get the idea that it is useless to complain about promotions or that to get a promotion, deserved or not, one should "raise the roof," damage will be done for a long time to come. Hence a given case should be handled so that all parties, whether directly or indirectly interested, are convinced of the fundamental integrity, honesty, and square dealing of the management.

2. DANGERS OF LOSING CONFIDENCE. Another truth to be remembered in the process of handling grievances is that it takes a long time to gain the confidence of employees and that, once gained, it can be lost overnight by a foolish decision or inept handling of a single case. In other words, eternal vigilance is the price of good labor relations. Every grievance must be considered important, no matter how irrelevant or insignificant it is or seems. If an executive is tired, in a bad temper, or otherwise feeling out of sorts, he will be much smarter to ask for a postponement of a grievance hearing; but it should be done courteously, apologetically, and with an apparent attitude of regret. Although delays are undesirable, they are to be preferred to the risk of saying something that would incur the distrust or enmity of the aggrieved employee. It is harder to overcome the results of hot-headed blundering, for example, than those due to delays.

3. HUMAN NATURE. In the long run, too, it is well to remember that human nature will not change much, if at all. People will become neither much better nor much worse. In handling grievances, people

should be taken for what they are—their strengths and their weaknesses. In other words, to assume that grievances can be postponed until people "see the light" themselves; that harsh decisions are good for employees, as they will learn later on; or that being easy with them now can be made up for by cracking down later is to forget that people do not change a great deal. Fairness has been desired for ages past and will be for ages to come; hence the question will always be "What is fair to all concerned?" It will be standards of fairness that largely change much more than the degree of desire for fairness.

4. EFFECTS OF THE PAST.   This leads to the thought that a long-run attitude should not only extend into the future but also give consideration to what has happened in the past. Often, when an employee complains, the source of his complaint may actually not be found in present conditions. The source or cause may be something that happened in the distant past; but to make his complaint sound credible, he may blame some present condition. For example—and this has actually happened—an employee complained about his wages when what he really was angry about was the fact that six months previously he had been spoken to rather harshly by his supervisor. In short, grievances of today often have their roots in the acts of yesterday and their branches in the effects of tomorrow. The roots are sometimes difficult to locate, and how the branches will grow, difficult to forecast. But difficult though the task, it must be tackled as best one can, else grievance handling becomes grievance fighting.

JOINT HANDLING OF GRIEVANCES

It is well to note again that handling grievances is a task that all levels of an organization must assume. Undoubtedly, in a settled organization, the line executives will do most of this work. Hence emphasis has been placed upon the work of line executives in this chapter. Of course, the labor relations department in its work must adopt and use the same methods and principles of handling grievances as line executives would. Indeed, the most constructive job that a labor relations department can do is to train line executives to handle as many grievances as possible.

However, all grievances are not subject to the sole jurisdiction of management. Where unions are concerned, grievances will usually be handled through some agreed-upon procedure and may even be taken to arbitration. The principles and practices discussed thus far are basic to either individual or joint handling of grievances. It is desirable now to describe joint handling of grievances, in terms of, first, grievance machinery and, second, arbitration.

GRIEVANCE MACHINERY

An example will suffice to illustrate the point that joint-action grievance machinery does not differ radically from basic principles of individual action. The following excerpt shows the care with which such machinery may be designed (note how each step, who is involved in each step, and time limits are precisely spelled out):

1. Any difference between the employer and employee involving the meaning of the provisions of this agreement shall constitute a grievance and may be taken up in the manner hereinafter set forth.
2. The company may utilize the following procedure upon any grievance against the union or any of its members:
   First—Presentation of complaint in writing to the officials of the union.
   Second—If no satisfactory adjustment is obtained within seven working days, then the company shall have the right to have the matter handled in accordance with the procedure outlined above for appealing grievances to the impartial referee.
3. The union and the company shall establish and maintain joint committees to review by mutual agreement hourly wage rates of employees in each department upon completion of each individual's six-month period of continuous employment with the company. Each wage review committee shall consist of six members, three from the union and three from the company, who are company employees. One of the union members shall be rotated so that the union committeeman of each department can serve as a member of the committee during the time the rates of his department are being reviewed. If a wage review committee fails to reach an agreement in regard to any case brought before it, then and in that event, the matter in question shall be referred in writing within twenty-four hours to a general wage committee, consisting of three men from each party to this agreement. Within five days after the general wage committee has received a deadlocked case, a decision shall be handed down. In the event the general wage committee is unable to reach an agreement, the matter shall be submitted to arbitration as provided for in this agreement. In accordance with past practice, the company will approve interim individual increases when justified by proof of the individual involved that he has been performing work, which work calls for a higher rate, job, or wage classification, to the satisfaction of his foreman. In all such cases, the foreman and the union committeeman shall be consulted prior to the granting of such increases.
4. The umpire, to whom any grievance shall be submitted in accordance with the provisions of this section, shall have jurisdiction and authority to interpret and apply the provisions of this agreement in so far as shall be

necessary to the determination of such grievance. But he shall not have jurisdiction or authority to alter in any way the provisions of this agreement.

5. The company may discipline or discharge any employee for just and proper cause, except that before any employee is disciplined or discharged, there shall be a hearing and mutual agreement between the shop committee (of the union) and a representative or representatives of the management appointed for such hearings. The decision, if mutually agreed upon, shall be final and binding upon both parties.

ARBITRATION

Ideally, labor and management should solve their difficulties through the processes of bargaining and negotiation. Practically, this does not always happen. Hence it is invariably the practice to provide for the services of third persons to aid in resolving grievances (or, for that matter, other types of disputes, too), such as contract interpretations. A summary of available methods is contained in Table 21. Here it is seen that the intervention of third parties may range from simple suggestions to irrevocable decisions of arbitrators or the courts.

The relative advantages and disadvantages of these methods are subject to much controversy. For example, some students favor arbitration as an excellent means of resolving disputes, claiming it to be a quick, inexpensive, and impartial method. Others contend that management gives up its rights of final decision to outsiders, who, no matter how experienced, cannot understand the problems of the company. Conciliation and mediation likewise have their opponents and proponents. Some favor their discretionary features, and others criticize them as being "lukewarm and ineffective."

1. A CASE EXAMPLE OF ARBITRATION PROCEDURE. An interesting clause covering arbitration is the following, because it takes up in detail the steps by which disputes may be resolved:

All disputes and grievances arising under the terms of this Agreement shall be adjusted in the following manner:

The Union Grievance Committee shall consist of five members, each of whom shall be responsible for grievances in a zone of the plant. The entire plant, for purposes of this Article, will be separated into five zones.

First Step. A grievance will be taken up by the employee and the Shop Steward or Committeeman with the foreman of the department.

Second Step. If a satisfactory adjustment is not reached, the Shop Steward will refer the grievance to the member of the Grievance Committee responsible for that zone. This member of the Grievance Committee, with or without the Shop Steward, will take the matter up with the department superintendent.

Third Step. If a satisfactory adjustment is not reached, the member of the Grievance Committee herein referred to will refer the grievance to the Business

TABLE 21

Comparison of Procedures to Settle Industrial Disputes*

	How and by Whom Initiated	Procedure	Administrator	Who Selects Arbitrator, Mediator, Board, etc.	Decision	Appeals	Conclusion
Voluntary arbitration	By mutual agreement, or on demand of one party pursuant to prior agreement	Under rules chosen by the parties	The parties themselves or AAA, or any other agency set up or chosen by parties	The parties, by mutual agreement	Award, based on evidence presented by parties at hearings and which parties agree in advance to accept	To court for enforcement or judgment, if good faith fails, or for correction of errors or misconduct	Execution of award in all but rare instances
Compulsory arbitration	By government agency or decree	As provided by government agency, or improvised by arbitrator	Whatever government agency orders the arbitration, or the arbitrator himself	Usually appointed by government agency	Enforceable award	To the courts	Acceptance of award, or strike or lockout, or seizure
Conciliation	By invitation of parties or initiation of outside person or agency, or by conciliator, or government agency	Improvised—no set procedure	None	Named by government, agency or outside person; parties may or may not agree to accept his services	None; result is compromise, agreement, or rejection	To public opinion	Compromise, agreement, to arbitrate, or strike or lockout, or seizure
Mediation	By agreement of parties, or in initiation by outside efforts, or by government order or government agency	Improvised	The mediator, or the agency chosen to mediate	Named by mediation agency or chosen by parties	Compromise, or recommendation which parties are at liberty to reject	To public opinion	Compromise, agreement to arbitrate, or strike or lockout, or seizure
Fact-finding	By government agency or decree, or by agreement of the parties	As set by government agency, or the board	The Board	Government agency	Recommendation	To public opinion	Acceptance or recommendation, compromise, or strike or lockout, or seizure
Litigation	By summons of one party to other to appear in court	Rules of the Court	The Court	The Court	Decision of the court	To a higher court	Enforcement of eventual court decision

* Prepared by the American Arbitration Association.
Source: William Sheperdson, "When Reason Takes Over—Arbitration," *Modern Management*, April, 1946, p. 7. Reprinted by permission of the Society for the Advancement of Management.

Agent of the Union, who will present these grievances to the Company each day at 10:00 A.M. The Company at that time will return to the Business Agent of the Union in written form any grievances which have been investigated.

The Grievance Committee of the Union will meet with the Labor Relations Manager or his assistant or someone of higher authority in the Industrial Relations Department of the Company each Tuesday and Friday to discuss grievances which the Union feels require clarification and/or additional investigation.

Fourth Step. If a satisfactory adjustment is not reached, grievances may be referred in writing to arbitration.

Time limits on these procedures are as follows:

First Step. One day or twenty-four hours.
Second Step. One day or twenty-four hours.
Third Step. Five days, or sooner if answers are available.
Fourth Step. One week for submission

Any dispute or grievance arising under the terms of this Agreement which cannot be settled between the parties involved may be submitted by either party on written notice to the other party to an arbitration committee for their determination.

The Arbitration Committee shall consist of three representatives of the Company and three of the Union, the seventh and impartial arbiter to be selected by the six members designated.

If no agreement can be reached as to the seventh and impartial arbiter within three days after the first meeting of the six members of the Committee, then they shall jointly petition the American Arbitration Association to make the appointment within five days after notification has been received.

The decision of the seventh and impartial member of the Committee shall be final and binding upon both parties to this Agreement. Every effort shall be made by the impartial arbiter to render his decision to both parties within ten days after the conclusion of the hearing.

The parties shall equally bear the expense of the impartial arbiter.

2. ARBITRATION CLAUSES.   Arbitration clauses, to be complete, should provide the following:

1. Grievance machinery
2. The elimination of strikes and lockouts during submission of disputes to grievance procedure and arbitration
3. A clear definition as to what is and what is not arbitrable
4. A statement as to how arbitrators are to be selected
5. If the contract provides for arbitration by a board, an exact definition of the number of members on the board
6. Rules of procedure under which arbitrators are to operate
7. Time limits on each step of the grievance procedure and for the handing down of the arbitrators' award
8. If the contract provides for arbitration by a board, provision for decision by either majority vote or by the impartial arbitrator alone
9. A declaration of whether the award of the arbitrator is to be final or reviewable by the courts

QUESTIONS AND PROBLEMS

1. In a given company, a "grievance" is defined as a complaint expressed in writing and presented to the supervisor. What are the arguments for and against such a definition?

2. Employees in a particular company cannot take a grievance to the personnel department until it has been discussed with the supervisor. What do you think happens to grievances that are against the supervisor? How would you handle such grievances?

3. It is said that some unions prefer to have all grievances reported to them so that they can "build them up" if necessary. What do you think of this accusation? What might the unions well reply?

4. Does the existence of grievances imply anything radically wrong with employees, the company, or the union? Explain.

5. In a given company, a group of employees in the office complained one wintry day that the office was too hot, and another group at the same time complained that it was too cold. How would you attempt to resolve these conflicting grievances?

6. In general, are employees more often satisfied with or dissatisfied with their companies? What does this imply for the future?

7. Is it possible to handle grievances to the complete satisfaction of everyone? If not, does this imply that labor and management can expect little more than warfare?

8. A given personnel manager said he did not approve of formal grievance machinery because it "created" grievances. Comment upon such views.

9. Suggest methods by which information about grievances may be obtained. Is an employee attitude survey likely to provide information about grievances or possible sources of grievances? Can grievances be group as well as individual?

10. Why is it difficult to obtain "facts" about grievances? If all the facts cannot be obtained in a given case, is it possible to reach other than makeshift settlements? What ingredient must be present in relations between labor and management under such circumstances if grievances are to be settled with an effective degree of success?

11. Do not executives apply their decisions in grievance cases without being told to do so? Can you illustrate that they sometimes do not?

12. Would you advise that all grievances and how they were handled be written up? What would be the advantages and disadvantages of such practices? Do you think that supervisors, let us say, would be prone to disregard grievances if they have to go through the motions of writing them up?

13. Why is it desirable to encourage employees with grievances to talk freely and fully? What must the executive not do if he wishes to encourage frank and complete talk? Where are the executives to find time to listen?

14. Is it possible for an interviewer to avoid giving an employee a clue to how he feels about the merits of a grievance before a decision is reached? Need

the executive be entirely "poker-faced"? Under what conditions might it be desirable to let the employee know almost at once that the grievance is a good or bad one?

15. Over what jurisdiction does a supervisor have authority to render decisions in regard to grievances? How about subject matter such as wages, hours, and working conditions?

16. A given supervisor complained that the general manager of his company made too many promises and got the employees excited about too many plans. Why would these be sources of grievances? What could the supervisor do about them?

17. Distinguish between mediation, conciliation, and arbitration.

18. Select a case in which two students are in disagreement. Undertake to arbitrate the case. What disadvantages do you find in arbitration? What are its advantages?

19. Investigate the work of the American Arbitration Association. Write a report on your findings.

20. List the factors and forces that you believe will tend to increase grievances and those that will tend to decrease grievances. What types of grievances are likely to increase?

Disciplinary Action

INTRODUCTION

Management's job would, indeed, be pleasant if employees never had any grievances against the company or the company never any against the employees. Such an ideal situation has never been known to exist. Therefore, management must be prepared to handle such unpleasantness. In the foregoing chapter attention was directed to the handling of grievances, or situations in which the employees are dissatisfied with the company. The present chapter is concerned with what to do when the employee is, or is alleged to be, at fault. The term covering this phase of management's work is "disciplinary action."

Since disciplinary action has the implication of penalties and since dealing out penalties is full of dangerous possibilities, management must be fully aware of when, how, to whom, and why the disciplinary action should be taken. Only then will this action, however unpleasant to take, likely gain its purposes with a minimum loss of employee good will. Even when an employee fully deserves punishment, he invariably accepts it with some amount of ill feeling. Nevertheless, to forego negative and drastic action when it is deserved is to ask for trouble. We all tend to become spoiled when we can "get away with things." But to deal out penalties when they are not deserved or when the reasons therefor are not clearly understood is doubly dangerous.

In the discussion that follows, it has been deemed advisable to examine the meaning of discipline and disciplinary action. Second, the steps to be taken in disciplinary action are studied. Third, fundamental and practical principles to be followed in taking the steps of disciplinary action are listed.

However, in the case of disciplinary action, as with grievances, management may deal in joint action with unions. Later in this chapter, therefore, mention is made of this phase of disciplinary action.

Disciplinary action in most companies is taken by line executives. Occasionally, the personnel department is made responsible for taking final action on such serious penalties as discharge of employees. In any event, the personnel department has a heavy responsibility to aid all executives in taking disciplinary action. Hence in this chapter the emphasis is on methods and principles of discipline which may be disseminated to executives as well as used by the personnel department.

DEFINITION OF TERMS

Perhaps the chief complaint that most companies have with their employees is that they sometimes do not do what they are told. Why do they fail to follow orders? There are several possible explanations. The workers may be ignorant; they may misunderstand orders and instructions; they may be careless either in receiving or following them; they may just not care, having little sense of responsibility; or they may purposely and with malice disobey orders or destroy or waste property. These explanations indicate that employees approach their work with a variety of attitudes toward their fellow workers, supervisors, and the company. The attitude they hold toward company regulations and supervision is given the name "discipline." Discipline is said to be good when employees follow willingly the rules of their superiors and the various rules of the company. Discipline is said to be bad when employees either follow rules unwillingly or actually disobey regulations. Thus employees develop attitudes, favorable or unfavorable, toward company rules and executives. But how do they develop or attain the kind or degree of discipline that exists? If discipline is good, it may be due to excellent handling of grievances or positive motivation of the workers, or it may be that cases of disobedience have been capably handled. Poor discipline, however, no matter what the cause, suggests the need of correction.

The type of correction depends, of course, upon the cause of poor discipline. If the attitude is unfavorable because the company is at fault, the action to be taken involves, first, removal of the cause and, second, convincing the employees of the desire of the company to be fair. Such correction comes under the heading of handling of grievances, general surveys of company policies and practices, and following up employee suggestions that pertain to such matters.

When the attitude is unfavorable due to faults in the worker, however, the action to be taken is known as "disciplinary action." It involves warnings, suggestions, and other penalties by the company to the worker. The correction, it must be noted, implies some degree of force and penalty. When the fault of the employee is due to misunderstanding or mistakes stemming from causes in company practices or policies, the action to be taken is not disciplinary but, as noted above, something else. Disciplinary action has two major aspects: first, the employee is at fault because of some failing of his own, and, second, some form of penalty is to be applied.

Although the two words are often used interchangeably, it is well to keep clear two ideas about discipline and disciplinary action. "Discipline," used as a noun and preceded by the adjective "good," means that the worker willingly abides by company rules and executive orders. When discipline is "bad," it means that the worker, through some fault of his own, is not being obedient. "Disciplinary action" or "to discipline" means the steps taken to attempt to correct the disobedience.

In handling disciplinary cases there are two major aspects that must be watched: first, the steps to be taken and, second, the principles to follow in each step. The two must be considered together in actual practice; but, for purposes of discussion, it is simpler to take up each separately. Attention is now directed to the first of these aspects.

PROCEDURES OF DISCIPLINARY ACTION

Although it is not always possible or practical to follow a set routine in taking disciplinary action, nevertheless there are certain steps or stages to which attention must be directed at one time or another. These steps include the following:

1. Accurate statement of the disciplinary problem
2. Collection of full information on the case
3. Selection of tentative penalties to be applied
4. Choosing among the alternative penalties
5. Application of the penalty
6. Follow-up of the case

STATEMENT OF PROBLEM

Perhaps no more important step can be taken in the whole process of disciplinary action than to make absolutely certain about the problem that calls for discipline. There should be no guesswork in this step, else mistakes accumulate through all the other steps.

In general, there are five questions that must be answered in arriving at a statement of a disciplinary problem:

1. Is this case one calling for disciplinary action?
2. Exactly what is the nature of the violation?
3. Under what conditions did it occur?
4. What individual or individuals are involved?
5. When or how often have the violations occurred?

1. DETERMINING THE NATURE OF THE VIOLATION. The first of the foregoing questions can seldom be answered first. Nevertheless, it is stated first because that question should run through all the proceedings. Falsely including a case under the heading of one calling for disciplinary action is bound to have unfortunate repercussions. Right from the start, it is a wise executive who does not jump at conclusions or misinterpret circumstances, for a slight delay in taking disciplinary action is not so serious as delays in handling grievances. After all, if a subordinate is in the wrong, the case will "keep"; but if he is not and is falsely accused, the insult will smoulder in his memory for some time. In so far as possible, executives must assure themselves that a violation has occurred and that the violation is entirely or in part the fault of one or more subordinates.

2. STATING THE VIOLATION. With this in mind, the next step is to state precisely and objectively the nature of the alleged violation. The specific rule, regulation, policy, request, or order that was broken and the degree to which it was broken must be determined. There should be no generalities or vaporizing here; or certainly the less, the better. For example, the following statement, "My request that the materials on his workbench be moved immediately was not obeyed until the next day," is much better than "He didn't follow my orders." There is a specificness about the former that gives a quantitative as well as a qualitative measurement of the violation, which the latter lacks.

3. DETERMINING THE CIRCUMSTANCES. Of course, a violation may be excusable or not, depending upon circumstances. In the example just cited, it might have been that the order was given shortly before quitting time. The worker might well have felt that he was not expected to work overtime but could finish the next day. Thus the worker might be excused for violating the order because the conditions, in the mind of the worker, justified quitting on time. After all, most employees leave their workplaces without reporting before leaving—in most instances this is customary practice.

Moreover, in examining the circumstances, it might be desirable in serious cases to make a critical analysis of a person's background and make-up. This is done on the healthful assumption that people are not "lawbreakers" inherently but that there may have been something that disposed a particular individual to break a rule. If the cause is found, its elimination will go much further in improving discipline than any penalty ever would. Viewed in this fashion, taking disciplinary action has a constructive and positive foundation rather than the negative force of punishment. It partakes somewhat of positive motivation discussed in the next chapter.

4. INDIVIDUALS INVOLVED. It is also significant to know exactly what individual or individuals were involved in a violation. For example, if one individual has broken a safety rule, he alone should be punished; but if someone else has been involved in the case, he too should be included in the penalty. Thus a given employee may have cut himself, let us say, while sharpening a tool against company rules, which state that only a toolmaker shall perform this operation. Yet the toolmaker might have refused to do the job for one reason or another when requested to by the injured employee. Of course, the injured employee had no right to proceed with the sharpening, but the toolmaker should also be included for possible discipline. Such multiple aspects of discipline must not be overlooked.

5. NUMBER OF REPETITIONS. And, finally, it is desirable to state as precisely as possible when or how often the alleged violations occurred. Here, again, the seriousness of a violation is dependent upon the number of violations. For example, a person who has been absent without excuse several times in a given month deserves a more serious reprimand than one who has been absent but once. Or, again, if a violation occurs during a particularly busy or rush period, it should be weighed more heavily than one that takes place during a lull. However, these things will not be known unless specifically included; hence time or times of violation should be cited.

To summarize, statement of the case requires careful examination of several aspects. It may involve some effort, but the results are worth while. First, the dangers of false or inaccurate accusations are reduced. Also, when presented with a clear statement of the case, employees learn that the superior is not making a hasty decision after a superficial examination but is desirous of being fair in dealing out penalties. In addition, the superior himself will feel more sure of himself in whatever decision he reaches. Moreover, a careful statement of the problem will indicate whether it is a case he himself should handle or whether it should be referred to his superiors. If the latter, a clear statement of the case will enable the superiors to take immediate disciplinary action with no lost time or waste motion in compiling the statement themselves.

GATHERING FACTS

Gathering facts is essentially supplementary to the preceding step as well as others to follow. Nevertheless, as in the case of handling grievanccs, pertinent data and information are essential. How these may be collected was discussed rather fully in the preceding chapter; hence it is suggested that a review of that material be made. It is worth while here to highlight some of the significant aspects of fact gathering.

As noted in the preceding chapter, fact gathering is often a process of fact sifting. Which are facts, and which are opinions? If opinions are mistaken for facts, it is easy to reach the wrong conclusions. For example, a given clerk's output declines, and the clerk is acting somewhat rudely to others in the office. It might seem that a simple warning and reprimand is called for—at least, so it might be argued, it cannot do much damage. But the case of the clerk's shortcomings might be much more deeply seated than just casual carelessness. Illness, fatigue, or worry may be the cause. Hence a reprimand might be worse than useless.

A thorough examination of every case is always suggested. When an executive has worked with a group of persons and has appraised them individually and as group workers, the "search of facts" period can be greatly shortened. Such practice in "sizing up" one's workers, by the way, is an excellent course of study for an executive to pursue, since it is often possible thereby to forestall or minimize grievances and disciplinary action. But until employees have been "sized up," it is advisable to go slowly before determining what disciplinary action should be taken.

The facts of the case should be so well culled that the superior is willing to produce them and has confidence in them if they should be called for. If some of the information is a bit questionable but nevertheless seems of some value, it should be so labeled; "backtracking" will be saved later if the information is questioned. It is wise, also, at least in any case that has any possibility of being important, to write down (informally, if not formally) the information, opinions, and facts that have been collected. Even the opinions should be noted because these may have a bearing upon the case; besides, so long as they are definitely marked as opinions and used as such, they cannot detract from the fairness of the ultimate decision.

One more word of warning about this step: Beware of the charge of spying in gathering information, because that is a sure way of losing the confidence of employees. It may sometimes be considered advisable to search for information unobtrusively. It may be undesirable to reveal that management's suspicions are aroused for one reason or another. After all, an executive might be completely wrong about his suspicions. To reveal them would undermine morale in such instances. On the other hand, after a case is in the open, management should certainly leave no stone unturned either to find or to elicit all pertinent information.

ESTABLISHING TENTATIVE PENALTIES

Tentative alternative types of disciplinary action should now be formulating themselves in the mind of the executive. The peremptory adoption of a given course of action is invariably undesirable. It suggests a predisposition toward a prejudiced mind and may lead to incorrect discipline. Moreover, if the first disciplinary action is shown to be inappropriate, a rehash of the case and a delay in its handling would result.

In the selection of tentative disciplinary actions, it is perhaps well, first, to have a list of all types of disciplinary actions permitted by the company; second, to have a list of those types that various executive levels are permitted to take; and, third, to compile a list that is pertinent and restricted to the case at hand. An example of increasing penalties as the number of repetitions grows is shown in Figure 77 (p. 472).

A list of all types of disciplinary action is a desirable tool. It can be used to make certain that no possibility is overlooked. Thus the executive involved can run down the list, actually written out or from memory, and see which might be pertinent. Having a list that divides penalties according to rank is desirable because executives will know which cases should be referred to others and which can be passed upon by themselves. For example, discharge is a very serious penalty and should be used only as a last resort. Moreover, a discharge may involve the company in a lawsuit, in which case the company, as well as the supervisor, would be affected. As a consequence, it is desirable for others besides the supervisors, for example, to pass upon such penalties. The recommendation of the supervisor invariably counts very heavily in such instances and would in all likelihood be the deciding factor so long as no governmental regulations were involved. This example illustrates the wisdom of having at least a tentative list which classifies penalties in accordance with the person who or department which normally handles them.

The third list is the one that would be worked up for each case that seemed to call for disciplinary action. It could be developed very quickly after the other two were compiled. It need not, of course, be a written list, although this is desirable.

FIGURE 77. Disciplinary Penalties*

►19. Posting or removal of any matter on bulletin boards or company property at any time unless specifically authorized by Industrial Relations Department.	1 day off	3 days off	Discharge		
►20. Theft or removal from the premises without proper authorization of any company property or property of the government or of any employee.	Discharge				
►21. Gambling or engaging in a lottery on company premises.	Discharge				
►22. Misusing, destroying, or damaging any company property or property of any employee.	Discharge				
►23. Deliberately restricting output.	Discharge				
►24. Making of false, vicious, or malicious statements concerning any employee, the company, or its product.	Warning	3 days off	1 week off	Discharge	
►25. Provoking, or instigating a fight, or fighting during working hours or on company premises.	1 week off or discharge	Discharge			
►26. Drinking any alcoholic beverage on premises or on company time.	1 week off	Discharge			
►27. Reporting for work obviously under the influence of alcohol or drugs.	1 day off	3 days off	1 week off	Discharge	
►28. Engaging in sabotage or espionage.	Discharge				
►29. Violating a safety rule or safety practice.	Warning	1 day off	3 days off	1 week off	Discharge
►30. Immoral conduct or indecency.	Discharge				
►31. Interfering or refusing to cooperate with Plant Protection officers in the performance of their duties.	Discharge				
►32. Sleeping on job during working hours.	Discharge				
►33. Entering restricted areas without specific permission.	Warning	3 days off	Discharge		
►34. Refusal to show badge at the request of any member of supervisison or Plant Protection.	Discharge				
►35. Leaving plant during work shift without permission.	1 day off	1 week off	Discharge		
►36. Insubordination.	1 week off or discharge	Discharge			
►37. Failure to observe parking and traffic regulations on premises.	Warning	1 day off	3 days off	1 week off	Discharge
►38. Mistakes due to lack of knowledge.	Warning	1 day off	Demotion		
►39. Leaving work area without permission before final whistle blows indicating end of shift.	Warning	3 days off	1 week off	Discharge	
►40. Failure to report for overtime work without good reason after being scheduled to work according to overtime policy.	Warning	1 day off	3 days off	1 week off	Discharge

* Source: "Simplifies Discipline Procedure," *Factory Management and Maintenance*, Vol. CVIII. No. 10, p. 458.

TYPES OF PENALTIES

At this juncture, it might be well to consider, at least in outline form, the various types of disciplinary action that are available. Perhaps the most common type is the simple reprimand. This is sufficient in most instances to change the attitude of an employee who has broken some regulation. After all, most of us do not like to be criticized, no matter how gently, and will seek to avoid incurring such disciplinary action. Such reprimands, by the way, need not always be given directly by an executive. For example, an executive who is experienced in judging people knows that some of them can be relied upon to reprimand themselves. He subtly points out their mistakes, and they give themselves a much more thorough "going over" than the executive could have done directly. Indeed, with some people such treatment is very effective because a direct reprimand is taken to heart much too seriously.

Another form of discipline is the mild penalty, but nevertheless a penalty. The penalties may be financial or nonfinancial. For example, tardiness may subject the employee to a small loss of wage. Or an excessive number of tardinesses or absences may remove the possibility of a merit increase. On the other hand, nonfinancial penalties may involve loss of preference for a transfer, various privileges, and assignment to favored jobs or tasks.

And, finally, there are the more drastic penalties. These include demotion, temporary layoffs, and outright discharges. As noted earlier, such disciplinary actions are so serious that they require authorization by the personnel department as well as the immediate executive. This does not weaken the hand of the executive because an executive who has carefully considered such a decision will seldom be overruled. Moreover, the best interests of the company may be better served sometimes by transferring a man to another department rather than by outright discharge. Removing him from his present department protects the accusing foreman; and sending him to another department saves the investment in the employee.

CHOOSING THE PENALTY

After a case calling for disciplinary action has been thoroughly examined and alternative penalties considered, the particular penalty to be applied should be chosen. This should be done fairly and fearlessly. To overpenalize an employee is unfair, but to be unduly easy may lead to a series of broken rules. It may sound farfetched, but the old adage, "sparing the rod spoils the child" has its industrial applications.

Every possible effort should be made to prevent the occurrence of disobedience; but, if drastic action is necessary, it should be taken unhesitatingly. Infractions of rules that go without penalty not only encourage the rule breaker to continue on his way but also convince others that it is not worth while to keep on the "straight and narrow." Even the "good citizens" of a community lose respect for its leaders when laws are not enforced. When good labor becomes scarce, management hesitates to discipline people for fear of losing them. Yet a temporary loss is far preferable to the decline in morale and respect for management that takes place when obviously serious violations go unpunished.

To repeat, the choice of a penalty should be made fairly and fearlessly. When uncertainty holds up a decision, it is a sign that further search for facts or consultation with others is called for. Indeed, after a number of tentative solutions have been selected, further study of each is invariably necessary. Of course, such information, opinions, and data will already have been available. In addition, executives should have their own experience and the experience of others to call upon for comparisons of the case at hand with previous cases. So the search for information at this stage need not consume too much time. On the contrary, it should require no more than a recheck of the available facts.

Also, it is wise to consult with others, particularly when a case evidently falls outside of the jurisdiction of a given executive. But even on matters that come completely within one's scope, outside consultation can be very helpful. Thus the supervisor who talks over a troublesome case with his own superior, some other superior, or the personnel department gets the benefit of their advice, and he also gives himself an opportunity to recheck himself as he presents the case to the others.

In the choice of a penalty, it should be remembered that it will serve somewhat as a precedent if a similar case has never been handled. Employees are quick to compare current decisions with what has gone before. When the kind or degree of penalties to be assigned for particular types of disobedience, for example, are indeterminate, employees will conclude that management is wishy-washy and unreliable.

APPLYING PENALTIES

The next step, the application of the penalty, involves a positive and certain attitude on the part of management. If executives are to convey the idea that they are sure of themselves in reaching decisions, their very attitude and conduct should be in accord with the decision.

In other words, if the disciplinary action is a simple reprimand, an executive should calmly and quickly dispose of the matter. When drastic action is called for, a forthright, serious, and determined attitude is highly desirable. On the one hand, the case is not overdone; nor, on the other hand, is the severity of the case minimized. In this regard it is highly desirable to minimize one's personal feelings or desire to dramatize. Reprimands and penalties are always unpleasant to hand out; hence the quicker and more impersonally the matters are handled, the fewer the undesirable effects.

In taking action, too, this step should not be delayed. Penalties are most effective when the punishment is closely associated in the mind of the wrongdoer with the act that brought it on. If a penalty is delayed unduly, the employee involved may have forgotten the case or considered it closed and, therefore, conclude that the company is "picking on him."

FOLLOW-UP OF DISCIPLINARY ACTION

The ultimate purpose of disciplinary action is, of course, to help develop good discipline. Its aim is to make certain, so far as possible, that employees do not willfully or carelessly break rules or disobey instructions. The disciplinary action cannot repair the damage done. Hence disciplinary action must be evaluated in terms of its effectiveness after it has been applied.

Too often, follow-up is a matter of assuming that disciplinary action has been effective so long as there is no recurrence of bad discipline. Of course, that is all right so long as rules are not being broken. A far better practice is to check closely employees who have been subject to disciplinary action. Their performance and attitudes should be subject to review, openly or with subtle casualness, as the seriousness of the case may suggest.

To be sure, employees who are being checked may resent it. However, since they did cause trouble, it will further serve the purpose of discipline for them to know that they have lost some of the management's confidence. This does not mean that management should "pour it on" indefinitely. In serious cases a checkup may be more or less formal, in less serious cases casual checkups may be all that are desirable, and in simple reprimands subtle observation ordinarily will be sufficient. If further repetitions are to be prevented, care obviously should be exercised at the points where difficulties have been encountered.

The personnel department should be informed of serious penalties, so that it, too, may follow up ultimate effects. A record of discipline cases should be filed here to provide evidence that misdeeds leading to severe penalties were of a continuing nature.

PRINCIPLES OF DISCIPLINARY ACTION

Although it is essential to know what steps should be taken in handling disciplinary cases, of equal importance is knowing the whys and wherefores of the steps being taken. There is yet much to be learned about the underlying principles of disciplinary action. However, much useful material is available on this subject, which the personnel department should be ready to supply to executives.

Executives cannot make the mistake very frequently, for example, of failing to recognize the differences that exist in individuals. It would be foolhardy to assume, however, that people are so different that nothing that one learns about a given case can be applied to others. On the contrary, people are more alike than they are different. It is foolish to let the differences blot out the similarities. Hence, in taking disciplinary action, it is wise to follow certain rules and to assume certain attitudes toward employees in general.

In addition, executives should be taught to recognize their place in the company as a whole. To act as though one's own department is all that matters is to invite crosscurrents of trouble. After all, there are broad company rules and policies that presumably have been thought out for the benefit of all. Hence the personnel department can pass on to each executive the benefit of company-wide experiences.

The personnel department can also aid executives by supplying them with a miscellany of disciplining principles. Included here are comments pertaining to the desirability of disciplinary action, dealing with the workers, implications of disciplinary action, and union-management relations in disciplinary action.

DESIRABILITY OF DISCIPLINARY ACTION

The fundamental reason for taking disciplinary action is to correct situations that are unfavorable to the company. At the moment, an employee may dislike to be criticized, reprimanded, or discharged; but it may be good for him over a period of time. However, it certainly should be good for the company both now and in the future. Later it will be shown that disciplinary action is at times undesirable for employees who have "broken the law."

1. RESPONSIBILITY OF PERSONNEL DEPARTMENT. Executives should be convinced that disciplinary action is a tool that must be used for the company's benefit, even though it would be temporarily more pleasant if such action were not taken. Hence the personnel department can do much good by training executives not to shrink from taking disciplinary action when it is justified. That is one of their responsibilities as executives. It is one of their unpleasant duties and one for the assumption of which they are compensated.

2. RESPONSIBILITY OF LINE EXECUTIVES. Executives must be "sold" on the need of discipline from the company's viewpoint. After all, to be profitable, the company must be efficient. To be efficient, it must, among other things, have employees who do not excessively disregard rules, disobey orders, or work carelessly. Hence, to protect its own interest and those of the customers it serves, disciplinary action is essential to the company. Obviously, an employee who "kills time" is not helping the company; yet he was hired to do a fair day's work, presumably at a fair day's pay.

3. CONFIDENCE IN COMPANY POLICIES. What if an executive believes that certain rules of the company are unfair? Several angles must be discussed regarding such a situation. In the first place, he should, nevertheless, continue to enforce it as though he had confidence

in it. An executive who in any way leads employees to believe that he has no confidence in the company will soon find that the subordinates do not trust him. In the second place, he should make certain that he knows precisely why the rule was established. Often we do not like what we do not understand, even though the lack of understanding may lie in our own failure to take steps to find out the meaning and reason for rules. If, after the second step, an executive is convinced that a rule is wrong, then he should attempt to clear up the matter by presenting his side, as he sees it, to his superiors with a view to suggesting a change. And finally, if a change is not made and the executive remains convinced of the inequity of the rule, he should either accept the rule notwithstanding or seek another position.

This does not mean that every time an executive disagrees with his superiors he should resign. After all, no matter where or with whom one works, there will always be points upon which agreement is not unanimous. Hence some disagreement does not mean disloyalty. But, if after going through the steps outlined in the foregoing, an executive disagrees with some company rules, he nevertheless should follow them implicitly or give up his position.

Asking a supervisor to do this is no more than the supervisor asks of his workers. The reasonable executive knows that he may be wrong at times but that he must continue to do his job as best he can. And in this vein, he must attempt to explain rules and regulations to all subordinates. If his views are not seen clearly after reasonable effort, the executive must refer the case elsewhere or take steps to close the case himself. Similarly, in dealing with his superiors about company policy, an executive cannot expect to see through the implications of all rules.

4. DEVELOPING CONFIDENCE IN EMPLOYEES. These remarks about the attitude of executives toward company rules and policies have been somewhat extended because bad discipline is bound to result when executives do not have or fail to display confidence in company rules. Furthermore, it is inevitable that executives will fail to see clearly the need for some rules or penalties. Nevertheless, they must not permit an irreducible number of conflicts to ruin their attitude toward rules, at least in the eyes of their subordinates. For example, the supervisor who says to an employee, "Well, that rule was figured out by some brass hat who doesn't know what's going on down here," is doing an injustice to the company. He is also doing the employee, and himself particularly, a serious injustice. He is not only "passing the buck" but also inviting other violations. The employees will be led to conclude that neither the supervisor nor the rules need be respected.

ATTITUDE TOWARD EMPLOYEES

To confidence in company policies on disciplinary matters must be added confidence in the innate goodness of the worker. It is essential to believe that employees can be trusted even though they occasionally break rules. After all, even the best workers make mistakes of omission and commission. To be sure, it is hard to trust employees when, at times, a wave of rule breaking takes place. Unless a fundamental faith is held in the trustworthiness of labor, management will have little else to look forward to than a future of watching for and disciplining lawbreakers.

1. IMPORTANCE OF ATTITUDES.   All of us influence people not only by what we do but also by the innumerable mannerisms that are inadvertent expressions of our feelings. In other words, our attitudes toward others show through our actions and behaviorisms. Hence, when an executive assumes that employees are untrustworthy, that attitude will be discovered by the employees, and they will return in kind.

The point is that even though some penalizing is inevitable, all employees should not be considered as inveterate lawbreakers. On the contrary, an underlying current of confidence in the fundamental integrity of employees must run through all disciplinary action.

2. THE VALUE OF DISCIPLINARY ACTION.   On the other hand, executives must be convinced that disciplinary action is needful and effective. In particular, they must feel that any penalties assigned in given cases were not only merited but also beneficial to employees. If, in the future, wrongdoings are reduced, the resulting harmonious atmosphere can be in part ascribed to earlier instances of negative motivation. Such a happier state can be achieved because most people prefer to conform. The effectiveness of disciplinary action in attaining this goal can be increased by adding to penalties constructive suggestions of how transgressions can be avoided.

3. THE USE OF FEAR.   Good does not derive from correcting the damage done—that is a loss, more or less. It must come from a changed attitude toward the company's rules and regulations. It is too bad that some employees are willing to obey rules only for fear of penalties. But if it is to their benefit to have jobs and if fear keeps them on the "straight and narrow," then the use of reasonable penalties is of benefit to the employees themselves. It must be remembered that, to some degree, fear rules in the lives of all of us. The wise man can get along with a minimum of fear; yet he, too, recognizes that it acts as a spur in his activities.

This brief comment upon fear, upon which penalties essentially rest, is not intended as justification for irresponsible employment of it. Although the role of fear should be restricted, nevertheless, when its use is called for, executives should be trained to employ it intelligently.

4. INDIVIDUAL DIFFERENCES. Moreover, executives should be impressed with the fact that some people are very thin-skinned, whereas others have the hide of an elephant. As a consequence, it is essential to adopt disciplinary practices that fit the case. That is why such rules as "reprimand in private" are often cited. Not that some people should not be penalized publicly. Rather there is greater danger in using an occasional public reprimand than when private penalties are always assigned. Indeed, with some employees a good all-out airing in public works best, but one cannot always be certain that such a reprimand is best for the person in question. Hence, in dealing out penalties it is wise to be conservative and gradually to step up the penalty, if need be.

IMPLICATIONS OF DISCIPLINARY ACTION

Disciplinary action can be successful only if an executive takes into account the implications of such action upon himself, upon others, and upon future relationships.

1. DISCIPLINARY ACTION AS A TOOL. An executive must, to begin with, consider disciplinary action as a tool, not as a weapon of supervision. He should see penalties and reprimands in the same light as brakes on a car. They "slow down" employees when needed, they act as a preventive, but they cannot cure an accident.

Hence, when a penalty is applied, it should be in the manner of using a tool and not as a threatening gesture. The penalty is bad enough; the executive gains nothing, indeed often losing prestige, when he becomes emotional or dramatic. Employees will accept penalties in good grace only when an executive does not gloat over the occasion, and they will tend to restrain themselves when they have confidence in the reasonableness of an executive's action. When disciplinary action is used as a club, an executive had better prepare himself for a period of intentional, willful, and perhaps vicious disobedience.

2. CO-OPERATION WITH OTHERS. Moreover, the executive's attitude toward disciplinary action can be seen in his attitude toward the efforts of fellow executives. Any indication of laughing at, ridiculing, or undermining the work of others will encourage repercussions from other executives and result in a loss of prestige in the eyes of one's own subordinates. When a man does not have respect for his own profession or those in his profession, he had better expect little respect for his own work in that profession. To destroy confidence in one's own

efforts, one need only go about destroying confidence in those who are doing similar work.

3. AFTEREFFECTS. In taking disciplinary action, it is also imperative to remember that disciplinary action has its aftereffects. This comes about in two major ways. In the first place, a given penalty does or does not serve to change the employee's attitude toward company rules. This aspect has already been discussed. In the second place, a given penalty in a given case is considered as a precedent. In the future, therefore, when similar cases are to be disciplined, the penalty should not be changed except for a good reason.

As an example, if some infraction previously has been punished lightly, such as reprimanding a person found smoking in areas where smoking is not permitted, an extreme penalty such as discharge should be used with hesitation and with warning. It is far better to announce that thereafter the rule is going to be enforced strictly. Although the "legal" right to fire in such cases without warning seems to exist, some companies have found to their sorrow that an unannounced change in policy toward the enforcement of company rules was considered a subterfuge by the National Labor Relations Board, for example, to obstruct collective bargaining. Thus rules should be applied in the same way all the time, or there is danger of losing the confidence of employees or having some outside agency criticize the company and its management.

UNION-MANAGEMENT RELATIONS

Most companies take the stand that disciplinary action is a prerogative of management. They contend that management must have unrestricted right to discipline employees, else it will be impossible to produce the right quality of goods economically and effectively. In essence, the argument is that in accepting the responsibilities that go with operating a business there must be a counterbalancing weight of authority. This attitude is held so strongly by some companies that they will neither relinquish any aspects of discipline to joint action with unions nor include any phase of it as a subject for collective bargaining.

On the other hand, there are companies which accept the offices of the unions in various aspects of disciplinary action. To begin with, some have agreed that the union may challenge cases in which it feels that punishment has been excessive, partial, or misdirected. In other cases, unions are given the right to participate in hearings in which the type of disciplinary action to be taken is being considered. And in still other cases, the union itself may take disciplinary steps, such as layoffs or a reduction of status on a priority list. While direct participation in disciplinary action is not common, it does indicate how far some companies have gone in accepting union action in this area.

What stand a particular company should take is not a question to be answered here. It should be noted here merely that there is precedent for sole company action or joint action. Which method is better depends upon the individual situation and the philosophy of the company and union executives. These are factors that cannot easily be analyzed.

As time goes on, it is probable that unions will play a larger role in disciplinary matters. In the final analysis, such participation must be based on good principles and procedures. It is as much to the advantage of the union to be fair to employees as it is to management. Hence, if good principles must prevail eventually, it would seem to be the wise thing for management to adopt such plans and practices before they are forced upon management by outsiders. When outsiders force changes, they take credit for them; yet it is management which must make them work.

QUESTIONS AND PROBLEMS

1. A given company takes the stand that disciplinary action is a prerogative of management that in no wise is to be diluted by the union. Why might it take this stand? Should union help ever be sought in such matters? Explain.

2. A supervisor and one of his employees are discussing a question with the personnel manager in the latter's office. While there, the employee lights a cigarette, and the personnel manager says nothing about it. Later the supervisor criticizes the employee for smoking and tells him not to do it again. Was the supervisor within his rights? Was he justified? Explain.

3. If individual differences are allowed for in taking disciplinary action, how can those treated harshly be prevented from developing the feeling that they were unjustly disciplined as compared to those treated with relative leniency for the same type of offense?

4. A given executive does not mix socially with his employees because he feels that he won't be able to administer penalties effectively if he does. Comment upon his opinion.

5. In your opinion are employees essentially "good" or essentially "bad"? How must your actions differ depending upon the stand you take?

6. What division of work would you suggest between the personnel department and line departments regarding the handling of disciplinary cases? How much would this division depend upon a definition of disciplinary matters?

7. What is meant by "good" discipline? Does this imply undue subservience by employees? What has this to do with the process of integration of interests?

8. In the case of disciplinary action, management must take negative or punitive steps. Is there any room for positive motivation in such instances? Explain.

9. Although it is suggested that undue haste in handling disciplinary cases should be avoided, how do you reconcile this with the claim that it is unwise to allow such cases to become stale?

10. If a number of employees are involved in an infraction of rules, should disciplinary action be taken individually or collectively? Explain.

11. What steps should executives take to minimize the possibility of allowing their opinions to take on the clothing of facts when dealing with disciplinary cases?

12. Would you recommend any degree of spying on employees in order to catch rule breaking?

13. Why do most executives dislike applying disciplinary action? How would you handle a conference intended to improve executives in this aspect of their work? What material would you include in such a conference?

14. What if a given executive seems to be or has the reputation of being unduly "tough"? What steps would you, as personnel manager, take? Explore the various possibilities.

15. Should management agree, assuming that it can avoid being forced to agree to the contrary, to a clause in a union contract that the union will discipline certain types of infractions? What might such an agreement lead to?

16. Has a company the right to publicize the names of rule breakers and thus hold them up to public scorn? Explain.

17. A given supervisor complained to the workers that the policies of the company were unsound. What effect are such complaints likely to have upon the supervisor? If you, as a supervisor, cannot understand certain policies in regard to disciplinary action, what should you do?

18. A personnel manager stated that he noticed that executives who had to discipline often were either poor executives or had an inferiority complex. Do you believe that this explanation is sound? What other reasons might there be? Do your suggestions fall in with those of the personnel manager's explanation?

19. Is it possible to follow uniform policies or patterns of disciplinary action and still make allowance for individual differences? Why or why not?

20. Under what circumstances would you suggest that the personnel department be given the responsibility of disciplining employees?

24 | Positive Motivation of Employees

INTRODUCTION

"An ounce of prevention is worth a pound of cure" is a saying with much to commend it, provided that there is a choice between prevention and cure. During physical illness, for example, a pound of "cure" is invariably worth the cost. And when employees are dissatisfied with their companies or their companies with them, the costly "cures" of handling grievances or of taking disciplinary action are unavoidable. However, when employees and the company are reasonably satisfied with each other, it is preferable to administer ounces of prevention. The foregoing two chapters have been concerned with "cures"; the present chapter is devoted to means of preventing in so far as possible the development of ills.

Part of the task of minimizing employee or company dissatisfactions lies in management's development of the ability to foresee cases of company ineptitude or employee disobedience. Perhaps the most hopeful prospect for pleasant and continued good labor-management relations lies in the development of a self-stimulating desire on the part of all groups to do their best to make the whole organization more successful.

Appealing to the desires rather than the fears of employees constitutes the basic idea of positive motivation. Negative motivation is based upon the drive of fear—a drive which certainly does bring some results. After all, most of us are driven and repelled by various fears. However, in the long run and in terms of greatest satisfaction, our greatest deeds are those that are accomplished through positive motivation—those that we really enjoy doing.

This chapter is concerned with the practices and principles of positive motivation. In order to have a fuller understanding of the implications and meaning of positive motivation, the first part of this chapter is taken up with definitions and meanings. Then essential steps in a program of positive stimulation are listed and described, some principles of stimulation are discussed, and, finally, a few comments are made on union-management relations in this area.

MEANING OF POSITIVE MOTIVATION

1. POSITIVE AND NEGATIVE DRIVES.   As already noted, all employees are spurred by negative and positive drives. On the one hand, they fear to lose their jobs or earning power because of the economic consequences to their families and themselves. It is unpleasant to contemplate the loss of prestige, the destruction of hopes and dreams, and the reduction in standards of living that can come from the loss of one's job or by demotion. Since most people have this fear, which forces itself sometimes vividly and sometimes weakly into their conscious behavior, they "watch their step" more or less carefully.

This type of drive is not completely satisfactory, but neither is it eradicable. It will always be with us. Its role in personnel management has been discussed in the preceding two chapters.

Opposing the drive of fear is that of positive motivation. It means doing things because of a liking for the tasks at hand. But do people like to work? Can we actually grow to like coming down to the shop or office, day in and day out? Is it as good as fishing, or hunting, or just staying in bed when you want to? Satisfactory answers to these questions are prerequisite to any discussion of positive motivation.

2. WORK AND PLAY.   "Variety is the spice of life" expresses a very profound truth. None of us wants to do one thing all the time. For example, out-and-out loafing becomes a very boring experience after awhile, or an unvarying diet of even a favorite dish soon proves distasteful. Whatever the reason may be (no one seems to know exactly why), we require a certain amount of change and a certain amount of variety to "spice" our existence.

Hence, in its place and in its proper proportion, work as opposed to play is relatively necessary and enjoyable. Indeed, without some work even play becomes uninteresting. So when we speak of "liking" work, it is a relative evaluation of work to other activities of human life. The statement assumes that an employee has other interests in some balance and proportion. Too much of any activity is as bad as too little. Therefore, in talking about liking work, it is not assumed that it has to be liked above other activities. It assumes that work is an essential ingredient in any well-rounded life. The gossip columns carry ample proof that absence of work leads to trouble.

Moreover, in discussing the matter of liking work, it must be recognized that the intensity with which different people like their work can and does vary. The degree of satisfaction one gets from his work depends, among other things, upon his inherent capacity to do the job. Hence it is highly desirable that individuals be placed in jobs for which they are fitted. With this placement as a good beginning, the degree of satisfaction and therefore the desire to work better are increased.

And, finally, in this general approach to the question of relative desires, attention is directed to the nature of satisfaction which one gets out of a job. There are varieties of satisfaction, and perhaps all of them are felt in working. A person may find sheer joy in working; he may like to see things "grow," he may like his companions, and he likes to earn the money with which to buy the goods that determine his standard of living. In general, all workers are stimulated by nonfinancial as well as financial rewards.

3. SUMMARY. In summary, the phrase "desire to work" when used as an explanation of what motivates people to work has relative rather than absolute meanings. It implies that a job has its place in a balanced scheme of life. It recognizes that work can be enjoyed when seasoned with play and when selected in accordance with our interests, likes, and dislikes. And, finally, the statement implies that a liking for work may flow from the work itself and from the compensation received for working.

STEPS OF POSITIVE MOTIVATION

As noted above, positive motivation comes from the expectation of financial and nonfinancial rewards. It will be assumed here that financial rewards are satisfactory. Attention is devoted accordingly to the nonfinancial methods of stimulation.

The major steps to be taken in the use of positive motivation include:

1. Develop a working set of motivating tools
2. "Size up" individuals that require motivation
3. Select the appropriate motivating tool
4. Apply the appropriate motivating tool
5. Follow up the results of the application

TOOLS OF MOTIVATION

It makes little sense to tell executives to use methods of positive motivation unless they have knowledge of the various types of positive motivations and can apply them as occasion demands. Hence the personnel department can make a real contribution by providing executives with, and educating them in the use of, these methods. The intention here is to review the major groups of positive motivations and to suggest conditions under which their use might be desirable.

Tools of positive motivation can be divided for purposes of discussion into two large groups. There are, first, appeals based upon the interests and needs of the company and, second, appeals based upon the interests, likes, and satisfactions of the employee. The first of these is perhaps most fundamental because, if the company does not succeed, there is no need to discuss the second group. Nevertheless, the first group is the hardest to understand and to put across because it is concerned with seemingly impersonal interests. The second group of interests is usually better understood and more often applied.

1. COMPANY INTERESTS. This group of appeals is based upon the argument that employees should exert themselves for the good of the company. It is based upon the very simple proposition that a worker can like to, and therefore will, exert himself for someone else. Without mincing words, is it true or not?

a) Working for Others. Obviously, you or I may refuse to work for somebody because we do not like that person; but, just as obviously, we may "work our fingers to the bone" for those whom we like a great deal. Indeed, many have made the supreme sacrifice for those they loved. All this is not intended as a buildup for a "do-or-die" spirit—it is intended to prove that people will and do work for others. Now, then, does or can "the others" include a business corporation?

To answer this it is perhaps better to inquire why we like to work for others. Here there are a variety of reasons. We may do so because we do not want to see others suffer. We may do so because we want to be associated with successful, happy, and progressive individuals; it gives us prestige. Or we may do so because our ego is expanded through the realization that our efforts have brought about a desired condition. All these explanations, it is notable, turn out to be personal reasons. We work for others because, in one way or another, our own interests are served thereby.

Apply the reasoning of the foregoing paragraph to the proposition that it is good to work and to work diligently for a corporation. Why should the worker exert himself? If he does, the corporation stands that much better chance of being successful. If it does succeed, the employee has minimized the possibility of losing his job with the economic consequences to himself or his family. He has increased his own prestige by being associated with a sound organization, and he can take pride in having helped to build the successful results.

b) Identity of Company and Personal Interests. The fundamental explanation for the soundness of an appeal based upon company interest is that the company's interests are in a sense also the interests of the employees. But consider the argument, which one often hears, that the interests of management and labor are opposed.

This question has two angles which the askers seldom take the effort to make clear. In the first place, it is impossible for the employees in the main to have satisfactory employment unless their company is successful. Success of the company is indispensable to the success of the employees. A company that does not "make money" (profits) cannot long continue to keep its employees in full force on the payroll. The company declines, and so do the rewards to labor. In this sense, then, there can be no opposition between labor and management—either both succeed or both fail; the failure of one will most certainly not help the other to succeed.

In the second place, however, it is possible that one party or the other, having contributed its efforts, may try to get more for its share; and thus the other will lose proportionately. For example, management may seek to gain an unfair share of profits, in which case labor would have a smaller amount to divide; or labor may seek excessive wages, in which case the risk taker would not get a fair return on his capital investment. That such "grabs" have taken place on both sides in the industrial history of the United States is beyond argument.

But even in this latter instance, the interests of labor and management are not opposed in the sense that each does not respect the right of the other to receive a return for its efforts. Difference of opinion does exist, however, as to how much each thinks the other should get. This is where "interests are opposed."

c) Absence of Precise Measuring Tools. Why not figure out exactly what management's and labor's contributions are worth? Unfortunately, there does not exist a yardstick, a thermometer, or a set of micrometers that will measure precisely the value of management's or labor's contributions to the common result. There are measuring devices that are more or less accurate and exact, but they are not precisely accurate. When it comes to such a sensitive nerve as the pocketbook nerve, the accounts must be cast accurately, or there is a controversy. The best hope for a reduction in controversies over the relative shares of labor and management lies in the development of confidence in the inherent fairness and in the desire to be fair of labor in management and management in labor. Unfortunately, in the past each has often given the other reason for distrust.

The trouble lies, not in the opposition of interests, but in a common human failing to see the other fellow's position. Management's and labor's interests are not opposed. They are similar in terms of both wanting, first, to see both succeed and, second, to have both receive a fair share of the revenues. There often is, however, disagreement as to what a fair share is. And there have been times when one or the other tried to outdo the other. Lack of agreement on a fair share or lack of standards of honest dealing should not be used as an argument for saying that the interests of labor and management are opposed.

d) Relation of Standards of Fairness and Confidence. To sum up, there are valid and good reasons for appealing to employees on the grounds that upon them depends the success of the company. However, this appeal cannot be used until two points are clarified in the minds of the employees. They must, first, understand why the success of the company is a necessary preliminary to their own success. They must also be convinced that their efforts in making the company successful will not result in somebody else getting rich at their expense. The first of these two is more difficult to prove than the latter.

It is, of course, easy to say, "Be fair," but it is hard to do it in such a way that the other person is convinced of your fairness. The fundamental rule that management must follow if it is being fair is: Keep at it. Confidence in the company is not developed overnight—it may be lost overnight, but it grows ever so slowly. It is often discouraging to keep at a program when the workers do not seem to appreciate its value, but unceasing efforts are the price that must be paid.

The appeal to company interests presupposes that, in everything management does, it is as fair as it knows how to be. Only then will employees "work their heads off" for it. And that is the kind of effort which, curiously enough, gives the deepest satisfaction to the worker and which is so earnestly desired by the company.

2. PERSONAL INTERESTS. The appeals that can be made to employee interests are numerous and varied. Perhaps all of them can be boiled down to the factor of pride. Practically everyone desires some kind of prestige. It may be that we pride ourselves in our accomplishments, our independence, our keenness of judgment, or our personality. Without any feeling of boastfulness, it is a natural reaction to take such pride. The real question for management to answer is which type of accomplishment gives workers the feeling of prestige. Hence management should be aware of the various types of accomplishment.

a) The Gregarious Factor. One of our fundamental drives is gregariousness—the desire to identify oneself as a member of a group. Following closely is the desire to be recognized as a significant member of the group. We are all more or less gregarious—we like to mix with fellow beings—and the degree to which we can be gregarious depends upon how well others accept us. And so we try to do those things that make us acceptable. That is why we hate to be laughed at—it is an unmistakable sign that our efforts (and consequently ourselves) have been rejected.

Unfortunately, in some companies for an employee to be accepted by his fellow workers, he must "hate" his company or his supervisor. When this state of affairs exists, the employees have some deep-seated grievances which must be removed before more constructive steps can be taken. Assuming, however, that the employees are not "down on" the company, how can the idea of "acceptance" be developed as an appeal?

b) *Gaining Acceptance.* It is not intended here to digest all the possible ways in which any of the positive appeals can be put into effect. Hence these are only suggestions. In the case of gaining acceptance, an early step should be that of a proper introduction of a new employee to his fellow workers. Many executives have forgotten how strange they felt when they first came to their jobs, but that strangeness is very real to the new employee. The quicker he is made to "feel at home," the quicker he becomes accepted and hence the sooner he becomes a better worker. And one more example, sincere compliments paid so that others can unobstrusively be made to overhear them certainly helps to increase the prestige and, therefore, the acceptableness of good workers. Of course, needless and repetitious compliments are soon recognized as "soft soap" and may hinder rather than help an employee.

c) *Pride in Craftsmanship.* Closely akin to acceptance, because it has something to do with being accepted, is the desire to be recognized for craftsmanship or workmanship. So long as an employee considers his task merely a routine job, it will fail to stimulate him to greater action. But when he feels that his accomplishments are due to some personal skill which others do not possess or have not developed in the same degree that he has, his pride will make him more productive and more satisfied. Present-day industry may be monotonous, but some of this feeling of drudgery arises out of a total lack of feeling that anything personal is required to do the job.

d) *The Factor of Significance.* Similarly, employees like to feel that they are doing something worth while. Lack of interest in a job can often be traced to a feeling that what a person is doing is insignificant. And here is where industry can learn an important lesson from the war effort. The boost in spirit which many workers got when they learned that they were, for example, building the tools to bomb Tokyo was astounding. No matter how small the task, everyone got an emotional lift. It may be impossible and impracticable to supply a similar lift in peacetime. Nevertheless, the old joke about "I've got a job putting on bolt No. 747" is an implied recognition that someone has failed to prove that, in its place, bolt No. 747 is the "lost nail, that lost the shoe, that lost the horse, that lost the message, that lost the kingdom." A tremendous amount of good can come from building a recognition of worth-whileness.

e) The Factor of Competition. Besides such direct appeals to the likes and dislikes of a given worker, it is possible to use indirect appeals. For example, the competitive urge can be developed sometimes by making wise comparisons of the output or progress of one worker with that of others. Or subtle hints may be dropped to the effect that when a vacancy occurs, it will be filled by an employee of given qualifications. Or, again, direct examples of how other workers have succeeded may serve to stimulate a worker to imitate them. Of course, more formal methods, such as prizes for suggestions, have sometimes been used with success in this connection.

Briefly, then, the personnel department should develop a list of the things that serve to stimulate people. Here a few of the more basic approaches to positive motivations have been noted. Such a list will be invaluable to all levels of executives, particularly those who deal with operative employees.

ANALYSIS OF INDIVIDUAL DIFFERENCES

All the foregoing suggestions would most certainly not have the same effect upon all employees. It is essential, therefore, to learn the nature of each employee. In this way, the stage is set for a more appropriate selection of a motivating tool. This step does not imply spying or figuring out what will "fool" the employee. Positive motivation depends absolutely upon the sincerity of management—upon a real intention to be absolutely honest with the employee.

However, since people differ, we should try to learn how they differ. It most certainly is fairer to deal with them as individuals than to try to fit all of them into one mold.

How does one find out how people differ and how they will react to different suggestions? In short, the answer is careful observation. Employees are constantly "telling us" what they like, dislike, hope for, etc. Unfortunately, we do not always "listen" to them. But the successful executive is very observant. He is a keen student of people; he watches them carefully; and, as a result, he gets along with them, and they like him. Hence the personnel department can be of help in showing executives how to observe their employees and to review their relations with them. For example, it can hold conferences to check over their experiences in handling employees. The past may seem to contain a lot of failures, but it is also a gold mine of useful information. As a result of such training, executives will be in a better position to know what techniques to use with each employee.

SELECTING MOTIVATING TOOLS

The selection of the most effective motivating factor can be made much more intelligently after a careful analysis of an employee's personality. There is little use in appealing to the motive of loyalty if he does not go for "flag waving." Yet this appeal is rather strong with most people, because they do not want to be considered disloyal and, therefore, fail to be accepted by the group.

Moreover, the selection of a motivating tool should give due consideration to timing. It is undesirable to appeal, for example, to craftsmanship when the stress at a given time has to be upon output. Or it is not wise to appeal to the competitive urge when a great deal of stress has to be placed upon high quality. The demands of the situation should have much to do with the selection.

Also, the selection should be made in terms of a long-run program of employer-employee relations. Selecting one motive today and another tomorrow is likely to confuse the situation; but a program of appeals, worked out in advance, is likely to succeed because timing considers the future. Obviously, what will be done in the future is conditioned by the past, and the present is tomorrow's past.

APPLYING THE MOTIVATION

The next logical step, applying a motivating tool, might seem to be obvious, and so it is. However, it is sometimes easier to decide upon a course than actually to follow it, and this is particularly true in the case of positive motivations. It is so easy to say, "Why should I appeal to his desire for prestige, can't he see it for himself?"

The trouble is that we all have the human failing, more or less, to backslide. Or, as the old saying goes, "The path to perdition is paved with good intentions." So employees do know that they ought to spur themselves, but they forget. Therefore, the motives must be emphasized and re-emphasized and re-re-emphasized.

Application of motives requires, of course, careful wording and approach. One does not just "appeal to an employee's loyalty." Here, the personnel department can be of service by providing courses in public speaking, private speaking, and interviewing. Such studies are well worth while. Perhaps the key to "selling" the employee is a very sincere attitude plus a simple statement of the case. This is when, by the way, current slang is much more effective than "big words."

FOLLOW-UP

A course of action, once taken, should not promptly be forgotten. Subsequently, and perhaps frequently, it is desirable to see how the effects of the stimulation are holding up. Indeed, the follow-up may consist of more than a routine checkup. The "treatment" may be continued; a series of shots-in-the-arm may be called for. Unless such a program of follow-up is decided upon as soon as a stimulator is first applied, there is danger that subsequent action may be overlooked.

Follow-up also has the decided advantage of serving to convince the worker in question that the executive's interest in him is more than temporary. A series of consultations, visits, and "pep talks" is real evidence that the interest is deep. And much as a worker likes a pat on the back, he likes two or more much better. One often hears some remark such as this: "The supervisor told me I was doing a good job— twenty years ago!" Perhaps the worker in question deserved only one compliment. However, in most cases more frequent compliments are earned and better serve the purpose of motivation.

A program of follow-up has the additional advantage of stimulating the executive himself. If he knows that certain steps must be taken in the future, he tends to become more observant, more discriminating, and more interested in his subordinates. Through such developments, the executive becomes a better executive.

FUNDAMENTALS OF MOTIVATION

Although the primary purpose of the preceding section was to outline the steps to be followed in positive motivation, a few common-sense rules were also discussed that should be remembered when taking the steps in question. In this section the aim is to discuss more fully some fundamentals that should underlie positive action. In other words, this section gives recognition to the fact that the personnel department should help executives to know not only how to do things but also why they are done that way—the "know-why" of the "know-how."

IMPORTANCE OF SELF-INTEREST

The list of appeals contained in the preceding section can be said to be built largely upon human selfishness. Of course, selfishness is bad when it extends into greediness. Nevertheless, it is justified so long as it stays within the borders of reasonable self-interest. Difficulty arises out of knowing exactly when reasonable selfishness becomes unreasonable. Individual standards for determining this must be developed, because there does not exist a universally accepted process of measurement.

But why is self-interest justified? To answer this we must first admit that if a tendency or characteristic is a part of that which we call "human nature," then we must be realistic and accept it as we do our environment. And self-interest is undoubtedly one of the strongest forces in the human being. Granted that it is, the conclusion follows that it should be used (and we all must hope that it will be used) reasonably, intelligently, and wisely.

When an appeal is made to an individual's pride, for example, there is danger of a person becoming egotistical. The activity must be carried on so that overmotivation does not result, and careful judgment is required to recognize the turning point. Appeal to self-interest, then, is similar in character to all good things—they remain good only in moderation. However, the risk of overmotivation must be taken if the desired results from appeals to selfishness can be hoped for at all.

IMPORTANCE OF ATTAINABILITY

The interests to which appeals are made must be attainable. This rule implies the elements of quantity, quality, and time of attainability. When we, for example, promise that by doing a good job a given operator will receive a particular amount of recognition, then that promise must be fulfillable.

The employee must be able, for example, to feel the pleasures of accomplishment if that is held out to him. He must be able to feel the satisfaction of a job well done. He must like to know that his superiors and fellow workers think highly of him for what he has done. He must, to put it simply, have an appreciation of other things besides the financial reward. (As pointed out earlier, the financial reward is not being discussed here.)

Moreover, if the employee in question has the ability to appreciate the reward, it must be given to him when it is earned. To claim that an employee will have more prestige is one thing, to see that he gets it is another. Some symbol must be used to identify prestige. Service ribbons, medals, and stripes are military devices for granting recognition to deserving soldiers and sailors. And industry, too, must distinguish, by buttons for example, the meritorious from the average worker.

Such "badges of distinction," whether formal or informal, are not window-dressing. Of course, some people do not like to wear their medals because they think it makes them conspicuous. In such cases, as was pointed out earlier, the reward should be handled with due consideration to individual likes and dislikes. But most people like their medals; they may "show off" a bit, but that is why they work hard. Besides, a reasonable amount of "showing-off" is accepted by most of us. We only dislike the fellow who struts too long and too often.

Finally, the rewards of recognition, craftsmanship, worth-whileness, etc., must be attainable within some reasonable length of time. The average worker does not want to wait until he retires to hear himself eulogized. He wants to know that he is good during his years and months of service. He does not want his efforts taken for granted or appreciation of them to go without saying. Because such neglect is practiced so often, he loses faith in everything but his own pay check— that comes at a definite time after performance.

PROPORTIONING REWARDS

The degree to which people exert themselves is not the same; therefore, their rewards should not be the same. This implies that an executive must be taught to measure how much "worth-whileness" or "recognition," for example, he will ladle out. This may sound unrealistic, but, figuratively speaking, that is what he must do.

It is possible to pay one individual, let us say, two dollars more per day than another. But if the first individual outproduces the second one, ten to eight, how are we going to measure out, let us say, an extra two units of compliments? The obvious answer is that it cannot be done precisely. If an attempt is not made, however, to measure out varying amounts of praise, the employees in question will notice it. They may not be sensitive in terms of thousandths of an ounce, but they can sense differences, nevertheless.

So, in using positive motivation, intangible though the rewards may be, executives must, nevertheless, make a serious effort to distinguish between the relative importance of the contributions that various people make. If they expect a uniform "thank you" to suffice for everyone, they will be disappointed sadly in the results. The reward must be proportioned to the contribution, to the individual, and to the conditions.

INTANGIBLE MOTIVES

The whole subject of positive motivation is concerned with the fact that we are feeling, as well as thinking, individuals. Hence, in using positive motivation, the factor of emotions is given great weight. This does not discount the rational and mental processes of labor, for both must be considered.

Appeal to intangible motives is another way of taking advantage of the well-recognized fact that most of us reach decisions largely upon the basis of how we feel rather than how we think. This does not mean that employees are foolish—they are no more foolish than the general run of any class or level of people. Assuming they are foolish is a sure way of underestimating their intelligence and their strength. One might fool them for awhile, but not always.

Indeed, our emotions are sometimes better guides than our reasoning powers. It is often difficult to calculate quantitatively what to do. In that event, the alternatives are to toss a coin or let our emotions decide. Since tossing a coin has no logical connection with the decision, we might just as well let our intuition decide.

The point being made here is that dealing with the emotions and feelings of people is a fair and honorable and justified practice so long as it stays within the bounds of honesty and decency. Hence it is a needful duty of management to learn how to work with the emotions of people as well as their reasoning processes. It does not denote meanness, stealth, dishonesty, or smallness when we appeal to an employee's emotions. He comes to work with them—he cannot leave them at home; so they should be considered a part of his equipment, just as the physical skills he possesses.

COMBINATIONS OF MOTIVES

The emphasis through this entire chapter has been upon nonfinancial appeals to the interests and likes of the employee. Of course, this emphasis has been for purposes of restricting reasonably the scope of discussion. It is impossible to talk about all aspects of a given problem at one time, however desirable that might be.

1. IMPORTANCE OF FINANCIAL REWARDS. It is now appropriate to state that appeals to intangible motives must be made with due consideration to the financial or other objective rewards that are also being granted or withheld. For example, there is little use to appeal to an employee's sense of loyalty if he has the feeling that his pay check is too small. The latter must be satisfactory before the former can be successfully employed. In short, positive motivation presupposes a satisfactory condition in the mind of the employee to whom the appeal is made that his wages, hours, and working conditions are fair. Unless this is true, the appeals to workmanship, recognition, etc., are largely a waste of time.

But what if a given worker is unreasonable? What if he does not think that wages, for example, are fair when they really are? The answer here is that the employee has a grievance, whether justified or not and whether imagined or not. And, like all other grievances, it must be "handled." Suggestions for such handling were taken up in an earlier chapter.

The point is that appeals to personal, intangible interests must be made only upon a satisfactory base of accepted wage and other objective rewards. In conjunction, the two make a strong incentive. When one is used without the other, the incentive is weakened. And when one is mishandled, an attempt to use the other usually brings failure.

2. CHANGES IN INTENSITY AND VARIETY OF MOTIVES. Moreover, the intensity of motivation may have to be increased and changed. The same old tune, played over and over again, does not bring the same results that it did at the beginning. Executives must change their "song-and-dance" routine. It is hard, but to get the best results it must be done. It is sometimes pathetic to hear employees remark among themselves, "Well, here comes the boss. I'll bet he's going to give us the such-and-so line today." Everybody knows what is coming, and the well-intentioned efforts not only fail but become the butt of a joke. Dealing with people cannot be routinized—it must go on, but with a change here and a change there.

In this connection, it would also be well for the company to read what is being printed in the union newspaper. Here will be found a current statement of changing demands, desires, and hopes. So if management expects to change motivators, suggestions can be found here.

3. THE ROLE OF THE PERSONNEL DEPARTMENT. The rules to be followed in taking positive action are never fully learned. Executives must forever be students. And all of this for the simple reason that personalities never remain static and never are quite completely open to examination. So the job is more difficult, but it is also, for that very reason, more interesting. And the personnel department can make a worth-while and significant contribution to the education of all executives in this matter of positive motivation.

UNION-MANAGEMENT RELATIONS

Inasmuch as unions are playing a more important role in labor relations, it is only realistic to examine briefly the possibilities of union-management co-operation in advancing positive motivation of employees. This possibility is generally overlooked because of the emphasis given to instances of labor-management strife. Yet, in the final analysis, more unions and companies get along better for longer periods of time than those that do not. Certainly, periods of labor-management peace are much more frequent than periods of strikes and strife.

On what grounds can unions and management co-operate to enhance positive motivation? None better than one in which both have a vital interest—higher and better standards of living. In this country, an increase in the necessities and "luxuries" of life is as much the responsibility and desire of one group as it is of the other. And their best joint action is indispensable to the attainment of desired goals. Hence the union, for example, has as much good reason to propagandize employees to increase productivity as does management.

Unfortunately, other issues have been so important at times to unions that enough effort or resources have not always been available to concentrate substantially upon positive motivation. In their desire to gain organizational recognition, increased wages, and protection from insecurity—all defensible goals—other positive areas of joint action have been sidetracked. But there is room for believing that after some of the urgent matters are settled, there will be a strong movement for strengthening the industry or the company in which a union has bargaining interests. And the best basis of adding strength is through a laboring force that wants to do the best job possible. This desire must be instilled through the joint offices of unions and management, as it has in some cases.

QUESTIONS AND PROBLEMS

1. As you review industrial progress, would you attribute such progress more to the pressure of fears or more to the liking which people have for their work? Explain and illustrate.

2. As union-management relations mature, do you expect to see unions participate more or less as a positive force in promoting industrial efficiency? Can you cite any evidence in support of the trend that you forecast?

3. "Blue Mondays" are not uncommon to factories or offices. Can you suggest any positive motivators to minimize such conditions?

4. It is said that an individual's desire to do a good job is sometimes inhibited by what fellow workers will think of him if he works too hard. Why might the group think thus? Is there anything that can be done about such inhibiting forces?

5. During the war years, a group of employees who were enthused about their jobs gradually lost much of their drive because output was constantly being impeded and delayed by numerous engineering design changes. What

would you have done, had you been a supervisor there? The personnel manager?

6. A given executive said that if he wanted his employees to follow a particular course of action, he began to condition them five years in advance. What did he mean by this statement? Is this not a pessimistic prospect for successful management of subordinates?

7. What is the basic appeal of programs of positive motivation of employees? How can positive motivation be applied in cases of grievances and disciplinary action?

8. Recently an advertisement appeared in a large city newspaper stating that a retired executive had tired of retirement and was seeking to make his executive services available for employment. What lessons are there in this case?

9. What has job placement to do with positive motivation of employees? Is it possible that, if all employees were placed in jobs that they really liked and were equipped to perform, they would be self-motivating?

10. Recent investigations point to the importance of sociological factors in determining the contentment or unrest of employees. Distinguish between psychological and sociological factors and principles.

11. An employee said that he liked his boss because he (the employee) was made to feel like an important person. What is the moral of this case?

12. A given company had lost money for a number of years after an earlier history of high profits. And the morale of its employees, as well as it could be measured, seemed to be definitely declining. Would you consider the lowered morale cause or effect, in relation to the trend of profits?

13. If employees are convinced, rightfully or wrongfully, that the company is keeping to itself an unfair share of profits, is there much use in attempting to appeal to them to work for the company? What is a fair share of profits for the company to keep?

14. Why is it difficult to follow the seemingly simple rule, "Be fair"?

15. An executive said, in reply to the suggestion that more praise be given to employees, that he found this practice made them too contented with themselves. How would you analyze this result?

16. Assume that you go to work for a company in its personnel department and find that the employees "hate" the company and its supervisors. How would you proceed in your attempt to change this state of affairs?

17. Is it possible to stress the aspect of workmanship and craftsmanship in this day of mass production and highly routinized jobs? What of the future?

18. How does the factor of timing enter into the process of positive motivation? Cite examples of good and bad timing.

19. It is sometimes stated that the principle of self-interest has failed in connection with business relationships. What is meant by this principle? Has it really failed? Explain.

20. If emotions are often more important than reasoning power in working with employees, what specific suggestions would you make to the management of your company if you were personnel manager? Illustrate your answer in connection with such matters as training programs, interviewing techniques, and company newspapers.

CHAPTER

25 | Physical Security

INTRODUCTION

Of significance to both employer and employee is the sense of security which surrounds the employee. The security may be of a physical or of an economic nature. Attention is devoted in this chapter to the former and in the next chapter to the latter.

The physical well-being of the employee is here studied in terms of working conditions, health, and safety. These phases have been chosen because of their universal importance and common acceptance as major areas of security activity. These phases are not independent divisions, for in actual practice they become interrelated and interaffecting. Moreover, each has drawn heavily upon or is affected by such professions as medicine, engineering, psychology, and management to a degree that exhaustive treatment here is impossible. All that can be done is to review various practices and principles in these areas that have contributed to better working conditions, improved health, and increased safety. Before discussing these topics, it is worth noting, first, the objectives of improved physical security and, second, the general trend of development in dealing with physical security.

OBJECTIVES

Numerous objectives may be attained by proper attention to working conditions, health, and safety. From the viewpoint of the individual, the importance of the objectives can hardly be overstated. For example, looked at, first of all, from the viewpoint of losses, how can anyone estimate the value of lives lost in industrial accidents? Or estimate the loss to the individuals involved in accidents resulting in loss of some member of the body? Of course, insurance benefits may be proportioned arbitrarily in order to provide some relief to these individuals or their beneficiaries, but the individual sufferings and losses are inestimable.

On the other hand, the healthy and safe worker gains personal satisfactions which alone make the effort to improve health, safety, and

499

working conditions worth while. A more co-operative spirit, higher morale, better workmanship, better use of materials and equipment, and better discipline are reflected in such workers. They not only gain more enjoyment from their work but also make the working day of their fellow workers and superiors more agreeable. All in all, the personal satisfactions, earnings, and progress of such workers are higher. And, of course, what happens to the individual—either negatively or positively—is of interest also to his family, relatives, friends, and the community.

To the company the objectives are many and significant. As an example, a quarter of a million working days, and the production thereof, are lost annually by fatal and disabling industrial accidents, according to estimates of the Bureau of Labor Statistics. The corollary losses of idle machinery, working capital, and space; of extra efforts to rearrange schedules and working crews; and of delayed shipments are beyond calculation. In the face of these facts, it is easy to see why industry now places a high priority on the effort to meet the challenge of safer and healthier working conditions.

TRENDS

Despite these obvious advantages, positive impetus to the development of a real interest by industry in the physical well-being of workers stemmed originally from the passage of industrial compensation laws by the various states. Prior to that time, which centers around the turn of the century, industry paid little attention to these matters because their burden and cost fell largely upon the worker, his family, or the community. Although industry, theoretically, could be held responsible for accidents, practically there were enough legal loopholes to make it immune to unfavorable lawsuits. In the common law, under which earlier employee-employer relationships were determined by precedent of previous court decisions, industry could escape financial responsibility for accidents under any of the following conditions:

1. An employee's own carelessness (known as the "contributory negligence rule")
2. The actions of a competent fellow worker (known as the "fellow-servant rule")
3. The risk connected with the work which the worker was willing to take when he accepted employment (known as the "assumption of risk rule")

Of course, the employer was expected to operate his business in a reasonably safe manner, to provide reasonably safe working conditions, and to employ workers competent to perform the tasks assigned to them.

1. DISADVANTAGES OF COMMON LAW. The results of such legal rules and administration were unsatisfactory. In the first place, when accidents just "happened" so that the cause could not be assigned to employer or employee, the latter had no recourse. Second, the loopholes in the common law were so wide that there were few occasions when the employer could not escape through them. Third, since court actions were the only medium by which responsibility could be established legally, they often dragged out so that employees gained little, even in the event of a favorable conclusion. And, last, industry itself never knew when a heavy judgment might be levied against it. Thus unfavorable though common-law principles and procedures were to employees, they also had risks for the employer.

2. ENACTMENT OF STATUTORY LEGISLATION. However, the demand for changes in legal rules came largely from labor, although some social-minded industrialists also favored changes. After much agitation, various states enacted laws covering compensation for accidents and illness arising from occupational hazards. These statutory enactments replaced the common-law decisions. By now all states have passed some such legislation.

The fundamental advantage of industrial compensation laws is that, irrespective of what or who causes an accident, except in instances of outrageous disregard of safety rules, the employee is compensated for financial losses which he incurs. Compensation is paid in a variety of ways. In the case of death, lump sums or weekly allotments may be paid to dependents. In the event of total or partial disability, the individual may be paid a lump sum and also provided with periodic subsistence payments. And in the event of accidents or illness which result in temporary losses of earning power, weekly allotments of varying amounts are provided.

3. FINANCIAL ARRANGEMENTS UNDER STATUTORY LAW. The funds for such compensation are obtained by charges against the employer. This is done through payment of premiums to insurance systems of private ownership in some states and to state-operated systems in others. Administrative machinery is provided by which the amount of liability can readily be determined, though in all cases recourse may be had to the judicial branch in the event of disagreement with administrative rulings.

The charges against employers will tend to vary with the number and severity of compensable accidents and illnesses. Hence it is to the interest of management to reduce them to the lowest possible number. Such efforts cost money, to be sure, but accident reduction programs are nevertheless followed because of the principle that to make or save money it is invariably necessary to spend money. Here is an important explanation of many safety programs that industry has promoted: It has been found that they are financially less costly than accidents.

4. MERIT RATING. Further incentive to reduce accidents and hazards is provided by the practice of adjusting insurance premiums in accordance with "merit ratings" of health and safety practices and results. The most common way of doing this is to adjust an employer's insurance rate in accordance with his accident record. This is known as "experience merit rating." Another plan is to adjust rates according to degree of risk which is present on an employer's premises. Obviously, a factory or office which maintains and safeguards its equipment is likely to have fewer accidents than those in which the reverse is true. This system of adjusting rates is known as "schedule merit rating."

In short, the trend in better conditions of employment and toward positive safety programs can be ascribed largely to the fact that industry has been forced to assume the burden of financial losses. After the dollar value of accidents and illness was forced home, it was not long before efforts were exerted nearly everywhere to reduce the losses. Whereas many companies may truthfully contend that their safety and health programs are based upon humanitarian motives, the financial responsibility serves to provide a strong bulwark to their good intentions.

WORKING CONDITIONS

GENERAL CONSIDERATIONS

When pictures or descriptions of factories as they existed prior to the turn of the century are contrasted with the physical arrangements of modern plants, there can be little doubt about the importance which management attaches to good working conditions. These conditions are apparent, on the one hand, in the technical tools of production. Machines and equipment used directly in production are designed with a view to the comfort and effective employment of the skills of the operator. For example, levers by which operators make adjustments to the machines are placed with a view to anatomical features of the human body and not to mechanical demands alone.

And, on the other hand, various features that might simply be said to add to the comfort of the worker are designed and installed with due care. Lighting and air conditioning, locker and personal facilities, and hazard controls exemplify the types of features that management considers as indirectly affecting production and costs through their direct influence upon the comfort and physical well-being of employees.

Although the actual work of design and maintenance of working conditions is largely the work of the engineering and plant maintenance departments, nevertheless the personnel phases of such work are significant. To begin with, the personnel department has a stake in such matters because of their effect upon the loyalty and attitude of employees. This department should therefore have an advisory relation to the departments that may plan for and maintain physical conditions. In the second place, unions often make an issue of physical conditions. Hence the personnel department should be attentive to such matters so that such disputes or frictions do not have cause for arising. And, third, the personnel department should keep abreast of new developments in order to be able to advise management on steps that might be taken so that desirable improvements will not be overlooked.

PHASES OF WORKING CONDITIONS

This is not to imply that the personnel department must have technicians on its staff. Rather it should be acquainted with technical working conditions merely to the extent that any shortcomings might be detected, corrections requested, and improvements suggested. In the following discussion attention is therefore directed to various important phases of working conditions; and pertinent suggestions regarding design, maintenance, and use are noted.

1. MATERIAL HANDLING. Material handling is the source of the greatest number of injuries in industry. Hence the flow of materials in all of its phases should be carefully planned. First, handling of materials and parts at machines and benches should be studied, to the end that physical handling is reduced to a minimum and adequate protective devices are provided. Second, the flow of work between machines and departments should be facilitated by proper equipment and be provided with well-designed and well-marked storage spaces and aisles and roadways. An interesting example of how a study of hazards can be tied in with the design of flow of work is illustrated in Figure 78 (p. 505).

2. MACHINE GUARDING. Protection of the worker by the strategic placement of mechanical guards and electronic controls is another essential of good working conditions. Various devices can be provided to protect workers, first, from the many parts of all equipment that transmit power and, second, from the hazards at the point of work. The

FIGURE 78. A Safety and Process Chart*

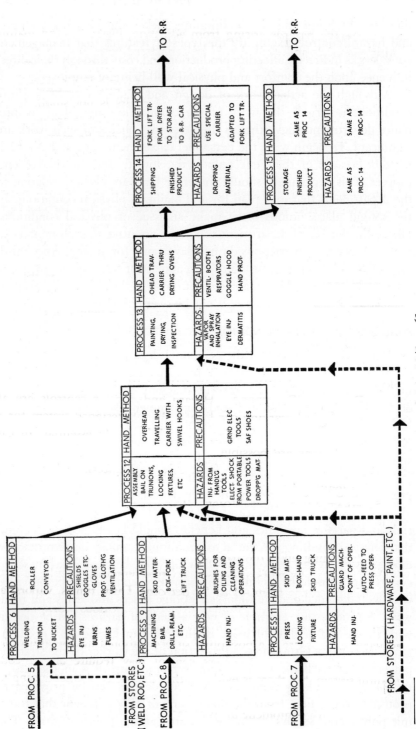

* Koller, George, "The Challenge of Post-War Safety," *Personnel*, July, 1945, p. 65.

dangers arising from the mechanical devices that surround the worker as well as the hazards arising from adjusting, inserting, and manipulating materials and tools should be considered here.

3. FACTORS OF THE WORKPLACE.   The comfort and efficiency of workers is also affected importantly by the physical factors at the workplace. For example, the influence of chairs is not small. In one company, chairs in the factory have been designed that are adjustable to differing sizes of individuals. The chair seats can be moved up and down, the backs both up and down and in and out, and the footrests up and down. Moreover, the chairs have foam-rubber seats and backs. In another company the installation of chairs that can be easily moved on operations that require considerable stretching and movement has increased production 25 per cent and decreased fatigue noticeably. Such adjustable chairs are particularly desirable when women as well as men are employed on similar operations.

Other factors of the workplace that deserve mention are the level of work surfaces and clothing or safety devices that should be worn. Adjustment of the level of the work surface to the height of the person using it, by providing platforms or adjustable chairs, can reduce fatigue and hence increase productivity. In relation to clothing and safety devices, rules regarding these should be established with a view to employee comfort and tastes, or co-operation will be difficult to secure.

4. DISASTER CONTROLS.   Hazard and disaster controls are also essentials of good working conditions. A well-designed system for detecting, inhibiting, and fighting fires is absolutely essential. In cases where explosions are possible, a program of control should include periodic inspections, isolation from other operations, and devices for reducing igniting factors.

5. HEAT, LIGHT, AND NOISE.   The importance of heat, light, and noise control are commonly recognized. In the matter of atmospheric conditions, temperatures should be controlled between 65 and 85 degrees, depending upon the nature of the work and season of the year. Unless required by work processes, relative humidity should be maintained in the range from 45 to 50 per cent. Dust, fumes, vapors, and gases should be removed from workplaces, obnoxious workplaces isolated, or workers supplied with protective devices, such as masks, particularly when there is a possibility of occupational disease and illness. Temperature and air cleanliness control may require an air conditioning system, but there is evidence that the value of maintaining personal efficiency during the summer months, for example, outweighs the cost of such equipment in most cases. The effect of lighting should

also be carefully determined. Good illumination is a factor not only in productive efficiency but also in accident reduction. Hence standards of illumination based on the advice of illuminating engineers should be adopted. Necessary goggles, shields, and glasses should be provided where there is danger to the eyes.

The factor of noise is also of significance in promoting employee comfort and efficiency. In factories the noise of many operations are at present seemingly beyond control. But it is possible to segregate excessively noisy equipment, to dampen vibration, and occasionally to redesign machines that are particularly annoying. In offices, however, much has been done to soundproof walls and ceilings as well as equipment and machines. The results in such cases have more than offset costs.

Since excessive noise can also lead to hearing injuries, which may be compensable under industrial compensation laws, noise measurement surveys are suggested if there is any question about noisy conditions. The threshold of painful noise begins around 110 decibels, the unit used to measure sound. An idea of sound and noise intensities may be gained from the following list of sound conditions:

Rustle of leaves	20 decibels
Average office	30
Stenographic room	60
Average conversation	60
Average machine shop	70
Newspaper pressroom	90
Subway train	110
Boiler factory	110

6. COLOR. Proper use of color may also have a constructive influence on safety and efficiency. One company reported that cost of accidents was reduced from $1.21 to $0.18 per employee after old machinery was painted to conform with safety recommendations instead of a uniform gray. A production increase up to 20 per cent was also noted. Suggested colors are as follows: yellow or orange for dangerous materials or parts of machinery; green, white, gray, or black for safe materials; blue for protective materials; and red for fire protection materials and equipment.[1]

7. PERSONAL NEEDS. Good working conditions also call for adequate provision of conveniences of a personal nature. Good drinking water, properly cooled, and made available through well-located dispensers should be supplied. Adequate toilet facilities that are well located, lighted, and ventilated and carefully cleaned and disinfected should be provided. Facilities such as shower rooms are also indis-

---

[1] *Management Review,* Vol. XXXVII, No. 5, p. 266.

pensable when working conditions may lead to skin diseases or contamination. And, finally, dressing and rest rooms should be provided if women are employed.

8. FACTORY LANDSCAPING AND LAYOUT. The outside of the factory should also be given attention in the matter of employee comfort and attitudes. First, the general appearance and landscaping cast an impression upon employees for good or for bad. Second, strategic arrangement and pleasing appearance of approaches, streets, sidewalks, gates, and entrances can be a part of "good working conditions." And, third, arrangements for parking of automobiles and areas for waiting for transportation—private or public—can put the employee into the right (or wrong) attitude toward his working day.

VARIATIONS IN WORKING CONDITIONS

Although there is general agreement on the standards that should govern heating, lighting, and air conditioning, practices differ widely on the other phases of working conditions. In more farsighted companies, all conditions are designed and maintained with meticulous care. In some factories that have dusty, oily, or grimy operations, all surfaces are painted light colors, walls and ceilings are cleaned frequently, and floors are swept carefully, so that they appear as neat as food-producing plants. Or, to combine maintenance with safety, various parts of machines are painted contrasting colors—green for nonmoving parts, yellow for parts that have a minimum of hazard, and red for dangerous parts. As these practices are adopted universally, it will be possible for the employee to adjust himself to new jobs with an increased sense of security, just as he now accepts and expects good lighting.

Moreover, arriving at and keeping up good working conditions can be of interest to employees as well as to the maintenance and engineering departments. For example, in some factories, operating employees are brought into the task of maintaining good physical conditions by providing bonuses or prizes to employees of departments adjudged to be cleanest and neatest during some preceding period. Thus the originality and contributions of employees can be added to the task of developing and maintaining conditions of such significance to themselves and the company.

HEALTH

PERTINENT FACTOR

The health of employees may be influenced by a number of factors. Off-plant living conditions and habits, medical services, environmental conditions, and past personal history are of vital significance. These phases are seldom considered within the domain of management influence, so are not considered here. A few companies, to be sure, have interested themselves in off-plant phases—and increasingly others are likely to—but at present the numbers so concerned are small. Health is also significantly influenced by working conditions and safety practices. This is discussed in other sections of this chapter, so no detailed mention of these phases need be made here. Of interest here are two commonly encountered health programs, first, medical examinations and, second, various health services. Discussed in this section, too, is the matter of organizing medical services.

MEDICAL EXAMINATIONS

Most companies give due recognition to provision for and performance of adequate medical examinations. This may be seen by reviewing (1) coverage of examinations, (2) facilities for examinations, and (3) medical and health records.

1. COVERAGE OF EXAMINATIONS. A useful survey of the subject may be made by noting who may be examined, when, and how. A list of those who may be examined would include the following:

1. Applicants for employment or re-employment
2. Employees who return from extended leaves of absence
3. Employees who are returning from sick leave
4. Employees who have been absent, excused or not excused, for a specified number of days, usually six to twelve days
5. Employees engaged in occupations with exposure to disease or illness
6. Employees whose work might endanger the life or health of customers or fellow workers
7. All employees, periodically or as new developments in medicine warrant

The periodicity of, or frequency with which, examinations may be given also varies. A list of the variations follows:

1. An examination of employees only when they enter the employment of the company
2. Nonperiodic examinations for those returning from sick leave, etc.
3. Periodic examinations
   a) Voluntarily assumed by the company for all employees or those engaged in hazardous or health-affecting occupations
   b) Required by law for those engaged in occupations affecting the health or security of customers or patrons

A list of types of examinations which may be given follows:

1. Medical examinations of general physical condition
2. Examinations for communicable disease, e.g., syphilis or tuberculosis

3. Visual and dental examinations
4. Psychiatric examinations
5. Visits to the homes of employees

Of course, few companies include all of the foregoing in their examination programs. This for the reasons that, first, opinions differ as to how far a company should delve into a person's physical and mental make-up and, second, facilities and staff are not always available or are beyond the resources of some companies, particularly the smaller plants.

There is a strong tendency, however, toward expansion of such programs. To cite but one example, there is a growing interest in the benefits of psychoanalysis and psychiatry. Various companies have moved slowly and with satisfactory results in this direction. The aim here is not so much to eliminate the obviously unbalanced but rather to help employees and executives who have minor troubles to minimize blocks and obstacles to more effective and satisfying living. Without doubt the constructive benefits derived by companies adopting such services will lead more and more to similar action.

2. FACILITIES FOR EXAMINATIONS. Most companies provide excellent facilities for physical examinations relative to their size and needs. Usually facilities are provided adjacent to the personnel department office, since most examinations are given in connection with various personnel procedures; e.g., new employees, transfers, employees returning from sick leave, or those absent without permission who are returning to their jobs. This location is also desirable because it gives applicants an opportunity to get a favorable impression of the company. Moreover, it is sufficiently removed from factory operations to make its location favorable for medical work.

Next to medical and professional staff, the equipment is invariably the most important part of the medical department. What it should contain depends upon the examinations to be given, the hazards that exist in the company, the policy of the company, and the number of workers to be served. Usually, facilities are provided for handling minor injury cases, taking chest X-ray pictures, making syphilis tests, urinalysis, and cursory eye, ear, nose, and dental examinations. Some of the larger companies also have completely equipped operating rooms and hospital units. A few have eye and dental dispensaries.

3. MEDICAL AND HEALTH RECORDS. All medical, health, and accident procedures should be properly implemented with adequate records and reports. Since vital decisions are based on them, it is doubly essential to gather and report information so that those who use them will be able to interpret them properly. The records which may be

kept are so varied that no more can be done here than to list the major categories.

Records that may be kept include the following:

1. Medical examinations
2. Dispensary cases handled
3. Reports of accident occurrence
4. Investigations and surveys of working conditions
5. Trends of accidents, occupational illness, and first-aid cases

HEALTH SERVICES

In addition to examining candidates and employees, health services may be expanded to include (1) surveys of plant conditions and (2) off-plant medical care.

1. PLANT SURVEYS. Plant surveys are essential in order to maintain healthy working conditions. They serve to reveal sources of occupational disease, unsafe working conditions, and conditions conducive to the development of fatigue. The surveys should be made periodically or upon special occasions. They should be conducted by skilled technicians operating out of the medical department of the personnel division, since this will insure freedom from interference by or condonance of undesirable conditions by line executives. In addition, the skills of properly trained technicians and professional talent will be brought to play in this important work.

In order to appreciate the types of surveys and checks, some of the more common types will be noted. An important phase of such surveys is that of checking operations that tend toward occupational disease or illness. Examples are making dust counts in core rooms and checking the percentages of carbon monoxide in the air of certain baking rooms.

The foregoing types of surveys pertain particularly to factors or conditions that can be detected without too much difficulty because they cover physical matters. As important, but less obvious to the observer, are factors leading to the development of excessive fatigue. Surveys of fatigue must be made indirectly in terms of the effect fatigue has upon output, scrap, absenteeism, illness, and accidents. Deducing the existence of fatigue and hence of factors conducive to fatigue from such studies is difficult and uncertain because other causes may induce lowered production, etc. Nevertheless, until better measures of fatigue are developed—indeed, until the nature of fatigue itself is ascertained by the scientists themselves—the foregoing types of surveys constitute the best methods.

2. EXTENSION OF HEALTH SERVICES. In some companies the health and medical services, originally provided only to serve the in-

ternal needs of the company, are now being extended to families of employees. Such extensions are not to be confused with health and medical service insurance, to be described in a later chapter, which provide for financial assistance to those who require such services from their own doctors. Medical facilities have been made available to employees and their families usually in cases where community facilities are inadequate or where company officials take the view that employees must be given such opportunities or they will not seek medical services, even when financially able, until too late.

The expansion of health services usually takes place by providing visiting-nurse service to employees away from work due to illness. After this, provisions are made for giving free physical examinations to all who desire them. Also, the services of company doctors or hospital facilities are made available in the case of emergency operations due to causes outside of the employment contract. From these extensions it is a simple step to provide free examinations and at-cost, or even free, service in connection with the prevention or cure of visual, aural, dental, as well as general physical ailments.

How far companies should go in these matters is debatable. On the one hand, it can be argued that such services are beyond their reasonable responsibilities and constitute a form of unfair competition to community service. But, on the other hand, such aid serves the whole community as well as the individuals concerned and often goes beyond the services available in any community. Thus far, the case is academic because relatively few companies have extended their services in this manner.

Less controversial are extensions of health service which are of an educational nature. For example, first-aid courses have been sponsored by many companies. Their effects have external as well as internal value, for the records are replete with cases in which lives have been saved and serious pain and losses have been prevented by those who had completed Red Cross first-aid courses. Home nursing courses are another example of training along these lines sponsored by some companies. Company sponsorship has also extended to allied subjects, such as nutrition. Instruction material in this field includes the theory of good nutrition as well as practical applications, such as suggested menus.

ORGANIZATION FOR MEDICAL SERVICES

In most large companies the medical department is made a part of the personnel division. Its work is so closely related to the objectives that are sought by the personnel function that the union is a natural one. Moreover, to keep an organization from having too many independent units which would overload the top executives, many units must be combined, even though there may be on occasion some reason for independent action. For example, some companies believe that the relation between doctor and employee is so private that the doctors should report to no one but the chief executive of the company. That the privacy of the relationship must be guarded is true, but to conclude that confidential information can be entrusted only to the chief executive is not. Such arguments reflect upon the ability and fair-mindedness of other executives, who, if the charge is true, should be discharged and replaced by men with trustworthy characteristics.

However, it is essential for the personnel director to have the utmost confidence in and respect for the opinions of the medical unit. For this condition to prevail, the medical staff should be selected and trained so that they understand the relationships involved in industrial medicine. It is necessary to define, therefore, their relations to the following groups:

1. To employees, with whom they should deal strictly in terms of matters arising out of the employment and industrial situations. If it is the policy of the company to offer services and aid beyond this, the doctor, employee, and executives should be informed of the exact nature and extent of available services.
2. To community physicians and local health agencies whose availability to workers should be respected and whose co-operation in attacking health problems should be sought, since outside factors are often as significant to physical well-being of workers as plant conditions. Local and state health departments, such agencies as the Red Cross, and medical doctors are as much in the fight for good health as company staff members.
3. To management, through whom medical staff must frequently work to gain the co-operation necessary to "sell" health and accident programs and whose proficiency can be increased in reducing hazards to health and safety.

This discussion does not imply that medical organization is a problem of large companies solely. Disabling injuries are about 50 per cent higher in small than large plants. While the smaller plants cannot individually support medical departments, there is no reason why several plants cannot employ doctors and nurses on a co-operative basis.

This is being done in several cases and is working out satisfactorily at a reasonable cost. One plan of co-operation provides for the establishment of a central clinic for three companies having a total of 800 employees. At the central clinic a doctor spends three hours a day, and a nurse five. The nurse spends an hour a day at each of the three plants. In another plan operated by eight companies having a total of 4,000 employees, a full-time nurse is employed in each plant, while a full-time doctor visits each plant each day.[2]

SAFETY

IMPORTANCE AND SCOPE

In no other phase of physical security has management shown greater application than that of accident prevention. The excellent attitude which industry generally has toward safety work, when compared with the lax standards once maintained, would lead one to believe that accidents are relatively infrequent. Although great progress has been

TABLE 22

ACCIDENT RATES FOR ALL AND REPRESENTATIVE INDUSTRIES
FOR SELECTED YEARS*

INDUSTRY	1939		1945		1949		1953	
	Severity Rate	Frequency Rate	Severity Rate	Frequency Rate	Severity Rate	Frequency Rate	Severity Rate	Frequency Rate
All industries.	1.42	11.83	1.16	13.63	1.02	10.14	0.83	7.44
Automobile...	0.70	6.95	0.62	10.29	0.57	6.35	0.38	3.39
Chemical.....	1.26	7.48	1.06	10.08	0.60	5.72	0.81	4.53
Construction..	3.14	28.81	2.27	19.84	2.15	19.48	2.06	15.68
Food.........	1.21	16.70	1.25	22.80	0.90	16.05	0.79	13.42
Lumbering....	3.70	45.46	5.08	64.85	4.67	47.72	3.90	33.91
Mining, coal..	12.75	46.36	11.94	63.06	6.84	41.48	4.79	25.81
Steel.........	1.79	6.57	1.75	7.23	1.49	12.40	1.08	3.90

* Source: *Accident Facts—1954 Edition* (Chicago: National Safety Council, and *Monthly Labor Review*).

made, there is much room for improvement. For example, data on accident frequency and accident severity rates shown in Table 22 are not commendable in some industries. Although the frequency rate was as low as 3.90 in the steel industry, it was 25.81 and 33.91 in the coal mining and lumbering industries, respectively, in 1953. Mining also shows up poorly in the accident severity column. It is understandable, therefore, why union leadership in this industry has recently demanded that a fund be set up to take care of accident losses.

These trends, though improving, are evidence of why safety activities are still strongly supported by industry. To appreciate better the nature of such activities, the following phases are here studied:

1. Measures of accidents
2. Mechanical aspects
3. Human aspects
4. Organizational aspects

---

[2] *Factory Management and Maintenance,* Vol. CIX, No. 9, p. 122.

1. MEASURES OF ACCIDENTS. As already noted in the foregoing sections, accidents and safety may be measured in indirect and direct terms. Indirect measures include such information as effect upon various aspects of production as a result of accidents and illness. For example, data on losses to production, lowered quality of output, and increases in costs of absenteeism and turnover are commonly collected and reported.

The more direct measures are the frequency and severity rates of accidents. The frequency rate is determined by multiplying the number of lost-time accidents during any selected period by one million and dividing the result by the total number of man-hours worked during

FIGURE 79.   A Chart of Accident Rates*

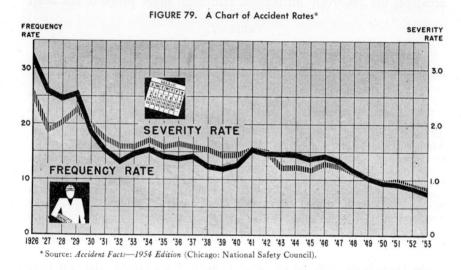

* Source: *Accident Facts—1954 Edition* (Chicago: National Safety Council).

the same period. The severity rate is computed by multiplying the number of days lost due to accidents during any selected period by one thousand and dividing the result by the total number of man-hours worked during the same period. The charting of such rates is shown in Figure 79. Although it is contended by some that these formulas are arbitrarily established and that they do not reflect the real pains and losses of accidents, nevertheless they have the advantages of almost universal acceptance and of comparability.

2. MECHANICAL PHASES OF SAFETY. Much has been done to make work mechanically safe. This phase of safety is largely the province of the engineering department; so the discussion here is limited to examples of what has been done along these lines. Some very ingenious devices have been developed to help protect workers. Examples are the use of handcuffs which automatically pull the operator's hand from the danger zone on the down stroke of the ram of a punch press;

electronic devices that prevent machines from operating so long as hands or arms are in the danger zones; safety masks to save the wearer from serious and painful injuries when hot metals splash; portable air pumps to supply fresh air during the cleaning of large tanks; and "safety" shoes in which is built a steel toe plate to guard against falling objects.

The emphasis upon safety in the design and use of devices of work is essential and commendable. High output with a minimum of accidents cannot be attained unless workplaces and tools are designed so that risk exposure is reduced. Hence the work of the engineering department must be carried on at all times with one eye wide open to the matters of safety. That most companies have done this is a matter of record.

3. HUMAN PHASES OF SAFETY. If mechanical aspects of safety work have been handled so well, why is the rate of accidents still relatively high and the financial loss so great? The answer is that employees, and supervisors particularly, are not sufficiently safety-conscious. To counter this through an effective safety program, the following aspects must be properly handled:

1. Accident-prone employees
2. Selection of employees
3. Training
4. Discipline
5. Supervision
6. Organization

a) Accident-Prone Employees. First, let us look at the record of accidents from the viewpoint of the individual. Almost without exception, it will be found that a few employees in every plant have the most accidents. So widely is this recognized that the term "accident-prone employee" is generally understood to mean an employee who, in spite of all efforts to educate him, continues to have more accidents than his fellow workers. Indeed, the number of accidents that employees will have can almost be predicted when a "normal" working force, from which accident-prone employees have not been eliminated, is studied. Studies of large numbers of accident reports of such "normal" populations, when plotted, produce a curve that looks like a "J" and hence are sometimes referred to as "J" curves. What should be done about such employees depends upon the underlying factors. Perhaps discharge is the only "cure" in some cases, training work in others, whereas psychiatric analysis may be necessary in still other cases. In any event, such employees should receive special attention and perhaps care.

b) *Selection.* An ideal approach to reductions of accidents is by elimination of accident-prone candidates in the selection process. Unfortunately, devices of screening the undesirables are not reliable. It is possible to do some good through interviews and examination of work histories. If this is done, some evidence can be gathered regarding the accidents which candidates have caused or have been involved in during

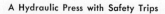

A Hydraulic Press with Safety Trips

Courtesy: Curtiss-Wright Corporation

In using two operators the hazard is eliminated by forcing both of them to utilize both hands to operate four trips, two on either side.

previous employments. By way of emphasis, such points, if pursued in the hiring process, would be much more useful to an employer than the time-wasting and ineffective practices that are presently indulged in by too many companies in their selection processes. While some good can be accomplished in screening poor accident risks, increased safety must be sought through other methods.

c) *Training.* High on the list of a good safety program is the function of training. This has a number of possibilities. Perhaps the best time to start safety training is when a new worker is being inducted.

Through the use of carefully designed lectures, visual aids, demonstrations, and conferences, a lasting impact can be made upon the employee when he is in a very receptive frame of mind. How well this works out is seen in the experience of one company that reported a reduction in accident rates of 78 per cent, as compared to the situation before such a program was in effect.[3]

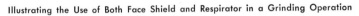

Illustrating the Use of Both Face Shield and Respirator in a Grinding Operation

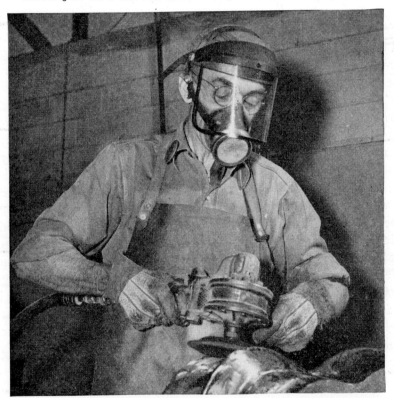

Courtesy: Curtiss-Wright Corporation

The worker is finishing a drop hammer die.

Second, courses completely concerned with safety have been effective. Employees are lectured on, or participate in conferences concerned with, major causes and examples of accidents, ways and means of prevention, proper use of safety devices and clothing, the services of the medical and accident departments, and what the individual can do to "build" safety in work.

---

[3] Asa P. Lombard and William D. Noa, "Cut New Worker Accidents 78%," *Factory Management and Maintenance*, Vol. CXI, No. 2, pp. 98–101.

In the third place, into training courses primarily concerned with other matters can be built safety lessons and principles. For example, while discussing how a part should be processed, a trainer may point out the dangers of which to be aware in each step of the process, how accidents have happened on such work, and safety practices which deserve especial mention. Or while inducting a new man, the supervisor may point at hazards of work, precautions that have been established, and the responsibilities that the employee himself should accept.

In the fourth place, it is desirable to publicize accident records and safety programs. Talk or words alone are insufficient to bring home to all employees the full importance of accident prevention. Hence most companies implement their programs by various techniques to dramatize their purposes.

The devices employed have been so many and varied that space here permits only reference to a few. A rather common plan is to use large displays to illustrate the safety records of various departments or divisions of the plant. The theory of such displays is that a competitive attitude to keep down accidents will develop. Another device which utilizes the principle of competition is that of contests in which the best or worst departments are rewarded or penalized. Comical awards are made, such as pictures or statutes of "white elephants," intended to ridicule the losers and hence stimulate them to do better. Bulletin boards are also commonly employed to draw the attention of employees to unsafe working practices and desirable safety precautions.

Other techniques are also used in connection with direct training in accident prevention. In recent years sound movies have been increasingly employed for this purpose. They are particularly effective in presenting convincing, lasting, and easily assimilated lessons. The use of charts and graphs to illustrate safety training lessons is also effective.

d) Discipline. Another tool used in safety work is the function of disciplinary action. It is particularly applicable in instances in which employees willfully break safety rules or in which an impartial penalty is pre-established as a warning to employees. As an example of the former, some companies assess penalties after analyzing the cause of an accident and find that an employee is at fault, who can be expected to be more careful only if penalized by such means as a layoff, loss of privileges, or demotion. At times discharge may be resorted to, but this is an implied recognition that the offender can be "cured" only by complete removal.

As an example of the latter, definite penalties may be posted in advance. Thus it may become a company rule that employees who participate in horseplay with air-pressure guns shall be subject to immediate dismissal. Or those who fail to wear assigned safety goggles or clothes, let us say, shall be laid off for a specified number of days. And those who come to work under the influence of liquor will be sent home immediately, or in some cases discharged.

The foregoing have some effect—upon some people. But, as a gen-

Operator Using Respirator while Spray Painting

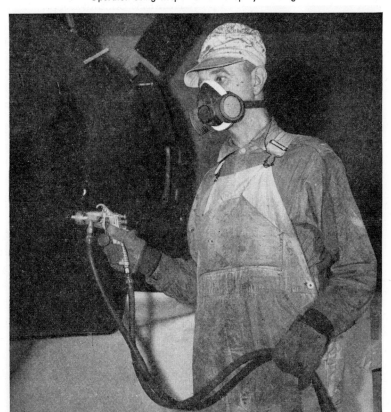

Courtesy: Curtiss-Wright Corporation

eral rule, the negative approach has the weakness of all "fear" techniques—most employees must be motivated positively to seek desired goals. Particularly in times of labor shortages does the fear of discharge, for instance, lose much of its effectiveness. However, as noted above, disciplinary action is another tool—not the only one; and, when judged applicable, it should certainly be used.

e) *The Role of the Supervisor.* Perhaps even more culpable than the individual is the supervisor and his superiors. When management is lax in safety matters, its attitude is reflected all down the line. However, when management is strict in enforcing safety measures, the records improve strikingly. Indeed, workers who, through their own carelessness, have had accidents are often loudest in their criticism of supervisors for having failed to make them "toe the mark" on safety practices.

A Spray Attachment Inserted in the Bomb-Bay Mechanism of an Airplane to Prevent Its Being Activated and Injuring Mechanic Working in the Bomb Bay

Courtesy: Curtiss-Wright Corporation

Thus the records, on the one hand, and the complaints of workers, on the other, bear witness that supervision is the key to the problem of accidents. All the work of the engineers and of the safety trainer are of little consequence if supervision is weak in these matters.

Obviously, the answer to this aspect of accidents is the development and maintenance of a high sense of safety-consciousness on the part of supervisors. To begin with, appointments to supervisory positions should not include candidates in whom can be detected a lack of appreciation for, or a poor record of, accident prevention. Second, all supervisors should be constantly impressed with the importance that top management places upon safety work. Third, not only should supervisors be given specially designed safety courses, but safety suggestions should also be incorporated in all of their training. Fourth, supervisors should be encouraged to show employees by example, by precept, and, indeed, with occasional dramatics, their intense belief in and demand for adherence to safety rules and practices. And, last, supervisors who have excellent records for safety should be rewarded appropriately and openly, to prove to them that their efforts are appreciated and so that the recognition receives the benefits of public acclamation. If all these steps are followed, there is little probability that a company will have an excessive accident rate, no matter what other practices it fails to incorporate in its program.

f) Safety Organization. Finally, good safety work depends upon proper organization. On the one hand, this means that every company should have someone or some department to whom sufficient authority is given to carry out an effective program. In most companies, a safety department in the personnel division is the answer to this question. On the other hand, intracompany co-operation and education calls for efforts by industry-wide organization. As a consequence, various industries have established safety committees in their trade associations to investigate unsafe conditions, to suggest methods of improvement, and to develop educational materials.

Perhaps most influential among the outside agencies is the National Safety Council, organized in 1911, as a nonprofit, nonpolitical, co-operative organization. Its purpose is to reduce the number and severity of all kinds of accidents. It covers the fields of industrial safety and health; traffic and transportation; other public safety; school and child safety; and home, farm, and general safety.

The Council serves as a national and international clearinghouse to gather and distribute information about causes of accidents and ways to prevent them. Through its headquarters and regional offices and its state and local units, it carries on a continuous and unified program of accident prevention.

The Council has 250 full-time employees and 1,000 volunteer workers. Its membership of 7,500 is made up of industrial and government corporations, civic organizations, insurance companies, firms, and individuals representing over 25,000 establishments and more than 15,-000,000 workers.

The Council receives safety information from its members and through the constant research of its own staff of statistical, educational, and engineering technicians. These facts and figures are tabulated and broken down to show where, when, how, and why people are injured. The information shows whether various safety measures are getting results and what needs to be done.

Example of One of a Series of Safety Posters

In regard to the particular field of industrial health and safety, the Council investigates and compares ways of making equipment and working conditions safer. It helps the plant management, the foreman, and workers to locate hazards and guard against them, as well as to recognize and prevent occupational diseases. It outlines programs for stimulating and maintaining safety interest both on and off the job.

Safety information is disseminated in various ways. The Council prepares and distributes a wide variety of publications, pamphlets, booklets, posters, and other employer and employee educational materials. It also has worked out and supplies material on a complete accident prevention plan applicable to any industry or organization. In addition, the Council works with newspapers, radio stations, magazines, and motion pictures in presenting safety information.

Other outside agencies interested in safety work include such groups as the American Society of Safety Engineers, the International Association of Industrial Accident Boards and Commissioners, and individual industry and trade associations.

QUESTIONS AND PROBLEMS

1. Can you prove that good working conditions are a good investment from a personnel point of view? In your own community what would be the correlation between the kinds of working conditions in various plants and the quality of morale?

2. How can you explain the fact that when some companies have put in an air conditioning system or fluorescent lighting, employee grievances increased?

3. If the work in many offices and factories is monotonous, can anything be done about working conditions to offset in some degree the negative aspects of monotony? Explain.

4. It has been said that people who work in noisy places don't mind the noise. If this is so, why bother to do anything about such noise?

5. Landscaping a factory location may have a favorable effect upon public relations, but can you cite any specific examples to prove that it has any effect upon employees?

6. In offering free periodic medical examinations, some companies have found that a number of persons are reluctant to avail themselves of this service. Why would this be so? How would you proceed to encourage the reluctant ones?

7. A given employee had a perfect safety record for ten years. One morning while operating a punch press, he cut off part of a finger. How would you determine the "cause" of this accident?

8. To do well on a piece-rate job, employees often disregard safety devices which tend to slow them. Is the rate set incorrectly, is supervision poor, or are employees unworthy of trust?

9. Why should the personnel department be assigned the task of correlating the work concerned with working conditions, health, and safety?

10. Upon what assumptions of liability are statutory laws of industrial compensation based?

11. Would you conclude that reductions in industrial accidents have reached an

irreducible minimum? If not, from what sources must pressure be exerted to lower the rates?

12. Why are good standards of working conditions desirable? To what extent are these intra- or interindustry standards?

13. In what ways would the location and layout of medical facilities for a small plant differ from those of a large plant?

14. What right has a company to prescribe a physical examination as a condition to employment? Is not this an intrusion upon individual privacy?

15. Are such health services as operating facilities and dental service to members of an employee's immediate family beyond the reasonable obligations of a company? What is your reasoning in connection with your answer?

16. To whom should the medical staff in a given company report? What safeguards must be adopted to protect their professional status?

17. Define the terms "frequency rate" and "severity rate" as used in connection with accidents. What shortcomings do these measures have?

18. Inasmuch as mechanical aspects of safety have received so much expert attention, how do you explain the numerous accidents that nonetheless take place? What suggestions do you have to offer to reduce industrial accidents?

19. When a given employee has an accident, there is often a series of like accidents among other employees. What can be done to keep accidents from "catching"?

20. How would you explain the success that such a voluntary group as the National Safety Council has had in helping industry to reduce accidents?

26 | Economic Security

SCOPE

Protecting the physical well-being of the employee finds a counterpart in measures designed to provide him with financial aid or subsidies to meet various contingencies. Disabling accidents, loss of health, old age, and death are the particular events which remove or minimize an employee's capacity to earn his livelihood or that of his dependents. For a long time, the losses associated with these events were generally held to be the concern of the employee, his family or friends, or community charity. Certainly, they were excluded from the "responsibilities of industry."

But changes have occurred. On the one hand, some employers have voluntarily established plans whereby benefits to employees, their dependents, or beneficiaries are paid when these contingencies occur. On the other hand, pressures have been exerted on more and more employers to assume various obligations. The states, for example, have rather universally imposed the responsibility for underwriting accident losses upon industry. The federal government has moved into the fields of unemployment compensation, discussed in an earlier chapter, and of old age and survivors' insurance, discussed in the present chapter. In both instances, much of the burden is borne by industry. And organized labor has in recent years made much headway in getting industry to increase retirement benefits and is increasingly pushing for protection from losses because of accidents and ill health.

These changes have met with much opposition and also support. Much has been made of the argument that efforts of labor and government to develop these welfare programs is full of danger. The initiative of employees to look out for their own needs, the growth of a "welfare" state, and the excessive costs of operation are cited as results that can lead only to the weakening of the individual and the ultimate destruction of our national way of life. Countering are claims that individuals cannot provide for these contingencies themselves, that our nation and its industries can and should support such worthy causes, and that human values are above materialistic property claims. These arguments pro and con are deserving of the most careful study, evaluation, and appraisal. This, however, is not the place for a study of these matters.

Having warned the reader of the imposing questions that must be weighed and pondered and having noted the important forces at work in connection with them, the present purpose allows only a consideration of various plans for providing certain types of economic security. Discussed here are the following:

1. Insurance plans for death, accidents, and ill health
2. Federal old-age and survivors' insurance
3. Private pension plans

INSURANCE PLANS

RISKS COVERED

The insurance programs installed by various companies or employee groups cover losses arising from death, illness, and accidents. Life insurance, for example, has long been a favorite in the programs of most companies. Perhaps this is due to the fact that the insurance companies have provided services at relatively low cost that are easily administered. Moreover, many companies have found that such insurance is most helpful at a critical time. The other types of insurance are far less common but nevertheless growing in popularity. Thus general hospital insurance and disability income plans have taken the popular interest in some companies to the extent that 100 per cent coverage has been obtained in a short period of time. Various examples of these plans will serve to show how they are operated and financed.

LIFE INSURANCE

As already noted, life insurance is one of the oldest and most common plans of providing economic security. How such plans are operated, coverage, eligibility, cost, and benefits may be seen in the following provisions of one company:

THE PLAN PROVIDES—

Standard group life insurance protection while employed at Farm Bureau.
Additional benefits in case of accidental death—loss of certain limbs and other disabilities as specified.

Waiver of premium in event of total disability before the age of 60 if proper requirements are met.

Privilege of exchanging Group Policy for certain other life policies without physical examination in event of leaving the Farm Bureau.

WHO IS ELIGIBLE?

All employees and district managers, regardless of age, are eligible at the end of a waiting period. This waiting period is 90 days for new salaried employees and six months for new hourly wage employees except that the Personnel Department may at its discretion shorten or eliminate this waiting period. No evidence of insurability or physical examination is required provided the employee's election to be insured is made within his eligibility period. This period expires 90 days after insurance has been offered to the employee.

WHAT IS THE COST?

A substantial part of the cost of the insurance is borne by the employer. Employee's cost each month for complete coverage is 65 cents per thousand of insurance carried and is deducted monthly from the employee's pay check. This cost will not increase from year to year and is usually reduced through the payment of dividends.

HOW MUCH CAN YOU CARRY?

The amount of insurance you may carry is determined by the amount of your annual basic salary. The following table will tell you how much insurance you are eligible for:

Employee's Annual Salary	Amount of Insurance
$ 0–1,500	$1,000
1,501–1,800	1,500
1,801–2,160	2,000
2,161–2,520	2,500
2,521–3,180	3,000
3,181–3,900	3,500
3,901–4,799	4,000
4,800 and over	5,000

PAYMENT OF PROCEEDS

Proceeds of your policy will be paid to the beneficiary you have designated in event of your death. Upon special request, however, arrangements can be made to have proceeds paid in monthly installments.

HOW TO TAKE OUT YOUR POLICY

This is not a compulsory insurance plan. It is provided as a service to all employees who desire low cost insurance protection. Interested employees should apply to the Personnel Department for full information and details of the policy. This department will furnish you with necessary forms and accept your application. When your application has been approved you will receive a certificate describing the details of your insurance.

FOR OTHER INSURANCE SERVICE

For the convenience of employees and residents of Central Ohio, an insurance service office is maintained in Room 309. A sales representative is always available to serve you in connection with any of your personal insurance needs. Arrangements can be made through this office to have any of your Farm Bureau Life Insurance policies placed on the "Salary Deduction Plan," whereby monthly premium deductions will be made from your salary checks.

HOSPITAL AND SURGICAL PLANS

Although there is a drive on to provide a federal plan of medical aid and health insurance, these phases of economic security are as yet left to individuals and to industry. Such plans as the Blue Cross Hospital Plan or private insurance company plans are available to individuals who wish to take advantage of them. Since most employees fail to do this and because the need is great, more and more companies are helping to underwrite such programs or are shouldering the cost themselves. As an example of details of operation and coverage, the following provisions of one plan are typical:

1. *Eligibility.* The amount of insurance is restricted because rates are low and the insurance company cannot select its risks as in ordinary lines of insurance.

2. *Indemnity for Hospital Confinement.* If an employee is confined in a legally constituted hospital upon the recommendation of a doctor for a period over eighteen hours because of injury or disease, benefits are payable as follows:
   a) Hospital costs for a period up to thirty-one days
   b) Other hospital charges, such as x-ray, laboratory, etc.
   c) Benefits shall not be paid for injuries or diseases payable in accordance with workmen's compensation laws
   d) Benefits shall be paid—
      1) While the employee is insured
      2) Within three months after leaving employment, if the confinement began on or before termination
      3) Within nine months after leaving employment, if the confinement is due to pregnancy

3. *Surgical Fees.* Benefits are payable for any operation resulting from nonoccupational injury or disease, during any one period of disability, not to exceed a maximum of $150.

4. *Indemnity for Dependents.* Similar in nature for dependents are the hospital confinement benefits cited for employees.

5. *Schedule of Benefits:*

	ANNUAL EARNINGS		
	Class I Less than $2,400	Class II $2,400 to $4,800	Class III $4,800 and Over
Daily hospital benefits for—			
Employees.....................................	$ 4.00	$ 5.00	$ 6.00
Dependents...................................	3.00	4.00	5.00
Surgical benefits for employees....................	150.00	150.00	150.00
Monthly cost for employee cover only.............	1.00	1.15	1.30
Monthly cost for employee and dependents' cover...	1.90	2.35	2.80

Such insurance plans as the foregoing are increasingly being financed by company contributions. Earlier plans were usually handled by "mutual benefit associations," which are essentially associations formed by employees for their own benefit and protection. Their early popularity may be ascribed to the fact that employees were acquainted with such associations in the many private mutual benefit associations that flourished in this country at the turn of the century. However, as insurance companies have developed group insurance plans, first, to provide death benefits and, later, health, accident and surgical benefits, the insurance type of protection has grown in popularity.

FEDERAL OLD-AGE ASSISTANCE

Approved by the President on August 14, 1935, and with the latest amendments coming in August, 1954, various parts of the program of the Social Security Act went into effect at different times. It provides for aid and assistance to a wide variety of groups, with a view to minimizing the losses due to a number of different problems. The subheadings of aid and assistance include the following:

a) Unemployment compensation
b) Old-age and survivors' insurance
c) Old-age assistance
d) Aid to dependent children
e) Services for crippled children
f) Child welfare services
g) Maternal and child health services
h) Aid to needy blind
i) Retraining for disabled workers
j) Public health services

Of interest here are the old-age provisions. Their basic aim is to aid the aged worker and his dependents.

This aid is financed by means of taxes shared equally by the employee and the employer. Thus employers deduct 2 per cent of the wages (up to $4,200 a year) earned by each employee, match this with an equal amount, and pay over the sum to the Bureau of Internal Revenue.[1] This payment is credited to the account of each employee, to which is assigned a social security number. The sums thus deposited determine in large measure the benefits to be paid out.

There are two kinds of benefits—retirement and survivors'.[2] Retirement benefits are payable to the wage earner and his family when the worker retires at sixty-five or later. Survivors' benefits are payable to the wage earner's family when the worker dies, no matter at what age. The worker must have had a job long enough, however, to build up an insured standing.

RETIREMENT BENEFITS. Monthly retirement benefits are payable to:

1. The wage earner when he is sixty-five or older and stops work
2. His wife when she is sixty-five
3. His unmarried children under eighteen

Retirement benefits are payable to the wage earner and his wife until death and to unmarried children until the age of eighteen. To qualify for these benefits a worker must be "fully insured." He becomes "fully insured" after he has been paid at least $50 in wages in covered employment in each of at least six calendar quarters before he attains the age of sixty-five or dies.

1. *The Worker's Benefits.* Benefits are a percentage of the worker's average monthly wage. The exact amount of a benefit cannot be calculated until a claim is filed. But the approximate amount can be figured on the basis of customary pay and the number of years expected to be worked.

To arrive at the approximate amount of the average monthly wage, add all wages up to $4,200 a year paid the worker in covered employment from January 1, 1937 (when the program began), or after either 1950 or June 30, 1953, whichever would result in a higher average monthly rate, up to the calendar quarter in which the worker files his claim or dies. Wages received for employment not covered by the Act must not be counted. Also, in figuring total number of months, those worked in noncovered employment and those when the worker was ill or unemployed must not be counted.

---

[1] The rate was 1 per cent until 1950, 1½ per cent until 1954, and is scheduled to be 2½ per cent in 1960; 3 per cent in 1965; and 3¼ per cent thereafter.

[2] Taken from "Federal Old Age and Survivors Insurance," Federal Security Agency.

Then take 55 per cent of the first $110 of the average monthly wage. Add to this, 20 per cent of the next $240. The resulting total is the monthly retirement or "primary" benefit. Any primary benefit which comes out less than $20 is raised to that amount.

As a computational example, assume that a worker is sixty-five and ready to retire. His average monthly wage was $350. His benefit would be figured as follows:

55 per cent of the first $110...................................	$ 60.50
20 per cent of the next $240...................................	48.00
Total retirement or primary benefit....................	$108.50

2. *The Family's Benefits.* Benefits for members of the worker's family are based on his primary benefit amount, whether he retires or dies. A widow's benefit is three fourths of her husband's benefit amount, as is that of a dependent parent of the deceased worker. For all others the monthly payment is equal to half the worker's primary benefit. However, the total monthly benefits that may be paid to a family on one worker's account, while never less than $40, may not be more than 80 per cent of the worker's average monthly wage, or $168.75, whichever is the least.

The lump-sum death benefit is 300 per cent of the monthly benefit to which the worker would have been entitled. However, when it is not paid to a survivor, but in reimbursement for funeral expenses, it is limited to the amount of the funeral expense.

To illustrate how to figure a family's monthly benefits, suppose that you retire and receive a primary benefit of $47.25 a month. Suppose, also, that your wife is sixty-five or more and you have one minor child. Benefits for the family would be:

Wage earner's benefit.......................................	$47.25
Wife's benefit (½)...	23.62
Child's benefit (½)...	23.63
Monthly total for family...............................	$94.50

Or, for example, say you leave a widow with two children. If your primary benefit is $47.25, your family would get the following:

Widow's benefit (¾).....................................	$35.44
Children (½ each)..	47.25
Monthly total for family............................	$82.69

To any person who is eligible for more than one benefit, the larger amount will be paid. For instance, a woman who works in a covered job and has a social security account of her own may, of course, qualify for benefits at the age of sixty-five on her own account. If she is a wife or a widow eligible for benefits also on her husband's account, she cannot get both; but she will get whichever amount is larger.

SURVIVORS' BENEFITS. Monthly benefits are payable to the following survivors of "fully insured" workers:

1. *Children* (*including adopted children and stepchildren in most cases*). These receive monthly payments until they are eighteen.
2. *Widow, regardless of age, caring for a child entitled to benefits.* If she does not remarry, she receives monthly payments until her youngest child is eighteen. The payments stop then, but begin again when the widow is sixty-five and continue until death.
3. *Widow without a child in her care.* She receives monthly payments when she reaches the age of sixty-five, provided she has not remarried.
4. *Dependent parents.* Where the deceased worker left neither widow nor child who might ever become entitled to monthly benefits, his parents may receive monthly payments when they reach the age of sixty-five if chiefly supported by the wage earner at the time of his death.

1. *Currently Insured.* For children under eighteen and widows with such children in their care the law provides monthly benefits even when the covered worker was not "fully insured." A worker is said to have died "currently insured," i.e., only partly insured, if he worked in a covered job roughly half of the last three years of his life. Neither the widow without young children nor the dependent parents of a worker who died "currently insured" receive monthly payments at sixty-five.

A lump-sum death benefit (one cash payment) is payable in the case of either a "fully" or a "currently insured" person when he leaves no survivor immediately eligible for monthly payments at the time of his death. If the worker died before January 1, 1947, the lump-sum payment may go to the widow, widower, child, grandchild, or parent, in the order named. If the worker is not survived by any such relative, the lump sum may be paid to other relatives or friends who paid the burial expenses. If the worker died after December 31, 1946, the lump sum may be paid to the worker's widow or widower if this spouse was living with the worker when the worker died; if there is no widow or widower, or if the surviving widow or widower was not living with the worker at the time of his death, the lump sum may go to the person or persons who paid burial expenses.

2. *Benefits for Veterans' Survivors.* Under one of the 1946 amendments to the old-age and survivors' insurance program, the families of qualified veterans of World War II were given social security protection

for a period of three years following the veteran's discharge. This protection is only for the survivors of qualified veterans; the amendment creates no retirement rights for the veterans themselves.

In order to afford such survivors' protection, ex-servicemen to whom the amendment applies are given a fully insured status and are granted wage credits of $160 a month for each month of military service. In addition, the basic benefits are increased by 1 per cent for each year in which the serviceman had a minimum of thirty days of active service in the armed forces after September 16, 1940. The types of survivors' benefits payable under this amendment are the same as those payable under the program for wages and salary earners in commerce and industry.

Survivors of veterans who die as the result of service-connected causes will not receive social security benefits under the veterans' amendment. Provision is made for compensation or pensions to such survivors in the program of the Veterans Administration; and the social security benefits provided by the veterans' amendment are not payable in cases where compensation or pensions are payable by the Veterans Administration. However, if a veteran has an insured status under the Social Security Act by reason of actual employment in jobs covered by the Act, the survivors may qualify for social security benefits even though eligible for compensation of pension under the Veterans Administration program. It should be noted that national service life insurance payments are not considered "compensation or pensions." Receipt of such payments does not prevent the payment of the social security benefits provided by the veterans' amendment.

Benefits under the amendment, like other old-age and survivors' insurance benefits, are payable only when claims for them have been filed, and they are payable retroactively only for three months prior to the date of filing.

PRIVATE PENSIONS

INTRODUCTION

Within the past few years, pension plans—payments to those who have retired from employment after extended years of service—have grown phenomenally in numbers and interest therein. Prior to 1900 only a few private pension plans in business concerns had been installed. During the first decade of the present century, 152 plans were established; during the second decade, 221 plans; and during the third, 130 plans. By 1938, over 1,000 plans were in existence. But by 1950, over

13,000 plans, covering about 7,000,000 employees in all types of businesses, were in effect.[3] And at present the number of plans is approaching 20,000.   *pension plans*

The reasons for this shift from slow growth to rapid acceptance are not difficult to ascertain. Earlier plans were underwritten voluntarily by companies which either took a farsighted view of the need for protecting the time when employees retired or felt, in their paternalistic philosophy, that pensions were good for their employees.

But in recent years the impetus has been provided rather largely, first, by employers who desired to attract workers during World War II by means other than those restricted under the Wage Stabilization Act of 1942 and, second, perhaps more significantly by union demands. Pension plans seemed to be out of the scope of collective bargaining, when the Supreme Court in the J. I. Case Company Case of 1944 excluded hospital, welfare, stock purchase, and pension plans. Such plans were included in the area of collective bargaining by the National War Labor Board. This view was taken in 1945, when the Board ruled that a voluntary pension plan, requiring no employee contributions and in effect for a number of years, constituted a condition of employment. In another case, the Board ruled that the continuance of a pension plan, in effect on a voluntary and noncontributory basis was a subject about which a union could bargain. As late as 1947, the Board also ruled that welfare plans fell within legitimate areas of collective bargaining.

The legal situation was made final in October, 1948, by the U.S. Supreme Court in the Inland Steel decision. Here it was ruled that pensions were not bargainable only if the union contract expressly excluded the issue. But if nothing was said, the issue was bargainable. As a consequence union after union—in the auto industry, the steel industry, the telephone industry, and in the coal mining industry—demanded and won pension plans.

Thus the floodgates of private pension arrangements have been opened. Expansion undoubtedly will accelerate. Hence it is desirable to examine methods of planning and operating such plans. In this connection, the discussion will be based upon the following points:

1. Who is eligible for pensions?
2. What is the amount of benefits?
3. What are supplemental provisions?
4. How are pensions financed?

---

[3] "Welfare Plans and Collective Bargaining," Chamber of Commerce of the United States, 1950, p. 6.

5. Who contributes to the financing?
6. How are plans administered?

ELIGIBILITY

Since pensions are paid to retired employees, the significant question to unretired employees is: Am I eligible to receive a pension? This depends upon the rules established. Eligibility is usually governed by (1) waiting periods, (2) length of service, (3) age, (4) work factors, and (5) nature and amount of compensation.

First, most pension plans establish a waiting period before employees become eligible. This may be anywhere from one to five years. The longer period tends to penalize "floaters" and turnover. The shorter period tends to give the newer employee a feeling that he is part of he plan. It may serve to reduce turnover and increase the morale of new employees. In recent years the trend has been toward the shorter eligibility period, perhaps because of union pressures.

Second, the length of service affects eligibility. This is particularly important so far as amount of pensions received is concerned, provided that other tests of eligibility are met. Thus a minimum number of years of service must be completed at a before-retirement age if full benefits are to be paid. Lesser service results in smaller payments. The minimum period may be from fifteen to thirty years. Thus an employee with thirty years' service may be eligible to retire with full pay at the age of sixty, or one with twenty-five years' service at the age of sixty-five. The service may have to be continuous, or breaks may be allowed for sickness, military leaves, and layoffs.

Third, the question of lower and upper age limits must also be answered. Some companies limit eligibility to those over twenty-five or thirty years of age. This is done because of the higher rate of turnover among younger employees. As a consequence, the clerical cost of administering the plan for such employees offsets any possible advantages the plan might have for the company or the employee. The upper limit, on the other hand, raises important problems. To include old employees raises the cost of the plan; but to exclude them may arouse employee and community antagonism. Or the plan may fail to qualify under the requirements of the Bureau of Internal Revenue, in which case costs of the plan would have to be written off after—not before—federal income taxes. The upper limits should be checked with the Bureau to get its approval.

Fourth, the working situation may also determine eligibility. Employees in certain types of work or locations may be excluded. Or only salaried, clerical, and executive ranks may be included. Or again, non-union employees may be excluded from a plan negotiated by a union. In any event, exclusions should be logically justifiable, or again employee enmity may be incurred or the approval of the Bureau of Internal Revenue not forthcoming.

Fifth, the nature and amount of compensation may be determining factors in eligibility. Salesmen on commission, part-time employees or those earning less than some set figure—$3,000 a year—and all hourly rated employees may be excluded. The general trend is, however, away from such "compensation" exclusives. Certainly, collective bargaining has improved the position of hourly rated employees who were once rather generally excluded.

AMOUNT OF BENEFITS

Another matter of major concern is the level and amount of benefits. To the employee this is significant because it determines what he will receive—and perhaps contribute, if the plan is contributory. And to the employer it is significant because it determines in part how costly the plan will be. The answer to this question may be sought here in terms of, first, what an adequate level of benefits is and, second, how amounts are actually calculated.

The question of an adequate pension is obviously a matter of judgment—and hence of argument. It can be contended that a pension should permit an employee to retire without undue hardship. But an amount that might be tantamount to "semiluxury" for a given employee might be out of the question for another whose standard of living is much higher and "cannot" be reduced.

Private pension plans have in recent years been rather uniform in their answer to this question—again, perhaps because of union influence. The minimum is about $100—made up of social security payments plus those of private plans. The CIO set up, for example, a monthly minimum of $100 for employees in the steel industry with twenty-five years of employment (this includes Social Security payments). The CIO in September, 1949, settled with Ford on a similar basis except for a thirty-year employment provision. In the glass and rubber industry similar settlements were reached. The United Mine Workers secured $100 a month pensions, exclusive of Social Security benefits. A few plans, such as the Sinclair Oil Company plan, calls for benefits of $125 a month. In all likelihood the trend will accelerate toward greater minimums in the years to come.

The calculation of the actual benefit is usually related to years of service and a certain period of earnings. In addition, a maximum limit may be placed on earnings which would be recognized in computing pensions. A few examples will illustrate a few of the methods of calculation.

In one case, an employee is permitted to earn an annual retirement income, based on 1 per cent of his average compensations, times the years of service. Thus an employee who had averaged $2,800 a year for thirty years would receive

$$1\% \times \$2,800 \times 30 = \$840 \text{ yearly, or } \$70 \text{ monthly .}$$

Instead of total average earnings, the average earnings for the last two to ten years of service may be used as the basis. This results in a higher cost to the contributors, although the employee benefits from a higher pension.

The benefits may be based only on a maximum amount of wages. For example, only the first $3,000 of earnings may be used in computations. Some limits go into the tens of thousands, but this is usual only in the case of executive or technical employee plans.

The question of amount also raises the question of whether or not a minimum pension will be paid even though seniority and earning requirements are not fully met. Unions particularly like such a floor for everybody. But if it is granted, the cost will be higher than an "earned" plan because the payments exceed the earnings by an amount which cannot be actuarially determined. Yet the contributions must be high enough or, as in the case of the coal miners in recent years, the funds for payments will be at times exhausted.

SUPPLEMENTAL BENEFITS

In addition to pension payments, provision may also be made for, first, severance payments and, second, death benefits.

Severance payments refer to the fact that after a certain number of years or after a certain age, or both, an employee acquires a right to a payment, now or in the future, even though he should leave the company before the regular retirement age. This right is referred to as a "vested right" or a "vesting of benefits."

The vested right depends upon the method of contributing. It is generally agreed that an employee's contributions are returnable upon severance. Whether or not interest should be paid, and how much, is a matter of company policy. As to the employer's contributions, practice varies. Some companies provide for full vesting (and immediately) of company contributions. This is done to set at rest any rumors that the company will discharge eligible employees just before retirement age. Others provide for delayed vesting; leaving employees may receive, at what would have been their retirement age, the pension to which they would have been entitled, or receive a paid-up insurance policy. And in some companies, those who leave of their own accord lose all benefits of company payments. The latter plan is followed by only a very small minority.

The advantages of forfeiture are that it discourages turnover and that, when severance does occur, the cost to the employer is reduced. On the other hand, forfeiture may make some employees fearful of and hence less loyal to management and may make the plan disallowed under the provisions of the Bureau of Internal Revenue.

When death occurs before retirement, benefit payments must take another form. Either a lump sum or annuities may be paid to survivors or the employee's estate. This must be provided for, or again the plan will not be qualified by the Bureau of Internal Revenue, which requires that a pension plan be for the benefit of employees or their beneficiaries. The employee has the right to select his beneficiaries, and his wishes in this must be respected. If the employee has selected no beneficiaries, the plan may provide for an order of priority as follows: the employee's wife, children, parents, brothers and sisters, and his estate. The company cannot be a beneficiary in this listing and still qualify the plan.

As in the case of severance, the amount of payment will vary with the particular nature of the plan. This should take into consideration age of deceased, length of service, earnings, employee's contributions, company contributions, interest factors, and rulings of the Bureau of Internal Revenue.

FINANCING

Before discussing who contributes to paying for a pension plan, it is desirable to note the various ways in which provision is made for assuring payments. The simplest plan of providing funds is the "current expenditure" method, in which payments are made out of general cash at the time employees retire. How much must be paid out can be quickly ascertained by listing the pensioners and the amounts due to each. The plan has disadvantages; cash or assets may not be available when needed, tax advantages may be lost, and the actuarial basis of pensions may not be followed. So, with few exceptions, a plan of advance provision or underwriting of funds is adopted. These are the so called "funded methods" and include insured or trusteed plans.

1. INSURED PLANS. Insured plans are those in which future pension liabilities are assumed by a commercial insurance company upon payment of premiums by the company. These plans are of four types: individual policy, group permanent policy, regular group policy, and deposit administration.

Under the indvidual policy plan, the employer makes an annual payment to a banker or trustee. The latter then has an insurance policy for each employee. Provision is thus made for a certain insurance or retirement benefit at retirement age. This plan has been favored by the small employer because of its simplicity in operation and because a minimum number of employees is not required.

Under the group permanent plan, individual policies are provided but paid for under the group insurance plan which requires some minimum number in the group. Moreover, no trustee or bank is required as an intermediary.

Under the regular group plan, pensions are provided for through insurance companies. Instead of individual policies, a master or blanket insurance policy is written to cover all employees. And each year the company's premium buys a unit of retirement income for each employee. Under this plan, the economies of the group insurance principle are obtained and also the clerical costs of writing and administering individual policies are reduced. This plan is usually used with a larger minimum number in the group.

Under the deposit administration plan, payments are not made to buy benefits for any particular employee until he reaches retirement age. At that time, from previous over-all annual payments based on actuarial computations, the necessary payment to buy each required annuity is made. This plan is more flexible than the others and is particularly useful to larger companies.

2. TRUSTEED PLANS. Under trusteed plans, the employer acts as his own insurance company or pays over each year's fund accumulations to a trustee. Under either system, funds are accumulated and invested and the earnings added to the capital. As needed, payments to pensioners are made from the fund. This fund, in cash, securities, or other assets, is kept separate and distinct from all others.

Trusteed plans have been used only by the larger groups of employers. They have felt that they were equipped to do the work that the insurance companies do in such matters, thereby saving the overhead cost which is loaded into the premium charged by the insurance company. But, if followed, this plan should be administered with great care so that all actuarial features are observed, that funds are wisely administered, and details of employee tenure and earnings are meticulously recorded.

CONTRIBUTIONS TO COSTS OF PENSIONS

Funds may be accumulated by joint payments of employees and employers (the contributory plan) or by payments by the company alone (the noncontributory plan). Which plan should be used has been subject to much debate, and it is improbable that universal agreement will ever be reached.

Proponents of the noncontributory plan cite various arguments. On the one hand, it is claimed that this is the general trend at present. Certainly, so long as unions are strong enough to demand this plan, the trend will so continue. Others claim that noncontribution leaves control in the hands of the employer himself. This may have been true once, but union interest in such matters does not stop because somebody else is paying the bill. It is also argued that, since such plans cover all workers, there won't be any employees electing to stay out and thus become, perhaps, public charges. And still others claim that the benefits that the employer derives from pension plans in the form of more loyal and effective workers is reason enough for asking him to shoulder the cost. Miscellaneous arguments of possible tax savings and no reduction in take-home pay are also cited.

Proponents of contributory plans are quick to rebut and add new arguments. They claim that in sharing costs employees become more interested in the plan and, indirectly, in other affairs of the company. Employees appreciate more the pension and other welfare plans. They claim that employees thereby save funds they might otherwise not spend so wisely. They also claim that greater pension benefits are also thereby provided. They claim, too, that the charge of paternalism cannot be leveled when employees as well as employers participate. They also claim that in any event employee contributions are never large, amounting to no more at most than 5 to 6 per cent of earnings. And, finally, they point out that the principle of contribution has been established in federal social security plans.

Perhaps it might be noted that, in the final analysis, the customer underwrites the program. The 40-cent-per-ton royalty basis of the welfare plan of the coal miners is a case in point. Hence it might be well for both the employee and employer groups to raise their sights to the ultimate source of funds—the customer—and render greater service to him. Also, each must answer the question of how much of present satisfactions each is willing to forego in order to underwrite a better future individually. For either to attempt to make the other underwrite his present and future seems unfair beyond a doubt. If fairness is sought by both parties, as each claims, an impartial analysis of the questions asked would be more appropriate than shallow claims.

ADMINISTRATION

The administration of a pension plan involves a number of phases. Among these are (1) control of funds, (2) review of details of operation, and (3) determination of basic rules.

1. CONTROL OF FUNDS. Of popular interest, and for good reason, is how pension funds shall be controlled. To begin with, it is well to take cognizance of legal requirements. Tax laws, as already noted, must be observed, else important income tax privileges will be lost. Also, the Taft-Hartley Act requires joint representation of employer and employee with respect to plans in which the union or its appointees are directly involved in fund administration (usual insurance or trusteed plans apparently are exempt). Then, too, plans must conform to the registration requirements of the Securities and Exchange Act; the insurance and trust provisions of state laws; the wage provisions of the Wages and Hours Act; and various estate and inheritance tax laws.

Thus the final plan of control may call for various representations and interests. Company executives, union executives, private insurance company executives, and various state and federal agencies may all have a direct or indirect role to play. And the services of such technical specialists as lawyers, accountants, actuaries, tax experts, labor relations experts, corporate and financial experts, investment counselors, and statisticians will also be required.

In brief, control of funds will necessitate not only appropriate company organization but also relations with unions, government, and various technical experts. This is one reason why pension plans that are sound cannot be created overnight or administered by unseasoned or semiskilled help.

2. REVIEW OF DETAILS OF OPERATION. Much detail is involved in the operation of a pension plan. These may be grouped for discussion here under the heading of, first, actuarial details and, second, routine records.

Since retirement and factors affecting severance can be estimated with a high degree of accuracy, this should be done if the benefits entailed by future obligations are to be offset by appropriate current premiums or investments. This involves actuarial calculations of what the probabilities of payments are in terms of the nature of one's working force. What are the probabilities of mortality, severance, disability, and retirement for a working group of certain ages, sex, types of occupation, etc.? And as the working group changes, the estimates must be rechecked so that over- or underpayments are to be avoided. Unless such probabilities are checked by sound actuarial methods, the administration of a pension plan will either cost too much or have insufficient funds for future needs.

The routine records that are to be kept must also be worked out in detail. These will include information on the following:

1. Accession of new employees
2. Voluntary severance of old employees
3. Disability severance of old employees
4. Employees going on retirement roles
5. Earnings of employees
6. Changes in positions or wage rates of employees
7. Various details of fund investments, changes, and earnings
8. Premium payments
9. Pension and supplementary benefit payments
10. Tax computations
11. Costs of operating the plan

3. SUGGESTED RULES OF OPERATION. Perhaps the subject of pensions can be best summarized by suggesting some points which should be given careful consideration in their operation. Perhaps it is trite to say that a pension plan should be carefully planned with the assistance of qualified experts. Since this takes time and since unions often "spring" pension demands without warning, it is well to work out such details in advance, whether a company wants a pension plan or not. If a plan is contemplated, it should be adequate to meet retirement needs and fair to employee and employer. Hence it might be wise to precede the installation of a program with a series of indoctrinating communications, so that a plan that will be adequate and fair can be adopted.

As already noted, a plan should be devised in terms of the needs and conditions of a particular company. It should be actuarially and legally sound. It should be built with due consideration to a firm's future possibilities and its place in the industry and the market. Perhaps above all, it should be an integral part of a company's total objectives and programs—and not just an adjunct tacked on by outside pressures.

For example, interchangeability of pension privileges between companies might well be considered on a voluntary basis, else they may be forced by government on a mandatory basis.

QUESTIONS AND PROBLEMS

1. From what sources have pressures been brought to bear upon industry to underwrite or pay for various welfare programs? What does this augur for the future?

2. Industry claims that it cannot afford to pay for various welfare schemes, but, when forced, it always seems to be able to. Is there a limit? What may be the straw that will break the camel's back?

3. Life insurance programs have been supported by industry for a long time. Why have such programs had an appeal, whereas such programs as health and accident insurance were late in arriving?

4. If a hospital and surgical plan is being considered for one's employees, what questions would have to be considered? Would you take your employees into your confidence during the developmental stages? Why or why not?

5. If there is a Blue Cross plan in operation in your community, find out whether it seems to be working to the satisfaction of the employees and the company.

6. How do you explain the recent trend toward private pension plans? What lessons does this have for the personnel manager?

7. What factors are generally given consideration when writing rules governing eligibility for private pension plans?

8. If pension plans are matters legally subject to collective bargaining, does this not lead to the conclusion that it would be wise to be prepared to bargain on almost any subject, including such things as salaries of executives and prices of one's products? Explain.

9. What effect do you feel the extension of pension plans, both private and public, is likely to have upon the hiring of older employees? What can be done about this?

10. As a personnel manager discussing with employees the question of amount of pensions, what would you tell them is a reasonable pension? How would you prove your contentions?

11. What are "supplemental benefits" in a pension plan? Why are they justified?

12. Why do such governmental agencies as the Bureau of Internal Revenue concern themselves with private pension plans? Be specific.

13. Rate the various methods of financing a pension plan according to (*a*) safety, (*b*) accuracy, and (*c*) simplicity. Which method would you adopt if you had your choice?

14. Do you know whether or not employees object strenuously to helping finance a private pension plan? If possible, conduct an attitude survey on the subject.

15. If you were an employee, in whose hands would you prefer to see the custody of pension funds placed? What lesson has this for personnel management?

16. What advantages does the Social Security pension plan have over private plans? Private pension plans over the federal plan? Which do you think will prevail? Why?

17. What are various economic risks to which all employees are more or less subject? In our technological society, are the average employer's chances of handling these risks himself increasing or decreasing? Explain.

18. Who may be beneficiaries under the Social Security Act? Against what type of risks has protection been provided by the Act?

19. What are the old-age provisions of the Social Security Act? Upon retirement, what is the most that a pensioner can receive under the Act?

20. To what types of workers are pension plans most likely to appeal? How can pension plans be "sold" to the younger employees? Need they be? Why or why not?

Service and Participation Programs

SCOPE OF PLANS

Over the years, a miscellany of plans has been offered to employees which fall outside the borders of that which is strictly pertinent to the affairs of business. Some, such as social and athletic programs, seem fairly well removed from the business of producing and selling goods. Others, such as medical plans and company stores, are more closely related, in that they provide services which might otherwise be unavailable. And still others, such as company newspapers and suggestion systems, can help significantly to relate the employee to the working environment and its reasons for existence.

In any event, whether or not any of these plans should be installed can be argued back and forth. Some companies contend that the ones they adopt raise employee morale, group teamwork, and productive effectiveness. Others argue that these plans deal with affairs that are not related to the business and represent interferences in the private lives of employees or compete with legitimate sources of community enterprises. And, finally, some see a day when most social and athletic activities may be taken over by the unions, noting that some unions are already making a strong bid in this direction.

The debate will not be continued here. The issues involved must be considered in terms of each company's philosophy, its community environment, its union relations, and forces pressing for or against adopting particular plans. It is apparent, however, that such plans have been adopted by many companies. Hence a description and analysis of such programs is justified here. This is done under the following headings:

1. Recreational, social, and athletic programs
2. Participation programs
3. Services of convenience or personal necessity
4. Organization of programs
5. Rules of adoption and operation

RECREATIONAL, SOCIAL, AND ATHLETIC SERVICES

Recreational, social, and athletic services have a double purpose. They make for a well-rounded life for employees, and they provide the company with employees who are better equipped to perform their daily tasks. How intensively and extensively any company should undertake to provide facilities for and to stimulate interest in these services are matters of company policy. Some companies feel strongly that workers are interested only in wages, hours, and working conditions. To them, this category of services is simply a luxury and a superfluity. At the other extreme are companies that feel that employee morale is significantly influenced by the services a company provides; hence these companies establish impressive plants and programs. In between are programs of varying degree and size.

Of course, company policy must be based upon interpretations of objectives, morale, and environmental factors. Thus, whether or not a given company concludes that a recreational plan, for example, should be established will depend, if the matter is examined logically, upon answers to such questions as the following:

1. Are any objectives of the company being missed because facilities for recreation are not available?
2. Does the community provide adequate and usable recreational facilities?
3. Is a union offering such plans or facilities?
4. Is employee morale, and hence willingness to co-operate, weak due to a lack of adequate recreational facilities?
5. If recreational plans are established, will the employees in sufficient numbers take advantage of them?

Assuming that favorable answers are derived, a wide range of programs is available from which to make selections. In describing these plans, only a superficial attempt is made to group them in recreational, social, and athletic categories. After all, such plans as bowling leagues have aspects of all these: they provide physical exercise, the athletic aspect; they provide a change in the tempo of living that brings renewed vigor to employees, the recreational aspect; and they encourage gregariousness among employees, the social aspect. Or a company symphony orchestra, for example, may be to one individual a recreational opportunity, and to another a social event. Hence the groupings here are for purposes for convenience rather than indicative of exclusive categories.

RECREATIONAL AND SOCIAL PROGRAMS

1. SOCIAL GET-TOGETHERS. Occasional events such as company-sponsored dances and picnics are the usual way in which recreational

and social programs are initiated. Whereas dances may be operated with relative ease because participation of those who attend the event is assured, such programs as picnics and outings call for a good deal of planning and organizing. Games and contests should be planned for all age groups and for both sexes. The events should be scheduled so that they neither drag nor overlap. Small prizes, too, are a desirable feature for winning contestants. And it is important that the executives attend and participate with unconcealed enjoyment.

Parties organized to suit the season serve to promote interest. Beach parties in the summer, Halloween and Thanksgiving parties in the fall, and Christmas and New Year's parties in the winter are examples of such occasions.

2. INFORMAL ASSOCIATIONS. Other recreational activities are provided by informal get-togethers of employees in clubrooms of their own. During rest periods, lunch hours, or before or after going to work, employees may gather in the club for refreshments or dancing. More elaborate arrangements provide facilities for athletic activities of various kinds.

3. MUSICAL GROUPS. A miscellany of other recreational plans has been adopted. The employees of one company have been unusually successful in organizing a symphony orchestra. This activity began with the formation of an orchestra for playing popular music, which evolved after a few years into a symphonic group. Of interest is the fact that this orchestra has been a success not only for the participants but also for nonparticipating employees who have learned to enjoy classical music. More popular among musical activities are dance bands, glee clubs, and military bands.

4. DRAMA CLUBS. Many companies also have drama clubs. These seem to be very attractive because they provide employees opportunity to produce and stage plays as well as act in them. Such groups have given plays on the stage and also have presented radio dramas. Thus this activity provides a variety of opportunities to attract employee participation.

5. FLYING CLUBS. Flying clubs have been organized by the employees of some companies. This is a relatively expensive activity, but the cost for the individual can be reduced considerably by the formation of clubs. Ordinarily, such clubs can be organized only in large companies. The number of potential fliers must be large enough to support a continuing turnover of learners and participants.

6. FLOWER AND GARDEN CLUBS. Gardening, from time to time, has proved of wide interest. During war years vegetable gardening was

Production Area during Working Hours

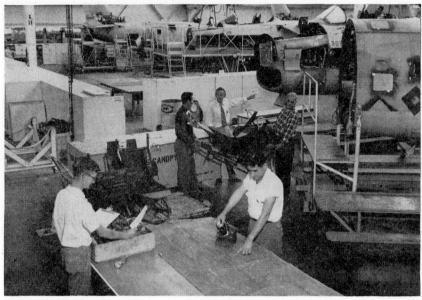

Courtesy: North American Aviation, Inc.

Recreation Area during Lunch Hour

Courtesy: North American Aviation, Inc.

Production Aisle during Working Hours

Courtesy: North American Aviation, Inc.

Play Area during Lunch Hour

Courtesy: North American Aviation, Inc.

a very successful employee service. Such programs can be made more effective by planning shows at which vegetables and canned goods are to be displayed and judged. Some companies have also had success on a more permanent basis through smaller-scale flower clubs. Here, too, periodic shows help to stimulate employee interest and activity.

7. NOON-HOUR PROGRAMS. The noon hour provides a real opportunity for providing employees with recreation. Horseshoe pitching and softball are popular in many companies. Other companies prepare elaborate programs of noon-hour entertainment, occasionally using professional talent from the entertainment world, famous figures in the sports world, and visitors of public renown. The latter type of program, on a large scale, can ordinarily be established only by the large company. The inexpensive nature of some of these programs is illustrated in the accompanying pictures showing how production space and aisles are used for noon-time recreational purposes.

9. SPECIAL INTERESTS. Groups with special interests may also be served. Chess and checkers clubs, camera clubs, and bridge clubs are examples. These groups, though small, will nevertheless be found to be among the most active that can be established.

10. PHYSICAL FACILITIES. Recreational and social plans must often be implemented by physical facilities. When community facilities are adequate and conveniently located, it is desirable to take advantage of them. However, it will ordinarily be found necessary to provide some space on or near the company premises. Arrangements for social events can be provided with relative ease when company restaurants are designed for all types of occasions. Thus the restaurant building of one company is used for dances, parties of all types, educational meetings, and meetings to pass out rewards for seniority and suggestions. In some cases the recreation building is separated from the company building. This has the advantage of removing the employee completely from the working atmosphere. Unusual facilities for various sports and social gatherings are provided by the 180-acre park established by the National Cash Register Company of Dayton for these purposes. Such arrangements are, of course, the exception.

ATHLETIC PROGRAMS

1. THE POPULAR SPORTS. Athletic programs are widely used to engage employees in after-hours activities. Bowling and softball, in season, are particularly popular with many companies. The former has grown widely in employee acceptance because it is a good mixer sport and can be enjoyed by the tyro as well as the expert. Softball teams have

grown in popularity, too. Some companies stress intramural teams, whereas others sponsor intercompany leagues. The former provides opportunity for a large number of employees to participate in athletics, while the latter gives employees an opportunity to cheer for their company, thus providing institutional pride. Basketball teams require more skilled participants and are usually restricted to intercompany competition, but they do provide much spectator entertainment. The merit of these programs sometimes has at least one serious detraction. As one company official noted, the costs of industrial compensation for accidents were higher in the case of recreational programs than for factory operations.

2. THE MINOR SPORTS. A variety of other athletic sports is also sponsored. Tennis and golf tournaments or parties are planned by some companies. In a few instances, skeet, trapshooting, and pistol ranges have been provided. Swimming facilities are also provided by some companies by renting community facilities at stated times and under qualified supervision. Gymnasiums may also be rented under similar conditions in some cases. In a few instances, companies have built such facilities for the exclusive use of employees.

Horseshoe pitching is also of interest to some employees. This game possesses possibilities in any program because facilities can be provided easily and the playing time of the game is relatively short. Hence it furnishes an excellent sport for the lunch hour. Continuing interest can be derived by keeping cumulative records and setting up interdepartmental teams. Other sports that have been established in a few instances include ice and field hockey, cricket, squash, and badminton. Because of the skill required by most of these sports, they have been less popular.

Enough enthusiasts can usually be found in most companies to organize a fishing club. In addition to organized outings, meetings to discuss fishing and outdoor recreation and to swap "lies" may be planned.

MUSIC IN THE PLANT AND OFFICE

Although music in business is a twilight case of a recreational or social program, it is included for discussion here, because music does have an aesthetic or emotional appeal that is more related to the recreational or enjoyment capacity of the employee than to his physical nature.

For many decades, music, as well as other forms of discussion and entertainment such as reading of stories, has been employed during working hours in various foreign countries. Until recently, such practices were almost nonexistent in the United States. But in the past several years there has been a small but growing trend toward the use of music as a means of improving production by relieving monotony and by providing employees with a "lift." Various studies both here and abroad have shown that production has been increased from 5 to 15 per cent after the introduction of music. The results in terms of lessened fatigue, cheerier dispositions, and increased emotional stability are equally favorable, if not measurable.

The introduction of music in the plant had to await the development of satisfactory equipment. Modern developments now make possible the distribution of music from central stations to strategically located loudspeakers at reasonably low cost. The musical equipment need not be located in the factory. Such services, in large communities, may be purchased from companies established solely for this purpose.

Another significant factor in the use of music is the building of programs that will not interfere with working rhythms and will appeal to employees. The music suitable for a punch press department may be distracting to a central stenographic department, and vice versa. Usually some experimentation will be necessary before programs suited to various departments are established. Similarly, experimentation will be be necessary to select programs that the majority of employees prefer.

The equipment for sending music may also be employed to broadcast various messages. Although some companies frown upon this practice, others favor it. The latter use the system to make special announcements, to describe lost-and-found items, to welcome new workers, to send birthday and anniversary greetings, and to broadcast such public events as World Series baseball contests, football games, news reports, and addresses by the President of the United States.

PARTICIPATION PROGRAMS

Although the inclusion is somewhat arbitrary, company periodicals and suggestion systems are discussed here in connection with employee services because both attempt to relate the employee to his working environment. Either might be dispensed with, as some companies have, on the grounds that periodicals are ineffective and suggestion systems are likely to bring about disputes and controversies between employees and employers. On the other hand, the supporters of such plans see much good in them as means of improving the ties between the two groups.

COMPANY PERIODICALS

Company periodicals are publications such as newspapers or magazines issued regularly to employees. Their widespread use is seen in the fact that three out of four companies with assets of five million dollars and over have such publications.[1] They are discussed here because their contents in most cases is devoted to social and personal items of interest to employees. But they also are used for instructional purposes of a general nature and to disseminate information regarding company products, policies, rules, and regulations. However, the latter must be heavily sugar-coated with personal items, else they are not likely to be read.

1. OBJECTIVES. The fundamental purpose of company publications of this type is to bring employee and employer closer together. The larger organizations in particular must have recourse to as many devices as possible in order to personalize employee-employer relationships. Company magazines are one of the tools that serve this purpose. Employees become better employees, so the theory of company magazines goes, because they get the feeling of worth-whileness and integration. Employees who "get in the news" are thereby made "public figures" in their company. This publicity imparts a sense of importance to employees so cited that they react favorably to their work situation. They have thereby been recognized publicly as a part of the organization. And such recognition is a reward of which few employees seldom get enough.

Publication of company rules and of explanations of procedures and plans also can serve indirectly to make employees feel that they are an important part of the organization. In the first place, they are taken into the confidence of the company, and, second, their ignorance regarding various aspects of company operations is removed. Hence, when properly handled, which means writing from the employee's viewpoint, company news can be as effective a morale builder as personal items.

2. LAYOUT AND FORM. To be effective, company periodicals must be made up with care. Much thought and study should be given to such matters as technical form, content, periodicity, method of distribution, and staff for gathering and editing materials. Some companies invest very small amounts in mimeographed sheets, whereas others publish magazines that compare favorably with the finest magazines found on the newsstands. In either event, the important point is to determine carefully what type of magazine will serve the conditions and needs most appropriately.

As already noted, a company magazine cannot be published until some thought is given to technical form. Such matters as size of magazine, type of paper, manner of printing, size and kind of type, and margins and headings will have to be studied carefully. There is no one standard for these matters that is best for all companies. However, sev-

---

[1] According to an address of Dr. Claude Robinson before the American Association of Industrial Editors, *Personnel,* March, 1953, p. 452.

eral points are well worth remembering. The size of magazines should be such that they are easy and convenient to handle. Type should be selected that is easy to read, and headings should both attract and guide the reader. And, perhaps above all, the style of writing should be somewhat on the "breezy" side, interesting and appealing to the average workman.

3. CONTENT. In regard to the content, it is generally agreed that personal items, social events, and recreational and athletic news should make up the greatest part of a magazine. Some contend that nothing else should go into a publication intended for employees. Perhaps it would be better to argue that nothing should be included unless it is written or translated for employees. After all, the opening of a new office building, for example, may be company business, but it is also of real interest to employees. Or news about new products, new processes and other technical matters are of interest to employees; but they must be described in nontechnical language.

News of personal interest, however, should lead all the rest. New additions to the staff, transfers and promotions, marriages and births, unusual happenings to employees, hobbies and activities, awards and recognitions, leaves of absence, and serious illnesses are examples of items that should be reported. A liberal sprinkling of pictures, particularly of children, is also desirable. After this, social events of personal interest, both within the company and within the community, such as dances, parties, and gatherings should receive attention. Then, too, the various sports activities of employees, such as standings of teams, personal performances, and game schedules should be highlighted. Although some people may state that they do not care whether or not they get their names in the paper, there are few indeed who actually do not like such mention, insignificant though the occasion for it may be. The old rule of the small-town newspaper that each subscriber's name should be mentioned at least twice a year in the paper also holds true of the company periodical.

4. PERIODICITY AND DISTRIBUTION. How often magazines should be issued and how they are to be distributed must also be considered carefully. In most cases, magazines are published once a month. Periods of greater or lesser time are selected infrequently. A month provides a convenient interval as well as one that whets the employees' interest and does not overwork the publication staff.

The question of how often is comparatively easy to answer, but the question of distribution is difficult. There is wide difference of opinion as to methods. Some companies prefer to mail the magazines to the homes of employees. In this way, there is greater assurance that the families will read the magazines. Some pass out the magazines as the employees "punch the clock," and others distribute them through the departmental supervisors. The last two methods are used primarily because of their convenience and secondarily because each employee is given his own copy on the company premises, providing another direct contact between employee and employer.

The real problem is, of course, to have the magazine read, else it may as well not be issued. This can be accomplished by including various features such as puzzles, rewards for those who notice special items scattered through the magazine, and contests for such suggestions as names of new sections of magazines or comic characters that are used to depict safety lessons and other instructions that may be run in the magazine from time to time. Emphasis upon personal items serves to promote reader interest.

5. NEWS GATHERING AND EDITING. Finally, arrangements must be made for gathering and editing the content of magazines. A popular method is to hire a full-time magazine editor and to rely upon selected employees from various departments to gather and report the news. This arrangement has the advantage of expert direction and of employee participation, but it suffers from the possibility that the employee reporters will not do a thorough job of news gathering. This may be circumvented by frequent "staff" meetings in which the departmental reporters are made to feel the importance of their jobs and, at the same time, are instructed in what news to gather and how to do it. In some companies a full-time staff to do all of the work is hired, members being selected from present employees or from sources outside the company. In this way the technical competence of gathering and preparing news items is assured. Whether or not a sense of employee participation is lost depends upon how closely reporters get in touch with employees and how well they ferret out and report their activities.

SUGGESTION SYSTEMS

General education and communication may also be improved by means of a good suggestion system. Although some companies have had unfavorable experience with suggestion plans, favorable results are more common. To be effective, however, suggestion plans should be designed with care in regard to the following aspects:

1. Objectives of suggestion plans
2. Procedures for collection and evaluation
3. Policies of compensation

It is invariably necessary to precede the inauguration of a suggestion system with a campaign of publicity designed to acquaint employees with the values of the system and how it is to operate. Specific notes should be made regarding the gains to the employees. In this connection, it is important to stress that laborsaving suggestions will not result in layoffs.

Then it is important to publicize the procedures of the system. In particular, employees should be informed as to how suggestions should be made, where they should be deposited, and how they are to be judged. Every effort should be made to indicate how the employee who makes a suggestion is to be protected in any rewards or recognition which may arise from the suggestion. In this connection, some companies have found it desirable to establish judging committees made up of employees as well as executives and technical assistants.

Rewards for acceptable suggestions is a matter of argument. Some companies frown upon any rewards except expressions of congratulation. Others conclude that some form of financial compensation is indispensable. In the latter event, practice varies. Some companies establish maximum rewards of $25 to $50, whereas others use formulas by which employees may be paid up to 25 per cent of the first year's savings derived from the suggestion. In the latter case, bonuses have been paid in thousands of dollars in some instances.

Although suggestion plans are largely concerned with ways and means by which production, sales, and office procedures may be improved, they are sometimes used to obtain the views of employees regarding management methods and policies. The latter objective, while desirable, is perhaps better handled in connection with grievance machinery. By making this separation, the suggestion plan can be used to keep the sight of employees upon positive improvements of mutual advantage to employer and employee. Complaints, disputes, and dissatisfactions should be channeled through appropriate executives or an effective and accepted grievance machinery.

CONVENIENCE SERVICES

"Convenience services" refers to the facilities or assistance that are ordinarily available in the community and arranged for by employees themselves, but for one reason or another are provided for employees by the company. Among such services are restaurants, company stores, company nursing and medical assistance, and counselors of various types. Unless made available in convenient form—so it is contended by those that offer these plans—employees will not take advantage of plans that are significant to their health, well-being, or state of mind. When properly installed, the morale and effectiveness of employees can be raised sufficiently to pay for the cost of these services.

RESTAURANT FACILITIES

Perhaps no employee service plan has received as much attention in recent years as that of restaurants. During the years of World War II, many war plants were constructed at sites away from available dining facilities. These companies, faced with the need of providing these services, gave considerable thought to methods of serving good meals at reasonable prices. Most companies concede that their restaurants are operated at cost or even at a loss, but they conclude that such losses are more than offset by the benefits of increased production and decreased absenteeism resulting from better health.

The biggest advances in eating services have been made in physical facilities and planning of diets. Considerable thought has gone into the design and location of restaurants and eating facilities. The technique of layout planning is being adapted to the design of factory cafeterias. In addition to fixed restaurant sites, more and more companies are adopting mobile and automatic dispensing food units. These units are used by some companies to serve employees who are located at inconvenient distances from the regular restaurants of the company. Other companies use these devices to reach workers during working hours and provide them with soft drinks, milk, candy, and sandwiches.

Careful study has been made of the dietary needs of workers. Industrial dietitians and nutritional experts have become permanent members of the personnel staff of many companies. The dietitians must plan meals that not only are well balanced but also will entice employees to buy them. Various plans have been devised to attract employees to the planned menus. The most popular method is to offer the planned meals as "specials" at a relatively low price. One company has gone so far as to serve free meals to employees so that they have no problem of "selling" their balanced diet. Another good method is to feature items that are deemed good for the diet. Thus one company stresses salads by serving them up attractively and well chilled. Another headlines salads on its printed menus, adding jingles that describe nutritional value. An example of how items are pushed is provided by the company which took all soft drinks out of the restaurant so that milk would not have that competition. Another company has used the idea of contests among employees to attract attention to balanced menus. Employees have responded not only by offering menu suggestions but also by buying more of the balanced menus than they did when the company alone decided what the menus were to be.

A final word on nutrition has reference to the practice of some companies supplying employees with vitamin pills as a supplement to possible dietary deficiencies. Of course, the practice of providing salt tablets to those who work under very hot conditions has for a long time been known to be desirable in replacing body salts lost by perspiration.

COMPANY STORES

Company stores have had widespread adoption. In some instances they have acquired a poor reputation because they have been used as a means of making excess profit. This has been possible when employees have had to rely upon company stores for their purchases. Either outside stores have not been available, or purchases from them in some instances were almost prohibited by drawing employee checks on the company stores. Company stores have also been used to keep employees in debt, thereby assuring the company of little, if any, labor turnover. These instances, although infrequent, occurred often enough in the past that unions frequently raise the issue in collective bargaining agreements. Moreover, the Wages and Hours Administrator has laid down rules governing how employees shall be paid so that employees will not fall victims to unscrupulous company stores practices. Company stores have also been opposed by community retailers, who feel that such profits logically should go to them. And some states have outlawed them.

The foregoing is intended to set a warning signal regarding the dangers of misuse of company stores. However, they can be an effective service. Certainly, in communities where stores are not of the best or where excessive prices are being charged, they are an excellent means of building employee good will. The offerings to employees can be exceedingly wide, covering food, clothing, sports equipment, automobile supplies, and household furnishings. Many of these items may be available on the company premises. Others may be offered through discount arrangements with wholesale dealers, only samples being shown at the plant.

The charge that company stores are exacting excessive profits can be avoided by turning over their operation to employees. In one company, the store is run by the employees for the purpose of financing various employee activities. The profits are used to support various recreational, social, and athletic activities. As a consequence, these programs are run and supported by the employees themselves. The company lends a minimum of support by providing store space at a minimum charge.

CREDIT UNIONS

Facilitative services include a variety of plans, only a few of which can be mentioned here. An interesting example is the "credit union," which has had a phenomenal growth in the United States. The credit union is essentially a small-loan institution operated by employees for their own benefit. Its purpose is to have a source from which short-term loans may be obtained for personal needs at rates far below those that are charged by the "loan sharks." Since some employees are hard pressed for funds occasionally, the credit union offers a worth-while service to them. And to the employees who invest in the credit union, it offers a combination savings and interest-earning plan, and also a life insurance program based upon savings and age of the member.

The losses in credit unions are remarkably low, having averaged about 7 cents per $100 loaned. In the first place, the officers of credit unions review applications for loans from a restricted group with whom they are well acquainted, since they are all fellow-employees. Hence losses are reduced at the source by careful screening of applications. In the second place, most plans have established an upper limit above which loans will not be made to any given individual. In this way, risks are spread over a large number of borrowers. In the third place, credit unions are subject to state and federal regulations, depending upon how the unions are established. Since 1907, when the first state law was enacted, forty-four states have enacted legislation governing the operation of credit unions; and in 1934 provision was made for federal incorporation.

Some idea of the pace with which credit unions have grown may be seen in the fact that there were about 5,000 credit unions in 1936 and over 14,000 in 1954. In that year, loans outstanding amounted to $1,454,146,000 on 5,000,000 loans. The majority of these unions are in the industrial states, with California, Illinois, Massachusetts, Michigan, New York, Ohio, Pennsylvania, Texas, and Wisconsin each having over 600 credit unions. In California and Illinois, the membership exceeds 600,000.

Assistance to employees in purchasing homes is also a popular plan of employee service. Such assistance is usually provided by a building and loan financial plan. This combines a savings plan, for employees who want to invest their savings, with the loan feature, for those who wish to build or buy homes. The borrower then repays to the loan association a fixed amount each month or payday. In other cases the company itself provides the financial assistance and deducts a fixed amount, covering principal and interest, each payday. Both plans make it possible for employees who so desire to procure long-term loans at reasonable rates with a minimum of red tape. Indeed, some companies make the loans at extremely low rates as an encouragement to homeownership, believing that such acquisitions make for stable employees.

MISCELLANEOUS SERVICES

An unusual type of employee service is exemplified by the practice during war years of providing nursery service, to encourage more women with preschool-age children to seek war work. By providing space, facilities, and trained attendants for children, a service was provided that was expedient to the war effort and helpful to the families of servicemen. In many cases, women with young children could not otherwise accept war work. Unless they could leave their children in safe and capable hands, their entrance into war employment was out of the question. And until company nurseries were opened, baby and children "sitters" were simply not to be had.

MEDICAL SERVICES

In recent years there has been a tendency for more and more companies to provide employees with medical service. Such service usually has started with visiting-nurse service for sick employees. It has gradually been extended so that varied medical service is available not only to employees but also to their families. Thus hospital and surgical facilities are available in some companies for all types of illness and operations. Also, the services of the dentist and optometrist are offered in some cases.

Obviously, providing such facilities goes beyond the normal concept of company responsibilities. Generally, provision of first-aid facilities on company premises and subsequent hospital needs of injured employees is unquestioned practice. But to go beyond this and offer facilities for treating illnesses, for taking care of injuries and ailments acquired beyond the company gates, and to accept nonemployees as well as employees is an innovation. Companies that have extended such services feel more than compensated. They find employee morale improved by the fact that the minds of employees are set at ease because they no longer dread the possibility of being faced with medical costs they may not be able to bear. In addition, they find that employees no longer hide symptoms but seek treatment of illnesses before dangerous stages are reached. They become, therefore, better workers, more loyal and dependable, and less irritable.

Opponents of these plans, or those that hesitate to underwrite them, have some important questions to ask. Why, for example, do employees who are paid high wages not seek and pay for such services themselves? Is this not an unwarranted intrusion upon the personal lives of employees? Will this not lead to company domination of employees, or at least a mild form of fascism? Is this not but a step on the road to socialized medicine?

It is not proposed to undertake to argue these questions pro or con here, but it is important to point out their significance. Certainly, such extensions of services to employees have potentialities for great good; but what of the cost? Maybe there should be political and social changes in the relations between employer and employee. Maybe there should not be. The point to be stressed here is that, when industry takes such drastic steps, it should do so with a clear understanding of the end to which innovations are likely to contribute and of what precautions to take as a corollary to prevent undesirable repercussions. It is by no means implied here that industry should not take pioneering steps. It has done so in technology; it has often not done so in the field of social relations and has found, as a consequence, that social changes have occurred, notwithstanding, with detriment to itself in its relations with employees.

CONSULTATIVE SERVICES

Included among the facilities offered by some companies are consultative services of various kinds. For example, some companies have opened their legal departments to the personal problems of employees. In most instances this is restricted simply to giving initial advice as to what to do if threatened with legal suits, for example, or what rights one has in various difficulties that may present themselves. In other instances help is given in instituting a suit, in selecting legal counsel if protracted court action is necessary, and in suggesting the nature of action to be taken. Of course, except in minor cases or actions, the legal departments are not offered to carry on court actions or extended cases. However, limited service is highly desirable because most employees do not have the slightest conception of what to do or what not to do when faced with legal difficulties. Hence the availability of this service will be of great aid to them, at very little cost to the company, unless perchance it should have an unusual number of troublemakers on its payroll.

Other companies have made arrangements whereby employees may discuss various problems with vocational guidance experts, psychologists, psychiatrists, and family relations experts. Such services, too, can do much to find and eliminate sources of trouble that disrupt an employee's ease of mind and, therefore, his capacity to produce efficiently and effectively.

ORGANIZATION FOR SERVICE PLANS

In most companies the various service plans are operated under the jurisdiction of the personnel department. Within this department a section is established to inaugurate and direct the service plans. This section is often called the "employee service department," but it is also known by such names as the "welfare department," the "recreation and athletic department," the "insurance department," and the "benefits department."

In performing its duties, this unit may rely upon the assistance of others. Thus, in the establishment of pension plans, for example, the service department would call upon the legal, financial, and statistical departments for advice on technical aspects of pensions. And, in the operation of the recreational plan, for example, it would rely in most companies upon the help and co-operation of formal committees or organizations of employees.

EXAMPLE OF SERVICE ORGANIZATION

To illustrate how the company organization ties in with employee organization, it is well to describe the plans in use by a few companies. Of interest, to begin with, is the plan used by a company employing 10,000 workers in a large city location.

In this case a recreation club, operated by the employees, serves as a nucleus for all social and athletic events within the company. All employees may join, the dues being 25 cents a month. The management of the club is in the hands of officers who are elected by the members. Activities include baseball, bowling, golf, skeet shooting, model auto racing, roller skating, dances, and other social affairs. Annual Halloween and New Year's parties are sponsored. The annual Christmas party is an outstanding event, being given for the children of employees.

The officers are advised and assisted by an activities director, who is on the staff of the personnel division. The director also plans and operates special entertainment and activities for the company. Noon-hour entertainment is an example of such activities. The activities director also has charge of the distribution of tickets for special events held outside of the company, such as operas, sports events, and a circus. Thus much of the work done here is by the company, but the employees are made to feel that they are running the show.

ORGANIZATIONAL PLAN UNDER DECENTRALIZED OPERATIONS

In another case an employees' club has been established at each of the several plants operated by the company. The general plan of organization is the same at all of these, but the program and activities of each plant are determined by the people located in them. Each of the clubs is made up of departmental groups averaging from about fifty to one hundred members, thus providing a well-knit working unit. The supervisor of the department is a member, but he can neither vote nor hold office.

In each department employees elect their own president, vice-president, secretary-treasurer, social chairman, athletics chairman, and welfare chairman. It is noteworthy that the greatest interest is in the social activities—dances, parties, picnics, and the functions of hobby and special-interest groups. The athletics committee plans activities which the employees desire the most—archery, table tennis, basketball, softball, golf, swimming, etc. Bowling, by the way, has proved the most popular sports activity. Among the activities the welfare committee carries on are: building of a fund to buy flowers for hospital patients, distribution of Christmas baskets, organizing first-aid or home-nursing classes.

The departmental presidents are then organized into the Executive Council, and the departmental chairmen into councils for the plant. Thus the social chairmen form the Social Council, and so on. Each council elects its own officers and meets once a month.

Dues vary from 10 to 50 cents a month, as the members of each department determine. The funds go into the departmental treasury. In addition, a central club fund, administered by the club's Executive Council, is built up from vending-machine profits, admission to central club dances, cafeteria profits, other plant-wide social or athletic events, as well as company contributions. Most club affairs are, therefore, self-supporting. Any employee, however, whether or not a member of the club, may attend any of the central parties or dances.

At most of the plants, the employee club has a clubhouse or rooms —the typical one has an auditorium, kitchen, game room, reading room, and one or two meeting rooms. The company provides and owns this property and buys all permanent facilities. The funds of the club are used only for current expenditures.

These clubs, like those in most companies, are not incorporated. Hence, to insure officers against the unlimited liability which may accrue from such organizations, the company has arranged to protect the officers from damage suits by means of a rider on the company's public liability insurance policy.

COMPANY EXPERTS

Another case of organization is illustrated by an employees' club in which the company supplies expert advice and guidance. A member of the staff of the Industrial Relations Department, who is known as the "Activities Director," helps organize and counsels the employee organizations which are a part of the Employees' Activities Association. This is a nonprofit association, organized and supported by the employees. Membership begins automatically for every employee at the time of employment. No dues are paid, the organization's activities being financed by the profits from vending machines.

A board of directors governs the association. It is composed of one representative from each club or activity represented in the association; the Activities Director, who is an ex officio member; and one other appointed by the president of the company. The latter appointee is an accountant who keeps the books and serves as treasurer of the association.

Whenever at least fifty employees participate in an activity, a petition may be made to the board of directors for representation in the association. Among the activities represented are a band, baseball, basketball, bowling, boxing, camera club, chess and checkers, fishing, riding, golf, gun club, horseshoes, mixed chorus, and tennis. The company provides and maintains an athletic field with night lighting, where baseball and softball games are played. It also provides a darkroom for the camera club and facilities for the gun club and casting club. It also pays the salaries of the Activities Director and his secretary and allows for time spent by the other company representatives on work of the Employees' Association. Beyond these expenditures, the employees carry the financial burden. The management feels that employee interest in recreational and social activities has a direct relationship to the extent to which employees plan, manage, and support their own activities.

The Activities Director also counsels the girls' club, to which all women employees belong automatically and which raises money through social activities for charitable purposes, the employees' relief association (a mutual benefit association), and the employees' credit union.

RULES OF OPERATION

If such plans are to yield the fullest returns, several suggestions are in order regarding the plans and their operations. Worthy of careful consideration are the following points:

1. PRIMACY OF WAGES, HOURS, AND WORKING CONDITIONS. In the first place, service plans will do little good if a company's wages, hours, and working conditions are not considered satisfactory by the employees. These are the foundation, without which all else is futile. Employee service plans cannot support a weak or unfair structure of wages, hours, and working conditions. Hence the first principle in establishing service plans is to review the basic values of employee relationships. Until any questionable features are removed, the installation of service plans should be delayed.

2. THE FACTOR OF NEED. In the second place, employee service plans should not be installed unless there is a real need for them. They should not be viewed from the "moralistic" angle of being "good for the employees." Rather the question must be: Do the employees want the services? To establish playgrounds, athletic fields, and recreational facilities, for example, just because some executive feels that these will turn employees away from the corner saloon to the "good life" will almost inevitably lead to failure. Of course, a company should not install features that would lead to moral deterioration, but neither can it succeed in making employees tread the "straight and narrow path."

3. EMPLOYEE SUPPORT. In the third place, a service plan should not be sponsored unless the employees are willing to support it with their time, effort, and sometimes money. To "give" employees facilities is dangerous to long-run success for the simple reason that those things that are easily obtained are seldom appreciated. But when employees help to build facilities, such as softball diamonds or vegetable gardens; to manage activities such as dances or parties; or to finance activities through monthly dues, for example, their attitude changes from that of an outsider to one of personal ownership. Hence it is invariably wise to provide for employee participation; whether by contributions of time, effort, or money should be determined by particular circumstances.

4. STIMULATING EMPLOYEE INTEREST. In the fourth place, the company need not wait for employees to "need" particular service plans or to display willingness to participate in them. Steps can be taken to suggest, directly or indirectly, the desirability of various plans. One company, for example, has contended that all its plans have been established

at the request of its employees. However, it has not been averse to dropping hints where they will do the most good. In one case, the company was "surprised" by the request of employees for financial aid in building low-cost housing; but its surprise was only superficial, because company executives had hinted months before to a few key employees that low-cost housing would be a desirable thing for many employees. The idea was subsequently presented at a meeting of the employees' club and soon snowballed into a company-aided program. Such steps must, of course, be taken with caution, lest any sign of company interference undermine the employees' feeling of possession.

5. OVER-ALL COVERAGE. In the fifth place, service plans should be developed so that all employees have some service or facility in which they have an interest. Not all employees want to participate in or watch softball games, bowling, or fishing, for example. However, if opportunities are provided in a variety of fields, most employees will find some service plan that will interest them. Unless breadth of offerings is sought, the result will be that only a few employees will participate. The service plans in that case are useful only to a restricted part of the payroll. For example, "varsity" athletic projects have that shortcoming. These should be strenthened by encouraging employees to be spectators at contests or by providing intramural sports that will permit mass participation.

6. SOFT-PEDALING EXPENDITURES. In the sixth place, it is desirable to operate plans with a minimum of financial fanfare. Otherwise, there is real danger that employees will tend to wonder whether or not the plans are being financed at the expense of lower wages. If employees begin to ask such questions, it is usually certain that trouble is bound to follow. Although costs of such programs are invariably low, they may seem high to employees who note elaborate recreational and sports equipment. Moreover, expenditures for these affairs tend to become a subject of collective bargaining, with consequent loss of control over them by management. Hence it is well to build facilities conservatively, to indoctrinate employees regarding their low cost, and to encourage employee participation in their management and financing. Under these conditions, the facilities will be accepted rather than suspected.

7. RELATING COMPANY AND PERSONAL OBJECTIVES. And, finally, service plans should be organized and operated so that employees become a more integral part of the company because of them. In other words, the bowling league should not only result in recreation and

exercise but also build company *esprit de corps.* Any activity or event should be designed so that a tie-in with company objectives and aims is made. This is not easy, but, unless accomplished to some degree, the employee service plans will represent an unconnected appendage that serves no useful organizational purpose. And wholesome and enjoyable though some activities may be, if they are not related to company objectives, they have no reason for taking up company time, resources, or energy.

It is worth repeating in this respect that unions are increasingly interesting themselves in social and athletic programs. They are conducting parties and dances, organizing athletic teams, and operating recreational activities. Whether or not this trend will continue to an extent which will ultimately see unions assuming a predominant role is as yet uncertain. But if it does, management will have lost an opportunity of substantial proportions to build employee relatedness and loyalty.

QUESTIONS AND PROBLEMS

1. As more and more service and participation programs are underwritten, how can the personnel manager be sure that the point of diminishing returns has not been passed? Have you any evidence that in some companies such a program has reached a state where the "tail wags the dog"?

2. Suppose an employee said to you, "Since you can get my recreation for me 'wholesale,' here's my whole pay check—do the same for me on food, clothing, and shelter. I'll get more for my money that way." How would you answer him? Why is it highly improbable that employees will come to this point?

3. How would you determine whether or not employees need a particular service plan?

4. The employees of a given company complained that the recreational facilities provided by the company were making an uncalled-for dent in their pay envelopes, but they agreed that the program was a good one. What might have been done to prevent the development of this reaction?

5. In one company the policy was against having any parties for employees and similar affairs because of the fear that drinking might become excessive and the affair get out of hand. Comment upon this policy. What suggestions have you to offer to avoid undesirable results?

6. If a company sponsors such athletic programs as softball and bowling, should executives participate with employees? What are the advantages? The dangers? How may the latter be minimized?

7. Visit a company that has installed music programs during the working hours. Report on your findings.

8. In one company, nothing except personal items and "human interest" sub-

jects are included in the company newspaper. Do you think that the company is getting its "money's worth" by eliminating references to company items?

9. Many companies provide restaurant services. Upon what grounds is this justified? Do not community businessmen have a right to object to such competition?

10. Some companies provide free meals to employees. What do you think of this practice? Consider the viewpoints of the shareholder and the ultimate customer in your answers, as well as the employee.

11. What is your opinion of the practice of installing nurseries for working mothers? Is the existence of such services an implied criticism of society?

12. When a company underwrites or provides complete medical, dental, and hospital services for its employees and their families, has socialized medicine and paternalism been attained indirectly? Explain.

13. When a company provides services such as those of psychiatrists, are not employees almost forced to use them whether they want to or not? Does this not lay the groundwork for revolt rather than for better relationships between labor and management?

14. When the personnel department is responsible for service plans, how can it gain the co-operation of the employees in operating them?

15. What are the advantages of having employee clubs in connection with various service programs? Is there danger that the efforts of employees in such affairs may lead to amateurish mistakes?

16. One company turns over all recreational and social affairs to the employee's club but makes available the services of a trained recreational and social counselor. What are the merits of such an arrangement?

17. If you were an employee, would you participate in the operation and management of employee service activities? Poll your fellow students as to their attitudes in this matter. Write a report giving your conclusions on the results of the survey.

18. Many companies have very few, and in some cases, no employee service activities or employee clubs, yet morale seems to be very good. How would you explain such situations?

19. If you were the owner and manager of a business, would you prefer to be rid of employee service activities and clubs? Explain.

20. As an employer, what percentage of your employees would have to participate in or show a desire to participate in employee service activities before you would feel justified in underwriting them?

28 | Women in Industry

INTRODUCTION

In this and the next chapter a number of special labor problems are discussed. They are "special" in the sense that they occur only occasionally or that they are so pressing in nature that they call for particular mention. Thus, for a period of time and in some companies, there will be a problem of re-entry of the returned veteran to industry. And in recent years more has been heard about "fair employment practices," referring to minority groups and their treatment in industry. Then, too, there are questions of policies regarding such groups as the handicapped and aged workers. Striking hard, at times, is the problem of fringe issues. Also, there are problems connected with women in industry that must increasingly be faced, as many companies learned during the war years, when great reliance had to be placed upon this source of labor supply. The problem of women in industry is taken up in this chapter, and in the next chapter a miscellany of special problems is discussed.

INDUSTRIAL BACKGROUND OF WOMEN WORKERS

Some of the difficulties in handling women workers are ascribed to their relative newness in industry. After all, any newcomer in any situation experiences strangeness, feels at a loss, and needs special attention. However, after adjusting to the new situation, the newcomer becomes an old-timer and needs no special or unique treatment.

In a sense, the characterization of women as "new" workers has a humorous and, to the men, an embarrassing slant. In the Dark Ages women were the "factory" workers—they were the slaves and did the "dirty" work. In the early days, the men went to the parties (bear hunts and scalping "teas"), while the women performed the menial tasks. But the women, seeing the error of their ways, then put the men to work while they attended the parties. Having been "out-slickered" once, the men should welcome the opportunity that presents itself now that women seem to want to return to the yoke of labor. Perhaps the men can regain their long-lost leisure.

In terms of modern industry, women are, of course, "immature." The Civil War in the United States records the first significant entrance of women into industry. However, this was largely in office work, not factory work. The number employed during World War II in all types of work rose to sixteen million. By the end of 1953, the number of women

Illustrating Safety Lock to Be Inserted in the Landing Gear Mechanism to Prevent Accidental Retracting of Landing Gear while Mechanic Works in Wheel Well

Courtesy: Curtiss-Wright Corporation

working was estimated by the U.S. Bureau of Labor Statistics to be around nineteen million. Thus about a third of the total working force was estimated to be made up of women. About half of the women were in clerical or factory work, areas in which once there were no women employed. Obviously, such changes in the laboring force are notice to personnel management to take heed of problems that may arise in connection with handling women in industry.

In each company, personnel management should undertake two major tasks. First, it should ascertain in what respects, if any, female employees differ from male employees. Second, it should prepare suggestions for executive consideration of these matters and establish personnel practices that will improve the handling of women employees. A description of factors significant in handling women workers is taken up in the first half of this chapter; in the second half, suggestions regarding the second of these tasks are outlined.

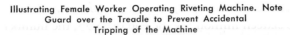

Illustrating Female Worker Operating Riveting Machine. Note Guard over the Treadle to Prevent Accidental Tripping of the Machine

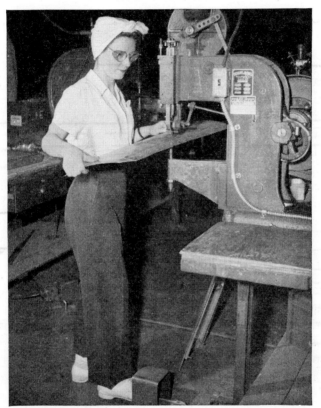

Courtesy: Curtiss-Wright Corporation

REQUIREMENTS OF MODERN INDUSTRY

Have modern industrial methods changed significantly the requirements for labor? This question is difficult to answer in general terms. It is really best answered in terms of particular jobs, but that is impossible to attempt here. On the average, though, the capacities now required of people in industry are not entirely different from those required before the Industrial Revolution.

To be sure, factories and offices have many more and complex machines, but operating them is different from "inventing" them. Almost anyone can drive a car, but few could have invented one. So in modern industry the vast majority of people use the same human qualities that their great-great-great-grandparents did. We have to put in time—but the hours are less. We have to be skillful—but not in so many different crafts as our forebears. We have to be resourceful—but we have many more experts on whom to rely. We have to expend physical energy— but the machines help out considerably.

Work today is thus "easier" than it was. Of course, some will point out that it is perhaps more monotonous and the worker is often nothing more than a cog in a machine. There is some truth in these arguments; but, on the other hand, we must recognize, first, that we work fewer hours and, second, that the span of life of factory workers has increased considerably. Moreover, correct placement of workers will help, because monotony means largely that workers have been placed in jobs they do not like or which fail to challenge their capacities.

So, all in all, the burdens of modern industry impose (with only few exceptions) no requirements upon women that would tend to exclude them. It is more logical to say that modern industry is much better for women (and for men) than it once was.

MALE AND FEMALE DIFFERENCES

PHYSICAL CHARACTERISTICS OF WOMEN

There are some differences in the physical make-up of women to which attention must be given in adjusting them to their work and their work arrangements to them. However, the differences are not so wide as to be sound reasons for excluding women as workers. For example, the complaint that women cannot lift heavy objects as well as men can may be rebutted by the argument that the use of manpower to lift heavy objects is very wasteful. What if women are physically unable to compete with men as weight lifters? Men should not be hired for this purpose in industry either.

In terms of bodily proportions and construction, there are certain facts that should be recognized. Women in general are smaller than men. Their trunks are relatively longer and their legs relatively shorter. They are relatively more knock-kneed and knock-elbowed than men. Their hips are relatively broader, but their shoulders narrower; and their fingers are somewhat longer, but their thumbs shorter.

These bodily differences explain why women are better in some things and poorer in others. Women are usually better than men at jobs requiring finger dexterity because they are not "all thumbs." The knockelbowedness helps them to do some factory jobs better but slows them down on tasks that require straight, as opposed to circular, motions. And their shorter legs are a disadvantage in jobs requiring considerable walking but a help in those requiring bending down to pick up materials. So, in selecting employees for given tasks and in arranging workplaces, these differences in men and women should be taken into consideration.

Women also differ from men somewhat in physical strength. Men have more muscle than women; and, on the average, women are only about 65 per cent as strong as men. Women do not have the strength of grip that men do. Because of such differences, women should not be expected to act as trucks or strong-arm workers. (In this mechanical age, neither should men.) They are weaker in physical strength than men; but that is not a vital point, because most jobs in industry today are not excessively demanding in physical strength.

MENTAL CHARACTERISTICS

Concerning mental differences, women workers in general have no cause to feel inferior to the men. Studies have disclosed no significant differences. The woman worker is, on the average, just as intelligent as the average male worker. This refers, of course, to native intelligence.

When it comes to acquired knowledge, the male worker has an advantage over the woman worker, but the superiority is not inherent. This means that with the same study and the same opportunity to acquire knowledge of technical matters, the knowledge of women employees would parallel that of men employees. Two deductions are worth drawing from this condition. First, men should generally be given preference to women on jobs in which technical knowledge is required. Second, the preference should be removed in cases in which individual women have caught up with the men.

Specifically, the matter of mental skills should be approached— whether men or women are being considered—in terms of given mental traits. If a job requires problem-solving skills, attention should be devoted to finding a person with, or training a person in, that skill. If it requires a good memory, attention should be focused on that element. When judgment is at stake, the aim should be to find a person with that quality. Mental skill, like physical skill, is too broad to be talked about in general—it must be divided into its components.

EMOTIONAL CHARACTERISTICS

1. DEFINITIONS. The emotional responses of women workers have been a subject of serious controversy. One often hears such com-

ments as the following from management: "Women are too sensitive"; "They cannot take a 'kidding' "; "They are too emotional"; "They blow up quickly"; and "They are too interested in personal matters." Such opinions occur too frequently to pass off as superficial prejudice, although there is some underlying bias.

The term "emotions" is hard to define to the satisfaction of everyone. It has to do largely with our feelings, our likes and dislikes, our fears and joys, and our smiles and our tears. Whatever they are, emotions are important because they are results and also causes. Obviously, we like the result of being happy—our emotions are in a desirable state, and we try to keep them that way. On the other hand, if we are depressed, anxious, or unhappy, we try to do things that will make us "snap out of it." Hence in industry, when the emotions of employees are in an undesirable state, the employees will do something about it— and what they do may not always be good for themselves or the company.

It is obvious, therefore, that the emotional status of employees is something to be watched carefully. And it is also obvious that the ability to maintain or return to a good emotional status is a quality to be desired in employees. In other words, emotional balance is a quality to be sought after.

When, therefore, it is said that a particular group of employees is less balanced than another, this is a condition that must be examined carefully. Such an investigation is very difficult to make because universal yardsticks for measuring emotions are nonexistent. So, when talking about the greater emotionality of women, we have to be cautious.

2. FEATURES OF EMOTIONAL STABILITY.   Are there physical, mental, or organic features that tend to make a woman "go to pieces" faster than a man? In some respects yes, and in others no. Here are some of the aspects that make women slightly more emotional. The thyroid glands of women are larger and more active, which accounts for a somewhat greater excitability. Their lung capacity is somewhat less; hence they tire sooner in continuous exercise. Their stomachs are a bit smaller, and, unless they eat more frequently, they become fatigued a bit sooner. Their nervous system is more sensitive, and therefore they are quicker to detect differences. On the other hand, their blood pressure is somewhat lower than that of men. And they have more fatty tissue, and hence more reserve energy. The foregoing aspects are not intended to be exhaustive; they suggest that there are some reasons for a degree of higher excitability.

3. DIFFERENCES OF DEGREE.   The foregoing differences are of degree, not kind. Men, too, are excitable, but not quite so much as women. However, their industrial education has taught them how to hide or sublimate some of their excitability, but most everyone could cite examples of men "frothing at the mouth" in their industrial activities.

4. NEWNESS IN INDUSTRY.   Probably the element that serves to explain (and which needs explanation in turn) the greater degree of emotionality in women is their greater self-consciousness. Anyone who is overly self-conscious is also hypersensitive, and so any comment of the supervisor is interpreted too personally, weighed too heavily, and considered too seriously. What, then, makes some people—in this case, women in general—somewhat more conscious of themselves than are others?

For one thing, many women have gone to work for the first time. Although their great-great-grandmothers were hardened veterans, many women of the present generation are babes in the industrial woods. And it is an acknowledged fact that most new employees are hypersensitive. Any visitor to a city, for example, "sees" many more things than the old-time dweller. New workers, too, see and feel many things and take many of them too seriously. The newness of the situation results in tenseness, and so we should expect the new workers to be somewhat self-conscious, embarrassed, and prone to make mistakes.

Unfortunately, the mistakes of newcomers are usually not condoned, and in women they are too often received as inherent. Instead of solving these difficulties, there is a tendency to give up in disgust. The new woman employee loses confidence, continues in erring ways, and, finally, convinced of the hopelessness of ever learning, gives up trying. What would happen to new men workers if they were treated as clumsy oafs? They would likely stay that way—as the spirits of some men have been broken. However, this aspect or cause of their self-consciousness may be expected to be reduced in most cases as time goes on.

SOCIAL CHARACTERISTICS

Another characteristic that is considered to weigh more heavily in the case of women is that of social or group relationships. These relations may take a variety of angles. For example, it is claimed that women are much too interested in their fellow workers, their activities, and other subjects of gossip. All this is presumed to interfere with their work. That there is more or less truth in this cannot be denied. But, again, such activities are evidence of a defense mechanism of the newcomer, who hopes to protect herself while adjusting to a new environment. And so long as any employee is given to understand that she is an interloper—even the gray-haired veteran of twenty-five years' service—she will act to protect her job.

Somewhat similarly, women employees get "clubby" or form groups. It serves to give them a feeling of solidarity that is otherwise lacking in the work situation. The women may not be aware of the reason for their clubbiness, but this fact of uncertainty is fairly well recognized as a cause.

Women workers are also accused of getting unwarranted "crushes" on fellow women workers, male workers, or the supervisors. Here, too, is a reaction which can be undesirable and often takes place. Attempting to seek a cause is difficult. Some students argue that the female—from childhood on—has her crushes. Unfortunately for this argument, boys and men, too, are known to indulge in hero worship. But, of course, the women are said to be guilty even more so. Some of the explanation in industry, undoubtedly, goes right back to a desire for encouragement, security, and backing. The feeling of uncertainty makes all of us look for bulwarks. And what is more certain or better than a friend in need?

DEPENDABILITY

Women are sometimes considered to be less reliable than men. This conclusion has some good evidence to back it, but it can be carried too far. In some cases, women have proved to be less reliable. To be sure, women are prone to quit their jobs after marriage in order to make homes. To what degree this can be a source of unreliability is an open question. If the trend of the past, in which more and more married women have decided to keep working, continues, the charge due to this factor will be minimized. If a high rate of turnover among women employees continues because of marriage, the employer obviously cannot be blamed for seeking less mobile workers.

On the other hand, women have been superior to men in some cases when it comes to reliability. In several companies, studies have shown the attendance records of women to be better. Women were absent less frequently, tardiness was less, and attendance during critical work periods more certain.[1] They tended to break fewer company rules. Their acknowledged better memories served to make them somewhat indis-

---

[1] General studies show women at a disadvantage on the score of absences. The Second Progress Report of the Research Council for Economic Security shows that on "prolonged absences" of four weeks or over, there were 62 absences per 1,000 of female production workers as compared with 32 for male workers (*Modern Industry*, December, 1953, p. 173).

pensable on certain types of jobs. And their willingness to perform many routine duties made them more reliable in these otherwise "thankless tasks." So these offsetting aspects of reliability make less tenable the position of those who accuse women of unreliability.

MISCELLANEOUS QUALITIES

1. MECHANICAL APTITUDE.   There are a number of other ways in which women differ somewhat from men. Women are at present less apt mechanically than men. Whether this is due to inherent or acquired reasons has not as yet been proved. Some people claim that women do not have the natural aptitude to compete mechanically with men. There is some truth in the fact that the bodily proportions and physical strength of women are not so adaptable to mechanical duties as are the corresponding physical characteristics of men; but others claim that the mechanical shortcomings are due solely to the fact that girls are started with dolls instead of mechanical toys. The latter argue that, were girls given mechanical toys, they, too, would be found to possess mechanical aptitude. The point is that they are admittedly less proficient mechanically, but whether or not they will continue to be so is an open question.

2. RELATIVE FEAR.   Some claim, too, that women are more fearful than men. They are supposed to be unwilling to take physical or economic risks. They are afraid—so it is said—to get hurt and, hence, do not work so hard as men do. And they are afraid to accept transfers or changes of jobs because of the uncertainty of making good. These claims seem to be justified. However, one employer has argued that he preferred people who were afraid of accidents because they had fewer of them. And as to the fear of changing jobs, that, too, has a stabilizing influence, since the laboring force is a little more settled. In other words, this fear complex has its advantages as well as its disadvantages.

3. SUSCEPTIBILITY TO PRAISE.   Another general trait of women employees is the abundance of favorable comment that they require. Some superiors have claimed that it is necessary to flatter them constantly. Here, again, it is apparently true that women are more susceptible to praise (as they are more sensitive to criticism) than are men. Again the explanation for this may be found in their relative industrial immaturity. They have not become so hardened to these things as men. Their sensitivities have not been tempered as have those of men. And, as will be noted in the next section, knowledge of this sensitivity to praise can be very useful to management.

4. SENSITIVITY.   Somewhat along these lines, women are more sensitive to and aware of physical matters such as dress. Indeed, where

men are satisfied (the women would say too satisfied) to wear the same old outfit until it falls apart, the women are said to be overconscious of this feature. Moreover, some claim that the desire of women to be different leads them to select factory and office clothes that seriously impede their work. Again these charges have more than a figment of truth in them. But it has been found that, when management is reasonable and unbending, standard practice in clothing and dress can be enforced. But how about the cause of this flair for exhibitionism? Again there is no proof that it is inevitably true of women. When this problem has arisen, some employers have handled it so that good, rather than grievances, resulted.

5. ECONOMIC DIFFERENCES. The economic treatment accorded women in industry often, though not always, differs from that accorded men. In many companies, women are paid at lower rates than men for the same jobs. This practice is condoned on the grounds that women cannot produce so effectively as men, are not so dependable, and cannot perform all the duties that men can. When these charges are factually true, then the case for lower wages is indisputable. The difference in wages, then, is ascribable not to differences in sex but to differences in capacities.

These reasons, though offered in support of wage differences, are often of historic but not of current significance. Since most factories are now designed to supplant human power with machine power, since many women are making factory and office work a career, and since most jobs are specialized tasks rather than crafts, more and more jobs are falling into the category of jobs that can be filled equally well by men or women. Many states and cities have laws regulating the hours during the day and the number per day or week that female operators may work, thereby restricting the employment of women and making them less desirable to industry as employees. But leaders among women in industry are contending that such legislation is often intended to discourage the competition of women rather than to protect their health and welfare.

The trend in the economic treatment of women in industry seems to be toward equality with men. More and more companies are adopting the policy of "equal pay for equal work." Some companies follow only the letter of this policy by claiming that women, even on the same jobs, do not do equal work because they must have help in lifting parts, adjusting machines, and meeting emergencies. But, on the whole, the adoption of this rule usually leads to the following of it in spirit as well, sooner or later. For the present, it must be admitted that, while a large number of companies have rules (formal or informal) differentiating between the economic status of men and women, all signs point to a diminution of these differences. However, it must be noted that avenues leading to higher-paying administrative, professional, and technical positions are not opening very rapidly for women.

6. STATUS DIFFERENCES. There is no doubt that the position assigned to women by both men and women is lower in the business world than that of men. This is a "custom" of the social group and may, or may not, be changed much for a long time. Certainly, this lower status tends to reflect upon those supervised by women executives. That is one reason why both men and women do not ordinarily like to be supervised by women. And where women supervisors are found, it is usually also found that the woman in question is much more efficient than any male who might have been in competition for the executive position. Until this group custom of looking down upon women in the business world is changed, it must be admitted that this factor of status is very powerful in molding relations between women and their working environment, as well as in reducing the economic value placed upon women workers.

LEGAL ASPECTS[2]

Women in industry are usually subject to restrictive regulations that do not apply to men. These regulations are on a state or municipal basis. The variations are so great that it is possible here only to give a few selected illustrations.

For example, the rules in Ohio cover such matters as enforcement, occupational restrictions, health requirements, hours of labor, and minimum wages.

In the enforcement of the Ohio rules, it is required that employers of female help post conspicuously the schedules of hours for such help. Records must also be kept for each female employee. Penalties for violation of any of the provisions of the Ohio law may include fines or imprisonment or both.

Various occupational restrictions are stated by the Ohio law. For example, women are prohibited from employment as bellhops, taxi drivers between 9:00 P.M. and 6:00 A.M., meter readers, and baggage handlers. Moreover, females may not be employed at work that requires

---

[2] It may be noted that similar types of regulations are also usually found in many states and cities covering the employment of minors, whether male or female.

frequent or repeated lifting of weights over twenty-five pounds. And any female under twenty-five years of age may not be employed in work that compels her to remain standing constantly.

A number of health requirements are also specified. For example, suitable seating arrangements must be provided. Also suitable toilets and dressing-room facilities shall be provided. Again, if a separate lunchroom is provided, at least a half hour shall be allowed for lunch, whereas a minimum of one hour shall be allowed if the employees must leave the premises. And the lunch period must be given after not more than five hours of work.

As to hours of work, the day must not exceed nine hours. Hours a week must not exceed forty-eight and must be worked within six days. The total number of working hours must fall within ten consecutive hours. And for those who have more than one place of employment, the aggregate number of hours worked must not exceed eight a day or forty-eight a week.

Minimum wages are set for most occupations. As examples, women restaurant workers, 55 cents an hour; cleaning and drying workers, 35 cents an hour; and beauty operators (depending upon the size of city in which they work), 40 cents. Of course, women employed in interstate commerce, come under the provisions of the F.L.S.A., which sets the minimum at 75 cents an hour.

PRINCIPLES OF SUPERVISING WOMEN

PRACTICES AND POLICIES

The foregoing discussion seemingly has favored the employment of women. Certainly the differences between women and men have been minimizd rather than inflated. The reasons for taking this tack lie in the facts that have been gathered about women in industry generally. Of course, what may be true in a given factory or office may differ from general trends and relationships. Hence this discussion is really intended as a guide to the factors about which personnel management should seek information as a basis for decisions in a particular case. Having made such studies, personnel management may then suggest practices and policies as follows:

1. In those respects in which no differences should exist in handling women and men
2. In those respects in which methods should be adjusted to types of women employees, just as they should be adjusted to types of men
3. In those respects in which methods should be adjusted to known differences between women and men

4. In those respects in which methods should be adjusted for probable, but not proved, differences between women and men

SIMILARITIES

Perhaps the most serious mistake that management can make in dealing with women employees is to start with the assumption that they are radically different from men. Immediately, in that case, it starts with a problem on its hands. It begins to read problems into situations where no problems really exist. It is suspicious where no suspicions are warranted. As a consequence, women employees begin to sense the attitude of suspicion and to return suspicion and lack of confidence.

After all, in dealing with people it is always desirable to know what they want and then offer them the opportunity to earn these desired rewards. For example, it is well understood that most employees want fair treatment, security, a feeling of worth-while accomplishment, recognition for work done, good leadership, good work equipment, and pleasant surroundings and fellow workers.

Looking over this list of basic wants, what is there in it that women employees do not also want? Obviously, they are just as desirous of obtaining these things as men are. There may be differences in intensity of desire among individual women, but such differences exist in men, too.

An illustration of the need for uniform treatment can be found in the question of whether women should be paid wages equal to men's. The answer must be determined upon the basis of contribution. If a woman can contribute (in the fullest sense of the word) as much as a man on a given job, the answer must be "yes," else the women will be dealt with unfairly. Of course, if for one reason or another a woman cannot contribute as much, is less reliable, or is not as stable, the wage or salary should be less. But it is significant that, so long as conditions are equal, the answer is bound to be in favor of equal wages. An arbitrary decision to pay less is an invitation to unnecessary grievances.

A recognition of the fact that, as employees, women are more like men than they are different supplies women with an incentive to live up to this belief. The vast majority of employees are bound to try to keep up with their assigned place. Pride is a strong factor, not only in men, but also in women. Use of this positive technique of stimulating more efficient workmanship in women is good management, therefore.

Uniform treatment also has the advantage of impersonalizing relations with women employees. As soon as management lets any group of employees know, directly or indirectly, that it intends to be business-like, it will tend to get better results. And it is hard to see how women employees can be made to feel that they are considered a significant part of the organization unless management tends to treat them exactly as they do men. In addition, by acting uniformly, management mini-mizes situations in which some women consider themselves privileged characters or try to use their femininity to secure special privileges.

Uniform treatment, in so far as possible, also has the added ad-vantage of reducing the possibility of blaming women employees for what, in reality, are mistakes of poor supervision or poorly devised rules and regulations. It is easy to place the blame, when things go wrong, on women employees, on the grounds that they are women and require special treatment. However, if the emphasis is placed upon uniform treatment, it will be easier to detect whether difficulties arise as a result of the rules or of the fact that women are being supervised.

But how are the men going to react if women are given equal and uniform treatment? One answer is that the treatment will not be en-tirely uniform, as will be noted later. The aim is to attain uniformity, not arbitrarily to develop a "single standard." Another answer is that the men are not going to like it if an attempt is made to approximate immediately a uniform basis of treatment. Perhaps this is the biggest obstacle to the tasks of management in attempting to deal uniformly with women employees. There is no sense in being unrealistic in regard to the objections of the male employees. Only through the passage of time can it be hoped to overcome their suspicions that women are taking away their opportunities.

In this regard, it might be well to digress to examine briefly this question of the competition of women for men's jobs. In a sense, it can be argued that the woman worker is taking a place that could be filled by a man. This is true only when there is an unemployed man available who is qualified to fill the job and for whom no other job is available. So long as people demand more goods and services, increased produc-tion is the only way to raise our standard of living. And the working force must be augmented with women if the desired standard of living cannot be attained with male employees alone.

In conclusion, there are very sound reasons for seeking to treat women employees the same as male employees. Management not only will save itself needless trouble but also will gain the confidence and trust of the women. Attempts to adopt uniform rules, however, will tend to make men employees somewhat less satisfied. There is reason to believe, however, that the men are more likely to become accustomed to equal treatment for women than the women are to accept a lesser position. For example, companies that have insisted upon a standard wardrobe for workers have found that men and women work together with almost imperceptible friction and fewer disciplinary problems as a consequence of this factor.

DIFFERENCES AMONG WOMEN

Another general mistake that is sometimes made is to assume or conclude that all women employees are alike. This conclusion is usually reached after management has a couple of women employees "act up" under approximately the same circumstances within a short period of time. It is so easy then to conclude that women are certainly a nuisance in the office, let us say. This conclusion is wrong if it overlooks the fact that there are also individual differences among men. And some managerial troubles have stemmed directly from a failure to recognize individual differences among women.

A few illustrative cases are in order: A given office supervisor was having trouble with a particular woman employee who was constantly flirting with the male workers. During a layoff period he managed to get rid of her. He was somewhat soured on women, but his distaste grew greater when he had the same experience during the next rush period. The next time he refused to hire a woman employee because this experience with two women led him to conclude that all women were flirtatious. In this case, the personnel manager slyly asked the supervisor if that applied to his wife, too. That stopped the supervisor. He was ready to listen to the suggestion to select his women employees more carefully and to "lay down" the law as soon as the first irregularities took place.

In another instance, a supervisor was having difficulty with a woman employee regarding her absentee record. Irrespective of the importance of her work assignments or of the warnings regarding her record, the employee continued in her irresponsible way. The supervisor, of course, was enraged and finally recommended that she be discharged, giving as his reason "unreliable female employee." When the personnel department investigated the case, it turned out that the employee was ill, had been taking treatments, and did not wish to have her illness known. She just happened to be of a retiring nature, her illness was not peculiar to women, and the case was finally straightened out. The difficulty here was not that "women are all alike"; there was an individual problem that merely required sympathetic investigation and handling.

And, finally, one supervisor had concluded that all women employees were unsatisfactory because they could not keep pace with the men in his department. The work in this case was not heavy, and the working conditions seemed to be satisfactory. The supervisor had even insisted that the workplace be studied when the first woman had been hired. Closer investigation revealed that the arrangements of materials, height of work desks, and type of chairs had been standardized upon the basis of that first girl. Afterward, as many additional girls were hired, nothing was done to allow for individual differences. It had merely been assumed that all women were alike.

HANDLING DIFFERENCES BETWEEN MEN AND WOMEN

As noted earlier, a number of differences (although in some instances very slight) between women and men are known. Perhaps the first group of differences to which attention should be paid are the physical differences. These, in a way, can be handled more easily. Moreover, the attempt to handle these differences will serve to develop confidence in management when the settling of emotional differences comes up.

1. PHYSICAL DIFFERENCES. The best practice in regard to the physical differences (these first having been ascertained) is to make a study of the jobs in one's department. The following questions should be considered: Under what conditions is each job performed? What are the requirements? Is it heavy or light work? Is it fatiguing? Does it involve gripping of work? Is it routine? Does it require the making of many decisions? Etc. The study, to repeat, should be made in terms of the known physical differences of women employees.

Having studied the jobs, they should be classified into the following groups: those which women should not be permitted to do; those which they should be permitted to do only for short periods or only after thorough study of the woman herself; those which will require redesigning or re-engineering before women can be permitted or expected to do them; and those to which they can readily be assigned immediately.

It would consume too much time to illustrate each of the foregoing, but a few examples are in order. Thus it is well agreed that women should not be permitted to do any heavy lifting. There is too much danger of injury to them, and also they are inefficient in performing such tasks. Again, long hours are highly undesirable because women become fatigued more easily, and they must have more periods of rest and food replenishment.

Women are known, too, to be less satisfied and more highly excitable on jobs that require numerous decisions. If they have to stop to figure out what should be done, they prove to be somewhat less efficient and less satisfactory. As a consequence, they should not be selected for such jobs as a rule; but, when specific women employees indicate their liking and their aptitude for performing such tasks, there is absolutely no reason why they should not be assigned to them. The key to the situation is whether or not specific individuals are fitted for such tasks. As a rule, it is best to go slowly. A few mistakes on the side of conservatism are better than many on the side of haste.

2. EMOTIONAL DIFFERENCES. When it comes to emotional differences, women are slightly less stable than men. Hence such differences should be watched for and handled with great care. This warning is made for the simple reason that emotional differences can be reduced, but only if employees are handled positively. To frighten the "patient" or to inform him that he is undesirable are certainly dangerous methods of approach.

Thus, if we agree that women are somewhat more excitable, more easily led to tears, and more sensitive, then the suggested answer to such problems is that management must be more patient, tolerant, and considerate. A favorable and stable disposition can be maintained and developed. To accomplish this it is absolutely essential that the supervisor maintain an even-tempered attitude.

For example, some of the sensitivity of women can be ascribed to their self-consciousness due to their relative newness in industry. With this in mind, it is imperative for a supervisor to assume an attitude of uniformity and impartiality. When an employee is given the impression that she is assumed to be a capable and acceptable employee, she is more likely to strive to prove worthy of the confidence. It is difficult to fight self-consciousness and an expressed lack of confidence at the same time.

Or, another example, if women are self-conscious or belligerent because they are considered to be intruding in a man's world, the case will not be helped by fighting them. Indeed, the belligerency, for example, will take some curious twists. The woman employee who purposely attempts to embarrass the supervisor by "turning on her feminine charms" may be, as a new employee, using the only technique available at the moment to fight the one who dislikes supervising women employees. She proves her strength over her boss, although she selects an inappropriate way to do so. In other words, if women are given a fair and impartial opportunity to prove themselves in a businesslike way, there is that much less reason for them to bring their feminine wiles into the office or shop.

Moreover, emotions are not a complete loss; they may be employed through the medium of positive motivation. If women are more sensitive to criticism, they are also more sensitive to praise. Thus an executive who is a bit more lavish with his complimentary remarks will in all probability develop a much more friendly and loyal group of employees. If women are more sensitive to social manners and relationships, there is no reason why an improvement in this direction would not serve the general good. If women cannot take a kidding as well as men, there is no reason why this desire for a more businesslike attitude should not be complimented. Too much of the "joking" among men is backbiting and horseplay. So it may well be that in these respects the position of women is more commendable than that of the men.

In summary, the known differences of women do not involve any radical changes or startling innovations in personnel management and executive practices. They merely call for the common-sense application of practices that are already well known. Perhaps the most important change that is called for is the mere recognition that management is dealing with people—something that it at times overlooks in dealing with men. Hence the entrance of women in business in increasing numbers may be a boon to all concerned.

ADJUSTING PRACTICES TO UNPROVED DIFFERENCES

There are, of course, some aspects of dealing with women employees that may or may not be due to differences between men and women. Most of these unproved differences are in terms of particular jobs and occupations. But facts that indicate specifically in which jobs or under what conditions women are superior, equal, or inferior to men employees are few and far between.

As a consequence, it behooves management to assume in any given instance that women are equal to men until proved otherwise. The history of woman's entry into American offices about the time of the Civil War is well known—how this move was looked upon with disfavor by women and men alike. Yet, with the passing years, women have proved their superiority in general over men in many office occupations, so that it would be a rash person who would now suggest their removal.

Furthermore, in the two world wars, women took over many jobs that previously had been filled exclusively by men. Some of these jobs were handled so proficiently (to the surprise of many men) that women are likely to compete successfully with men in them from now on.

All this points to the moral that the safest course for management to pursue in supervising and dealing with women is to give them the benefit of the doubt. A fair trial should be allowed. Should women prove unsatisfactory in given cases, management will at least have proved its sincere desire to be fair from the beginning. If women do prove capable in other cases, any resentment will be cushioned by the basic fairness of having provided opportunity for a trial.

In general, it may be noted that personnel management can make a significant contribution to the task of dealing with women in industry by being prepared to supply management with good advice and suggestions. Moreover, a good personnel department should include women on its own staff for such purposes as hiring, counseling, and training women employees and supervisors of women employees. Indeed, in some companies the top position in the personnel department is held by a woman. Although this is relatively infrequent in industry, the number of women personnel executives in offices and distributive businesses, for example, is increasing.

QUESTIONS AND PROBLEMS

1. How do you explain the contradiction of the high esteem in which women are held in the community but the lower position assigned them in industry?

2. In your opinion which aspect—sociological, psychological, or technical— is most significant in explaining how women are received in industry? Explain.

3. Are there any geographical, vocational, or historical differences in the status accorded women in industry? Cite evidence.

4. What is your opinion on the hiring of married women in industry? Under what conditions do you, and do you not, favor such practices?

5. As time goes on, do you expect the relative number of women in industry to increase or decrease? What has been the trend thus far? What is the lesson of this for personnel management?

6. Upon whose shoulders would you place the greatest responsibility for effective supervision of women employees? What must be done to make such supervision really effective?

7. Poll your class to determine whether the students classify women in industry as problem cases or not. Classify the students' answers according to whether they have industrial or office experience, neither, or both.

8. Women are often paid lower base wage rates than men. Why are such practices followed?

9. It is often claimed that women cannot perform physical work on an equal basis with men. Should they or men have to in the light of the expensiveness of human effort?

10. Some women claim that differences are claimed between men and women

merely to keep the women in an inferior position in industry and business. Would you agree with this contention? Explain.

11. For what types of jobs are women better? For which types less efficient? It is not true that not all men are equally well suited for all jobs?

12. Are there any significant mental and emotional differences between men and women for working purposes? If not, why do men often complain that women are prone to break into tears when they are criticized?

13. If it is true that women are more conscious of social and group relationships, what factors should management watch carefully when selecting, inducting, and training women workers?

14. As a supervisor, what steps would you take (assume that you are a male supervisor) if a woman employee got a "crush" on you? What should be done to minimize the occurrence of such situations?

15. Many companies claim (although some contend to the contrary) that women are more reliable and dependable than men. If these claims are correct, for what types of work would such characteristics be desirable?

16. List the factors that should be given careful consideration in supervising and dealing with men. Are there any factors that would not apply to women? Are there any additional ones required in the case of women?

17. If women employees are given to understand that they are problem cases, what results should one be prepared to expect?

18. What should be done if in a given case men refuse to work for a woman supervisor, just because she is a woman? Analyze such attitudes on the part of some men.

19. Some contend that women, too, prefer to work for male supervisors. When such instances occur, is it wise to put in a woman supervisor? Explain.

20. What advice would you give in regard to the use of humor in supervising women? Would the same rules apply to men? Is there not room for a sense of humor in business? Explain.

| # Miscellaneous Phases of Personnel

INTRODUCTION

In this chapter a miscellaneous group of phases and problems of personnel is studied. They are grouped here because their inclusion elsewhere would be somewhat strained, yet to exclude them would be to overlook some significant phases of the subject. Moreover, study of this miscellaneous group provides an opportunity not only to examine some new as well as old problems and some commonly encountered problems but also to review various phases of personnel illustrative of the whole field. Included here for study are the following: public relations, fringe benefits, handicapped workers, minority groups, older employees, retirement of employees and executives, automation, and cybernetics.

PUBLIC RELATIONS

The development and maintenance of attitudes on the part of the general public which are favorable to a company and sympathetic toward and understanding of its objectives, programs, and activities are tasks growing in importance. This is so for a number of reasons. Various companies have found themselves attacked or misrepresented at times from a number of sources; or they have found that the general public simply was ignorant about the company. Yet, when attempting to protect itself from attack or when seeking the aid of the general public on some deserving project, the companies found themselves being held in low esteem and often viewed as malignant culprits.

After such experiences and after analysis of the causes, some pertinent conclusions have been reached. At the outset, it is apparent that a company cannot assume to be a thing apart from its community, local or national. Nor can it assume an attitude of separation at one time and, at others, seek out desirable relations. Again, it cannot rely upon good services alone, good intentions, and just good business practices, to counteropposing forces and propaganda. In short, it must seek to develop and maintain good public relations as a conscious and practiced program.

How this should be done has not been universally agreed upon. Some companies have organized major divisions for this purpose and staffed them with experts of various kinds. Some have merely left the task up to each executive to accept public relations as a part of his own job. Others have fallen somewhere in between. Again, some companies interpret public relations as being an integral part of every phase of a company's business—production, sales, finance, accounting, etc. Others see the job of holding public good will as a separate function.

Although there is much difference of opinion, the subject is discussed here because there is a growing body of students who feel that good public relations begins at home, with employees, and expands outward. Certainly, employees can do much good or damage to a company's reputation in its own community. For example, if employees are disgruntled to begin with and, in addition, are misinformed about some dispute or other, they will not support in their private conversations the newspaper advertisements that a company may be running to inform the public. As these employees visit friends, gossip at taverns, and discuss matters at various group meetings, their negative attitudes will serve to offset any good the newspaper advertising might have done.

Before spreading outward, good public relations should therefore establish a sound foundation at home. This requires, to begin with, a thorough review of basic company policies, programs, and objectives. Are these in line with good practice and generally accepted standards of social values and ethics? If not, they must be revised: if they are, next steps can be taken. The program of employee education can then be undertaken; first, by various educational methods and, second, by being certain that a company's deeds and actions measure up to their words.

Since general education and communications have been discussed earlier, only a brief review is needed here. By such means as training sessions, conferences, movies, bulletin boards, newspapers, letters and booklets sent to the home, and personal interviews, the company's position and problems should be explained to employees. This cannot be a "one-shot" plan; it must be construed as a continuous and perpetual program.

As important, if not more so, than words are the actions of a company. How supervisors and executives talk to their subordinates can bring about a feeling of friendliness or of enmity. How grievances and disciplinary cases are handled will influence employees' feelings of fairness or unfairness. How disputes and collective bargaining are conducted will determine whether or not a company is acting in good faith and with fairness and equity. How individuals are transferred, promoted, and granted various increases will serve to influence employee thinking. And so on the list could go.

Once employees are convinced by words and deeds, the program can be turned outward with excellent chances of success. The details of such programs are numerous and varied; newspaper advertising (as already mentioned), public speeches, participation in community visits, open house or plant tours, traveling technical exhibits, booklets and pamphlets, company movies, financial reports, participation in community affairs, and co-operation with trade and commercial groups.

As to the nature of information to be disseminated, the list could be equally long and varied. The subject can be summed up in two sentences: Be prepared to discuss in the open any and all phases of the operations of the company. Be prepared to discuss them in terms of reasons and explanations that will be convincing. For example, it is not enough to report on profits; they must be explained in terms of why they are reasonable and justified. Nor is it enough, to cite another instance, to talk about the high quality of company products unless this is commingled with explanations of why this is important to the community and the employees. And to mention one more point, it is not enough for executives just to appear at public gatherings, they must evidence a sincere and wholesome attitude of appreciation and of obligation to the group. Thus public relations requires that the subject rather be colored by reasoning; that physical appearances be colored by emotional and mental sincerity; and that the desire to gain good will be balanced by an open recognition of the company's obligation to do what is right.

To sum up, public relations has three major tasks:

1. To plan a program by which the views of the company may be correctly presented to the public and to employees
2. To devise ways and means for presenting company policies, practices, and organization in the best possible light
3. To appraise and control the public relations program in the light of public reactions and desired results

As a final word of caution, to do the most good, such work must be undertaken before "trouble" develops. A message may be accepted when relations are good; the same message will be rejected in the stress of a strike, for example. A good deed in time builds for the future; a good deed too late antagonizes because of its obvious belatedness.

FRINGE BENEFITS

In recent years there has been a trend on the part of unions to make demands which increase the return to employees in ways other than wages. Examples are vacations with pay, sick leave with pay, establishment of funds to assist employees injured in accidents, and provision of medical services. Such demands would provide employees with services or returns that they otherwise would have to finance themselves out of their own wages. As a consequence of this tie-in with wages, they are popularly called "fringe" benefits.

The cost of "fringes" is by no means insignificant, averaging in many cases 10 per cent and over of the direct labor payroll. In a survey conducted by the Chamber of Commerce of the United States the cost in cents per hour worked amounted to 23.7. The details are shown in Table 23. These data are averages, hence it is apparent that some com-

TABLE 23

NONWAGE PAYMENTS AS PER CENT OF PAYROLL
OF 690 COMPANIES, 1949*

Items	Per Cent
Employer's share of compulsory old-age insurance, unemployment compensation, and workmen's compensation..	2.9
Employer's share of agreed-upon payments for pensions, insurance programs, separation pay allowances, and miscellaneous payments to employees.......	5.0
Pay for rest periods, lunch periods, wash-up time, etc.....................	1.4
Payments for vacations, holidays, voting time, National Guard duty, time off for personal reasons, etc..	5.2
Bonus, profit sharing, special awards, etc.................................	1.5
Total	16.0

Nonwage payments as	
Per cent of payroll.....................................	16.0
Cents per hour worked................................	23.7
Dollars per year per employee..........................	477

* Source: *Wage Supplements* (Washington, D.C.: Chamber of Commerce of the United States).

panies must have paid out more than $477 per employee per year. Some instances have been reported in which payments amounted to over $700 per employee per year.

It is to be expected that employees will ask for more from employers, so this trend should not be surprising. What the employer should and can do about them is to prepare for changes in demands. It should be one of the jobs of the personnel department to anticipate the direction that employee demands are likely to take and to be prepared to meet them or to show employees why they cannot be met. One of the saddest sights in labor relations (from the viewpoint of management) is to see labor make a demand upon management which catches the latter entirely unprepared. In this matter of strategy and tactics, management too often seems to be off balance. Hence it can neither defend itself from demands put upon it nor start an intelligent counteroffensive.

The best preparation is to make studies of various possible demands, so that, if they are presented, a reasonable reaction can be established immediately. For example, the demand that employees should be paid for sick leave or that their sick-leave allowances should be increased cannot be deflected by words alone. Such countercharges that the cost of the program would be excessive or that malingering would be increased excessively must be supported by facts. Displaying a chart such as that illustrated in Figure 80 will carry weight in support of a claim

FIGURE 80.   An Analysis of Sick Claims*

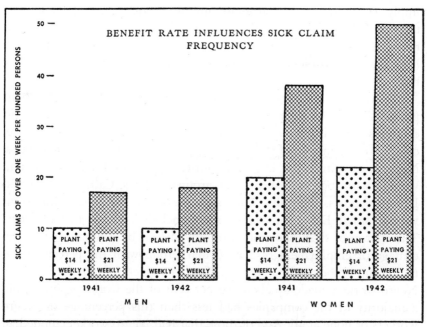

* Source: *An Analysis of the Paid Sick-Leave Plan* (Detroit: General Motors Corp.).

that an increase in sick-leave allowance will tend to increase malingering. Information, gathered in advance, analyzed for principles, and aptly illustrated, is the substantial basis upon which management can fight fringe demands, anticipate them, or agree gracefully that they are warranted, when once presented.

MINORITY GROUPS

1. SCOPE OF PROBLEM.   One of the questions that more and more companies are having to answer is what to do about various minority groups. Although the issue is, by and large, a voluntary one at present, over a dozen states have passed laws of varying degrees of compulsion

requiring that employment of labor be free of partiality concerning race, color, and creed. During World War II the federal government established a Fair Employment Practice Committee to see that executive orders relative to impartial employment practices were observed. Thus the trend seems to be toward governmental elimination of discriminatory practices unless, of course, the problem is handled satisfactorily upon a voluntary basis.

In this brief survey of discriminatory practices, no attempt is made to evaluate the claims of those who wish to employ as they please or of those who seek to eliminate discrimination. Nor is it intended to imply or suggest which course an employer should pursue. These matters call for more space than is available here. The discussion is limited to a description of what is considered to be discriminatory practice and how some companies have inducted minority groups into their labor ranks.

2. NATURE OF DISCRIMINATION. "Discriminatory employment practices" may be defined simply as those practices which result in decisions regarding the employability of workers upon the basis of race, color, or creed instead of skill, ability, and capacity. In the United States, Negroes constitute the largest minority group. In lesser degree and varying with localities, such other groups as Jews, Catholics, Seventh-Day Adventists, Jehovah's Witnesses, Mexicans, and immigrants from various small European countries are included within this category. The charge of discrimination is usually shown by comparing the percentage of employment of a particular group with the percentage of that group in the total population. Thus in a given community in which Negro workers made up about 10 per cent of the working population, a majority of the companies had less than this percentage of Negro workers or none at all. And of those that had Negro workers, none had relatively equal percentages of Negroes and whites in all kinds of jobs. The Negroes held the poorer and less desirable jobs and seldom were given anything above a minor supervisory position and were the "last to be hired and the first to be laid off." Discrimination has also been noted in respect to wages, seniority rights, and union membership.

3. EVIDENCE OF DISCRIMINATION. Ordinarily, such evidence as the following is cited as proof of discrimination upon the part of an employer:

a) The policy to hire members of a minority group as laborers or in custodial work only, regardless of their particular skills

b) The recruitment of a substantial number of skilled workers from a technical school with Jews and Negroes, but hiring a proportionately small number of Jews and no Negroes

c) An advertisement for labor containing racial or religious specification
d) Racial or religious specifications to the United States Employment Service
e) Discharge of employees who refuse to salute the American flag or to stand during the playing of the national anthem
f) A preference for employees of a particular race to be intrusted with hiring
g) A refusal to hire a Negro craftsman unless he obtains a permit from a labor organization which bars him from membership on a parity with white craftsmen
h) Hiring under a quota system

4. GOVERNMENTAL INTERVENTION. Impetus to the movement to combat discriminatory practices was provided by the federal government during World War II by two executive orders.

Executive Order 8802 was issued on June 25, 1941, because of "evidence that available and needed workers have been barred from employment in industries engaged in defense production solely because of considerations of race, creed, color, or national origin, to the detriment of workers' morale and of national unity." This order forbade discrimination in public and private employment and also ordered the administration of government-sponsored training programs to be free of discrimination. A Committee on Fair Employment Practice was appointed to investigate complaints in violation of the order and to redress grievances.

Executive Order 8802 was replaced by Executive Order 9346 on May 27, 1943. A new seven-member Committee on Fair Employment Practice was appointed, with headquarters in Washington, D.C. Under its direction were twelve regional offices.

The most effective sanction conferred upon the committee by the President's orders was the requirement that contracting agencies of the government insert a clause in all defense contracts prohibiting contractors from discriminating against minorities in employment. Although some employers have attempted to violate this clause, others have complied with it. As a consequence, many minority-group workers gained entrance into companies that had previously been closed to them.

Although there has been much agitation to enact antidiscriminatory legislation by the federal government since the end of World War II, these efforts have as yet failed.

A number of states have, however, passed such legislation. New York's Law against Discrimination, passed in 1945, is of typical interest. Its purpose is to guarantee every applicant for employment and every employee the right of equal treatment without regard to race, creed, color, or national origin. In administering the law, the State Commission against Discrimination has promulgated the rules that it shall be unlawful—

A. For an employer to—
  1. Discriminate in hiring, upgrading, or discharging employees because of race, creed, color, or national origin
  2. Ask questions before hiring which directly or indirectly would disclose race, creed, color, or national origin
  3. Print or circulate matter which directly or indirectly indicates discrimination because of race, creed, color, or origin
  4. Discriminate against anyone who files a complaint or testifies in connection with the Law against Discrimination
B. For a union to—
  1. Discriminate against members or applicants for membership because of race, creed, color, or national origin
  2. Discriminate against employers on the same grounds
C. For an employment agency to—
  1. Discriminate in registering or referring applicants
  2. Ask questions before hiring which directly or indirectly would disclose race, creed, color, or origin
  3. Disclose such information to employers
  4. Print or circulate matter which directly or indirectly expresses discrimination because of race, color, creed, or origin
  5. Discriminate against anyone who files a complaint or testifies in connection with the Law against Discrimination
D. For Employees to—
  1. Offer resistance to the hiring of anyone on grounds of race, creed, color, or national origin
E. For anyone to—
  1. Compel, help, or incite or to attempt such acts which would lead to discrimination on account of race, creed, color, or national origin.

5. INTRODUCING MINORITY GROUPS. In those instances in which companies have employed members of minority groups after strict enforcement of policies of exclusion, success attended the efforts only of those which followed a carefully developed policy of assimilation. This was necessary because the opposition of the existing working force had to be overcome and the natural belligerence of the minority members had to be prevented from coming to the surface.

The specific steps which have been found helpful in facilitating introduction of any minority group include the following:

  a) Careful selection of the representative of the minority group to be introduced; characteristics of personality, emotional stability, and understanding of obstacles to be met are as significant as technical job qualifications
  b) Thorough indoctrination of the representative of what he is likely to encounter in going into the working situation and how he must handle himself therein
  c) Careful selection of the area or department into which introduction will

be made; it is usually better to start slowly and thus show other areas
that the introduction presents no unusual difficulties

d) Counsel key employees regarding the contemplated introduction, indicate
why it is necessary, and gain preliminary willingness to "give it a trial"

e) It also seems better to initiate the program with only one representative,
so that no "group" of minority members can form at the outset; after
the "ice is broken," more than one at a time can be employed

f) Whether or not separate toilet facilities should be provided is debatable,
although better practice here seems to be against separate facilities

g) Follow up reactions closely, to ward off trouble and to tackle unforeseen
difficulties or obstacles.

As an example of how this was done, the case of a company that
was faced with a shortage of labor during the war years is of interest:

When the hiring of nonwhites was first suggested, it was not considered
advisable by management because of opposition on the part of certain individuals
and because it was believed that most workers in the plant were opposed to this
policy. Recognizing the necessity for opening the way for hiring from this
group, several meetings were held with labor-management committee. Throughout these negotiations, the management took the stand that the emergency called
for the utilization of all groups and that there should be no discrimination.
It was also pointed out that failure to follow this course could result in the
closing of the plant because of the federal executive order on discriminatory
hiring. After an agreement had been reached, a general meeting was held with
the employees on each shift and they were advised of the policy which the labor-
management committee had determined to follow.

The integration of colored workers was gradual, and was accomplished with
much less friction than had been anticipated. They were accepted into the Union
and accorded plant-wide seniority rights. The Union impressed all workers with
the fact that there would be no racial discrimination. Physical examinations were
provided for all their employees. There were no separate toilet facilities for
nonwhites. The hostile attitude of the majority of white workers was soon overcome. Instances have even been cited in which white workers in a certain department have protested the transfer of colored workers out of their department.

THE HANDICAPPED WORKERS

The handicapped worker also represents a problem that industry in
general must face if charity is not to be the answer. Whether crippled,
defaced, partially or totally blind, deaf, dumb, or otherwise handicapped, this group contains a source of labor which many companies
have found to be very desirable. The case for the handicapped workers
is summed up very well in the following instructions which one office
of the United States Employment Service issued to its Employer Service
Representatives, whose job it is, among others, to find jobs for handicapped workers:

Techniques in Selling the Employer on Use of Handicapped

a) In approaching an employer in behalf of a handicapped applicant the Counselor or Employment Service Representative never mentions the handicap first, as "I've got a one-armed man here, but he can do the work"; rather, he stresses the man's good points, building up in the employer a desire to hire the man. Then he can mention the limitation casually, adding that it does not hinder the applicant's performance on the job.

b) The Counselor and ESR use a specific name for the disability such as "lame" or "hard of hearing" rather than a general term like "handicapped," "disabled," or "a limited person," since the specific term does not produce a mental image of a person with a more serious handicap than that of the applicant and is less likely to arouse prejudice against him.

c) The initial approach to an employer regarding the hiring of the handicapped concerns a specific individual or group of individuals qualified for definite jobs in the employer's business rather than the handicapped in general. This enables the Counselor and ESR to get down to cases, to show by physical analysis of his applicant and physical-demands analysis of the employer's job that the applicant's limitation is not a work limitation. Thus, the employer may be led to conclude that he will hire qualified handicapped applicants for any jobs they can perform.

d) The Counselor or ESR stresses advantages in the employment of workers with certain types of handicaps for specific jobs; i.e., deaf workers may prove more efficient under noisy working conditions than persons with normal hearing.

e) He emphasizes the fact that disabled persons usually put forth more effort to hold their jobs, are less likely to leave their employment, and seem to be less prone to accidents.

f) The use of references from previous employers is often helpful because they cite specific examples of successful performance.

g) The Counselor or ESR develops a dependable relationship with the employer by referring only suitable applicants, whether handicapped or non-handicapped. If this is done, the employer is more likely to accept the recommendations of the Counselor or ESR.

Answers to Possible Employer Objections to Hiring of Handicapped Workers

Counselors and ESRs should be prepared to reply courteously and intelligently to the objections against hiring handicapped workers which will be raised by employers.

a) *Objection.* The employment of handicapped persons means higher accident cost and compensation insurance rates.

Answer. Two factors are involved in a satisfactory answer to this question. First, employers usually assume that a handicapped person is more liable to a second injury than nonhandicapped persons. Various studies have been made which indicate that this is not true. In a study made by one company involving 685 handicapped workers employed during the period from 1929 to 1931, it was found that only 23.5 per cent of the handicapped group were injured, whereas 39.1 per cent of the control group of nonhandicapped persons employed during the same period were injured.

Second, placement workers must be thoroughly familiar with the workmen's compensation law in their state in order to inform the employer of any special provisions which may have been made covering second-injury benefits for handicapped persons. In addition to any special provisions for second-injury benefits, it should be pointed out that the rate of compensation insurance for any employer is based upon the relation of accident cost to the total payroll. No information is required concerning the physical condition of the employees. There have been no known studies which indicate that the employment of handicapped persons increase the number of accidents, whereas there have been studies which indicate that handicapped persons are not so liable to accidents as the nonhandicapped. This fact is probably due to greater caution on the part of handicapped workers in avoiding accidents. In the states that have set up special funds for compensation to persons receiving second injuries in industry, the number of claims reported has been negligible.

b) *Objection.* The employment of handicapped persons will strain sick benefit or group insurance plans.

Answer. As regards sick benefits, the assumption here is that the handicapped are more liable to illness, injury, or accident than are nonhandicapped persons. In addition to the accident statistics reported from this company, records were kept of the sick leave taken by handicapped and nonhandicapped workers. During the period covered by the study, it was found that 60 per cent of the nonhandicapped were absent during the period, while only 53 per cent of the handicapped were absent.

In group life insurance, the rate is based solely upon the age and sex of the employees and not upon physical conditions. Companies issuing such insurance say that physical disabilities are not considered.

c) *Objection.* Handicapped workers are frequently absent because of weather conditions or illness. They cannot work regular hours.

Answer. This is similar to objection (a). The same answer may be used. It is a prevalent misconception that the handicapped, especially the crippled, are usually in delicate health. This, of course, may be just as true of applicants not classed as handicapped as of those who have some obvious disability. Where the interviewer requires a medical statement to assist in determining the restrictions necessary to safeguard the health of the applicant, the employer who does not normally require examinations actually has better protection in employing handicapped workers than in employing other applicants who are not under medical supervision.

d) *Objection.* Disabled persons are not so efficient as normal workers.

Answer. In answering this question, the Counselor or ESR should stress that handicapped persons are referred only to jobs where they can com-

pete satisfactorily with nonhandicapped workers. The interview ~~his~~ has selected the applicant for the job because analysis of his capacities reveals
he can meet the physical demands of the job.

e) *Objection.* Handicapped workers cannot be shifted so easily to other
jobs in slack times.

Answer. The answer to this question must be determined by what the
"other jobs" are. Within the scope of the physical qualification of the
applicant, the answer is "yes"; otherwise "no," and no general answer
can or should be given since everything depends upon the individual
case.

Records of one company during the period of their survey showed
that the percentage of nonhandicapped workers laid off for lack of work
was 2.6 per cent less than the percentage of the handicapped. This indicates that, in general, handicapped workers are successful in competition
with nonhandicapped workers, even during slack periods.

In addition, in slack times, when the employer, after careful study,
finds no suitable position open to which he can transfer the handicapped
worker, he should feel free to let him go as he would any other worker
in a similar position.

f) *Objection.* Other employees do not like to see them around; they make the
office look like a charity concern; customers do not like to see them or
ask them for service.

Answer. This is an expression of the social attitude which for centuries
has denied handicapped persons an equal opportunity to develop their
capacities. The feeling that other employees object probably looms larger
in theory than in fact. When the handicapped person has a normal attitude, most people will become accustomed to him. The sales manager of
a very successful New York department store uses a cane because of a
limp and finds no difficulty handling staff or customers.

g) *Objection.* Crippled persons need special attention; they expect special
advantages and consideration from the employer.

Answer. There may be handicapped persons who have not been taught
to develop self-reliance and who need special supervision in making a
vocational adjustment. On the other hand, there are many disabled persons who have made good, who have been years with the same employer,
who have been promoted to responsible positions, and who get along
well with other people. In placing handicapped applicants, references
from former employers may help to break down this objection. Wider
publicity concerning the favorable experiences of other employers is also
helpful. A study of 1,506 jobs held by the deaf showed that 46 per cent
of the jobs were held for over one year and 16 per cent for over five
years.

h) *Objection.* We provide for our own employees who become disabled
and cannot, therefore, employ others.

Answer. The answer to this objection is that the applicants are placed on
the basis of qualifications and are seeking jobs, not as charity, but on a
competitive basis which is economically sound from the employer's point

of view. Furthermore, if a person is disabled between jobs, or before his first job, such a policy would tend to keep him out of the labor market permanently, depriving employers of much qualified labor.

i) *Objection.* The entrance physical examination required by our company rules out all persons with physical disabilities.

Answer. The physical examination is commendable if used in a discretionary way to assure that applicants have no disabilities which prevent proper job performance, that they are in good health, and as a means of protecting the employer against future damage claims, such as for hernia which may have existed prior to the time of employment. On the other hand, to use the physical examination as a means of eliminating all but "perfect" physical specimens is an unfair discrimination against many who are in every way qualified for the job to be filled.

THE OLDER EMPLOYEE

The older employee during the depression years of the thirties threatened to become a serious problem to industry and society, but since then he has largely removed himself from the problem category. In the extreme reductions in staff which were made in almost every company during the depression, it was not unexpected that the older employee fell into the category of those that could not be considered as the backbone of the organization and so were laid off among the first. And perhaps the older workers were also hit harder than others because some employers may have felt that their individual taxes under the Social Security Act would be less if their accounts were not charged with the soon-to-be-paid pensions of older workers. Hence one often heard during these years that the older worker was not as good an employee as the younger worker.

The experience of the war years and the removal of the fear of excessive social security payments have proved rather conclusively that the older worker is no more a problem than other groups of workers. Indeed, the record of the older worker seems to be better than that of younger groups. Whereas older employees cannot perform the heavy work that younger employees can, this is offset by the following:

1. Greater versatility, with an ability to handle a variety of jobs
2. Greater dependability, with a better record of absenteeism
3. Fewer accidents
4. Less volatile; hence, more stable
5. Fewer grievances and fewer occasions for disciplinary action.

Thus older workers make up in steady workmanship and craftsmanship what they may lack in ability to spurt for short periods or to handle heavy jobs. Inasmuch as our population pattern shows a change toward a higher percentage of older people, the place of the older worker in industry must be given more favorable attention.

Employment of older workers should invariably be handled with thought, as should all employment matters. To begin with, a long-range program of hiring will serve to build a well-balanced force so that a predominance of age groups of any bracket will not result. In the second place, a variety of procedures may be established for the older workers. Among these are the following:

1. Review of occupations best suited to accommodate employees of advanced years
2. Review of occupations that lend themselves with some modification to the accommodation of employees of advanced years
3. Training to increase and prolong their productivity within a given occupation
4. Training for other occupations more suited to one of advanced years
5. Adoption of a pension plan as a bridge between active employment and retirement
6. Arranging the pay of the employee in keeping with his productiveness and charging the balance to the pension account

RETIREMENT OF EMPLOYEES AND EXECUTIVES

Almost all private pension plans establish an age at which retirement is compulsory. The age may be as low as sixty for women or up to sixty-five for men. In favor of an arbitrary age limit are the claims that, first, it serves to remove from the payroll those who, though obviously ineffective because of age, would not voluntarily quit, and, second, it provides opportunities for younger employees and executives. On the other hand, opponents of such arbitrary limits argue that all people do not show the same degree of decreasing powers at the age sixty-five, let us say. And as we learn more about the science of geriatrics—which is concerned with the physical, mental, emotional, and social manifestations of growing old—there is reason to believe that flexibility in age limits may be the better practice.

One of the most interesting phases of the whole question of compulsory retirement has been along the lines of dealing with the problems of those who retire. While much has been done to alleviate at least the minimum financial requirements of retirement, only recently has attention been directed to what an employee or executive shall do with his free time after he retires. While it may seem that most of us would welcome such a problem as having free time, it has been found that an abrupt change from work to unplanned retirement finds the individual at loose ends.

To minimize these problems and to give a "pensioner" a feeling of significance, some constructive efforts have been made regarding the transition required by retirement. Three phases of retirement may be noted: pre-retirement, at retirement, and post-retirement.

In the pre-retirement phases, it has been found desirable to discuss with employees and executives their approaching retirement. Problems they are likely to encounter in readjusting, possible plans they may make, and financial changes that will be forced upon them, are examined. Each is counseled to consider the new way of life that he and his family will soon be facing. And help may be given to plan for new hobbies, to investigate possible activities, and to prepare for changes gradually.

In the "at-retirement" stage, it has been found desirable to establish a formal program of leavetaking. Such affairs as banquets, with their gifts and speeches, at which are gathered associates and executives, show the appreciation of fellow workers and the company. Making the rounds of one's associates, particularly when accompanied by a high executive, adds to the prestige of the individual and his pride in the significance attached to this tradition by the company. And a careful explanation of the formal plans and services to which the pensioner is now entitled should also be made at this time.

In the post-retirement stage, various activities may be undertaken which serve not only to tie in the pensioner with the company but also to build good will throughout the organization. Literature such as house organs, letters, and periodicals should be sent to pensioners. Participation in social and recreational clubs should be encouraged. Use of company facilities, advisory services, and medical aids should be extended. And the right to visit the plant or office may well be granted. Indeed, in this latter respect, some companies have found it very useful to continue key employees or executives as consultants on a part-time, extra-fee basis. A few have provided special areas where pensioners may continue to come to work or use for their private hobbies. And a small number of companies are experimenting with progressive retirement, that is, a person is given a month off when he reaches a certain pre-retirement age, and each year thereafter an added month or two of vacation time is granted until full retirement is reached.

In all cases the idea is to ease the transition from working habits to retirement activities, to keep the good will of those being retired, and to prove to others that management has a sincere interest in its working force through all its days. This is a far cry from the day when industry threw people "into the ash can" without regard for their financial or personal needs when old age overtook them.

AUTOMATION

Of unique interest to personnel management is the incipient movement toward the automatic factory. The problems which the "pushbutton" factory—or "automation," as it is popularly known—raises should be considered carefully by management. What happens when production, material handling, assembly, and inspection are highly mechanized and self-regulating?

A number of production units have moved in this direction so that available experience provides the basis for some tentative comments. Generally, automation will likely increase the importance of personnel management. To begin with, the skills of the work force in any given company will be much higher. Drudgery and monotony will be minimized, and jobs will be less boring and more interesting. Personnel will be of a higher caliber, more alert, better trained, and more highly educated. Consequently, the job of human relations will have to be on a higher plane. And very serious will be the problem of technological unemployment and that of how the products of industry are to be distributed to the consuming public.

Briefly, the following shows the variety of subjects which will have to be re-examined or re-emphasized:

1. Automation involves complicated equipment and processes. The need is great for highly skilled technical and maintenance personnel. Selection and placement techniques must be perfected to assist in securing capable employees who can operate such plants proficiently.
2. Redesign of plants will call for completely new job and man specifications. Job analysis and job studies will be prime necessities, if selection, placement, and training are to be conducted successfully.
3. The importance of training will increase as automation increases. More people will require longer periods of training. Engineers and other technical personnel will need supplementary training; maintenance workers will require additional skills and better technical background; and operative employees will have to convert to maintenance and control skills.
4. Automation will not eliminate the need of good relations with organized labor. Indeed, their co-operation will be needed in order to gain acceptance of layoffs and job changes and transfers.
5. The problem of compensation will have to be reviewed again all the way from basic theory to specific wage plans. The basis of incentives is likely

to change from that of individual effort to that of over-all results. Undoubtedly, too, supervisors will be included in the incentive plans.

6. It may be necessary to change from a line-and-staff type of organization to a functionalized scheme. The specialists who are required in such an operation must have a more direct control of operations.
7. Employee attitude changes must be expected. Better employee communications, idea sharing, and education are indicated. This will all place a bigger burden not only on the personnel department in designing better plans but also on executives who must carry them out.
8. Automation should tend to reduce safety hazards, because machines will do the work and because such devices as television can be used to view dangerous operation.
9. Better housekeeping will also be required in the automatic factory.

These are formidable matters. If management is to avoid the mistake of being derelict in its consideration of the human aspects of such technological changes, it should weigh the human problems raised thereby as carefully as it considers mechanical innovations.

CYBERNETICS

Cybernetics is another recent development which has great implications for personnel management. Cybernetics—a coined term—employs complicated electronic machines to permit automatic and continuous computing, checking, and correcting of mechanical processes. This explains why it has been referred to as the "brain" of the automatic factory.

Although cybernetics cannot act as a substitute for human judgment and creative thinking, it can perform many routine mental tasks, thus freeing people for more creative work. Moreover, it can do routine tasks faster, more accurately, with exact timing, and at less cost than can the human worker. As a consequence, the whole work force will be upgraded and the lower skills will tend to be eliminated. As drudgery of office work is reduced, interest and morale of employees should be increased. Human relations will have to be on a higher plane to deal correctly with the resulting better-educated, higher-type employee.

Because it acts as a substitute for many human mental and physical skills, cybernetics may contribute to technological unemployment. As has been the case in the past, such unemployment may be temporary—with the long-run effect being in the direction of an increase in total jobs—nevertheless it would raise a current problem for personnel management. Some companies have tried to solve the problem by putting in such improvements during times when employment generally is high, so that displaced workers can more readily find other jobs. And some have expected their own increase in volume to serve to keep all their present workers.

Other personnel problems will be raised, too. It is probable that such factors which increase productivity will lead to demands for a shorter workweek. How these demands will be met, as well as corollaries of wage determination, will require high levels of administrative thinking. Shortened workweeks certainly will call for more company-sponsored recreational and educational programs.

Cybernetics will place more emphasis on the selection of personnel. It can even aid scientific selection. The Defense Department has used electronics to search out needed skills and abilities. It will also be invaluable in validating and scoring psychological tests.

Cybernetics will have a dual role in training. Its use will require more specialized training by personnel and line executives. But it can serve to expedite communications. And it will supplement, but not supplant, the need for personal contact with employees on an individual basis. And it can contribute greatly to personnel research by facilitating the gathering and keeping of personnel records. The science will be useful, too, in safeguarding the health of employees. Electronics can serve to analyze such matters as human blood, diagnose incipient diabetes and tumors, and check the heartbeats of patients. And it can serve in a better selection of healthier employees.

QUESTIONS AND PROBLEMS

1. Assume that the employees in your company through their elected representatives place before you a demand for a particular fringe issue that would amount to 5 cents an hour for each employee. How would you handle this situation?
2. Under what conditions are fringe demands more likely to be made than outright wage demands?
3. What, if anything, can management do to make employees feel more related to and identified with the company when such fringe demands as paid vacations, pension programs, and health insurance plans are granted? Or must the union always get "credit" for such benefits?
4. What subjects would you exclude from discussion with employees? Why? Won't it follow that what is kept hidden will be suspected?
5. In many companies the head of the public relations department is someone experienced in newspaper work. What are the advantages and disadvantages of such a background?
6. Show how public relations can be built into a selection procedure; a training program; and a recreational program.
7. To whom should responsibility for public relations be assigned? Is it not

true that all executives have to keep public relations in mind? If so, how is it possible to assign this task only to one executive?

8. Describe some projects that might be established in order to cultivate good public relations.

9. What preparations should management make in order to be in a position to counter fringe demands if they are warranted or to grant them if they are reasonable?

10. What is a "minority" group in industry? Upon what theory are laws passed that aim to prevent so-called "unfair unemployment practices"?

11. Are discriminatory practices limited to race, color, and creed? Can you cite examples of other types of discrimination?

12. Some employers contend that they have no objection to hiring Negroes but that many of their present workers object. Is this a legitimate reason? Explain.

13. What is your opinion of the argument that, if minority groups took constructive action among themselves to remove the causes of objections to them, there eventually would be no discrimination practiced against them?

14. In what respects is a handicapped worker a problem of industry? In what respects are they not a problem?

15. Relate the contributions that job analysis, job placement, and job training make to the solution of the handicapped in industry?

16. Some contend that handicapped workers are better risks than the nonhandicapped. In what ways?

17. In what respects have older workers proved themselves superior to younger employees? What policies should be followed in connection with the older worker?

18. What are suggested practices for preparing employees for retirement? What do you think of post-retirement plans suggested in the text.

19. What problems will have to be solved when a factory is converted to automatic processes?

20. What is meant by "cybernetics," and what effect is it likely to have upon personnel management?

CHAPTER

30 | Personnel Research and Evaluation

INTRODUCTION

At the outset of this text it was noted that personnel management has to do with planning, organizing, and controlling various tasks of procuring, developing, maintaining, and utilizing an effective work force. And throughout the foregoing chapters, principles and practices related to these functions have been described and examined. A useful review of the work of personnel management may be accomplished by emphasizing the research aspects of the function of planning and the evaluation aspects of control. Each chapter of this text could well have had sections on research and evaluation, were space no object; but much duplication is eliminated by this final summary. It contains a point of view, however, which is fundamental to every function of personnel management discussed in earlier chapters.

The first section of this chapter is concerned with research, an activity without which planning must be hit and miss or based upon what others have done. Neither of the latter is very satisfactory because the cut of the cloth seldom fits the particular situation or problem at hand.

The second section is concerned with evaluating what has been done. One learns from the past only by reviewing the actions taken in the past. The lessons so learned can brighten the future. Thus evaluation has as its purpose, not recrimination, but rather minimizing of future errors and thereby maximizing of future benefits.

PERSONNEL RESEARCH

NATURE AND SCOPE

"Personnel research," defined simply, is the task of searching for and analyzing of facts to the end that personnel problems may be solved or principles or "laws" governing their solutions derived. Its scope is all-inclusive. There are no subjects in personnel about which so much is known that no further research is justified. On the contrary, our tested

608

knowledge of basic relationships in personnel is so meager that it is a wonder that we get along as well as we do in working with labor.

Even in fields in which industry has been working for many years, a sound and balanced basis of action is not available. Witness the following remarks on industrial training:

> There is, then, little dependable research data published on industrial training. By dependable research data, I mean conclusions concerning a problem which are based on investigations which control, statistically or otherwise, all variables. This, of course, is not conclusive evidence that training men are not using a research approach. My contacts with industrial training, other than in my own organization, are not so broad as I would like. Yet these contacts have given me little evidence that an extensive use of research techniques is being made in industrial training.[1]

The absence of adequate research in every other field of personnel could similarly be observed. Hence the problem of research is not that of duplicating what others have done. Rather the problem is determining which of the many pressing problems should be studied first. It is a problem of determining how available resources and time can best be allocated. It calls for a determination of a priority list of research, not a listing of subjects covered as opposed to those to be covered.

Obviously, it is impossible here to survey the fields of needed research or what has been done. Suffice it to say in repetition that every phase of personnel is in great need of the fruitful and light-giving services of research. All that can be done here is, first, to comment briefly upon some basic considerations in research and, second, to illustrate with an example or two the task and value of careful data gathering.

BASIC CONSIDERATIONS

A number of comments are in order regarding how and why research should be carried on.

1. USES OF RESEARCH. The objective of research is the truth. This simple statement should be sufficient to support the claim that research is for the use of everyone concerned with a personnel problem. Labor, management, the general public, governmental agencies, and the consumer are its beneficiaries. Each gains or none does. Unless this attitude is accepted by the "researcher," whoever he may be, the results will be rejected on the grounds that "figures may not lie, but liars may figure." It is imperative, therefore, that in undertaking re-

---

[1] William McGehee, *The Research Approach to Training* (American Management Association, "Personnel Series," No. 117), pp. 32–33.

search, investigations should be conducted in the hopes of finding the correct answer—not the answer some particular group wants.

If research is conducted with a view to impartiality, each step of the research should be acceptable to and reviewable by any unbiased student. With this premise guiding one's research, the results will be useful to all concerned because they will be truthful.

More specifically, uses of research would be related to the following aspects of personnel management, human relations, and labor-management relations:

   a) To measure and evaluate present conditions
   b) To predict future conditions and events
   c) To evaluate effects and results of current policies, programs, and activities
   d) To provide an objective basis for revising current policies, programs, and activities
   e) To appraise proposed policies, programs, and activities

2. RESPONSIBILITY FOR RESEARCH. The foregoing suggests, in turn, that research is not the sole responsibility or within the sole jurisdiction of any particular group, interest, or department. To be sure, for present purposes it might be argued that a research section should be established in the personnel department of most companies. This is a fine practice because it serves to focus attention on research, to help establish a research program, and to provide for experts and facilities of research.

But others, too, can and should be brought into the fold. Line supervisors and executives at all levels can help with research projects as well as carry on their own projects. Where unions are in the picture, that help and co-operation should be sought. Nor should such outside organizations as educational institutions, private research groups, endowed foundations, and governmental agencies be overlooked.[2]

The importance of co-operation is evidenced by the growing use of operations research. This involves the solution of personnel problems by the use of teams of specialists who combine their talents, skills, and techniques in an interdisciplinary, scientific group effort. The group considers and weighs which among several alternative answers is best, giving due consideration to the dynamic character of the variables in a problem. Obviously, such co-operative effort provides a force of

---

[2] Invaluable is the work of such organizations as the American Management Association, National Industrial Conference Board, Bureau of Labor Statistics, Bureau of Foreign and Domestic Commerce, National Office Management Association, and the Society for the Advancement of Management.

analysis which few, if any, personnel managers can hope to attain individually.

The extent of co-operation depends upon a number of factors. Some problems may be of an individual and confidential nature, whereas others may be of universal interest. The former may desirably be attacked on a private, individual, and intracompany basis. The latter may be attacked with all the outside help that can be obtained. In most cases it is well to adopt the rule that the problems are so difficult that the room is ample for all who wish to contribute their talents and resources.

3. FACILITIES OF RESEARCH. And the suggestion is in order that extensive facilities, desirable though they may be, need not be provided in order to carry on much useful research. The records of every company contain a wealth of information. All that is needed is the effort to examine them. For example, a simple survey, such as that of why employees have left the company, will serve to improve personnel practices. In one company that made such a survey, it was found that a majority of quits occurred in two departments. Following up this trail by an attitude survey, poor supervision was discovered to be the cause. After this was cleared up by retraining the supervisors, the quits in these departments fell to a normal figure. When personnel management takes advantage of the information at its disposal, much research can be carried on without excessive cost or effort.

On the other hand, some research techniques involve high skill and considerable outlays for equipment. Some tabulating equipment falls into this category. Or "linear programming," a mathematical and graphical method, is useful (but complicated) in arriving at decisions involving situations where several choices, with variations of degree in each choice, are available. And cybernetics involves skills and expenditures of a high order. But in complicated and important problems, the use of such techniques is indispensable.

4. IMPORTANCE OF PURE RESEARCH. One of the lessons that industry in general as yet must learn about personnel research is that "pure" research in this area is as useful as it is in physics and chemistry. It is not uncommon to read reports issued by various companies announcing the projected opening of new and complete facilities for research and testing in the physical sciences, but provision of facilities for research in personnel problems is rarely made. Yet human problems of industry, it is generally agreed, are far more complex and numerous than physical problems. Unfortunately, research in human problems seems to many to be frosting on the cake, whereas technical research leads to direct results in the competitive battle for markets.

Failure to learn how to handle labor problems, however, may eat most of the profits that technical research may be providing. Where or when the impetus to pure research in personnel relations will come is uncertain; but, until it does, industry will stumble along in its methods of approaching human problems.

5. RELATION OF RESEARCH AND COLLECTIVE BARGAINING. Another lesson that industry must learn is that it must undertake research if it is to bargain successfully with unions. The latter, in some instances, are so far advanced in their researches on wages, economic trends, bargaining processes, and labor relations that the efforts of management to refute labor's arguments are often ludicrous. No other road will lead to stable labor relations but that which is paved with facts, information, and statistics. Until industry travels that road, it can look forward to nothing but emotional bombast, name calling, and pressure politics. If intelligent labor relations is the goal, then the roadway of intelligence—factual information—must be sought.

6. PRIORITY LISTS. Earlier it was noted that establishing a priority of research projects is perhaps of greater practical significance than determining subjects of research. The tests of priority should be importance of problems and timeliness. During the war years, such problems as absenteeism commanded a great deal of attention because they were both important and timely. At the present, much good could be done by research in such matters as methods of improving collective bargaining, better techniques for evaluating jobs and personal efforts, procedures for disseminating rules and information to employees, and programs for improving co-operative efforts of labor and management.

A useful way of developing such a list is to sample executive judgment. For example, a list such as that illustrated in Figure 81 could be sent to various executives. They could be asked to number, from the sample list, the first ten—or any other number—projects which they considered most significant. The results would be most helpful in determining where money, talents, and time should be allocated.

7. SPECIALISTS AND THEIR TECHNIQUES. And, finally, a word more is in order on the importance of looking to various fields and their tools for help. To begin with, research emphasizes a search for facts. It is quantitative, therefore, in nature. Perhaps the most useful tool in this connection is statistics. Hence, in gathering data, in analyzing them, and in their interpretation, reliance upon and understanding of statistical methods are indispensable. This does not mean that involved and intricate formulas and calculations are the test of good research. It does

FIGURE 81.   Suggested Research Projects

Please check the areas which you consider worthy of research efforts.

Area

— a.   Discovery of new principles of human relations
— b.   Application of known principles of human relations
— c.   Human characteristics and attributes
— d.   Measurement of human characteristics and attributes
— e.   Forecasting future of company with reference to its human relations position

— f.   Personnel policies
— g.   Labor market
— h.   Job analysis and evaluation
— i.   Recruitment, selection, and placement
— j.   Individual testing

— k.   Operator training
— l.   Supervisor training
— m.   Administrator training
— n.   Performance rating
— o.   Employee services

— p.   Personnel records and reports
— q.   Promotions, demotions, transfers, layoffs, and separations
— r.   Health
— s.   Safety
— t.   Communications

— u.   Employee attitude
— v.   Adjustments and social relationships
— w.   Wages and salaries
— x.   Hours of work, rests
— y.   Working conditions

— z.   Production standards
— a'.   Labor turnover
— b'.   Absenteeism
— c'.   Measures of effectiveness of personnel program
— d'.   Legislation affecting human relations

— e'.   Relationship with union
— f'.   Collective bargaining
— g'.   Clauses for union contracts
— h'.   Grievance procedures
— i'.   Mediation and arbitration

— j'.   Other (*Please specify.*)

_____

_____

mean that, relative to the nature of each particular research project, the quantitative tools should be adequate.

And the range of specialists from whom help may be sought is broad indeed. The assistance of psychologists has, of course, long been sought and generally respected. And the statistician, too, has contributed much. Recently the services of others have proved most useful. For example, the psychiatrist has been called in to help solve individual problems of an emotional and mental character that were disturbing company efficiency and individual happiness. And in the last few years, the sociologist and anthropologists have carried on significant research and investigations concerning group relations, customs, and status in industry.

The moral is obvious; the field of research requires the services of numerous types and tools. To seek answers through the methodology and principles of a single specialty is to build upon a weak foundation. Rather, research calls for a cosmopolitan attitude and interdisciplinary co-operation. The specialist who tries to build a fence around all aspects of research does himself and industry a serious disfavor.

EXAMPLES OF RESEARCH

To show the usefulness of research, its application will be illustrated in relation, first, to the problem of absenteeism and, second, to sociological contributions.

ABSENTEEISM[3]

1. IMPORTANCE OF PROBLEM.   Absenteeism is one of the most serious problems that beset industry from time to time. During periods when production is at a peak and labor is scarce, the absence of some workers from their appointed stations can be disruptive to production and morale. How serious the problem sometimes is may be seen in the following case. In a certain company there were, in one department, eight absentees on one day after payday, and four others were sent home on the same day because of hazardous "hangovers," making a total of twelve men (or 25 per cent in this instance) absent from their work. This case is of interest because it shows how departments with high turnover may reduce production much more than the average figures of absenteeism for an entire factory might indicate. In the chart in Figure 82, for example, absenteeism in the worst departments is

---

[3] Tardiness is a problem similar to that of absenteeism. Its treatment might well follow the general pattern accorded absenteeism.

FIGURE 82. Chart of Absenteeism

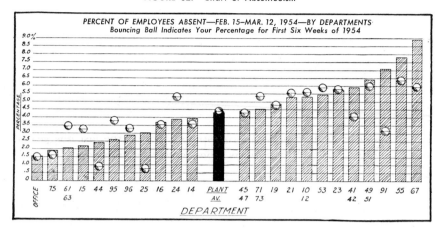

about five times as high as in the best departments, and this unbalances production in the latter as well as the former departments.

2. MEASUREMENTS OF ABSENTEEISM. To combat absenteeism, it is necessary to determine the extent of absenteeism and its causes. To do this, a definition of absenteeism should be established and records kept by departments for various causes of absenteeism by such divisions as seniority, sex, days of the week, and classes of jobs. Although there is no standard definition of absenteeism, the following definition of the Bureau of Labor Statistics is widely used:

"Absenteeism" is the failure of workers to report on the job when they are scheduled to work. It is a broad term which is applied to time lost because sickness or accident prevents a worker from being on the job, as well as unauthorized time away from the job for other reasons. Workers who quit without notice are also counted as absentees until they are officially removed from the payroll.

In order to have a common and comparable basis for measuring absenteeism in various plants, the Bureau of Labor Statistics suggests the following formula:

$$\text{Absenteeism} = \frac{\text{Man-days lost}}{\text{Man-days worked plus man-days lost}}$$

To help the companies in one community to gather uniform data, the United States Employment Service found it desirable to make the following suggestions in computing absenteeism:

It is important that all reporting firms have a uniform method of reporting absenteeism so that the information will be comparable. The following method is suggested by USES:

1. A worker is not an absentee if he is not scheduled for work. For example, he is not scheduled to work if—
   a) He is on leave of absence
   b) He is ill and the illness is of such duration that his name is removed from the list of active employees
   c) He is on vacation or annual leave
2. Illness and deaths of members of the worker's immediate families should constitute reason for excused absence only if arrangements have been made by the worker prior to the absence.
3. Any worker absent from work for a period of six days without reporting to the company should not be included as scheduled to work. (There may be some exceptions, as when the employee indicates, upon investigation, that he intends to return to work shortly after the six days off.)
4. Handicapped workers, not able to work the designated full shift, should not be considered full-time workers. They should appear on the payroll as part-time workers scheduled to work —— hours per week.

It is recognized that this procedure is for uniform reporting purposes only, and there is no intent to change Management-Labor agreements or company payroll and leave regulations.

3. CAUSES AND DISTRIBUTION OF ABSENTEEISM. The specific causes of absenteeism are numerous and devious. To attribute absenteeism in a given case to illness, for example, may result in overlooking the fact that incorrect job placement may have led first to boredom, then to fatigue, and then to physical illness. Hence, in listing the following causes, no attempt is made to determine priority or immediacy of cause and effect. This can only be done by study of individual cases.

a) *Reasons for Absenteeism.* Among the reasons for absenteeism, the following list contains those cited frequently:

1. Ordinarily, illness is high on the list of absenteeism causes. Colds, headaches, run-down condition, and aches and pains of various kinds are the cause of as high as 50 per cent of the absenteeism in some cases.
2. Industrial accidents and occupational disease bring on much absenteeism. In one year the equivalent of the production of a million men for one year was lost due to industrial accidents. Obviously, when labor is scarce, the loss in production (not counting the personal misery) was high.
3. Poor production and material control can result in absenteeism. Unless the flow of work between departments is balanced and maintained, workers may stay away from their jobs because they lose interest in their work and lose the feeling of the importance of being dependable. Herein is a major explanation for much of the absenteeism that occurred during the war years.
4. Hours of work can contribute to absenteeism. In one war plant, for example, it was found that scheduled increases in overtime hours were almost entirely offset by hours of absenteeism. In another case, absenteeism dropped from 20 per cent to 8 or 9 per cent when hours of work were

cut from 73½ to 55 hours. And in another plant, men working 7 days a week, 7½ hours a day, lost twice as much time as men working 6 days a week.

5. Wages are at times a contributor to absenteeism. During the war years, it was often found that, particular among newer workers, high wages led some to lay off work after accumulating funds during part of the week to carry them through the remainder of it.

6. Lack of interest or of a feeling of responsibility and worth-whileness are fundamental causes of absenteeism. It has been found, for example, that campaigns intended to show employees the significance of their efforts have cut absenteeism as much as 50 per cent.

7. After-payday sickness and "hangovers" contribute to absenteeism, particularly when combined with poor working conditions, lack of interest in work, and high wages. Many contend that drinking aggravates absenteeism but is seldom a primary cause.

8. A miscellaneous group of causes would include such factors as bad weather, lack of transportation, looking for another job, taking care of personal business, oversleeping, and friends visiting from out of town (see Fig. 83, p. 618).

9. Attitude of mind—caused by environmental factors, sociological factors, or opinions of neighbors—may condition some to develop a feeling of irresponsibility about coming to work.

b) *Factors in the Problem.* Study of the incidence of absenteeism will usually show some significant trends. In the first place, there seem to be absence-prone workers, just as there are accident-prone workers. From 10 to 20 per cent of the workers will be found to be responsible for as high as 75 to 80 per cent of the absences. Such workers may be more susceptible to illness, lack a sense of responsibility, or use absenteeism as their expression of vindictiveness. Second, such groups as women, new employees, and older employees are reported by some companies to have higher absence rates than other workers. This is not a general tendency because other companies claim that women and older workers are more dependable in this respect than the average worker.

Absenteeism is also related to the time factor. The first and last days of the week and the day after payday are usually the worst. When a plant works seven days a week, Sunday has been found to have the highest absence rate in some companies. Monthly trends are also discernible. November and December, with their year-end holidays, are usually the months with the poorest records, in some cases running two to three times as many absences as the average of the other months.

Departments or geographical areas also vary in their absence rates. Departments or locations distant from the homes of workers will usually have higher rates than others. There is occasional but not indisputable evidence that departments that call for heavy exertion or have

FIGURE 83*

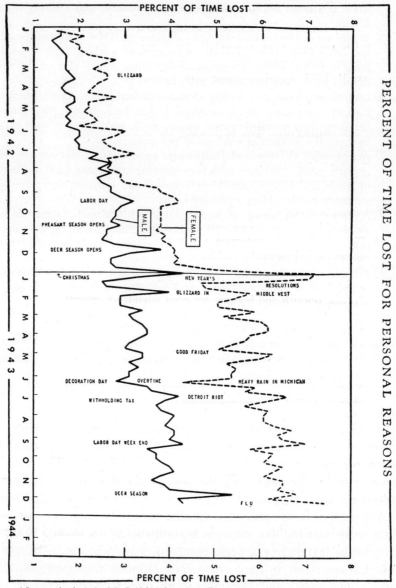

* Source: *An Analysis of the Paid Sick-Leave Plan* (Detroit: General Motors Corp.).

monotonous operations and obnoxious conditions tend to have higher rates of absences. What the rates are in any company must be determined by statistical analysis.

4. CONTROL OF ABSENTEEISM. The control of absenteeism depends upon its causes. When these are uncovered by study and analysis, steps can be taken to eliminate them. Some of the cases are relatively

simple to isolate and attack, but all are difficult to eliminate. For example, if it is discovered that illness of employees in a few departments
is the major source of absenteeism, there is a real problem of how to
combat the illness. Some companies have found vitamin tablets of use
in such cases; others have insisted upon health examinations; and others
have installed job rotation plans with success. In other words, there is
no one sure cure for absence causes, once discovered.

All that can be done here is to list a variety of plans that have been
used in this connection. The following are examples of control efforts:

1. Experiment with hours of work per day and per week to find the number
   at which absenteeism is reduced to reasonable limits.
2. Select employees with greater care to eliminate at the beginning the irresponsible, the illness-prone, and the unreliable.
3. Induct new employees in such a way that their critical attitude is reduced
   as quickly as possible and, with it, absenteeism from this source.
4. Plan the flow of production and materials so that workers do not on
   occasions find themselves without work.
5. Discipline chronic offenders by means of reprimands, layoffs, discharges,
   and loss of promotions and other privileges.
6. Provide rewards and bonuses for good attendance records.
7. Strengthen the hands of supervisors so that they know how to and can
   handle absenteeism.
8. Ridicule chronic offenders by publicizing names.
9. Interview all absent workers upon their return to determine causes and
   to impress upon them the seriousness of their absence.
10. Work with unions or labor-management committees so that the force of
    labor is applied against absenteeism.

In brief summary, absenteeism, except for what might be called excusable or noncontrollable causes, finds its source in the feeling of employees that their absence will not make much difference. This may be
strikingly shown by comparing the rates of absenteeism among supervisors with those of operative employees. In the former group, among
whom the feeling of responsibility ordinarily runs high, absenteeism
will usually be near the zero mark, as compared to the usual 3 to 6 per
cent general average of absenteeism among the latter. Hence the moral
is obvious: Develop in employees a sense of individual importance and
worth-whileness, and their absenteeism too will go down drastically. On
the contrary, whatever causes the employee to feel insignificant or useless will tend to increase the absentee rates.

SOCIOLOGICAL RESEARCH

The famous Hawthorne experiments are an example of research
which illustrates the unpredictable sources of valuable information that
may be uncovered. During experiments conducted at the Hawthorne

Works of the Western Electric Company to ascertain the effect of working conditions upon output, it was found that social and organizational relationships between employees are a most potent force in influencing employee output and morale. The status which an employee enjoyed because of the job he held had much to do with his productivity, perhaps more than had ever been previously realized. As a consequence, there has been much to-do in recent years about the need for developing satisfactory group relationships in industry. Thus to industry there has been brought the principles and methods of sociology as another contribution to the tools of personnel management, as in past years psychology, psychiatry, medicine, statistics, and economics, to mention only a few, have made their contributions.

To summarize, personnel research is an indispensable function of personnel management. It includes every field and activity of personnel relations. All that can be done here is to note a few principles and types of research. However, the point should be re-emphasized that the future of personnel management depends more upon research than any other factor. This phase of management must gain the standing accorded other scientific fields or incur the risk of being discredited along with phrenology, palmistry, and other pseudosciences.

EVALUATION

NATURE AND SCOPE

Closely akin to research is personnel evaluation. It has to do with, first, measurement of the effectiveness of personnel programs and activities and, second, as a result of such measurements, determination of what should or should not be done in the future. Its effectiveness, as with research, is dependent upon information. And, like research, its scope is as broad as the field of personnel management. The significant problem here, too, is what phases of personnel activities should be given priority. Available resources are seldom sufficient to permit an evaluation of all functions to an equal degree.

In this discussion of evaluation, it is impractical to examine various methods of evaluation. All that can be done is:

1. To comment upon some basic considerations
2. To summarize the subjects and methods of evaluation

BASIC CONSIDERATIONS

Evaluation of personnel and policies may be backward- or forward-looking. Since evaluation is concerned with a comparison of what happened with what was expected, there is a tendency to turn the process into faultfinding. The intent is that of finding scapegoats. Everyone begins to expect to be called "on the carpet." And as offsets, each begins to have alibis ready, to shirk responsibilities, to "pass the buck," and to mistrust others. Under such conditions, the evaluation has become worse than useless.

Forward-looking evaluation still has the determination of faults, mistakes, and errors in mind. But the purpose is not to assess penalties—although that may be done on occasions. The purpose is to find out what went wrong so that the mistake won't be repeated. In such an atmosphere, the wrongdoer is as much interested in unearthing causes of failure as anyone else. With improvement being emphasized, pride in making progress is enlisted. The eyes of all turn forward to goals of accomplishment, and not backward on the errors of the past. The philosophy is positive—not negative.

Another consideration in evaluations is that of how often they should be made. A number of alternatives are available. Perhaps the most common plan is the annual evaluation or audit. At the end of the calendar or fiscal year, a report covering such information as activities performed, results achieved, costs and expenditures, statistical displays, and comparison of objectives and accomplishments is presented. The reports are passed on to various executives and levels. Individual or group conferences are then held to discuss and appraise the contents.

Since too much water can pass over the dam before corrective action can be taken, other companies prefer monthly summaries of significant or exceptional developments. For example, the report illustrated in Table 24 (p. 622) provides much useful and current information on personnel activities. As a consequence, appropriate and timely action can be taken. Moreover, responsible executives are more likely to keep abreast of their personnel duties so that undesirable exceptions will not have occurred to make such reports necessary.

In addition to periodic audits, there is the practice of conducting special studies as needed. For example, attitude surveys on particular topics may be conducted as occasion demands. Or special reports may be prepared on such matters as grievance cases, workings of seniority rules, or effect of overtime practices, for use in forthcoming bargaining sessions. Or new laws or administrative rules may necessitate a review of a company's practices to see what changes, if any, need be made.

Along similar lines is the question of who should conduct evaluations and audits. Some hire outside consultants to make such reviews, whereas others perform this task themselves. The former course has the advantage of being conducted by disinterested specialists. They have no axes to grind and can evaluate a particular set of practices against a broad background of experience. They can present their findings without respect to "fear or favor" of any individuals. On the other hand, the outsiders are not always in the plant a sufficient length of time to get a

TABLE 24

SAMPLE PAGE OF PERSONNEL REPORT*

INDUSTRIAL RELATIONS INDEX, OCTOBER	MONTHLY CUMULATIVE AVERAGE		MIDLAND
	Year to Date	Previous Year	Month
Employees, wages, and hours:			
Number of wage employees....................	6,782	...	6,612
Total employees.............................	7,618	...	7,470
Total man-hours (1,000)......................	1,334	...	1,595
Average weekly wage.........................	$ 85.34	...	$ 78.05
Average hourly rate (including overtime)..........	$ 2.16	...	$ 2.15
Premium overtime cost per hour.................	$ 0.07	...	$ 0.03
Premium overtime cost........................	$81,728	...	$36,565
Employment:			
Applicants†..................................	42.8	...	8.4
Accessions†.................................	25.5	...	6.7
Separations†................................	30.6	...	53.0
Percentage turnover rate per month.............	2.7%	...	2.1%
Labor relations:			
Grievances pending first of month†..............	4.4	...	5.6
Grievances filed during month†.................	1.0	...	1.5
Total grievances settled during month†..........	0.7	...	0.4
At second step†...........................	0.1	...	0
At third step†.............................	0.3	...	0.1
At fourth step†............................	0.3	...	0.3
Arbitration†......	0	...	0
Grievances pending end of month†..............	4.7	...	6.7
Work stoppages—man-hours lost................	8.9	...	0
Safety:			
Frequency rate..............................	1.54	...	1.69
Severity rate...............................	0.56	...	0.09
Compensation cost per 1,000 man-hours..........	$ 3.76	...	$ 8.06
Supervisory training:			
Average hours in training......................	1.7	...	2.1
Suggestions:			
Received†..................................	2.0	...	1.3
Adopted†...................................	0.6	...	0.9
Declined†..................................	2.0	...	0.9
Tangible savings............................	$ 5,561	...	$ 6,723

* Seward H. French, Jr., "Measuring Progress toward Industrial Relations Objectives," *Personnel*, March, 1954, pp. 338–47.
† Per 1,000 employees (total).

complete and balanced picture of what is going on. And after they have presented their report, there may be no one to carry on the threads that will tie into future practices. However, the good in most cases outweighs the shortcomings, so that outside help is often used in conjunction with other plans, through seldom alone.

Most companies conduct their own audits. The examinations are most frequently assigned to the functional heads of the personnel division, although occasionally an audit and research unit is formed. The latter practice is limited to the larger companies. Under the former practice, the employment manager reports on the achievement of hiring goals, the training manager reports on training accomplishments, and the labor relations manager reports on progress in collective bargaining. This seems to make the executive his own judge; but there are offsetting "juries." The conclusions of the various reports will be inconsistent and require reconciliation and explanation. Superior executives will find that reports do not agree with their own interpretations of past events. And employees, through attitude surveys or expressed conflict, may enter counterevidence to the story told by reports.

But the personnel division need not be the sole appraiser of personnel practices. It is well to adopt the policy followed by some companies of having each line executive incorporate as a part of his annual or monthly report, a section on personnel accomplishments and shortcomings. This has the advantage of underlining the sound premise that every executive is a personnel manager. It has the further advantage of interpreting personnel policies and practices at their most vital point, and not solely from the viewpoint of a staff bystander.

In short, evaluation can embrace the services of several groups and levels. The warning that must be called out here is: If many are made responsible, no one may tie all the loose ends together. Hence, whatever plan is followed, some one individual or organizational unit—senior vice-president or personnel manager or personnel evaluation division— should have the tasks of, first, bringing together all audit reports; second, arranging meetings for their discussion; and, third, following up action taken on recommendations of such meetings.

SUBJECTS AND METHODS OF EVALUATION

As in the case of research, there is no subject that is being performed so well that evaluation is unnecessary. Rather all phases of personnel practice should be audited. In this way, it can be determined more accurately whether or not a company is getting the most out of the practices it is pursuing. But, on the other hand, audits are desirable to ascertain whether all practices that might be of advantage to a company are being pursued. Each of these is now reviewed.

1. APPRAISING CURRENT PRACTICES. The field of evaluation is so broad that all that can be done here is to outline the areas and methods of evaluation. Certainly, if the accompanying list of records, statistics, and methods of analysis are employed (Fig. 84), it should be

FIGURE 84.   Outline of Personnel Audit and Appraisal through Records and Statistics*

Major Function	Records and Statistics	Methods of Analysis and Interpretation
1. Job analysis (including time and motion study)	A. Job Specifications B. Personnel inventories, manning tables C. Time standards; output records D. Costs of job analysis	A. Compare minimum personal requirements before and after study B. Compare with other plants C. Compare: 　With other plants 　From time to time 　Before and after motion study D. Compare with other plants: 　Note savings from job breakdown, dilution, lowered personal requirements, reduced training time, etc.
2. Recruitments	A. Application blanks and check lists B. Numbers of applicants: 　By source 　By means of recruitment 　Advertising 　Scouting, references, etc. C. Costs of recruitment: 　By source 　By means	A. Classify applicants by sex, age, experience, education, marital status, other personal characteristics B. Comparison by source or means of recruitment, in terms of: 　Output 　Service ratings 　Promotions and transfers 　Test scores 　Labor turnover 　Length of service 　Accident frequency, severity, proneness 　Attendance 　Necessary training, time, type C. Compare to show: 　Savings from changed sources or means
3. Selection and placement	A. Bases for selection (personal characteristics): 　Test scores 　Interview check lists, ratings, training, education 　Experience 　References 　Marital status, etc.	A and B. Correlate with: 　Labor turnover 　Length of service 　Absenteeism, tardiness 　Service ratings 　Output, spoilage, inspection reports 　Necessary training period 　Accident frequency, severity, proneness 　Transfers and promotions 　Morale scale 　etc.

* Presented by Professor Dale Yoder at a meeting of the American Management Association.

FIGURE 84.—Continued

Major Function	Records and Statistics	Methods of Analysis and Interpretation
	B. Follow-up and progress reports and ratings C. Personal employee records D. Costs: Interviewing Testing and test analysis Induction and follow-up	C. Same as application blank above D. Compare: With other firms By source of employees Before and after changed selection procedure With savings from lower turnover and other conditions in A and B above
4. Training	A. Numbers and individuals trained, by type of training B. Training grades, scores C. Training time required D. Costs of training, by type of training	A. Compare: Output, spoilage, inspection costs before and after training and with control group Rate of promotion, trained and control group B and C Compare: Grades and length of training by source and personal characteristics (2A, above) Length of training with other firms Length before and after change in program D. Compare: Unit costs by type, with other firms Unit costs by source Costs before and after change in program Costs with savings from increased output, lower overhead, reduced accidents, turnover, and spoilage, etc.
5. Employee rating	A. Service rating scores B. Costs of rating program	A. Compare or correlate with: Output, spoilage, inspection costs Personal characteristics (3A, above) Training experience Morale scales B. Compare with: Possible savings in training costs Possible reductions in turnover Improved output reasonably attributable to rating
6. Systematic promotion and transfer	A. Records of promotions and transfers, by types	A and B. Compare: Grievance records before and after systematization Length of service with output, spoilage

FIGURE 84.—Continued

Major Function	Records and Statistics	Methods of Analysis and Interpretation
		Promotions and transfers by departments Promotions and transfers before and after systematization Promotions and transfers by source and personal characteristics
	B. Seniority lists	Length of training necessary before and after systematization Turnover rates before and after Morale level before and after
	C. Cost of systematization	C. Compare: Output before and after Training costs before and after systematization Savings from unnecessary transfers avoided Savings from turnover reduction before and after Possible savings in increased usable output, before and after Savings from possible reduction in grievances, before and after
7. Maintaining interest, morale, and discipline	A. General measures and records: Morale scale scores Disciplinary actions by type Grievances Counseling records Employee use of services, publications, cafeterias, etc. Suggestions Attendance reports	A. Compare each by departments: From time-to-time Before and after modifications By source of employees By employee personal characteristics By possible interrelationships—e.g., grievances and morale, use of cafeteria and absences, etc. Analyze output by hours and fractions of hours
	B. Costs, by type of activity	B. Discover possible savings from improved procedures; e.g., grievances settled at lower level, or with more favorable results, lessened absenteeism, lower turnover, lessened monotony
8. Health and safety	A. Health records: Visits to medical service Illnesses, by type Days lost from illness Physical defects discovered	A. Analyze by department, source, and personal characteristics: Compare output with types of physical defects Compare records before and after change in services provided Compare with general population, other firms Compare with morale scales

FIGURE 84.—*Continued*

Major Function	Records and Statistics	Methods of Analysis and Interpretation
	B. Accident records: Frequency Severity Type of accident	B. Analyze by department, time of day: Source of employee, personal characteristics, length of day, morale scale Compare with other firms, industry reports
	C. Costs	C. Estimate savings in accidents prevented, days lost, overhead, workmen's compensation costs, improved placement
9. Employment stabilization	A. Employment records: Total employment Time cards, hours worked	A. Compare fluctuations (seasonal, cyclical) after stabilization devices compare output by length of day, overtime versus regular time, and by shifts
	B. Turnover rates	B. Analyze by department, trend, source of employee, personal characteristics, cause of separation
	C. Costs of stabilization and security devices, severance compensation, etc.	C. Show savings from reduced unemployment compensation premium, improved shift arrangements, reduced overtime, selection of workers for certain shifts, reduced turnover
10. Wage and salary administration	A. Payroll data: Wage rates Incentive bonuses Earnings B. Job ratings C. Cost of living D. Unit labor costs	A, B, and C. Compare job rates, differentials, wage structure, and earnings with other firms Maintain check on real earnings, take-home D. Compare with other firms: Compare before and after modifications in wage system
	E. Costs, including job evaluation, administration of incentive plans, etc.	E. Show savings effected through change in system, lower unit labor costs, reduced inspection, spoilage, overhead
11. Collective bargaining	A. Check-off lists	A. Compare union members and nonmembers, by departments, sources, personal characteristics, ratings, morale scales, earnings, promotions
	B. Arbitration awards	B. Analyzing subject, delay, department involved, employee characteristics
	C. Work stoppages	C. Show time lost, department, cause, costs, union involved
	D. Contract clauses	D. Before and after comparisons of disputes, absenteeism, illness, earnings, grievances, etc.
	E. Costs of bargaining	E. Show savings resulting from improved contract terms, reduction of stoppages, lost time, grievances, etc.
12. Research records	Detailed above	Detailed above

FIGURE 85

CHECK LIST ON MORALE BUILDING

	Yes	No

I. Does the company—

A. Explain to all employees the rules and policies of the company?
(Necessary to prevent misunderstanding of rules and possible later disciplinary action. May increase employee participation in insurance, safety, health and other programs.)

B. Explain the labor policy of the company?
(To avoid misunderstandings and maintain better relations.)

C. Show employees the importance of being at work every day as scheduled?
(May prevent employee becoming an absentee.)

D. Promote the feeling of employee's personal participation in work?
(Every worker is an important cog in the production wheel.)

E. Show all employees the use to which their products are put?
(Employees are interested in final use to which products are put.)

F. Appeal directly to workers by means of posters, bulletins and speakers of importance of their work?
(These programs usually help in utilization of manpower.)

G. Have a merit rating plan?
(Employee is given an incentive to make a good record.)

II. Does company have an organization for the sympathetic discussion of employee problems in order to help solve them?
(Employee counsellors properly trained can analyze employee problems and propose programs to improve morale.)

III. Are the following investigated as possible employee problems?

A. Housing?

B. Child-care?

C. Transportation problem?

   1. Share-the-ride?

   2. Mechanical service to employee's car?

D. A legal problem?

E. A medical or dental problem?

F. An eating facility problem?

G. Fatigue due to too long working periods?

H. Misunderstandings due to material shortages?
(Lowered morale of employees is often caused by a problem on which employee needs advice.)

IV. Does the company have program of providing recreation to employees such as—

A. Morning and afternoon recess periods for women?

B. Definite schedule of vacations?

C. Interdepartmental baseball?

D. Interdepartmental football?

E. Interdepartmental basketball?

F. Bowling team?

G. Family picnics?

FIGURE 85.—Continued

		Yes	No

V. Does the company have a commissary for employees to purchase—

   A. Small tools? _____ _____

   B. Wearing apparel? _____ _____

   (Convenience in buying shop needs is often considered important.)

VI. Does the company have dispensing machines for—

   A. Women's needs? _____ _____

   B. Beverages? _____ _____

   C. Cigarettes? _____ _____

   D. Confections? _____ _____

   E. Vitamin tablets? _____ _____

   F. Salt tablets? _____ _____

   (Many plants provide these items for employees feeling it is a necessary part of human relations.)

VII. Does the company have a public address system throughout the plant to give employees—

   A. Music during working hours? _____ _____

   B. News commentators? _____ _____

   C. Talks by nationally known people? _____ _____

   (Considered part of program to break monotony and fatigue. May be considered recreational. Most employees appreciate these programs.)

VIII. Has the company used labor-management committees in their morale building programs? _____ _____

IX. Does the company keep in contact with men in military service and post letters from them? _____ _____
(Builds good will.)

X. Are the various programs delegated to persons with definite authority and instructions to carry them out? _____ _____
(To make a success of any program, responsibility for its operation must be delegated to persons with ability and authority to carry it out.)

XI. Does the company publish a shop paper or bulletin giving interesting news items of employees? _____ _____
(Many concerns find this is an excellent medium and obtain good results.)

XII. Does the company publish an annual financial statement in terms understandable by the average employee? _____ _____

XIII. Does top management receive a report of the results of various morale building programs? _____ _____
(Management should approve and support morale building programs and keep in touch with them through progress reports.)

possible to assure oneself that his company is getting the most out of the personnel practices it is pursuing.

2. ADEQUACY OF PROGRAM.   In the matter of determining whether or not a company is pursuing all practices which are of advantage to it, two major alternatives are available. First, outside consultants may be called in to review a company's program. This is a highly desirable way because it is difficult for any company to examine itself. But an outsider who knows the practices of others and particularly the breadth of programs found elsewhere can do a good job of sizing up inadequacies, weak points, and gaps.

If a company desires to do this job itself, check lists such as the selected illustration shown in Figure 85 (pp. 628–29) may be used. In this system of check lists, emphasis is placed upon the use of questions that may be answered either "yes" or "no." On the surface this may appear to be an oversimplification. However, it must be remembered that problems cannot be solved or plans laid for their solution until they are uncovered. Hence the use of such audit forms is desirable, in that they serve to reveal areas of personnel practices in which improvements may be desirable. Once ascertained in this manner, the next step—and a very significant one, of course—is that of determining what is to be done about practices in question.

Another interesting aspect about such check lists is that they focus attention upon the wide range of personnel policies and practices that various companies have found it desirable to include in their programs. The mere fact that these plans are cited in the check lists is sufficient to cause some employers to wonder whether or not they, too, should take a broader view in their personnel practices.

On the other hand, it is well to guard against unnecessary dissatisfaction with one's personnel program because of the use of such check lists. As one reviews his practices against a list which is a composite of numerous plans, it is easy to conclude that one's present program is inadequate. While it is well to have plans for future expansion, it is perhaps more undesirable to undertake an overly ambitious program which is likely to fail because of hurried installation than it is to proceed with a limited personnel program that is gradually expanded.

In any event, the following check lists do perform a function of indicating a type of practice that is useful in auditing personnel practices. It is simple, yet comprehensive. As a consequence, such a plan of auditing is more likely to catch the attention of busy top executives than extended descriptive reports.

SUMMARY

Perhaps it can be said in summary that research and evaluation reflect the philosophy of personnel management adopted by a company. In the last analysis, the particular attitude taken toward how problems of labor-management relations are to be solved will determine more than anything else the quality of a company's labor relations. This is so, but not because one's solutions are bound to be accurate—such an ideal state can scarcely ever be expected. However, this is so because others soon become impressed with the attitude management takes.

If the attitude is that of searching for the truth—let the chips fall where they may—labor will grow to respect and to co-operate. If the attitude is self-seeking, labor will reflect a similar attitude. These developments may not come at once, but come they will. Perhaps that is why so often management despairs. It does what it considers good but sees no immediate tangible results. It does not realize that in personnel, time—much time—must elapse before we can reap what we have sown. But reap we will; so, if a harvest is expected, the seeds must be planted early and with patience cultivated.

QUESTIONS AND PROBLEMS

1. How much money should a company spend on research? Can you state a principle by which a solution to this question may be derived?
2. Is there any significant difference between pure research and practical research? Why is pure research in personnel not subsidized to the same extent as pure research in the so-called "physical sciences"?
3. One hears executives boast about physical laboratories for research but not about their personnel research. Does this explain why many companies have so much labor trouble?
4. Discuss the significance of linear programming, cybernetics, sociometrics, and tabulating equipment to personnel research.
5. What is the record of absenteeism among executives as compared to employees? How do you explain the difference? Is it possible that the reasons that executives are infrequently absent could be used with the same result among employees?
6. If a large number of absences are attributable to overindulgence in liquor, why are such workers retained?
7. A company reported that on the first day of the hunting season in one year, over half of the male employees were absent. Would you recommend a holiday on that day each year? Or would you try to eliminate absenteeism? How would you go about this?

8. An executive stated that his company had much labor trouble because the supervisors had so many different types of details to handle that they often overlooked aspects that eventually led to difficulties. What type of research would have been helpful in this case?

9. What kind of research would you suggest in order to help a company establish an effective training program?

10. A company decided to develop the abilities of its supervisory staff. How would you go about determining what specific abilities need developing?

11. If a company follows the program of rating employees, what information should be gathered in order to determine which supervisors are prejudiced (and to what degree) in their ratings?

12. Inasmuch as no company can undertake all the research projects that it might desire, what tests should be adopted in order to determine which projects should be given priority?

13. An employer feels that some of his employees are dissatisfied with their work because their wives are dissatisfied with the reputation of the company. How could the employer set out to find whether his assumptions are correct?

14. Study the population data for your community. Can you deduce any conclusions regarding possible difficulties of labor supply that may develop? Why are such census figures useful in other ways to the personnel manager?

15. A company desires to measure the effectiveness of its promotion policies. What research should it undertake to do this?

16. A given company takes pride in the fact that its personnel practices are audited once a year by an outside concern. What is your opinion of this practice?

17. A personnel manager stated that he never proposed a personnel plan of any kind without accompanying it with suggestions regarding its control and evaluation. What is your opinion of this practice?

18. An executive stated that he planned his personnel practices so carefully and indoctrinated all employees in them so thoroughly that the plans controlled themselves. Are you inclined to believe this claim? Why or why not?

19. It is usually found that, when a company decides to install personnel records and reports, it often goes "overboard" on such matters. What rules should be established in order to keep the records from becoming red tape?

20. Organizationally speaking, how should personnel research and control be established in order to get the most good out of such tasks with a maximum of co-operation from other departments?

APPENDIX

A

Instructions for Filling

Out the Job Analysis Schedule[1]

1. *Headings.* Items 1–14 on the Job Analysis Schedule (Fig. 15) are included in the term "headings." This part of the schedule provides for naming and locating the job industrially and for recording of certain identification data which are needed for every job.

2. *Item 1, Job Title.* Here should be entered the name by which the job being analyzed is commonly called in the establishment (plant title). All job titles (Item 1) or alternate titles (Item 8) should be written in capital letters in the singular and in the natural form as used in industry, such as BARTENDER, not TENDER, BAR. The only exception to this rule is that the words "assistant," "helper," and "apprentice" should not be used to begin a title. A descriptive word should precede these such as MACHINIST APPRENTICE, PRESSMAN HELPER.

3. *General Terms.* Such general terms as "manager," "foreman," and the like should always be editorially qualified by a descriptive phrase if these titles stand alone. For example, FOREMAN (BRICKLAYING); but BRICKLAYER FOREMAN would require no editorial qualifications.

4. *Agreement with Dictionary Form.* Extreme care should be exercised to make all titles other than plant titles in the Job Analysis Schedule and in the *Occupational Dictionary* agree in form; that is, if a title appears in inverted form in the *Occupational Dictionary,* it should be used in inverted form in the Job Analysis Schedule. A few titles are always used in inverted form, to avoid unreasonable alphabetic placement. The words "assistant," "helper," "apprentice," and "foreman" always follow the descriptive portion of the title showing the type of assistant, helper, apprentice, and foreman.

5. *Item 2, Schedule Number.* This item is used for identification and filing purposes primarily.

6. *Item 3, Number Employed.* Here is entered the number of workers engaged in jobs identical with the job being analyzed in this particular establishment.

7. *Item 4, Establishment Number.* This entry is used for identification and filing purposes.

8. *Item 5, Date.* Enter here the date on which the job analysis is completed.

9. *Item 6, Title of Verified Job.* This entry is left blank until the job under consideration is verified as to content.

10. *Item 8, Alternate Titles.* All names by which the job is known, other

---

[1] See form illustrated on pp. 92–97.

than the one entered in Item 1 above, should be entered in the space opposite Item 8. These job names should not include slang terms unless such terms are widely used and recognized in the industry.

11. *Items 10 and 11, Dictionary Title and Code Number.* If the job which is described in this analysis is defined in the *Dictionary of Occupational Titles,* enter the specific dictionary title and code number here.

12. *Item 7, Industry.* Here enter the accepted name of the industry in which the analyzed job is observed.

13. *Item 9, Branch.* A branch represents a larger division of an industry, made according to type of activity carried on, as contrasted with a department, which represents a division made according to phases of a single activity or process.

14. *Item 12, Department.* Enter here the name of the department of the industry in which the analyzed job is found. The analyst is responsible for specifying either the division in which this job exists, or the fact that no division exists.

15. *Item 13, Analysis Prepared by.* Here is entered the name of the person who is responsible for preparing the job analysis.

16. *Item 14, Field Office.* Enter here the name and the code number of the field office which services the area in which the industry is located.

17. *Item 16, Job Summary.* The job summary presents in concise form the essential and distinguishing characteristics of the occupation. Since it is a summary of all of the information collected by the job analysis, it is not written until all of the job analysis has been completed. Hence the details for preparing the job summary will be discussed in paragraph 53 of these instructions.

18. *Minimum Qualifications.* The source of information included in Items 16 to 19 is the person responsible for hiring workers for the job under analysis. This person should define the minimum acceptable standards for employment. It should be recognized, however, that employers generally have a tendency to demand higher qualifications when discussing jobs than when they actually hire workers. It is the problem of the analyst to determine tactfully and accurately the actual minimum requirements and to record these rather than the ideal standards.

19. *Minimum qualifications for employment* always remain the minimum requirements for success on the job, even though an employer may at the moment prefer applicants of a certain nationality and of higher educational requirements than necessary. He may feel that these requirements are necessary to meet the needs of other jobs in the plant when promoting or transferring workers from one job to another. Minimum qualifications for employment at the time of analysis are not necessarily permanent hiring factors, since hiring requirements readily fluctuate with changes in the labor market. If other than actual minimum job requirements are noted, the entry should be qualified with an explanation.

20. *Item 16, Sex.* Enter here the answer to the question, "Does the employer hire men exclusively, women exclusively, or either men or women, for this job? Enter "M" for male, "F" for female, and "O" if there is no preference.

21. *Item 16, Age.* Enter here the minimum and maximum age which the employer will require in hiring people for this job. If no special range is desig-

nated, enter a zero (0). Thus if the employer is willing to accept people between the ages of eighteen and twenty-five only, the entry in Item 16 appears as "18–25."

22. *Item 17, Necessary Physical Requirements.* Here are entered any special physical requirements that are necessary to adequate performance of the job. If average, ordinary, not unusual requirements are specified, the entry should be zero (0). The data should include all necessary characteristics, such as: "Small and agile to climb between girders"; "Not under 5'10" tall to reach high shelves"; or, "Strong and husky, weight 160 pounds or over, to carry heavy lumber."

23. *Item 18, Education.* Encircle "S," "R," or "W," or all three, to indicate that the ability to speak, read or write English, respectively, is the minimum literacy requirement for employment. If the minimum education required is more than ability to read and write, it should appear after "Other"; as "8 years elementary school"; "business-school secretarial training"; "college graduation with major in chemistry."

24. *Item 19, Experience.* Here indicate any prior work experience which may be required of the applicant. When questioning the employer, it is important to determine exactly what he considers as minimum experience requirements in the light of the normal labor market situation.

25. *Item 20, Relation to Other Jobs.* Item 20 is intended to provide information with reference to the job from which qualified workers come to the job under analysis, as well as the jobs to which qualified workers may be promoted. It points out ways in which workers are or can be interchanged between jobs within the establishment, as well as the manner in which interindustry transfers may readily be made.

26. *Item 21, Supervision Received.* Here enter a rating of the degree of supervision received by the worker, by marking an "X" in the space after the appropriate item: "general," "close," or "medium." It is essential that the analyst indicate the amount of responsibility placed on the worker for the quality and quantity of his product or performance. The term "general" indicates the usual type of overseeing which most workers receive. "Close," at the other extreme, denotes a constant overseeing of the worker by the supervisor, with almost no responsibility placed on the worker. "Medium," between these extremes, indicates that the worker is given specific detailed instructions, particularly at the beginning of a task and, hence, is assigned a certain amount of responsibility.

27. *Item 22, Supervision Given.* If no supervision is given to other workers by the worker under observation, an "X" should be entered in the space after the word "none." If the worker whose job is being analyzed has, as part of his duties, the supervision of others, the number of workers supervised should be entered following "No. Supervised." The titles of the jobs supervised should be entered following the word "title." Where the titles of the job supervised are numerous, an indication of the group supervised is sufficient, but it should be possible to ascertain the title from the statement made, supplemented by a note in Item VIII, Comments, if necessary.

28. *Item 23, Seasonality.* In certain industries, as in canning, the number of workers employed is closely related to the season of the year. In canning, the greatest number of workers are employed during the months of September and

October and the smallest number in February. If the job being analyzed, or the industry in which it exists, is affected by seasonal fluctuations, the weeks and months in which the hiring and the laying-off occurs should be recorded. The weeks or months during which employment is above normal are known as the "peak" of employment, and the period during which employment is below normal is known as the "trough."

Filling Out Supplementary Sheets

29. Certain kinds of information which are needed to describe a job fully, vary so much in form, extent, and content, that little more than a heading and a general explanation can be given. Of such a nature are the eight items of the supplementary material. These items are:

I. Work performed	V. Hazards
II. Equipment	VI. Special information
III. Material	VII. Definitions of terms
IV. Surroundings	VIII. Comments

30. Not all of these eight supplementary items will be of value on every job. On some jobs the detailed treatment of work performed may be unnecessary, especially if ample descriptive material is contained in the job summary. In jobs in which no hazards exist, or in jobs which involve few or no special terms, these items will not be required.

31. *Work Performed.* The primary purpose of this supplementary item is the description of the duties of the job concisely, precisely, and explicitly so that a reader may be able to visualize the tasks composing the job, preferably in the sequence of steps taken, and may be able to recognize the skills, knowledges, and judgments or responsibilities involved, with a minimum of reorganization of the data in his own mind after reading. The purpose of the information on work performed is to furnish the interviewer with enough detail about the job to enable him to do effective interviewing, selection, and placement work.

32. In *Supplementary Item I* should be entered a statement or description of what the worker does in a series of either chronological or logical steps, setting forth what he does, how he does it, and why he does it.

33. A statement of work performed will usually consist of a series of numbered statements, each comprising a description of a task or major step in the job. The statements should be brief, and the job title of the worker is implied as the subject of each sentence.

34. *Knowledges and Judgments.* It is not enough to record simply a description of the motions performed by the worker; it is generally of greater importance that the interviewer have a record of the knowledges, training, and experience necessary to perform these motions at the right time, in the right order, and in the right manner. Consequently, it is vitally necessary in every instance that the analyst determine whether execution of the motions depends on any skills, knowledges, exercise of judgments, or other intangible factors, and that he make specific statements emphasizing the significance of such factors. This comment applies to each separate task in the job, as well as to the job as a whole.

35. *Rating of Per Cent of Time.* After each numbered element of the work

performed, in the column headed "Per Cent of Time" should be indicated the percentage of the worker's time that the element occupies as compared with the job as a whole.

36. *Rating of Degree of Skill.* After each element in the second column headed "Degree of Skill," should be indicated a rating of the skill that is required of the worker to perform the element. Expressions of the degree or rate of skill are indicated by the figures "1," "2," and "3"; "1" being used to express the lowest amount of skill, and "3" the highest amount. When assigning the ratings to job elements, only the job being analyzed is to be considered. This practice must be followed strictly because it is not possible to compare the skills involved in different jobs, since what might be rated a "3" skill for the element of one job might deserve only the rating of "1" in another job.

37. The *"Work Performed"* item should include a statement of the duties that are performed infrequently, as well as in the normal work cycle. Such tasks as the occasional setting up of a machine, occasional repairs, infrequent reports, and the like, should here be included. In each case a notation should be made concerning the frequency of occurrence of the performance.

38. *"May" Tasks and Alternative Tasks.* If a task may be performed by one worker or by another, the description of it should be introduced with the word "may." All alternative methods of performing a task should be stated: "Either . . . (the one) . . . or . . . (the other) . . . ."

39. *Simultaneous Tasks.* In cases in which a worker may start several tasks at the same time, none of which is completed for several days, each task should be completely described before beginning the descriptive of a second task.

40. *Miscellaneous Cautions.* In preparing the "Work Performed" item, care should be exercised to avoid the simple listing of the tasks performed by the worker without any explanation of how they are performed. The inclusion of too many duties in one work element should be avoided. Even closely related duties should be broken up into more than one element if the item has become too long and involved.

41. *Equipment.* Under this item enumerate, in the order mentioned under "Work Performed," all machines and all special or unusual equipment used by the worker on the job that is being analyzed.

42. Under *Description of a Machine* should appear the following: a statement of the function of the machine; a description of the physical appearance of the machine and its essential parts; and a description of the operation of the machine and its relation to the worker. Only essential features of the mechanical equipment should be included in the description. Structural details, such as gear ratios, types of power drive, and other technical features, need not be included unless some specific job duties are performed in relation to these features.

43. *Tools.* For simpler devices, particularly for hand tools, it will be necessary to include only a definition of the device rather than a complete description. In every case the purpose for which the device is used should be shown.

44. *Relating the Description to the Drawing.* If a drawing has been included in the Schedule, all descriptions of equipment should be related to the drawing by placing the letters appearing on the drawing in parentheses after the names of the component parts of the device to which they refer.

45. *Material.* Under this item should be listed and described the components used by the worker to make a finished product, if such activity is being performed on the job. For example, a baker makes bread from flour. A core maker makes cores from sand, but a cab driver or elevator operator does not use material in this sense.

46. *Surroundings.* Under this item will be described the physical conditions under which the job is performed. The statement should show the nature of the conditions and the manner in which they affect the worker. The statement of the surroundings may begin with the word "inside" or the word "outside" if this fact is not obvious from the statement to follow. Three situations may arise in analyzing surroundings. These are: First, situations in which the analyst determines that no significant entries need to be made concerning surroundings, such as might be typified by a large group of clerical workers who perform their duties in "normal office surroundings." In preparing schedules for such jobs, a zero (0) should be placed after Item IV, Surrounding. Second, situations in which the surroundings are significant and inherent factors on the job. Third, situations in which the analyst is in doubt whether the significance of the surroundings or their inherent identification with the job adds to the job analysis. When in doubt, the analyst should include the data as reference information, leaving to others who use the information the decision as to its relevance.

47. If the job is of such a nature that its performance involves possible injury, death, or damage to health, these dangers should be described. Only those hazards that can be connected with the job itself should be included. For example, traffic hazards to which everyone is subjected are not considered occupational hazards for most jobs, but in the case of a traffic patrolman, the danger of being struck by a passing vehicle is a very real occupational hazard.

48. The material in this section should enumerate the factors in the job, the presence or absence of which may have a direct bearing on occupational classification or on placement. A substitute heading for this item might be "Registration and Placement Aids." This item should be used to emphasize characteristics in which the job under analysis differs in important respects from other jobs of its kind. It should assist in anticipating variations in the job which may occur in different establishments.

In this item two main headings are kept in mind, "Basic Requirements" and "Variable Requirements."

Basic requirements are the "performance" characteristics—those qualifications which are definitely required by the nature of the job itself. These may be beyond or aside from any qualifications of "evidential" nature which may be demanded by individual employers in keeping with their labor policies. Such factors as "the ability to do art work," or "the possession of engineering training," should be mentioned here. The analyst must be careful in all cases to state the minimum rather than the maximum qualifications for success on the job. Even when no experience is required for the job, some knowledge or ability may be specified as needed for its successful performance. For example, the employer may specify one of the following: "Eighth-grade education or its equivalent, to provide ability to solve problems involving multiplication and division of fractions"; "Sufficient physical strength to stand continuously and lift articles weighing approximately 50 pounds from the floor into the feed hopper at frequent intervals"; or "Worker must possess or obtain a food-handler certificate."

The description of variable requirements should bring out the differences that may be expected between workers, all of whom are employed in the same job, in either the same or in different establishments. This information should guide interviewers in obtaining supplementary information that will indicate a worker's fitness for a specified position after it has been determined that he is qualified to perform the duties of the occupation. Here would be noted such factors as wide variation in procedure followed, equipment used, or the number of workers supervised.

49. *Information for the Applicant.* In Supplementary Item VI, information should be included such as the applicant might request concerning the job. Obviously, all factors listed below will not necessarily apply to any one job, nor does the list include all of the possible items that might apply. Among the more common types of information requested by applicants are: specialized knowledge of machine operation which is required, use of attachments, tolerances or accuracy required, rate of production required by employer, opportunities for training on the job and in the community, length of the learning period, base rate of pay hours of work shifts, transportation to and from the job, housing and boarding facilities in the neighborhood of the plant, etc.

50. All unusual or technical terms that are used throughout the analysis should be underlined as they are used. In Item VII, these technical terms should be listed in the order in which they appear in "Work Performed." Each term should be defined. The definitions will vary with the terms to be explained. Each definition should include a clear statement or explanation of the word or thing by describing the attributes, properties, or relations which distinguish it from all other words or things. The term may be defined by stating its use.

51. The style to be used in preparing "Definitions of Terms" is illustrated in the following examples derived from an analysis of the job of polisher in an establishment where costume jewelry is produced:

Gloss: A high-luster finish produced by polishing with fine abrasives; also, a term applied to the operation of producing such a finish.
Satin: A soft finish produced with a wire-brush wheel.
Cut and Gloss: The process of smoothing metal surfaces with a medium fine abrasive compound which requires little oil, and the immediately polishing or high luster on another wheel with a fine abrasive.

52. This item contains miscellaneous material not elsewhere classified. It should be used for footnoting all other parts of the job analysis. If the space allotted in the printed form is insufficient at any point, the information to be entered may be continued in Item VIII.

53. *Job Summary.* Refer again to paragraph 17 of these instructions. The job summary presents in concise form the essential and distinguishing characteristics of the occupation. It should be so constructed that it characterizes the job accurately. The job summary must be an abstract of the entire analysis; hence, it is written after the Job Analysis Schedule proper has been completed. It should be so complete that it can be used independently as an adequate presentation of

the essential facts about the job. It should be a concise over-all definition of the job, and not simply a summary of the work performed. Such items as the following should be taken into account in determining the content of the job summary:

What the worker does

How he does it

Why he does it (for what purpose) and his place in the process

Under what conditions he does the work

The degree of his responsibility

The kind of establishment in which the work is done (if the industry includes more than one)

Considerations controlling his trade judgments or decisions

The special qualifications which he must possess

Undesirable Differentiations

ADJUSTER.—Receives complaints from customers in person or by telephone concerning merchandise and bills; investigates complaints and makes adjustments.

ADJUSTMENT CLERK.—Notes complaints made by customers; as TRACER and informs customer what adjustment will be made.

Desirable Differentiations

ADJUSTER.—Receives complaints from customers concerning qualities of merchandise, credits to be allowed for defective merchandise, and the like. Investigates complaints, decides what adjustment is to be made, and authorizes replacement of merchandise or the giving of credit.

ADJUSTMENT CLERK.—Receives complaints of customers concerning routine matters such as nondelivery of merchandise and erroneous charges. As TRACER ascertains reason for the complaint, what adjustment will be made, and informs customer.

Another example is cited of an unacceptable job summary and an acceptable revision:

Unacceptable Job Summary

CORE PASTER.—Mixes paste; removes baked core from rack; cuts vent holes through sections; applies paste, presses sections together; spreads flurry on seams, checks dimensions.

Acceptable Job Summary

CORE PASTER.—Assembles baked-sand core sections to form a core by brushing the adjoining surfaces with flour paste, to make them adhesive, and fitting the sections accurately together, smoothing the surfaces with a plastic mixture and inspecting the dimensions for accuracy.

Two acceptable job summaries are cited in conclusion:

PUNCH PRESS OPERATOR. Sets up and operates a punch press to punch or shape small aircraft pieces from sheet aluminum. Checks dies against blueprints and fits dies into press, bolting them securely in place. Sets gauges and makes trial run to test position of dies and gauges, making adjustments so that the completed work conforms to specifications recorded on blueprints. Places piece of aluminum stock in position against gauges on the punch press and operates the machine by stepping on a pedal, periodically checking completed pieces to be sure they are according to requirements. Supervises a PUNCH PRESS OPERATOR HELPER.

ROAD PAVER OPERATOR. Operates a one-yard capacity gasoline-powered road paver to mix wet concrete and spread it on a roadbed by manipulating hand levers and foot treadles to lift and dump the ingredients from the skip (loading hopper) into the rotating mixing drum of the machine. Empties the drum contents into a bucket, moves the bucket horizontally along the boom, and distributes the contents of the bucket onto the roadbed as the bucket is being emptied. Moves the road paver on its crawler treads during the paving process.

APPENDIX · B

CONFIDENTIAL

B. L. S. 1219
U. S. DEPARTMENT OF LABOR
BUREAU OF LABOR STATISTICS
Washington 25, D. C.

Budget Bureau No. 44-R 290.6.
Approval expires January 31, 1947.

REPORT ON LABOR TURN-OVER

(Please read instructions on reverse side before filling out report)

This copy is our permanent office record.   Please return before the 5th of each month, using No. 6 return envelope

A separate report for each establishment is requested.

------------|------------|------------|------------
(State) | (Area) | (Industry) | (Group) | (Establishment)

LOCATION OF ESTABLISHMENT COVERED IN THIS REPORT

City ------------
County ------------
State ------------

(ABOVE IS MAILING ADDRESS, INCLUDE POSTAL ZONE NUMBER—CHANGE IF INCORRECT)

Section A.—ALL EMPLOYEES

MONTH	Employment in pay period (preferably 1 week) ending nearest 15th	SEPARATIONS (During calendar month)					Accessions except transfers during calendar month	TRANSFERS		Period covered by this report (preferably 1 calendar month)	
		Total	Quits	Discharges	Lay-offs	Miscellaneous including military		To other establishments of company	From other establishments of company	From	To
(1)	(2)	(3)	(4)	(5)	(6)	(7)	(8)	(9)	(10)	(11)	(12)
1945—Dec.											
1946—Jan.											
Feb.											
Nov.											
Dec.											

Section B.—ALL WOMEN EMPLOYEES

MONTH (13)	Employment in pay period (preferably 1 week) ending nearest 15th (14)	SEPARATIONS (During calendar month)		Accessions except transfers during calendar month (17)
		Total (15)	Quits (16)	
1945—Dec.				
1946—Jan.				
Feb.				
Dec.				

Section C.—VETERANS

Employment in pay period (preferably 1 week) ending nearest 15th (18)	SEPARATIONS (During calendar month)		Accessions except transfers during calendar month (21)
	Total (19)	Quits (20)	

Section D.—MAJOR PRODUCTS OR KIND OF WORK DONE.—Please list in order of importance indicating percent of employees engaged in each product

1946—Jan. .... July. ....

Feb. .... Aug. ....

June .... Dec. ....

Section E.—COMMENTS.—Please indicate the main factors responsible for any unusually large number of quits, discharges, lay-offs, transfers, or accessions

1946—Jan. ....

Feb. ....

Dec. ....

....

(Signature of person making report) .... (Position)

(See over for "Instructions")

GPO   16-46879-1

INSTRUCTIONS

I. PERIOD COVERED BY THIS REPORT.—In order that comparable labor turnover information may be obtained from all employers, the items of turnover (quits, discharges, etc.) should cover the full calendar month or a period closely covering the calendar month. The dates for the period covered should be entered each month. Employment figures, as noted below, should relate to the pay period (preferably one week) ending nearest the fifteenth of the month.

II. EMPLOYMENT (Items 2, 14, and 18).—Report all classes of the designated employees who worked or received pay for any part of the pay period (preferably one week) ending nearest the fifteenth of the current month. Include in these sections employees engaged on force-account construction and those on paid vacation. Exclude pensioners, members of the armed forces, and persons on leave of absence without pay.

III. QUITS (Items 4, 16, and 20).—"Quits" are terminations of employment initiated by employees for such reasons as acceptance of a job elsewhere, return to school, ill health, marriage, maternity, dissatisfaction, or for unknown causes. Quits for the purpose of entering the armed forces should be reported under miscellaneous separations. Unauthorized absences (whether for illness or other causes) for seven consecutive workdays (the seventh of which falls within the period covered by this report) should be reported as quits.

IV. DISCHARGES (Item 5).—"Discharges" are terminations of employment initiated by the employer for such reasons as incompetence, violation of rules, dishonesty, insubordination, and laziness.

V. LAY-OFFS (Item 6)—"Lay-offs" are terminations of employment (expected to last more than seven days) initiated by the employer, without prejudice to the workers, for such reasons as lack of orders or materials, conversion of plant, release of temporary help, and introduction of labor-saving machinery or processes. A termination of employment with definite instructions to return to work within seven days is not to be regarded as a lay-off. Vacations or suspensions of operations during inventory periods are likewise not considered lay-offs.

VI. MISCELLANEOUS SEPARATIONS (Item 7).—"Miscellaneous separations" are terminations of employment due to permanent disability, death, retirement on pension, or to enter the armed forces or women's auxiliaries (voluntary enlistment or Selective Service) and should be reported here, whether or not the workers' names are retained on the pay roll.

VII. ACCESSIONS (Items 8, 17, and 21).—"Accessions" are all additions to the work force during the month, whether of new or rehired employees. Returns to work after a short lay-off (not exceeding seven days) or after vacations should not be reported as accessions.

VIII. VETERANS (Section C).—"Veterans" are all persons with discharges from the armed forces or women's auxiliaries of World War II.

IX. TRANSFERS (Items 9 and 10).—Transfers from one establishment to another within this company should not be included in separations or accessions.

Suggestions for Selecting
Additional Readings

A number of sources are cited here to which the instructor or student may turn if he wishes to find additional materials on subjects whose study he desires to pursue further than this text permits. The sources are classified according to (1) general and selected bibliographies, (2) governmental legislation and rulings, and (3) current magazine articles.

I. BIBLIOGRAPHICAL SELECTIONS

Excellent lists of readings, classified by subjects, may be found in the following:

1. BAKER, ALTON W. *Sources of Information on Personnel Management and Labor Relations.* Monograph No. 62. Bureau of Business Research, Ohio State University, Columbus 10, Ohio.
2. *Bibliography for Office Managers.* National Office Management Association, Lincoln-Liberty Bldg., Philadelphia 7, Pa. April, 1945. Also Supplements of April, 1946; April, 1947; and April, 1950.
3. SCOTT, CLOTHIER, and SPRIEGEL. *Personnel Management.* McGraw-Hill Book Co., Inc., New York, 1954.
4. WALTERS, J. E. *Personnel Relations.* Ronald Press, New York, 1945.
5. WATKINS, DODD, MCNAUGHTON, and PRASOW. *The Management of Personnel and Labor Relations.* McGraw-Hill Book Co., Inc., New York, 1950.
6. YODER, DALE. *Personnel Management and Industrial Relations.* 3d ed. Prentice-Hall, Inc., New York, 1948.

II. GOVERNMENTAL LEGISLATION AND RULINGS

To keep abreast of current legislation, judicial rulings, and interpretations and rulings of administrative bodies, the loose-leaf and reporter services of such organizations as the following are desirable:

1. Bureau of National Affairs, Inc.
   24th and N Streets, N.W.
   Washington 7, D.C.
2. Commerce Clearing House, Inc.
   Empire State Bldg.
   New York 1, N.Y.
3. Prentice-Hall, Inc.
   70 Fifth Ave.
   New York 11, N.Y.
4. Research Institute of America, Inc.
   292 Madison Ave.
   New York 17, N.Y.

III. CURRENT LITERATURE

Trade magazines and the learned journals carry innumerable articles of current interest in personnel management. The first one in the following list is a standard reference for magazine articles, while the remainder are a few of the more pertinent journals carrying personnel articles.

1. *Industrial Arts Index.* H. W. Wilson Co., 950–72 University Ave., New York 52, N.Y.
2. *Advanced Management.* Society for the Advancement of Management, 84 William St., New York 7, N.Y.
3. *Business Screen.* Business Screen Magazines, Inc., 150 East Superior St., Chicago 11, Ill.
4. *Factory Management and Maintenance.* McGraw-Hill Publishing Co., Inc., 330 W. 42nd St., New York 18, N.Y.
5. *International Labour Review.* International Labour Office, 3450 Drummond St., Montreal 25, Canada.
6. *Journal of Industrial Training.* American Society of Training Directors (Secretary-Treasurer, C. A. McBride), 5401 Hamilton Avenue, Cleveland 14, Ohio.
7. *Manage.* National Association of Foremen, 321 West First Street, Dayton 2, Ohio.
8. *Management Record.* National Industrial Conference Board, Inc., 247 Park Ave., New York, N.Y.
9. *Management Review.* American Management Association, 330 W. 42nd St., New York 18, N.Y.
10. *Dun's Review* and *Modern Industry.* 99 Church St., New York 8, N.Y.
11. *Modern Management.* Society for the Advancement of Management, 84 William St., New York 7, N.Y.
12. *Monthly Labor Review.* Bureau of Labor Statistics, U.S. Department of Labor, Washington 25, D.C.

13. *Personnel.* American Management Association, 330 W. 42nd St., New York 18, N.Y.

14. *Personnel Journal.* Personnel Research Foundation, 60 E. 42nd St., New York, N.Y.

15. *Sales Management.* Sales Management, Inc., 286 Fourth Ave., New York 16, N.Y.

16. *Sociology and Social Research.* University of Southern California, 3518 University Ave., Los Angeles 7, Calif.

17. *Social Research.* New School of Social Research, 66 W. 12th St., New York 11, N. Y.

Case Problems

The following case problems have been adapted from actual practice and are presented in relatively short form. (Of course, names used herein are fictitious.) It is strongly felt that more will be gained by full discussions and intensive analysis of brief case problems than by cursory study of extended descriptions. It may be noted, too, that, while it is often said that a short statement does not contain all of the facts about any case, the same can also be said about the long statement. The long statements, as users of such material can testify, are never long enough. Hence the cases given here have been digested to a point where the student can visualize an actual situation, yet do so without complaining that the cases require so much reading time that little time is left for critical analysis.

The order in which the cases are presented follows broadly the chapter outline of the text. A regular *plan* of problems, exclusive for each chapter, would be difficult to provide because the actual business world does not produce such neat arrangements. Hence the instructor should use his judgment in assigning problems and in interpreting the solutions in the light of his own standards of how much the students should be expected to cover and accomplish.

In regard to solutions to these problems, the author prefers to see what imagination and good sense each group of students can bring to bear upon the materials. However, it is recognized that the student will usually bring to the analysis of these cases what he has learned from his readings, classroom lectures, and discussions. In each instance, therefore, the instructor should be the best judge of the standards of comparison which he will apply in reading the submitted reports. The questions at the end of each case are merely suggestive; the instructor and student may well prepare and propound others.

Nor does the author have a rigid plan of assigning case problems. Sometimes few, and sometimes many, are assigned. This must always be a matter to be decided in the light of particular conditions. It is felt, however, that problems should not be assigned merely to keep students busy; a problem should be assigned only when it serves a definite objective in the instructor's plan of advancing the student's knowledge and critical powers.

CASE 1. NATIONALITY GROUPS

The Steel Foundry and Machine Company, located in a large eastern city, does job work in iron and steel for the other industries in the city. The firm started a "flying-squadron" type of training program for its young executives. From unfortunate past experience, the personnel director of the firm found that the college graduates they employed were quick to learn but ignorant as to the operation of this type of plant. When such men were placed in executive positions, they failed to do as good a job as was expected of them, owing to their lack of experience and understanding. It was for this reason that any inexperienced college graduate employed was sent on a six months' training program throughout the plant.

The "flying-squadron" training idea was a good one; but in actual practice it ran into some real difficulties, particularly in the foundry department of the plant. The foundry department employed Polish workers exclusively. The plant happened to be in a Polish section of the city, and most of those who applied for foundry jobs were Polish. There was a strong racial feeling in the department; yet, as long as only Polish men were employed, the department operated efficiently. The workers did a fine job where physical labor was required; however, the educational background of the group was poor. Unfortunate past experiences had discouraged management's attempts to employ workers other than those of Polish descent.

The foreman in the foundry department was a good one. He was respected by the men and succeeded in getting the work done. The only objection that his superiors had was that he could not do the paper work involved with his job because he had had only a sixth-grade education. All his paper work was turned over to a secretary in another department. This was an inconvenient procedure, but the department seemed to operate efficiently under such an arrangement. The foreman was rather sensitive on this point because the other foremen in the plant did not need this additional help.

When the trainees were introduced into this department, they were met with a "cold shoulder" by both the workers and the foreman. The workers soon found out, from the trainees' actions and language, that the trainees did not consider themselves on the same social level as the workers. In addition, the fact that most of the trainees were not Polish increased the tension and mistrust between the workers and the trainees.

The trainees had difficulty in adapting themselves to the dust, heat, and hard manual labor of the foundry. The workers were not friendly, and the tight clique maintained by them was impossible for the trainees to break.

The foreman was suspicious that his superiors were trying to train one of these college graduates to take his job, owing to his inability to do the paper work involved. For this reason, the foreman succeeded in making it as hard as possible for the young men by giving them the most menial and dirty jobs.

Many of the trainees quit at this stage in the program. At first, the personnel director thought that he had found a way to eliminate the trainees who did not have the "intestinal fortitude" to finish the training program. However, it was not long thereafter before the personnel director discovered that these same men who quit were doing fine jobs in executive positions in other plants similar to the Steel Foundry and Machine Company. The personnel director then realized that his training program was at fault.

Since the foundry was one of the most important departments in the firm, the personnel director felt that the trainees should have an opportunity to work in it for a few weeks in order to be able to understand its operations and problems before being placed in an executive position elsewhere in the plant. On the other hand, he did not want to disturb the efficient operation of the foundry department by bringing in other workers to break the Polish clique, nor did he want to lose the foreman.

QUESTIONS AND PROBLEMS

1. Outline a plan which would serve to make the training program of the company effective. If you think this cannot be done with the present training program, what type of executive training program would you suggest? Outline your suggested plans.
2. Would you recommend breaking up the nationality front in the foundry? Explain.

CASE 2. PERSONNEL PHILOSOPHY

The Smith Woolen Mills produces woolen fabrics for automobile upholstery, overcoats, women's suits, blankets, and other uses. Rayon, cotton, nylon, and other synthetic fibers are sometimes incorporated with wool to produce the desired fabric characteristics. The firm receives virgin or secondhand wool supplies. To produce finished fabric or cloth, it then performs such processes as scouring, sorting, dyeing, picking, carding, spinning, weaving, carboning, and inspection. Some 1,500 workers are employed in the various departments. The firm was founded and operated initially by Mr. Smith. Later, in 1920, the firm became incorporated. The controlling stock was purchased by Mr. Smith and his family—thus the company became a "close corporation." In 1940 Mr. Smith retired from active management and his son, Jim Smith, became the general manager. At this time, a personnel department was established. A Mr. Rand, who had married Jane Smith (Jim Smith's sister), was appointed as the personnel director. He had quit college in his sophomore year in 1930 to work in the ragpicking department of the mill. Until 1940 Mr. Rand had continued in the rag department and had attained the position of foreman during this period.

During the war Mr. Rand, who was on a leave of absence from the mill, contracted a lung condition while serving in the Navy. Because of this condition, Mr. Rand, who returned to his personnel duties in 1946, was anxious to train someone who could take over his job in a few years. He hired a Mr. Jones, a high-school teacher, aged 35, as his assistant in March, 1946. Mr. Jones was immediately placed in charge of employment interviews. He used job description cards and his own opinion as the basis for hiring new employees. The personnel department comprised: Mr. Rand, Mr. Jones, and three secretaries.

In August of 1948, Mr. Rand interviewed a Mr. Robert Morris. Morris had received a Master's degree in personnel from a leading university and was seeking employment in personnel work. Mr. Rand told Mr. Morris that he was not satisfied with Jones. In October, Mr. Rand requested that Mr. Morris visit the mill (at the firm's expense) for further interviews. Mr. Morris was hired with the understanding that he would work through the mill as a textile technician. After acquainting himself with the various departments and their operations, job requirements, etc., he was to replace Mr. Jones. Mr. Rand explained to Mr. Morris that he should keep the nature of his assignment confidential so that neither the employees, foremen, nor Mr. Jones would know what was "in the wind."

Mr. Morris started to work on October 28, 1948, in the wool-receiving department. When the departmental foreman communicated to Mr. Rand that he thought that Mr. Morris was prepared to enter another unit, Mr. Rand conducted Mr. Morris to another department, introduced him to the new foreman as a textile technician trainee, and requested that he be given a chance to work on all jobs in the department.

Except for these "new department introductions," Mr. Morris saw little of Mr. Rand during his first three months of employment. Mr. Morris seemed to get along well with other employees and received good recommendations from the foreman. On January 10, 1949, Mr. Morris went to Mr. Rand's office after working hours. The following discussion ensued.

MORRIS: I dropped by to tell you that the men in the ragpicking department are dissatisfied. They believe that a new water cooler for their department has been in storage for several months. Also, many of the old hands complain because they say that other mills in this area pay twenty cents an hour more for comparable work.

RAND: I don't know about the water cooler. I'll have to check on that. About wages—sure, these men can get twenty cents an hour more, but we have the only mill that can give them steady employment.

MORRIS: Perhaps a booklet or some company literature explaining these offsetting advantages would be desirable. Also a clear-cut statement of company policy.

RAND: I've thought about it, but we don't want to get all tied up in policies. We're far more flexible this way. Anyway, these men soon pick up rules and company policy from other employees.

MORRIS: Speaking of policy, Mr. Rand, all of the employees smoke in the rest rooms, and yet they say it is against the rules. Wouldn't it create less friction to have regular smoking rooms and enforce the policy elsewhere—or abolish it?

RAND: Well, they know it's against the rules to smoke anywhere in the plant but, darn it, when they get caught they know what to expect. Well, Morris, what do you think of Smith Mills now?

MORRIS: Well, sir, I have every desire to become better acquainted with you and also to meet those members of management I don't know. You have an unusual degree of loyalty on the part of the executives I've met; they certainly have devoted all of their energies and the major portion of their interest to the mill. I think this is fine—I want to feel the same way.

RAND: You mean that you don't already? Why, from the first day that I started here I knew that there was nothing else for me. I even quit college to start. Of course, I want to get to know you better—how you think, your politics, and how you feel about unions. As you should know by now, we're going to fight them to the last man if they ever try to organize us.

MORRIS: No, I didn't know this, Mr. Rand. I came here with the impression that you wanted someone trained in personnel administration to help expand your department. I don't mean to imply that I expect to take over responsibilities here until I've received considerable training; but it would be difficult for me to fight unionism if it were voted in here.

RAND: This is quite a surprise, Morris. I thought that by this time you'd be more loyal. The stuff you get in school is all right to a certain point, but that's all. We're running this business to make money. Jones had a few too many ideas of his own as to how things should be run around here—that's one reason I'm getting rid of him.

MORRIS: To be frank, Mr. Rand, I'm not sure that Smith Mills is the place for me. I'll think this matter over very carefully and give you a definite answer within a week.

RAND: All right, Morris, I've had good reports on you. I'm sure that we can work this thing out.

Morris resigned one week later. Mr. Rand tried to talk him out of it by, telling him among other things, that it would be very difficult to find opportunities in personnel work elsewhere.

QUESTIONS AND PROBLEMS

1. Compare the "philosophies" of the various men.
2. What are your recommendations in this case? Why?
3. What is your suggestion on how to co-operate with "old-time" executives?

CASE 3. TIME-OFF PROBLEM

The City Railway Ticket Office is engaged in the selling and handling of ticket reservations. The personnel consists of two men, one woman, and Mr. Brown, the office manager, who is also the city ticket agent.

The working hours are from 8:30 A.M. to 5:30 P.M. daily, except on Saturday, when the office is closed at 3:00 P.M. However, Saturday is the busiest day of the week because of week-end traveling.

The young lady working the office is a popular girl, quite active socially, and a member of different clubs and societies. One evening this young lady was asked by a former classmate to take part in her wedding, which would take place on a Saturday in about two months. She accepted the invitation, and the next day asked Mr. Brown if she could have that Saturday off so that she could be in the wedding. He told her that he would have to take her request up with the chief city ticket agent, but also added that she probably would have nothing to worry about.

A few days prior to the day of the wedding the girl reminded Mr. Brown of her request. It so happened that he had forgotten all about it, and he reprimanded the girl for not reminding him of it sooner. Consequently, he was forced to take the girl's request immediately to the chief city ticket agent. The girl, not being accustomed to the harsh words used by Mr. Brown, began to feel very uneasy about the whole matter. Finally, she was granted the day off. After this incident, the office manager and the young lady have not been very friendly to one another.

A short time later, she was again asked to be in a Saturday morning wedding and again she accepted. This time, however, she said nothing to the office manager and simply took off work when the day arrived. She offered no explanation when she reported to work the following Monday. When questioned, she simply remained silent on the subject, and even went out of her way to avoid the other employees. She began to report late for work and became slipshod and indifferent toward her work.

QUESTIONS AND PROBLEMS

1. What would you do if you were sent in from the home office personnel division to straighten out the present state of affairs?
2. Should all companies have a policy concerning time off for such reasons as this one? Should it be promulgated?
3. What would your time-off policy be if you were the chief ticket agent?

CASE 4. ENFORCING POLICIES

In July, 1947, John Martin applied for a job as insurance underwriter at a large insurance company. He had had no previous experience in that line, but a battery of aptitude tests indicated that his chances for success on that job were high. Information on his employment questionnaire showed that he was a veteran, twenty-four years of age, who had completed two years of college and had had varied experience in retail selling as well as several office jobs. No attempt was made to get information about his early life or current private life.

The employment office passed him and sent him to the underwriter supervisor for acceptance. The supervisor approved him and sent him back to personnel, where he was instructed on company policies, rules, and procedures, and where he was told when to report for work.

After he became adjusted to the job, his work was satisfactory. He was extremely fast and efficient in his work but not very accurate. However, after working for a month, he started dating a girl in the department. This, as he well knew, was against the rules set up by the company. The company did not expect to prevent employee dating by this rule but did expect to reduce some of these distractions. In Martin's case, his supervisor knew of the romance but said nothing about it. But, as time progressed, the love affair did also; and the couple showed their affection openly. They exhibited their feeling not only during the lunch hour but also during office hours. Martin would leave his job several times during each working day to visit with her. It was at this point that the supervisor intervened. He said nothing to the girl but took Martin aside and reminded him of the rule concerning dating of employees.

When the supervisor warned him about neglecting his work to visit the girl, Martin became indignant saying that he was not neglecting his work and that he was getting out as much, if not more, work than any other underwriter.

The warning, however, served its purpose; and, if any more romancing occurred in the office, it was done when the supervisor was gone.

Martin became belligerent toward the supervisor. He did not openly disobey the supervisor but would not follow customary procedures in the performance of his work. Because Martin got his work done as well as any other underwriter, the supervisor said nothing to him about the breach of procedure.

This condition existed until June, 1948, when Martin and the girl announced their engagement. It was at this point that he showed open revolt when the supervisor reminded him of the policy that prevents two members of the same family from being employed by the company. Martin "blew up," releasing all his pent-up hostility and expounding on the worthlessness of policies in general and that one in particular. And while he was in the mood, he proceeded to "cuss out" the supervisor.

The supervisor, thus provoked, sent Martin to the personnel department with a "recommendation for discharge," charging him with poor quality work (this was partially true, but obviously not the immediate cause of dismissal). Later, after tempers had cooled down, the supervisor, Martin, and the personnel department made an arrangement whereby the case would be recorded as resignation by mutual consent. This was done in order to avoid prejudicing Martin's chances for getting a job elsewhere.

QUESTIONS AND PROBLEMS

1. What is your opinion of this company's policies relative to (*a*) dating and (*b*) not hiring both husband and wife?
2. When should the supervisor have stepped into the Martin case? How would he know when the couple was "falling in love"? Would he not be running a foolish risk very often if he interfered too soon?
3. Should a company change the reason for discharge, as was done in this case?

CASE 5.   ORGANIZATIONAL LINES

Jim Krall, seventeen years old, had quit school when he was in the tenth grade. He had worked at various jobs in different factories and for the government. Nine months previous to the present incident he had been hired by the Specialty Products Company.

The present case arose when Mr. A. B. Bonkey, president and general manager of the company, needed a man to make a special electrical oven to bake paint.

Howard Bowser, the superintendent of the light department, said that, since his force was working to full capacity, he could not spare anyone to build this oven.

Mr. Bonkey asked John House, superintendent of Plant No. 2, to send him a man who he thought was capable of doing some special electrical work. It so happened that Mr. House selected Jim Krall for this assignment and sent him to Mr. Bonkey. Plant No. 2, where oil burners were made out of sheet metal, was working on a short shift.

Bonkey told Jim that he need a special oven to bake paint and that he had been selected to build it. He then took Jim to Mr. Bowser, the superintendent of the light department.

Mr. Bowser showed Jim a couple of pencil sketches and explained to him that the oven was to be heated with light bulbs. Bowser then made out and gave Jim a bill of materials for the materials with which to build the oven.

Jim was then assigned a corner of an assembly room to work in. He was provided with a vise, pliers, knife, and other equipment and was told to start work on the following Monday.

What happened subsequently is perhaps best described in the following dialogue:

Monday, 10:00 A.M.

Jim went to Mr. Bonkey's office and asked if Mr. Bonkey had a minute.

MR. BONKEY: Yes, Jim, what do you wish to see me about?
JIM: Mr. Bonkey, I can't build the heating units with the wire furnished me if you expect them to work.
MR. BONKEY: What do you mean? What's the matter?
JIM: That wire is too brittle for one thing; and then another thing is, that wire won't carry the current.
MR. BONKEY: Why see me? See Howard about the wire, he's in charge of building the oven.

Jim left Mr. Bonkey's office and went to Mr. Bowser's office.

JIM: Mr. Bowser, you'll have to get me some better wire.
MR. BOWSER: What's the matter with the wire you have?
JIM: Too brittle and won't carry the current.
MR. BOWSER: Nonsense! Quit stalling, and get the job done. We need it.
JIM: O.K. You're the boss.

The rest of that day Jim proceeded to make the casings for the heating units.

Tuesday, 1:00 P.M.

Mr. Bonkey was passing through the shop, and went over to Jim's corner.

BONKEY: Jim, how are things coming along?
JIM: I'm coming along on the casings, Mr. Bonkey, but I won't promise anything on the wiring.
BONKEY: What did Howard say about the wire?
JIM: He said to go ahead with the wire I have.
BONKEY: Well, let me know when you're through here. I have another job I want you to do.
JIM: Yes sir, Mr. Bonkey, but I won't promise anything about the wire.

Thursday, 10:30 A.M.

Mr. Bowser went to Mr. Bonkey's office and told him that Jim had broken and wasted a lot of wire. He also said Jim was unnecessarily slow in getting the job done.

Mr. Bonkey called Jim on the intercommunication system, telling him to report immediately to his office.

BONKEY: Jim, Howard tells me you've wasted wire, and he says you're too slow.
JIM: Mr. Bonkey, sir, I told you that wire was too brittle and won't work.
BOWSER: What do you mean? I selected that wire and designed that oven.
JIM: I don't care who designed that oven. It won't work with that wire.
BOWSER: Are you saying that you are a better judge of that than I am?
JIM: I'm sorry, Mr. Bonkey, may I go back to Plant 2?
BONKEY: What makes you think that wire won't work, Jim?
JIM: I talked to a couple of electricians and they both said that that wire won't carry the current necessary. And, besides I can't work fast with that brittle wire.
BOWSER: I'll finish the job myself; it won't take me very long.
BONKEY: I did have another job up here for you, Jim, but you'll have to go back to the lower shop. Tell John (House) that I want to see him after lunch.
JIM: O.K., sir.

It was noon before Jim saw John House and was able to tell him that Mr. Bonkey wanted to see him.

JIM: Johnny, Mr. Bonkey wants you to see him after lunch. He told me to come back here and go to work.
JOHNNY: You through with your job up there already, Jim? I thought that job would take the rest of the week to finish.
JIM: No, that Bowser gave me wire that wouldn't work and was mad when I told Bonkey about it.

JOHNNY: Jim, someday you'll learn to do as the man says and let him take the blame if anything is wrong.

Thursday, 1:30 P.M.

Johnny House just arrived at Mr. Bonkey's office.

JOHNNY: You want to see me, Bonkey?
BONKEY: Yes, Johnny, come in. I want to ask you some questions.
JOHNNY: Is it about Jim, or something else?
BONKEY: How does Jim get along in your shop?
JOHNNY: He does his work all right, but he's hard to keep on one job.
BONKEY: Hard to keep on one job?
JOHNNY: Yes, he moves from one job to another when he feels like it.
BONKEY: Why didn't you let me know that before? I would have laid him off.
JOHNNY: Well, Bonkey, I'll tell you, it's like this: Jim takes time out for smoking when he feels like it, he changes his jobs when he feels like it, and he takes a day off when he feels like it; but he gets more done than the average worker. He can do any job in the shop; he does them all well. I don't want to lose him.
BONKEY: Well, Johnny, that's about all I wanted to know for now.

Mr. Bowser and another worker finished building the oven on Saturday; and, when they tested it, the wires burned out. The whole oven had to be rebuilt with larger, better wire the next week.

QUESTIONS AND PROBLEMS

1. In what respects did the several conversations fail to bring out the facts necessary for an executive to make a decision? Specifically, what facts are needed in each case?
2. Have organizational lines of communication been followed properly in all cases? What of the "open-door" policy that seemed to be in use here? Is it helpful or harmful?
3. Should an employee follow orders even when he knows that the results are bound to be unsatisfactory?
4. What is your opinion of an employee who is an excellent worker but takes liberties with rules and regulations?

CASE 6.   JOB REQUIREMENTS

This case concerns Ted Lyons who was laid off during the summer of 1948 by an electrical products manufacturer. He went to the State Employment Service and filed for unemployment compensation. He had received one week's compensation when the employment service sent him to the local branch office of the ABC Company, to be interviewed for a position as a stockman. The ABC Company, a home-equipment manufacturer, whose home office was in New York, had branches in principal cities throughout the country. The company handled all types of home equipment, from electrical appliances and silverware to rugs and mattresses.

Mr. Snyder, branch manager of the ABC Company, conducted the interview. He asked Ted a few questions and then told him the duties of the job. Ted was to work in the stockroom and issue merchandise to the salesmen who took orders by door-to-door stops. After they returned to the branch office, the salesmen would requisition merchandise from the stockroom and make their own deliveries. The larger items were shipped by truck.

Ted accepted the job and reported for work the next day. He waited for Mr. Snyder, who arrived about 10:00 A.M. Mr. Snyder took Ted to the stockroom for his training period and left Ted with the present stockman. The stockman informed Ted that he worked in the credit office and was just helping in the stockroom until a man could be hired. For about ten minutes he showed Ted where various items were stocked and how the requisitions for merchandise should be filled out. Then the man left saying, "You'll get along all right."

Ted started issuing stock to the salesmen. When he could not get an item, the men would get it for themselves. Mr. Snyder came in while several of the men were in the stockroom, and reprimanded Ted bitterly for allowing this. He also informed Ted of a new duty: to sweep all the floors, including the offices and empty the wastepaper baskets. Ted also was told to keep the stockroom neat.

Ted struggled through the first day, but the second proved no better. He was reprimanded this time for issuing irons, pop-up toasters, and other hard-to-get items. These were only to be given to those salesmen that Mr. Snyder called his "ace salesmen."

The ABC Company was having a summer sale on blankets. They came in six colors, but some of the shades were not as attractive as the others. When some of the men wanted white or light blue blankets, Ted was told to issue them as they came or he would be stuck with all of the bad colors. However, when this happened to Mr. Snyder's "Aces," he was told to issue to them what ever they wanted.

The third day Ted found himself very discouraged with his new job. As the day went on Mr. Snyder told him that he was to clean the rest rooms daily from this time forward. He told Mr. Snyder that he wasn't hired as a porter, and after a few days Ted quit.

He went back to the Employment Service and told them of his experiences at the ABC Company. A form was sent to Mr. Snyder, and he wrote back that Ted was informed of all phases of the job before being hired and for no apparent reason he voluntarily quit. Ted was refused further compensation by a reviewing board.

QUESTIONS AND PROBLEMS

1. Evaluate the decision of the reviewing board.
2. Should Ted have quit when he did or should he have gone to the Employment Service first?
3. Were job specifications impractical in this company with all its branches?
4. Appraise the personnel management skills of the manager.

CASE 7.   A TURNOVER PROBLEM

This problem occurred in a rather large manufacturing plant located in a large metropolitan area. The plant embraced many acres of buildings. The employees of this company were members of an independent union which bargained directly with the company. Seniority and merit rating were the factors considered in job promotions. This was done by a system called "job bidding." Whenever a vacancy occurred, the job in question was posted on the factory bulletin board, and employees interested in the vacancy applied in writing to the service department. The applicant with the most seniority was usually selected. However, the company had the prerogative of refusing an employee of greater seniority in favor of one with lesser service if it was deemed that the ability of the former did not meet the requirements established by the job. Under this system, it was very unusual for a new employee to begin on a "choice" job, because there were many who had a greater amount of seniority and were constantly alert for openings to better jobs.

The factory was composed of many departments, but the one concerned in this case was the plant protection department. This department operates 24 hours a day, 7 days a week. Patrolmen had a planned route to cover all floors in all buildings over the entire factory area. Although this was a job that required a good physical condition, because of the walking and climbing of steps, other skill demands were minor in character. Consequently, it was among the lower-paid groups.

This department experienced a turnover problem which was due, for the most part, to the low level of compensation. Added to this was the undesirable aspect of Saturday and Sunday work. When a new employee was hired, he received an orientation in factory plans and policies by the personnel department. In addition, he was given a talk by the department foreman and approximately a week of on-the-job training with a regular employee. This meant that the company paid one and one-half to two weeks' salary to each new employee in this department before regular work began.

This system seemed to function quite well in itself. However, after a month or two, the newly hired employees in this department might see on the bulletin board a job which was open in another department. The job in question could be in the lower classification of the department concerned, yet the rate range may be higher than that of a patrolman. Also, Saturday and Sunday work would not be involved. In most instances, patrolmen would bid on the job and often receive it.

This was constantly causing a shortage of personnel in the plant protection department. So the circle of hiring and training for this department went on without interruption. Moreover, the department was unable to function effectively because the turnover in personnel was not conducive to the amassing of experience necessary to cope with the various departmental problems that occur from time to time. In sum, the operating cost of the department was greater, whereas its effectiveness was lower, than it should have been.

QUESTIONS AND PROBLEMS

1. What suggestions do you have to offer that would help in solving this turnover problem?
2. Would added remuneration remove the objection to Saturday and Sunday work?
3. Should the company change its seniority and merit rating to avoid the turnover problem?

CASE 8.   ESTIMATING MANPOWER REQUIREMENTS

In a manufacturing company, at a given date, production schedules showed a load of work amounting to approximately 50,000 man-hours as measured in direct labor. Shortly thereafter, an additional 20,000 man-hours of work were received, and delivery promises were made by the sales department. The step-up in production required many additional workers to meet the delivery dates. It was some two weeks later, however, before the plant superintendent was notified. Moreover, another two days passed before the superintendent notified the personnel department that an additional 35 new employees would be required. Most of the men that had to be hired fell into semiskilled and skilled classifications, such as welders, machinists, assemblers, burners, and some general laborers.

At the moment skilled help was scarce in the labor market. As a result, the personnel department needed twice as much time as usual to fill the labor requisitions. In the meantime, the production line fell behind in its schedule. Shipping dates were already a week behind when the general manager called the plant superintendent to task, demanding to know why the deadlines were not being met. The superintendent blamed the personnel department. The personnel manager told the general manager that labor was scarce, and qualified workers could not be obtained in the limited time given him.

The general manager told Joe Mallon, the personnel manager, "We will have to sacrifice product quality and lower employee qualifications in order to meet production. We just cannot afford to let down on this job. It means future orders." Joe Mallon did not agree that future orders would be received if the quality of the work was sacrificed, but soon he had the requisitions filled, and things returned to normal.

After the boom was over for awhile, the superintendent began to complain that he was stumbling over all the help in the plant. Less than a week later he told the personnel department to lay off 25 men at 4:30 that afternoon. Mallon argued against this action, claiming that the men had been trained for the company's type of work, and, with labor getting tighter every day, they could not afford to lose them. But the superintendent replied that they had no promise of any job which would require more than a normal working force as far as he could see. He deemed it an excellent opportunity to cut costs.

So Joe Mallon checked each man out that evening, fully realizing that he would never get this same group of men back again. There were too many openings for these people elsewhere.

About 12 days later Joe Mallon answered his phone to hear the superintendent say, "Joe, I hope you have been in touch with some of those men we had to lay off a few weeks ago; we're going to need all of them and more besides. There is a big job coming up for the plant next week. I'll send you a requisition."

Joe Mallon realized that something had to be done about the company's policy. The turnover was already up to a ridiculously high figure.

QUESTIONS AND PROBLEMS

1. Outline the course of action that Joe should pursue.
2. What could be done about the policy of management?
3. List the salient personnel management principles that should be used to convince management.

4. What effect would this layoff policy have on present employees and prospective employees?

CASE 9. A SELECTION PROBLEM

A meat-packing company had an opening for a foreman on the second shift in its orders department. The orders department was in a large refrigerated room. The operational set-up to fill orders was as follows: there were about eighteen "desks" or stands, each having a "desk man" and three to four "runners," that is, a carrier of items from stock to the "desks." Promotion from "runner" to "desk man" was on a seniority basis.

The foreman in this department was considered to be part of management. The job presented a good opportunity and increased base salary. However, the take-home salary discouraged eligible men from accepting the position. No overtime was paid to the foremen, whereas employees could make as much money as the foreman through added overtime. Coupled with this objection was the increase in responsibility and work for the foreman. After several men had turned down the offer, Roger Davis, an employee who had been with the company for over twenty-five years, accepted.

Davis was an earnest worker and a relatively good man, but he was rather a slow learner. He was trained for the foreman position and then returned to the department around July 1.

Many employees already had the idea that Davis was incompetent, and as far as they were concerned he was not the man for the job. This handicapped him in his work. In the following weeks there was virtually continual complaining by the men due to the many errors on the part of Davis. Many employees, even those with a long tenure, often talked of quitting. The employees finally decided to take action. This was done in the form of a "slow down," and only about 10 per cent of the usual number of orders were filled. Davis could do absolutely nothing, so he turned to his superior for help. Davis was told to stick with his work and to expect some trouble in his first few months as a foreman, to work hard, and the men would gradually come around to his way of thinking.

QUESTIONS AND PROBLEMS

1. Do you think that the men will "come around"?
2. How would you develop "sources of supply" of potential foremen?
3. Could it be possible that training was not adequate in this case?

CASE 10. A PLACEMENT PROBLEM

This problem occurred in the plant department of a Telephone Company. In the plant department there is an installation force consisting of installer groups, each having from fifteen to forty-five men, depending upon the size of the district. Each of these groups has a foreman in charge, who is directly responsible to the assistant district superintendent.

It is the duty of these groups to install house telephones, pay-telephone stations, key equipment, and other miscellaneous apparatus leased to subscribers by the equipment company.

Wages are dependent upon the length of service. Top salary is reached after eight years, if no "reprimands" or "stays" in salary occur during that time.

Advancement and higher schooling result from the individual employee's will to get ahead and other factors, such as past records of efficiency, neatness of work, compliance with company rules and regulations, and his personal appearance.

Installers must know how to meet the public and satisfy the subscriber. Company specifications must be met. Since the training of a telephone installer is expensive, the company suffers a considerable financial loss if the employee does not succeed.

The installations force in one city consists of a group of twenty men, the majority of whom are World War II veterans. All employees are well screened, interviewed, and tested before they are hired. However, in a concern as large as this, men are sometimes employed who do not meet the company standards.

Each man in the group is paired with another installer to make an installations team. They are "issued" a truck which they are to keep stocked with equipment and in an orderly arrangement as well as keeping the cab of the truck clean. The employee with the longer service is usually in charge of the vehicle. These two men must work as a team so as to fulfill the orders efficiently, safely, and in the shortest period of time, since every job is given a company rating.

The case in point developed when a veteran with more than three years of overseas duty in the Armored Infantry was employed in the installation group. Prior to his discharge from the service, this employee had spent six months in an Army mental hospital to overcome a neurosis developed in combat. Normally, he seemed a little above average in intelligence, but at times he lapsed into a gloom that permeated any individual or group that was forced to work with him. Because of the actions he had seen in the service he had developed a bitter attitude toward all men who had not seen similar front-line duty. In his brighter moments he was a good worker and measured up to standards. But when he lapsed into one of his depression periods the group's rating suffered.

None of the men wanted to work with him because he constantly needled them, asking if they were company men. He told them that they were sticking too close to the book of specifications.

The foreman did not know how to handle the situation. Should he fire this man? After all, the man could be a valuable asset to the company. It was known that he could do good work. He was sent to a psychiatrist without any success. The employee did not feel as if there was anything wrong with himself, and probably at the time he visited the physician, he was quite normal. However, at work he was the same as in the past.

QUESTIONS AND PROBLEMS

1. What action should the company take now?
2. What is the limit of the company's social responsibilities here?
3. Would it be desirable to give the employees who work with this veteran any special instructions? What might they be?

CASE 11. EMPLOYMENT OFFICE LOCATION

A company placed its employment section and personnel office in a one-story temporary structure behind the main plant. The building was known to all the plant personnel as "the Barn." Management was responsible for the name, since various executives were accustomed to speaking of "going out to the Barn," in connection with it.

In the "Barn" were the offices of the personnel manager and the employment manager. The employment section operated there. New applicants were interviewed for positions in the "Barn." The union sent its grievance committee to meet with management representatives there because management was glad to keep the committee out of the main office.

The grievance committe called the hard benches in the employment office "the bull pen" and made many insulting remarks about them. The grievance committee members would talk excitedly among themselves about difficulties that were bothering them. At the same time, job applicants were often present in the same room and could hear the complaints being aired while they were waiting for interviews.

The committee was frequently kept waiting for some time in the employment office. Often they became quite noisy, perhaps to show company officials that they wanted to be heard without so much delay. On one particular day, the committee was in the office, talking loudly as usual. The personnel director sent word to the union representatives to control the committee or have them "leave the 'Barn.'" He asked that they go back to work and wait to be called. But, evidently not hearing the instructions, they left the premises of the plant.

When the employees found that they had been "docked" for the day, they instituted a grievance through their union.

QUESTIONS AND PROBLEMS

1. If you had been an arbitrator called in to adjudicate the issue, what would your decision (and reasons) be?
2. Assume you were a consultant called in to suggest improvement. What improvements would you recommend, and how would you substantiate your recommendations?

CASE 12.   PLACEMENT, TRAINING, AND MOTIVATION

In 1944, the Mid-State Hotel Equipment Company was established by two brothers, James and Robert Roe. Both were successful wholesale salesmen. James took charge of the office, while Robert retained control of the sales department. Principally because of the clientele that Robert had built up in this area, the company expanded rapidly and soon attained a prominent position in the local trade. By the middle of 1945, the company employed three men in the shipping room, four girls in the office, and three salesmen. A large part of the sales of the Mid-State Hotel Equipment Company were composed of complete installations of equipment. These installations required considerable skill and experience. Robert found that it was almost impossible for him to lay out and control all of the installations the company was making. He therefore decided that it would be necessary for him to hire and train an assistant. On July 1, 1945, he placed the following advertisement in a local newspaper: "Wanted—a young man interested in a future as a skilled sales engineer. Will train. No experience necessary. Give full particulars. Write % Box 210."

Of the men who answered the advertisement, a man named William Axe interested Robert. Axe seemed to have the qualifications Robert desired. He was twenty-five years old, married, and a veteran. Before his induction into the Army Air Forces, he had been a casualty insurance salesman. While in the Air Corps, he served as a photographer. His letter was neat and well composed. Robert arranged for an interview.

Mr. Axe arrived at the appointed time. After a brief discussion of Mr. Axe's qualifications and the job, Robert started to describe the opportunities the position offered:

ROBERT: Laying out an installation is a skilled job, Mr. Axe. It requires hard work, experience, knowledge of the equipment, and, most important, a lot of ingenuity. Now, I think that you have the basic stuff. If you're interested in the field, I can give you the necessary training.

MR. AXE: It sounds very interesting, Mr. Roe. I've always been able to learn quickly, and I think I'll be able to catch on without too much trouble.

ROBERT: Well, there's a real future here. There are so many people trying to do this work who don't know what's going on, that a good man who knows his stuff is really appreciated. Why, look at me! I have so many installations here that I can't handle them all myself. That's why I need a good young man to help me. This organization has grown rapidly, and it's going to keep right on growing. I've got to get someone in now—someone who can grow right with the company. After all, I'm not so young any more; and I can't keep up this pace. I'm going to have to take it a little easier in the future. Well, how does it sound, Mr. Axe?

MR. AXE: It sounds very good to me, Mr. Roe. I think there's a lot to be learned, and I'm pretty sure I can handle it. I've always wanted the chance to start with a young company and grow with it. This sounds pretty good to me.

ROBERT: Well, then, I guess it's settled. Be here around 8:30 Monday morning, and you can start right in.

MR. AXE: Thank you very much, Mr. Roe. I'll see you Monday.

On Monday, Axe reported for work. His first assignment was helping with sales on the display floor. As Robert told him, "The first thing you have to do is get some idea of what the equipment is like. If you aren't busy selling, I want you to spend your time reading and studying some catalogs."

For several days, Axe had a great deal of trouble, since he did not know the names, uses, or even the location of the merchandise on the display floor. However, gradually, he began to "find his way around."

On Saturday, Axe received his first pay check for $39. Immediately he went to see Mr. Roe.

MR. AXE: Look, Mr. Roe, I know we didn't talk very much about salary, and that's a fault of my own; but I can't support my family on this! I can't work for $39 a week.

MR. ROE: I'm very sorry, but I thought you understood that this is an on-the-job training setup. Now, your forms are all in at the VA; and within a month or two, you'll start getting a check from them.

MR. AXE: Well, I didn't understand, and I don't see how I'm going to be able to manage until they come through.

MR. ROE: Well, I'll tell you what we'll do. Suppose we have the company loan you, say $50 a month until the VA comes through. When their first check comes, you can pay us back. All right?

MR. AXE: Well, that's O.K. I guess there isn't anything else better to do.

That afternoon, Robert spent two hours and more with Mr. Axe, explaining the various classes of merchandise sold by the company. Mr. Axe listened intently, and this talk seemed to rekindle his enthusiasm. For the next two weeks Axe continued to work in the display room and continued to have informal talks with Mr. Robert Roe on Saturdays. At the end of this time, Robert asked him to help temporarily with stock control. Axe worked at this job for approximately two weeks. Throughout this period, Axe's enthusiasm and interest seemed to be lagging. Nor was Robert very happy with his progress. As Robert said to his brother, "I don't know what's wrong with Bill. He just doesn't seem to use his common sense, and then he's wasting a lot of time talking to the office help. I'm going to start him working with me. Maybe he'll straighten out then."

Thereafter, Axe began to work with Robert. He sometimes accompanied him on calls to customers. He redrew layouts to Robert's specifications. At first, Axe seemed to enjoy his work very much. Shortly thereafter, the Saturday afternoon talks had to be dropped because a number of important installations were pending and Robert was kept very busy. About this time, too, Robert went to Chicago to attend a convention. He left Axe to "look after things." During the three days Robert was gone, Axe spent a good deal of time out of the office, supposedly at one of the company's installations. When Robert returned, Axe approached him and said, "Look Mr. Roe, I know that you aren't very happy with the way I've worked out on this job. Frankly, I'm not very happy either. Why don't we just call it quits?" Robert did not urge him to stay.

On the following Saturday, Mr. Axe quit.

QUESTIONS AND PROBLEMS

1. Could the outcome case have been prevented? How?
2. Would you, if you were Robert, try to get Axe to change his mind about quitting? Remember your "investment" in him.
3. What has been done, if Axe quits, to prevent a recurrence? What should be done?

CASE 13.   TESTING SUPERVISORS

A company is experimenting with tests to be given to office supervisors with the hope of obtaining measures that may prove valid in predicting successful and unsuccessful supervisors. One of its tests, now in its initial stages of validation, consists in part of several examples of personal problems that arise in office situations. Each example is accompanied by a series of statements, and the testee indicates the degree to which he agrees or disagrees with each of the statements.

The personal problem described below is taken from the test and is intended to be a typical example of the effect of unsatisfactory home conditions upon a worker's output, attitude, and morale.

Jim Lake, seventeen-year-old copy boy for the *Daily Tribune,* reached for the outgoing mail on the desk of Mr. Wilson, business manager for the *Tribune.* Just as Jim was about to leave the room, he paused, turned to Mr. Wilson, and said he wished to be transferred to another job. Mr. Wilson asked Jim why; and, after much hesitation, Jim told Mr. Wilson that he was constantly having trouble with his girl friend who did nothing but "nag" at him, telling him he was lazy and good for nothing and joking about his being a mere "office stooge." Mr. Wilson discovered, through the course of the conversation, that what Jim Lake really wanted was a job with more responsibility. Mr. Wilson told Jim that, although he was sorry about his home conditions, his recent work had not been too satisfactory and he had better be contented with his present status.

The supervisors taking this test were rated by their department heads as "satisfactory" or "very satisfactory." After the results of these two groups were tabulated, it was found that 58 per cent of both groups disagreed with Mr. Wilson's solution to the problem. Of various alternative solutions open to the supervisors, the majority of supervisors agreed that Mr. Wilson should have had a man-to-man conference with Jim Lake and explained to him the importance of his present job, since this would have tended to make Jim more satisfied with his position. Both groups agreed that, as in Jim's case, a worker is often justified in blaming his home conditions for unsatisfactory work; however, they felt that this alone does not merit a worker a better position.

The supervisors who were rated "very satisfactory" strongly indicated that they felt Mr. Wilson should have discussed Jim's personal problems with him. In fact, 95 per cent of these supervisors felt that the only real solution to this problem is to take a personal interest in the home problems of the worker and discuss these problems with the worker.

Sixteen per cent of the supervisors who were rated "satisfactory" stated that they would keep their office clear of employees' personal problems, since it is difficult to maintain respect and authority if the relationship becomes too personal. They would refer all employees with personal problems to the personnel office.

Many of the supervisors felt that, had Mr. Wilson talked over the problem with Jim Lake's girl friend, Jim's home conditions, as well as his work on the job, would have improved.

None of the supervisors agreed with the suggested solution that an employee with unsatisfactory home conditions is likely to become dissatisfied and should be gotten rid of as soon as possible.

The results described above were obtained from a sample of only forty supervisors, and further validation is in the offing.

QUESTIONS AND PROBLEMS

1. What usefulness would you expect from tests of this type?
2. Do you find any validity in the sample test?
3. Would you include such tests in a selection procedure? Where and how?

CASE 14. A PLACEMENT TEST

The following took place in a large office of a war plant. It concerned a girl who was hired to work in the accounting department. The girls in this department worked in groups. Each group of six girls was responsible to an assistant supervisor and a head supervisor of the department. Each girl was given an opportunity to prove she was capable of handling the job in other ways.

When this girl was hired, she was given the same opportunities as any other girl. The senior clerk explained the work to her, but she paid little attention to his instructions. Her work in the next few days showed the same attitude, with no improvement whatsoever.

The senior clerk was compelled to tell the assistant supervisor of the girl's indifference. The assistant supervisor had the girl work immediately under him, thinking this would help. But it was to no avail.

To give the girl a third opportunity, she was interviewed for another department where skill requirements were lower. This was to be a last resort. But after careful consideration she was refused the transfer.

The personnel department thought that everything had been done to help the girl. It came to the conclusion that the girl lacked education and ability for office work, so there was no alternative but to discharge her.

QUESTIONS AND PROBLEMS

1. Do you think the personnel department made the correct decision in discharging the girl?
2. Does this give evidence of a poor selection job?

3. Could this be a case of blind reliance on aptitude tests bringing unsatisfactory results?
4. What motivational tools were used? Were not used?

CASE 15. WHO GETS THE JOB?

This case involves a problem of promotion in which two qualified and able men are considered for the job. The job is that of department head of a governmental agency, which has the responsibility for the administration of the supply and procurement of coal.

The job has the following general duties:

1. Computing requirements for coal for governmental agencies
2. Initiating procurement action for all coal purchases
3. Preparation of the coal budget
4. Supervision over the expending of government funds for coal
5. Arranging transportation for coal
6. Maintaining supply records and stock control over coal supplies
7. Initiating conservation measures in the use of coal
8. Supervision of a working force of about thirty employees
9. Frequent attendance at conferences in respect to coal policies and coal supply as a representative of the department and the government

A policy of promotion from within was usually followed, but applications were accepted of all who felt qualified to handle the job and who at the same time appeared to possess the necessary qualifications. After careful consideration and review of all applications by the personnel branch, the list of names was reduced to two, Mr. Joe Blow and Mr. John Doe. Mr. Blow was currently the chief of a major unit in the coal department and Mr. Doe was a technical consultant to the department chief.

Following are the background and qualifications of the two men:

1. Mr. Blow has been employed by the government for twelve years and has been very much interested in getting a promotion to a higher grade. He has just purchased a new home and has a family of five children to support. The additional money would help him in paying for his home and to maintain a moderate standard of living for his family. He is forty years of age and expects to work until retirement age. A promotion would increase his retirement income, which makes him all the more eager to have the higher-paying job.

Mr. Blow belong to a religious "minority" group. He has worked his way through college and went on to earn a Master's degree in Business Administration. In 1935, he accepted a job with the government in order to take advantage of the security and retirement benefits it offers.

He started his career in the same department as a clerk and has worked himself up to his present position.

After several years of experience in this department he became an expert in the supply of coal for the government and, during the war, was of valuable assistance in establishing procedures and initiating policy for the supply of coal. He spent long hours in his office without extra pay in order to accomplish his work.

His supervisors regard him as a very capable man. Oftentimes he is consulted by other agencies on coal problems and helps them to make policy decisions that affect the government. His co-workers respect his ability, admire his efficiency, and enjoy working for him. His department chief has often told him that he would be considered for promotion at the first available opportunity.

Mr. Blow has one shortcoming, which is that of excessive talking over minor detail and the use of flowery language. Whenever he explains something, it takes excessive time to get to the salient points of the conversation because of the unnecessary explanation of detail. He has been cautioned about this trait, but to little avail. His work required that he frequently attend important conferences, but it was necessary to relieve him of this duty because the conferrees complained of his wasting time by arguing over minor details. His intimate knowledge of coal supply is still respected, but he must submit his opinions in memorandum form.

2. Mr. Doe is approximately upon the same plane of government service, although he is a consultant rather than a supervising executive. He is about forty-five years of age and has no children. He enjoys his work and desires to stay on in the government service in order to take advantage of retirement benefits.

Mr. Doe is a graduate mining engineer and has about twenty years' experience with private coal firms. He has held various jobs in industry, both technical and administrative.

During the war, he volunteered his services to the government and was accepted as an expert in the coal industry.

As a technical consultant, he also attended many conferences and is noted for giving clear, concise, and exact reports. He is well liked and respected by higher officials, and his superior rated him as a key man of the organization.

If Mr. Doe is turned down for the job, he will remain with the agency for an additional year and then return to a job with a private coal company. It will be very difficult to find a replacement for him, but his services will be available during the transition and reorganization period.

If Mr. Blow is turned down, he might think that he is being discriminated against because of his religion, that he is not being rewarded for the additional work he did without pay during the war, and that his long and loyal service is not appreciated.

QUESTIONS AND PROBLEMS

1. In terms of the available information, which man would you select? Why?
2. Is there any other information that you feel is needed for a correct decision? What is it, and how would you get it?
3. Is there anything that could be done to induce the rejected candidate to stay with the agency?

CASE 16.   MERIT RATINGS

Persons Involved

Mr. A. B. SWAN.........Vice-president in charge of manufacturing
Mr. J. O. SEALS............................Personnel manager
BILL.................................Spot welder, Dept. A-36
JOE..................................Spot welder, Dept. A-36
Mr. WILLIAM MARLON...................Industrial consultant

The Situation

The Bland Manufacturing Company, located in Wheatfield, a small Midwestern city, recently instituted a system of paying hourly rated employees on the basis of merit-rating scores. The objectives of the plan are as follows:

1. Eliminate unwarranted inequalities in pay
2. Provide information for transfers, promotion, layoffs, and dismissals
3. Indicate potential promotion possibilities
4. Develop and increase a sense of fairness and impartiality on the part of the supervisors
5. Stimulate interest in self-improvement on the part of the employees

The vice-president in charge of manufacturing, Mr. Swan, had been sold on the idea of the plan at a convention. Upon his return from the meeting, he decided to put the plan into effect at once because he felt certain that the plan would prove to the employees that the company was stressing fairness in its administration of wages. He also felt that it would minimize haggling over wage disputes as well as encourage workers to do their best.

Mr. Swan and Mr. Seals talked over the program and decided that the best thing to do at the outset would be to publicize the program so that every employee would know its purposes. Moreover, they decided to "sell" the union on the idea by stressing the fact that no one would receive less than he was getting at the start of the merit-rating program. Mr. Swan and Mr. Seals further decided that:

1. A rating sheet utilizing the following factors would be used:
   a) Quantity of work
   b) Quality of work
   c) Dependability
   d) Versatility
   e) Co-operation
   f) Use of machines, tools, and materials
2. The foreman must be convinced that they are the key to the success of the plan.
3. Fairness must be the test at all stages in the operation of the plan.
4. Ratings would be made once every three months to get the base rate for each employee for the next three months.
5. Employees would be permitted to talk to their foreman about their ratings. The foreman would point out good and bad points of the rates.

A year before, all jobs had been rated under a job evaluation plan. It was decided, therefore, to divide the rate range for each job into five divisions. The merit rating for each employer would then determine into which division of his rate range he would be assigned for the forthcoming period. Thus the division or group assignment would be made as follows:

Group	Merit Ratings
1	91 to 100
2	81 and under 91
3	71 and under 81
4	61 and under 71
5	60 and below

How this worked may be seen in the case of an engine lathe operator, grade A. This job had been rated with a range from $1.40 to $1.60 an hour.

The following method for setting daywork, or base rates, in terms of employee ratings as illustrated by the engine lathe operator, grade A, is to be followed.

1. Any group 1 employee should be entitled to receive the maximum rate specified for that job. In the case of the engine lathe operator, grade A, this would be $1.60 an hour.
2. Any group 2 employee should be entitled to receive three-fourths of the difference between the maximum and minimum rates in the rate range. Thus, a group 2 man on the grade A engine lathe job would then be entitled to $1.55 an hour.
3. Any group 3 employee should be entitled to receive one-half of the difference in the spread. For the lathe operator this would be $1.50.
4. Any group 4 employee should be entitled to receive one-fourth of the difference in the spread. For the lathe operator this would be $1.45 an hour.

5. Any group 5 employee would be entitled to receive only the minimum rate specified for the job. For the lathe operator this would be $1.40 an hour.

The plan went into effect on January 1, 1948. The first rating of employees was to be made on April 1, to go into effect on April 15. On March 22, Mr. Seals called the foremen into his office and had a short conference. "Gentlemen," he said, "we have to get your ratings to coincide for the same type of men in the various departments. In other words, it is just as important to secure consistency in employee rating between departments as it is in job rating. A group 1 man in one department should mean the same thing as in another." Mr. Seals went on to add that, if discrepancies developed between departments and individuals within departments, the whole plan might have to be scrapped.

A couple of weeks after the employers had been rated and their base rates re-established, trouble began to brew. For example, the following conversation between two spot welders in Department A-36 were overheard by Mr. Swan.

SPOT WELDER BILL: Joe, did you know that most of the girls down in Department B-4 are making more dough than we are? Yeh, and the work is identical. Just who are they tryin' to kid with their new plan?

SPOT WELDER JOE: You're right. D'you know that we produce as much if not more than they? I know 'cause I checked with one of the inspectors that used to work down there. It must be those rating scales I've heard about.

BILL: I think you're right. The guys at my table are ready to walk out right now. The union or management had better do something about this or we go out after payday.

As a result, Mr. Swan called in William Marlon, the consultant. He was pretty well liked by the union and was known as a "square shooter."

Mr. Marlon studied the situation and submitted the following report to Mr. Swan:

Dear Mr. Swan:

In compliance with your request to investigate the variations of merit-rating scores between departments, I submit the following report.

I recommended that the steps listed below be taken:

a) Appoint the foreman and the assistant foreman in each department to fill out rating scales on all men in the department.

b) Train these foremen in the art of merit rating. A training program of an hour a day every other day for two weeks should suffice.

c) Have the foreman make up a summary of his ratings after he has rated every man. Have the foreman check all the quality ratings of his men to be sure he has been consistent in rating them all on quality. Then, have him check all the ratings on quantity on all the men. Do this for each of the remaining factors. The purpose of this is to help the foreman to be more consistent by considering the ratings for each factor on all of his men, thus checking his previous judgment when he rated each man on all the factors. Ratings by foremen should be reviewed and checked by the superintendent or industrial relations manager.

d) Each employee's rating should be kept confidential. Under no circumstances should one employee be shown another's rating.

e) Raters should not have access to previous ratings when rerating.

f) Plot the scores of each foreman and assistant foreman on the same graph for one department at a time.

g) Determine the average score for each department, and then plot the departments on another graph. Compare departmental curves to determine which are out of line and should be corrected.

h) Thus the equivalent groups will be in the same bracket, or nearly so. Since the rating procedure itself is not too accurate, the use of a more refined statistical procedure would accomplish very little.

i) It must be kept in mind that only departments of comparable functions and job requirements can be compared.

I would recommend that the merit-rating plan remain in effect. As each person concerned with rating the employees becomes more proficient, the value of the plan will become much more apparent.

WILLIAM MARLON

QUESTIONS AND PROBLEMS

1. What is your opinion of this plan of merit rating? Be specific.
2. In what respects did the company fail in establishing the plan?
3. What is your opinion of the consultant's report?

CASE 17.   APPRENTICESHIP PROGRAMS

In the Blank Company, a four-year training program exists for tool- and diemakers. Ordinarily this program rotates the apprentices at short intervals to various types of jobs so that they may acquire the various skills that will eventually be required of them.

Any interruptions or adverse changes in the rate of rotation would reduce the amount of knowledge and skill that otherwise could be acquired within the time period of this program.

However, slight production problems of a few weeks' or perhaps even a few months' duration would have no large effect on this program; but longer periods that necessitate maximum production (such as those in World War II) would decrease the development of the apprentices if the program were not properly controlled to meet such emergencies.

In the Blank Company during World War II, the supply of labor was short, as in many other war-production industries, with the majority of the machinery running at maximum capacity.

With its objective to increase production, the company retained apprentice tool- and diemakers on specialized types of jobs for extended periods of time; and, although the apprentices supposedly increased their skill on particular jobs through specialization, they did not acquire the diversified skills and knowledge for which the training program had been established.

QUESTIONS AND PROBLEMS

1. How could the company meet its objective in such emergency periods and, at the same time, protect its training program?
2. Would it be advisable to cancel such a training program for the duration of the high-production period? Why or why not?
3. Is it advisable to postpone such a training program during a severe depression? Give consideration to the interests of nontrainees as well as those of the company and the trainees.

CASE 18.   VACATION PERIODS

This problem is concerned with the employees of the mail department of a large steel concern. The positions in this department hold little room for prestige. In fact, the future, so far as advancement is concerned, is not too bright. Most of the work is routine but calls for accuracy in seeing that the mail reaches its destination and is received without delay. Mail service is important to the company, so efficient and economical operations are important.

To attain these objectives the company pays its mail room employees well and provides them with various privileges. The company also provides the mail room department manager with prerequisities, equivalent to other company executives of comparable level. This executive reports directly to the office manager, who in turn reports to the controller.

The office manager is "efficiency-minded." He is continually looking for better ways of doing things. Because of his approach to various problems in the past, the men of this mail department were not very favorably disposed toward him.

The head of the mail department has been with the company for a quarter of a century in the same capacity. He is efficient in his work, but, except for some supervision, his job could be performed by a mail boy. The next man in seniority, a bachelor, has been with the company for twenty years and is the driver of the mail truck. He is a likeable fellow but knows little beyond truck driving and following the schedule outlined for him. A third man has been with the company about fifteen years. He is married and is entirely dependent on his income; his only child has been ill since birth. Two other men have been with the company for fifteen years. Each is married, but neither has children.

All of these employees have worked solely with this one company. They know no other trade and fear to demand any privileges, lest they lose their current status. While job prestige is lacking for them, their long service with the company, favorable working conditions, and relatively satisfactory earnings have kept them working.

Recently a company-wide reduction in costs has affected them adversely. These men feel, however, that the office manager is being unfair to them despite their long service with the organization.

The pertinent facts are these. Although the office in general worked eigth hours, the mail room operates on a ten-hour day. This is necessary because the mail must be picked up, sorted, and distributed before the office workers come to work, and it must be collected and sent out after the office workers finish work. Before passage of the Fair Labor Standards Act, these mail room employees worked ten hours a day, five days a week, or a total of fifty hours a week. Although the extra ten hours was at straight time, it was an incentive to stay on the job. After the passage of this act, the men were placed on a forty-hour week, and a girl was hired to take care of the excess work that resulted from the reduction of hours. During World War II, however, the men were allowed fifty hours a week with full overtime allowances. For a number of years after the war, the privilege of earning overtime was continued.

In addition, these four men earned additional overtime sums during the vacations of each year. When one of the men was off, the others worked added overtime hours. The vacations were split so that each man took one week in the summer and one in the winter.

To reduce costs in the mail room, the office manager has initiated a policy whereby all the men in this department will take their two-week vacations in successive periods during the summer and a girl will be hired to fill in, thus reducing overtime costs. The savings expected are shown as follows:

	New Plan	Old Plan
Number of employees..........	5	4 (1 on vacation)
Earnings per week............	$50.00 ($1.25 per hour)	$68.75
Total cost per week..........	$250.00	$325.00 ($275 plus $50)
Hours per week..............	40	50
Total hours per week.........	200	200

The total cost of $325 when the one man is on vacation includes his paid-vacation salary. The weekly difference amounts to $75. With five men each taking two weeks' vacation, it means a gross saving of $750 to the company for the ten weeks the men are on vacation. If a girl is hired to fill in during this period, she would be paid $35 a week; in ten weeks she would earn $350. Thus, by doing away with the overtime by taking the vacations in succession for ten straight weeks, a net saving of $400 would result for this company.

However, the men resent this move. Besides losing their overtime pay, they lose the prestige of being able to take split vacations.

QUESTIONS AND PROBLEMS

1. What is your opinion of the projected move of the office manager?
2. Is there any way for providing opportunities for employees in such "blind alley" jobs?

CASE 19.   TRANSFERS AND PROMOTIONS

The A.B.C. Laboratories manufacture and market a complete line of pharmaceutical products. In addition, they operate a chemical manufacturing plant that produces many chemical intermediates used in compounding various medicinal products.

The company has been in business for fifty years, during which time it has gained a national reputation in its field. The company employs approximately five hundred persons and has a moderately strong company union. In promotions and transfers of employees, the union is always consulted before a decision is reached.

The company, in promoting an assistant supervisor to a major supervisor, passed over John Tinker in favor of a younger man with less experience.

Tinker is forty-one, has only a grade-school education, and has been an employee of the company for twenty-two years. He has been an assistant supervisor in the production department for twelve years. He is a steady worker, dependable, slow, and deliberate, well respected in the company and the community. A year ago Tinker was given a trial as supervisor when the regular supervisor was on a month's sick leave, and his work left much to be desired. Because of his lack of formal education, he was unable to do the clerical work necessary to handle a supervisor's job.

The man finally selected for the promotion to supervisor was Bill Johnson, who is thirty-three, has two years of college, and has been employed by the company for fifteen years. He has been an assistant supervisor for eight years in the same department. He is exceptionally bright, has an unimpeachable record, gets along with everyone, and has made valuable contributions to the company.

The union has approved the promotion of Johnson, and the management informed him of his duties on the new job. However, the next day Tinker, hearing of the promotion, was very much disappointed because he did not receive the promotion. He immediately left his job and went to the personnel manager's office and threatened to quit. Because of his experience in the pharmaceutical business, he would be a difficult person to replace.

QUESTIONS AND PROBLEMS

1. How would you explain why he was not promoted, and prevent him from quitting?
2. In your judgment what mistakes were made by management?
3. Outline a possible approach the company can use in straightening out this problem now.
4. State how the situation should have been handled in the beginning.

CASE 20.   SENIORITY

This problem took place in an industrial firm in the Cincinnati area. The firm employed approximately two thousand people—fifteen hundred shop and five hundred office. Personnel consisted of both men and women in the shop and office. The problem concerned only those employees within the bargaining unit. The collective bargaining contract (with a CIO union) had specified that seniority was to be considered on a group-wide rather than a plant-wide or a departmental basis. This meant that, by mutual agreement, the company and the union had set up eight groups within the shop; each group consisted of from five to ten departments which had common characteristics and job interchangeability.

Any layoff was to be governed by seniority within the respective groups. When a layoff became necessary, the following problem was encountered.

Seniority lists had been prepared, from which it was decided that certain people in each group were to be laid off. However, it was discovered that there were four or five job classifications that were to be found in almost every group. These were porters, laborers, helper, and industrial truck operators. To lay off by group seniority meant laying off a porter in Department A with 5 years' service, while a porter in Department B had only 6 months' service. All this because Porter A in Department A was the only porter in that group and that group faced a small reduction. Porter B in Department B was safe because no reduction in his group was necessary. What could the personnel manager and the department foreman do to make a fair layoff of a porter? Transfers from one group to another were out of the question, because, according to the contract, any employee transferred from one group to another must be in his new group for one year before he could transfer his hiring date seniority with him.

QUESTIONS AND PROBLEMS

1. What could be done now to rectify this problem?
2. In what respect did the company fail in establishing the plan of seniority?
3. What should a company be completely sure of in promulgating their seniority system?
4. How would you incorporate merit rating along with seniority in this company?

CASE 21. RATES AND CLASSIFICATIONS

Jane Smith was employed in the central offices of the X Company during World War II in the sales department as secretary to the manager. She had come up through the ranks, starting at the bottom of the classification and working to the top. These classifications are as follows:

1. Junior typist
2. Senior typist
3. Junior stenographer
4. Senior stenographer
5. Secretary

Jane served as secretary for twenty-three months and then quit to marry an ex-G.I., who was attending a university in another city.

After his graduation, the couple moved to a city in which the X Company had a branch plant. Jane, now Mrs. John Brown, applied for employment. She was told that it was not the company's policy to hire married women in the front office, although she would be accepted in a factory office. In the latter, there were two jobs available—one as a billing typist in a large production department and another as a stenographer in the traffic department. She accepted the latter position. When her personnel cards were received in the traffic and shipping department several days later, she discovered that the actual classification of her job was that of a typist. Jane then went to the personnel director's office and explained her former ratings with the same company's central office, but the personnel director explained to her that in the factory offices there were only two classifications for women. One was that of a billing typist who operated only the billing machine and did some filing. The other was that of a typist who kept all departmental records, did all correspondence, and general office work. After this discussion with the personnel director, Jane decided to continue on with the job. At the end of three months, she had reached the top of the typist's pay bracket. The traffic manager complimented her on her efficiency, friendliness, and cooperativeness many times. He was happy to have Jane because in four months, before Jane took the job, three different girls had quit.

After two years of employment, Jane asked the traffic manager (for about the third time) if he could get her a better classification or a higher pay bracket because it had become discouraging working with the other girls in the office who were all receiving the same amount of pay without having comparable responsibilities. She had taken on many new duties as time had passed. He said that he would visit the works manager (his supervisor) and present her case. The works manager asked the traffic manager to submit a written report of the case and his recommendations.

The traffic manager submitted the following report:

In accordance with your request of this date, we are listing below the duties of Mrs. John Brown who is currently classified as a typist on an hourly job.

1. Dictation for department (five men) and composes many letters.
2. Typing
   Statistical
   Claims and follow-up letters
   Correspondence
   Routings and follow-up
   Personnel report
   Salary payroll
   Shipping schedule each day
   Daily car requirements
3. Filing
4. Opens and distributes mail for department
5. Reservations (hotel, in and out of town, rail and air)
   Consists of making reservation, arranging for pick-up having accounting department issue a check, checking rates, typing envelope for tickets, and delivering.
6. Picks up and distributes checks to supervisors
7. Corrects tariffs from supplements issued

8. Corrects back car shortage each day
9. Records (all involving employees)
Attendance (salary time statements and extended workweeks, and daily attendance of hourly employees)
Transfers and releases
Seniority, classifications, amount earned by each hourly employee
All increases
Floor check
Check overtime for each employee in department
Check gasoline used in the traffic department against receiving department's records
Compute and record all outbound weights
Records repair to company cars and trucks
Records periodic gradings

In view of the many duties performed by Mrs. Brown that an ordinary typist cannot do, we respectfully request she be placed on a salary basis or an hourly classification that has a higher maximum rate of pay.

We advise that Mrs. Brown's attendance on an hourly basis has been exceptional and believe that if she were placed on a salaried job her attendance would remain the same. Also the employee in question has the knowledge to perform to some extent various traffic functions such as tracing, expediting, and routing.

We suggest the following alternatives for your consideration:

1. Change the policy of classifying factory clerical workers. There is one girl in each factory office with much the same problem as that of Mrs. Brown. They are doing stenographers' jobs while they are classified as typists. If the policy were changed so as to set up a stenographic rating in the factory offices, this problem would be solved.
2. If the policy is to remain the same, the maximum rate of pay could be increased, which would give the supervisor of the department an opportunity to reward the deserving employees. The policy at present allows a thirty- and ninety-day automatic increase of five cents per hour, with a maximum of four five-cent merit increases. If the rate were raised to include payment for exceptional functions performed, it would serve the same purpose as putting in a stenographer's rating.
3. Lastly, if the policy is to remain as it is, I think Mrs. Brown's job could be put on a salary basis and be known as "clerk in charge of reservations," as long as making reservations for the local company's employees who go to other plants and those visiting the local plant take up about half of Mrs. Brown's time. I think this classification would be justified. She could still perform her other functions; or some may be dropped, and more traffic functions added.

Respectfully yours,
TRAFFIC MANAGER

QUESTIONS AND PROBLEMS

1. Which of the recommendations do you favor? Why? What are the objections to the others?

2. Are there any alternatives that the traffic manager overlooked?

3. What is your opinion of the policy toward married women?

CASE 22. FIRST-LINE SUPERVISION AND ORGANIZED LABOR

The Steel Products Company, operating in a small town, is divided into two plants, A and B. Both are line organizations, and each plant is in charge of a plant superintendent who reports to a production manager. Most production is that of special order.

The problem in this case culminated in a strike by the union against the company. It centers around the superintendent of Plant B, who shall be called "Mr. Smith."

Prior to the unionization of the two plants by a national union, Mr. Smith was assistant superintendent of Plant B and the leader of a movement which led to the formation of a company union. He was, and is, a man who believes strongly in fair and honest treatment of labor. He helped to organize the company union as a means of collective bargaining; and for three and one-half years, the union seemed to operate satisfactorily for all concerned.

During these years Mr. Smith worked on a lathe, side by side with the men he supervised. He handled the functions of transfer and layoff and passed upon the hiring of new workers. He has known, respected, and liked by all. He instructed new workers for Plant B. He handled grievances which were within his capacity. Disciplinary action, when needed, was taken by the production manager of both plants on advice of his superintendents.

During the course of these years, Mr. Smith became acting superintendent, owing to the ill health of the superintendent.

At the start of World War II, Plants A and B were organized by a national union. The vote in these two plants was very close because of the hard work of Mr. Smith and other members of the company union who were satisfied with the situation as it existed.

After the union had been certified as the legal bargaining agent, Mr. Smith tried to conduct the shop as he had done before. Mr. Smith had tried, in what he always called the "good old days," to lead his workers. He now found that he was no longer allowed to work at a machine, that the welders and machinists started to do things as they saw fit, and that production in the machine welding and assembly departments fell off. His attitude toward the union became one of negative leadership. When asked to solve a problem, he would do the job himself and in such a manner that it tended to ridicule the man who had asked for help.

An example of such an instance is worth citing. One of the welders made a remark that Mr. Smith was just "talking through his hat" if he thought he could weld eighty inches in thirty minutes. Mr. Smith heard about it through the grapevine and, when the opportunity arose, he did the job for an absent union man much quicker than the other welders.

This, of course, did not set well with the men and was evidence of Mr. Smith's opinion that he could do any job in the plant faster and as good as, if not better than, any union man. His ability to produce was undoubtedly the primary reason for his being made plant superintendent.

In another instance, the method of exercising leadership used by Mr. Smith was well illustrated. A union man who had been working on a rush order was absent. Mr. Smith received permission from the union to operate the machine of the absentee. He completed twice the amount of work that the union man usually did. This, of course, made the other union workers and the steward angry. When the sweeper came to clean up the shop the next day, he was told by the other workers not to sweep under Mr. Smith's machine. The sweeper followed their suggestion. Mr. Smith noticed this and asked the sweeper why he had not swept under his machine. The sweeper replied that Mr. Smith was not a union man; therefore, he was not supposed to sweep up his mess. Thereupon, Mr. Smith asked the sweeper who his boss was. He replied that it was Mr. Smith. Mr. Smith then told him to get a scoop shovel from the storage closet, which he did with much grumbling. When the sweeper returned with the shovel, Mr. Smith asked him what his job was; he replied that it was to sweep all the floor. Mr. Smith then went to his machine, shoveled the shavings all over the floor, and ordered the sweeper to sweep the floor.

After this incident, a feeling of unrest developed to a degree that the employees went out on strike. The strike was called for the announced purpose of gaining a general wage increase.

QUESTIONS AND PROBLEMS

1. What steps should have been taken, and by whom, to develop the necessary leadership qualities of Mr. Smith?
2. If the company union had been so successful, why did the outside union win out?
3. Would you have advised the formation of a personnel department in this case? If so, indicate the form of the structure. If not, how should personnel policies and programs be handled?
4. How would you have handled the case of the welding dare? The case of the sweeper?

CASE 23.   EDUCATING AN EXECUTIVE

This problem occurred in a supermarket which is a member of a large supermarket chain having branch offices and a number of stores in the Midwest. This supermarket employees approximately 20 full-time employees and 6 part-time employees.

This company offers excellent opportunities to promising young men in their organization. In the summer of 1953 the manager of this particular store was selected by the company to attend a midwestern university to study for a Master's degree in merchandising. This super-market did not have a co-manager so it was necessary for the company to transfer in a new manager.

The old manager left the store on September 5, but the new manager did not take up his duties until September 21. This left a two-week period for both to take their vacation but also left the store without a manager.

When the new manager arrived, he found the store in a deplorable condition. One wall had been replastered, the shelves were not stocked, and chaos in the working plan was apparent. The company had sent in trainee managers to do the ordering of the merchandise from the warehouse during the vacation period of the managers, and it seemed that they had overordered every item in the store. To make the situation worse, three of the summertime stock clerks had returned to school and were now working only part time. This depleted the work force and helped keep the shelves unstocked.

Business was extremely good during the following months of October and November. During this time, every week's gross income for the store was greater than in any week in the past. It took this period of two months before the manager was able to straighten out the poor stocking condition and the work force to handle the new influx of business.

The relationship of the manager toward the employees was poor from the start. The manager tried to be a high-pressure executive, always keeping everyone hurried and harried. He barked his orders, boomed his commands, and grew very irritated at the slightest delay in carrying them out. His unpleasing personality became the concern of everyone. He even lacked the common courtesy that one person will give to the next.

Many of the full-time employees have been with the company for several years, working for a number of managers. As might be expected, in their opinion of managers, this one rated lowest with them. They became increasingly dissatisfied with their work. Some left the company, while others just remained discontented and pursued each task disgruntledly. With all the employees suffering from the same attitude toward this man, the group morale was at a very low ebb.

The company conducts a store inventory every four weeks, which divides the year into thirteen periods rather than the usual twelve months. For the first two periods under the manager, shortages were found by the inventory. In the company three to four of these shortages out of thirteen periods is usually grounds for dismissal. This put the manager under extreme pressure and only made the situation at the store more acute. He put many restrictions on the employees for fear that part of the shortage could have been caused by shaving the prices on what other employees would purchase as well as what they might be shoplifting. All such changes just caused the already poor attitude of the employees to be lower than ever. This poor mood was the precipitating cause of constant friction among all of them.

Finally, after the third-period inventory was taken and found to be satisfactory, the manager became more friendly toward the employees. In fact, he seemed to be a companion. It was also about this time that the manager asked the head cashier what the employees thought of him. She told him just what he had been hearing and that he had three department heads that did not like him as a person or as a manager. Upon hearing this and also having the pressure reduced from the good inventory, there seemed to be a complete change in the man. He no longer hounded everyone to see that the work was done and that the employees were working as hard as possible. He stopped making cutting remarks and started giving consideration to the individual problems of the employees.

The change in the individual employee's attitude was immediately observed to be better. The change in the morale could be judged in comparing the man-hours of work per $100.00 intake. The company has a policy of so many man-hours of work per $100.00 intake, which is computed weekly by each store. For the first five months the new manager's hours for the store were far above what they should have been. But now the work is being done with company specifications on man-hours of work per $100.00 intake. The man-hours now are 40 to 50 less per week for the same volume of business.

It is now the seventh month with the new manager, and all the employees are well satisfied with their working conditions. They like to think back to see how things have changed and delight in realizing that they now feel more like working. And they think their production is higher.

QUESTIONS AND PROBLEMS

1. Is the new manager inherently a good manager or not? If he is, why didn't he show it in the first five months?
2. If you were the divisional manager, how would you have handled the induction of the new manager?
3. What do you think of the manager's method of finding out the attitude of employees toward him?

CASE 24.   THE FIVE-DAY WEEK

The principal in this case, John Williams, works for a large manufacturer of capital goods. He is a graduate engineer and has worked for the company for over three years. He is well liked and seems to be happy with the work he is doing. He has received an extensive training in all the major departments of the company. His present job is the beginning of an interesting career with almost unlimited chances for advancement.

This company is a very progressive company, providing many fringe benefits, such as medical care, low-cost cafeteria, recreational facilities, pension plan, performance dividends, and liberal vacations. The labor turnover indicates good employer relations.

But, even so, one day John went into his supervisor's office and told him that he was going to leave the company. This was quite a surprise to the supervisor, who regarded John as potentially one of his better men and had encouraged him in his work. The following discussion ensued.

SUPERVISOR: Why are you thinking of leaving? Are you dissatisfied with your work, your pay, or your advancement?

JOHN: No, I'm satisfied on that score, but I don't like to work on Saturday morning.

SUPERVISOR: What's wrong with working on Saturday morning?

JOHN: Well, there's a number of reasons. All of my friends have Saturday off, and when they plan picnics, golf games, and other things, my family is left out. My wife and my friends can't understand why I have to work. They always invite us to their social gatherings, and it has become embarrassing to refuse all the time. Besides, I just bought a new home, and it needs all sorts of minor improvements which I could do myself if I had the time. I'd even be willing to work a nine-hour day in order to make up those five hours. I just don't want more than a five-day scheduled workweek.

SUPERVISOR: Give me a few minutes to explain why we are working five and a half days instead of five. It started in the shop. As you know, this business requires some degree of skill in all its shop men. It is not a mass-production industry and the workers, instead of being trained for one repetitive operation, must be trained on the job for relatively long periods of time before they become producers. Many of our men are skilled machinists and mechanics, and we cannot hire and train enough people to meet the heavy demands of the defense load. Also, if it were possible to double the work force overnight—would it be advisable to do so with the possibility that some might have to be laid off in six or eight months? It is not possible, but if it were—would you recommend that we do it? To produce as much as possible with the work force available, we are working longer hours in the shop. Because of the work our department does, it is advisable for us to be available at least during the time the shop force is here. This same thing applies for other office personnel. As things return to normal we will, in all probability, go on a five-day week.

JOHN: I am not satisfied with the explanation; I still want a five-day week.

QUESTIONS AND PROBLEMS

1. Do you think the company should talk to John about his future and sell him on this until arriving at an equitable solution? Explain.
2. Should the company want to keep a man who is apparently as unco-operative as John?
3. Is this company's time policy in fault in any way, or does it conform good personnel principles?
4. Should this company attempt to find out whether this feeling is company-wide? How could this be done?

CASE 25. DOWNGRADING

Plant C is located in a town of about 13,000 population. It is the largest plant in town, employing about 2,000 workers. Its products are widely used in electrical equipment, both consumer and industrial.

The workers are mostly home-town native-born; a few are from surrounding villages and farms.

Because of the plant's reputation for fairness, labor troubles have been conspicuously absent. The UEW of the CIO, after several unsuccessful elections, finally succeeded in becoming the recognized bargaining agent; but the workers support their union apathetically.

Conditions in the plant are good in so far as accident prevention is concerned. However, owing to the nature of the product processing, much of the work is dirty (handling graphite, chemicals, oil, carbon, etc.), and working conditions are unhealthful.

The personnel program, in view of past successful employee relationships, has been relatively simple. Its more important parts include: high hourly wages and incentive rates, a forty-hour week, paid vacations, medical service, a retirement pension plan, an employee savings plan, annual picnics, and Christmas parties.

Plant C's hiring procedure consists of filling out an application blank, an interview by the personnel director, a physical examination, and the job assignment. There are no tests given, nor is there formal induction to the job.

The policy of Plant C concerning transfers and promotions is informal. Promotions have been made on the basis of seniority and recommendations by supervisors.

A check on the work of new employees is made periodically. The policy has been, if a worker receives an unfavorable report, to transfer or downgrade him and eventually, if his ratings continue unsatisfactory, to release him.

The problem here is to find a way to reduce the time and morale lost by transferring or downgrading a worker because of his unsuitability to a particular job.

A specific case of this sort is that of Edward Smith. Smith had worked previously in four different departments in seven months. In none of them did he get a rating better than "fair."

According to the information available from his application blank and interview record, the personnel director thought Smith should have done much better.

Yet Mr. O. L. Wade, Smith's present and fifth supervisor, reports that Smith is "soldiering" on the job, stepping out for frequent smokes, and indifferent in his attitude.

Wade called Smith into his office for a talk, his intention being to find out why Smith didn't work more effectively. The conversation, generally, was as follows:

WADE: Smith, how do you like the job you're on?
SMITH: Oh, it's all right.
WADE: Well, I've noticed you seem to have a lot of spare time on your hands. Seems you might put out a little more.
SMITH: I think I do as much as anyone else on that job.
WADE: You don't keep yourself very busy.
SMITH: There's nothing else to do; if you look at the charts, you'll see I carry out as many or more cans than the guy on the shift before me.
WADE: Well, let's see if we can't keep a little busier in the future.
SMITH: O.K. (*He leaves.*)

A review of Smith's application blank and work record revealed the following information:

Age: 20
Experience: None in factory, previously
Education: One year of college; studied art; couldn't afford to continue

Military status: 4-F; perforated ear drums
Days lost: None
Late to work: None
Accidents: None
Production record: Average
General characteristics: Quiet, slow-moving, defensive when talking with
                         superiors, lacks initiative

A review of job reports was as follows:

First job: Carbon cutting; broke in with "Old Harvey." Didn't make much
               effort on the job. Department supervisor asked to transfer him
               out.
Second job: Carting saggers; temporary during vacation period for regular
               man. Did the job all right.
Third job: Piecework in forcing department, traying carbons. Earned
               above-average hourly rate regularly. This job was a vacation
               fill-in, also.
Fourth job: Helper in mixing room; worked slowly.
Fifth job: Transferred to new C.W.S. plant as helper in calcining room,
               where he is presently employed.

The question arises as to where to send him now.

QUESTIONS AND PROBLEMS

1. Comment upon the interview between Mr. Wade and Smith.
2. From the available facts, is this a disciplinary case or one of placement? Why?
3. Does the personnel program seem to call for strengthening? Where and why?
4. Of what use are the job reports as written?
5. Why does the company keep Smith on the payroll?

CASE 26.   SPREADING THE WORK LOAD

This problem occurred in a plant employing approximately three
hundred people. Of the employees, seventy-five to one hundred were
skilled craftsmen, the balance being semiskilled craftsmen and regular
labor. Its working force was equally divided between male and female
employees. Its building was modern, with good locker facilities, a cafeteria, and other conveniences for the employees.

Wages paid to all employees, especially the skilled craftsmen, were
higher than the wages normally paid in the community where this plant
was located. This was due both to the high standards that the company
maintained in the manufacture of its product and the highly organized
craft union.

The company was largely family-owned, but a small percentage of the stock was held by a few of the employees. The plant was managed by a works manager and a superintendent of production, assisted by departmental foremen.

The union in the plant was a craft union, originally having only the highly skilled craftsmen as members. But a few years earlier, when outside unions tried to organize the semiskilled employees, the craftsmen union changed its rules and admitted all employees of the plant. This was done to keep other unions out. If the other unions had organized the semiskilled labor, having a majority of the employees, they could enforce their wishes over the smaller craft union. As it worked out, the skilled employees were in virtual control of the union.

The company had a very good record for steady business and regular employment even in the poorest times. So it was quite a surprise, a number of months before, when new orders ceased. Although back-log orders kept production running at the usual rate for three months, it became apparent that even these orders would soon be finished. The company desired to keep all its personnel active at least two or three days a week, both from a point of fairness and to cut to a minimum the loss of trained employees. Therefore, the company apportioned out the available work.

This apportionment worked out satisfactorily everywhere except in the press department and the screen department, as the work shortages were most acute in these departments.

The personnel of the press department was composed of the journeymen pressmen, three apprentices, feeders, helpers, and fly girls. In the screen department there were set-up men, the screen machine operators, and the laborers.

The press department, especially, had a high number of skilled craftsmen that could handle any job in either the press or the screen department. But the unskilled workers could not handle their jobs.

When the work shortage developed and the work was apportioned among the employees as planned, the skilled craftsmen complained about the arrangement. They felt that the less skilled classes should be laid off and the skilled men should take over their jobs. As they expressed it, no skilled men should be laid off as long as an unskilled employee was working. This would require the release of the lower-skilled worker so that only the more skilled would be working steadily. If this plan was carried out, the company stood to lose practically all of its laborers and many of the semiskilled workers, who were trained and experienced in their work. And when work loads increased, time would be lost in finding replacements, and training costs would have to be incurred.

The company further objected to the worker's complaint because it had been found in the past that skilled workers did not effectively handle these unskilled jobs. This was due to the purely mechanical nature of the jobs, on which success came only after repetition and experience. Also, some of the jobs were of an undesirable character and hence distasteful to the craftsmen.

To follow the suggestions of the craftsmen would cause loss of workers, lower production, lower quality, and increased costs. Moreover, the company would be in a poor competitive position to expand quickly when work loads increased.

The complaining craftsmen were informed of the foregoing conditions. They were asked to bear with the company and allow them to be fair to all the workers, as the company believed all would benefit by its plan. But the complaining craftsmen immediately submitted their grievance to the union. The union backed up the craftsmen's complaint at first, saying that the company should keep the skilled men working in preference to the unskilled employees. When the balance of the workers heard of this decision, they also complained to the union and to the management, for they were in favor of the company's apportionment plan.

During another conference between the union and the company, the union had not decided as yet which course it should follow, as its members were divided into two different groups. The company then informed the union that it would follow its original plan of apportioning the work, until or unless the union could submit a better plan satisfactory to all the workers and to the company.

QUESTIONS AND PROBLEMS

1. What do you think of the company's plan?
2. Should this policy of layoffs have been written into the original union contract?
3. Is the union or the company in the most difficult situation in your opinion? Explain.

CASE 27. A TIME PROBLEM

This case concerns a printing company established in 1905 by a group of union printers. These men planned to emphasize speed and quality of production.

After the company was organized, the president acted as supervisor until his death, whereupon his son became president. This young man, with modern ideas, immediately divided the plant into nine departments with a foreman at the head of each. These foremen were selected on tenure of service with the company. All of the departments in time began to function smoothly except for Department B.

Department B is supervised by a man of some twenty years' experience in this particular field. This department has increased its operations and now employs ten men on the day shift and six on the night shift. There is only one foreman, and he works on the day shift. All the employees for this department are hired by the foreman.

This is constant friction between the day and night shifts regarding the daily work quota and the handling of equipment. The men feel that a "night foreman" should be hired to help correct this situation. The foreman refuses to do so, fearing a loss of prestige and responsibility for himself.

At first, each of the two shifts overlapped, so that the foreman could leave a few sketchy instructions for the night shift. At present, the night shift begins half an hour after the day shift quits. The foreman uses the intervening period to lay out the night's work.

Each of the two shifts claims that it does the greater amount of work. Neither one will clean or adjust the machinery so that the next shift can begin with production immediately. As a result, each shift begins with a poor attitude and with much loss of production time. Furthermore, on the night shift work is done as each man feels like doing it, because there is no one to tell him whether or not production is on par with company standards. As a result, if the night shift turns out bad work, the day shift must rework it instead of starting on new work.

The company's periodic efficiency survey in each department shows that Department B is carrying overtime hours in excess of what "standards" show to be necessary. It also shows that waste is more than normal.

The men on both shifts claim that they are not properly instructed on doing the work. This, they claim, increases waste of time and material. There is no specific pattern or method used in the shop. Each of the journeymen have served a six-year apprenticeship, and, in addition, each has worked in a variety of shops in this city. Each realizes that all work in a given shop must follow a certain pattern if production is to increase. Since no method is established by the company, each man does the work his own way.

The foreman seems to resent any constructive thinking on the part of the men working under him. Any ideas or suggestions they present for improving conditions and procedures are completely ignored by him rather than being discussed with the front office or being given a trial. However, in a few weeks or months, the foreman will present some of these same ideas as his own and receive due credit from the executives.

This foreman believes that a man is hired to do a given job and there should be no credit given for exceptional work or any thanks given for personal contributions to the effectiveness of the organization. On the other hand, the foreman never misses the opportunity publicly to ridicule a man's mistakes. Because of his attitude, the department is averaging the loss of one man per month.

QUESTIONS AND PROBLEMS

1. What is your opinion concerning this company's working hours arrangement?
2. Can you outline a working schedule that would be an improvement over the existing one?
3. What would you do with the foreman in this department if you were the manager for this company? What help would you expect from the personnel manager?

CASE 28. WORK ASSIGNMENTS

Early in 1947, Harry Black and Ralph Rope applied for work at the Smith Manufacturing Company. During the course of the morning both were interviewed and given several tests. Both were rated about the same by the interviewer, and as a result both men were hired. Rope requested that he and Black be placed in the same department. He explained that the two had been close friends since their high-school days and would like to work together. The employment manager granted this request and placed them in the machine shop. The employment manager noted on the record that Rope's mechanical aptitude was slightly higher than Black's.

The men were sent to the machine shop and instructed to report to Sam Oldster, an old-line foreman. They eventually found their way to this department. Oldster said that he didn't need anybody but that, if they were sent over, he supposed he'd have to put them to work. By this time both Black and Rope were somewhat confused. However, they attributed their uneasiness to their newness in the company.

After grumbling a few more minutes, the foreman finally told Black to "come along" and placed him on a semiskilled job. His duties were to place a sheet of metal in a jig and bore a hole two inches from the side. This piece was later finished by Dick Roe, a skilled machinist, and attached to the finished product. The foreman instructed Black on how to turn the machine on and off, and how to place the metal in the jig.

The foreman then took Rope to the same machine; however, Rope's duties were to carry the sheet metal from Black to Dick Roe, the other operator. In addition, Rope was instructed to sweep up around the two machines at certain designated periods during the day.

Both Rope and Black were started at 90 cents an hour. Rope asked the foreman at the time if he couldn't have a different job, and Oldster said that he would have to wait and see what "turned up." He told Rope that it didn't make any difference since both he and Black were getting the same pay. Rope seemed to be satisfied and said nothing more about it.

Rope felt that his job was below his abilities, but he stuck with it and performed his tasks daily. However, he found that he could handle both of his duties in about half of the allotted time. Consequently, he spent his spare time talking and joking with the other operators.

Not long after Rope and Black were hired, the company was organized; and both men became union members. As a result of the contract that was signed, a general wage raise was granted. However, this raise was on an individual and not a blanket basis. In the case of Black and Rope, for example, Black was raised from 90 to 95 cents and Rope was raised from 90 to 92½ cents an hour. As a consequence, Rope reported to his foreman that he had the same amount of seniority as Black and felt that he should have the same raise; however, Oldster said that nothing could be done about it.

Because of Rope's conversations and horseplay, neither Black nor Rope could maintain their schedule; and the production records of both dropped off. Oldster warned Rope about interfering with the other workers, and Rope retorted that it wasn't his fault, since he was doing his work. Rope again asked the foreman for a better job, and Oldster again replied that he would see what he could do. However, Rope did not stop with this. He also went to his union representative and asked him to do something about the matter. The steward had other problems to deal with and forgot about Rope's request.

A short time later the company's business increased, and it began hiring new employees. One of the new workers was placed in the machine shop, and the foreman immediately placed him on a semiskilled job similar to Black's. When this happened, Rope came over to the foreman and the new employee and told them that the job rightfully belonged to him, and that he was going to take it. He then pushed the new worker away and started to take his place; at this, the foreman grabbed Rope's arm and tried to pull him away. Rope then turned and swung at the foreman and would have hit him, had the foreman not ducked. Oldster fired Rope as a result of this altercation.

When Black learned of this, he asked the foreman to reconsider; and, when he refused, Black quit. At this point, both Rope and Black called on the shop steward and explained the situation to him. After listening to their story, he suggested that all three go up and talk to the personnel director. This they did.

They told the story to the personnel director as it has been described above. He then called the foreman who corroborated the story with these exceptions: (*a*) He had spoken to Rope several times for loafing and for interfering with the other workers. (*b*) Rope had grown sullen after these instances and had made several caustic remarks about Oldster.

After talking with Oldster, the personnel director told the complainants that he would make a further investigation. He advised Black and Rope to go home and wait for the outcome.

Then the personnel director called the employment manager and asked for the men's records. After reviewing the records, he conferred with the employment manager and learned that the only reason the company required employment tests and records was that "it was the thing to do."

From the records, the personnel director learned that the native intelligence of both men was relatively high. Rope, particularly, had an active mind and a great deal of initiative. In high school he had participated in many activities and had varied interests.

The personnel director also had a conference with Dick Roe, the machinist. It was Roe's opinion that Rope had received a so-called "raw deal." After Rope and Oldster had tangled the first time, Roe had heard Oldster say that "he'd pin this kid's ears back."

QUESTIONS AND PROBLEMS

1. Were the assignments made correctly?
2. Could Rope claim that he was doing his work and not interfering with the efforts of Black and Jones?
3. To what extent are Oldster and the personnel department co-ordinating their efforts?
4. Is the personnel director very well acquainted with the work of his department?
5. What would your decision in this case be, and why?

CASE 29.   CONTRACT INTERPRETATION

The present case is concerned with a grievance filed by two truck drivers who claimed that their wages were incorrectly computed to their disadvantage. In support of their claim, they cite the following two clauses of their union agreement:

Article I: Layover shall commence following the fifteenth (15th) hour after the end of the run. If the driver is held over thereafter, he shall be guaranteed two (2) hours' pay in any event for layover time. If he is held over more than two (2) hours, he shall receive layover pay not to exceed eight (8) hours' pay in each twenty-four-(24)-hour period.

Article II: On breakdowns or impassable highways, drivers on all runs shall be paid the minimum hourly rate for all time spent on such delays, commencing with the first hour or fraction thereof, but not to exceed more than eight (8) hours out of each twenty-four-(24)-hour period, except that, when an employee is required to remain with his equipment during such breakdown or impassable highway, he shall be paid for all such delay time at the rate specified in this agreement.

The situation that brought about the grievance occurred as follows: On August 8, 1947, at 9:00 P.M. drivers A and B departed from the Cincinnati terminal of the X Y Z Company on a run to Cleveland. At 2:00 A.M., August 9, the drivers claim, such heavy fog was encountered in the vicinity of Columbus, Ohio, that they were forced to park along the highway until conditions had improved enough at 7:30 A.M. to permit them to continue on their trip. They arrived in Cleveland at 3:00 P.M., August 9.

On August 10 at 6:15 A.M., they departed from Cleveland on the return trip to Cincinnati. Upon reaching their home terminal, the drivers turned in time tickets claiming pay for the entire time en route, plus two hours' layover pay. When they received their pay, they saw that they had been paid neither for the time lost due to fog nor the layover pay. They immediately went to the employer, who told A and B that they were not entitled to that pay and would not receive it.

The drivers then reported the incident to the business agent of the local union, who the following day discussed the matter with the employer. The employer refused to alter the position he had taken.

The next step set forth in the grievance procedure is that "all complaints not settled shall be referred to an impartial arbitrator." This step was then taken.

The union contended here that, according to Articles I and II of the agreement, the drivers were entitled to the pay that they claimed. To strengthen their claim, it was asked that the employer submit the trip tickets for drivers A and B. These tickets showed that the aggrieved employees had been held in Cleveland fifteen and one-fourth hours.

To strengthen the claim further, the union submitted a report certified by the Weather Bureau. The report showed that surface weather conditions were such that traffic was slowed up and halted generally. Traveling conditions were hazardous.

The employer countered with two arguments. He contended that the drivers had been held in Cleveland the full fifteen hours as disciplinary action and had been so notified when they had arrived in Cleveland. This disciplinary action was taken because of the late arrival of drivers A and B.

The employer stated further that he refused to pay for time claimed for delay en route because "several other drivers traveled the same highway at approximately the same time and experienced no difficulties."

QUESTIONS AND PROBLEMS

1. In the light of the union agreement, the union's arguments, and the company's arguments, what would you decide if you were arbitrator? Why?
2. Would it be wise to define delays more accurately? Write a definition that would (a) make the company liable for drivers' wages, and (b) that would absolve the company under defined conditions.

CASE 30.   DEALING WITH UNIONS

This problem occurred in a frozen-food plant which employed approximately one hundred people, who were union members, in its meat-packing department. Production was on an incentive basis, and several times during the year in question new records were reached in production for this department. Management was pleased and decided to initiate a retroactive system of merit raises for those individuals responsible in large for the successful production results. The company house organ was used to announce the system of merit raises, and a special assembly was called to give a detailed explanation of the system to the employees. The employees welcomed the company's plan and expressed their complete approval.

However, the department steward and the factory steward, in their report on the system to the local officials, opposed it on the grounds that the company must first bargain with the union before granting merit raises to individuals. The local officials upheld them in their contention and at the next meeting with management argued the matter "pro and con," but without a settlement. The situation was next discussed at the meeting of the international association of the union, which resulted in the union restating their position. But management refused to capitulate and after discussing the problem with their associates, decided that the problem was one for the court to solve.

The U.S. Circuit Court of Appeals reviewed the case and decided that the company must bargain with the union on merit raises. The company then decided to take the matter to the Supreme Court with the request that it review and overturn the Circuit Court's decision. The Supreme Court denied the company's request, which had the effect of upholding the Circuit Court's decision.

The attorney for the company then asked the Supreme Court to reconsider its denial, with the plea that "to deny an employer the right to give individuals unsolicited pay increases plunges the poisoned dagger of collectivism into the heart of our system of economics." However, the Supreme Court refused for the second time to review the decision of the Court of Appeals.

Management instructed its legal counsel to drop the matter and began bargaining with the union for the merit raises. The company, in calculating the merit raises, felt justified in deducting the high litigation costs, with the result that extra amounts to be paid to the employees were reduced considerably. But since the original system of merit raises had received so much publicity in the house organ and in the special assembly, the new low rates were creating a poor attitude with the workers, resulting in a drop in current production.

QUESTIONS AND PROBLEMS

1. Evaluate management's relations with the union.
2. How does the ruling of the Circuit Court tie in with the National Labor Relations Act? Could such a "ruling" have been included in the union contract with the company?
3. What are the ethical and logical aspects of deducting litigation costs from the merit raises?
4. Outline the approach that management should have used in the beginning and show how such a procedure would have been better economically.

CASE 31.   MOTIVATION

This case concerns a young man who had worked part time for three years, and upon graduation from high school started full-time employment as head produce clerk in a supermarket which was a member of a large supermarket chain. His ability and effectiveness had been praised by both his store manager and his district manager. A very co-operative young man, he often did more than his job required. For these reasons he received pay raises and steady promotion until he was made head produce clerk. His personal qualifications made him a definite asset to the company.

John had enlisted in the Army and, after his discharge, had reapplied for his original job. He was interviewed by both the store manager and the district manager at the place of his previous employment. He was informed that, because he was not employed full time for more than six months as the produce manager, he had lost the title to his original position. This position was now held by another man of equal ability, who was to be transferred to another store. The district manager told him that if he would accept the job as stock clerk, with a reduction in salary from what he was previously earning, he would be promoted to his original job with an increase in salary within a month. John accepted the offer and returned to work.

When the month had passed, no change appeared, and John waited until another week had passed. Then he consulted the store manager regarding the proposed change. A week later, he was informed that the matter had been taken to the district manager and at present nothing could be done about the situation.

During the next month, John came persistently late for work. At first his tardiness was attributed to possible accident, but when it reoccurred, the store manager reprimanded him for it. In reply, John said, "Our closing time is six o'clock, but many a night I work until six-fifteen or six-thirty without pay because there is no provision for overtime. Therefore, I have the time due me."

John also refused to accommodate produce customers asking for service. The manager asked him about this and he replied, "My job title is stock clerk, not produce clerk, and the union contract stipulates that I perform my job title only."

After a week or so, John's title was transferred from stock clerk to produce clerk. He protested the transfer and objected to his union representative on the supposition that he would accept the transfer only if his job classification and wages were improved. The representative told him that nothing could be done to prevent such a transfer. However, after he held the produce job a month, he received an automatic time raise. From this time on his tardiness declined and a better attitude was noticeable.

This did not last long. In a few weeks the district manager let it be known that he and the store manager had rated and evaluated the employees. The store manager and district manager held a meeting in the stock room and discussed the ratings with the employees. John's rating was taken last, and he was told that he had the lowest rating in the store. John was quick to question such a rating, for he claimed he did his work well with a maximum efficiency, and often had done more than his job required. The district manager told him, "Before you entered the service we had great respect and hope for your future, but since you have returned, our impression of you has fallen." John replied, "Before I joined the Army my respect for you was also high, but since I returned my impression of you has fallen. What of your unkept promises? Since I believe that you had no intention, now or later, of fulfilling them, I wish to withdraw from employment in this company." The district manager accepted his withdrawal.

QUESTIONS AND PROBLEMS

1. What were some of the "mistakes" in personnel management made in this case? How should it have been handled?
2. Shouldn't employees understand that a company cannot keep all of its promises precisely as made? Conditions do change, and the future cannot be forecast exactly.
3. What opinion would other employees cultivate from the principles used by management?
4. How much weight should be given the personnel procedures involved and the man's attitude in considering why an able employee was lost from the company?

CASE 32.   THE DISCONTENTED SEWING MACHINE OPERATOR

The company involved in this case was part of a large corporation which had decentralized some of its "job-shop" operations. The job-shop company, located in a town with a population of about 8,000, employed approximately 190 people, mostly women. The work involved the handling of canvas goods. Approximately ninety women were sewers, who were located in three different rooms within the plant for better utilization of space and productive facilities. A recent contract of considerable size had forced the company to expand its complement; thus it was decided by management to hire twenty new employees and, in hiring, to limit the age group to between twenty and thirty. Management believed that business would remain steady enough so that the twenty could be kept as permanent employees, and they wanted young employees who could be trained in the company's methods. Of the twenty hired, ten were sewers. Average age of the sewers was forty-four before the ten new employees came into the shop.

This case is based on an incident that occurred shortly after the new people were hired, and it was the first complaint involving any of the new employees.

Mr. Smith had the job of "employee relations" in addition to other duties. Actually, he discharged all the functions of a recognized personnel director.

Miss Brown was a new employee (twenty-seven years old, recently divorced, and the mother of two children) who had been with the company only three months when she complained to her supervisor, Mr. White, that she did not like the work and thought she would quit. Mr. White, a man of limited background, asked her to "stop by" and see Mr. Smith before making a decision.

The First Meeting

SMITH: Come in, Miss Brown. Won't you sit down?

BROWN: Thank you, Mr. Smith. I hate to bother you because I know you are a busy man, but I'm thinking about quitting my job unless I can find out —reach some definite understanding with you.

SMITH: Well, what seems to be your problem, Miss Brown?

BROWN: Well, I sew more awnings than any of the other women, but I don't make as much money as a lot of them. I haven't any friends left in the shop, and I don't mind telling you that it is a very unpleasant situation.

SMITH: Could you be a little more definite, Miss Brown? We have established the work in your shop on a piecework basis, and you are being paid at the same rate as the other women there. Is there something that I'm not aware of?

BROWN: Well, all I know is that Mr. White said that the more awnings I sew, the more money I make. I don't know, I guess they have some kind of a chart or something.

SMITH: Do you know for a fact that you have done more work than someone else who received more money than you?

BROWN: Well, I'm not sure because I don't know how many the other women have sewed, but I've overheard them talking. And the group leader even said to me: "What was I trying to do, make it rough on the other girls who have worked here a long time and know a lot more about making good awnings than I do?" And I just said: "Well, I'm here to make money. I don't know about you."

SMITH: Have you talked this over with your supervisor?

BROWN: Yes, and he said my work passed inspection fine and that I sewed more awnings than anybody else. 'Course, that was just for one day, but I work just as hard one day as the next. I don't know how much the other girls are making, in fact—

SMITH: Just a minute, Miss Brown—

BROWN: In fact, they don't even talk to me except to tell me that I'm sewing wrong. Now I know I'm the youngest there, and I haven't worked here as long; but that doesn't mean I can't sew good awnings, does it? If they wouldn't spend so much time criticizing me, maybe they'd sew more themselves.

SMITH: Miss Brown, I want you to give me time to look into this problem; and if you will come back at two o'clock, I think we can straighten this out.

BROWN: Well, that sounds fair enough; but I don't want to make any more enemies down there than I have already, you understand that! And if you want me to sit around and talk like the others do and sew their way instead of mine, it's all right with me. Just as long as I draw the same pay check I am now. 'Cause that's what I'm working for—the money. At the same time, I'm not happy working here if I have to listen to the criticisms of the older girls all the time.

SMITH: You let me look into this situation, Miss Brown; and, if you will come back at two, I'll have some answers for you.

BROWN: Yes, I'll be back at two and thank you very much. I appreciate this. Thank you.

In the interval, Mr. Smith checked with Mr. White, supervisor of the sewing shop, who stated that, although Miss Brown was a good worker, she could not seem to get along with the other workers. A check of the records of the women in Miss Brown's section revealed that the woman nearest Miss Brown's age was forty-three years old. Mr. Smith suggested to Mr. White that perhaps if Miss Brown were transferred to Section 3, where there were several girls in their twenties, she might get over her antagonistic attitude. Mr. White seemed delighted at the suggestion and said that he would go along with it. It was agreed then that Mr. White would arrange for the transfer of Miss Brown's equipment and would introduce her to the girls in Section 3.

Mr. White left after agreeing to sit in on the meeting at two o'clock between Miss Brown and Mr. Smith.

The Final Meeting

WHITE: Hello, Miss Brown. Won't you sit down?

BROWN: Thank you very much.

SMITH: Miss Brown, I believe we have the answers to your problem. First of all, I want to explain the piecework system so that you will be able to determine your pay each day as you work. Each day you are paid at the following rate: 50 cents each for the first 10 awnings; 60 cents each for the next 5; and 75 cents each for every awning above 15. Your average per day for the last two months has been 14, which is fourth highest in the plant; and you can be proud of your record—more so because you are our newest employee in the sewing shop. Do you have any questions on the piecework?

BROWN: No, Mr. Smith, you make it sound very simple. I never had it explained to me that way before.

SMITH: As to your lack of friends in Section 1, we feel that perhaps the difference in ages may have been an influence; therefore, a transfer to Section 3, where there are several younger girls, might be in order. Do you know any of the girls in Section 3?

BROWN: I met two girls on the bus just the other day from Section 3, and they seemed real nice. It sounds good to me. The sooner the better.

SMITH: Mr. White, will you have Miss Brown's equipment transferred immediately? And Miss Brown, suppose you go with him now and let him introduce you to some of the girls in Section 3.

BROWN: All right, Mr. Smith; and thank you very much. I'm sorry if I bothered you.

SMITH: Not at all, Miss Brown. And please let us know if you run into any more problems. We are here to do all we can for you.

QUESTIONS AND PROBLEMS

1. What organizational confusion exists in this case? How should it be cleared up?
2. What suggestions do you have to offer regarding the handling of this case?
3. Was the interviewing conducted in accordance with good principles? Explain.
4. Why is the matter of wage rates, which seem to be in error, passed over so lightly?
5. How much weight should be given to the opinions which fellow-workers have for each other?

CASE 33. SAFETY

The Motor Manufacturing Company makes auto parts, which are sold to various automotive companies in and around Detroit. The company employs approximately five hundred men. It was unionized in 1940 by the UAM.

The company uses punch press and drop hammer operations in the manufacture of some of its products. There are about fifty employees in this department who operate approximately twenty machines in two shifts. Operation of these machines is extremely hazardous unless all safety rules are strictly observed. It is the responsibility of the foreman to enforce these rules. He is aided in the enforcement by group leaders.

The accident rate in the operation of these machines has been very high. A check of the safety rules shows the following procedure is to be followed in the operation of the machines: The operator picks up the unformed part with his left hand, grips it with tweezers in his right hand, and places it in the machine. The machine is set in motion with his foot. After the machine completes its cycle, the operator removes the part with the tweezers and, at the same time, grasps an unformed part with his left. The cycle of operations is then repeated.

The operators are on incentive work and tend to disregard safety in an effort to boost their earnings. Consequently, they have developed the habit of grasping the unformed part with the left hand and placing it in the machine while they remove the formed part with the right hand.

In an effort to reduce the number of accidents, the safety engineer had the machines equipped with a sweep-motion mechanical guard. The guard brushed the operator's hand aside when the machine was set in motion.

This brought a complaint from the operators that the guard was removing their hands far enough to clear the descending die but that their hands were being hit with the guard. The complaints continued, and it was eventually agreed to discontinue the use of the guard provided that the workers used the tweezers.

However, the rule of using the tweezers was disobeyed and the accidents continued.

The safety engineer investigated other safety devices in an effort to reduce accidents. The investigation disclosed a device, which was being used for similar machines in other plants, that automatically pulled the worker's hands away from the machine when it was set into operation.

At a safety committee meeting of the department, the safety engineer explained the device and went into detail as to how it functioned. The foreman of the department opposed the device on the grounds that he had seen it in operation at other plants and had found that employees co-operated reluctantly after such devices had been installed.

The committee, because of the foreman's objections, voted against the use of the safety device.

Later, in a further investigation of the same device, the safety engineer conferred with a representative of the firm that manufactured the device. At his suggestion, it was decided to experiment by installing the device on a machine. The foreman agreed to permit the installation on a machine that was used for odd jobs. At his suggestion, the device was installed without any notice to the workers or to the union.

Several men tried the device, which proved to work satisfactorily, but reserved their opinions on it. Others refused even to try the machine.

At this point, the union steward saw the device and requested that it be removed at once. He objected to it for two main reasons. First, he maintained that the device was not actually foolproof and, second, that the device would restrict the worker's actions and make him less efficient.

All efforts by the safety engineer to disprove these beliefs were rejected by the steward. The machine remained in the shop for several days and finally, upon the insistence of the steward, was removed.

In the light of the facts given, the problem still remains of how to cut down an excessively high accident rate. The problem is accentuated by the fact that the attempts to install various devices have been rejected by the employees, the union, or the foreman.

QUESTIONS AND PROBLEMS

1. Who is responsible for safety?
2. Why has management failed to take positive action?
3. Why do employees seem to have insufficient regard for their own safety? What is the moral?
4. What should management do in this case?

CASE 34.   ABSENTEEISM

Recently, in the Style Shoe Company, absenteeism rose to a rate of 20 per cent. This rate was maintained for the first six months of 1949, whereas previously the rate had not gone above 5 per cent.

The Style Shoe Company employs about seven hundred persons, about evenly divided between men and women. Of the women personnel, one hundred were employed within the last year. The plant is nonunionized and operates on a forty-hour week. It is divided into three departments: setup, assembly, and furnishings.

In examining the possible causes of absenteeism, the company has attempted to answer four questions. First, where does absenteeism occur? Second, who is absent? Third, when does absenteeism occur? Fourth, why do people not come to work?

Three steps were involved in studying the question of where absenteeism occurs. The first step was a study of the situation as a whole. This showed, as already noted, an increase of absenteeism from 5 to 20 per cent in the preceding six months. The next step was to find out in which department absenteeism seemed to prevail. After an extensive observation of clock cards from each department for two weeks, it was found that most of the trouble was in the assembly department. Here absenteeism averaged about 30 per cent for about three hundred women employees of this department. A study of individuals here revealed that 75 per cent of those absent ranged in age from twenty-three to thirty and most of these were married. Further absenteeism occurred mainly at the beginning and the end of the week.

Chronic absentees were then interviewed personally. It was found that most of the absenteeism fell on Mondays and Fridays for a number of reasons. First, women who failed to come to work on Mondays generally stayed away because they had home duties to perform. Second, those who did not show up for work on Fridays usually spent the day downtown shopping or in the local markets doing the household shopping. Third, other reasons varied from sickness to bridge parties.

Sickness and poor health accounted for a small amount of absenteeism. However, the most important causes were related to household and home obligations, which caused over 60 per cent of all absenteeism.

The company felt that some absenteeism might be management's fault. Therefore, the study also covered regulations governing employees and the work expected from each employee. The only significant fact uncovered was that there tended to be a weakness in the knowledge the employee had of the job and where this particular job fitted into the entire picture. This fault was attributed to the lack of employee-management planning.

QUESTIONS AND PROBLEMS

1. What is your opinion of this plan of analysis of absenteeism?
2. As a result of the facts disclosed here, what should be done?

CASE 35.   GETTING THE FACTS

The Steel Alloy Tool Company had been having considerable trouble with turnover in most of its jobs. It hired a consulting firm to make an investigation. Among the studies conducted by this firm was one in which a consultant masqueraded as an employee, having himself hired as a night watchman. Part of his report on his experience is summarized in the statement that follows:

On September 20, 1948, I was hired by the employment clerk as a night watchman. I was told to contact the regular watchman when he came to work at 4:30 P.M. in the afternoon. I was not told where to contact the man or what he looked like, but I was told that I would learn the job by making the rounds with this individual and thereby learn where the "boxes" were located.

At 5:30 P.M., after some searching, I found the man who was to be my instructor. He was not told that I was hired or that he was to teach me the routine of the job. However, after getting the facts of the situation and what he was expected to do, we started the training process.

I learned that my duties consisted of making a round of the plant every other hour while I was on duty. This consisted of registering, by key signal, thirty boxes situated throughout the plant. These boxes had to be punched in rotation for the signal to register at the private detective agency office downtown, and each box had to be registered at a certain precise time. This insured the company that the watchman was covering the whole plant on each round. On the hour that the other watchman was registering the boxes, I was in charge of the main gate to see that no one entered who was not supposed to be in the plant.

The job consisted of two shifts of watchmen, with two men on each shift. The hours for the first shift were from 4:30 P.M. to 12:00 A.M. and for the second shift, from 12:00 A.M. to 7:30 P.M. The work schedules were staggered throughout the week in order to give each man one night off a week. This meant that each man on the job had to work with every other man sometime during the week. The watchmen included four men who had long service with the company, an older man with about one year of service, and myself.

There had been high turnover for the two positions not occupied by the long-term employees. The older employees complained constantly to the plant superintendent, who was the sole supervisor of all the watchmen, about the new men on the job. They would claim that the new men were not making rounds properly, or that they failed to do the duties expected of them at the gate. The attitude of the plant employees toward these two long-term employees was not favorable. They believed that the old watchmen served as plant spies for the superintendent and would report to him any infractions of rules and policies (minor or major).

When I came to work, they had just succeeded in getting a man transferred who had been a watchman for six months. The employee with only one year of service also feared and hated these two older employees. The man who had been transferred was his friend, and now he felt that he would have to battle these two men alone. Therefore he tried to enlist my aid in his personal fight with the older employees and also told the men in the plant that the long-term watchmen were telling the superintendent everything that happened on the second and third shifts. On several occasions the plant superintendent left certain instructions with the two old-timers, and this information was to be transferred to us when we came to work on the third shift. These instructions were not relayed on two occasions, but the old-timers claimed that they had told them to us and we had deliberately ignored them.

Actually there was no written instruction of the duties that this job entailed. The job was constantly being given new duties as the need for these actions occurred. However, these additions were not written but were told to one watchman, and he was to inform the others of the new tasks to be performed. Whenever a new problem arose and the procedure for handling it was unknown, the superintendent had to be called at his home for guidance. There was no supervisor present to take over and solve the problem. In instances when the superintendent was not home, then the man with the new problem had to work out a solution in a manner which he thought was adequate.

Another problem that was becoming serious was the increase in thefts of company property. The watchmen were supposed to inspect articles carried from the plant to insure against stealing. However, employees were allowed to bring their cars through the gates, and inspection of cars when the men left was superficial. Also, there was a second gate which was not guarded, by which the employees could enter or leave. Yet the watchmen were blamed for the increase in thefts and were told that they were not sufficiently careful in their inspections when the workers were leaving.

In selection and induction of watchmen, there was no set policy. Records showed that most of the men hired for this position were transferred from factory jobs because they couldn't do the work required or were older employees given this job instead of a pension. I was one of the few outsiders hired for this job. The induction process as practiced in my case was evidently normal. The complaints of the older watchmen seemed to be a common characteristic of most other older employees against the younger employees in the other jobs as well.

QUESTIONS AND PROBLEMS

1. Do you think that the consultant made a wise selection in the job in which he desired to masquerade? Why or why not? Is the masquerade justifiable?
2. Specifically what aspects of selection, induction, training, grievance handling, and disciplinary action required attention?
3. How do you explain the attitude of the older employees toward the younger ones? Does this seem to indicate a problem in social status? Economic status?

CASE 36. RACIAL PROBLEMS

This problem occurred in a governmental agency employing approximately five hundred persons. Promotion and reassignment was based almost entirely on seniority, efficiency being the only other factor applied. If an employee had an efficiency rating of good or better and he was on the top in seniority, he was to receive prior consideration regardless of race, color, or creed.

This particular agency had three major divisions. These divisions were broken down into units and subunits. All three divisions pooled their personnel for consideration when promotions were made. When there was an opening in one of the divisions, all eligible personnel were considered.

Recently, one of the higher clerical positions was vacated. The personnel division was contacted and asked to supply the division supervisor with a list of the eligible candidates. The person who filled this clerical position would also be the supervisor of a stenographer.

The "number one" candidate was a Negro whose efficiency rating in the past had always been good or better. However, the division supervisor was warned that the man was arrogant and haughty in his mannerisms. Several times in the past, minor personnel difficulties had resulted from his attitude. Fellow employees had complained that he carried a chip on his shoulder and seemed to look for arguments.

The man had to be accepted for the position because of his seniority.

There was a white stenographer already assigned to this man when he took the position. Although the stenographer resented this arrangement, she was asked by the division supervisor to go along with it for awhile. Reluctantly she agreed, but after a few weeks she began to complain about the man's attitude. The supervisor decided that something should be done and decided on a plan of action.

In this same unit there was a situation in which there was a white clerk and Negro stenographer. There had been no trouble with this stenographer in the past, and she was contented with her position as well as the clerk under whom she was employed. So the supervisor had decided to switch the two stenographers. Their positions were similar, and very little training would have been required. The supervisor notified his personal secretary to convey this information to the parties concerned. When the Negro stenographer heard of the new arrangements, she immediately became very indignant and complained to the personnel division of unfair employment practices. As a result of this complaint nothing was done about the original problem. It seemed to have straightened out itself.

QUESTIONS AND PROBLEMS

1. What is your opinion of the problem in this case?
2. Should the supervisor's secretary convey the notice of the transfer to the employees?
3. Is this problem still boiling under the surface? Why or why not?

CASE 37.   PERSONNEL EVALUATION

This case concerns a manufacturing company employing between fifty and sixty people. Most of the workers are highly skilled because of the nature of the work. By the same token, the wages are above the average scale in the community.

This small company has no personnel manager, the hiring being done by the general manager. All prospective employees are screened before being allowed to see the general manager. Only the most undesirable are turned away, the rest being interviewed by the general manager and, if found satisfactory, are then taken to the shop superintendent. Here a candidate is actually given a technical phase of the work to perform relating to his claimed specialty, such as welding, shearing, or operating a punch press. In this way, the fast-talkers and apprentices are weeded out.

The factory is equipped with the latest machinery, and the working conditions are as pleasant as can be maintained in any small shop manufacturing a diversified line of products. The wages, union set-up, hospital-care coverage, working hours, and paydays are explained to the employee when he is hired. The employee is then told when to report to work.

Operator X was hired after having been interviewed in this manner. He was found to be, from the very first, a "super"mechanic, a rare find. X was a press brake operator and could easily do the normal week's work in three days. He had excellent knowledge of the "set-up" and short cuts used in the work. His work was fast and accurate as well as flawless.

After working about three weeks, he was absent from work on a Monday morning. As a matter of fact, he didn't show up until Thursday, and then in such an intoxicated condition that he was not fit to work. Being such a high-class worker he was given another chance, but in a few weeks he was off again. Still, against the general manager's better judgment, he was allowed to come back to work only because he would be hard to replace. At the time he was taken back, he was counseled on his waywardness and impressed with the responsibility of his job to himself and the company.

Two weeks later X was absent again. By this time management was beginning to believe that he was a confirmed drinker and there was little chance for him to reform.

QUESTIONS AND PROBLEMS

1. What would have been your course of action on this latest absenteeism of Operator X?
2. What is the real problem in handling this type of case, as far as the morale of the company is concerned?
3. Can you suggest a method of avoiding the hiring of such employees and how would you fit it into the hiring procedure of this company?
4. Would such screening be good personnel procedure?

Index

713

This book has been set on the Linotype in 12 and 10 point Garamond No. 3, leaded 1 point. Chapter numbers are in 14- and 18-point Gothic No. 2 and chapter titles are in 18-point Gothic No. 2. The size of the type page is 27 by 46½ picas.